Past, Present, and Future Contributions of Cognitive Writing Research to Cognitive Psychology

Past, Present, and Future Contributions of Cognitive Writing Research to Cognitive Psychology

Edited by Virginia Wise Berninger

 Psychology Press
Taylor & Francis Group

New York   London

Psychology Press
Taylor & Francis Group
711 Third Avenue
New York, NY 10017

Psychology Press
Taylor & Francis Group
27 Church Road
Hove, East Sussex BN3 2FA

Printed in the United States of America on acid-free paper
Version Date: 2011908

International Standard Book Number: 978-1-84872-963-6 (Hardback)

**Visit the Taylor & Francis Web site at
http://www.taylorandfrancis.com**

**and the Psychology Press Web site at
http://www.psypress.com**

This book honors three pioneers who helped create and sustain research on the cognitive processes of writing—John R. Hayes, Michel Fayol, and Pietro Boscolo—and a pioneer in the social constructivist tradition of writing research—Charles Bazerman. All are leaders in creating a global network of writing researchers across many disciplines and countries in which cognitive psychologists participate.

Contents

PART III   THE CHANGING NATURE OF TEACHING, LEARNING, AND ASSESSING WRITING ACROSS THE LIFE SPAN: K–12, ADOLESCENCE, HIGHER EDUCATION, AND THE WORK WORLD

PART IV   LEVELS OF LANGUAGE PROCESSES IN WRITING: WORD, SENTENCE, AND TEXT

PART V   COGNITIVE PROCESSES IN WRITING

PART VI   APPLICATIONS OF TECHNOLOGY TO
STUDYING AND TEACHING WRITING

PART VII EMERGING COGNITIVE NEUROSCIENCE OF WRITING

VISIONS OF THE FUTURE OF WRITING RESEARCH: PERSPECTIVES FROM THE NEW GENERATION OF WRITING RESEARCHERS AND CONTEMPORARY LEADERS

Preface

The idea for this book was generated in Santa Barbara, California, in February 2008 at the second Writing Research Across Borders II, organized by Charles (Chuck) Bazerman. In the editor's separate conversations with three presenters at the conference, John R. (Dick) Hayes, Michel Fayol, and Pietro (Piero) Boscolo, each expressed regret that writing research had not become an established topic within mainstream psychology, especially cognitive psychology. Although writing researchers have applied concepts and methods from cognitive psychology to the teaching of writing and other topics within the field of writing research, the contributions of mainstream writing research have not, in turn, influenced cognitive psychology. Each man had a vision of writing research enriching and being further enriched by a greater presence of the field of writing within the fields of cognitive psychology and cognitive science.

Moreover, each of these pioneering writing researchers expressed a strong belief that the future of cognitive writing research will depend on collaboration that reaches beyond a single discipline, single tradition of research within a discipline, or a single country. Indeed, all three have modeled these beliefs in their own work over the years. Not only does Charles Bazerman, the organizer of the 2008 global writing conference, which was attended by writing researchers from more than 40 countries, share their beliefs, but he has also been a leader in helping writing researchers cross those borders between disciplines, traditions within disciplines, countries in which they live and work, and the languages they speak and write. In addition, he has made pioneering contributions to the development of the sociocultural and historical traditions within the field of writing. He is open to building productive links between the cognitive and the sociocultural and historical traditions within writing research.

The goal of this book on the past, present, and future of cognitive writing research is, therefore, to honor these four pioneering leaders and contributors to the fields of writing research and cognitive psychology, while at the same time to provide the readers with an overview of the contemporary leading edge work in the cognitive psychology of writing, with visions of what the future of this field might be. Those honored pioneers in writing research include Europeans as well as North Americans, as do the contributors, who are French, Italian, Portuguese, Belgian, German, Dutch, and British, as well as Canadian and American (United States). The intended audience includes those who are contemporary contributors to the fields of cognitive psychology, cognitive science, and even cognitive neuroscience, and their students—the future generation of contributors—as well as consumers of the research findings, including but not restricted to elementary, secondary, and university educators, those engaged in writing in the workplace or professional development for professional writers, and anyone who uses computer and other technology tools for constructing, sending, and receiving written-language communication.

Credit for encouraging the editor to pursue a book on writing research and for helping her bring it to timely completion goes to Gert Rijlaarsdam, a contemporary leader in writing research who describes himself as one who delights in balancing on the rope of time. The editor is also deeply grateful to George Zimmar at Taylor & Francis, the parent company for Psychology Press, for introducing her to Paul Dukes. She thanks Paul Dukes for his respect and enthusiasm for basic as well as applied cognitive psychology research and commitment to publishing quality work in the field of writing. Paul, who grew up in Britain, lived in France, and currently lives in the United States, has resonated with the goal of international writing researchers writing for an international audience about the past, present, and future of the cognitive psychology of writing. Both Paul and his able assistant Lee Transue made it possible to launch and culminate this writing collaboration among numerous scholars from different streams of cognitive writing research in many countries of the world. She also acknowledges the contributions of Marc Johnston of Cenveo Publisher Services and Robert Sims of Taylor & Francis; their expertise and guidance helped bring this book to final production.

Editor

Virginia Wise Berninger received her PhD in psychology from Johns Hopkins University in 1981 (specialization in cognitive psychology and developmental psycholinguistics). She has been on faculties at Harvard Medical School (1981–1983), Tufts New England School of Medicine (1983–1986), and the University of Washington (1986–present), where she is currently Professor of Educational Psychology (Learning Sciences). She was Principal Investigator of National Institute of Child Health and Human Development-funded research projects on writing—*typical writing development and effective writing instruction for at-risk and disabled writers* (1989–2008, Literacy Trek and brain imaging of typically developing writers and children with dysgraphia) and *specific written language learning disabilities* (1995–2006, University of Washington Interdisciplinary Learning Disabilities Center, family genetics, brain imaging, and treatment studies). She directs the University Brain Education and Technology group, which is currently investigating computer-assisted instruction in writing with support from the Binational Science Foundation in collaboration with Dr. Zvia Breznitz, Director of the Edmond J. Safra Brain Research Center, University of Haifa, Israel. She teaches courses in normal brain development and educational applications, brain disorders in learning and behavior, and writing (and reading and math) instruction with the brain in mind; she also advises PhD students in Learning Sciences. Her research interests include the bidirectional cognitive ← → linguistic translation processes involving four functional language systems (language by ear, mouth, eye, and hand), each organized by levels (subword, word, syntax, text), and three word forms (phonological, morphological, and/or orthographic) as the human brain interacts with the social and physical environment.

Contributors

Denis Alamargot
Research Center on Cognition and
    Learning
National Center for Scientific Research
University of Poitiers
Poitiers, France

Rui Alexandre Alves
Department of Psychology and
    Educational Sciences
University of Porto
Porto, Portugal

Barbara Arfé
Department of Developmental
    Psychology and Socialization
University of Padua
Padua, Italy

Anna L. Barnett
Oxford Brookes University
Oxford, United Kingdom

Christopher Barry
University of Essex
Colchester, United Kingdom

Charles Bazerman
Gevirtz Graduate School of Education
University of California, Santa Barbara
Santa Barbara, California

Céline Beaudet
University of Sherbrooke
Sherbrooke, Quebec, Canada

Bianca De Bernardi
University of Verona
Verona, Italy

Patrick Bonin
LEAD-CNRS
University of Burgundy and
    Institut Universitaire de France
Dijon, France

Gaelle Borchardt
Laboratory of Cognitive Psychology
    and Neuropsychology
Paris Descartes University
Paris, France

Pietro Boscolo
Department of Developmental
    Psychology and Socialization
University of Padua
Padua, Italy

Marta Branco
Department of Psychology and
    Educational Sciences
University of Porto
Porto, Portugal

Gilles Caporossi
Groupe d'Études et de Recherche en
    Analyse des Décisions
École des Hautes Études
    Commerciales de Montréal
Montreal, Quebec, Canada

São Luís Castro
Department of Psychology and
    Educational Sciences
University of Porto
Porto, Portugal

Lucile Chanquoy
University of Nice
Sophia Antipolis, France

David Chesnet
Centre for Human and Society
    Sciences
National Center for Scientific Research
University of Poitiers
Poitiers, France

Vincent Connelly
Department of Psychology
Oxford Brookes University
Oxford, United Kingdom

Juliette Danjon
Laboratory of Cognitive Psychology
    and Neuropsychology
Paris Descartes University
Paris, France

Helene Deacon
Dalhousie University
Halifax, Nova Scotia, Canada

Bianca De Bernardi
University of Verona
Verona, Italy

Julie E. Dockrell
Institute of Education
University of London
London, United Kingdom

Michel Fayol
University of Clermont Blaise Pascal
Clermont-Ferrand, France

Carmen Gelati
Department of Psychology
University of Milano Bicocca
Milano, Italy

Steve Graham
Vanderbilt University
Nashville, Tennessee

Roger Graves
University of Alberta
Edmonton, Alberta, Canada

Karen R. Harris
Vanderbilt University
Nashville, Tennessee

John R. Hayes
Department of Psychology
Carnegie Mellon University
Pittsburgh, Pennsylvania

Harriet Jisa
University of Lyon
Lyon, France

Perry D. Klein
Department of Education
The University of Western Ontario
London, Ontario, Canada

Bertrand Labasse
Department of French
University of Ottawa
Ottawa, Ontario, Canada

Tracey L. Leacock
Department of Education
Simon Fraser University
Burnaby, British Columbia, Canada

Mariëlle Leijten
Research Foundation Flanders
University of Antwerp
Antwerp, Belgium

Christel Leuwers
University of Chambéry
Chambéry, France

Eva Lindgren
Umea University
Umea, Sweden

Charles A. MacArthur
School of Education
University of Delaware
Newark, Delaware

Audrey Mazur-Palandre
Dynamics of Language
National Center for Scientific
    Research and University of Lyon
Lyon, France

Deborah McCutchen
College of Education
University of Washington
Seattle, Washington

Debra Myhill
Graduate School of Education
University of Exeter
Exeter, United Kingdom

Guido Nottbusch
Human Sciences Faculty
University of Potsdam
Potsdam, Germany

Thierry Olive
University of Poitiers and National
    Center for Scientific Research
Poitiers, France

Sébastien Pacton
Laboratory of Cognitive Psychology
    and Neuropsychology
Paris Descartes University
Paris, France

Ascension Pagan
Research Center on Cognition and
    Learning
National Center for Scientific Research
University, Poitiers
Poitiers, France

Margherita Pasini
University of Verona
Verona, Italy

Francesca Poeta
University of Verona
Verona, Italy

Virginie Pontart
Research Center on Cognition and
    Learning
National Center for Scientific Research
University of Poitiers
Poitiers, France

Kathleen O'Brien Ramirez
Research Center on Cognition and
    Learning
National Center for Scientific Research
University of Poitiers
Poitiers, France

Todd L. Richards
Department of Radiology
University of Washington
Seattle, Washington

Gert Rijlaarsdam
Research Institute of Child
    Development and Education
University of Amsterdam
Amsterdam, the Netherlands

Paul M. Rogers
George Mason University
Fairfax, Virginia

Sébastien Roux
LEAD-CNRS
University of Bourgogne
Dijon, France

Karen Schriver
KSA Communication Design &
  Research
Oakmont, Pennsylvania

Mark Torrance
Division of Psychology
Nottingham Trent University
Nottingham, United Kingdom

Huub van den Bergh
Utrecht University
Utrecht, the Netherlands

Luuk Van Waes
University of Antwerp
Antwerp, Belgium

Åsa Wengelin
Lund University
Lund, Sweden

Introduction

VIRGINIA WISE BERNINGER and GERT RIJLAARSDAM

> If you don't know the past, then ye will not have a future. If ye don't know where your people have been, then ye won't know where your people are going.
>
> Carter, *The Education of Little Tree* (1990), p. 40

Ironically, although researchers place considerable emphasis on citing names of researchers who author publications, they seldom address who the author is—the person who is writing about the research and its findings. To honor four pioneers in the field of writing research, the editor of this volume encouraged others to tell their stories—their professional journey as a writing researcher. The resulting stories in the first four chapters provide not only a glimpse into the history of the writing field from its earlier times to the current issues and unfinished work for the future, but also provide a model of programmatic writing research across a career for the new generation of writing researchers. David Olton at Johns Hopkins University emphasized to graduate students in psychology the importance of systematic programmatic research in addressing research questions in a meaningful, productive way, which often does not follow linear progression. With the current obsessive focus on the number of single-article publications and citations, we often lose sight of how the contributions of systematic, sequential studies address changing questions, based on the outcome of prior investigations, to build a cumulative body of scientific knowledge, and verify findings across variations in methods or samples. The three chapters in Part I and first chapter of Part II (Chapter 4) of this book offer an opportunity to learn to know the author, that is, the person who is the researcher behind the systematic and programmatic writing research and to learn about that researcher's personal professional journey in conducting a lifetime of programmatic research, which has made significant contributions to the field.

In Chapter 1, Hayes tells of his transformation from a physicist to behavioral psychologist to cognitive psychologist, his application of think-aloud protocols to the study of cognitive processes in writing, evolving models of the cognitive processes in writing, and discovery of language bursts marked by pauses in written production. In Chapter 2, Fayol describes his journey from writing teacher in a small French village to university cognitive researcher who studied writing from developmental, psycholinguistic, and experimental perspectives, and introduced the concept of online experiments, based on production rather than reaction times, and in the process mentored students who are now leading writing researchers. In Chapter 3, Boscolo, who also began as a writing teacher, shares a personal account of his developmental and instructional research, which considered both cognitive and affective/motivational variables, and in the process makes the important case that writing research has as much to learn from writing teachers as writing teachers have to learn from cognitive, developmental, and educational psychologists who study writing. In Chapter 4, Charles Bazerman introduces cognitive psychologists to the sociocultural and historical traditions in writing, which take into account affective as well as cognitive variables, and tells the story of his professional trajectory as writer, teacher, researcher, and theorist of writing.

Not only has each of these four pioneers contributed to the research literature on writing but each has also made major contributions to the professional organizations in the field of writing: Hayes to teachers of English at the college level and professional writers; Fayol and Boscolo to the special interest group (SIG) for writing of the European Association for Research on Learning and Instruction (EARLI); and Bazerman to Across-the-Borders, an international organization he organized and launched, which to date has brought writing researchers from over 40 countries together three times (in 2005, 2008, and 2011) to share their work. The professional careers and contributions of the four writing pioneers were celebrated in a symposium at the Writing Research Across Borders II, in February 2011 in Virginia.

Moreover, collectively their careers tell a story of great importance in the global age. These four honored researchers form a complementary quartet that has made remarkable music around the world in the field of writing research. To celebrate their collective contributions, the continuing global story is now told from the European perspective.

Pietro Boscolo and Michel Fayol were the founding fathers of the SIG of EARLI. This association was founded in 1985, and Boscolo participated from the very beginning in establishing this international group of scholars. Fayol and Boscolo took the lead to establish the SIG Writing Conference, which stood out among the other SIGs and had themes such as "Learning and Development in Early Childhood" and "Social Interaction in Learning and Instruction." Fayol and Boscolo were the first SIG Writing coordinators, and they started the biennial series of SIG Writing Conferences, which met in Padova (Italy 1988) and then Paris (France). The first conferences were attended by invitation only. Since 1994 (Utrecht, the Netherlands), conferences have had about 200 participants, from all over Europe, with a small contingent from other continents, especially from North America. Even after Fayol and Boscolo left their SIG coordination position after 4 years (EARLI regulations), they supported the SIG actions by establishing (a) the book series "Studies in Writing" (started in 1996, 21 volumes and more in progress), (b) the *Journal of Writing Research* (first publication 2008), and (c) international networks, including the COST network (Denis Alamargot, chair). Both inspired many young researchers in the tradition of psycholinguistic-inspired ingenious experiments with developmental factors, including educational interventions (Pietro Boscolo in Padua). They inspired master's and PhD students who continue the efforts, and both are respected advisors for national scientific research boards.

When Boscolo and Fayol established the SIG Writing Conference in the 1980s, Europeans were conducting writing research, based in linguistics, psycholinguistics, text linguistics, cognitive psychology, and educational psychology. Rijlaarsdam, Van den Bergh, and Couzijn (1996a, 1996b) and Levy and Ransdell (1996)[1] note that national papers or papers in English were cited most often, but references to other European works were beginning to be added. Most European researchers at that time published primarily in their home languages. The establishment of the SIG Writing Conference stimulated writing researchers to publish internationally, and the SIG Writing Conference peer-reviewed book series served that goal.

Much writing research in Europe and North America has been inspired then and now by the two chapters written by John Hayes and Linda Flower in a book based on papers from a symposium edited by Gregg and Steinberg (1980). These chapters stimulated thinking about how think-aloud protocols could support and test theory building and proposed a model of cognitive writing processes (components with a monitor that could fit various configurations and deal with recursiveness). These chapters generated research on understanding the writing process using a new methodology for studying these processes and designing educational interventions. John (Dick) Hayes was invited for a sabbatical in Utrecht in the early 1990s where he learned that in Europe many writing researchers borrowed from his model and supported the cognitive approach. His participation in SIG Writing Conferences was much appreciated, especially his approachable nature; he was well known yet so interested in what other researchers do and think. His presentations at these conferences are examples of how work in progress can stimulate thinking in the participating audience.

The influence of Bazerman's work in Europe occurred later. The scientific attention in Europe for writing in higher education and in the disciplines is relatively recent. During the past two decades, as access to higher education became a major educational policy of Europe, attention to writing also grew: Teachers in higher education found that students' basic skills in composing longer texts based on sources were not always strong enough once they reached higher education levels. Even in the SIG Writing group, the interest in learning to write was far more pronounced than for writing to learn (although see Tynjälä, Mason, & Lonka, 2001). Therefore, another European network was set up to inform teachers in higher education about writing: The European Association for the Teaching of Academic Writing (EATAW) was established as a formal association in 2007. This association has strong links to the U.S. networks on Writing in the Disciplines (WID) and Writing Across the Curriculum (WAC). As Dick Hayes had, Bazerman also detected the wealth of writing research in Europe and participated in the SIG Writing Conferences. He combines a wide interest in current issues with a strong

---

[1] Michael Levy and Sarah Ransdell, who were among the first U.S. researchers to attend a SIG Writing Conference (Utrecht, the Netherlands, 1994), were quite surprised that in Europe the cognitive approach was still a major research area because in the United States it had fallen into disfavor. They decided to edit a volume for Erlbaum on the cognitive tradition in writing, with United States and European research included.

voice in his commentaries; one of his scientific missions, to which he devotes much time and energy, is organizing cross-nation and cross-linguistic activities to bridge the various communities. Both Hayes and Bazerman are internationally oriented writing researchers.

The story of the cognitive psychology of writing research is also one that is currently being told by contemporary leaders in the field, including established and up-and-coming researchers. The rest of this book is their story and a story that all contributors hope will continue to be told and written in the future. One emerging theme across the remaining chapters in this volume is that in creating a specialization in writing research within mainstream cognitive psychology, researchers should draw on multiple disciplines.

In keeping with this theme, Part II provides examples of interdisciplinary collaboration between the cognitive psychology and the sociocultural traditions. In Chapter 5, Beaudet, Graves, and Labasse share their separate lines of writing research with adults, including both undergraduates and professionals in the world of work. Collectively these studies serve as a reminder that learning to write is a lifespan task, and adult writing is not just scaled-up children's writing—rather, it is qualitatively different, with different goals, requirements, and applications. In Chapter 6, Klein and Leacock introduce the concept of distributed cognition, which is a currently influential paradigm in both adult and child writing and draws attention to writing as a shared, collaborative activity rather than merely a solo activity of an isolated individual. In Chapter 7, Gelati considers the effects of gender, a salient individual difference variable with social implications, on writing development.

Part III illustrates how writing—how it is learned, effectively taught, and validly assessed—changes across the lifespan at home and school from early to middle childhood to adolescence to adulthood (in higher education and the world of work). In Chapter 8, Graham and Harris pay tribute to the pioneering cognitive researchers featured in Part I as they describe their own 30-year programmatic research on teaching and learning self-regulated writing. In Chapter 9, McCutchen makes the case for more research focus on language processes in writing and shows how phonological, orthographic, and morphological word-level processes contribute across levels of text generation during the writing process. In Chapter 10, Connelly, Dockrell, and Barnett tackle the important topic, which deserves more research attention, of children who struggle with not only writing but also reading and oral language and/or motor problems. They provide conceptual frameworks for asking assessment and treatment questions for both research and practice. In Chapter 11, Myhill demonstrates how metalinguistic knowledge, which is becoming a cutting-edge topic in writing research, is relevant to writing assessment and instruction for adolescents. Not only language but also awareness of and reflection about language contribute to writing. In Chapter 12, Shriver fleshes out the picture of lifespan writing with a focus on the adult professional writer and writers in the work world, where not only writing but also design are fundamentally important. Note that although Chapters 5, 6, and 7 are in Part II because of their social cultural grounding, they also contribute to understanding of lifespan writing development from elementary

(Gelati, Chapter 7), to middle school, to adolescent and adulthood (Klein & Leacock, Chapter 6), and to adults in college and the workplace (Beaudet et al., Chapter 5). Likewise, Chapter 12 draws on sociocultural influences in Shriver's work with real world writers.

Part IV, which focuses on language processes in writing, is considerably longer than Part V, which focuses on the cognitive processes in writing, in keeping with the emerging vision among writing researchers in this volume that more attention should be paid to language processes, but with cognitive processes in mind (see Vision "Looking Into the Text Generation Box to Find the Psycholinguistic (Cognitive–Language) Writing Processes" and Chapters 9 and 11). The first three chapters of Part IV focus on *word level*: lexical access and retrieval (Chapter 13, Bonin et al.), graphotactic and morphological regularities in spelling (Chapter 14, Pacton et al.), and spelling in a shallow orthography, which appears in a groundbreaking new study, reported here for the first time, to share common, heretofore overlooked linguistic features with morphophonemic deep orthographies (Chapter 15, Arfé et al.). The next three chapters take into account transcription mode and language processes at different levels of language in cutting-edge studies: bursts (Chapter 16, Alves et al.) and single words and sentences (Chapter 17, Torrance & Nottbusch). The final chapter in the language section (Chapter 18, Mazur-Palandre et al.) reports results for macrolevel language variables such as text types (genre) and modalities of output. This line of research is likely to expand as writing researchers investigate how different kinds of technology, used for either written or oral output, may interact with the language and cognitive processes in translation.

Of the chapters in Part V on cognitive processes in writing, only one deals with translating (Chapter 19, Alamargot et al.), in this case how subject–verb agreement is managed during online translation. The cognitive ← → language translating process is sufficiently complex and timely and is discussed in greater depth in a related book (Fayol, Alamargot, & Berninger, 2011). Chapter 20 by MacArthur provides a lively up-to-date account of the evaluation (review) and revision processes with suggestions for future research directions on this important topic. Revision of writing is increasingly the norm now in educational contexts, as it always has been in professional writing. The final chapter in this part (Chapter 21, Olive) provides an overview of past, current, and future directions in research on working memory and writing. Not only does working memory support the writing process, but individual differences in working memory explain why individual writers vary in how easily they learn to write or why they may struggle with the writing process. Hopefully the research on the cognitive processes of writing will expand in the future with fresh new approaches, perhaps inspired by one or more chapters or visions in this volume. For example, time emerged as a dimension of considerable promise for learning more about the cognitive processes in writing. To an earlier preoccupation with reaction times, contemporary cognitive writing researchers are adding production times or pauses (to support inferences about online processing) (see Parts IV, V, and VI and Visions "Through the Models of Writing: Ten Years After and Visions for the Future" and "The Future Is Bright for Writing Research") and in measurement of writing products (see Vision "Writing Research: Where to Go To?").

Part VI on technology tools has one chapter (Chapter 22, Van Waes et al.), but it is one that cognitive psychologists who become interested in writing will find extremely valuable. Here the available technology tools for writing research are compared, contrasted, and discussed for writing instruction. Thus, in an era of increasing use of technology in all aspects of life and work, this chapter is an important resource for those who teach writing in middle or high school, higher education, or the work world.

Part VII on the emerging cognitive neuroscience of writing also has only one chapter (Chapter 23, Berninger & Richards). It explains what is known about the cognitive, language, sensory, and motor systems that operate within a working memory architecture to support the writing process as the writing brain interacts with both its internal mental and external physical and social environments. As such, this chapter also serves as a synthesis of important points made by the authors of all the prior chapters in the volume. Also, in keeping with the volume's theme of interdisciplinary collaboration in cognitive writing research, this chapter models how a cognitive psychologist could be partnered with a neuroscientist in interdisciplinary research.

The volume concludes not with an ending but with visions for the future. Vision "Through the Models of Writing: Ten Years After and Visions for the Future" foresees a future of less model building of the entire writing process and more empirical research on specific research questions focused on just a few aspects of the complex writing process. In a similar fashion, Vision "Looking Into the Text Generation Box to Find the Psycholinguistic (Cognitive–Language) Writing Processes" recommends attending less to the text generation box and more to the interactions of the cognitive and language processes, especially at the higher levels. Vision "Writing Research: Where to Go To?"—setting the research agenda to improve writing education and in turn cognitive writing research—calls for intervention studies conducted in close collaboration with teachers and designed to include process and product measures and individual learner variables that inform writing practice and theory. Vision "Evolving Integration and Differentiation in Cognitive and Sociocultural-Historical Writing Research" looks forward to more cross-tradition collaborations across the cognitive and sociocultural traditions as well as longitudinal and instructional studies. Vision "The Future Is Bright for Writing Research" predicts a bright future for writing research, which draws on cognitive and linguistic processes and technology tools for experimental, developmental, and instructional research, with acknowledgment that the future is unknown, for the current generation, standing on the shoulders of those who came before, to discover.

For readers who are new to the field of writing research or writing researchers who wish to update their knowledge of writing research across traditions (Bazerman et al., 2010; Grigorenko, Mambrino, & Preiss, in press) and countries (EARLI writing series editor, Rijlaarsdam), lists are provided at the end of this Introduction of current sources of writing research, which began near the end of the 19th century but increases in volume and scope at the beginning of the 21st century. Hopefully this volume will inspire further reading, reflecting, researching, and 'riting—the four R's of the information age.

REFERENCES

Bazerman, C., Krut, R., Lunsford, K., McLeod, S. Null, S., Rogers, P.M., & Stansell, A. (Eds.). (2010). *Traditions of writing research* (pp. 365–377). Oxford, UK: Routledge.

Carter, F. (1990). *The education of Little Tree*. Albuquerque: University of New Mexico Press.

Fayol, M., Alamargot, D., & Berninger, V. (2011). *Translation of thought to written text while composing: Advancing theory, knowledge, methods, and applications*. Psychology Press/Taylor & Francis Group/Routledge.

Gregg, L. W., & Steinberg, E. R. (Eds.). (1980). *Cognitive processes in writing*. Hillsdale, NJ: Erlbaum.

Grigorenko, E., Mambrino, E., & Preiss, D. D. (Eds.). (in press). *Writing: A mosaic of perspectives and views*. New York: Psychology Press.

Levy, C. M., & Ransdell, S. (1996). *The science of writing: Theories, methods, individual differences, and applications*. Mahwah, NJ: Erlbaum.

Rijlaarsdam, G., van den Bergh, H., & Couzijn, M. (Eds.). (1996a). *Effective teaching and learning to write. Current trends in research*. Amsterdam: Amsterdam University Press.

Rijlaarsdam, G., Van den Bergh, H., & Couzijn, M. (Eds.). (1996b). *Theories, models and methodology in writing research*. Amsterdam: Amsterdam University Press.

Tynjälä, P., Mason, L., & Lonka, K. (Eds.). (2001). *Writing as a learning tool. Integrating theory and practice*. Dordrecht: Kluwer.

RECENT WRITING HANDBOOKS
OR OTHER COLLECTIONS

Bazerman, C. (Ed.). (2008). *Handbook of research on writing: History, society, school, individual, and text*. Mahwah, NJ: Erlbaum.

Beard, R., Myhill, D., & Riley, J. (Eds.). (2010). *International handbook of writing development*. London: Sage.

Connelly, V., Barnett, A., Dockrell, J., & Tolmie, A. (Eds.). (2009). Teaching and learning writing. *British Journal of Educational Psychology Monograph Series II*, 6.

Gregg, L., & Steinberg, E. (Eds.). (1980). *Cognitive processes in writing: An interdisciplinary approach*. Hillsdale, NJ: Erlbaum.

MacArthur, C. A., Graham, C., & Fitzgerald, J. (2006). *The handbook of writing research*. New York: Guilford.

Rijlaarsdam, G., Van den Bergh, H., & Couzijn, M. (Eds.). (2005). *Effective learning and teaching of writing: A handbook of writing in education* (2nd ed.). New York: Kluwer.

Sullivan, K. P. H., & Lindgren, E. (Eds.). (2006). *Studies in writing 18: Computer key-stroke logging and writing: Methods and applications*. Oxford: Elsevier.

Troia, G. (Ed.). (2009). *Instruction and assessment for struggling writers. Evidence-based practices*. New York: Guilford.

EUROPEAN ASSOCIATION FOR RESEARCH
ON LEARNING AND INSTRUCTION

EARLI Writing Series (Gert Rijlaarsdam, Editor)

Alamargot, D., & Chanquoy, L. (2001). *Through the models of writing*. Dordrecht: Kluwer.

Alamargot, A., Terrier, P., & Cellier, J. M. (2007). (Eds.). *Written documents in the workplace*. London: Emerald.

Allal, G., Chanquoy, L., & Largy, P. (Eds.). (2004). *Revision. Cognitive and instructional processes*. Dordrecht: Kluwer.

Björk, L., Bräuer, G., Rienecker, L., & Stray Jörgensen, P. (Eds.). (2003). *Teaching academic writing in European higher education*. Dordrecht: Kluwer.

Camps, A., & Milian, M. (Eds.). (2000). *Metalinguistic activity in learning to write*. Amsterdam: Amsterdam University Press.

Courier, P., & Andriessen, J. (Eds.). (2000). *Foundations of argumentative text processing*. Amsterdam: Amsterdam University Press.

Hidi, S., & Boscolo, P. (Eds.). (2007). *Writing and motivation*. London: Emerald.

Kostouli, T. (Ed.). (2005). *Writing in context(s). Textual practices and learning processes in sociocultural settings*. New York: Springer.

Le Ha, P., & Baurain, B. (Eds.). (2011). *Voices, identities, negotiations, and conflicts. Writing academic English across cultures*. London: Emerald.

Olive, T., & Levy, C. M. (Eds.). (2002). *Contemporary tools and techniques for studying writing*. Dordrecht: Kluwer.

Ransdell, S., & Barbier, M. L. (Eds.). (2002). *New directions for research in L2 writing*. Dordrecht: Kluwer.

Rijlaarsdam, G., Van den Bergh, H., & Couzijn, M. (Eds.). (2005). *Effective learning and teaching of writing. A handbook of writing in education* (2nd ed.). Dordrecht: Kluwer.

Shum, M., & Zhang, D. L. (Eds.). (2005). *Teaching writing in Chinese speaking areas*. New York: Springer.

Sullivan, K. P. H., & Lindgren, E. (Eds.). (2006). *Computer keystroke logging and writing*. London: Emerald.

Tolchinsky, L. (Ed.). (2001). *Developmental aspects in learning to write*. Dordrecht: Kluwer.

Torrance, M., & Galbraith, D. (Eds.). (1999). *Knowing what to write. Conceptual processes in text production*. Amsterdam: Amsterdam University Press.

Torrance, M., & Jeffery, G. (Eds.). (1999). *The cognitive demands of writing. Processing capacity and working memory effects in text production*. Amsterdam: Amsterdam University Press.

Torrance, M., van Waes, L., & Galbraith, D. (Eds.). (2007). *Writing and cognition: research and applications*. London: Emerald.

Tynjälä, P., Mason, L., & Lonka, K. (Eds.). (2001). *Writing as a learning tool. Integrating theory and practice*. Dordrecht: Kluwer.

van Waes, L., Leijten, M., & Neuwirth, C. (Eds.). (2006). *Writing and digital media*. London: Emerald.

Part *I*

The Cognitive Tradition in Writing Research

1

My Past and Present as Writing Researcher and Thoughts About the Future of Writing Research

JOHN R. HAYES

T he invitation to write this chapter came with a request to write the story of a research career and the researcher who was the main character in that career story. Thus, in this chapter, I describe my research career as it unfolded in real time: my past—how I became a cognitive psychologist and brought my cognitive perspective to writing research; my present—what I am doing now; and, finally, my thoughts about future directions for the psychological study of writing. To tell the story, the chapter will contain bits of history, snippets of current events, and fragmentary personal opinions, all loosely tied together by experiences I have lived through during a long career. In short, don't expect conventional organization.

THE PAST: HOW I BECAME A COGNITIVE PSYCHOLOGIST

As is true of many of my cognitively oriented colleagues, I came to psychology by way of the physical sciences. In high school, I was fascinated by physics. I was first hooked on the subject when I happened to read a brief history of atomic physics. The important thing, I think, was that the topic was presented not as a body of facts, but as a narrative about real people asking hard questions about nature and then struggling, sometimes against adversity, to answer them. Intrigued, I read biographies of Madame Curie, Galileo, Copernicus, and other scientists and began serious study of college physics texts. I had no doubt that my future lay in physics because I was having such a wonderful time building spectroscopes and vacuum pumps in my cellar laboratory.

Everything about physics was magical to me. I expected to love physics even more in college, but a peculiar thing happened. It soon became clear to me that the professors at Harvard whom I so admired and whom I wanted to model myself after had no interest in involving undergraduates in research or even in talking to them very much. They were too involved in earning their Nobel prizes. I didn't understand until years later why my interest in physics faded and why I instead became fascinated with psychology. I'm sure that it had nothing to do with the subject matter. Rather, I'm convinced it was because I found psychology professors who were, willing to let me get involved in doing psychology. I knew I had found a home when my professors let me have my own rat lab. Later reflection on these events that changed me from a physicist into a psychologist made me acutely aware of the important impact teachers can have on their students' lives simply by paying attention to them.

Harvard psychology at the time was dominated by Skinner and his radical behaviorism. I bought into it enthusiastically. I was happy to work with pigeons and rats because I accepted the behaviorist dictum that psychology is best pursued "bottom up." Behaviorists believed that you have to understand the simple things first: conditioning in rats and pigeons before language and learning in humans. Basic research questions were strongly favored over applied ones. They believed that to be "scientific" you could deal only in observables. Observables included stimuli—the palpable environment of the animal, and their responses—what the animal could be seen to do. Observables did not include thoughts, images, memories, or any other experiences that could not be confirmed by an outside observer. And they definitely did not include models of what was going on inside. The behaviorists were certainly an interesting group and they had a very definite set of attitudes. I accepted all of these attitudes as truth and criticized Skinner's enemies, or as I saw it, "our enemies," for their fuzzy-headedness, for their mentalism, for their failure to define their concepts operationally; in short, for their failure to be doctrinaire behaviorists. This "we know the one real truth" attitude that I reveled in at the time may be great for promoting in-group solidarity and enthusiasm, but, as I discovered later, it not only narrows the perspective of individual researchers "within the faith," but may also act to disadvantage others peacefully pursuing other approaches.

I carried my behaviorist enthusiasm with me when I went to graduate school at MIT, where I studied with George Miller and was able to take courses with Jerome Bruner and anthropologist John Whiting. And I carried that enthusiasm through to my thesis, a study of the motivation (read persistence) of preschool children when playing games. I started my thesis believing that I could account for children's motivation for play in terms of Skinner's schedules of reinforcement. I designed games in which young children would be rewarded by viewing pictures, intended to reinforce them, according to various Skinnerian schedules.

In one way, my results were consistent with the Skinnerian point of view. The children's interest in my games was related to the schedules of reinforcement, roughly as I had predicted. In another way, though, my results were radically at odds with the Skinnerian point of view. The children were not treating the reinforcements, the pictures, in the way I expected. They weren't attending to them in the way that rats or pigeons in a Skinner box would snap up morsels of food. Actually, they hardly gave my pictures a glance. But they did show a lot of interest in discovering the rules of the game. What I found was that the children weren't being conditioned; they were enjoying the cognitive activity of solving problems.

My experience with the nursery school children made it clear to me that there were some very interesting phenomena that fell outside of the behaviorist world-view. I began to look for a new, more inclusive psychology. This was 1955. I didn't have long to wait. The events that led to the birth of cognitive psychology were already under way.

One of these events was the publication of Chomsky's (1959) devastating critique of verbal behavior, Skinner's (1957) book about language. Skinner had attempted to extend his conditioning studies of rats and pigeons to human language and had failed disastrously. I realized that perhaps the behaviorists' bottom-up approach wasn't such a good idea after all. Another event was the publication of George Miller's (1956) "The Magic Number Seven, Plus or Minus Two." This precedent-setting article offered the first important cognitive model. The model was cognitive in that it explained memory in terms of unobserved mental structures and processes (a sort of mentalism the Skinnerians completely rejected). The model was important because the limitations of short-term memory that Miller described constitute a bottleneck through which many human thought processes must pass.

The event with the most far-reaching effect, though, was Newell and Simon's powerful computer metaphor for thought. The metaphor was made concrete in their programs that carried out activities usually believed to require human intelligence, such as proving mathematical theorems (Newell & Simon, 1956) and solving problems (Newell, Shaw, & Simon, 1959). Oddly, the computer metaphor had the effect of encouraging psychologists to study human thought. The behaviorists believed that it was unscientific to talk about internal thought processes because they were not directly observable. Seeing that computer scientists discussed the internal information processes of their machines in respectable scientific ways, however, gave psychologists courage to disregard behaviorist strictures and consider the same kinds of process models for the descriptions for human thought.

THE EFFECT OF THE PARADIGM SHIFT

With the paradigm shift from behaviorism to cognitive psychology, important things changed for researchers. First, new areas for research were opened up. Researchers could now explore topics such as memory, planning, problem solving, imagery, and creativity—explorations that the behaviorists would certainly have discouraged. Second, two powerful new research tools became available: cognitive process models and protocol analysis. Cognitive process models allowed researchers to theorize about the internal mechanisms that the behaviorists refused to consider and to think through the implications of these mechanisms for what people did. Such models have been widely used by psychologists for understanding the nature of memory, problem solving, decision making, and other complex human activities. Protocol analysis is a technique in which a person is asked to think aloud, that is, say what is on the "top of their mind" while performing a task. What the person says is used as one set of cues to identify the processes underlying his or her task performance. Protocol analysis has been used in studying how people perform a wide variety of complex tasks such as playing chess, theorem proving, and writing.

The paradigm shift to cognition clearly shaped my later career as a writing researcher. It allowed the use of protocol analysis with which my colleagues and I identified the major cognitive processes people use to write. It allowed us to postulate internal processes such as planning, translation, and evaluation and to represent the relations among these processes in cognitive process models. But, while essential, these features of cognitive psychology were by no means the only tools that I gained from my training in psychology. The paradigm shift changed a lot about psychology, but it didn't change everything. Over a century and a quarter, psychology has developed a rhetorical tradition—an accumulation of methods and standards for making convincing arguments based on data. I call it rhetorical because it is centrally concerned with persuasion and the construction of arguments. It is the set of strategies that guides psychologists when they try to convince an audience of peers that their claims are plausible.

The rhetorical tradition is a work in progress. Each paradigm has made contributions to the tradition, and these additions were passed on to the next. To become professionals in the field, students must become fluent in this tradition. They must learn to design studies, to use control groups, randomization, and counterbalancing, and to be concerned with the reliability of measurement. They must learn how and when to use a variety of statistical methods—the rhetorical tools par excellence in empirical research. And they must develop a heightened awareness of "lurking variables" (of which there are many) that may fool one into making inappropriate inferences from data. Teachers sometimes use puzzles, such as the following, to illustrate the importance of lurking variables:

> Teacher: Did you know that there is a strong correlation between writing ability and foot size?
> Student: Really, how could that be?
> Teacher: Well, very small children tend to have small feet and they also don't write very well.

Students are expected to be able to look at a result reported in an article, consider the myriad lurking variables that might have caused that result, and judge whether or not the author provided appropriate controls for these variables. Of course they are expected to exercise the same critical standards when they design their own studies. Researchers who do not meet the standard—by failing to recognize lurking variables, by omitting needed control groups, or by using inappropriate statistical methods—are criticized or, more to the point, their arguments are rejected as unconvincing. This tradition, in addition to the cognitive paradigm shift, has been invaluable to researchers in designing and carrying out persuasive studies, whether on writing or on other topics.

HOW I BECAME A WRITING RESEARCHER

Since I already had a satisfying career studying decision making and problem solving, you may be wondering what led me to change my research direction and take up the study of writing. In retrospect, it seems to me that writing was and is an excellent topic for cognitive researchers. First, it is a *generative* language activity. For this reason, it offers more interesting challenges and possibilities than does reading, which is a *receptive* language activity. Reading is certainly an important topic and it is easier to study than writing, but, in the long run, I believe that the study of writing will yield more important insight into the human psyche. Second, writing is a social activity that has the goal of influencing other humans. Thus, it is a kind of crossover study that could and should be jointly explored by cognitive and social psychologists as well as cultural researchers. Finally, it is a socially important developmental activity. We expend major resources to teach students to write from first grade to graduate school. Understanding how to do that well is important. To me, these are compelling reasons why writing should be a very attractive topic for psychologists. But so far, it has attracted relatively little attention within mainstream psychology. For myself, I must admit, these reasons were not the ones that led me to take up writing research. Rather, my reasons for taking up writing research were more or less accidental. There were two major reasons.

The first was my work with Herbert Simon. Newell and Simon had created General Problem Solver (GPS), a computer program that could solve a variety of problems such as Tower of Hanoi and Hobbits and Orcs. When people solve problems, they typically have two tasks. The first is figuring out the real nature of the problem—what really needs to be done, what are the means for doing it, and what information is or is not relevant. Then, when they have answered these questions, that is, when they have represented the problem clearly to themselves, they can try to solve it. GPS could take a well-represented problem and solve it but, unlike humans, it could not form that representation. Simon recognized that this was an important link that was missing in our understanding of human problem solving and initiated a project to fill in the gap.

I was lucky enough to work with Simon on this project. The work produced two running programs that are, in effect, very concrete theories about how humans form representations. Both programs took descriptions of problems written in English as their inputs. One of the programs (Hayes, Waterman, & Robinson, 1977) separated information in a written problem that was relevant for solving the problem from information that was not. The other (Hayes & Simon, 1975; Simon & Hayes, 1976) used the relevant information in the problem to form a problem representation that could be used by GPS to solve the problem. The importance of this work for my career in writing was that it was the occasion for me to use the tools of cognitive psychology, cognitive modeling, and protocol analysis for understanding human language use.

It was at this point that I met Linda Flower. Linda had been teaching writing strategies to students, so studying cognitive processes made sense to her. We decided that it would be interesting to apply cognitive methods—protocol analysis and cognitive modeling—to the analysis of writing. This decision led directly to the development of our first writing model (Hayes & Flower, 1980). Very supportive administrators and faculty members fostered a positive environment for writing research at Carnegie Mellon University. Lee Gregg and Irwin Steinberg (1980) organized the first symposium on cognitive processes in writing. The English Department, chaired by Richard Young, established a PhD program in rhetoric and document design and over the next 20 years produced 50 PhDs whose theses focused on empirical studies of writing.

Many of the students coming to English graduate programs did not have a background in empirical research. They tended to like language but not numbers. As a result, students were often unfamiliar with statistical methods and the rhetoric of empirical research that I mentioned earlier. To help fill this gap for Carnegie Mellon students, Richard Young and I developed a course tailored to the needs of aspiring writing researchers. Generally, the course worked well. However, we ran into an interesting pedagogical problem. An essential part of the training was to help students to become critical of studies by recognizing lurking variables, missing control groups, inadequate samples, and so on. In the course of this training, some students became hypercritical. No study appeared adequate to their critical eyes. The perfect had become the enemy of the good. To deal with this problem, we compiled, with the enthusiastic collaboration of four graduate students, what we called the "neat studies" book (Hayes et al., 1992). This book presented 18 of our favorite studies illustrating for students what we considered examples of very valuable professional quality research.

The book also attempted to deal with another problem. Some students were the opposite of hypercritical. In their published form, studies seemed so perfect to them that they couldn't imagine being able to do them themselves. To counter this tendency, we asked the writers of the articles to describe how the article had come about. Starting with the first idea or puzzlement that initiated the study, they described errors, false leads, and lucky breaks that occurred on the way to the final article. We hoped that these frank statements would humanize the research and help students to see it as an activity that they could engage in. I believe that the book was reasonably effective as a teaching tool, but, in any case, the collaboration that produced it was great fun.

WRITING RESEARCH: BOTH THEORETICAL AND APPLIED

Between 1978 and 2000 I engaged in a wide variety of theoretical and applied inquiries. On the applied side were numerous studies using protocol analysis to improve functional documents such as insurance policies and consumer electronics manuals (Bond, Hayes, & Flower, 1980; Flower, Hayes, & Swarts, 1980; Schriver & Hayes, 1994; Swaney, Janik, Bond, & Hayes, 1981). The underlying idea was that by studying protocols of people reading documents we could pinpoint the features that confused or misled them. This information could then be used to revise and improve the documents. Other lines of practical research involved evaluating reading on-line (Haas & Hayes, 1986) and assessing the consistency with which teachers graded essays (Hayes, Hatch, & Silk, 2000).

On the decidedly more theoretical side were efforts to develop general writing models. These included the Hayes-Flower model (Hayes & Flower, 1980) and my revision of that model (Hayes, 1996), designed to broaden its scope by adding working memory and motivation and to accommodate numerous research results obtained after 1980. Also my article with Nash on the nature of planning in writing was primarily theoretical (Hayes & Nash, 1996).

However, most of the studies I have engaged in have involved a mixture of collecting data about a practical writing problem together with modeling those data to provide better theoretical understanding of the problem. For example, an empirical study of how people paragraph (Bond & Hayes, 1984) yielded a model of a writer's use of linguistic and spatial cues to determine paragraph boundaries. Similarly, a set of empirical studies of text generation (Kaufer, Hayes, & Flower, 1986) resulted in a model of sentence production. And an empirical study of how people revise (Hayes, Flower, Shriver, Stratman, & Carey, 1987) inspired a model of revision. A theoretically oriented study of how freshmen revise (Wallace & Hayes, 1989) led to the development of a quick teaching procedure that demonstrably improved students' revision skill. A purely theoretical study of how we perceive the personality of others through their writing (Hatch, Hill, & Hayes, 1993) produced concrete suggestions about how students applying to college could better impress the adult audience they were addressing. This study inspired another study (Schriver, Hayes, & Steffy, 1995) that explored why teenagers are not persuaded by drug education literature that is written by adults.

Along with many of my colleagues, I believe that mixing theory and application is good practice. Concern with application keeps us grounded in what is important to people. Creating theories and models helps us to understand our data and guides us as to what we should explore next. It helps us to see the big picture and avoid getting lost in "dustbowl empiricism."

MY CURRENT INTERESTS

At present, I am involved in two major research activities: One is a search for bottlenecks in the composition process. The other is an effort to model text production in young children.

Searching for Bottlenecks

In an earlier study (Kaufer et al., 1986), I had been struck by the discontinuous way in which adults composed text. They seemed to spill out part of a sentence in a sudden burst of language and then pause to consider what to say next. It is as if some aspect of the composition process had been exhausted. Figure 1.1 illustrates this phenomenon. It shows a protocol of a writer composing a sentence to include in an essay about her job. Dashes indicate pauses of 2 seconds or more. In segment 1, the writer proposes a burst of language to serve as the beginning of a sentence but then pauses, not sure how to continue. Then, at segment 4, she proposes another language burst to serve as a continuation of the sentence and pauses again to consider how to continue.

1   2   3
The best thing about it is that – what? Something about using my mind –
         4   5
it allows me the opportunity to – uh – I want to write something about my
              6   7   8
ideas – to put ideas into action or to – develop my ideas into – what? –
              9   10   11   12   13
into a meaningful form? Oh, bleh! – say it allows me – to use - na! –
    14   15   16
allows me –scratch that – The best thing about it is that it allows me to
                 17
use – my mind and my ideas in a productive way.

Figure 1.1   Think-aloud protocol of a writer composing one sentence of an essay.

Writing protocols reveal that writers typically compose in this way. However, in roughly 10% of cases, language bursts are terminated by a revision rather than a pause. For example, segments 9 and 12 appear to be terminated by revisions. We differentiated between these two types of bursts, calling the first *pause bursts* and the second *revision bursts*. We made the distinction because the pause bursts seemed to reflect a language creation process running to exhaustion, whereas pause bursts seemed to reflect an interrupted creation process. As it turned out, the distinction was an appropriate one. Variables, such as memory load, influence the two very differently.

This phenomenon—pause bursting—seemed to me to reflect a bottleneck in the writing process. However, although I always had it in the back of my mind, I didn't begin to investigate just where that bottleneck might be until nearly 15 years later. In 2001, Ann Chenoweth and I began a series of studies that is still under way. All of these studies focus on the length of the language bursts that writers produce in various circumstances.

In the first study (Chenoweth & Hayes, 2001), we compared students writing in their first language (L1) with the same students writing in a second language (L2). Students produced significantly longer bursts (about 60% longer) in L1 than L2. Clearly, linguistic experience was an important factor influencing burst length.

In our next study (Chenoweth & Hayes, 2003), we explored the impact of restricting verbal working memory on burst length. Participants were asked to write a sentence describing a wordless cartoon. In the experimental condition, writers repeated the word tap 120 times a minute in time to a metronome. This activity, called articulatory suppression, has been shown to interfere with the writer's verbal working memory. Writers in the control conditions tapped a foot in time to the metronome or did nothing. Writers in the control conditions produced bursts that were about 50% longer than bursts of writers in the articulatory suppression condition. Clearly, the availability of verbal working memory was also an important factor influencing burst length.

Our next question was, which specific writing processes are responsible for producing language bursts? To guide us in exploring this question, we used the

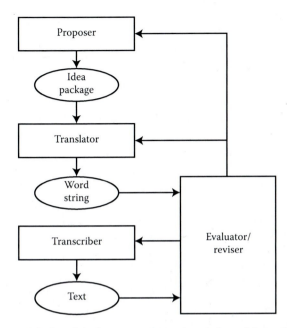

Figure 1.2   A simplified model of written composition. (Adapted from Chenoweth, N. A., and Hayes, J. R., *Written Communication*, 20, 99–118, 2003.)

simplified model of cognitive writing processes shown in Figure 1.2. According to this model, ideas for text are generated by the *proposer* who sends an idea package, either in verbal or nonverbal form, to the *translator*. For extended texts, the *proposer* would also provide planning and goal-setting functions. The *translator* then creates a new language string based on the idea package. The language string is then vetted by the *evaluator/reviser* and, if accepted, is passed to the *transcriber* to be turned into text. The *reviser* can call for change at any point in the process from idea generation to transcription. The *reviser* makes changes by calling recursively on the other writing processes.

Our question, then, was which of these processes could be responsible for pause bursts? We argued, on logical grounds, that revision was unlikely to be the source of language bursts, since, by definition, the revision process was not active during pause bursts.

We then asked, could the transcription process be a source of bursts? To answer this question, we asked participants to do a simple transcription task (Hayes & Chenoweth, 2006). We found that essentially no bursts occurred while participants were simply transcribing text without composing it. The transcription process itself did not appear to be a source of bursts. Thus, we had narrowed the possibilities down to the proposer and the translator.

The observation that burst length is sensitive to linguistic experience (Chenoweth & Hayes, 2001) suggested to us that the translation process was likely involved in creating language bursts. Thus, in our next experiment, we (Hayes & Chenoweth, 2007) searched for evidence that the translation process by itself, that is, without the proposer, could be a source of bursts. To test this idea, we asked participants to perform a task that involved translation but not idea generation. Specifically, we asked them to translate passive sentences into active form. Thus, they had to create new language but not new ideas. We found that in this task, participants routinely produced bursts while carrying out the translations from passive to active voice. These results are consistent with the position that the working memory limitations of the translation process cause language bursts and that these memory limitations constitute a bottleneck, limiting writers' fluency. A more detailed summary of these results may be found elsewhere (Hayes, 2009). The studies I have described so far do not rule out the possibility that the proposer could also be a source of language bursts. The answer to this question awaits new studies.

Modeling Children's Writing Processes

Recently I have turned my attention to modeling children's writing processes. I believe that by providing specific models to account for children's writing behavior at various ages, we can make it easier to identify the specific changes in process that are involved in writing development. My first effort has been to try to model the processes by which children create text at various ages.

In their classic work, Bereiter and Scardamalia (1987) proposed two models of text production—*knowledge-telling*, a relatively primitive procedure most characteristic of children's writing, and *knowledge-transforming*, a more sophisticated process characteristic of skilled writing. In knowledge-telling, the writer chooses a topic and then creates a series of statements about that topic. Bereiter and Scardamalia proposed the model, shown in a simplified version in Figure 1.3, to characterize the knowledge-telling process. Figure 1.4 shows the kind of text that a writer using the knowledge-telling process could produce. As the name suggests, this process is focused on presenting the writer's knowledge and not at all on adjusting that knowledge to the readers' needs. Thus, we can characterize it as a nonrhetorical writing process. In contrast, writers using knowledge-transforming engage in a rhetorical process in which they try to shape their knowledge to meet the readers' needs. These two models are the most widely accepted models for describing writing development.

In preparing myself to explore the issue of modeling children's writing, I read extensively the work of Virginia Berninger and her colleagues. In particular, I read Berninger and Swanson's (1994) article, about adapting the Hayes-Flower model

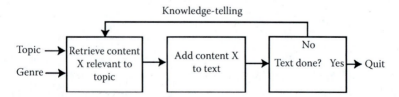

Figure 1.3   A simplified version of Bereiter and Scardamalia's knowledge-telling model.

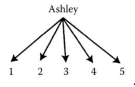

I like Ashley cus she is nice. (1)

I like Ashley cus she plays with me. (2)

Ashley is my friend. (3)

I like people and Ashley is one. (4)

She is nice. (5)

Figure 1.4   A text from Fuller (1995) consistent with the knowledge-telling model.

to describe children's writing, and the article by Berninger, Fuller, and Whitaker (1996). The latter article reported observations from the dissertation of Francis Fuller (Fuller, 1995), a student of Berninger. Fuller analyzed the structures of children's texts collected by Berninger and Swanson (see Berninger & Swanson, 1994) that were written in response to both expository and narrative prompts. Fuller's analysis led me to suspect that perhaps children produced text structures that could not be accounted for by Bereiter and Scardamalia's (1987) two models.

Following this lead, I reanalyzed the 540 texts presented in Fuller's thesis. As a result of this analysis, I concluded that there is a distinct intermediate strategy between knowledge-telling and knowledge-transforming, a strategy that I call *knowledge-structuring*. The knowledge-structuring model is shown in Figure 1.5. This model differs from knowledge-telling because it contains a loop that allows writers to expand on subtopics, something that the knowledge-telling model does not allow. Figure 1.6 shows a text written by a third-grade child that could be produced by the knowledge-structuring model but not the knowledge-telling model. Changes in the distribution of the text structures that children produce suggest that knowledge-structuring replaces knowledge-telling as young writers' most used strategy roughly between the fourth and fifth grades. The knowledge-structuring model is nonrhetorical (it has no mechanism for adjusting to the readers' needs) and, in this way, it clearly differs from the knowledge-transforming model.

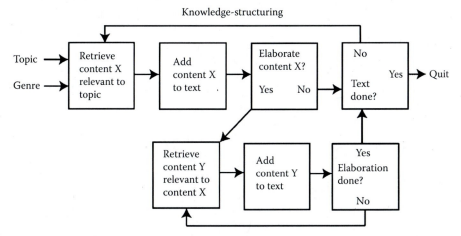

Figure 1.5   Graphic depiction of knowledge-structuring model.

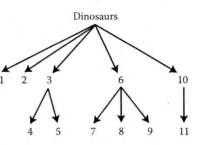

Dinosaurs

I like dinosaurs because they are big. (1) And they are scary. (2) I like Rex. (3) He was very big. (4) He ate meat. (5) Triceratops is a very nice dinosaur. (6) He ate plants. (7) He had three horns on his fass [sic]. (8) He had a shield on his neck. (9) Stegosaurus was a plant eater too. (10) He had (unfinished) (11).

Figure 1.6   A third grader's text from Fuller (1995) that could be produced by the knowledge-structuring model but not the knowledge-telling model. Note that the misspelling of "face" as "fass" appeared in the original child's essay.

I believe that the use of knowledge-structuring depends on the child's acquiring the ability to use subgoals in the task of writing. I speculate that this acquisition initiates a sequence of events that results between the fifth and seventh grades in a major change in the way they plan their texts. This work was described in a paper presented at WRAB in 2011 (Hayes, 2011). I am hoping to expand this work by modeling other aspects of the writing process as it develops from first grade through high school.

MY THOUGHTS ABOUT THE FUTURE OF WRITING RESEARCH

Below I discuss five areas that I believe writing researchers should pay more attention to. I argue that advances in each of these areas can provide substantial benefits for writing research. Some of these areas, such as brain-scanning studies, are relatively certain to blossom because of the obvious usefulness of the information they can provide. For other areas though, the future seems less certain. For example, although I believe that greater emphasis on motivation and greater mutual respect among writing researchers in different paradigms would be very beneficial, it is less clear that these changes are likely to occur. In any case, here are my arguments for what I believe would be helpful changes in our field.

Brain Scanning Studies

Brain imaging techniques, such as positron emission tomography, functional magnetic resonance imaging (fMRI), electroencephalography, and magnetoencephalography, are currently transforming research in cognitive psychology and spurring a new paradigm shift toward cognitive neuroscience (see Chapter 23, this volume). Such techniques are useful, not only for locating brain injuries and anomalies, but also for understanding cognitive processes in the normal brain. For example, the logician Boole (1854) proposed abstract syllogisms such as:

All A are B
All B are C
Therefore, all A are C

as models of human reasoning. However, psychologists have found that people seem to reason differently when dealing with such abstract materials than when reasoning about concrete information such as "All poodles are dogs." Psychologists suspected that different cognitive processes might be involved in the two kinds of tasks. An fMRI study by Goel, Buchel, Frith, and Dolan (2000) revealed that reasoning about concrete materials actually took place in different brain regions than reasoning about abstract materials, thus confirming the suspicion.

Brain imaging studies are also yielding insights into the writing brain, both its acquired and developmental disorders and its normal development. Studies described in Chapter 23, this volume, review interesting brain scanning studies comparing normal writers with writers who are dyslexic or dysgraphic. These studies clearly illustrate the promise of brain scanning studies for helping us understand the nature of writing processes. Imaging studies, which can generate data at the brain level of analysis to test hypotheses, in conjunction with data at the cognitive and behavioral levels, are likely to expand exponentially and increase in sophistication as technology continues to advance.

Research on Development of Text Produced So Far

Kaufer et al. (1986) showed that adult writers pay considerable attention to the text produced so far (TPSF) as they are composing. Attending to the TPSF can serve several functions. It can promote internal coherence by reminding writers of their choices of number, tense, and wording. It can serve as a source for idea generation by providing the writer with opportunities to trigger associations with earlier content. Further, it can be a valuable occasion to revise what has just been written. In contrast to adults, very young children appear to pay little attention to what they have just written. Presumably, the child's inclination to attend to the TPSF develops over the school years. If we were to study the development of children's attention to the TPSF, we could potentially obtain valuable insights into the increasing coherence of children's texts and the increasing effectiveness of revision in children's writing. Such studies might be carried out using technology such as that developed by Alamargot, Chesnet, Dansac, and Ros (2006).

Creation of Frameworks

Throughout my career, I have found the creation of frameworks very helpful for summarizing relations in data and for promoting new research projects. By a framework, I mean any representation designed to help us think about complex processes (see Hayes, 2006). A framework can be as simple as a list to remind us of a set of categories. For example, anthropologists have used this list—*bands*, *tribes*, *chiefdoms*, and *states*—as one framework to describe the organization of human societies. In contrast, a framework may be as complex as theories in physics or engineering that specify precise quantitative relations among variables.

In writing research we are more likely to encounter frameworks (often called models) that specify the direction of relations among variables but typically do not do so with quantitative precision. The Hayes-Flower model (1980) is an example

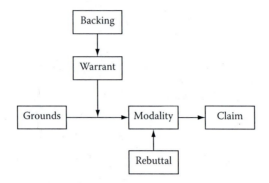

Figure 1.7   Toulmin's model for argument. (Adapted from Toulmin, S., Rieke, R., and Janik, A., *An Introduction to Reasoning*, Macmillan, New York, 1979.)

of such a framework, as is the framework by Toulmin, Rieke, and Janik (1979), for describing arguments, as shown in Figure 1.7.

Frameworks help for a number of reasons, and new ones are likely to be proposed and developed in future writing research. First, they can provide a common language for discussion and for teaching. The anthropologists' framework mentioned above can obviously serve these functions. Second, frameworks can help us notice relations in data. For example, a teacher grading student papers might notice that some of the arguments are less effective than others. However, without the framework by Toulmin et al. or one like it, she might not notice that a common feature of the less effective papers was that they failed to provide backing for the argument. Recognizing this common feature could lead to improvements in the teacher's instructional strategies. Third, frameworks can embody empirical predictions. For example, Hayes et al. (1987) proposed a model for revision that included "the reviser's definition of the task" (p. 186) as a major component. Using this framework, Wallace and Hayes (1989) predicted and then demonstrated empirically that training in defining the revision task in an appropriate way significantly improved first-year college students' revisions. Fourth, creating frameworks can encourage us to commit to a specific view of the world. Without the focus provided by commitment to a view, we are less likely to notice whether or not observations fit that view. For example, the anthropologists' framework commits to just four forms of organization that societies can assume—not three or five. In the context of this framework, the discovery of a fifth form will be seen as significant. The kind of clear commitment that is promoted by creating frameworks helps us to increase knowledge in our field.

To elaborate on the fourth advantage of models, creating models of writing activities forces us to speculate in specific and productive ways about what writers are doing. These specific hypotheses, right or wrong, provide the opportunity to check our ideas against observation and in the best cases set us off in search for data to check our hypotheses. This process of hypothesis formation and testing results in the accumulation of tested ideas that we can rely on in designing applications and further scientific explorations.

As a note of caution, we should recognize that not all frameworks are equally effective in promoting new knowledge. The terms of a framework must be defined sufficiently clearly so that those using the framework can be confident they are using a common language. For example, it is important for anthropologists to be able to agree on the distinction between a state and a chiefdom.

The Importance of Motivation

My most serious concern with the cognitive paradigm is that it has paid insufficient attention to motivation. Hilgard (1987) noted that with the advent of the cognitive paradigm there was a decline in attention to motivation. He attributed the decline in part to the fact that cognitive theories were not based in physiology, and that the study of physiologically based drives, such as hunger, thirst, and sex, had been a traditional source of interest in motivation. Whatever the reasons for the omission, cognitive psychology definitely has not focused on motivation. However, because motivational issues are a common concern in the field of writing, writing researchers can ill afford to ignore it. (See Hidi and Boscolo, 2006, for an account of the recent emergence of interest in motivation and writing.)

I have argued (Hayes, 1996) that it is appropriate for writing researchers to expand the cognitive perspective to an individual perspective that integrates cognitive and motivational factors. To illustrate how this might be done in a concrete case, I will discuss modeling of the relation between transcription and other writing processes in the context of an essay-writing task.

In the past decade and a half, there has been a tremendous advance in the understanding of the role that transcription plays in the development of writing. Pioneering work by Berninger and her colleagues (Berninger et al., 1992; Berninger, Cartwright, Yates, Swanson, & Abbott, 1994) showed that individual differences in handwriting and spelling were related to composition length and quality. Their instructional studies showed that the relationships were causal. When they were given training in handwriting or spelling, children wrote better compositions. Similarly Jones and Christensen (1999) found that handwriting practice improved the quality of children's texts written by hand. And Christensen (2004) showed that typing practice improved typed text quality, but not length or quality of handwritten texts, in eighth and ninth graders with low typing skills. Connelly, Gee, and Walsh (2007) compared fifth and sixth graders' essays written by hand and by keyboard. Students wrote significantly faster by hand than keyboard. Berninger, Abbott, Augsburger, and Garcia (2009) found that children wrote longer essays and wrote words faster by pen than by keyboard. De La Paz and Graham (1995) found that primary school children's texts improved significantly in quality if they dictated rather than wrote their texts. Studying second-, fourth-, and sixth-grade students, Hayes and Berninger (2010) found that older children included more ideas in their essays than younger children when composing either by handwriting or typing. We can summarize these results as follows:

1. The more demanding the transcription mode, the more transcription will interfere with other writing processes (mode effect). Thus, typing produces more interference than handwriting, and handwriting, in turn, produces more interference than dictation.
2. The more experienced the writer is with the transcription task, the less transcription will interfere with other writing processes (experience effect). Thus, older children and children with training in a particular transcription mode will tend to experience less interference than other children.

Typically such effects have been interpreted in cognitive terms. For example, Berninger and Swanson (1994) argued that transcription interferes with other writing processes because it requires substantial working memory resources that are therefore not available to other writing processes. In a study of the relation of transcription to idea generation, Hayes and Berninger (2010) concluded that their results were "consistent with the view that transcription processes may interfere with children's ability to express ideas in written language" (p. 178). These theoretical ideas may be summarized as follows:

1. Less practiced or more difficult transcription modes tend to require more cognitive resources.
2. As writers get more experience with a transcription mode, the amount of cognitive resources required by that transcription mode decreases.
3. The more cognitive resources used by transcription, the more transcription will interfere with other writing activities such as idea generation, translation, and revision because there will be fewer cognitive resources available for carrying out these activities.

In this cognitive perspective, it is easy to envision how heavy demands on cognitive resources could slow composition. Lack of cognitive resources could slow writing processes or force writers to execute these processes in sequence rather than in parallel. However, it is less obvious, from a purely cognitive perspective, how reduced cognitive resources could lead writers to write less. For example, why should a child write a shorter essay while typing than while handwriting? If a young child is using a knowledge-telling strategy (see Figure 1.3), each sentence is produced in essentially the same way as the previous one. Demands on cognitive resources will be cyclical. These demands may vary during a production of a sentence: starting at some baseline value, perhaps peaking for young writers during transcription, and then returning to baseline. During production of the next sentence, demands on cognitive resources go through a similar cycle. The critical point is that *demands on cognitive resources do not accumulate over sentences.* If the child can produce one sentence, whether she is speaking, handwriting, or typing, there is no reason, based on cognitive resources alone, why she could not be able to produce any number of sentences. Thus, a purely cognitive perspective may not offer an easy account of the fact that children produce longer essays when dictating than when handwriting than when typing. I believe the most natural way to account for the effects of transcription mode on the length of children's essays is with a perspective that integrates cognitive and affective factors. This perspective holds that the transcription process may, in some cases, act not so much to interfere with children's *ability* to carry out other writing activities as it does to reduce children's *willingness* to carry out those activities.

A motivation-focused theory is proposed to account for interference between transcription and other writing processes. With the motivation-focused theory, we assume that the child's motivation for producing text depends on a balance of positive and negative factors. Positive factors may include a desire to please the teacher or to avoid the teacher's disapproval, and perhaps an intrinsic interest in the task. Negative factors, as Berninger and Swanson (1994) suggested, include the difficulty of spelling and handwriting for transcribing text. Presumably, the heavy demands that transcription places on cognitive resources such as working memory and attention contribute to the perceived effortfulness of these activities. However, these are not the only negative factors. Somatic factors may make transcription unpleasant as well.

Data reported by Kos and Maslowski (2001) (shown in Figure 1.8) indicate that the discomfort of holding a pencil can contribute to the unpleasantness of transcription for young children. A central assumption of the theory is that these negative factors can cumulate. That is, they can become more intense with the continuation of the activity. Thus, a second-grade child may be willing to write out three sentences for her teacher but perhaps not six. We assume that when the negative factors outweigh the positive ones, the child will decide to stop. Just when the tipping point is reached may depend on a kind of negotiation between the teacher and the child. I hypothesize that the child examines the text she has written so far to determine whether or not she has produced enough text to satisfy the teacher. Here, the child is responding to the teacher not as reader/audience but rather as taskmaster. The child's estimate of what the teacher will accept presumably depends on the child's history of interaction with the teacher, and perhaps with other teachers, over a period of time. In turn, the teacher's estimate of what the child can be expected to produce is the product of experience with the child and with other children of the same age and circumstances.

The theory accounts for the mode effect as a result of the relative unpleasantness of the various transcription methods. For young children, handwriting is difficult and typing is even more difficult (Connelly et al., 2007). Indeed, some children might avoid transcription entirely if their teachers did not encourage them to do it. In contrast, as many parents will attest, it is the rare child who tires of speaking.

Lysbeth: My finger hurts. See right here, my finger hurts. (She has redness at her middle knuckle where she is holding her pencil.)

Teacher: Do you want to change anything? Why not?

Carol: 'Cause I like it and I don't like writing that much, 'cause I got a bump where I been writing a lot.

Figure 1.8   Evidence that writing can be physically painful for second-grade children (Based on Kos, R., and Maslowski, C., *Elementary School Journal*, 101, 567–585, 2001.)

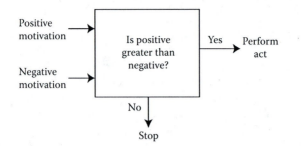

Figure 1.9   Structure of an affective decision mechanism.

The motivation-focused theory accounts for the experience effect as a result of children's increasing facility, and hence, reduced difficulty, with handwriting and keyboarding. As children's motor skills improve, it becomes easier for them to handle a pencil (or strike a key) and to form letters. As their knowledge of the written language increases, spelling becomes less onerous. As a result of these changes, the unpleasantness of transcription will lessen.

Notice that, although the theory emphasizes motivation, it also includes roles for practice, demands on cognitive resources, physical development, and social interaction. The theory makes specific empirical predictions. For example, it predicts that if a teacher encourages a child to produce more text after she has decided to stop, then the child will typically write more sentences. This prediction is confirmed in data collected by Berninger and Swanson (1994). The theory also predicts that a child will produce more text if she observes that other children have produced long texts. Indeed, the theory predicts that any manipulation that increases or decreases the writer's motivation will influence the amount of text that writers will produce.

Because I have presented the motivation-focused theory in narrative form, one may ask how one would actually include affective factors into a formal cognitive model. I propose that a convenient way to integrate affective factors into cognitive models is to use *affective decision mechanisms* (ADMs) such as that shown in Figure 1.9.

An ADM is a mechanism that takes in information about the positive and negative motivations for performing an act and decides to perform the act if the balance of motivations is positive and not to perform the act if the balance is negative.[1] An affective-cognitive model to account for the effects of transcription mode on text length might include an ADM as the front end of a cognitive model of the writing process such as a knowledge-telling or a knowledge-structuring model.

To summarize, I suggest that we may better be able to understand writing by making use of models that integrate affect and cognition. I am not asserting that every writing phenomenon requires the inclusion of motivation for its explanation. I am simply asserting that for some phenomena, an integrated cognitive-affective

---

[1] One can also imagine cognitive decision mechanisms that use cognitive information about alternative courses of action. For example, chess-playing programs that compare the probability of success of alternative move sequences could be thought of as including cognitive decision mechanisms.

model may be helpful. I believe such models can be especially useful for predicting writers' persistence in activities, such as planning, idea generation, and essay writing.

Relations Among Paradigms

There are multiple perspectives among current writing researchers. Some focus on culture, others on linguistics, and still others on power relations among groups. Although there is no necessity for these perspectives to be anything but complementary and mutually supportive, it is a fact that turf wars are not uncommon.

A while ago, I was involved in a project on creativity that revealed a great deal to me about the interaction among different perspectives. The project was inspired by the work of Chase and Simon (1973). These authors estimated that chess players, by the time they reached the level of grand master, had learned approximately 50,000 chess patterns. For even the most precocious players, this learning required about 10 years of intensive practice. I wondered if a similar effect might be observed in creative activities such as musical composition or painting. So I set about examining the biographies of great composers to find out when they first became seriously involved in music and when they produced their most notable works. The question was, would the great composers of the past three centuries need years of practice before they began to produce the works for which they were famous?

To get advice about my research, I went to an experienced musicologist and explained my project to him. He was not impressed. He told me, in a nice way, that my study was not worth doing. The aesthetic goals of musicians, who composed in different centuries and in different artistic traditions, were so diverse that there could be nothing in common among them. Therefore, no consistent results could be expected.

The musicologist's argument was certainly a reasonable one. However, I didn't agree with it. He came from a perspective emphasizing the importance of cultural and historical influences. I came from a perspective emphasizing the importance of individual factors such as practice. It is not surprising that he guessed that the effects of cultural differences would mask the effects of practice and that I guessed the opposite.

In fact, I found the results shown in Figure 1.10. Of the 76 composers I studied, 73 had had 10 or more years of practice before they wrote the first work for which they became famous, and the remaining three had either 8 or 9 years. I found similar results for painters. Practice, then, clearly had an impact on creative performance, even though cultural factors must surely have been operating as well.

My point here is not that one perspective won out over another. Indeed, I don't think that happened. Both the musicologist and I agreed that practice and cultural factors are important, but we disagreed on their relative importance. Perhaps if I had broadened the range of cultural differences, say by including Middle Eastern, African, and Oriental music in my study, cultural factors might have had a greater impact. The most important point, though, is that if my study had failed to produce robust results, the musicologist's perspective would have helped me to interpret the outcome. I would have been alerted to the need to take account of cultural

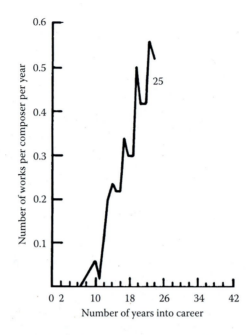

Figure 1.10 Average numbers of compositions produced for each year in the compos-er's career. (Based on Hayes, J. R., in *Thinking and Learning Skills*, 391–405, Erlbaum, Hillsdale, NJ, 1985.)

differences in looking for answers to the questions I was asking. Perspectives can be mutually supportive in this way. When different perspectives make different predictions, each has the potential to enrich the other.

The importance of considering alternative perspectives is not limited to those cases where one perspective plays a dominant role. It is reasonable to believe that in many cases, both individual and cultural factors have significant impact. For example, a recent series of studies suggests that the symbols that various cultures choose to represent their language—their letters, logograms, signs—are strongly influenced both by cultural and cognitive factors. For example, Changizi, Zhang, Ye, and Shimojo (2006) carried out a sequence of studies on the topological forms of symbols used in visual communication systems. These systems included (a) symbols used to represent 96 ancient and modern nonlogographic languages, (b) Chinese logographs, and (c) nonlinguistic symbols such as traffic signs. Their first result was that the distribution of topological forms in the three systems was constrained (some forms were used much more frequently than others); and more surprising, the distribution of forms was quite similar in all three of the systems. The authors checked to see if the constraint might be due to random factors. For example, they wondered if just placing marks on paper at random or writing without the intention to communicate as in children's scribbling might also produce the same sort of distribution. It did not.

Second, the authors compared systems that were intended to facilitate writing ver-sus those intended to facilitate reading. In particular, they measured the distribution of forms produced by five shorthand methods. Shorthand is designed to make it easy to transcribe spoken language. It is not designed to produce text that everyone can read. They also measured the distribution of forms in trademarks—symbols that are meant to be read but not written. They found that the distribution for trademarks was very similar to that for the communication systems discussed above and very different from that for shorthand. The authors concluded that the distribution for communication systems appeared to be chosen to facilitate reading rather than writing.

Third, the authors found that the characteristic distribution of forms in signaling systems matched that of forms found in natural scenes. This final piece of evidence allowed the authors to construct a reasonable story about how our writing systems were shaped. Over millennia, evolution shaped our perceptual mechanisms to respond to important features of natural scenes—features that allowed us to identify objects important for our survival. Visual communication systems such as alphabets appeared about 5,000 years ago—not nearly enough time for us to evolve special perceptual mechanisms for perceiving written symbols. Rather, people employed the already evolved mechanisms for viewing natural scenes and used these mechanisms to read visual symbols. The particular symbols we use for communication depend on cultural choice. Clearly, different cultures have chosen different symbols to use for communication. However, for all cultures, the choice of symbols is constrained by human capacity to perceive and distinguish them. Over time, contrasts that are hard to make will be replaced by contrasts that are easier to make. That is, cultural choices of symbols will be subjected to a kind of natural selection. The symbol set that survives is the one that fits well with the preexisting human perceptual system. Symbols that are not easily discriminated by the perceptual system will be weeded out.

This is the story that Changizi et al. (2006) constructed and it is consistent with the data they have collected. The relevance of this story here is that it illustrates how cultural choices may be influenced by the cognitive makeup of the individuals within the culture. Part of understanding a culture is understanding the cognitive and motivational makeup of the individuals within that culture.

Unfortunately, although different perspectives can be mutually supportive, often they are not. Perspectives have a tendency to produce paradigm zealots, that is, people who believe that there is one best way to approach a topic and that other approaches are simply wrong or, in extreme cases, evil. As I noted earlier, I was a paradigm zealot when I first took up the behaviorist cause. The result was that I closed myself off from the interesting stream of results that the social psychologists on campus were discovering. Unfortunately, paradigm zealots don't just injure themselves. When such people occupy influential positions in granting agencies and journals, they can deny funding and publication to researchers who do not share their perspective.

It is not necessary that researchers pursue the same project, use the same methods, or embrace the same global theories. Diversity increases our chances of discovering productive paths. What is important, though, is that we respect one another as people who are all honestly trying to make sense out of a very confusing world, and that we are open enough to be able to make use of ideas from other perspectives when they are relevant to our own work.

REFERENCES

Alamargot, D., Chesnet, D., Dansac, C., & Ros, C. (2006). Eye and pen: A new device for studying reading during writing. *Behavior Research Methods, 38*(2), 278–299.

Bereiter, C., & Scardamalia, M. (1987). *The psychology of written composition.* Hillsdale, NJ: Erlbaum.

Berninger, V., Abbott, R., Augsburger, A., & Garcia, N. (2009). Comparison of pen and keyboard transcription modes in children with and without learning disabilities affecting transcription. *Learning Disability Quarterly, 32*, 123–141.

Berninger, V., Cartwright, A., Yates, C., Swanson, H. L., & Abbott, R. (1994). Developmental skills related to writing and reading acquisition in the intermediate grades: Shared and unique variance. *Reading and Writing: An Interdisciplinary Journal, 6*, 161–196.

Berninger, V., Fuller, F., & Whitaker, D. (1996). A process model of writing development across the life span. *Educational Psychology Review, 8*, 193–218.

Berninger, V., & Swanson, H. L. (1994). Modifications of Hayes and Flower's model to explain beginning and developing writing. In E. Butterfield (Ed.), *Children's writing: Toward a process theory of development of skilled writing* (pp. 57–81). Greenwich, CT: JAI Press.

Berninger, V., Yates, C., Cartwright, A., Rutberg, J., Remy, E., & Abbott, R. (1992). Lower-level developmental skills in beginning writing. *Reading and Writing: An Interdisciplinary Journal, 4*, 257–280.

Bond, S. J., & Hayes, J. R. (1984). Cues people use to paragraph text. *Research in the Teaching of English, 18*, 147–167.

Bond, S. J., Hayes, J. R., & Flower, L. S. (1980, April). *Translating the law into common language: A protocol study.* Report No. 8, Document Design Project, Pittsburgh, PA: Carnegie Mellon University.

Boole, G. (1854). *The laws of thought.* New York: Dover Press.

Changizi, M. A., Zhang, Q., Ye, H., & Shimojo, S. (2006). The structure of letters and symbols throughout human history are selected to match those found in objects in natural scenes. *American Naturalist, 167*(5), E117–E139.

Chase, W. G., & Simon, H. A. (1973). The mind's eye in chess. In W. G. Chase (Ed.), *Visual information processing* (pp. 215–281). New York: Academic Press.

Chenoweth, N. A., & Hayes, J. R. (2001 January). Fluency in writing: Generating text in L1 and L2. *Written Communication, 18*, 80–98.

Chenoweth, N. A., & Hayes, J. R. (2003) The inner voice in writing. *Written Communication, 20*, 99–118.

Chomsky, N. (1959). Review of verbal behavior, by Skinner. *Language, 35*, 26–58.

Christensen, C. A. (2004). Relationship between orthographic-motor integration and computer use for the production of creative and well-structured text. *British Journal of Educational Psychology, 74*, 551–564.

Connelly, V., Gee, D., & Walsh, E. (2007). A comparison of keyboarded and handwritten compositions and the relationship with transcription speed. *British Journal of Educational Psychology, 77*, 479–492.

De La Paz, S., & Graham, S. (1995). Dictation: Applications to writing for students with learning disabilities. In T. Scruggs & M. Mastropieri (Eds.), *Advances in learning and behavioral disorders* (Vol. 9, pp. 227–247). Greenwich, CT: JAI Press.

Flower, L. S., Hayes, J. R., & Swarts, H. (1980, March). Reader-based revision of functional documents: The scenario principle. (Report No. 10, Document Design Project). Carnegie-Mellon University.

Fuller, D. F. (1995). *Development of topic-comment algorithms and test structures in written compositions of students in grades one through nine.* (Unpublished doctoral dissertation). University of Washington.

Goel, V., Buchal, C., Frith, C., & Dolan, R. (2000). Dissociation of mechanisms underlying syllogistic reasoning. *Neuroimage, 12,* 504–514.

Gregg, L., & Steinberg, E. (1980). *Cognitive processes in writing: An interdisciplinary approach.* Hillsdale, NJ: Erlbaum.

Haas, C., & Hayes, J. R. (1986). What did I just say? Reading problems in writing with the machine. *Research in the Teaching of English, 20*(1), 22–35.

Hatch, J. A., Hill, C. A., & Hayes, J. R. (1993). When the messenger is the message. *Written Communication, 10*(4), 569–598.

Hayes, J. R. (1985). Three problems in teaching general skills. In S. Chipman, J. Segal, & R. Glaser (Eds.), *Thinking and learning skills* (pp. 391–405). Hillsdale, NJ: Erlbaum.

Hayes, J. R. (1996). A new model of cognition and affect in writing. In M. Levy & S. Ransdell (Eds.), *The science of writing. Theories, methods, individual differences, and applications* (pp. 1–27). Hillsdale, NJ: Erlbaum.

Hayes, J. R. (2006). New directions in writing theory. In C. A. MacArthur, S. Graham, & J. Fitzgerald (Eds.), *Handbook of writing research* (pp. 28–40). New York: Guilford.

Hayes, J. R. (2009). From idea to text. In D. Myhill (Ed.), *Handbook of writing development* (pp. 65–79). London: Sage.

Hayes, J. R. (2011, February). *Reevaluating knowledge-telling: Modeling early writing development.* Paper presented at Writing Research Across Borders II Conference, George Mason University, Fairfax, VA.

Hayes, J. R., & Berninger, V. (2010). Relationships between idea generation and transcription: How act of writing shapes what children write. In C. Bazerman, R. Krut, K. Lunsford, S. McLeod, S. Null, P. Rogers, & A. Stansell (Eds.), *Traditions of writing research* (pp. 166–180). New York: Taylor & Frances/Routledge.

Hayes, J. R., & Chenoweth, N. A. (2006). Is working memory involved in the transcribing and editing of texts? *Written Communication, 23,* 135–149.

Hayes, J. R., & Chenoweth, N. A. (2007). Working memory in an editing task. *Written Communication, 24*(4), 283–294.

Hayes, J. R., & Flower, L. S. (1980). Identifying the organization of writing processes. In L. Gregg & E. Steinberg (Eds.), *Cognitive processes in writing: An interdisciplinary approach* (pp. 3–30). Hillsdale, NJ: Erlbaum.

Hayes, J. R., Flower, L., Schriver, K. A., Stratman, J., & Carey, L. (1987). Cognitive processes in revision. In S. Rosenberg (Ed.), *Advances in psycholinguistics. Vol. 2: Reading, writing, and language* (pp. 176–240). Cambridge: Cambridge University Press.

Hayes, J. R., Hatch, J. A., & Silk, C. M. (2000). Does holistic assessment predict writing? *Written Communication, 17*(1), 3–26.

Hayes, J. R., & Nash, J. G. (1996). On the nature of planning in writing. In M. Levy & S. Ransdell (Eds.), *The science of writing* (pp. 29–55). Hillsdale, NJ: Erlbaum.

Hayes, J. R., & Simon, H. A. (1975). Understanding written problem instructions. In L. W. Gregg (Ed.), *Knowledge and cognition* (pp. 167–200). Potomac, MD: Erlbaum.

Hayes, J. R., Waterman, D. A., & Robinson, C. S. (1977). Identifying the relevant aspects of a problem text. *Cognitive Science, 1*(3), 297–313.

Hayes, J. R., Young, R., Matchett, M., McCaffrey, M., Cochran, C., & Hajduk, T. (1992). *Empirical research in literacy: The emerging rhetorical tradition.* Hillsdale, NJ: Erlbaum.

Hidi, S., & Boscolo, P. (Eds.). (2006). *Motivation in writing.* Amsterdam, Elsevier/Emerald.

Hilgard, E. R. (1987). *Psychology in America: A historical survey.* San Diego: Harcourt Brace Jovanovich.

Jones, D. A., & Christensen, C. A. (1999). Relationship between automaticity in handwriting and students' ability to generate written text. *Journal of Educational Psychology, 91,* 1–6.

Kaufer, D. S., Hayes, J. R., & Flower, L. (1986). Composing written sentences. *Research in the Teaching of English, 20*(2), 121–140.

Kos, R., & Maslowski, C. (2001). Second graders' perception of what is important in writing. *Elementary School Journal, 101*, 567–585.

Miller, G. A. (1956). The magic number seven, plus or minus two: Some limits on our capacity for processing information. *Psychological Review, 63*, 81–97.

Newell, A., Shaw, J. C., & Simon, H. A. (1959). Report on a general problem-solving program. In *Proceedings of the International Conference on Information Processing* (pp. 256–264). Paris: UNESCO.

Newell, A., and Simon, H. A. (1956). The logic theory machine. *IRE Transactions on Information Theory, IT-2*(3), 61–79.

Schriver, K. A., & Hayes, J. R. (1994). The impact of product complexity in using consumer electronics. *Performance Improvement Quarterly, 7*(3), 76–84.

Schriver, K. A., Hayes, J. R., & Steffy, A. (1995). *Reading the message of drug education literature: How teenagers' beliefs about the messenger shape interpretation.* (Interim report). Office of Educational Research and Improvement.

Simon, H. A., & Hayes, J. R. (1976). The understanding process: Problem isomorphs. *Cognitive Psychology, 8*, 165–190.

Skinner, B. F. (1957). *Verbal behavior.* New York: Appleton-Century-Crofts.

Swaney, J. H., Janik, C. J., Bond, S. J., & Hayes, J. R. (1981, June). *Editing for comprehension: Improving the process through reading protocols.* (Technical Report No. 14, Document Design Project). Carnegie Mellon University.

Toulmin, S., Rieke, R., & Janik, A. (1979). *An introduction to reasoning.* New York: Macmillan.

Wallace, D., & Hayes, J. R. (1989). Redefining revision for freshmen. *Research in the Teaching of English, 25*(1), 54–66.

2

Cognitive Processes of Children and Adults in Translating Thought Into Written Language in Real Time

Perspectives From 30 Years of Programmatic Cognitive Psychology and Linguistics Research

MICHEL FAYOL

A t the beginning of my career as a teacher, I worked in the village of Meaulne, the name of which corresponds to the title of the Alain-Fournier book *Le Grand Meaulnes*.[1] As a teacher, my aim was to improve the knowledge of my students, usually around 25 and 30 per school year, about facts (e.g., historical dates, geographical facts), procedures (e.g., addition, subtraction, multiplication, and division with carrying; subject-verb agreement), concepts (e.g., proportions, fractions), problem solving (e.g., arithmetic problems, some of which were very complicated), and composing (e.g., narrative and descriptive texts). I quickly realized that I was rather successful regarding the three first goals, but that I failed concerning the last two. More precisely, the students did not progress as much as I had expected, especially in composing.

To help them become better composers of text, I tried several approaches. One approach proved more efficient than the others, at least with the older students

---

[1] *Le Grand Meaulnes* by Alain-Fournier was first published in France in 1913 and is considered one of the great works of French literature. The only novel by Alain-Fournier, the book is narrated by the son of a school director in a countryside with sandy forests and lake; it deals with mysteries of bridging childhood and adulthood. There are many English translations available, including *The Lost Domain* and *The Wanderer*, as well as films and music

(10 to 14 years of age): collectively composing (i.e., with all the pupils of the class-room) a novel (about 30 pages). This activity motivated the students and led them to produce more and more accurate texts. However, their collective progress did not impact their individual attempts to produce texts.

My next strategy for improving students' composing abilities was to go to the nearby university, first in Clermont, then in Bordeaux, to seek out efficient inter-ventions to help children improve their composing (and problem solving) skills. It was shocking for me to discover that so little was known about effective instruction procedures in schools and student learning. What was even more concerning was that so few professors (and students) were interested in such topics.

I began to envision a specialized lab aimed at studying learning of academic skills: reading, writing, and math problem solving. I spent 7 years at the University of Clermont, from my first year (1970) to my first dissertation defense (1976), while at the same time a full-time teacher in charge of about 20 to 25 pupils every school year. I was recruited in 1977 by the Scientific University of Montpellier where I worked mainly on learning science and mathematics. In parallel, I was preparing my second dissertation on narrative production. The defense of this second disser-tation took place in Bordeaux in March 1981. I was then recruited to the University of Burgundy (Dijon), where I immediately started to work on a new lab devoted to learning and development.

Early in my university career, I was mainly interested in two topics: math and literacy (mostly written composition, which became my first priority). For written composition, I planned two complementary research lines. One line was devoted to studying in detail how text composition is acquired by children from 6 to 11 years of age and how it could be improved. Another line, much more ambitious and still in progress, aimed at studying the *on-line characteristics of written language production*. In this chapter, I will report the main results from these two research lines in that order.

THE EVOLUTION OF TEXT COMPOSITION FROM AGES 6 TO 11

The work that I conducted during the decade between 1980 and 1990 was charac-terized by two main aspects, one theoretical and the other methodological.

At the theoretical level, research was dominated by the model of Flower and Hayes (1980; Hayes and Flower, 1980), which primarily viewed written ver-bal production as a dynamic problem-solving activity. This model fell within the framework of cognitive psychology in that it postulated the existence of different representations, processes acting upon these, and a limited processing capacity (see Alamargot & Chanquoy, 2001, for a detailed description of the model and other models of text production).

The main criticism leveled at the Flower and Hayes model and the derivatives it spawned during the 1980s related to the very summary nature of the translation component (Fayol, 1991a), both in terms of the representations and the processes involved (but see Berninger & Swanson, 1994, for an exception). That is why my own research initially concentrated on the translation component. I attempted to study the production of written (primarily narrative) texts by focusing on dimensions specific both to the text and to the written modality. Two major themes were therefore addressed, initially using an offline approach (corpus analysis and experiments): the acquisition and implementation of connectives and punctuation marks and verbal forms of the past.

At the methodological level, data were collected using two paradigms. The first of these was corpus analysis, undertaken on the basis of criteria borrowed from linguistics. The cognitive processes were thus inferred from the observed linguistic markers and their arrangements. For example, the *connectives were considered to be the traces of cognitive and linguistic activities* and were used to establish and indicate the existence of *relations between both events or states and speech actions* (to tell or write a sentence, and then to tell or write another one; Caron, 1997). The second paradigm consisted of designing experiments aimed at testing precise hypotheses, most of them stemming from *corpus analysis*, for example, related to how children use punctuation marks when dealing with orally presented texts they must transcribe into writing. Note that, contrary to what had been done with adults and adolescents, we did not use oral thinking-aloud protocols mainly because this paradigm is difficult to apply with children, especially when they are composing texts, which is a difficult activity for their developing working memory (Gufoni, 1996).

Analyzing Already Produced Texts

I asked 265 6- to 10-year-old children to write a story about something that had happened to them. The textual organization of the stories was analyzed, especially regarding the concurrent development of the organization of content (i.e., what is written in reference to the topic: the events) and the implementation of the linguistic markers used to express the transformation of speech forms into story forms (Fayol, 1986, 1996, 2003). My analysis has shown that the evolution of the types of texts can be schematized in several steps (Fayol, 1991b). Some examples are provided in Table 2.1.

Evolution of Writing Skill

The earliest type of organization is found in the compositions of 6- and 7-year-old children (Table 2.1, Example 1). The child authors produce a series of *news announcements*, most of them in the perfect form (French: *passé composé*) and directly related to the time of writing, for example, *hier* (yesterday); *il y a x jours* (x days ago). No intratextual marking system is used: The sentences are not integrated in a whole but instead refer to an assembly of independent actions or states.

A more advanced step (not illustrated here) consists of establishing a kind of spatiotemporal frame (e.g., "One day, I went to my aunt's"), filling in this frame with several events, generally in chronological order. These texts are similar to scripts (Fayol & Monteil, 1988): They almost always relate to commonplace, everyday events. The first punctuation system ensuring cohesion appears (e.g., one day ... one hour later ... next Monday), with punctuation marks co-occurring

TABLE 2.1   Examples of Texts Composed by Children

1. Je suis allé à la piscine./Dimanche je suis allé au rugby./Samedi je suis (allé?) chez ma maman./
Le mercredi j'ai été au cathéchisme./Dimanche à huit heures je suis parti en colonie/et j'ai été
faire du ski (7-year-old)./
(I went to the pool./Sunday I went to rugby./Saturday I (went?) to my mom's./Wednesday I went
to church./Sunday at eight o'clock I left for camp/and I went skiing)

2. J'étais dans ma baignoire/j'ai fait tomber la chopine (= petite bouteille)/elle est un peu cassée./
J'étais dans mes escaliers/et j'ai tombé sur le nez/et j'ai comme un bouton (8-year-old);
(I was in my bathtub/I dropped the bottle/it's a little broken./I was on my stairs/and I falled on
my nose/and I have like a bump)

3. Un jour chez ma mémé j'allai(s) en vacances chez elle./Le soir je suis allé me coucher/j'ai rêvé./
Le lendemain matin je me suis levé tôt./J'ai pris mon vélo/et j'ai été en faire du vélo/C'était dans
une descente/je n'avais pas vu/qu'il y avait un hérisson/j'ai marché sur ses piquants/alors une roue
de mon vélo a été crevée./ (8-year-old);
(One day at my grandma's I was on vacation at her house./At night I went to bed/I had a dream./
The following morning I got up early./I took my bike/and I went for a ride/It was downhill/I
didn't see/that there was a hedgehog/I rode over his spines/so I got a flat tire.)

in them. Most of the time, the verbs are reported in the French *passé composé* (belonging to the speech system).

The last step corresponds to true narratives, including events and states centered on one or more episodes with at least one complication and one resolution (i.e., following the story schema described by Mandler & Johnson, 1977; Stein & Glenn, 1979; see Table 2.1, Example 3). The punctuation marks are clearly different from those found in previous steps and those emphasized in speech. The initial utterance generally sets up a spatiotemporal frame separated from the immediate situation of production (i.e., a displaced origin; Fayol, 1984) and related use of the *imparfait* (imperfect) and sometimes the pluperfect tense, referring to a past in the past (*il avait couru*; he had run) (Fayol, 1982). The present tense or the simple past tense are reserved for unexpected events. The connectives *soudain* (suddenly), *alors* (so), and *mais* (but) are regularly used. The punctuation marks are more frequent and more diverse, but become rarer when the story describes complication and resolution events (see Table 2.1, Example 3).

Experimental Studies

The evolution of the written narratives from age 6 to 10 was reminiscent of that of oral narratives in 4- to 7-year-old children (Applebee, 1978; Fayol, 2000), suggesting that moving from the oral to the written modality entailed a decrease of production abilities at least in the initial stages of writing acquisition (Simon, 1973). Especially intriguing was the sketchiness of the event frames and the rarity of connectives, despite the fact that an oral performance paradigm was used. One approach consisted of asking children to transcribe texts orally presented (to control for the textual organization) and illustrated (to be sure that children understood the sequence of events and their temporal-causal chaining) (Fayol & Mouchon, 1997; Mouchon, Fayol, & Gombert, 1989). One series of experiments had to do with connectives. Peterson and McCabe (1991) remarked that narratives include multiple clauses and cohesion devices regarding these two dimensions of connectives and multiple clauses. This observation led to a search for the reasons for such a difference of performance between oral and written modalities. One initial question regarding the concurrent evolution of the content of stories and of the linguistic marks was to determine whether concentration on a single event along with the expansion of that event into components following a temporo-causal organization is the prerequisite of the understanding and use of linguistic markers. I thus planned a series of simple experiments dealing with three topics: the use of connectives, the use of punctuation marks, and the use of verbal tenses.

Linearization or Nextness Principle

In the following series of experiments, I aimed at verifying that the mean trends observed in the corpus analysis remained true when most of the variables impacting composition were controlled for. The general conception was that all discourse refers to a mental representation (i.e., that which is described, related, argued about), which is always multidimensional, that is, has many elements and relationships linking them. However, oral or written language production is strictly linear and time-dependent. As a consequence, one of the main problems confronting a speaker or writer is to find ways to present information in a linear format. The linearization process functions according to the "nextness" principle (Ochs, 1979): Unless otherwise indicated, two linguistic items that are close "on the text/ discourse surface" have the same importance and are strongly related to each other. However, two consecutive statements in an oral or written discourse may (a) pertain to successive states or events that are strongly related to each other in the situation being described, or (b) pertain to states or events that are weakly related to each other in that situation, and thus (c) have quite different weight in the course of the events. Hence, the need for one or several systems of linguistic marks to indicate the strength, nature, and relative importance of adjacent statements and their links. Only a set of very specific marks is capable of governing (or controlling) the application of the nextness principle: the punctuation/connectives paradigm (Fayol, 1997a, 1997b) and the verbal tense paradigm.

Punctuation and Connections

In order to test this general hypothesis, several experiments showed how the linguistic elements of the text are linked to one another. They also pointed out that connectives have two complementary functions: They express both semantic (e.g., temporal, causal, etc.) and pragmatic (i.e., between speech acts) relations. The main connectives, the functioning of which had been explored, were as follows: *et* (and), *alors* (so), *puis* (then), *après* (afterward), *soudain* (suddenly), and *mais* (but). The goal of the following experiments was to determine whether children used these connectives in a relevant way when the content to be reported was controlled for.

Children (5- to 8-year-olds) were provided with series of both clauses and pictures (one per clause) associated with each of them (Table 2.2). Those series described sequences of events that were either commonplace (WO) or less predictable due to an obstacle (SO) or an event (DO). The experimenter simultaneously read the sequence of clauses without connectives and showed the corresponding pictures slowly to enable the children to understand what was occurring. After

TABLE 2.2   Example of Oral Frame Provided to Children to Assess Their Use of Connectives

---

Text with common beginning and different endings:

Common beginning
(a) Eric found his room sad.
(b) He decided to repaint it.
(c) He took a paint-pot and a brush.

Different endings
(a) WO (without obstacle): He climbed the stepladder. He painted all day. Eric did not find his room sad anymore.
(b) SO (static obstacle): The color seemed too sad for him. He did not repaint his room. Eric still found his room sad.
(c) DO (dynamic obstacle): He spilt the paint climbing up the stepladder. He no longer had enough of it to paint.

---

being read the sequence of sentences and shown each series of the corresponding pictures, children were given the pictures alone and asked to tell the story as exactly as possible, in the oral or in the written modality: They were not instructed to give a verbatim recall.

The written and oral productions were analyzed taking into account the connectives, their frequencies, and their positions in texts. The results showed the same trends regardless of the school level or the modality: The children systematically added connectives into their texts; the connectives were more frequent in texts reporting a complication (or obstacle), and in such cases, the connectives—*mais* (but), *soudain* (suddenly)—appeared before the complication and *alors* (so) before the resolution; by contrast, in WO texts, the connective (almost exclusively *et* [and]) occurred just before the last clause. The trends observed in the corpus analysis were thus documented using a more reliable experimental paradigm, enabling more precise control of variables likely to impact the choice and use of connectives. More important, when the content and the structure of the narratives were controlled for, the same trends appeared in both oral and written productions: The same connectives were used at the same positions and as a function of the narrative frames. The same approach has been used to study the role of connectives in reading and understanding texts (Mouchon, Fayol, & Gaonac'h, 1995). Using another paradigm to study the use of punctuation marks, Fayol and Lété (1987) gave children (and adults in other experiments) short sequences of sentences without punctuation marks, but sometimes included connectives (Table 2.3). The participants were asked to rewrite these sequences to produce texts. We analyzed the punctuation marks that were added, their nature (e.g., comma, full stop), and positions within the text.

The results showed that, very early, children used punctuation marks as a function of the degree of relatedness between successive events or states: The more related the two successive events were the less frequent and the less strong (e.g., comma) the punctuation marks that were used. Conversely, the less related the events, the more frequent and stronger (e.g., paragraph) the punctuation marks. Moreover, the connectives and punctuation marks fulfilled complementary functions: Strong punctuation marks occurred with some

TABLE 2.3   Example of Sequence of Events That Children Were Asked to Use to Produce Texts by Adding Punctuation Marks

Annie. (1) Annie ne savait pas quoi faire ce jour là (2) un joli petit chat entra dans sa chambre (3) Annie était surprise et très contente (4) elle voulut s'amuser avec le chaton (5) elle lui mit la tunique de sa poupée (6) elle reçut un coup de griffe sur la main (7) elle bouda jusqu'à la tombée de la nuit.

(1) Annie did not know what to do that day (2) a pretty little cat came into her room (3) Annie was surprised and very happy (4) she wanted to play with the cat (5) she put her doll's dress on it (6) she got scratched on her hand (7) she sulked until nighttime.

(a) Type 1 versions have no punctuation or connectives;

(b) Type 2 versions have the connective *et* [and] between propositions (3) and (4), or (4) and (5), or (5) and (6).

(c) Type 3 versions have either *et* [and], *alors* [so], or *après* [afterward] between constituents (5) and (6).

Source: From Fayol, M., and Lété, B., *European Journal of Psychology of Education*, 2, 57–72, 1987.

connectives (e.g., afterward) but not with others (e.g., and). Again, the most important determinant of punctuation and connective use was the strength of the relation between events or states evoked in two successive clauses. Several experiments confirmed these trends, in adults as well as in children (Bestgen & Costermans, 1994; Chanquoy & Fayol, 1991; Fayol & Abdi, 1988; Heurley, 1997; Mounier & Bisseret, 2001; see Fayol, 1997a, for an overview). Also, some experiments were devoted to the study of the impact of punctuation on understanding sentences (Roy, Gaonac'h, & Fayol, 2002).

Differential Weighting of Events

The final objective was to study how children discover and acquire the ways of giving different weights to the events reported in texts. In written French, verbal inflections simultaneously encode tense and aspect (in addition to person and number distinctions). Tenses mark the temporal relations between the situation reported by the speaker (or writer) and some reference point, most often the time of speech. The aspect marks the speaker's or writer's viewpoint regarding the temporal structure of the described event: Any event can be considered according to its characteristics or its completeness (e.g., the event can be viewed as accomplished, as with the past participle, or as ongoing, as with the present or the imperfect tense). Past inflections are dependent on the semantic properties of the predicates, for example (a) activity verbs, which describe durative and nonresultative actions such as *Les enfants jouent au football* (The children are playing football); and (b) achievement verbs, which describe punctual and resultative predicates, such as *Un pneu explosa* (A tire exploded). French past tenses belong either to the discourse set, for example, *présent, passé composé*, or to the narrative set, for example, *imparfait* (imperfect), *passé simple* (simple past) (Weinrich, 1973). When telling stories, people generally use the imperfect with events and states belonging to the background of the situation and the simple past (but sometimes the present tense) to refer to the foregrounded events. Used to contrast, the verbal past tense enables distinguishing between focused and nonfocused events or states (Hickmann, 1997). As a consequence, it is difficult for adults to select the tenses in texts and still more complex for children to learn and use them.

Verbal Past Tense

My colleagues and I conducted several experiments to determine whether and when children are sensitive to the different verbal past tenses (Bonnotte & Fayol, 1993a, 1993b, 1997, 2000; Fayol, 1985; Fayol, Gombert, & Abdi, 1989) and use them as a function of the textual contexts. A first series of results showed that children have memorized the associations of some verbs with some specific verbal tenses; for example, they employed *tomber* (fall down) mainly with the simple past and *marcher* (walk) with the imperfect tense (Fayol et al., 1989). However, these associations could result either from applying rules (e.g., to describe the background of any narrative or select the imperfect tense or the pluperfect) or from recalling specific instances memorized as such (e.g., in the past this specific verb is associated with this verb form). To disentangle these two possibilities, we designed an experiment in which adults and 10-year-old children had to choose verbal tenses in order to either produce an isolated sentence or to include this same sentence within a narrative frame in three positions: beginning, middle, or ending of brief stories (Table 2.4). Every sentence included one verb of a specific predicate type, varying from duration (either describing an enduring or a brief event or action) to results (activity verbs such as to play, to walk, to dance) to achievement (verbs such as to explode, to break, to knock over).

Three results were notable. First, children used the *imparfait* (imperfect) much more frequently (67%) than the adults (38%) in narratives. Second, the adults used the imperfect differently in relation to the types of verb, more often with activity verbs (65%) than with achievement verbs (0%); the difference was far weaker in children (73% and 58%, respectively). Third, and more important, the percentage use of imperfect varied significantly as a function of the position of the

TABLE 2.4   Example of Material Used to Study How Children and Adults Employ Verbal Past Tenses in Narratives

The task consisted of using a past tense instead of the infinitive form in order to produce a narrative. The verb was inserted within a sentence presented either isolated or to be included within a narrative.

Target sentence (isolated presentation)

Un pneu (*explose*) (A tire to explode)

Version 1

Insertion at the beginning: Mister Talon was on his way to work. A tire (to explode). The car (to go) in the ditch. The left front tire (to be) flat. Mister Talon (to change) the flat tire. The car (to start).

Versions 2 and 3

Insertion of the target sentence in the **middle** or at the **end** of the narrative, respectively.

Source: From Fayol, M., Hickmann, M., Bonnotte, I., and Gombert, J. E., *Journal of Psycholinguistic Research*, 22, 453–478, 1993.

target sentence in adults (58% at the beginning; 40% in the middle; 27% in the end position) but not in children (71%, 71%, and 60%, respectively).

To resume, predicate types had a strong effect on participants' selection of verbal inflections in both children and adults, in isolated sentences as well as in narratives. The imperfect was more frequent with activity than with achievement predicates. By contrast, only in adults did the position of the sentence in the narrative have an impact on the use of the imperfect tense. Children were not sensitive to this textual dimension of verbal tense use. Further experiments provided evidence that children do not understand the effect of verbal inflections on the representation of how the described processes unfold in sentences or narratives. Indeed, contrary to adults, even 10-year-old children seem insensitive to variations of meanings related to verbal forms: Children do not treat verbs in the imperfect as corresponding to ongoing processes or verbs in the simple past as corresponding to terminated processes (Bonnotte & Fayol, 1997, 2000). Consequently, French children use past verb forms in instances of memorized words and employed them as such, not for forms that changed as a function of aspects or shades of meaning.

Developmental Issues

Linearization in production leads to the necessity to juxtapose information that may be more or less closely related. Thus, it requires the use of a system of markers indicating the degree (punctuation), the nature (connectives), and the weight (verbal tenses among others) of the relation between statements (Fayol, 1997b; Heurley, 1997). This system of analysis supplies the reader with indications of the segmentation of information (i.e., separating facts from one another), integration of information (i.e., elaborating a unified representation from the set of propositions), and foregrounding information (i.e., whether or not an event is of special importance). Adults do indeed use the corresponding markers in a manner appropriate to these functions. What about children? Connectives are acquired very early and in an order that can be found in all languages (Kail & Weissenborn, 1991), and they are used in oral productions at an early age (French & Nelson, 1985; Hudson & Shapiro, 1991). We might therefore have expected them to emerge very early in children's initial written productions. Corpus analyses have shown that was not the case and often they do not appear until third grade (9 years old) (Fayol, 1991b). This "delay" is due to the facts that the event sequences that are recounted do not require the use of markers other than *and* or *then/after* and the texts produced by the youngest subjects have no thematic unity. Once these sequences comprise chronological-causal relationships between events, written compositions include the relevant connectives. It therefore appears that as far as the most elementary connectors are concerned, their occurrence in written narratives between the ages of 5 and 10 is not a developmental problem, but rather has to do with the degree of elaboration of the content reported in the text (Fayol & Mouchon, 1997).

Findings are very different when we consider punctuation marks. Both their forms and their functioning are acquired in parallel when children learn written language. This discovery continues from 6 to 12 years of age; from the outset, it follows the regularities characteristic of adult production. The occurrence of a full stop, with or without a capital letter, delimits episodes or blocks of information that possess a thematic unity. That conclusion is confirmed by the associated pause lengths (Foulin, Chanquoy, & Fayol, 1989). The comma appears later and is immediately applied to segmentations with a lesser level of importance. The other punctuation marks appear later (Ferreiro & Zucchermaglio, 1996).

Findings were again quite different with verbal forms of the past. Understanding and using French tenses in relation to past, present, and future appears relatively early, around 4 years of age. However, grasping the shade of meaning associated with different aspects of tenses (i.e., imperfect vs. perfect; duration) takes time: At the end of primary schooling, most children are not sensitive to such shades. Most probably children memorize verbal forms as instances, without understanding why and how to use them.

The study of punctuation, connectives, and verbal tenses in production and comprehension of texts has important consequences regarding the composition of technical texts (notices, instructions). Several experiments have been conducted in order to better understand why those texts are so difficult to process and to improve both their organization and their use by ordinary people (Fayol, 2002a, 2002b; Fayol & Heurley, 1995; Ganier, Gombert, & Fayol, 2000).

In the same way as for the *narrative superstructure* (Fayol & Lemaire, 1993), the results mentioned above suggest that the errors and difficulties of beginning writers in composing texts are often due not to an inability to plan or organize a sequence of events, but more likely as a result of inadequate contact with texts or the impossibility of performing in parallel the tasks of writing and marking the relevant relation between adjacent clauses. It may not be lack of knowledge, but rather implementation, that causes the writing problems. The next line of research described hereafter tried to provide evidence for that hypothesis.

Coordinating Low-Level and High-Level Processes

Both theoretical models and empirical data stress that composing requires efficient on-line coordination of both low-level and high-level processes (Alamargot & Fayol, 2009; Fayol, 1999). High-level processes include elaborating ideas and conceptual relations, processing thematic relations, maintaining coherence and cohesion, and respecting text-type constraint processes whatever the modality of production (i.e., oral or written) (Berninger & Swanson, 1994; Fayol, 1991a, 1991b, 1997b). Lower-level processes relate both to verbal production in general, for example, lexical access or syntactic frame construction (Bock & Levelt, 1994; Levelt, 1989), and to specific written language or transcription processes (e.g., spelling and handwriting).

In 1990 I implemented two series of investigations. The first one was devoted to studying in detail each of the theoretical components of composing: graphic transcription and its impact on composing; writing words; and producing morphosyntactic dimensions. The second one had to do with a new and risky topic: the study of on-line processing in composing. The following sections deal successively with each of these two topics.

Components of Composing

At the time I began these studies, anecdotal observations suggested that the processes of producing handwriting and spelling impact composing performance in children. For example, eliminating these letter- and word-writing demands of writing, by asking elementary school children to dictate the text they are composing to an adult acting as a secretary, may result in an increase in the amount of text generated (McCutchen, 1987; Simon, 1973). However, longer texts do not systematically result in improvements in text quality: Scardamalia, Bereiter, and Goelman (1982) found that both production rate and letter and word writing influenced the amount of text generated, but not the quality of the texts. In contrast, Graham (1990) reported that these transcription skills influenced both the length and quality of compositions in unskilled fourth- and sixth-grade writers. The confounding among different dimensions, modality, graphic transcription, and spelling could explain such discordances among the results.

Bourdin & Fayol (1994) decided to use a new paradigm to deal with the question of the potential impact of graphic transcription on producing language. We simply reasoned that all the language components and processes (e.g., accessing words, framing sentences, and connecting words through agreement processes) as well as the modality specific processes (oral vs. written) draw on a single attentional and memory pool that has limited capacity. That is, we were proposing a capacity theory of writing (Fayol, 1999; McCutchen, 1996, 2000). As a consequence, any increase in the amount required by one component reduces the cognitive resources available for the other components, for example, when the cost of handwriting (vs. spelling) is high, the resources potentially available for finding ideas, accessing the lexicon, or computing agreements are reduced, which could entail errors or decrease the quality of text composition.

The Graphic Component

Bourdin and Fayol (1994, 1996) then showed that in a serial recall task of unrelated words, as well as in a sentence production task, the performance of 7- and 8-year-old children, but not that of adults, was impaired in the written modality compared with the oral modality. The number of recalled words or that of sentences produced from the list of words was significantly reduced in the written modality as compared to the oral modality. This result suggested that the cognitive cost of writing hampered the children's ability to maintain the information in working memory. The same phenomenon did not occur in the oral modality due to the high automaticity of the production processes.

To support this hypothesis in adults, Bourdin and Fayol (1994) were able to show that adults' performance decreased dramatically when they had to write using capital letters. Using a rarely practiced graphic subsystem increased the load of the transcription process and led to a decrease in the working memory performance. Overloading the graphic component by increasing the difficulty of managing the output modality was thus shown to affect a higher-level component: the maintaining and recalling of a series of items, and even the production of short sentences from a series of provided words (Bourdin & Fayol, 1996).

More recently, Bourdin and Fayol (2002) have shown that, even in adults, if management of the narrative content of a story to be composed is made more difficult, oral productions were better than written productions. This result is in compliance with the capacity theory of writing: whatever the component, increasing the difficulty to deal with it entails increasing the management load, hence decreasing the resources available to the other components. As a consequence, most of the time, errors occur. Fayol and Miret (2005) provided further relevant evidence that French third graders having difficulty in transcribing quickly and legibly, made more spelling errors than did their peers of the same age, intelligence level, and general orthographic ability. Such a result is in compliance with results reported by Berninger (1999) and Graham, Berninger, Abbott, Abbott, and Whitaker (1997) in children and Connelly, Dockrell, and Barnett (2005) in university students.

Spelling: The Inflection Problem

The same reasoning was used regarding spelling. The French orthographic system is very complicated (see Berninger & Fayol, 2008; Catach, 1986; Jaffré & Fayol, 2005, for an extensive review) and difficult both to learn and to manage, even in adults (Fayol, 2008; Fayol & Jaffré, 2008; Fayol, Thévenin, Jarousse, & Totereau, 1999). Especially difficult is the management of inflectional morphology, more specifically the agreement of nouns and verbs. In written French, the marks of plurality for nouns and adjectives (adding -s at the end of nouns and adjectives), and for verbs (adding -nt at the end of verbs) are most often silent (they have no phonological counterparts): il chante (He sings) and ils chantent (They sing) are pronounced alike. Consequently, children only learn these inflection marks when they are able to read them and cannot rely on phonology to detect and transcribe them. They have to pay attention to the plurality meaning and to the distribution of the marks over the words of the sentences, which is more difficult when managing spelling while doing another activity.

In a series of experiments devoted to studying the management of agreement spelling in adults, Largy & Fayol (2001) conducted several experiments to provide evidence that the agreement process in written French (but far less in the oral modality) is easily disrupted when adding a secondary task, even though very simple (e.g., to keep in mind and recall a series of three to five words when transcribing a sentence with an agreement problem). For example, people tended to make the verb agree with the closest noun (N2) instead of the subject (N1) in sentences like Le chien des voisins aboie(nt); the correct spelling is Le chien des voisins aboie (Fayol & Got, 1991; Fayol, Largy, & Lemaire, 1994). Such attraction errors have been described in several other languages, even in the oral modality (Bock & Cutting, 1992; Bock & Eberhard, 1993; see Sandra & Fayol, 2003, for an overview), but they are far less frequent (Negro, Chanquoy, Fayol, & Louis-Sydney, 2005). In written French, these errors only occurred in those aged 9 to 10 years, when children have automated the noun and verb agreement processes (Fayol, Hupet, & Largy, 1999). Later, another kind of error appears. It consists of substituting a noun inflection for a verb inflection, or the reverse, for example, writing il les timbres (he them stamp) instead of il les timbre (he them stamps)

(Largy, Fayol, & Lemaire, 1996). Such inflection errors are especially interesting because they suggest that, in a highly complex orthographic system like French, people rarely compute the verb agreement by looking for the subject of the verb and matching it with the verb ending. More plausibly, they tend to retrieve the most inflected verbal forms from memory as a function of their syntactic position and frequency. Most often such a process leads to correct agreements. However, sometimes it fails and produces an error. This error can be detected and edited, but frequently it goes unnoticed (Hupet, Fayol, & Schelstraete, 1998), again especially when the writer is involved in an attention-demanding task.

To resume with the unfolding systematic research program, the management of inflectional morphology is very difficult in written French, even in highly educated adults: It is a resource-demanding process easily disrupted by secondary tasks (Fayol, 1994). An important question had to do with how 6- to 10-year-old children learn inflectional morphology (Fayol & Totereau, 2001).

Totereau, Thévenin, and Fayol (1997) published the first extensive study about the acquisition of morphological inflections in French. They showed that plural marks for nouns are acquired and automated earlier than plural marks for verbs. Moreover, they provided evidence that children easily acquire conceptual knowledge about the meaning of morphological marks (i.e., -s, -e, -nt), but that they keep on making omission errors (i.e., they do not put any mark at the end of nouns, adjectives, or verbs) in production until late in their primary schooling (about third grade). Largy (2001) extended these results by showing that second to fourth graders are able to detect and correct omission or substitution errors despite committing such errors. Thévenin, Totereau, Fayol, and Jarousse (1999) conducted an instructional experiment (using a pre- and posttest design with an experimental and a control group) with about 360 first to third graders to demonstrate that it is possible and efficient to teach young children to inflect nouns, adjectives, and verbs correctly through practicing how to do so (see also Fayol et al., 1999). They reported an impressive improvement in morphological use even in the youngest children.

They also observed the occurrence of a new category of errors: the overgeneralization of -s inflection to verbs, followed by the overgeneralization of -nt (the verb plural mark) to some nouns and many adjectives (Totereau, Barrouillet, & Fayol, 1998). Later research confirmed that overgeneralized use of -nt marks was more frequent than overgeneralized use of -s, and that such errors were due to the formal character of plural marks for adjectives and verbs (Fayol, Totereau, & Barrouillet, 2006). All these results have been interpreted in a theoretical framework prompted by Anderson's (1983, 1995) conception of declarative versus procedural learning. This theory is able to explain both the effect of training and the occurrence of different kinds of errors: omission errors (due to cognitive overload) and substitution errors (due to frequency effects; see Cousin, Largy, & Fayol, 2002; Largy, Cousin, Bryant, & Fayol, 2007).

These series of experiments clearly showed how difficult the mastery of inflectional morphology is in written French. They enabled us to understand both the length of the learning process (which necessitates explicit teaching over all the school years) and the existence of inflectional errors even in adults and in high-standard newspapers. However, they revealed only part of the spelling difficulties in French. Another domain had to do with the acquisition of lexical spelling.

Spelling: The Lexicon and Sublexicon Problems

The written French orthography has an incomplete one-to-one mapping between phonemes and graphemes. The result is that managing the system in the phoneme-to-grapheme direction is very difficult (Fayol, Zorman, & Lété, 2009). First, many phonemes can be spelled in more than one way (Lété, Peereman, & Fayol, 2008). For example, /o/ can be spelled *o, au, eau, ot*; and /ã/ can be spelled *an, en, and, ant,* or *ent*. Second, many letters do not have a phonological counterpart. For example, the final -*d* of the words *bavard* (talkative) and *foulard* (scarf) is unpronounced, as well as the -*h* in *théatre* (theater). Third, most often doubling a consonant (*bar* vs. *barre*) does not change the pronunciation. Consequently, in order to spell correctly, French children must acquire and deploy both lexical knowledge of specific word forms and general orthographic knowledge about sublexical graphotactic regularities (sequences of letters frequently co-occurring). A large series of studies has been conducted in order to discover when and how children and adults acquire and use such knowledge.

Pacton, Perruchet, Fayol, and Cleeremans (2001) used both judgment and production tasks with pseudowords to explore children's sensitivity to regularities concerning double letters. For example, children were presented with pairs of pseudowords such that one pseudoword in each pair included a consonant frequent in both single and double formats (*abolle*), whereas the other pseudoword included a consonant frequent only in single format (*abodde*). The target consonants appeared in single format in half of the pairs (e.g., *orile–oride*) versus in double format (e.g., *abolle–abodde*) in the other half. Children were asked either to select the "invented" word in each pair that looked most like a French word or to fill in the blanks in pseudowords such as *tuba__i* with single (e.g., *l* or *k*) versus double (e.g., *ll* or *kk*) consonants. In another series of experiments (Pacton & Fayol, 2004), children from Grades 2 to 4 were instructed to spell "invented" words such as /obidar/, /ribore/, or /bylevo/ in order to assess whether children varied their transcription of the sound /o/ (as *o, au, eau, ot, aut, ho,* etc.) according to its position in the word and its consonantal context. In French, -*eau* is frequently in the final position, rarely in a medial position, and nonexistent initially (Catach, 1986), -*eau* is also more frequent after the letter *v* than *f*.

From first grade onward, pseudowords with consonants frequent only in single-letter format were more often selected or produced when they occurred in single letter format (e.g., *oride* instead of *orile*) than in double format (e.g., *abodde* instead of *abolle*); this effect increased at the next two grade levels. Regarding the transcription of the phoneme /o/, even the youngest, second-grade French children varied their transcriptions of /o/ as a function of the context. More precisely, the sequence -*eau* was used more frequently in the final position, and more frequently following *r* than *f*, which signals the early sensitivity of children to graphotactic regularities. In French, transcription of the same sound can be governed by graphotactic constraints that are probabilistic in nature (e.g., at the end of words the sound /o/ is more often transcribed -*eau* after *r* than after *f*) and also by morphological constraints that are describable with a general rule (for example, /o/ is always transcribed -*eau* when used as a diminutive suffix). This dual situation allowed us to explore the combined influence of the two types of constraints on children's spelling. Eight- to eleven-year-old children's spellings of pseudowords were affected by derivational morphology, with pseudowords such as /sorivo/ more often spelled with -*eau* when they were dictated inside sentences like "a little /soriv/ is a /sorivo/" than when dictated in isolation or embedded in sentences in which /o/ did not function as a diminutive suffix (Pacton, Fayol, & Perruchet, 2005). Children's spellings were also influenced by graphotactic regularities when no morphological rule could be applied, with pseudowords such as /sorivo/ more often spelled with -*eau* than pseudowords such as /sorifo/. Importantly, this effect remained unchanged in conditions triggering the application of the morphological rule, and it persisted over grade levels.

Pacton et al. (2005) argue that even after massive exposure to print, children did not rely on abstract, rule-based, morphological knowledge. Children learn associations between abstract features like "diminutiveness" and "end in -*eau*," leading them to use *eau* more often when they encounter pseudowords like /sorivo/ in the context of a sentence like "a little /soriv/ is a /sorivo/." But associations between other features may also be established; specifically, because words with a final -*eau* preceded by -*r* are far more frequent than final -*eau* preceded by -*f*, the association between -*r* and -*eau* will be stronger than between -*f* and -*eau*. That is, the effect of such graphotactic constraints persists in the diminutive condition as well, because even though children encounter more and more words ending with -*eau* where the final /o/ stands for a diminutive suffix, the proportion of words with -*eau* after -*r* to which they are exposed remains higher than the proportion of words with -*eau* after -*f* (see Pacton & Fayol, 2004, for an overview and Pacton & Fayol, 2003, for another example having to do with inflectional morphology of adverbs vs. present participle).

To summarize, several series of experiments have been devoted to the study of spelling in French. The topic is highly complicated and requires taking into account (a) lexical-specific knowledge, which we are still exploring to understand why learning word forms is so difficult in some cases and so easy in other cases (Martinet, Valdois, & Fayol, 2004); (b) sublexical general knowledge (i.e., regularities) acquired very early through implicit learning and resistant to the influence of morphological knowledge, despite explicit instruction regarding the latter (Pacton & Fayol, 2003); and (c) morphological knowledge about both derivations and inflections. We have focused on the latter because it is very specific and important for writing in French, for children and for adults. One remaining question has to do with the impact of spelling management and performance when composing text, and conversely, the influence of different spelling capacities (i.e., lexical knowledge, general knowledge, and command on morphology) on the management and result of the composition process. A longitudinal study is currently being conducted with third to sixth graders to describe the interplay of spelling and composing in French (Slusarczyk, Bressoux, & Fayol, 2011).

COMPOSING IN REAL TIME: STUDYING THE COMPONENTS

The studies previously cited have been conceived in the framework of the capacity theory of writing (Fayol, 1999; McCutchen, 2000; Olive, 2004). In every case, the main assumption was that in a multicomponent activity, such as composing, all components make some demands on cognitive resources and any increase in the amount required by one component reduces the cognitive resources available for the other components. When a component (e.g., transcription) necessitates a lot of resources, one or several other components have their functioning hampered, which leads sometimes—but not always—to errors or a decrease in quality or quantity of written production (Bourdin & Fayol, 2002). However, errors or difficulties did not systematically occur, due to variations in task demands, skill mastery, and individual differences. It was realized that it was necessary to develop a more precise theoretical approach within the framework of the capacity theory of writing. In real time, at any moment during composing, people must deal with the management of the different processes in order to produce a coherent and cohesive message adapted to the audience. The successful production of the message depends on both the cost of the processes mobilized by the different components and the ability to manage (or orchestrate) the allocation of resources to these different processes.

The first hypothesis was that each of these components—lexical choices, grammatical encoding (Bock & Levelt, 1994), spelling, and handwriting—was cognitively costly, a fact that had to be demonstrated in the 1990s because so few data were available regarding the specific processing costs of the different components of writing. The second hypothesis was that composing is a goal-directed, highly costly activity, the management of which necessitates both different component subskills and coordinating their intervention in order to make the activity feasible. This orchestration demands focused attention and conscious mental effort devoted to the global control of the production processes and capacity to deal with each component process (Herrmann & Grabowski, 1995). An important goal is to prevent overloading or to regulate overloading when it occurs.

Two different mechanisms are potentially involved in the reduction of costs necessary to make composition tasks more manageable. The first mechanism is automaticity, which exploits the constancy of either task information or task operations: It is thus possible to automate or at least to reduce the cost of transcription, lexical access, and perhaps grammatical encoding. When a (sub)component skill is automated, it becomes faster, effortless, and noninterfering. As a consequence, it does not overload the limited capacity of the working memory system and can be conducted in parallel with other skills. The second mechanism is strategies: Writing enables controlling for the rhythm of production, slowing down, or speeding up as a function of goals and constraints. When writers encounter limited difficulties in integrating subcomponent skills in real time, they could adjust their writing speed by decreasing transcription rates or by increasing pause duration within and between words. They thus could *distribute the cost of the management among components*: Anticipating the cost of some of them by planning ahead and influencing the cost of others by temporarily simplifying the current task (e.g., not dealing with spelling difficulties).

At the beginning of the 1990s, few researchers were interested in such topics. I decided to have two lines of research in my studies, one devoted to the study of two components of writing—words and syntax—and the other to the on-line study of text production. I will deal with them in turn.

Producing Words

At the beginning of the 1990s, the oral production of an isolated word had been extensively studied through different paradigms and conceptualized by different models (Bock & Levelt, 1994; Dell & O'Seaghdha, 1992; Levelt, 1989, 1999). No corresponding data were available regarding the production of words in the written modality. Two main questions were raised: Is written word production systematically dependent on oral language (Bonin, Pacton, & Fayol, 2001; Bonin, Peereman, & Fayol, 2001)? Are the representations, the processes, and the costs of written language production the same as those involved in oral production?

The paradigms used were well-delineated situations that allowed strict control of the variables: the picture-naming task, the interference paradigm (Bonin, Fayol, & Gombert, 1997), and the priming paradigm (Bonin, Fayol, & Gombert, 1998; for an extensive description, see Bonin & Fayol, 2002). In every case, the dependent variables were the latency and accuracy of oral or written productions. The results (not detailed here) provided evidence that written word production in picture naming is very similar to spoken picture naming regarding the representations (semantic and orthographic-phonological) activated during the time course of lexical retrieval (Bonin & Fayol, 2000). In addition and more important, written word production was both relatively autonomous from phonology (producing an isolated written word from picture does not require the preliminary and systematic activation of phonological representations) and constrained by phonology at the sublexical level (Bonin, Fayol, & Peereman, 1998). This last point is especially important regarding the time course of written production.

Bonin, Fayol, and Gombert (1997) have studied the naming and writing of the same nouns on the basis of pictures depicting well-known objects. The nouns were either frequent or rare and the dependent variable was the latency (i.e., the time needed by the participants to produce the words). The results have shown that (a) latencies were longer in writing than in naming and (b) word frequency effects (WFE) were observed in writing as well as in naming from pictures (see also Bonin & Fayol, 2002). Lexical production was thus identified as a costly process in the written as well as in the oral modality. Its cost depended on the difficulty of retrieving more or less frequent or familiar words. Results of two more recent studies have qualified these results. The first had to do with the age-of-acquisition effect (AoA), the age at which words are first learned. When controlling for the estimated AoA, the classical and central WFE did not emerge as significant determinants of naming latencies, in speaking as well as in writing (Bonin, Fayol, & Chalard, 2001; Bonin, Chalard, Méot, & Fayol, 2002). At the moment, the WFE remains central for explaining many empirical results, but AoA could in the long run reveal more powerful effects.

Second, phonographic consistency impacts on latencies: The difficulty of spelling processing differs between spelling systems, depending on the consistency of the phoneme-to-grapheme correspondences (Bonin, Collay, & Fayol, 2008). Phonology-to-orthography consistency refers to the level of variability in the orthographic codes that can be assigned to a particular phonological unit (Lété, Peereman, & Fayol, 2008). That is, phoneme-to-grapheme consistency is lower when a number of different graphemes can be mapped to a particular phoneme, for example, /o/ in French is spelled /o/ in *mot* (word), /au/ in *saut* (jump), and /eau/ in *oiseau* (bird) compared to when a single grapheme is always associated with a particular phoneme (e.g., again in French, /u/ is always spelled /ou/ as in the words *fou*, *cou*, and *bijou*).

Bonin, Peereman, and Fayol (2001) manipulated sound-to-print regularities of picture labels to investigate whether phonological codes constrain the selection of orthographic codes in written picture naming. Participants wrote picture names, which were inconsistent or consistent at the sublexical level mapping. The position of the inconsistent units within the picture name (initial vs. middle or final) was manipulated. Only initial inconsistencies affected written latencies in the written picture-naming task, but middle or final inconsistencies influenced written latencies in a spelling-to-dictation task. These findings suggest that the buildup of orthographic activation from pictures is costly and phonologically constrained through the sequential operation of sublexical conversion.

An important question remains: How do children and adults integrate their knowledge of lexical items and sublexical units in real time to produce word spelling? Delattre, Bonin, and Barry (2006) used a spelling-to-dictation task to compare the written production of regular versus irregular French words matched on several dimensions (frequency, bigrams, etc.). They found that the latencies in the initiation of written production were reliably longer for irregular than for regular words. More important, the writing duration was also significantly longer for irregular than for regular words matched for length and bigram frequency. The authors interpreted these results within a cascaded model of written word production: Spelling irregular words should trigger some central conflict between sublexical processing (i.e., using phoneme-grapheme associations) and lexical processing (i.e., access to the word-specific orthographic form). Resolving this conflict would both delay the beginning of word transcription and slow down the writing rate of the words, thus suggesting that the conflict is still not resolved when writing begins. The results previously reported clearly show that the latencies and the writing rates of the written production of isolated words are sensitive to both the frequency and consistency and regularity of these words.

From Words to Sentences

A communicative intention leads to the activation of one or more lexical concepts that are to be expressed (Levelt, 1999; Levelt, Roelofs, & Meyer, 1999). The output of the conceptualization process is a preverbal message, which is passed on to the next stage of formulation. Formulation comprises the two main steps of lexicalization and grammatical encoding (Dell, 1986; Dell & O'Seaghdha, 1992; Levelt, 1989, 1999; Levelt et al., 1999). Grammatical encoding consists of assigning syntactic functions. Lexicalization is most often viewed as a two-step process. First, a modality-neutral lexical entry is activated and selected (i.e., a lemma), which provides syntactic information such as gender or grammatical class. Second, a lexeme (i.e., a phonological word form) is retrieved, which triggers the activation of segmental and metrical information. Lexemic information is then used by articulatory processes, which result in overt speech. Most current models of speech production assume that the processes involved in speech production work incrementally, that is, different parts of the utterance can be processed concurrently at the different levels previously outlined (Levelt, 1989). What is not as yet clearly understood is the scope of the units that are planned for any level of representation involved. At the moment, we know more about the spoken or written production of *isolated* words than about the production of *multiword* utterances, that is, sentences.

Two categories of studies have been conducted addressing this issue. The first one assumed that there is a hierarchy of linguistic units—paragraphs > sentences > clauses > phrases > words—and tested the hypothesis that the larger the unit, the longer the preceding pause duration (Foulin, 1998; Foulin, Chanquoy, & Fayol, 1989; Foulin & Fayol, 1988). Adults and second and third graders were videotaped while composing a report about a personal tour, a simple text type using a topic about which every participant was knowledgeable. Every pause (except the prewriting time and the pause following the last word of the text) was coded relative to its position. Five different positions were considered: initial pause of paragraph; initial pause of sentence; initial pause of clause; initial pause of phrase; and noninitial or intraunit pause.

The same pattern of results emerged in adults and children. The variations of pause durations have two determinants. First, there is a prevalent weight of the initial location in the temporal structure of the main grammatical units in writing: Whatever the grammatical unit considered, the mean duration of initial pause is significantly longer than the mean duration of intraunit pause. Second, whatever the writer's ability, the pause duration varies as a function of the grammatical level of the pause location: The higher the grammatical level of the pause location, the longer the pause. These results are in compliance with those provided by explorations of planning in spoken sentence productions. They have been confirmed by Nottbusch's (2010) data showing that producing a written subordinated noun phrase (e.g., The red stars with the blue circle) required longer initial pause than producing a coordinated noun phrase (e.g., The red stars and the blue circles). However, Foulin's (1998) data did not control for the number of arguments included in the sentences, which made it difficult to disentangle the respective impact of word characteristics and syntactic structure.

Several experiments were thus conducted and aimed at studying the production of two-word sentences in order to better understand the scope of planning and the nature of the representations and processes involved in such productions: Do the processing levels run in parallel or are the processes sequential? Which processes and representations are devoted to the first target completed before the processes devoted to the second one start (Bonin, Fayol, & Malardier, 2001; Bonin, Malardier, Méot, & Fayol, 2005; Malardier, Bonin, & Fayol, 2004)? Participants had to either speak aloud or write down the single nouns (Bonin et al., 2005), for example, Experiment 1, *aimant* (magnet) or *pile* (battery), or write down the noun phrases (determinant followed by the noun); and Experiment 2, *un aimant–une batterie* corresponding to two pictures that were presented side by side on a computer screen, always starting with the left one. Latencies were recorded. Certain properties, corresponding to the pictures themselves, the concepts depicted by the pictures, or the names associated with the pictures, of the first and of the second targets, were included as predictors in multiple regression analyses to determine which characteristics of the first target (vs. the later targets) were reliable determinants of spoken and written naming latencies.

The first result answered the question as to what extent the two words were planned before the beginning of production. The initiation of speaking aloud or writing down two target names from pictures depended to a large extent on the processing that takes place on the first target and, to a very small extent, on processing that takes place on the second target. Planning thus concerned mainly the first word to produce, but some impact of the second word emerged, though slightly. The second result enabled identification of the representations involved in the planning of each of the targets. Name agreement and AoA, but not word frequency, were the main determinants of latencies regarding the first target, which suggests that processing at the semantic and lexical levels is engaged before the initiation of writing or speaking. Only image agreement, a variable not involved in accessing word forms, was a determinant associated to the second target. These results are in agreement with those collected in spoken production. Interestingly, insofar as word forms of the second target were not accessed before the initiation of production, such word forms are most probably retrieved when articulating the first target. Certain linguistic processes are thus reflected in writing rate and within word pauses.

To summarize, several results from on-line studies have given us a better understanding of the representations, processes, and costs involved in the production of words, isolated or grouped by pairs, and in context of simple or complex sentences. More precisely, data provided evidence that the more complex the unit—word, words, phrases, clauses, sentences—the more the time required to plan the longer initial pause. However, every dimension was not planned from the start, as illustrated by the production of pairs of words. Only some dimensions were totally prepared when transcription began, whereas some others were planned on-line when the writer was already producing parts of the words or sentences. This type of result suggested that parts of the message—representations and processes—were planned before beginning to produce the following unit and other parts were prepared when transcribing the first part of the message. That is, people were doing at least three things at the same time in parallel: transcribing, maintaining in temporary memory information already planned, and preparing some remaining dimensions for the translation process. The question was thus to try to precisely determine what those dimensions were and the processes that were involved in their production.

Composing in Real Time: Producing Texts

From the very beginning, we were convinced that the study of composing stimulates development of two complementary lines of research. The first one, prompted by neuropsychology, consisted in defining components, their architecture, and the processes supposed to be involved in their functioning in order to construct models of producing words, sentences, and texts. Even if Hayes and Flower (1980; Flower & Hayes, 1980) did not refer to neuropsychological approaches and did not specify the translation processes precisely, their goal, like that of neuropsychologists, was to decompose the complex task of writing in order to analyze the mental representations and component processes that work together in composing. The second line of research aimed at trying to understand the dynamics of composing as it unfolds in real time, which is also necessary to understand the dynamics of reading. Addressing these dynamics requires research that studies complex activities and generates complex data. In particular, observing how isolated words or sentences are dealt with in real time is only a first step in determining how processing unfolds when words and sentences are processed in real time.

I, as well as my students and colleagues, have implemented these two research approaches since the beginning of the 1990s. The first on-line study (Foulin & Fayol, 1988) used a rough video-recording system with second- and third-grade children (12 at each school level), each of them producing one narrative text ("Tell us about a fright") and one expository text ("Tell about a tour") (Fayol, 1991c). To begin, we analyzed some linguistic marks in the texts, as described at the beginning of this chapter, pauses at different positions in the text, and variations in writing rates. The data were simple, but we were convinced that this kind of research was feasible. We found that third graders produced longer texts and wrote faster than the second graders. By contrast, no significant difference appeared regarding the mean length and the proportion of pauses. The pattern was very different from that described with adults. Gould (1978) observed that adults spent two-thirds of the composing time pausing while children spent the same proportion writing.

The next research program was far more sophisticated. Chanquoy, Foulin, and Fayol (1990) wanted to study the effects of the familiarity with the content, the type of text, and the syntactic complexity on the on-line management of composing short texts (i.e., text endings). Forty-eight participants (16 adults, 16 fifth graders, and 16 third graders) were asked to produce endings from oral text beginnings, which were either narrative (e.g., "Mary goes to the restaurant. She reads the menu. She goes in.") or expository (e.g., "It's a car. It is parked in the car park. It's shining."; Holmes, 1984). They were all required to produce endings that were either highly predictable (script-like endings, Fayol & Monteil, 1988) or unpredictable. The endings had to consist of three (for the adults) or two (for the children) events (in the narratives) or states (in the expository texts). The adults had to formulate the endings in either one or three sentences, whereas the children had to use either one or two sentences. To adapt the difficulty to the participants, the children produced eight endings (four narrative and four expository; one sentence or two sentences long; four predictable or four unpredictable), whereas the adults produced 16 endings (eight for each condition). All the participants, especially the children, were trained before performing the task.

The text productions were videorecorded and analyzed using a videotape recorder with an image reading accuracy rate of 1/10th of a second. Three dependent variables were analyzed:

1. The *prewriting duration* (PW), that is, the time lapse between the end of the instructions and the beginning of transcription;
2. The *between-clause pause duration* (BC), that is, the time lapse between the end of the nth clause and the beginning of the $n + 1$th clause (adults had two BC pauses, whereas the children had only one BC pause); and
3. The *within-clause writing rate* (WR) (in seconds/character), that is, the mean duration for the transcription of one character between the beginning and the end of the same clause.

The main results can be summarized as follows. First, the PW pause duration was significantly longer in the adults than the children; the WR significantly increased and the BC pause duration significantly decreased as a function of age or school level. Second, in the three groups, the familiarity with the content entailed a decrease in PW pause duration, as well as in the BC pause duration and an increase in the WR in adults and fifth graders, but not in the third graders. No effect of the text type (narrative versus expository) appeared for pauses or WR. Third, in adults and fifth graders, the WR increased in the last clause (i.e., the third or the second, respectively), thus suggesting that its management imposed a lower load on the participants. Overall, these results show that the speed and the flexibility of composing increase as a function of age or school level: With increasing age and experience, people become both more skilled in dealing with the low-level components of writing and more able to strategically distribute the management of the other components of composing (see Schilperoord, 1996, 2002; Van Hell, Verhoeven, & Van Beijsterveldt, 2008; Verhoeven & Van Hell, 2008, for similar results). However, no precise data were available regarding the processing of the low-level dimensions of composing: the WR provided only a rough indicator of the transcription process.

Thus, using a text-ending paradigm, we were able to provide evidence of some on-line production effects in adults as well as in fifth graders: The more predictable the endings are, the shorter the initial and the between-clause pause durations and the faster the writing rate. These effects did not appear in third graders, most likely because children at this stage of writing acquisition mainly devote their attention to the management of transcription and therefore have very few resources available for dealing with the higher dimensions of text production. Transcription skills contribute uniquely to composing in the early grades (Grades 1 to 3) but less so in the upper grades (Grades 5 to 6) of elementary school (Berninger & Swanson, 1994).

One possibility is that the cost of handwriting is so high and writing is so slow in young children that it is only during pauses that they are able to deal with other dimensions. To test this hypothesis, Fayol and Stephant (1991) compared the written composition and the written recall of the same text endings in children and adults. We assumed that the cognitive load associated with conceptual and linguistic processing could be measured by comparing the pauses and writing rate associated with each linguistic segment in composition and in transcription after rote learning (i.e., recall). As in the previous experiment, children and adults listened to the beginning of stories and were asked to compose two action endings for each beginning. The endings had to be either predictable or highly unpredictable, and the two actions had to be inserted in either one or two separate sentences. Each of the 12 third graders and 12 adults produced four endings each. After composing, each participant was asked to read every ending he or she has composed, memorize it thoroughly, and later write it down by rote. The participants were video recorded while composing and recalling the text endings. The films were then analyzed for temporal parameters relating to both composition and recall: initial PW pause duration (composition only); BC pause duration; within-clause pause duration; and within-clause WR.

As in the previous experiment, the mean PW pause duration was significantly longer with unpredictable than with predictable endings in adults but not in children. As already discussed, the times for composing text endings were always faster than composing the corresponding texts in both adults and children. There were dramatic decreases between the composition and the recall durations and rates: in BC pause duration, –5.55 s (–69%) in children and –1.76 s (–72%) in adults; in within-clause pause duration, –0.56 s in children (–39%) and –0.15 s in adults (–33%); and in WR, –0.13 s per character in children (–14%) and –0.04 s per character in adults (–10%). The decrease was unexpectedly of the same magnitude in children and in adults, which suggested that the *relative* cost of graphic transcription was approximately the same in children and adults. However, the pause durations and word transcription times were far longer in children than in adults. These results lead to the conclusion that exploring the on-line management of composing is necessary to better understand how children and adults deal with the multiple constraints of composing in real time.

Recently, we went a step further (Fayol, Foulin, Maggio, & Lété, in press) in the study of the dynamic of composing in order to examine the potential impact of two low-level dimensions—the length of words (indexing the frequency) and their spelling consistency. As previously reported, the WFE explains at least part of the variation in between-word pauses and hesitations in oral production and part of the latencies in written word production (Bonin & Fayol, 2000, 2002; Bonin et al., 1997). Given that word frequency is closely related to word length, a consideration of the impact of word length (in number of letters) should provide an easy and fast way to evaluate the effect of word frequency on composing. Phonology-to-orthography consistency refers to the level of variability in the orthographic codes that can be assigned to a particular phonological unit: Phoneme-to-grapheme consistency is lower when a number of different graphemes can be mapped to a particular phoneme than when a single grapheme is always associated with a particular phoneme. The results obtained by Bonin, Peereman, and Fayol (2001) as well as Delattre et al. (2006) clearly show that the written production of isolated words is sensitive to the consistency of these words.

One important point was to check whether this dimension also impacted pause duration and writing rate in text production. We first correlated the duration of the before-word pause (BWP) (excluding the initial PW pause already studied, the duration of which depended on familiarity for the content and syntactic complexity) and the writing rate of the corresponding word (WWR) (in seconds per character) for each of the words. This correlation was significant but very low in adults ($r = -.06$) and fifth graders ($r = -0.08$), and slightly higher in third graders ($r = -0.19$), suggesting that the BWP and WWR may index different phenomena and justifying the use of separate analyses for pause durations and writing rates. A number of different regression analyses were conducted using BWP and WWR as dependent variables to determine whether the length and consistency of words make a significant independent contribution to both BWP and WWR once the impact of other variables was controlled.

Lastly, a new series of experiments is currently in progress, aimed at investigating the production of words-in-texts in real time (Maggio, Lété, Chenu, Jisah, & Fayol, 2011). The reasoning in this study is prompted by reading research in which it has been shown that the processing of isolated words is quite different from that of processing the same words in the context of reading texts (Kliegl, Nuthmann, & Engbert, 2006). More precisely, it has been observed that some dimensions of words were processed before the fixation of those words and others after the eyes have moved onto the following word. To sum up, the assumption of the immediacy of processing was only partially attested. The same reasoning led us to explore what dimensions—frequency of word form, consistency, position in the text—were predictive of three parameters: pause duration before word, pause duration within a word, and writing rate of the word. Moreover, three loci of influences were studied: influences of word n (immediacy effects), influences of word $n - 1$ (delayed effects), and influences of word $n + 1$ (anticipatory effects). Children and adolescents have been asked to compose texts in the oral and the written modality (the order was counterbalanced) and all the temporal parameters were recorded and analyzed. The WWR and the intraword pause measures show both immediacy and anticipatory effects. However, the BWP measures show only delayed effects, which has not been reported in previous studies. As far as we know, this investigation is the first revealing that the linguistic processing of a word n can still occur while the pen has already moved to the next word $n + 1$ or can take place before, while the word $n - 1$ is being transcribed. Some other analyses are in progress.

CONCLUSIONS

The collection of studies and reviews of this chapter illustrate how far we have come in our understanding of adults' and children's composing products and composing processes. We started by analyzing children's written narratives, went through the experimental study of several components—lexical production, spelling, punctuation, transcription, and so on—and attempted to synthesize all the results into an integrative model of on-line composing that is still in progress and thus remains largely to be constructed.

Four points are worth noting. First, some dimensions have not been explored in depth. For example, grammatical encoding has not received as much attention as lexical production or spelling. This is a fundamental component of the composing process, the functioning of which is necessary to understand how people proceed to both package information and chain successive sentences. Punctuation and connectives are only a first step on the way to construct models of syntactic planning. Most of the time, the syntactic dimension was confounded with the number of lexical items, making it difficult to disentangle the impact of the former from that of the latter. A lot remains to be done, for instance, by using Bock's (1986) syntactic priming paradigm in tasks where the lexicon could be more or less controlled for. Another topic too rarely explored has to do with the role of content in composing. It is a well-known fact that the knowledge base of the topic to which one will compose about is a strong determinant of both the quantity and quality of text. However, the data remain sketchy, and more precise investigations are required: Bourdin and Fayol's (2002) paradigm looks promising; but it has not yet been extended to different topics and populations.

Second, few precise attempts have been made to link the study of composing processes to that of general cognitive processes such as working memory or processing speed. Kellogg's (2001) study as well as Berninger's (1999) work have provided both evidence and theoretical frames to better understand how working memory impacts individual differences in products and in the management of composing (see Alamargot & Chanquoy, 2001, or Olive, 2004, for overviews). However, there are multiple components of working memory, and we do not fully understand individual differences in strategic approaches to tasks loading on working memory. The role of speed of processing is still often ignored, despite its importance in individual differences and development (but see Chapters 5 and 6, this volume). A large research program could be devoted to these two dimensions, taking into account the role of knowledge of the topics.

Third, we have rarely conducted highly controlled studies about teaching and learning written composition. At best, we have explored the impact of teaching noun, adjective, and verb agreements on children's performances on spelling tasks (Fayol et al., 1999) and other tasks related to written word learning (Gombert & Fayol, 1992; Rieben, Ntamakiliro, Gonthier, & Fayol, 2005). Currently, Slusarczyk et al. (2011) are conducting a longitudinal study with children (8 to 11 years of age) in order to better understand if and how spelling performance impacts text composition and the reverse. But it was not possible to have precise and theoretically grounded indications about the teaching of both spelling and composing provided during the 3 years of the study. We are thus left with the challenge of elaborating an experimental design to investigate the effect(s) of teaching composing and its components on a large population.

Fourth, in written composition as well as in reading it is one thing to study the processing of each component in isolation and another thing to try to understand the dynamics of processing when all components are to be dealt with by the writer in real time, constrained or not. Until now, we have enlarged the knowledge of many of the components (the lexicon, spelling, syntax), including that of graphic transcription (Kandel, Herault, Grosjacques, Lambert, & Fayol, 2009; Lambert, Kandel, Fayol, & Esperet, 2008). However, the complexity of coordinating the functioning of all components is so high that we need to explore more precisely the on-line management of composing, using special devices such as eye-tracking, handwriting recording, and so on (Alamargot, Chesnet, Dansac, & Ros, 2006). Most probably, computer modeling will be necessary because of the impossibility of conducting all the required experiments. And, more important, theoretical progress is needed to raise relevant questions and plan further experiments.

Not only have I learned much about writing from these research studies, but I also value the opportunity to train graduate students who have gone on to pursue the same kinds of questions that motivated me early in my career. Over the years some have focused their research and subsequent professional activities on math and reading and other topics related to the cognitive and linguistic processes in learning, but in the Appendix to this chapter I call attention to those who have focused on writing research and celebrate their contributions. I end with a dose of reality regarding time and a sense of humor about reality of writing research. Several studies of many lives will be necessary!

APPENDIX

Former PhD Students of Professor Michel Fayol Whose Dissertation Focused on Writing Research

Isabelle Bonnotte (1989) – Maître de Conférences, University of Lille
Lucile Chanquoy (1991) – Professor, University of Nice
Jean Noel Foulin (1991) – Maître de Conférences, University of Bordeaux
Serge Mouchon (1992) – Maître de Conférences, University René Descartes (Paris), retired
Laurent Heurley (1993) – Maître de Conférences, University of Amiens
Vanda Gufoni (1993) – Private
Béatrice Bourdin (1994) – Maître de Conférences, University of Amiens
Pierre Largy (1995) – Professor, University of Toulouse Le Mirail
Patrick Bonin (1996) – Professor, University of Burgundy (Dijon)
Corinne Totereau (1998) – Maître de Conférences, University of Grenoble at Chambery
Isabelle Negro (1998) – Maître de Conférences, University of Nice
Frank Ganier (1999) – Maître de Conférences, University of Brest
Eric Lambert (1999) – Maître de Conférences, University of Poitiers
Sébastien Pacton (2000) – Professor, University René Descartes (Paris)
Nathalie Mallardier (2003) – Private
Marie-Paule Cousin (2004) – School Psychologist
Sandra Collay (2004) – Private
Bruno Boyer (2006) – Private

REFERENCES

Alamargot, D., & Chanquoy, L. (2001). *Through the models of writing*. Dordrecht, Boston, New York: Kluwer.
Alamargot, D., Chesnet, D., Dansac, C., & Ros, C. (2006). Eye and pen: A new device to study reading during writing. *Behavior Research Methods, 38*, 287–299.

Alamargot, D., & Fayol, M. (2009). Modelling the development of written composition. In R. Beard, D. Myhill, M. Nystrand, & J. Riley (Eds.), *The SAGE handbook of writing development* (pp. 23–47). Thousand Oaks, CA: Sage.

Anderson, J. R. (1983). *The architecture of cognition*. Cambridge, MA: Harvard University Press.

Anderson, J. R. (1995). *Learning and memory*. New York: Wiley.

Applebee, A. N. (1978). *The child's concept of story*. Chicago: University of Chicago Press.

Berninger, V. (1999). Coordinating transcription and text generation in working memory during composing: Automatized and constructive processes. *Learning Disability Quarterly, 22*, 99–112.

Berninger, V., & Fayol, M. (2008). Why spelling is important and how to teach it effectively. Retrieved from http://literacyencyclopedia.ca/pdfs/Why_Spelling_Is_Important_and_How_To_Teach_It_Effectively.pdf

Berninger, V. W., & Swanson, H. L. (1994). Modifying Hayes and Flower's model of skilled writing to explain beginning and developing writing. In E. Butterfield (Ed.), *Children's writing: Toward a process theory of the development of skilled writing* (pp. 57–81). Greenwich, CT: JAI Press.

Bestgen, Y., & Costermans, J. (1994). Time, space, and action: Exploring the narrative structure and its linguistic marking. *Discourse Processes, 17*, 421–446.

Bock, J. K. (1986). Syntactic persistence in language production. *Cognitive Psychology, 18*, 355–387.

Bock, J. K., & Cutting, J. C. (1992). Regulating mental energy: Performance units in language production. *Journal of Memory and Language, 31*, 99–127.

Bock, J. K., & Eberhard, K. M. (1993). Meaning, sound, and syntax in English number homophonic picture names. *European Journal of Cognitive Psychology, 14*, 289–313.

Bock, J. K., & Levelt, W. J. M. (1994). Grammatical encoding. In M. A. Gernsbacher (Ed.), *Handbook of psycholinguistics* (pp. 945–978). New York: Academic Press.

Bonin, P., Chalard, M., Méot, A., & Fayol, M. (2001). Age of acquisition and word frequency in the lexical decision task: Further evidence from the French language. *Current Psychology of Cognition, 20*, 401–443.

Bonin, P., Chalard, M., Méot, A., & Fayol, M. (2002). The determinants of spoken and written picture naming latencies. *British Journal of Psychology, 93*, 89–114.

Bonin, P., Collay, S., & Fayol, M. (2008). La consistance orthographique en production écrite: une brève synthèse. *L'Année Psychologique, 108*, 517–546.

Bonin, P., & Fayol, M. (2000). Writing words from pictures: what representations are activated and when? *Memory and Cognition, 28*, 677–689.

Bonin, P., & Fayol, M. (2002). Frequency effects in the written and spoken production of word interference experiments. *Journal of Memory and Language, 35*, 477–496.

Bonin, P., Fayol, M., & Chalard, M. (2001). Age of acquisition and word frequency in written picture naming. *The Quarterly Journal of Experimental Psychology, 54A*, 469–489.

Bonin, P., Fayol, M., & Gombert, J. E. (1997). Role of orthographic and phonological codes in picture naming and writing: An interference paradigm study. *Current Psychology of Cognition, 16*, 299–324.

Bonin, P., Fayol, M., & Gombert, J. E. (1998). An experimental study of lexical access in the writing and naming of isolated words. *International Journal of Psychology, 33*, 269–286.

Bonin, P., Fayol, M., & Malardier, N. (2001). Writing two words from picture. *Current Psychology Letters, 3*, 43–58.

Bonin, P., Fayol, M., & Peereman, R. (1998). Masked form priming in writing words from pictures: Evidence for direct retrieval of orthographic codes. *Acta Psychologica, 99*, 311–328.

Bonin, P., Malardier, N., Méot, A., & Fayol, M. (2005). The scope of advance planning in written picture naming. *Language and Cognitive Processes, 21*, 205–237.

Bonin, P., Pacton, S., & Fayol, M. (2001). La production verbale écrite: Evidences en faveur d'une (relative) autonomie de l'écrit. *Psychologie Française, 46*, 77–88.

Bonin, P., Peereman, R., & Fayol, M. (2001). Do phonological codes constraint the selection of orthographic codes in written picture naming? *Journal of Memory and Language, 45*, 688–720.

Bonnotte, I., & Fayol, M. (1993a). Comment apprendre l'emploi des formes verbales à l'écrit? *Bulletin de Psychologie, 46*, 645–652.

Bonnotte, I., & Fayol, M. (1993b). Le fonctionnement adulte des formes verbales dans des récits en Castillan, en Euskara et en Français. *Langue Française, 97*, 81–101.

Bonnotte, I., & Fayol, M. (1997). Cognitive representations of predicates and the use of past-tenses in French: A developmental approach. *First Language, 17*, 75–101.

Bonnotte, I., & Fayol, M. (2000). Gestion des relations sémantiques. *Syntaxe et Sémantique, 2*, 179–201.

Bourdin, B., & Fayol, M. (1994). Is written language production really more difficult than oral language production? *International Journal of Psychology, 29*, 591–620.

Bourdin, B., & Fayol, M. (1996). Mode effects in a sentence production task. *Current Psychology of Cognition,15*, 245–264.

Bourdin, B., & Fayol, M. (2002). Even in adults, written production is still more costly than oral production. *International Journal of Psychology, 37*, 219–222.

Caron, J. (1997). Toward a procedural approach to the meaning of connectives. In J. Costermans & M. Fayol (Eds.), *Processing interclausal relationships. Studies in the production and comprehension of texts* (pp. 53–73). Mahwah, NJ: Erlbaum.

Catach, N. (1986). *L'orthographe française*. Paris: Nathan.

Chanquoy, L., & Fayol, M. (1991). Etude de l'utilisation des signes de ponctuations et des connecteurs chez des enfants et des adultes. *Pratiques, 70*, 107–124.

Chanquoy, L., Foulin, J. N., & Fayol, M. (1990). The temporal management of short text writing by children and adults. *European Bulletin of Cognitive Psychology, 10*, 513–540.

Connelly, V., Dockrell, J. E., & Barnett, J. (2005). The slow handwriting of undergraduate students constrains overall performance in exam essays. *Educational Psychology, 25*, 97–105.

Cousin, M-P., Largy, P., & Fayol, M. (2002). Sometimes, early learned instances hinder the implementation of agreement rules. A study in written French. *Current Psychology Letters, 8*, 51–65.

Delattre, M., Bonin, P., & Barry, C. (2006). Written spelling to dictation: Sound-to-spelling regularity affects both writing latencies and durations. *Journal of Experimental Psychology: Learning, Memory, and Cognition, 32*, 1330–1340.

Dell, G. S. (1986). A spreading-activation theory of retrieval in sentence production. *Psychological Review, 93*, 283–321.

Dell, G. S., & O'Seaghdha, P. G. (1992). Stages of lexical access in language production. *Cognition, 42*, 287–314.

Fayol, M. (1982). Le plus-que-parfait. Etude génétique en compréhension et production chez l'enfant de 4 à 10 ans. *Archives de Psychologie, 50*, 261–283.

Fayol, M. (1984). La distanciation dans le langage: l'exemple du calcul de l'origine dans le récit écrit d'expérience personnelle chez l'enfant de six à dix ans. *Enfance, 1*, 5–19.

Fayol, M. (1985). *Le récit et sa construction*. Paris: Neuchâtel, Delachaux et Niestlé.

Fayol, M. (1986). Cohérence et cohésion: une revue. In M. Charolle, J. S. Petofi, & E. Suzer (Eds.), *Research in text connexity and text coherence: A survey* (pp. 125–146). Hamburg: Buske.

Fayol, M. (1991a). From sentence production to text production [special issue on writing]. *European Journal of Psychology of Education*, 101–119.

Fayol, M. (1991b). Stories: A psycholinguistic and ontogenetic approach to the acquisition of narrative abilities. In G. Piéraut le Bonniec & M. Dolitsky (Eds.), *From basic language to discourse bases* (pp. 229–244). Amsterdam: Benjamins.

Fayol, M. (1991c). Text typologies: A cognitive approach. In G. Denhière & J.P. Rossi (Eds.), *Text and text processing* (pp. 61–76). Amsterdam: North Holland.

Fayol, M. (1994). From declarative and procedural knowledge to the management of declarative and procedural knowledge. *European Journal of Psychology of Education, 9,* 179–190.

Fayol, M. (1996). La production du langage écrit. In J. David & S. Plane (Eds.), *L'apprentissage de l'écriture de l'école au collège* (pp. 9–36). Paris: Presses Universitaires de France.

Fayol, M. (1997a). On acquiring and using punctuation. A study in written French. In J. Costermans & M. Fayol (Eds.), *Processing interclausal relationships. Studies in the production and comprehension of texts* (pp. 157–178). Mahwah, NJ: Erlbaum.

Fayol, M. (1997b). *Des idées au texte*. Paris: Presses Universitaires de France

Fayol, M. (1999). From on-line management problems to strategies in written composition. In M. Torrance & G. Jeffery (Eds.), *The cognitive demands of writing*. Amsterdam, the Netherlands: Amsterdam University Press.

Fayol, M. (2000). Comprendre et produire des textes écrits. L'exemple du récit. In M. Kail & M. Fayol (Eds.), *L'acquisition du langage* (Vol. 2, pp. 183–213). Paris: Presses Universitaires de France.

Fayol, M. (2002a). La production du langage. *Encyclopédie des Sciences cognitives*. Vol. X. Paris: Hermès.

Fayol, M. (2002b). Les documents techniques: bilan et perspectives. *Psychologie Française, 47,* 9–18.

Fayol, M. (2003). Text and cognition. In T. Nunes & P. Bryant (Eds.), *Handbook of children's literacy* (pp. 181–198). Amsterdam: Kluwer.

Fayol, M. (2008). L'apprentissage de l'orthographe. Bilan. In Académie des Sciences (Ed.), *Education, sciences cognitives et neurosciences* (pp. 93–111). Paris: Presses Universitaires de France.

Fayol, M., & Abdi, H. (1988). Influence of scripts structure on punctuation. *European Bulletin of Cognitive Psychology, 8,* 265–279.

Fayol, M., Foulin, J-N., Maggio, S., & Lété, B. (in press). Towards a dynamic approach of how children and adults manage text production. In E. Grigorenko, E. Mambrino, & D. D. Preiss (Eds.), *Writing: A mosaic of perspectives*. New York: Psychology Press.

Fayol, M., Gombert, J. E., & Abdi, H. (1989). Use of past tense verb inflections in French: Developmental study of the interaction between types of process and context. *European Bulletin of Cognitive Psychology, 9,* 279–295.

Fayol, M., & Got, C. (1991). Automatisme et contrôle dans la production écrite. *L'Année Psychologique, 91,* 187–205.

Fayol, M., & Heurley, L. (1995). Des modèles de production du langage à l'étude du fonctionnement du scripteur. In J. Y. Boyer, J. P. Dionne, & P. Raymond (Eds.), *La production de textes* (pp. 17–48). Montréal: Ed Logiques.

Fayol, M., Hickmann, M., Bonnotte, I., & Gombert, J. E. (1993). French verbal inflections and narrative context: A developmental perspective. *Journal of Psycholinguistic Research, 22,* 453–478.

Fayol, M., Hupet, M., & Largy, P. (1999). The acquisition of subject-verb agreement in written French. From novices to experts' errors. *Reading and Writing, 11,* 153–174.

Fayol, M., & Jaffré, J-P. (2008). *Orthographier*. Paris: PUF.

Fayol, M., Largy, P., & Lemaire, P. (1994). Subject-verb agreement errors in French. *Quarterly Journal of Experimental Psychology, 47A,* 437–464.

Fayol, M., & Lemaire, P. (1993). Levels of approach to discourse. In H. H. Brownell & Y. Joanette (Eds.), *Narrative discourse in normal aging and neurologically impaired* (pp. 3–21). San Diego, CA: Singular.

Fayol, M., & Lété, B. (1987). Ponctuation et connecteurs: une approche textuelle et génétique. *European Journal of Psychology of Education, 2*, 57–72.

Fayol, M., & Miret, A. (2005). Écrire, orthographier et rédiger des textes. *Psychologie Française, 50*, 391–402.

Fayol, M., & Monteil, J. M. (1988). The notion of script: From general to developmental and social psychology. *European Bulletin of Cognitive Psychology, 8*, 461–475.

Fayol, M., & Mouchon, S. (1997). Production and comprehension of connectives in the written modality. A study of written French. In C. Pontecorvo (Ed.), *Writing development: An interdisciplinary view* (pp. 193–204). Amsterdam: Benjamins.

Fayol, M., & Stephant, I. (1991, August). *Assessing cognitive load in writing*. Paper presented at the Fourth Conference of the European Association for Research on Learning and Instruction. Turku, Finland.

Fayol, M., Thévenin, M. G., Jarousse, J. P., & Totereau, C. (1999). From learning to teaching to learning French written morphology. In T. Nunes (Ed.), *Learning to read: An integrated view from research and practice* (pp. 43–64). Dordrecht: Kluwer.

Fayol, M., & Totereau, C. (2001). Learning the written morphology of plural in written French. In L. Tolchinski (Ed.), *Developmental aspects in learning to write* (pp. 97–108). Dordrecht: Kluwer.

Fayol, M., Totereau, C., & Barrouillet, P. (2006). Disentangling the impact of semantic and formal factors in the acquisition of number inflections. Noun, adjective and verb agreement in written French. *Reading and Writing, 19*, 717–736.

Fayol, M., Zorman, M., & Lété, B. (2009). Unexpectedly good spellers too. Associations and dissociations in reading and spelling French. Monograph series 2: Teaching and learning writing. *British Journal of Educational Psychology, 6*, 63–75.

Ferreiro, E., & Zucchermaglio, C. (1996). Children's use of punctuation marks: The case of quoted speech. In C. Pontecorvo, M. Orsolini, B. Burge, & L. Resnick (Eds.), *Children's early text construction* (pp. 145–164). Mahwah, NJ: Erlbaum.

Flower, L., & Hayes, J. R. (1980). The dynamic of composing: Making plans and juggling constraints. In L. W. Gregg & E. R. Steinberg (Eds.), *Cognitive processes in writing* (pp. 31–50). Hillsdale, NJ: Erlbaum.

Foulin, J-N. (1998). To what extent does pause location predict pause duration in adults' and children's writing? *Cahiers de Psychologie Cognitive/Current Psychology of Cognition, 17*(3), 601–620.

Foulin, J-N., Chanquoy, L., & Fayol, M. (1989). Approche en temps réel de la production des connecteurs et de la ponctuation. *Langue Française, 81*, 21–39.

Foulin, J-N., & Fayol, M. (1988). Etude en temps réel de la roduction écrite chez des enfants de sept et huit ans. *European Journal of Psychology of Education, 3*, 461–475.

French, L. A., & Nelson, K. (1985). *Children's acquisition of relational terms: Some ifs, ors, and buts*. New York: Springer-Verlag.

Ganier, F., Gombert, J. E., & Fayol, M. (2000). Effets du format de présentation des instructions sur l'apprentissage de procédures à l'aide de documents techniques. *Le Travail Humain, 63*, 121–152.

Gombert, J. E., & Fayol, M. (1992). Writing in preliterate children. *Learning and Instruction, 2*, 23–41.

Gould, J. D. (1978). How experts dictate. *Journal of Experimental Psychology: Human Perception and Performance, 4*, 648–661.

Graham, S. (1990). The role of production factors in learning disabled students' compositions. *Journal of Educational Psychology, 82*, 781–791.

Graham, S., Berninger, V. W., Abbott, R. D., Abbott, S. P., & Whitaker, D. (1997). Role of mechanics in composing of elementary school students: A new methodological approach. *Journal of Educational Psychology, 89,* 170–182.

Gufoni, V. (1996). Les protocoles verbaux comme méthode d'étude de la production écrite: Approche critique. *Études de Linguistique Appliquée, 101,* 20–32.

Hayes, J. R., & Flower, L. S. (1980). Identifying the organization of writing processes. In L. W. Gregg & E. R. Steinberg (Eds.), *Cognitive processes in writing* (pp. 3–30). Hillsdale, NJ: Erlbaum.

Herrmann, T., & Grabowski, J. (1995). Pre-terminal levels of process in oral and written language production. In U. M. Quasthoff (Ed.), *Aspects of oral communication* (pp. 67–85). Berlin: de Gruyter.

Heurley, L. (1997). Processing units in written texts: Paragraphs or information blocks? In J. Costermans & M. Fayol (Eds.), *Processing interclausal relationships* (pp. 179–200). Mahwah, NJ: Erlbaum.

Hickmann, M. (1997). Information status and grounding in children's narratives: A cross-linguistic perspective. In J. Costermans & M. Fayol (Eds.), *Processing interclausal relationships* (pp. 221–244). Mahwah, NJ: Erlbaum.

Holmes, V. (1984). Sentence planning in a story continuation task. *Language and Speech, 27,* 115–134.

Hudson, J., & Shapiro, L. R. (1991). From knowing to telling: The development of children's script, stories, and personal narratives. In A. McCabe & C. Peterson (Eds.), *Developing narrative structure* (pp. 89–136). Hillsdale, NJ: Erlbaum.

Hupet, M., Fayol, M., & Schelstraete, M-A. (1998). Effects of semantic variables on the subject-verb agreement processes in writing. *British Journal of Psychology, 89,* 59–75.

Jaffré, J-P., & Fayol, M. (2005). Orthography and literacy in French. In R. M. Joshi & P. G. Aaron (Eds.), *Handbook of orthography and literacy* (pp. 81–104). Mahwah, NJ: Erlbaum.

Kail, M., & Weissenborn, J. (1991). Conjunctions: Developmental issues. In G. Pieraut le Bonniec & M. Dolitsky (Eds.), *From basic language to discourse basis* (pp. 125–142). Amsterdam: Benjamins.

Kandel, S., Herault, L., Grosjacques, G., Lambert, E., & Fayol, M. (2009). Orthographic vs. phonologic syllables in handwriting production. *Cognition, 110,* 440–444.

Kellogg, R. T. (2001). Competition for working memory among writing processes. *American Journal of Psychology, 114,* 175–191.

Kliegl, R., Nuthmann, A., & Engbert, R. (2006). Tracking the mind during reading: The influence of past, present, and future words on fixation duration. *Journal of Experimental Psychology: General, 135,* 12–35.

Lambert, E., Kandel, S., Fayol, M., & Esperet, E. (2008). The effect of the number of syllables on handwriting production. *Reading and Writing, 21,* 859–883.

Largy, P. (2001). La révision des accords nominal et verbal chez l'enfant. *L'Année Psychologique, 101,* 221–245.

Largy, P., Cousin, M-P., Bryant, P., & Fayol, M. (2007). When memorised instances compete with rules: The case of number-noun agreement in written French. *Journal of Child Language, 34,* 425–437.

Largy, P., & Fayol, M. (2001). Oral cues improve subject-verb agreement in written French. *International Journal of Psychology, 36,* 121–132.

Largy, P., Fayol, M., & Lemaire, P. (1996). The homophone effect in written French: The case of noun-verb inflection errors. *Language and Cognitive Processes, 10,* 217–255.

Lété, B., Peereman, R., & Fayol, M. (2008). Phoneme-to-grapheme consistency and word-frequency effects on spelling among first- to fifth-grade French children: A regression-based study. *Journal of Memory and Language, 58,* 952–977.

Levelt, W. J. M. (1989). *Speaking: From intention to articulation.* Cambridge: MIT Press.

Levelt, W. J. M. (1999). Models of word production. *Trends in Cognitive Sciences, 3,* 223–232.

Levelt, W. J. M., Roelofs, A., & Meyer, A. S. (1999). A theory of lexical access in speech production. *Behavioral and Brain Sciences, 22,* 1–75.

Maggio, S., Lété, B., Chenu, F., Jisah, H., & Fayol, M. (2011). Tracking the mind during writing: Immediacy, delayed, and anticipatory effects on pauses and writing rate. Manuscript submitted for publication.

Malardier, N., Bonin, P., & Fayol, M. (2004). Dénomination par écrit de paires d'images: La question de la dépendance. *L'Année Psychologique, 104,* 407–432.

Mandler, J., & Johnson, N. S. (1977). Remembrance of things parsed: Story structure and recall. *Cognitive Psychology, 9,* 111–151.

Martinet, C., Valdois, S., & Fayol, M. (2004). Lexical orthographic knowledge develops from the beginning of reading acquisition. *Cognition, 91,* B11–B22.

McCutchen, D. (1987). Children's discourse skill: Form and modality requirements of schooled writing. *Discourse Processes, 10,* 267–286.

McCutchen, D. (1996). Cognitive processes in children's writing: developmental and individual differences. *Issues in Education, 1,* 123–160.

McCutchen, D. (2000). Knowledge, processing, and working memory: Implications for a theory of writing. *Educational Psychologist, 35,* 13–23.

Mouchon, S., Fayol, M., & Gaonac'h, D. (1995). On-line processing of links between events in narratives: Studies on children and adults. *Current Psychology of Cognition, 14,* 171–193.

Mouchon, S., Fayol, M., & Gombert, J. E. (1989). L'utilisation des connecteurs dans les rappels de récits chez les enfants de 5 à 8 ans. *L'Année Psychologique, 89,* 513–529.

Mounier, E., & Bisseret, A. (2001). Usage de la ponctuation dans la description technique: marquer la partition de l'objet décrit. *Le Travail Humain, 64,* 363–390.

Negro, I., Chanquoy, L., Fayol, M., & Louis-Sydney, M. (2005). Subject-verb agreement in children and adults: Serial or hierarchical processing. *Journal of Psycholinguistic Research, 34,* 233–258.

Nottbusch, G. (2010). Grammatical planning, execution, and control in written sentence production. *Reading and Writing, 23,* 777–801.

Ochs, E. (1979). Planned and unplanned discourse. In T. Givon (Ed.), *Syntax and semantics* (XII): *Discourse and syntax* (pp. 51–80). New York: Academic Press.

Olive, T. (2004). Working memory in writing: Empirical evidence from the dual-task technique. *European Psychologist, 9,* 32–42.

Pacton, S., & Fayol, M. (2003). How do French third and fifth graders use morphosyntactic rules when they spell adverbs and present participles? *Scientific Studies of Reading, 7,* 273–287.

Pacton, S., & Fayol, M. (2004). Learning to spell in a deep orthography. In R. A. Berman (Ed.), *Language development across childhood and adolescence. Trends in language acquisition research* (Vol. 3, pp. 163–176). Amsterdam: Benjamins.

Pacton, S., Fayol, M., & Perruchet, P. (2005). Children's implicit learning of graphotactic and morphological regularities in French. *Child Development, 76,* 324–339.

Pacton, S., Perruchet, P., Fayol, M., & Cleeremans, A. (2001). Implicit learning out of the lab: The case of orthographic regularities. *Journal of Experimental Psychology: General, 130,* 401–426.

Peterson, C., & McCabe, A. (1991). Linking children's connective use and narrative macrostructure. In A. McCabe & C. Peterson (Eds.), *Developing narrative structure* (pp. 29–53). Hilsdale, NJ: Erlbaum.

Rieben, L., Ntamakiliro, L., Gonthier, B., & Fayol, M. (2005). Effects of various early writing practices on reading and spelling. *Scientific Studies of Reading, 9,* 145–166.

Roy, M., Gaonac'h, D., & Fayol, M. (2002). L'effet de la ponctuation et des connecteurs sur le traitement des phrases en lecture. *Le Langage et l'Homme, 37,* 139–161.

Sandra, D., & Fayol, M. (2003). Spelling errors as another way into the mental lexicon: Homophone intrusions in Dutch and French. In R. H. Baayen & R. Schreuder (Eds.), *Morphological structure in language processing* (pp. 485–514). Berlin and New York: de Gruyer.

Scardamalia, M., Bereiter, C., & Goelman, H. (1982). The role of production factors in writing ability. In M. Nystrand (Ed.), *What writers know. The language, process, and structure of written discourse* (pp. 173–209). New York: Academic Press.

Schilperoord, J. (1996). *It's about time: Temporal aspects of cognitive processes in text production*. Amsterdam and Atlanta: Rodopi.

Schilperoord, J. (2002). On the cognitive status of pauses in discourse production. In T. Olive & C. M. Levy (Eds.), *Contemporary tools and techniques for studying writing* (pp. 61–87). Dordrecht: Kluwer.

Simon, J. (1973). *La langue écrite de l'enfant*. Paris: Presses Universitaires de France.

Slusarczyk, B., Bressoux, P., & Fayol, M. (2011). *Does spelling performance impact on text production? A longitudinal approach*. Manuscript in preparation.

Stein, N. L., & Glenn, C. G. (1979). An analysis of story comprehension in elementary school children. In R. O. Freedle (Ed.), *New directions in discourse processing* (pp. 53–120). Norwood, NJ: Ablex.

Thévenin, M. G., Totereau, C., Fayol, M., & Jarousse, J. P. (1999). L'apprentissage/enseignement de la morphologie écrite du nombre en français. *Revue Française de Pédagogie, 126*, 39–52.

Totereau, C., Barrouillet, P., & Fayol, M. (1998). Overgeneralizations of number inflections in the learning of written French: The case of nouns and verbs. *British Journal of Developmental Psychology, 16*, 447–464.

Totereau, C., Thevenin, M. G., & Fayol, M. (1997). The development of the understanding of number morphology in written french. In C. Perfetti, M. Fayol, & L. Rieben (Eds.) *Learning to spell* (pp. 97–114). Mahwah, NJ: Erlbaum.

Van Hell, J. G., Verhoeven, L., Van Beijsterveldt, L. M. (2008). Pause time patterns in writing narrative and expository texts by children and adults. *Discourse Processes, 45*, 406–427.

Verhoeven, L., & Van Hell, J. G. (2008). From knowledge representation to writing text: A developmental perspective. *Discourse Processes, 45*, 387–405.

Weinrich, H. (1973). *Le temps*. Paris: Presses Universitaires de France.

3

Teacher-Based Writing Research

PIETRO BOSCOLO

A BRIEF AUTOBIOGRAPHICAL NOTE

*M*any years ago, before becoming a professor of educational psychology, I taught language skills at various grade levels, including primary, middle, and high school. These early teaching experiences have deeply influenced my writing research, which has mostly been conducted in collaboration with teachers at different grade levels. Recently, I have returned to teaching writing, by holding academic writing courses for undergraduate and graduate psychology students at my university. When, in the early 1980s, the cognitive models of writing became familiar to European researchers, I approached writing research from the perspective of a researcher who was formerly a teacher. Now, I have had the opportunity of monitoring, as a researcher, my teaching. This teaching can therefore be considered an atypical example of action research, or an example of "controlled" experience, in which the competencies of the researcher and the practitioner meld in one person.

The title of the chapter reflects the duality of this experience. The aim of the chapter is not to provide an exhaustive review of writing research conducted in the classroom, but to highlight the role of teacher-based writing research within writing research. After a definition of this type of research, some examples will be presented and discussed. These are related to the two basic questions about which teacher–researcher collaboration has been most fruitful in recent years: writing to learn and motivation to write.

LEARNING AND TEACHING WRITING:
A MATTER OF COMPLEXITY

Writing is commonly considered a general skill that is learned at the beginning of primary school, becomes automatic through school grades, and is adapted to different genres. This common-sense view of writing has been seriously questioned by the results of psychological research and the conceptualization of writing over the past three decades. On the one hand, cognitive research has shown that learning to write is quite a complex developmental process. On the other hand, the social-constructivist approach to literacy learning has argued persuasively that writing is not a general skill, but rather a socioculturally situated activity. In general, psychological research has demonstrated that in a student's life, learning to write is a recurring novel experience, in which the "skill" assumes different roles, functions, and meanings. Before schooling, writing emerges in the scribbles and pseudo-words used by children when discovering the basic tools of written communication. In early elementary school, children learn to code words and short sentences, through which they have their first, simple but meaningful, experience with various genres (Chapman, 1995). In the upper grades of primary school and in middle school, written expression is progressively shaped into the rules and constraints of academic writing, and more and more rarely used for recounting personal experiences. In high school, the elaborative function of writing is definitely emphasized. Writing becomes the tool used by students to elaborate and expose knowledge and, through their written expositions, to be evaluated by teachers.

Moreover, there is another important aspect of writing that psychological research has investigated, although rather late compared with the cognitive aspects, that the common-sense view, instead, neglects. Learning to write does not only regard a student's cognitive and linguistic development through various writing experiences; students also progressively learn to give a meaning to writing. For instance, they learn to view writing as a more or less relevant subject in the curriculum and as a source of interest or boredom, personal satisfaction, or failure: That is, they develop attitudes toward writing that include beliefs and motives.

The teaching of writing is a complex instructional endeavor to the degree to which it tries to take into account the cognitive and motivational complexity of learning to write. On the one hand, the different moments of learning to write imply different difficulties for learners, which require a teacher's careful use of appropriate instructional practices. On the other hand, as teachers of language skills know, students are often scarcely motivated to write, and lack of motivation may be a cause as well as a consequence of poor writing achievement. Thus, a teacher of writing should not only be concerned with the cognitive and linguistic skills to be learned, but also the affective components of learning a complex subject. The development of writing research over the past three decades has greatly contributed to making teachers aware of this complexity and improving their teaching practices, especially in primary school.

The impact on instruction of psychological models—in particular the cognitive ones—revolves around two aspects. First, based on the findings of cognitive research on writing processes, instructional tools, such as guidelines and teaching programs, have been elaborated and circulated with the aim of helping teachers deal with and overcome the writing difficulties of novice and struggling learners. Second, psychological models of writing have often inspired innovative teaching practices aimed at making writing more fruitful and engaging for students. The role of teachers in designing and testing the effectiveness of these practices is often crucial.

Of course there is a tradition of good practices in writing instruction based on composition and literary studies, preceding and even anticipating the psychological models of writing. This tradition, whose merits are well recognized, will be mentioned in the following section devoted to the instructional applications of writing research.

WRITING RESEARCH AND INSTRUCTION

Basic Versus Applied Writing Research

School writing provides a variety of topics and problems for empirical studies and theoretical reflection. The applications of writing research to instructional settings are numerous, but it is not easy, nor perhaps useful, to group them into definite categories. A traditional way of categorizing studies is by distinguishing between basic and applied research, which has been extensively used in the experimental-quantitative approach to cognitive processes. The two levels of research are not usually considered dichotomous, but as the extreme poles of a continuum, along which studies can be positioned according to their prevailing focus on cognitive processes, analysed independently of instructional applications, or, at the opposite pole, on the instructional uses of these processes. The main limitation of the continuum metaphor is the difficulty or impossibility of positioning on a linear continuum some types of study that not only differ in the contexts in which they are conducted—laboratory versus school—but also in objectives and methodology. In the case of writing, the continuum metaphor seems to be even less useful due to an unbalanced distribution of studies at the two poles. In fact it is quite difficult to find a study on writing without any, albeit generic, instructional implication! The continuum metaphor does not fit the social-constructivist approach either, in which research is conducted in "natural" contexts, in particular school and the workplace, and writing is studied in its authentic uses, that is, for true communicative or expressive objectives. This chapter will propose avoidance of the rigidity of the basic versus applied research distinction by shifting emphasis from the type of study to the researcher's attitude toward a writing problem: process—versus teaching—oriented.

Development of the Process Approach

When, in the early 1980s, European psychologists recognized the cognitive models of writing, the view of writing as an ability to be evaluated in terms of written products rather than processes was still dominant in schools and colleges. However, in the United States in the 1980s writing research was already active, as demonstrated by papers published in *College Composition and Communication* and *Research in the Teaching of English*. From the 1960s, before the cognitive "discovery" of writing as a problem-solving process, a new perspective based on the shift from a product- to a process-oriented view of writing was becoming dominant, although not yet supported by psychological research. The great innovation of the new perspective was called the *process approach*. This approach, with its emphasis on students' freedom in writing as opposed to the then current instructional practice of analyzing and trying to reproduce "model" texts (Calkins, 1986; Graves, 1983), has continued to be popular among teachers.

In the process approach, writing is viewed as consisting of a sequence of stages. Although given different names, these stages represent the transition from prewriting (generating ideas, reflecting on what to write) to writing the first draft to revising the written text (Emig, 1971; Rohman, 1965). In the 1970s, several scholars studied the writing processes of students, particularly at the college level (see Hillocks, 1986, for a critical review; see also Pritchard & Honeycutt, 2006), thus preparing the ground for Hayes and Flower's (1980) model. The expression *process approach* is clearly ambiguous, because the generic terms *process* and *approach* are used in relation to very different domains of research and instructional practice (Boscolo, 2008). In his seminal analysis of modes of teaching writing, Hillocks (1986) appropriately renamed this approach as the "natural process mode." It is characterized by free writing on a topic selected by students for a peer audience without impaired genre, conferencing with classmates and teachers, with an emphasis on rewriting and revising. In this instructional mode, the role of the teacher is to facilitate and be responsive to students' writing.

Of the cognitive models of writing, the process approach found a new and more precise conceptualization based on the view of process as a methodological tool for the analysis of writing behavior, on the one hand, and for its improvement in the school context, on the other. The instructional relevance of cognitive models of writing was immediately apparent in the early 1980s, due to several seminal essays that provided a view of writing that was no longer in terms of products, but rather of processes that could be trained, facilitated, and strengthened. Hayes and Flower's (1980) model was an invaluable conceptual frame for analyzing writing processes in their sequence and recursivity. Then Bereiter and Scardamalia (1982, 1987) insightfully described novice writers' strategies as well as their difficulties in using knowledge appropriately when writing. This new conceptualization of writing, which differentiated novice and skilled writers, strongly influenced both researchers and practitioners. Educational psychologists interested in literacy found that the cognitive models provided solid and illuminating frameworks for investigating writing processes and difficulties in writing. At the same time, the conceptualization of writing in terms of cognitive processes, working memory load, and the more or less expert use of knowledge suggested new ways for teaching writing and helping students manage writing processes. Over the next decades writing research developed remarkably in the direction of expanding theory and its application to school instruction.

The Process-Oriented Approach to Instruction

Following Hayes and Flower's (1980) and Bereiter and Scardamalia's (1987) models, numerous process-oriented studies have been conducted in which writing is viewed from a cognitive-developmental perspective. These studies usually have a dual valence. On the one hand, a researcher's interest is based within a theoretical framework in which writing processes are conceptualized and deserve to be investigated in greater depth. On the other hand, the researcher's interest is often triggered by an instructional problem—the difficulty of learning to write. Underlying this approach to writing research is the idea that writing is a demanding process, for which many students, due to individual or cultural differences, lack the tools with which to deal successfully. Therefore, the cognitive analysis often has a developmental dimension, aimed at identifying the malfunctioning of writing processes that emerge in school, and inevitably get worse through the school grades. Two examples of process-oriented studies can help clarify the relation between research and the instructional application of this approach.

In a series of studies conducted over the past two decades, Berninger and her co-workers have investigated the causes of young writers' difficulties and have investigated instructional interventions to prevent them. Berninger and Swanson's (1994) started from Hayes and Flower's (1980) model by modifying for beginning and developing writers the translation component, which in the original model for skilled writing was less relevant than the processes of planning and revising. According to Berninger and Swanson, translation includes two components: text generation and transcription. Deficits in transcription skills can interfere with the development of text generation. The automatic nature of transcription skills therefore makes working-memory capacity available for high-level composing skills. These studies focus on writing difficulties, and their findings often suggest strategies for overcoming them, such as the training of accurate and automatic transcription (handwriting and spelling) and fluent text generation (Berninger et al., 1997, 1998, 2002).

The second example can be found in a recent study on the relationship between discourse knowledge and elementary school children's writing performance (Olinghouse & Graham, 2009), which is a classic theme of the cognitive-developmental approach to writing. The authors' starting point was the prominent role of background content knowledge in the writing process as emphasized by the cognitively oriented model of writing. In general, the role of this knowledge has been recognized as influencing writing performance, but less attention has been paid to the role of discourse knowledge, which includes knowledge about genres and procedures as well as linguistic knowledge (McCutchen, 1996). The aim of the study, therefore, was to investigate how various types of discourse knowledge (story elements, substantive processes, production procedures, role of motivation in writing, and irrelevant knowledge) could account for a significant variance in students' performance in story writing. The findings showed that discourse knowledge can predict quality, length, and vocabulary diversity of stories written by participants. In discussing their findings, Olinghouse and Graham (2009) argued that, on the basis of their findings, writing instruction should include knowledge about writing, but they emphasized that the effectiveness of procedures used to improve students' writing knowledge "rests on a thin database" (p. 48).

These two research cases exemplify what we called process-oriented writing research. In both Berninger and Swanson's and Olinghouse and Graham's work, attention to theory as a starting point for research, and a condition for the cautious generalization of findings, is integrated with attention to young and even younger students' writing difficulties. Berninger (2008; Wong & Berninger, 2004) underlines the practical implications of improving low-level transcription (hand-writing and spelling) processes within the context of lessons that include authentic written composition, with explicit instructional guidelines for teachers. Graham, whose research work is conducted in collaboration with several scholars, including Harris, has devised an instructional approach named Self-Regulation Strategy Development aimed at teaching self-regulation in written composition to struggling writers and enabling them to write good, or at least acceptable, texts (e.g., Harris & Graham, 1996).

Teacher-Based or Teaching-Oriented Research

As argued in the previous section, in a *process-oriented* study the researcher works "inside" a theory and tries to apply or generalize findings to writing instruction by identifying strategies of writing instruction that can respond to writers' cognitive needs. In contrast, for a *teaching-oriented* researcher, the starting point is an instructional intervention whose validity is assessed through an empirical study. Thus, both types of study are aimed at fostering writing achievement, but for a process-oriented researcher this objective is pursued by improving the functioning of basic writing mechanisms, for example, planning, transcribing, revising, use of knowledge, or self-regulation. In a teacher-based study, on the other hand, the researcher is focused on the effectiveness of the instructional strategies that make writing a successful and meaningful activity for students. Subsequently, process-oriented studies tend to focus on relatively simple writing tasks through which processes can be appropriately investigated, whereas teacher-based or teaching-oriented studies tend to focus on more complex writing tasks and situations, through which students' writing achievement and attitude toward writing can be improved. Teacher-based studies are often aimed at devising and assessing teachers' "best practices" in writing instruction.

The two types of studies also have different relations with theory and the context of research. In a process-oriented study, the starting point is the researcher's aim to analyze specific writing processes or difficulties. The study provides the researcher with the opportunity to test a model in relation to a specific learner difficulty or an aspect of information processing related to writing. In teacher-based research, where the starting point is a complex instructional activity, the researcher views an instructional activity as a problem to be framed in a theoretical perspective, from which it can take meaning and coherence. A second difference is the context of research: location and collaboration. The location of a study is not a sufficient feature for distinguishing teacher-based from process-oriented studies, as both types of research may be conducted in the classroom. However, for a process-oriented researcher, the classroom is basically the place for collecting data and for a tryout, while teacher-based studies are closely related to the classroom context—the presence and role of teacher and peers—and the classroom's influence in students' writing achievement and motivation.

The collaboration between researchers and practitioners, which is a fundamental aspect of educational research, is particularly important in both process-oriented and teacher-based studies, although in different ways. Collaboration with teachers is an invaluable resource for psychologists interested in writing difficulties and the strategies for overcoming them. In fact, teachers are the first to experience student difficulties, and they can suggest interesting problems to a researcher. They also have the opportunity to test the applicability of new instructional strategies or interventions.

In teacher-based research, basically two types of instructional interventions are analyzed. In the first, the teacher can provide a researcher with the instructional material, the effectiveness of which needs to be tested by means of an empirical study. In contrast to other school subjects, learning to write does not imply the acquisition of a large amount of declarative knowledge, with the exception of the structure of the most common genres. Accordingly, a teacher's instructional creativity can be used to design and carry out innovative ways of teaching writing, thus improving students' writing competence as well as their motivation to write. In my experience as an educational psychologist interested in literacy—mainly writing—and motivation, I have interacted with excellent teachers of language skills, thus gaining the opportunity to appreciate their didactic work. In some of these interactions, I was impressed by the novelty of the instructional intervention devised by the teacher and its relevance to student learning and motivation. These observations were the starting point for studies aimed at assessing the effectiveness of interventions. Collaboration with a researcher is obviously not limited to the "invention" of an interesting teaching strategy. During a study, which may continue for several months, intensive collaboration is necessary for the researcher to monitor the intervention in the experimental and control groups.

In the second type, the problem investigated by teacher-based research is represented by classroom activities in which reading and writing are linked. In school, writing often takes on a secondary role in relation to various school subjects, for instance for taking notes, making summaries and outlines; that is, writing becomes a tool for learning as in writing-to-learn research. Writing is also often used as the concluding moment of reading and study activities, when students are asked to write a summary or comment based on what they have read and studied (reading-to-write research). Such studies are not aimed at testing innovation, but rather at analyzing the effectiveness of traditional ways of teaching or using writing.

The meaning of the term relevance is different for a practitioner and a researcher. From an instructional perspective, a practice or activity is relevant to the degree to which it addresses an important objective, for instance, facilitating students' approach to a new genre or getting them involved in elaborating knowledge in a written form. For a researcher, an instructional problem is relevant to the degree to which it can be meaningfully framed in a theory or model, and investigated through a psychological study, whose findings could hopefully expand the research field.

QUANTITATIVE AND QUALITATIVE APPROACHES TO TEACHER-BASED RESEARCH

From a methodological point of view, teacher-based research presents a variety of approaches, both quantitative and qualitative. Two recent studies are presented below to illustrate, at least in part, this variety. The first study, by Klein and Rose (2010), a qualitative study, focused on a basic problem of academic literacy: writing to learn, that is, writing as a positive factor in learning. Studies conducted over the past decades have shown inconsistent results regarding the utility of writing for learning. The aim of the authors, a researcher and a teacher, was to implement the knowledge transforming model (Bereiter & Scardamalia, 1987). Knowledge transforming is a metaphor indicating how expert writers, when exposing their knowledge about a topic, are able to use and integrate two "spaces": the space of knowledge and the space of discourse. "Transforming" means adapting, selecting, and organizing knowledge about a topic to reach a communicative goal, which is not only to inform the reader, but also to provide him or her with a clear view of the topic. The study was conducted under the assumption that two writing genres, argumentation and explanation, would be appropriate for teaching students to transform their knowledge. In the knowledge transforming model, a student who writes an argument adopts a rhetorical objective, which requires the elaboration (transformation) of knowledge, whereas writing an explanation requires making inferences and carrying out problem-solving operations. The instructional intervention included many classroom activities, aimed at making writing familiar to students, remedial practice, support of self-evaluation, and development of intrinsic motivation to write. The study was carried out using a design experiment in which one experimental and one comparison class of fifth graders participated.

A design, or formative, experiment is an appropriate method for developing theory and improving instructional practice (Cobb, Confrey, diSessa, Lehrer, & Schauble, 2003). Design experiments have several methodological characteristics that make them different from traditional experimental and quasi-experimental methods (Reinking & Bradley, 2004). First, they are aimed at improving learning and instruction and, therefore, conducted to achieve a relevant educational goal. For example, in Klein and Rose's (2010) study, the goal was to prepare junior students to use writing to learn. Second, the study must be framed in a solid theoretical model, to which the effectiveness of the intervention must be related. In the study cited, the theoretical framework was Bereiter and Scardamalia's (1987) model of knowledge transforming, which was tested and expanded with an instructional goal and includes reading and writing tasks not considered by the authors. Third, a design experiment includes a continuous cycle of data collection, aimed at determining which factors enhance or inhibit the intervention's effectiveness. Design experiments are therefore iterative. Lastly, this type of experiment is flexible and includes various ways to collect data in response to developments during the study. A design experiment is an appropriate method for studying the construction of a complex ability in that it allows the researcher flexibility in monitoring the phases of an intervention and the comparison of its results with a control group. In other cases, a researcher may be interested in exploring the performance of a complex writing activity in the classroom, not in terms of students' learning and achievement, but how they respond to the new experience and how it modifies the teaching-learning context. In this case, writing, and in general literacy, is better explored through the ethnographic method, which, according to Purcell-Gates (2004), aims "to discover, understand, and describe human behaviour holistically, as it occurs naturally within social and cultural contexts" (p. 92).

The second study, a qualitative study, is a recent ethnographic study by Bruce (2009a), who as a teacher-researcher, investigated a specific form of writing in the school setting: video composition. Unlike academic writing, video composition relies on multiple representational modes including music, sound effects, still and moving images, as well as text (Alvermann, 2005; Bruce, 2009b). Bruce adopted various methods of data collection: (a) an initial survey of all students of media literacy at his high school (Grades 10–12) to analyze their knowledge and attitude toward video composition and writing; (b) audio-taped think-aloud protocols, including a limited number of retrospective protocols for students involved in the production of a video; and (c) interviews with participants and videotapes. Bruce (2009a) summarized the processes students used to compose with video in a three-section model—visual conceptualization, visual production, and evaluation—which, in its structure and recursivity, is reminiscent of Hayes and Flower's (1980) model. Bruce also emphasized the different attitudes of students toward school writing and video composition, the former often being used in boring and demanding tasks, the latter being able to stimulate student creativity. Although there is no explicit reference to motivational constructs, the author emphasized as a positive result the engagement demonstrated by students in video production.

Teacher-based research not only evaluates alternative approaches for instruction, it also evaluates for motivation. In fact, when instructional strategies are aimed at the acquisition of complex abilities, such as those described in the two studies above, students feel more or less motivated to carry out cognitively demanding writing tasks. In the following section, factors that influence motivation to write will be considered, and a few studies on this topic will be presented.

TEACHER-BASED RESEARCH ON MOTIVATION AND WRITING

Constructs and Themes in Motivational Research on Writing

As I argued at the beginning of this chapter, students are often scarcely motivated to write, due to various interacting factors, such as low self-perception of competence and self-efficacy in writing, severe teacher evaluation of students' written productions, and boring writing tasks, which are often unable to stimulate their involvement in writing. As a demanding activity, writing has affective and motivational correlates to which, in the past two decades, several constructs of motivational research have been applied: writing apprehension (Daly & Miller, 1975a, 1975b), a forerunner of low self-efficacy, mastery, and performance goals; value, self-efficacy, and self-perception of competence; intrinsic motivation; and interest.

Research on the motivational aspects of writing can be grouped into three main themes (Boscolo & Hidi, 2007). The first theme regards students' engagement, that is, their positive or negative attitude toward writing, which has been conceptualized within different theoretical frames: often, interest (Hidi & Boscolo, 2006, 2007;

Hidi & McLaren, 1990, 1991), and more rarely, intrinsic motivation (Oldfather & Dahl, 1994; Oldfather & Shanahan, 2007). The second theme regards the writer's perception of his or her writing ability and efficacy in dealing with a writing task (Pajares & Valiante, 2006). In relation to writing as well as other school subjects, the constructs of self-efficacy and self-perception of competence are often used as synonyms, although their meanings are, in fact, different. The former indicates the individual's belief in being able to perform a task at a specific level, whereas the latter indicates an individual's evaluation of his or her competence in writing (Bong & Skaalvik, 2003). Lastly, the third theme regards self-regulation, that is, the cognitive, metacognitive, and motivational processes that a writer has to monitor and control during a writing task (Zimmerman & Kitsantas, 1999, 2002). Although student engagement and self-efficacy have been studied mostly in relation to academic writing, self-regulation in writing has been conceptualized by considering not only students', but also professional writers', writing behavior. This chapter's focus will be on student engagement.

In the past decade, several papers and reviews have tried to outline the conditions for motivating students to write, that is, for leading students to respond positively to writing assignments. In a seminal review, Bruning and Horn (2000) identified four basic conditions for motivating students to write. The first condition is nurturing positive beliefs in writers, that is, helping students view writing as a meaningful activity. The second is assigning authentic writing tasks, which students can consider really worth doing. The third condition is providing a supportive context for writing, in which the teacher is the most important element as a facilitator and a guide. Lastly, the fourth condition is creating a positive emotional environment, from which fear of teacher evaluation and competitiveness among students are put aside. Obviously, these conditions are also interrelated. Being engaged in writing is the main condition for the development of positive feelings about the value and utility of writing itself and for a good level of self-efficacy and self-competence in writing. A positive emotional environment is easier to attain when students are willing to carry out a writing task in which they feel challenged, particularly if the task requires peer collaboration. Although all these conditions are important, the second—engaging students in writing—seems to be the most important. The next section will outline the contribution of teacher-based studies to the conceptualization of student engagement in writing.

The Motivational Impact of Meaningful and Challenging Writing Tasks

In teacher-based research, writing tasks that are attractive to students are often emphasized. These are tasks in which students have the opportunity to use writing in novel and stimulating ways that are within their reach. These tasks have a high motivational potential, because they stimulate students' interest, and the instructional context in which they are assigned and carried out contributes to keeping students' self-efficacy beliefs reasonably high. Over the past two decades, numerous studies have analyzed the conditions that can make a writing task attractive, thus contributing to the conceptualization of motivation to write. At the end of the

1980s, several studies considered the topic of a writing task to be the source of situational interest. Hidi and McLaren (1990, 1991) hypothesized that how interesting a theme or topic was, which has been shown to facilitate comprehension, would also influence the production of expository texts. However, the authors failed to find a positive effect of topic interest on the quality and quantity of sixth graders' written expositions. Although Hidi and McLaren considered situational interest generated by a text topic, other researchers focused on interest in a topic as a long-standing interest, but with limited evidence of an influence of individual interest on writing quality (Albin, Benton, & Khramtsova, 1996; Benton, Corkill, Sharp, Downey & Khramtsova, 1995).

A broader perspective of engagement in writing emerged in the last decade of the 20th century, mainly due to the influence of the social-constructivist approach to literacy, on the one hand, and the development of studies on interest, on the other. In the social-constructivist perspective, writing is not conceived of as a process, but rather as an activity situated in a social and cultural context, from which it takes meaning and value. Although this approach does not usually consider motivational aspects, emphasis on the authenticity of the task and context of writing—writing for a "true" goal in a collaborative context—and, subsequently, criticism of the unfruitful nature of traditional writing tasks, particularly composition, have contributed to the conceptualization of writing as a meaningful activity (Gambrell & Morrow, 1996; Hiebert, 1994). In this approach, the communicative function of writing in the classroom context is emphasized. Through writing, students learn to be members of a literate community (Nolen, 2001, 2007), and from this perspective, an interesting topic is a necessary, but not sufficient, condition for motivating students to write. Interest research has explored the affective aspects of learning to write, and the concept of interest has been used to analyze the attitude of writers in classroom activities and tasks characterized by novelty, which appear to be quite different from those usually assigned in school. This view of motivation to write reflects a complex view of school writing as a tool for learning and elaborating knowledge rather than a rhetorical exercise and literary production.

In relation to this broader view of writing, various adjectives have been used to identify attractive writing tasks and activities. Among the most frequent are "interesting," "authentic," "meaningful," and "challenging," with partially differing meanings. The use of the term interesting has been justified and supported by research on interest, particularly text-based interest in which novelty, surprise, and liking have a dominant role. The adjectives authentic and meaningful have been mostly used by those who advocate the social-constructivist approach to writing, which emphasizes the communicative function of writing in a classroom context. Unlike the term interesting, these two adjectives do not emphasize novelty or liking, but rather meaning. Students can get involved in writing to the degree to which they can relate writing to peer relationships in the social context of the classroom.

In recent years, the adjective challenging has been associated with writing tasks that can fulfill the three basic needs of Deci and Ryan's (1985) self-determination theory: autonomy, competence, and relatedness. According to Miller (2003; Miller & Meece, 1999), a task can be considered challenging to the degree to which it stimulates a student's cognitive involvement in a collaborative context. Second, a challenging task requires students to assume increasingly higher levels of responsibility for learning, that is, autonomy in carrying out a task, which requires the elaboration, not only retrieval, of prior knowledge. A third feature is represented by the collaborative context, which facilitates and stimulates students' involvement. Thus, among the cited adjectives, challenging is perhaps the most precise, because it includes reference to students' cognitive commitment and self-efficacy.

Regardless of the varied terminology used, both meaningful and challenging tasks are used in research on motivation to write. Some writing tasks take meaning from the classroom activities to which they are linked. For instance, in a primary school class (Grade 5 or 6) students may be involved in identifying the rules for organizing group work, an objective they view as important to classroom life. Different writing genres may be required at different moments of this activity, for example, to record individual ideas and comments, summarize points of view, and write the rules (Boscolo & Gelati, 2007). In such a context, writing is a meaningful (or authentic) activity for students, who realize that writing can be used not only for traditional compositions, but also to clarify ideas and communicate them to others. In other school situations, writing can be used in unconventional ways, as when young students manipulate (modify and rewrite) texts. As we will see later in the chapter, manipulation of texts is an activity young students enjoy and appreciate. In this case, the writing task is a challenging one. Although demanding, young students deal with this task willingly and view it as within their reach.

Therefore, when related to writing tasks, the adjectives meaningful and challenging, although partially overlapping, are not synonymous. A meaningful writing task may not necessarily be challenging, whereas a challenging one is also meaningful because the writer views it as worth carrying out, either for personal gratification or collaborative attitude. In the following sections, examples of meaningful and challenging writing tasks will be presented and discussed. In the first example, related to the tradition of writing-to-learn studies (e.g., Klein & Rose, 2010; Langer & Applebee, 1987; Newell, 2006), writing is used as a meaningful activity, as a tool that can lead to a more productive and interesting study of literature for ninth graders. In the second and third studies, the challenging dimension of writing is considered in the rewriting "games" of fourth graders and in a reading-to-write activity for high school students.

TEACHER-BASED STUDIES ON MOTIVATION AND WRITING

The Uses of Writing in the Learning of Literature

The first example is a study on writing as a tool for learning literature I conducted with ninth graders in collaboration with a teacher of language skills in a scientific lyceum (Boscolo & Carotti, 2003). In Italy, the scientific lyceum is a demanding high school, in which both literary and scientific subjects have an important role. In the first year (Grade 9), the literature syllabus is flexible, without the chronological constraints (from the Middle Ages to contemporary Italian literature) of the following years. As a result of this flexibility, students can approach the study of literature in greater depth than in middle school, as teachers are free to select texts and poetry from Italian, but also from foreign literature (translated into Italian).

The instructional method adopted by the Grade 9 literature teacher consisted of assigning students the reading of a literary text as homework and fixing a date for reporting on the reading in the classroom. On the fixed date, the teacher checked students' literary comprehension of the assigned poem or novel in the classroom and asked them to propose questions emerging from their reading to be discussed in the classroom. The most interesting aspect of this approach to teaching literature was the role of writing that was used individually and in groups as a tool for linguistic and literary learning. Students were encouraged to use a variety of kinds of writing: to record their impressions and thoughts while reading at home and school as well as the teacher's comments; to identify key words describing characters and their relationships in the texts they were reading (a sort of card indexing); to summarize the text by highlighting specific aspects; and to write a final report, with subsequent classroom discussion. Some of the tools used for text analysis were applied to various literary texts.

The good results obtained by the teacher using this instructional approach to teaching literature stimulated me to plan and conduct a study. This study allowed the results obtained in terms of student achievement to be compared with those of teaching literature in a traditional way. Writing has been investigated several times, as a tool for learning various subjects, such as science (Mason & Boscolo, 2000) and history (Boscolo & Mason, 2001), whereas studies on the use of writing in the learning of literature are less frequent (Beach, 1998; Marshall, 1987, 1990). In literature teaching, writing seems to present even greater potential than in other subjects. It can be a tool for elaborating knowledge through a variety of genres, as well as a way of having students approach relevant questions, such as the relationships between parents and children (e.g., in H. James's "Washington Square"), or the role of irony in literary style in a personal way and through classroom analysis and discussion of literary characters' feelings and conflicts. From the students' perspective, writing is a stimulating experience in the study of literature, because very often in high school the two experiences of literary reading and writing are quite separate: Students are asked to read novels and poems, demonstrate they understand their meaning, and write compositions in which they are required to make comments on the literature.

According to our hypothesis, the instructional intervention should have a positive effect on students' attitude to literature, as well as writing. As the intervention was based on students' experiences with novel ways of writing, we wanted to ascertain whether these would modify students' orientation to writing as well as to literature. To control the effects of the intervention, a parallel Grade 9 class was selected as a comparison group. These students read the same literary texts according to a traditional teaching method; that is, the teacher presented the author and his or her literary framework, assigned reading passages to students as homework, and students presented individually a passage or content of a novel in the classroom.

Both the experimental ($n = 25$) and control classes ($n = 25$) completed the same cognitive and motivational measures before and after the intervention.

Regarding the cognitive measures, students read a short story by Chekov (one at the beginning and one at the end of the year) and wrote a summary of the text; they expressed in writing the meaning that could be drawn from the text, and wrote some comments relating the story to their personal experience. Summaries and comments were rated by the authors in terms of comprehension, formal correctness, and personal interpretation to generate three scores for each student. Regarding the motivational measures, the authors first applied a "content analysis" to the teaching of writing and literature in middle and high school and identified five crucial aspects that characterize it, although with different emphases according to different teachers:

- Traditional use of writing (summarizing a passage)
- Working with text (paraphrasing poems, analyzing the structure of a text or poem, recording personal reflections)
- Text manipulation (writing a new text from a model)
- Personal writing (writing letters, diaries, narrating personal events)
- Collaborative work (classroom discussion of a passage, collaborative writing)

In relation to these 5 aspects, 19 activities were identified (examples in parentheses above). Three questionnaires were then constructed:

1. *"Do you like?"*, in which students were asked to rate on a 5-point scale how much they liked doing each of the 19 activities
2. *Self-perception of writing competence*, in which students were asked to express on the same scale how well they felt able to perform the 19 activities
3. *Perception of usefulness*, in which students had to rate each activity in terms of perceived usefulness

In addition, participants completed an abridged version of Miall and Kuiken's (1995) response to literature questionnaire (32 items, regarding literary reading as a stimulation of thought and as relaxation, the relationship of literature to real life, criticism of the study of literature in school, importance of the plot, and the author's voice). Lastly, at the end of the school year, students were asked several questions, regarding their ideas or opinions of literature and their experience with writing. The intervention lasted the whole scholastic year, from September to May.

No significant differences were found between the two classes in the "Do you like?" and self-perception of competence questionnaires; however, the students in the writing-oriented group perceived academic and personal writing as more useful than the traditional students did. Regarding the written summaries and comments, the writing-oriented group attained better interpretation scores than the traditional group. Relevant differences between the groups were found in responses to the open-ended questions on literature and writing experience. Interestingly, students in the writing-oriented group emphasized the role of writing in expanding knowledge and its dual function in school: as an obligatory activity and a possible source of interest. Therefore, although responses to the "Do you like?" and self-perception of competence questionnaires were similar for the two groups, differences emerged when students were asked to write free responses.

Playing With Narrative Genre Through Challenging Writing Tasks

In Boscolo and Carotti's (2003) study, the opportunity of studying the effects on learning and motivation of a stimulating way of using writing in a relatively controlled setting presented a research challenge. However, in a more recent study the challenge was presented by an instructional intervention consisting of having students "play" with narrative genre (Boscolo, Gelati, & Galvan, in press). The study started with the creativity of an elementary school teacher, Nicoletta Galvan, who taught fourth graders to manipulate and rewrite narrative texts. A genre is defined and taught as a text type characterized by a set of discourse conventions or textual regularities and classifiable into clearly delimited categories. In learning to write, children practice the basic genres—the narrative, expository, and later the argumentative genre. In Galvan's classroom, children were led to view a genre not only as a structure comprising the features to be considered when composing a text, but also as a tool for making writing challenging and attractive. The verb "to play" was used to define students' activities, which consisted of modifying and manipulating texts by introducing variations according to specific rules. For instance, a story is the narration of an event, which is acted out by various characters, and characterized by a setting and one or more episodes. If, in the same structure, one or more characters or the setting is changed, a completely different story will be generated, although with the same structure. Obviously, this change can be simple routine, without any enjoyment for children and teacher. Alternatively, manipulating and modifying text can be a stimulating activity if children realize that through changes new and interesting texts can be obtained, according to a given constraint. An instructional intervention was therefore planned and carried out.

There were two basic assumptions underlying the study. The first was that, although carried out in a playful context, the tasks require students to analyze texts carefully, introduce changes, and monitor the coherence of the new texts. Through these tasks, students learn to regulate their own writing, in particular in regard to maintaining text coherence throughout the manipulations and changes. The tasks were also carried out in collaboration, and students compared their results of changing texts and revised collaboratively in a classroom climate in which the teacher had the role of scaffolding and suggesting, rather than evaluating. Modifying a text implies respecting certain constraints—for instance, changes cannot produce incoherence and the resulting text must be plausible—while also allowing students to find new and creative solutions. For instance, the alphabet exercise used in the present study required rewriting a text with the first letter of each sentence in alphabetic order. That is, for each sentence in the text, students had to find a word with a specific initial letter, in alphabetical order, which could plausibly start a sentence. This task, and the other writing tasks, required writers to carry out the basic processes of writing. They had to anticipate incoherence due to a change in part of the story, revise the modified text where incoherence is found, and use words and expressions appropriate to the new text. Basically, this type of writing is a problem-solving situation in which the student had to compose a new text while respecting the structure of the old one. This type of task can be considered play because students were faced with challenging problems without having to be concerned with the teacher's evaluation in terms of grades. However, it is a serious endeavor, because a narrative has a structure that must be maintained to attain an acceptable outcome at the end of the "play."

The second assumption concerned students' motivation. Playing with a genre (in this case, narrative) may help students become aware that a genre is not a static entity, but may be the source of new texts and meanings. This awareness, which is arrived at through writing and manipulating texts, should have a positive effect on children's motivation to write. It should help children view writing as an enjoyable and challenging activity if some conditions are respected (Boscolo & Gelati, 2007; Bruning & Horn, 2000). The first condition is that manipulating and transforming texts must not be too difficult a task, but within students' reach. Second, the task should be a challenge. Modifying a text according to a certain rule may seem a scarcely meaningful and routine task. However, it can lead children to understand that through writing they can create new stories, situations, and characters, that is, new meanings. A third condition regards the instructional context. This type of task can be very enjoyable if children's efforts in dealing with the linguistic and cognitive difficulties related to the task are supported by a classroom atmosphere in which efforts are appreciated without severe evaluation and results are attained though student collaboration. The motivating effect of "playing" with genre should also be valid for children with poor writing achievement. Although modifying a text is not usually an easy task, especially for less-skilled writers, a playful and collaborative instructional context appears to be a good approach for allowing struggling writers to view writing as a more enjoyable and less "threatening" activity.

Thus, it can be hypothesized that the intervention would increase students' awareness of the structure of a narrative text and the mechanisms through which it is constructed. This awareness should improve the ability to analyze, modify, and reconstruct a text and transform it into a new one, respecting the structure and constraints of the original. A second hypothesis was that the intervention would increase students' motivation to write, leading them to view writing as more enjoyable and themselves as more competent writers. Finally, because the intervention was conducted in classes with students of different levels of writing competence, it can be hypothesized that a writing condition with a collaborative atmosphere and pleasurable tasks would help struggling writers to enjoy writing and perceive themselves as more competent.

There were 66 participants in the experimental group, divided by gender into 28 struggling (M = 13, F = 15) and 38 skilled writers (M = 13, F = 25). The control group included 48 participants divided by gender into 26 struggling (M = 13, F = 13) and 22 skilled writers (M = 10, F = 12). An instructional intervention was planned and carried out that focused on challenging writing tasks, which consisted of manipulating and rewriting narrative texts. The intervention, conducted by two teachers, lasted 10 weeks, with weekly workshops of 90 minutes each. During the intervention, participants were involved in various language "games" in written form. All tasks required children to rewrite a short narrative text according to a specific rule. For instance, the "tautogram" game required rewriting a narrative text with sentences starting with the same letter, whereas in the "dialogue" game the change introduced dialogue in a narration between the characters, whose actions and ideas were described in the text. In this case, the constraint is represented by the character type, which required a coherent linguistic register and related lexical choices.

A self-perception of writing competence questionnaire and a liking writing questionnaire were administered to all participants before and after the intervention. In addition, the experimental group participants were asked to comment anonymously about their enjoyment and the usefulness of the intervention.

Despite the differences in text comprehension and vocabulary skills between the two groups, the experimental group, after treatment, attained higher scores than the control in a few games. In particular, the treatment seemed to improve students' ability to modify the sequence of events in a narrative while respecting the text structure and taking into account the constraints of the original text and the changes. No difference emerged between the two groups in ability to identify the structure of a narrative text. Regarding writing ability, the intervention had no effect on narrative writing, a result that is not surprising due to the difference between the tasks of rewriting and writing.

The second hypothesis regarded motivation to write. We considered the manipulation of narrative texts to form new ones, which is a challenging writing task if students work in a collaborative situation and without being concerned about teacher evaluation. Moreover, overcoming the difficulties related to text modification should also contribute to making students more confident about their writing competence. This second hypothesis was only partially verified. After the intervention, experimental group students, including those with lower writing achievement, enjoyed writing more. This result seems to indicate that children identified new reasons for liking writing, and this enjoyment was shared by both skilled and struggling writers. Instead, no effect on self-perception of competence was found. This result was unexpected, but not surprising. Students' self-perceptions, developed through years of writing experience, may resist change during a relatively short intervention.

Regarding less-skilled writers, differences between the two levels of writing competence emerged in the written narration and the alphabet and story change games, that is, writing tasks usually assigned in school, on the one hand, and rewriting tasks, on the other. As expected, the posttest task performance of skilled writers was globally better. However, no difference emerged between the two levels of ability regarding liking of writing or in self-perception of competence. A possible objection is that the linguistic games adopted in this study may be too difficult for struggling writers. Our study, although confirming the differences between various levels of writing competence, has shown that the intervention was appreciated by both subgroups of students, as the comments by the experimental group students after the intervention, regarding enjoyment and perceived usefulness of the writing tasks, also confirmed. Most students (90%) expressed favorable comments on the work. Both subgroups appreciated the intervention, which might mean that differences in students' levels of competence are not reflected in their views about writing or in their ideas of themselves as writers.

The Effects of Challenging Writing Tasks on Learning and Interest in a Topic: A Study of Reading to Write

In this study, writing was the conclusive step in a reading-to-write high school activity (Boscolo, Ariasi, Del Favero, & Ballarin, 2011). Although the previously described studies on writing as a learning tool for literature and on playing with narrative genre were aimed at assessing the effectiveness of instructional interventions carried out by teachers in their classrooms, the present study was not based on an innovative instructional activity. Instead, its aim was to reproduce a typical classroom literacy activity, quite common from the upper grades of primary school onward, in which students had to elaborate information obtained from reading in a written summary, report, or composition.

In this study there were 247 participants from Grades 11 and 12, who were divided into six groups according to a 2 × 3 (interesting vs. uninteresting topic: terrorism and globalization, respectively; type of writing task) design. Students were asked to read a text on a current topic: terrorism or globalization. Each phenomenon was described in a text containing three types of information: *conceptual information*, such as a definition of the phenomenon and its main characteristics; *description of events or activities*, which exemplified the phenomenon (e.g., in the text on terrorism, the description of a terrorist attack); and *evaluative comments* on the phenomenon from moral, political, or legal points of view. Two texts of about 1,500 words each, one on terrorism and one on globalization, were devised to include four paragraphs for each type of information: concepts, events or activities, and evaluations. Each text was therefore made up of 12 paragraphs. While reading, participants had to rate the paragraphs in the text according to five indices of the concept of interesting: novelty, curiosity, impressiveness, importance, and will to reflect. These indices were selected on the basis of literature on text-based interest and a preliminary study with high school students.

Finally, students were randomly assigned to one of three writing tasks regarding the text topic. Two tasks were considered challenging, whereas one was a traditional composition. The first challenging task was argumentation. Students were invited to justify and support their points of view about terrorism (or globalization) with the following words: "We are proposing an unusual writing task for you. Discuss, based on the passage you have just read, as if talking with a conversation partner, and sustain your point of view, also on the basis of your previous knowledge about the topic. Remember that in a discussion it is not always necessary to demonstrate that one is right. Sometimes discussion helps clarify your point of view to yourself" (Boscolo, Ariasi, Del Favero, & Ballarin, 2011, p. 473).

Arguing in written form requires a writer to take into account and compare different perspectives about a topic as well as reevaluate his or her perspective in the light of information obtained through reading. In this task, students were not required to argue in favor of one or other position, as frequently occurs in written compositions, but to view the information conveyed by the text as a position to be critically discussed. The challenging aspect of the task was that, on the one hand, it allowed more freedom to argue than traditional compositions; on the other hand, this freedom required the writer to select and adapt text information to the perspective adopted.

In the second challenging task, students were asked to design a passage about terrorism (or globalization) to be included in a textbook for high school students: "You should not write a full text, but indicate in detail the information units and their sequence. You can also suggest the inclusion of some figures or tables, briefly explaining the reason for your proposal. Remember that your text should be clear and interesting!" (Boscolo, Ariasi, Del Favero, & Ballarin, 2011, p. 473). This task was quite an unusual one, at least in Italian schools. From a motivational point of view, the challenging dimension of this task was requiring writers to "transform" their knowledge to make the topic understandable, and to take peers' perspective into consideration to make the text interesting.

Regarding the third characteristic of a challenging writing task, the collaborative dimension, all tasks were carried out individually. However, both the argumentation and the text design differed from the composition for their dialogic dimension. In fact, the argumentative task explicitly required students to "discuss" the text, while the text-designing task required students to plan an interesting text for a peer audience.

Lastly, students assigned to the traditional composition condition were asked to use information from the text to explain the meaning of terrorism (globalization) and the problems it implies for society. In all conditions, participants were told that, when writing, they could also make use of any prior knowledge about the topic. After writing, participants replied to open-ended questions regarding the text information, which was considered the learning measure. Interest in the topic (terrorism or globalization) was assessed three times: before reading, after reading, and after writing.

It was hypothesized that in argumentative writing, participants would use fewer concepts and would present events as well as evaluations to support their position, independent of their interest in the topic. For the second challenging task (text design), we expected that, when designing a passage about terrorism or globalization to be included in a textbook for high school students, participants would use more concepts based on their importance in the text, with events viewed as more interesting information in a text designed for students. We also hypothesized that students' interest would be apparent by an emphasis on specific information and the details selected to be included in the text design.

Regarding the effect of writing on learning from text, we hypothesized that students assigned to the challenging tasks would attain higher scores on the postwriting knowledge questions. Regarding topic interest, we hypothesized that, after challenging writing tasks, participants' interest in the topic would not decrease, whereas this effect should occur after a traditional composition, as emerged from a previous study with high school students, where writing about a topic turned out to have a detrimental effect on interest in that topic (Boscolo, Del Favero, & Borghetto, 2007).

Students' texts were analyzed in order to tackle explicit and implicit expressions of interest in the topic or in specific subtopics. Explicit expressions of interest are exemplified by comments such as "I found particularly interesting …" or "There is a sentence in the text which struck me," that is, the writer's explicit comments regarding the relevance, novelty, or impressiveness of the text information. In particular, we considered two types of explicit comments of interest:

1. Interest in specific paragraphs and, in the case of the text-designing task, suggestions to present them as graphics or tables. Two judges counted the number of times interest in specific paragraphs was expressed. Interjudge agreement was 88%. Disagreements were resolved through discussion.
2. Interest in the general topic, usually at the beginning of the written text. Two judges decided independently whether interest in the topic was expressed in each text. Interjudge agreement was 95% and disagreements were resolved through discussion. Implicit expressions of interest were considered as well as the writer's emphasis on specific text information, such as (a) the number of activities or events cited as examples of concepts, and (b) the number of paragraphs and subtopics cited by the writer.

Three indices of interest expressed in the text were identified, namely the number of paragraphs and subtopics cited when writing, the number of activities used to support an argument or to explain a concept, and the number of explicit comments of interest in specific paragraphs or suggestions to present them as graphics or tables. Three analyses of covariance were performed, one for each index, with the writing task and topic as independent variables, and writing ability, prereading knowledge, topic interest, interest in writing, and self-perception of competence in writing as covariates. Students in the argumentation condition cited a lower number of paragraphs, whereas a higher number were cited in the text-design condition. A main effect of the writing task was found for the number of events or activities cited when writing: Students in the text-designing condition cited a higher number of events or activities. No significant effect emerged for the number of comments of interest in specific paragraphs or suggestions to present them as graphics.

On the whole, the expression of topic interest and the number of paragraphs used in the text, especially paragraphs related to activities, seemed to depend on the type of writing task. Because students cited more events or activities in the text-design condition, the question was whether there were also differences in the number of concepts and evaluations used across different tasks. As previously shown, more events or activities were cited in the text-design condition, and fewer concepts were used in the argumentation condition. Students who wrote on globalization included more evaluations in their texts than students who wrote on terrorism. In the argumentation and text-design conditions, participants chose to include fewer concepts, which in the reading phase received lower scores for novelty, reflection, impressiveness, and curiosity compared with the events or activities and evaluations, but were rated higher in importance than the events or activities.

Thus, the hypothesis was confirmed that students who wrote an argument used different types of information.

Regarding the effects of the writing tasks on learning and topic interest, results showed a significant main effect of topic. Students who read and wrote on terrorism remembered more about the topic than students who read and wrote on globalization. No significant effect of the writing task was found. Lastly, a significant effect of the writing task was found for topic interest. As expected, students in the academic text condition reported lower topic interest scores after the writing task compared with the other two tasks. On the whole, topic interest increased from the prereading to the postreading phase, particularly for students who wrote the argumentation text. Thus, writing did not seem to exert a detrimental effect on topic interest, which increased progressively when students wrote an argumentative text.

The Role of Writing Tasks in the Development of Motivation to Write

The conceptualization of challenging writing tasks is an important step in research on motivation to write. The term challenging, as related to writing, is an adjective with a complex meaning, which includes the conditions under which a task can be motivating. In fact, challenging is not a characteristic of a task in itself, but the stimulating effect that a task produces on a writer, to the degree to which he or she has the cognitive tools for managing it and perceives it as within reach. Three aspects of this concept need to be analyzed and investigated in greater depth. The first is the attractiveness component of a task, which in Miller's (2003) conceptualization, inspired by Deci and Ryan's (1985) self-determination theory, seems to be less relevant than the cognitive and self-regulatory commitment. A challenging writing task is one in which a writer is cognitively involved and from which he or she expects success. However, a feeling of efficacy is a necessary, but not sufficient, condition for testing oneself in a demanding task. A challenging task must also be promising in terms of personal satisfaction or enjoyment. The concept of a challenging task, therefore, needs to be revised and integrated with other motivational components.

The second aspect has to do with relatedness, which seems to be the least relevant of the three components of a challenging task and appears to be linked to students' grade level. Although in primary and middle school the challenge of writing is also positively influenced by classroom climate (collaboration, supportive teacher attitude, good peer relationships), for a high school student a writing task carried out individually may also be challenging, and cognitive and self-regulatory components are probably more important than collaboration.

A final aspect involves the role of challenging tasks in a general view of motivation to write. Although students enjoy meaningful and challenging writing tasks when challenge is not undermined by a concern with teacher evaluation, this enjoyment seems to be linked to the specific tasks and does not affect students' general liking of writing, which tends to remain low. This finding, which consistently emerges from studies conducted at different school grades and with different tasks (Boscolo & Carotti, 2003; Boscolo, Gelati & Galvan, in press; Mason & Boscolo, 2000), seems to testify to the motivational "heaviness" of writing students have been experiencing for years through scarcely interesting writing tasks and severe teacher evaluation. Also, if the instructional writing intervention has been satisfying and successful, students do not seem to change their basic attitude to writing. They tend to value writing more, but do not find it more enjoyable. From a theoretical perspective, these findings pose the question of how motivation to write develops through school grades and levels (Boscolo, 2009). Although learning to write is a discontinuous process from a cognitive perspective, it seems to have a basic motivational, although sometimes negative, continuity.

TEACHER-BASED RESEARCH: A BRIDGE BETWEEN PROCESS-ORIENTED RESEARCH AND WRITING INSTRUCTION

Teacher-based research on writing depends on the combination and integration of two types of competencies. The first competence comes from psychological research on writing, which provides the theoretical framework and the methodological tools to be applied to the empirical investigation of teaching and learning to write. The second competence is provided by teacher experience with students' learning to write at different grade levels and the commitment to devising new ways of teaching writing. Therefore, teacher-based research may become a bridge between process-oriented research on writing and writing instruction. On the one hand, as argued throughout the chapter, writing instruction can provide both process-oriented and teaching-oriented research with problems to be analyzed and investigated. On the other hand, the findings of both types of research can contribute to improving writing instruction.

The bridge should be crossed from both directions, however; that is, not only from process-oriented research to teacher-based research and writing instruction, but also inversely. What is the contribution to process-oriented research from teacher-based research? When outlining the main features of the two types of research, I have stressed the different relationship to theory. While a process-oriented study is closely related to a theory and may provide a test or a possible expansion of it, in teacher-based research the complexity of instructional problems may exceed the scope of a theoretical framework. The cognitive models of writing can persuasively account for a poor use of strategies and some limitations of knowledge processing, but they are less able to account for the interaction of cognitive, linguistic, and motivational factors, which characterize complex writing activities, such as writing in a genre or the reading–writing connections. As I argued at the beginning of the chapter, learning to write is not an easy developmental journey and is discontinuously scanned into phases or moments related to different school, and personal, experiences. So far, writing research has clarified the early phases of this journey, but more research is needed on the subsequent ones.

There are at least two kinds of problem that teacher-based research analyzes and which can provide process-oriented researchers with fruitful suggestions for theorizing. One problem is the "content" component of writing. The cognitive approach has considered the processes by which texts are written, whereas the genres that give shape to writing have been considered less. Teacher-based research may provide elements for analyzing in greater depth the development of genres in learning to write. A second, and related, problem is motivation to write. Although much more relevant in Hayes's (1996) model, than in Hayes and Flower's (1980) model, the role of motivation is not analyzed in depth, particularly regarding its influence on energizing writing processes and phases. So far, the affective aspects of writing have not been a central aspect of the cognitive approach to writing, or to the social-constructivist approach, for different reasons. In particular, clarification is needed of the concept of a challenging writing task and the relationship between the various concurrent elements—classroom context, task features, and student motivational and cognitive variables—that make a task challenging. Motivating students to write is not just an instructional problem, which a teacher can resolve by planning and carrying out effective interventions, but fostering motivation to write is also more than merely a means of identifying which academic writing task(s) is(are) appropriate. The contrast between the cognitive discontinuity and the motivational continuity of learning to write, which was mentioned in the previous section and is apparent in teacher-based research, requires a more comprehensive conceptualization of writing. In addition, the more frequent use of nonacademic literacies in school and out, while raising questions about the meaning, utility, and limitations of academic writing, will also stimulate inquiry on the possible different roles of the basic processes cognitive research has identified in relation to academic writing.

To summarize, along the path toward a comprehensive model of writing, teacher-based research represents the challenge of complex writing tasks, a challenge that process-oriented research should accept.

REFERENCES

Albin, M. L., Benton, S. L., & Khramtsova, I. (1996). Individual differences in interest and narrative writing. *Contemporary Educational Psychology, 21*, 305–324.

Alvermann, D. E. (2005). *Adolescents and literacies in a digital world*. New York: Peter Lang.

Beach, R. (1998). Writing about literature: A dialogic approach. In N. Nelson & R. C. Calfee (Eds.), *The reading-writing connection* (pp. 229–248). Ninety-seventh yearbook of the NSSE—part II. Chicago: University of Chicago Press.

Benton, S. L., Corkill, A. J., Sharp, J. M., Downey, R. G., & Khramtsova, I. (1995). Knowledge, interest and narrative writing. *Journal of Educational Psychology, 87*, 66–79.

Bereiter, C., & Scardamalia, M. (1982). From conversation to composition: The role of instruction in a developmental process. In R. Glaser (Ed.), *Advances in instructional psychology* (Vol. 2, pp. 1–64). Hillsdale, NJ: Erlbaum.

Bereiter, C., & Scardamalia, M. (1987). *The psychology of written composition*. Hillsdale, NJ: Erlbaum.

Berninger, V. W. (2008). Evidence-based written language instruction during early and middle childhood. In R. Morris & N. Mather (Eds.), *Evidence-based instructions for students with learning and behavioral challenges* (pp. 215–235). Hillsdale, NJ: Erlbaum.

Berninger, V. W., & Swanson, H. L. (1994). Modifying Hayes and Flower's model of skilled writing to explain beginning and developing writing. In E. Butterfield (Ed.), *Children's writing: Toward a process theory of development of skilled writing* (pp. 57–81). Greenwich, CT: JAI Press.

Berninger, V. W., Vaughan, K., Abbott, R., Abbott, S., Brooks, A., Rogan, L., Reed, E., & Graham, S. (1997). Treatment of handwriting fluency problems in beginning writing: Transfer from handwriting to composition. *Journal of Educational Psychology, 89,* 652–666.

Berninger, V. W., Vaughan, K., Abbott, R. D., Begay, K., Coleman, K. B., Curtin, G., Hawkins, J. M., & Graham, S. (2002). Teaching spelling and composition alone and together: Implications for the simple view of writing. *Journal of Educational Psychology, 94,* 291–304.

Berninger, V. W., Vaughan, K., Abbott, R., Brooks, A., Abbott, S., Rogan, L., Reed, E., & Graham, S. (1998). Early interventions for spelling problems: Teaching spelling units of varying size within a multiple connections framework. *Journal of Educational Psychology, 90,* 587–605.

Bong, M., & Skaalvik, E. M. (2003). Academic self-concept and self-efficacy. How different are they really? *Educational Psychology Review, 15,* 1–40.

Boscolo, P. (2008). Writing in primary school. In C. Bazerman (Ed.), *Handbook of research on writing* (pp. 289–305). Mahwah, NJ: Erlbaum.

Boscolo, P. (2009). Engaging and motivating children to write. In R. Beard, D. Myhill, J. Riley, & M. Nystrand (Eds.), *The SAGE handbook of writing development* (pp. 300–312). London: Sage.

Boscolo, P., Ariasi, N., Del Favero, L., & Ballarin, C. (2011). Interest in an expository text: How does it flow from reading to writing? *Learning and Instruction, 21,* 467–480.

Boscolo, P., & Carotti, L. (2003). Does writing contribute to improving high school students' approach to literature? *L1–Educational Studies in Language and Literature, 3,* 197–224.

Boscolo, P., Del Favero, L., & Borghetto, M. (2007). Writing on an interesting topic: Does writing foster interest? In S. Hidi & P. Boscolo (Eds.), *Writing and motivation* (pp. 73–91). Oxford: Elsevier.

Boscolo, P., & Gelati, C. (2007). Best practices in promoting motivation for writing. In S. Graham, C. A. MacArthur, & J. Fitzgerald (Eds.), *Best practices in writing instruction* (pp. 202–221). New York: Guilford.

Boscolo, P., Gelati, C., & Galvan, N. (in press). Teaching elementary school students to play with meanings and genre. *Reading and Writing Quarterly.*

Boscolo, P., & Hidi, S. (2007). The multiple meanings of motivation to write. In S. Hidi & P. Boscolo (Eds.), *Writing and motivation* (pp. 1–14). Oxford: Elsevier.

Boscolo, P., & Mason, L. (2001). Writing to learn, writing to transfer. In P. Tynjälä, L. Mason, & K. Lonka (Eds.), *Writing as a learning tool: Integrating theory and practice* (pp. 83–104). Dordrecht: Kluwer.

Bruce, D. L. (2009a). Writing with visual images: Examining the video composition processes of high school students. *Research in the Teaching of English, 43,* 426–450.

Bruce, D. L. (2009b). Reading and writing video: media literacy and adolescents. In L. Christenbury, R. Bomer, & P. Smagorinsky (Eds.), *Handbook of adolescent literacy research* (pp. 287–303). New York: Guilford.

Bruning, R., & Horn, C. (2000). Developing motivation to write. *Educational Psychologist, 35,* 25–37.

Calkins, L. M. (1986). *The art of teaching writing.* Portsmouth, NH: Heinemann.

Chapman, M. L. (1995). The sociocognitive construction of written genres in first grade. *Research in the Teaching of English, 29,* 164–192.

Cobb, P., Confrey, J., diSessa, A., Lehrer, R., & Schauble, L. (2003). Design experiments in educational research. *Educational Researcher, 32*, 9–13.

Daly, J. A., & Miller, M. D. (1975a). The development of a measure of writing apprehension. *Research in the Teaching of English, 9*, 242–249.

Daly, J. A., & Miller, M. D. (1975b). Further studies in writing apprehension: SAT scores, success expectations, willingness to take advanced courses and sex differences. *Research in the Teaching of English, 9*, 250–256.

Deci, E. L., & Ryan, R. M. (1985). *Intrinsic motivation and self-determination in human behavior.* New York: Plenum.

Emig, J. (1971). *The composing process of twelfth graders.* Urbana, IL: NCTE.

Gambrell, L. B., & Morrow, L. M. (1996). Creating motivating contexts for literacy learning. In L. Baker, P. Afflerbach, & D. Reinking (Eds.), *Developing engaged readers in school and home communities* (pp. 115–136). Mahwah, NJ: Erlbaum.

Graves, D. H. (1983). *Writing: Teachers and children at work.* Portsmouth, NH: Heinemann.

Harris, K. R., & Graham, S. (1996). *Making the writing process work: Strategies for composition and self-regulation.* Cambridge, MA: Brookline.

Hayes, J. R. (1996). A new framework for understanding cognition and affect in writing. In C. M. Levy & S. Ransdell (Eds.), *The science of writing* (pp. 1–27). Mahwah, NJ: Lawrence Erlbaum Associates.

Hayes, J. R., & Flower, L. S. (1980). Identifying the organization of writing processes. In L. Gregg & E. R. Steinberg (Eds.), *Cognitive processes in writing* (pp. 3–30). Hillsdale, NJ: Erlbaum.

Hidi, S., & Boscolo, P. (2006). Motivation and writing. In C. A. MacArthur, S. Graham, & J. Fitzgerald (Eds.), *Handbook of writing research* (pp. 144–157). New York: Guilford.

Hidi, S., & Boscolo, P. (Eds.). (2007). *Writing and motivation.* Oxford: Elsevier.

Hidi, S., & McLaren, J. (1990). The effect of topic and theme interestingness on the production of school expositions. In H. Mandl, E. De Corte, N. Bennett, & H. F. Friedrich (Eds.), *Learning and instruction: European research in an international context* (Vol. 2.2, pp. 295–308). Oxford: Pergamon.

Hidi, S., & McLaren, J. (1991). Motivational factors in writing: The role of topic interestingness. *European Journal of Psychology of Education, 6*, 187–197.

Hiebert, E. H. (1994). Becoming literate through authentic tasks: Evidence and adaptations. In R. B. Ruddell, M. R. Ruddell, & H. Singer (Eds.), *Theoretical models and processes of reading* (4th ed., pp. 391–413). Newark, DE: International Reading Association.

Hillocks, G., Jr. (1986). *Research on written composition.* Urbana, IL: NCRE—ERIC.

Klein, P. D., & Rose, M. A. (2010). Teaching argument and explanation to prepare junior students for writing to learn. *Reading Research Quarterly, 45*, 433–461.

Langer, J. A., & Applebee, A. N. (1987). *How writing shapes thinking.* Urbana, IL: National Council of Teachers of English.

Marshall, J. D. (1987). The effects of writing on students' understanding of literary texts. *Research in the Teaching of English, 21*, 30–63.

Marshall, J. D. (1990). Writing and reasoning about literature. In R. Beach & S. Hynds (Eds.), *Developing discourse practices in adolescence and adulthood* (pp. 161–180). Norwood, NJ: Ablex.

Mason, L., & Boscolo, P. (2000). Writing and conceptual change. What changes? *Instructional Science, 28*, 199–226.

McCutchen, D. (1996). A capacity theory of writing: Working memory in composition. *Educational Psychology Review, 8*, 299–325.

Miall, D. S., & Kuiken, D. (1995). Aspects of literary response: A new questionnaire. *Research in the Teaching of English, 29*, 37–58.

Miller, S. D. (2003). How high- and low-challenge tasks affect motivation and learning: Implications for struggling learners. *Reading and Writing Quarterly, 19*, 39–57.

Miller, S., & Meece, J. (1999). Third graders' motivational preferences for reading and writing tasks. *Elementary School Journal, 100*(1), 19–35.

Newell, G. E. (2006). Writing to learn. How alternative theories of school writing account for student performance. In C. A. MacArthur, S. Graham, & J. Fitzgerald (Eds.), *Handbook of writing research* (pp. 235–247). New York: Guilford.

Nolen, S. B. (2001). Constructing literacy in the kindergarten: Task structure, collaboration and motivation. *Cognition and Instruction, 19*, 95–142.

Nolen, S. B. (2007). The role of literate communities in the development of children's interest in writing. In S. Hidi & P. Boscolo (Eds.), *Motivation and writing: Research and school practice* (pp. 241–255). Oxford: Elsevier.

Oldfather, P., & Dahl, K. (1994). Toward a social constructivist reconceptualization of intrinsic motivation for literacy learning. *JRB: A Journal of Literacy, 26*, 139–158.

Oldfather, P., & Shanahan, C. H. (2007). A cross-case study of writing motivation as empowerment. In S. Hidi & P. Boscolo (Eds.), *Motivation and writing: Research and school practice* (pp. 257–279). Oxford: Elsevier.

Olinghouse, N. G., & Graham, S. (2009). The relationship between the discourse knowledge and the writing performance of elementary-grade students. *Journal of Educational Psychology, 101*, 37–50.

Pajares, F., & Valiante, G. (2006). Self-efficacy beliefs and motivation in writing development. In C. A. MacArthur, S. Graham, & J. Fitzgerald (Eds.), *Handbook of writing research* (pp. 158–170). New York: Guilford.

Pritchard, R. J., & Honeycutt, R. L. (2006). The process approach to writing instruction: Examining its effectiveness. In C. A. MacArthur, S. Graham, & J. Fitzgerald (Eds.), *Handbook of writing research* (pp. 275–290). New York: Guilford.

Purcell-Gates, V. (2004). Ethnographic research. In N. K. Duke & M. H. Mallette (Eds.), *Literacy research methodologies* (pp. 92–113). New York: Guilford.

Reinking, D., & Bradley, B. A. (2004). Connecting research and practice using formative and design experiments. In N. K. Duke & M. H. Mallette (Eds.), *Literacy research methodologies* (pp. 149–169). New York: Guilford.

Rohman, D. G. (1965). Pre-writing: The stage of discovery in the writing process. *College Composition and Communication, 16*, 106–112.

Wong., B. Y, & Berninger, V. W. (2004). Cognitive processes of teachers in implementing composition research in elementary, middle, and high school classrooms. In B. S. Shulman, K. Apel, B. Ehren, E. R. Silliman, & A. Stone (Eds.), *Handbook of language and literacy development and disorders* (pp. 600–624). New York: Guilford.

Zimmerman, B. J., & Kitsantas, A. (1999). Acquiring writing revision skill: Shifting from process to outcome self-regulatory goals. *Journal of Educational Psychology, 91*, 1–10.

Zimmerman, B. J., & Kitsantas, A. (2002). Acquiring writing revision proficiency through observation and emulation. *Journal of Educational Psychology, 94*, 660–668.

Part *II*

The Sociocultural Plus Cognitive Traditions in Writing Research

4

Writing, Cognition, and Affect From the Perspectives of Sociocultural and Historical Studies of Writing

CHARLES BAZERMAN

I begin with a personal introduction. I am not trained as a psychologist; nor do I do psychological research, and I am not associated primarily with psychologically based theories. Rather, I am a writer, a teacher, a researcher, and a theorist of writing—working largely from sociocultural and historical perspectives. I have studied how writing forms relations and shares meanings with others and how writing creates new social realities with the historical changes in the tasks, forms, contexts, technologies, processes, and meanings of writing. Yet, as a writer, I spend much time with my thoughts, searching for emergent communicative impulses and identifying the ideas and emotions I want to communicate. I also go through roller coasters of emotions as I struggle with writing. As an observer of my growth as a writer I have witnessed six decades of learning, associated with expanding cognitive possibilities. I remember specific cognitive development episodes such as stylistic imitation in adolescent years, a curiosity about text structure in the middle of my undergraduate years, a fascination with metaphor during the summer when I was 22, and an obsession with genre and intertextuality in my 30s and 40s. These and many other episodes of focused thought and learning increased my ability to conceive new meanings and think new thoughts. Each engaged me with a broader set of writing resources and knowledge.

As a teacher, I see students invest great mental effort into writing, and I see them struggling with emotions evoked by both the contents and processes of their writing. Much of my instruction is to help them identify and develop thoughts they wish to express, how to think about constructing and interpreting texts, and how to monitor and sharpen their writing processes. I also help create an affective atmosphere that allows them to carry out the difficult work of writing. As a teacher,

I witness intellectual growth as students' literacy skills expand. As a historical and social scholar, I gain access to the thinking of people distant from me and see the emergence of new forms of thought as forms of writing and literacy emerge to mediate new forms of social relations.

On the bases of these experiences, in this chapter I will make some heuristic suggestions about how psychological phenomena might be understood in relation to other dimensions of writing. My hope is these thoughts might contribute to a cognitive and affective psychology with a multidisciplinary understanding of writing as an individual, social, cultural, historical, and textual phenomenon.

As a historian of academic and disciplinary writing, I am also aware how problematic introspective accounts are for some areas of psychological inquiry (Danziger, 1990). Yet, as a person deeply engaged in literacy, I realize how much the activity occurs while I sit in a chair, staring at a screen or page, thinking about meaning. This meaning connects me with the thoughts and actions of other people, but the immediate site of action is in my head. Literate meaning, though socially transmitted, negotiated, and transformed in interactive consequences, is evoked within individual cognition. The most direct access to the meaning evoked within individual cognition and to the processes by which those meanings are evoked and managed is through the report of the meaning maker. Further, the sources of the most skilled meaning-making processes are the most skilled meaning makers who have long histories of social interactions and social learning and who have developed large and complex internal processes. Unlike some other problem areas studied on the expert–novice continuum, publicly displayed behavior will not get us sufficiently into the cognitive processing to understand the choices and processes made by highly skilled writers, where so much of the work is done internally over long periods of gestation and intuitive processes, as situated responses to complexly perceived problems, embodied in implicit stances and roles.

In this chapter I will explore the intersections of cognitive studies of writing with cultural, historical, technological, and textual studies of writing and consider models of cognition that take into account social communicative practices. I will also discuss the ways in which human cognitive and physical architecture may have constrained and shaped the social and material history of writing. Although my goal is to present a broad-ranging view of writing and cognition while respecting the many traditions of thought, my presentation will inevitably be situated within my own sociocultural and sociohistorical views of cognition.

The production, forms of representation, interpretation, and possible meanings of writing are all shaped and constrained by human mental and physical capacities. Yet writing has only recently been utilized by most humans, whereas in earlier times only a few members of society were taught or expected to use this remarkable human invention, which enables communication between people across time and space. As writing developed across the past 5,000 years, humans have learned how to produce and arrange text, what to write about, and how to interpret what other people have written. We have invented new technologies that allow us to produce, transmit, store, and process written texts, presenting further cognitive challenges and opportunities. We have also learned to think the kinds of thoughts that writing enables us to think. Finally, writing facilitated the development of new activities and social groupings, which have led us to adopt new roles, to develop new knowledge and modes of thought, and to orient us to our world differently.

As a result of these advances, the cognitive apprenticeship necessary for skillful writing has extended from a brief orientation to a limited range of signs for categorizing agricultural products to a lifetime of learning. The study of the cognitive aspects of writing would benefit from consideration of the plasticity and cultural evolution of cognitive practices in relation to the artifices humans invented to use in writing and the changing social circumstances within which humans communicate.

SOME EVOLUTIONARY AND HISTORICAL CONTEXTS

Animals are social beings, responding to one another's presence and influencing one another's behaviors—visually, aurally, chemically, and haptically. Higher avians and mammals are communicative, sometimes even with conscious awareness and attention. The perceptual, cognitive, and affective underpinnings for these social developments have parallels in the complex, affectionate parent–child relationships we witness in advanced primates. As language evolved in humans, it further extended the possibilities and complexity of social relations, supporting higher degrees of coordination and sharing of attention, subtlety of stance, extended reports of information, refinement of social relations and hierarchies, and individualization of interaction even within larger populations in tribes, villages, and cities. Cooperation and task differentiation in meeting the needs and pleasures of life as well as more elaborate arrangements for group security were facilitated. The social arrangements that consequentially developed created new cognitive and affective challenges, which required postpartum psychological development of individuals as they became participants in their society and its tool-facilitated material practices.

The addition of written symbols to the human communicative repertoire, for which the exact time of appearance is still under debate by evolutionary geneticists, seems to have been built on prior biological, perceptual, psychological, and social capacities, which over time became deployed, organized, and retrained to carry out new kinds of tasks. In particular, the humans who produced modern complex literate systems beginning 5,000 years ago were, as far as we know, genetically equivalent to humans who existed for tens of thousands of years prior to modern literacy and are genetically equivalent to humans today. Although our brains support both reading and writing, learning and using reading and writing are never simply biological processes, but rather biological resources that are used and trained within culturally evolved practices.

Certainly the history of systems of literacy shows the multiplicity of technological inventions and cognitive processes for supporting literacy, the creative complexity, and the contribution of the social environment to its development. Writing seems to have been invented initially in a few different locations, each time through a substantially different written symbol system: in the ancient Middle East, evolving from a hieroglyphic system to a range of syllabic and alphabetic systems; in China, evolving from an iconographic system into a mixed ideographic system with phonetic indicators of a variety of spoken Asian languages; a no-longer used ideographic system in Mesoamerica; and an extinct and indecipherable system in the ancient Indus valley (Schmandt-Bessarat & Erard, 2008). All modern forms of literacy seem to have evolved through a series of further inventions from these few. These few initial inventions suggest how unusual an innovation the evolution of written language was, not merely a chimp poking a twig into a termite hill! A complex history of many turns and inventions has led to our current practices of writing.

Further, different forms of apprenticeship and schooling have developed in different societies. Thus, it is reasonable to assume that people manipulate and contemplate these symbols in different ways and then use them differently to facilitate the development and sharing of their thoughts. These differences are likely to occur not only among the major different systems of literacy but even among languages using the same systems of written symbols—as evidenced by the differences in learning between alphabetic languages with substantially different phonologies, such as English and Spanish (Tolchinsky, 2001). Comparative studies of emergent spelling suggest, however, regularities do occur and are the result of the processes of making sense of a system rather than the specific system itself (Scharer & Zutell, 2003). The emergent spelling process utilized by hearing-impaired children provides a particularly striking example of the continuity in sense-making processes (Mayer, 1998).

There are also reasons to believe there are great differences in individuals within the same language sharing similar conditions of learning. Skilled writers using the same language on the same topic take substantially different approaches, making different arguments with different information cast within different styles. In an educational context, although we would be quite happy if all students turned in the same answer in mathematics, using closely similar lines of reasoning and work, we would be quite unhappy and even suspect cheating if all students were to turn in the same essay with converging drafts, even with students in the same grade and with similar preparations and skills. Thus, writing should be considered not only as a problem-solving process, as envisioned in the early stages of the cognitive psychology of writing (Bereiter & Scardamalia, 1987; Hayes & Flower, 1980), but also as a constructive process in which thought is transformed, formulated, and constituted as new knowledge (Galbraith, 2009).

THE COMPLEXITY OF WRITING IN THE CONTEMPORARY WORLD

With literacy, human consciousnesses has moved from immediate interaction with material and social relations directly in front of us to complex distant relations mediated by texts (now including electronic texts with extended multimedia capabilities). Our understanding and interaction with the immediate material and social world is transformed by our representation of it in written documents, turning it into information and data. Even within the same language and the same levels of schooling, we have developed differentiated forms of writing that travel in differentiated social networks to serve different tasks, evaluated by different standards. The differences among genres of different disciplines, professions, and social practices are so great that a person highly skilled in one domain, for example, legal writing, may be at a loss in dealing with chemical or economics writing, or poetry, or literary criticism. Even within a single professional domain some people are highly skilled in some genres while comparatively weak at others. Some lawyers specialize in contracts and others in patents and yet others in appeals. They each require different skills, modes of expression, action stances, and processes of production.

In short, through literacy we have learned to think about different things in different ways. Learning to participate as an effective thinking being in any of these systems at one of these more advanced stages of literate history requires an extensive cognitive apprenticeship in the skills, practices, and knowledge associated with any particular literate domain. Brandt (2001) gave a striking picture of how demands and needs and uses for literacy change rapidly even in the same geographic region over a few decades, whereas Goody (1986) and Bazerman (2006) gave a broader view of the massive changes in human activity and social order that have come about as institutions have developed based on the infrastructure of literacy.

Detailed studies of workplace writing (Beaufort, 1999; Dias, Freedman, Medway, & Pare, 1999; Dias & Pare, 2000; Russell, 1997) indicate the great variety of writing practices that occur within specific material, social, and economic constraints and accomplish complex tasks embedded within specialized knowledge domains. Smart (2007) examined the complex distributed writing that creates the knowledge and decision making in a large government agency to monitor and regulate the economy. Studies of architects also identify the way cultural traditions, aesthetic imagination, intellectual movements, material constraints, and building codes can all enter into the projection of building designs to be realized in concrete (Medway, 1996; Medway & Clark, 2003). Klein (1999) noted that in studies of writing to learn, different forms of learning are foregrounded, based on the nature of the task, even in a laboratory setting.

The recent changes in writing technologies also remind us what has been true since the beginning of literacy—that the material, social, and economic conditions of text production and distribution influence what it means to write. Pencil on cheap paper supports revision better than ink on expensive parchment. In the past several centuries, the economics and social organization of printing have contributed to increasingly large distinctions between professional authors and consuming reading publics. The rise of white-collar work within bureaucracies, although generating much documentary work and supporting technologies of typewriters, stencil reproduction, and filing cabinets, has not been viewed as serious writing in either the school or publishing world. In the closing decades of the 20th century, however, the invention of computers, word-processing and publishing software, and the Internet has made revision, collaboration, multimedia, and page design much more convenient, has sped distribution and response, and has fostered new genres and venues for personal, informational, political, and commercial writing.

THE UNIQUENESS OF SCHOOL WRITING

To meet the needs of literate societies, extensive systems of schooling were formed within which youth have spent increasingly large parts of their time in organized learning activities, now extending from early childhood into early adult years (Haswell, 2008; Rouen, Goggin, & Clary-Lemon, 2008; Olson, 2008). These learning activities may at first have involved some direct relation to activities in the world, but have increasingly developed their own logic as school subjects and activities, directed by beliefs about learning and development. School writing activities are then organized for the transmission, practice, and assessment of what is to be learned. These activities frequently focus on correct linguistic forms, or, in a somewhat more sophisticated manner, the processes by which these correct forms are produced. The transmission, practice, and assessment of skills form the rhetorical and communicative situation of writing—with the curious effect that the very communicative and rhetorical character of writing may be obscured.

The impulse to write or communicate arises out of particular communicative circumstances that guide complex decisions about how to address those circumstances, which might be called the rhetorical dimension of reading and writing. Without a compelling rhetorical need to communicate, people would have little to say. Texts produced solely under the mandates of schooling and assessment do not engage the full set of skills of writing, do not display the expressive potential of students, and do not necessarily place the literate activity in relation to material resources and material consequentiality; nor do they place the writing in situations of social consequentiality beyond school evaluation. Further, because writing requires a high degree of concentration, mobilizing complex cognitive and affective resources over extended periods of time to solve fuzzily formed social problems, a high degree of exigency is useful to evoke the intensity of focus and to mobilize the extensive cognitive and affective resources needed to compose successful texts, from which, through repeated engaged practice, a writer develops. There must be the push to create and communicate important meanings to make one care sufficiently about writing, to do it well, and to develop as a writer.

When writing is embedded in significant social activities, people care about it and work on it. When writing is for a grade, students are more likely to feel work has ended when they have achieved an acceptable grade. The motives for higher levels of performance in school writing are few and specific, affecting only a subset of the school population, but looming large in the ideology of teaching—desire for understanding, a respect and admiration for the teacher as an audience, a desire to succeed in front of peers, or a deep engagement with ideas and knowledge one is contemplating. But even deep engagement must be channeled through topics and tasks related to school contents and subjects—that is, the student who loves geography may lavish great care on the geography assignment but perhaps less on the philosophy essay. All these are legitimate human motives, but they are different from the more typical writing situations outside of school that require effort. Within the school environment, these human motives tend to reflect oddities of school culture and roles typically available to only a few students. This need for creating more authentic functions and situations for the development of writing of *all* students is often at odds with mandated assessments and standards framed around decontextualized skills (Hillocks, 2002; Murphy & Yancey, 2008).

As writing has become essential to participation in almost every element of contemporary society, the disjunction between school uses of literacy and those in the rest of the world has grown. This lack of connection is not just a matter of pedagogy and motivation. It is a matter of our fundamental understanding of writing as a social, psychological, cultural, and economic process because most research into writing is determined by exigencies of schooling and advancement through the school curriculum of writing; most data are collected in school or school-like settings using school-like tasks outside of the complex conditions, intertextual and activity fields, motives, and tasks that frame the variety of writing in the world. In modern information-based societies most people spend much of their day contemplating the writings they create and receive. Even farmers now regulate their farming by informational systems and detailed agricultural and economic records by which they guide their decisions and actions.

In the literate-world consciousness, personal philosophies and commitments, moral and ethical behavior, or simply calculations and plans incorporate knowledge, stances, advice, and evaluations from literate resources. The desire to articulate a coherent personal view through writing can become particularly compelling for individuals, and thus there is a close association noted in the previous paragraph between affective and cognitive order with intellectual projects. Adam Smith (1759), 250 years ago, posited that the search for cognitive order drove the development of philosophy and science. More recently, studies of cognitive dissonance (Festinger, 1957) became an underlying theme of an influential pedagogy of writing (Young, Becker, & Pike, 1970). An inquiry into writing needs to extend far beyond the limited elements practiced in the elementary school curriculum to consider many advanced forms of complex thought and reasoning.

COGNITIVE AND AFFECTIVE COMPLEXITY OF SITUATED WRITING

Writing extends beyond a mastery of signs, forms, and procedures for language manipulation to the gathering and giving of shape to communicative impulses and thoughts, potentially in dialogue with all one has previously thought, read, and written. Further, the communicative impulses are responsive to more immediate experiences that give rise to and constrain the communicative impulse within the perceived rhetorical situation. Further, the social relations enacted in the immediate communicative moment may involve memories of previous relations, mental projections of interlocutors, and situations played out over the time frame for transmission and the repeated later use of a document. Writing may also involve interlocutors who are not known in any way in person, but are known only by their social systemic or activity system relationship and through institutional roles or engagement with certain topics. All this must be constructed mentally. Texts contain information, from memory, from other sources of knowledge, or from experiences, which then must be selected and deployed purposefully. This information must be gathered in ways trustworthy and credible for the intended audience.

The extreme case is in reports of scientific experiments carried out under controlled conditions with the implicit commitment that anyone who follows these procedures will get similar results, because some result has been proven under the special conditions of these experiments. Then each piece of writing is accountable to other texts forming resources and creating the dialogic moment, an intertext that lies behind the text. Sometimes intertextual accountability may be defined by expectations of others within a specialized activity system, as all credible experts in a scientific field need to be aware of and take account of certain standard texts that embody theories and findings as well as stay abreast of the evolving literature. A failure to align with or show reasonable awareness of the current literature, or a responsible stance toward it, reduces credibility and meaningfulness of one's claims. Similarly, lawyers must exhibit and operate within knowledge of the relevant law and precedents. Reasoning must then draw these resources and contexts of situation, action, facts, and intertexts together into credible and effective meanings that contribute to the evolving interaction.

Other forms of writing may require access to emotions or imaginative constructs that will reverberate with the imaginations and feelings of others or will provide surprise and novelty or comic incongruities. Locating those means of engagement with others and the sources of invention in oneself are also part of the choice making for effective writing. Engaging deep issues of content and approach, effective writing is far more than a matter of choosing and sequencing words—although that too is part of forging effective and forceful meanings that will impress themselves on other people's minds, both drawing on the resources of the author and anticipating the resources of the readers and how they will be gathered and activated into coherent meanings in the readings.

To accomplish the complex tasks of writing one needs to engage in extensive processes, some of which may be explicit and fairly close to the surface, visible in externalized behaviors of taking notes, planning, drafting, and revising; but others are more implicit and deep in the mind, involving what a writer is contemplating, considering, or eliminating. The latter are barely noticed in the case of spoken reports because these tasks often do not enter conscious awareness. At the other extreme may be deeply internalized, automatized behaviors that are unproblematic for the writer, but without which the writing might not be decipherable by others. Other more emergent meaning impulses may be realized in the gist or spontaneous ideas that seem to come from complex, even impulsive, dynamic activations in the brain.

An important component of the situated gathering together of one's resources for the purpose of writing is an embodied formation of a stance in a situation—a kind of organizing of the self to be responsive in a situation, as a ball player is attuned to the movement on the field, the state of play, one's position and body postures and sensations, and readiness to react to momentary developments. In a similar analogy, a musician brings to bear a lifetime of training, deep familiarity with a piece and style, and an immersion in the musical moment with only a few focused moments of monitoring thoughts floating on top. Because so much of the situation of the writer is reconstructed in the mind of the writer from distant clues and deep knowledge about audiences and activities, the elements of stance in situation may be in some cases even harder to recover, and may evolve over long periods of composition, so much so they become an enduring part of the person's disposition.

When a writer experiences fluency and flow, that is likely to be based on not only automatized behaviors, but also on a framing of the task and situation; a strongly composed sense of self, stance, and disposition; a coherent impulse to communicate; and easily accessed resources that seem to be falling into place, evoking one another in purposeful associations. The *fluency of the flow state* reflects a high state of complex problem solving at the limits of one's capabilities, leading to surprise at what one is able to accomplish. One deeply knows what one is doing and what one has to say, even if one cannot consciously report what one knows, particularly at the moment when all of one's cognitive resources are engaged in carrying out the task at hand, that is, writing the words one is impelled to communicate.

These views of embodied complex writing activity seem to be consistent with current views of the brain as engaged in complex, dynamic processes, enlisting multiple parts and dimensions simultaneously in fresh configurations in response to perceived situations, contexts, impulses, and actions (Kelso, 1995; Marinaro, Scarpetta, & Yamaguchi, 2008; Thelen & Smith, 1994). The meaning making of writing then requires a full enlistment of many parts of the brain in high states of activation (or low states of inhibition or irrelevant processes) and co-firing of parts that need to work together in concert like an orchestra. Although brain recording of writers in extended compositional episodes is not possible with current imaging technology, it is certainly the case that evidence points to multiple parts of the brain being involved in writing, which include not only structures associated with cognition and metacognition, language, and motor functions, but also social, emotional, and affective functions. (See an overview of the writing brain in Chapter 23, this volume.)

Given current knowledge based on imaging technologies that assess timing parameters and not just regions of activation, it is a reasonable hypothesis that there are likely to be changing patterns of which parts of the brain are activated at the same time and across different moments of time in the process of composition. In real time for real composing tasks, the writer moves from the deeply internal work during initial composing to coordinating communication of meaning, based on various forms of accessing, gathering, transforming, formulating, and externalizing knowledge, and then during written language production to monitoring, evaluating, considering and selecting alternatives, and revising, from the point of view of public standards and the potential readers in the audience.

With this amount of brain activity it is no wonder that writing is considered one of the most complex human activities and may be associated with high brain oxygen needs, depressed states of being, and headaches. At the same time, the brain also has pleasure centers that may be activated in moments of joy for writers, for example, when they find just the right way to express an idea or are able to communicate it to a reader. The high degree of complex brain activation in space and time that is likely with writing is manageable because the brains of skilled, experienced writers have developed over time specialized organization systems for accomplishing a variety of writing tasks.

WHERE CAN PSYCHOLOGICAL REGULARITIES BE FOUND?

The perspectives I have laid out of the variability and complexity of writing suggest that the search for a single psychological model of writing is chimerical, but that does not mean that there are no generalizations in writing. Rather than looking for a single set of writing processes, we might look for the *processes* that are activated, enlisted, coordinated, and transformed in the course of writing and over one's development as a writer. That is, rather than considering writing as an isolated modularized function, we might look at it as a complex accomplishment, enlisting varying assemblies of human psychological and material capacities that we have learned how to redirect and coordinate for these special purposes, and that over time might create more enduring or automatized assemblies that take shape in individuals, perhaps influenced by available social practices and organized instruction. Luria (1970) referred to these assemblies as functional systems or the working brain.

One direction for research is in identifying the range of psychological, perceptual, and affective functions that are activated, deployed, and used in writing: how these are activated in the course of different writing tasks; how their architecture constrains and affords human activity and shapes human engagement; and how these capacities grow and develop in engagement with writing. The most material perceptual and motor issues of written language, already substantially understood, provide examples of what I mean: Eyes and visual recognition must be trained to focus on small sequentially arranged marks and to notice the differentiations of letters and graphs in the locally used writing system, and young children must develop the fine motor control to transcribe, whether with stylus, pencil, or keyboard. At the other end of the literacy and abstraction spectrum, highly literate people must develop, from general human memory and conceptual capacities, very specific skills of holding extensive information in working memory (for overview see Chapter 21, this volume) over extended periods of time at various levels of consciousness so as to maintain the sense of textual coherence and argumentative or narrative flow over extended texts, while recalling and forming relevance judgments based on wide areas of their experience and previous reading so as to construct meaning within this coherence.

The human capacities and practices of writing are necessarily built on biological affordances and have emerged in ways compatible with them in the same way that tongs fit the hand, extend the reach, and utilize the fine motor capacities of the opposable thumb and hand for control and strength. Pencils and keyboards are made for the hand, and print is designed to be read at an arm's length. But well-crafted sentences contain no more than the mind can hold in current working memory, even as they move the minds to new mental configurations across the phrases and clauses. Well-designed texts display larger organizations in forms comprehensible to mental architecture.

A second direction for research would be to examine the multiple capacities and functions—such as memory, visual and auditory capacities, semantic and episodic knowledge, planning and organizational functions, and social and communicative functions—that must be coordinated for successful writing. How are these activated, synthesized, and brought together into externalizing motor actions of transcription where mind and meaning guide one's hand? How is that we can learn to engage and develop in such complex multidimensional practices? Further, how do we evaluate our words under multiple levels of simultaneous constraints to select the one that meets multiple considerations and to which we become committed? The power of this choice is so strong that it is often difficult for people to face revision, to reconsider the complex choices they made in order to pick apart the dimensions that went into the choices, and to review them consciously. We have a strong bias to let the words stand as we first struggled to compose them. Other writers may be insecure and not able to review or accept any criticism and correction. Skilled revision requires an ability to face one's composed words with a professional stance toward one's language and to impose and use specific criteria for review to look at one's own produced words with some equanimity and distance in order to improve them. Although we currently teach the writing process as a natural sequence, perhaps we should think of writing processes as a set of sophisticated cognitive skills to be developed and strategically deployed. Perhaps we also should help students overcome the emotional challenges of confronting one's words to make those words more concise.

As a complex, highly engaging activity requiring long training and varied skills, the writing process of activating, calling forth, and assembling complex capacities under heightened motivational states can be taught. A variety of pedagogic, rhetorical, and personal devices have been developed to awaken the self to the communicative situation and develop concentration, preparation of mind, and assembly of the self so as to be able to write. We can introduce students to the rituals and special spaces writers frequently develop and meditative practices they use to get in the right frame of mind. As teachers we can create strong writing prompts and a supportive atmosphere in class, employ warm-up exercises, and introduce heuristics for identifying rhetorical situations.

It would be worth examining the self-reported practices people have developed for assembling, ordering, and monitoring their skills in producing writing of different sorts. What range of practices and assemblages is created across different types of texts and situations for one individual? To what extent are certain practices for assembling or coordinating automatized for an individual? What is the longitudinal developmental path by which these coordinated assemblages of skills and practices develop? To what extent are these practices shared among people engaged in similar tasks or having gone through similar educational or cultural experiences? To what extent are automatized practices individualized and idiosyncratic? What accounts for similarities or differences among practices and assembled processes?

Writers also appear to be responsive to inchoate prelinguistic or nonlinguistic impulses, gists, feelings, and imagination that appear to be outside language. Writers report materials become organized in subconscious or preconscious ways, sometimes through graphic, musical, or geometric imagery. What is the nature of these nonconscious and nonlinguistic impulses and how are they brought to linguistic form? Further, how might this process of forming meaningful communications be animated by affective motivating states in response to our perceived environment? Conversely, how do the forms of externally received texts form the mental structures associated with the literate or intellectual mind? How is literate experience related to prefrontal cortical development and related intellectual, social, and identity processes among the educated, particularly during the intense experience of literacy in schooling, especially with preadolescents, adolescents, and young adults? On these issues, as with prior ones, the dimensions of variation and similarity are worth exploring.

A third direction to consider is the creation, maintenance, and development of mental projects over long periods of time. As production of texts can occur over extended periods, even over several years or decades for some books, slowly gestating in the minds of authors, there are issues not only of how these are held and built as mental constructs over time, but how they are viewed, evaluated, and monitored for further work. Within the extended period of text development, which can range from 10 minutes to 10 years, what is the relation and dynamic process between what is held and worked on internally and what has been externalized in text and can be manipulated as a graphic object, at a distance from the self? How, and in what form, is meaning maintained and transformed as it moves from an internal, and perhaps only partly and inchoately formed, impulse into an externally available public construction, dependent on the limits of the words chosen to give it expression?

A fourth direction to consider is the dynamic of externalization and social engagement and how that impacts the production of meaning. Forming one's thoughts to be interpretable for others in material situations, mediated by signs, entails conceiving oneself as a social actor, such as Mead (1934) or Smith (1759), which some have seen as the foundation of the self, and creating a linguistic presence, of which others need to make sense. Thus, the focus of the act of writing becomes socially integrative and interactional and an extension of the psychological impulses we have toward sociality and coordination. This social dimension also then raises questions about how our learning to use the common language is itself formative of the categories of our thinking, thereby integrating the individual mind into the social mind, even as the particularity and originality of our utterances, speaking to our perceptions of our needs, situations, and relevant actions, defines us as having particular social identities and relationships. Particularly as writing is associated with advanced education and specialization in disciplines or spheres of activity, such as law, business, or journalism, what might an inquiry into social externalization tell us about how we form modes of disciplinary or professional thinking? Such modes may draw on meanings, knowledge, and forms of expression and interaction of other participants in these social fields. What are the processes of our literate cognitive apprenticeships that transform us into particular literate human beings?

A fifth direction to consider is our reflective executive direction of these complex processes by which we produce text. How can we come to understand the welter of emotions and states of mind that surround, inhabit, and saturate the act of writing? It may be that this management is learned as we come to observe and reflect on our behavior and come up with plans about how best to manage our resources, being attentive to the smallest stirrings that might give us guidance, at the same time as not to be misled by transient doubts, exhaustions, or slow working processes that leave us waiting. In constructing our texts we also may be learning to construct ourselves as writers, reflecting not only about the texts and their effect but also ourselves as creators of texts, both in our internal workings and the external social presences we take on through the embassy of our texts. One might expect great variety in ways people solve these problems, but the processes by which these sets of problems come to our attention and how we go about solving them may hold clues about complex human cognition.

PSYCHOLOGICAL THEORIES RELEVANT TO SOCIOCULTURAL AND HISTORICAL WRITING TRADITIONS

In trying to understand the relevance of these issues for writing practice and writing education, even though I am not a psychologist, I have found two approaches to psychology useful for what they explain in themselves and how they conjoin with other knowledge: Vygotskian sociocultural psychology and pragmatist interpersonal psychiatry (most closely associated with Harry Stack Sullivan). Both accounts consider individuals with interpersonal purposes, developing within social worlds of others' responses and cultural tools available in their time and place. In this way both approaches are consistent with the idea that writing and literacy developed historically among humans for human purposes, and that writing is specifically a form of communication and interaction that is based on our understanding of human relations, stance, emotions, and anxieties. Both theories are also consistent with the idea that writing creates a public self, forming an identity that is potentially more durable, transportable, and public than most other forms of behavior and action. Even writing kept in a drawer can become a witness across time and space, and through tricks of cultural understanding, a witness to eternity—or a witness to ourself whom we imagine as the ideal reader.

Vygotsky (1978, 1986) sees learning occurring in interaction with cultural tools, with initial interpersonal use becoming internalized and transformed into personal tools and forms of thought. We then mobilize these internal resources under conditions of action. In this view we form ourselves within social interaction, moving from the interpersonal to the intrapersonal, but we also reform the social milieu by our actions and inventions in response to situations. This account allows for cultural invention and transformation of human consciousness through history as individuals develop new tools and interactions and actions within larger social systems—the type I sketched out earlier, where new genres and activity systems become sites of new relations and identities. On the basis of such reasoning I have made some proposals about how learning to write in some genres may be related to cognitive development (Bazerman, 2009).

This Vygotskian view is consistent with G. H. Mead's (1934) views of formation of self in an attempt to make ourselves understood by others and with John Dewey's (1947) view of life and society as experiments, constantly creating new selves. This tradition also gave rise to Harry Stack Sullivan's (1953) interpersonal theory of psychiatry, which proposed a more direct way to understand the emotional force of language in interpersonal relations and the turmoil that might surround the assertion of self through written statements (Bazerman, 2001, 2005). This theory focuses on the development of the self through interpersonal relations as we engage in the forms of interaction offered by our time, place, and sets of available partners in family and community. These relations are formed through positive affect of desire for integration and successful satisfaction of needs, but are also framed through the anxiety system we develop, which marks the boundaries of where we feel comfortable with those with whom we interact, based on our perception of their comfort and discomfort.

Our sense of anxiety is grounded in our earliest, preverbal interactions with caregivers, but evolves through our lives in interaction with new partners in new situations. As we mature, language takes a deeper role in our interactions, identities, and relations. Although writing as we mature frequently occurs in semiprivacy, it begins with face-to-face interactions, as we see the sense others around us make of what we have put on paper. As we get older and often face our writing alone, we are enacting relations of the imagination, wrapped in all our deeply embedded emotions surrounding communicative relations, unrelieved by any information from immediate face-to-face presence. Anxiety should be high on the research agenda for a psychology of writing for two reasons: (a) the reported great anxiety of writers along with the high degree of procrastination and digressive behavior associated with acts of writing; and (b) the practice of hiding one's personal writing from others, as utilized by most adults who use writing only for limited purposes within fairly restricted purposes. There has been a limited writing research agenda around the topic of writing apprehension, based on self-reporting surveys. This work provides a starting point, but more in-depth work is needed.

FINAL COMMENTS

Although writing has often been characterized as noncontextual because it could convey messages from one locale to another and had a greater burden of explicitness, I argue here that writing is psychologically challenging precisely because it is so contextual. However, context has to be understood internally—it is mentally constructed by reader and writer and it is mediated only by a few limited external visible signs that provide clues as to what is being communicated. Rather than a situation being apparent to perception, as filtered through our perceptual categorization and organization conditioned by language, the situation itself must be worked upon to become apparent. The high degree of imagination, information gathering, mental framing, and meaning making required for reading and writing suggests that literate processes are constantly adaptive to and constructive of situations, organizing the brain for situated action. Just as spoken language creates mutual alignment, coordination, and shared attention and cognition, so too does writing over greater communities, times, and spaces. Writing creates common intellectual heritages, within which we learn to participate over a lifetime of reading and writing, carrying on the human project of intelligent life as well as the follies of phantasmagoric creation of chimerical meanings.

REFERENCES

Bazerman, C. (2001). Anxiety in action: Sullivan's interpersonal psychiatry as a supplement to Vygotskian psychology. *Mind, Culture and Activity 8,* 174–186.

Bazerman, C. (2005). Practically human: The pragmatist project of the interdisciplinary journal *Psychiatry. Linguistics and the Human Sciences 1,* 15–38.

Bazerman, C. (2006). The writing of social organization and the literate situating of cognition. In D. Olson & M. Cole, (Eds.), *Technology, literacy and the evolution of society: Implications of the work of Jack Goody* (pp. 215–240). Mahwah, NJ: Erlbaum.

Bazerman, C. (2009). Genre and cognitive development. In C. Bazerman, A. Bonini, & D. Figueiredo (Eds.), *Genre in a changing world* (pp. 279–294). West Lafayette, IN: Parlor Press and WAC Clearinghouse.

Beaufort, A. (1999). *Writing in the real world: Making the transition from school to work.* New York: Teachers College Press.

Bereiter, C., & Scardamalia, M. (1987). The psychology of written composition. Hillsdale, NJ: Erlbaum.

Brandt, D. (2001). *Literacy in American lives.* New York: Cambridge University Press.

Danziger, K. (1990). *Constructing the subject: Historical origins of psychological research.* New York: Cambridge University Press.

Dewey, J. (1947). *Experience and education.* New York: Macmillan

Dias, P., Freedman, A., Medway, P., & Pare, A. (1999). *Worlds apart: Acting and writing in academic and workplace contexts.* Mahwah, NJ: Erlbaum.

Dias, P., & Pare, A. (Eds.). (2000). *Transitions: Writing in academic and workplace settings.* Cresskill: Hampton Press.

Festinger, L. (1957). *A theory of cognitive dissonance.* Evanston, IL: Row, Peterson.

Galbraith, D. (2009). Writing as discovery. *Teaching and learning writing: psychological aspects of education—current trends. British Journal of Educational Psychology Monograph Series, II* (6), 5–26.

Goody, J. (1986). *The logic of writing and the organization of society.* Cambridge: Cambridge University Press.

Haswell, R. (2008). Teaching of writing in higher education. In C. Bazerman (Ed.), *Handbook of research on writing: History, society, school, individual, text* (pp. 331–346). New York: Routledge.

Hayes, J. R., & Flower, L. (1980). Identifying the organization of the writing process. In L. W. Gregg & E. R. Sternberg (Eds.), *Cognitive processes in writing* (pp. 3–30). Hillsdale, NJ: Erlbaum.

Hillocks, G. (2002). *The testing trap: How state writing assessments control learning.* New York: Teachers College Press.

Kelso, J. A. S. (1995). *Dynamic patterns: The self-organization of brain and behavior (complex adaptive systems).* Cambridge, MA: MIT Press.

Klein, P. D. (1999). Reopening inquiry into cognitive processes in writing-to-learn. *Educational Psychology Review,* 11, 203–270.

Luria A. R. (1970). *The functional organization of the brain. Scientific American,* 222(3), 66–78.

Marinaro, M., Scarpetta, S, & Yamaguchi, Y. (Eds.). (2008). *Dynamic brain—from neural spikes to behaviors.* Basel: Springer.

Mayer, C. (1998). Deaf children learn to spell. *Research in the Teaching of English, 33,* 35–65.

Mead, G. H. (1934). *Mind, self, and society.* Chicago: University of Chicago Press.

Medway P., & Clark B. (2003). Imagining the building: Architectural design as semiotic construction. *Design Studies, 24*(3), 255–273.

Medway, P. (1996). Virtual and material buildings: Construction and constructivism in architecture and writing. *Written Communication, 13,* 473–514.

Murphy, S., & Yancey, K. (2008). Construct and consequence: Validity in writing assessment. In C. Bazerman (Ed.), *Handbook of research on writing: History, society, school, individual, text* (pp. 365–386). New York: Routledge.

Olson, D. (2008). History of schools and writing. In C. Bazerman (Ed.), *Handbook of research on writing: History, society, school, individual, text* (pp. 283–292). New York: Routledge.

Rouen, D., Goggin, M., & Clary-Lemon, J. (2008). Teaching of writing and writing teachers through the ages. In C. Bazerman (Ed.), *Handbook of research on writing: History, society, school, individual, text* (pp. 347–364). New York: Lawrence Erlbaum Associates.

Russell, D. R. (1997). Writing and genre in higher education and workplaces. *Mind, Culture, and Activity, 4*(4), 224–237.

Scharer, P. L., & Zutell, J. (2003). The development of spelling. In N. Hall, J. Larson, & J. Marsh (Eds.), *Handbook of early childhood literacy* (pp. 271–286). Thousand Oaks, CA: Sage.

Schmandt-Besserat, D., & Erard, M. (2008). Origins and forms of writing. In C. Bazerman (Ed.), *Handbook of research on writing: History, society, school, individual, text* (pp. 7–22). New York: Routledge.

Smart, G. (2007) *Writing the economy: Activity, genre and technology in the world of banking.* London: Equinox Press.

Smith, A. (1759). *The theory of moral sentiments.* London: A. Millar.

Sullivan, H. S. (1953). *The interpersonal theory of psychiatry.* New York: Norton.

Thelen, E., & Smith, L. (1994). *A dynamic systems approach to the development of cognition and action.* Cambridge, MA: MIT Press.

Tolchinsky, L. (Ed.). (2001). *Developmental aspects in learning to write.* Dordrecht: Kluwer.

Young, R., Becker, A., & Pike, K. (1970). *Rhetoric: Discovery and change.* New York: Harcourt.

Vygotsky, L. (1978). *Mind in society: The development of higher psychological processes.* Cambridge, MA: Harvard University Press.

Vygotsky, L. (1986). *Thought and language.* Cambridge, MA: MIT Press.

5

Writing Under the Influence
(of the Writing Process)

CÉLINE BEAUDET, ROGER GRAVES,
and BERTRAND LABASSE

*T*his chapter illustrates the trends toward global writing research across languages, integration of social with cognitive writing research, and increasing emphasis on adult writing research related to the workplace and professional development. In the first part of the chapter Roger Graves gives an overview of the cognitive approaches to writing studies in English Canada since the 1980s. Although writing studies in English Canada began with a focus on cognitive studies of writing processes, more recent work has focused on the social more than the cognitive part of social cognition. Most of the research done centers on professional writing by researchers in technical and professional writing. This work has become increasingly linked with genre study approaches that link social cognition, genre, and rhetorical studies in a multimodal research approach. In the second part of the chapter Céline Beaudet outlines 20 years of effort in French-speaking Quebec universities to move from a normative and prescriptive approach of writing to a comprehensive view of both writing products and the writing process. Research in Quebec draws from the French and English traditions of linguistic discourse analysis, cognitive research on written composition, and rhetoric studies. Thus writing studies incorporate a special twist different from that in English-speaking Canada. In the third part of the chapter Bertrand Labasse reflects on the results of 30 years of international research on the psychology of writing and its impact on professional writers and describes a four-axis pedagogical intervention based on his experience teaching advanced journalism and scientific popularization. Together, these three sections give a deep and broad picture of cognitive studies of writing in Canada.

WRITING STUDIES IN ANGLO-CANADIAN POSTSECONDARY CONTEXTS

Perhaps the most important moment in the development of cognitive studies of writing in Anglo-Canadian universities came in 1979 with the Learning to Write conference sponsored by the Canadian Council of Teachers of English. The book *Reinventing the Rhetorical Tradition* (Freedman & Pringle, 1980) includes several of the most important papers delivered at the conference on topics such as revision, sentence combining, and invention. In the Preface, the editors, Aviva Freedman and Ian Pringle, include cognitive psychology as one of many fields that participate in reinventing rhetoric in general and the "invention" aspects of writing in particular. They argue that the concept of inventing ideas—drawn from classical rhetorical theory—can be enriched by "drawing on fields as diverse as creativity theory, cognitive psychology, tagmemic linguistics and other fields" (Freedman & Pringle, 1980, p. vii).[1] This new rhetoric took as its starting place ideas from classical rhetoric, but it extended them and sought to place them in a research- and evidence-based context.

The rest of this section provides an overview both of early work in writing studies research on composing processes and the more recent turn to social cognition or writing processes in social context. Canadian researchers knew of the research on cognition in writing studies and drew on this knowledge to establish their own research agendas. Indeed, many of the key figures in early cognitive writing studies attended the Learning to Write conference.

Cognitive approaches to writing instruction, social-epistemic rhetoric, and expressionistic rhetoric were the three main "new" approaches that together formed the "new rhetoric" of writing studies in the late 1970s (Berlin, 1987). The "old" approaches generally referred to what Fogarty (1959) labeled the "current-traditional paradigm" for teaching writing: Current because it was used then and is now, and traditional because it reflected approaches to teaching writing that focused on grammar and modes of discourse (such as the compare and contrast essay) without attention to a philosophy of language (see also Young, 1978; Crowley, 1985). Current traditional approaches to teaching writing did not stem from a research base—they proceeded on the basis that we teach this way because we have always taught this way. From a current traditional perspective, the text is a fixed object subject to analysis but not revision. Cognitive approaches, in contrast, attempted to map the activities of the mind as an individual drafted, revised, and edited a text. From a cognitive perspective, texts under examination were alive, subject to extensive revision, and a product of the interaction of writer and materials.

Early studies in the 1960s and 1970s that established research into writing processes as an important object of study focused initially on invention, creativity,

---

[1] Tagmemic linguistics, developed in the 1960s, was important to rhetoric and writing studies because it valued the linguistic element in the context of the whole text being examined. This focus above the sentence level and at the level of the whole text fit with the rhetorical perspective, which itself also worked at the level of the whole text. These whole texts were always situated in a social context, and so the cognitive process of writing was always also situated.

and the generation of ideas (Emig 1977; Rohman & Wlecke, 1964). Rohman and Wlecke observed that student writers needed to engage in extensive "prewriting" to discover what they wanted or needed to write about. They referred to prewriting as "thinking as discovery," and used it to mean much the same as the writing across the curriculum movement phrase "writing to learn" (p. 103).

Emig (1971, 1977), who contributed a chapter to *Reinventing the Rhetorical Tradition*, cited Rohman and Wlecke in her work and grounded her claims about the importance of writing and discovery in the psychological work of Vygotsky, Luria, and Bruner. In her book *The Composing Processes of Twelfth Graders*, Emig posed research questions that have drawn attention in cognitive research in writing since then: If there are specifiable elements, moments, and stages in the composing process of students, what are these? Are elements organized linearly in the writing process? Recursively? What governs the choices students make? When and why do students have or not have a writing plan? What psychological factors affect or accompany portions of the writing process?

Emig (1971) found that established writers follow a much different writing process than was articulated in the textbooks of the time—that is, they did not follow a linear composing model. In an earlier study (Emig, 1964) she also found evidence suggesting that students generally do not follow a formal outline.

Sommers, who also contributed a chapter to *Reinventing the Rhetorical Tradition* (Butturff & Sommers, 1980), extended this work to the act of revising. Sommers's (1980) article "Revision Strategies of Student Writers and Experienced Adult Writers" starts by challenging the idea that writing is linear. She argues that both Rohman and Welcke and Britton proceed from a model of the writing process as a set of linear stages: "conception—incubation—production" (p. 378). For Sommers, what these models "fail to take into account is the recursive shaping of thought by language ... *revision*" (p. 378). Experienced writers use revision as an invention technique to "re-view" their work as they searched for ways to structure what it was they wanted to say. This re-seeing of the work encompasses all aspects of it from sentence-level changes to the reordering of the entire work. Sommers described how revision strategies change throughout the composing process as writers deploy their limited cognitive resources effectively.

It is important to note that both Sommers and Emig compared their studies of students to experienced, adult writers. As the field of writing studies expanded its reach into professional and technical writing, studies of adult writers in working contexts came to be of significant interest. Selzer (1983), for example, took the interest in composing processes but applied it to an engineering professional rather than a student.

Flower and Hayes, together and individually, began publishing articles on the composing process in 1977. The intense interest of the emerging rhetoric and composition field in writing processes from the early 1960s until Hayes and Flower turned their attention to writing drew from a wide variety of research backgrounds. Hayes brought his training as a psychologist to the study of writing processes (see Chapter 1, this volume). Flower and Hayes' (1981) "A Cognitive Process Theory of Writing" emphasized the use of protocol analysis and marked important turns, both in focus and methods through its focus on the entire writing process, not just invention, and on a relatively new method drawn from a field of research not shared by many other writing researchers.

In English-speaking Canada, the research interest in writing studies generally, and in cognitive approaches to writing specifically, deviated from the U.S. tradition. The first break concerns the subject of analysis: There is no first-year writing requirement at the vast majority of Anglo-Canadian universities. One consequence of this policy is that first-year writers are not considered a "problem" or object of analysis for writing studies, as has happened in the United States, for example. We do not seek solutions or ways to teach students in these courses because there simply are not many of them. Both Emig and Sommers took students in such beginners' writing courses at the undergraduate level as half of the object of their study. The other object of their study—adult or experienced writers—has been the concerted area of focus for Canadian researchers. Canadian universities did not adopt the U.S. first-year writing sequence as a model, but they have adopted professional writing as a subject of study and developed many professional and technical writing programs (Smith, 2006).

The second break from U.S. tradition involves the nature of cognitive activity under review. Writing studies scholars in Anglo-Canadian universities do not focus on individual cognition in the way that the early Flower and Hayes models do. Instead, Canadian scholars have turned their attention to social cognition and distributed cognition. Their exception to this turn toward social cognition involves researchers located in education faculties and schools. For example, Bereiter and Scardamalia (1987), whose book *The Psychology of Written Composition* is one of a series of important publications in cognitive research in writing from the 1980s to the present, were from the University of Toronto at the Ontario Institute for Studies in Education. They argued that there are two distinct composing processes: one used by unskilled writers and another used by expert writers. Writing strategies are linked intimately with thinking strategies, and in recent years their work has concentrated more generally on topics related to learning and knowledge rather than explicitly on writing. Other educational psychologists have also contributed to cognitive research on writing in Canada (Klein 1999a, 1999b, 2004; Klein, Piacente-Cimini, & Williams, 2007). Often this work focuses on K–12 students and contexts, however, and is presented at education-related conferences rather than writing studies conferences. The consequences of these different educational contexts for writing research have been that the research that is being done on cognitive approaches to writing tends to remain in the educational research community. (See Chapter 6, this volume, for an integration of the cognitive and social with educational applications.)

There is another explanation for the failure of cognitive research on writing to transfer from educational psychology domains to writing studies in Canada. Writing studies scholars, as far back as the mid-1980s, began exploring the role of social influences in writing. Early critiques of the Flower and Hayes (1981) model, while noting the contributions of the model, pointed out the lack of any social context for the writing process. Although subsequent versions of the model (Hayes, 1996) include social context, in the 1980s and 1990s researchers in writing studies in Canada focused on the social more than the cognitive part of social cognition.

Because many of the researchers worked in technical and professional writing educational programs, their work often drew on professionals who write and students in professional programs who aspired to jobs in those professions. As a consequence, much of the research summarized in the next section may seem like a summary of research in professional writing; nevertheless, this research does have as its goal the identification of writing processes very much related to the questions central to cognitive studies of writing.

Studies of writing processes in workplace writing contexts invariably encounter the "problem" of authorship: Many documents are written by teams, and some of the text included in these documents appears and reappears in many subsequent documents. An even more problematic situation occurs when these documents are understood as part of a broader set of social actions and as part of what has been termed a genre set (Devitt, 1991), genre repertoire (Orlikowski & Yates, 1994), and a genre system (for an overview, see Artemeva, 2006). In these cases, the focus of cognitive research shifts from the individual (as in Flower and Hayes and Bereiter and Scardamalia) to the group. In writing studies research in Canada, Dias, Freedman, Medway, and Paré (1999) give perhaps the clearest explanation of how social contexts affect the composition of texts. According to these authors, to understand *texts in contexts* we need to focus on how groups of texts work together. For them, "distributed cognition" refers to "the knowledge and knowledge-making on which a group within an organization depends in order to accomplish its activities" (p. 31). They adopt Lave's (1991) description of "distributed" as shared between people and Cole's (1991) sense of shared cognition as held in common and divided up between individuals. One key way that groups have of sharing knowledge is through genres of written communication: "Genres embody the experience of previous writers, allowing it to be reactivated on each new occasion of writing" (Dias et al., 1999, p. 31). Even reports that are written by one individual mind in a workplace embody "other people's contributions . . . through their experience as stored in genres, existing texts, and cultural forms" (p. 32). For this reason Dias et al. argue that we need to study the context from which documents are generated, including co-participants whether they are co-authors or not. The *connection between an individual writer and the community* that sponsors the writing (classroom or workplace) must be understood if we are to learn how people write.

Artemeva (2006) connects theories of genre and social cognition to activity theory and situated learning. Artemeva quotes Resnick's claim that "every cognitive act must be viewed as a specific response to a specific set of circumstances" (Resnick, Levine, Teasley, 1991, p. 35). That is, we can only understand cognitive acts if we examine them in their social context; we can only understand the writing of students if we place it in the context of the classroom they study in. Paré (2000) outlines the parallels between the development of the view of writing as social and the idea of social cognition. Both traditions of thought place cognition firmly within the context of others, both immediately available and present through texts. As Paré points out, if we view texts as artifacts of society, then they can be seen as just another aspect of the social activities that make up a culture. Other researchers see similar possibilities for the study of activity theory. Hayes (2006) identifies activity theory as a promising "framework" in much the same way that Flower and

Hayes (1980) worked as a theoretical framework from which to base further empirical studies of writing. Hayes (2006) commented that "activity theory is designed to describe purposeful actions that a person or a group of people undertake by relating the actions to the environments in which they take place" (p. 37). Paré and Smart (1994) argue that any study of composing processes must account for the actions Hayes refers to as they are embodied in genres of writing.

Artemeva (2006), citing Giltrow (2002) and Paré and Smart (1994), makes the important point that the resulting texts people write do not just respond to a context or environment; they co-create or change the environment through the process of their creation. Context is not stable or fixed; it is shifting, a moving target. Further, the texts students and workers produce are attempts to create documents in genres that are also shifting or "stable for now" (Schryer, 1993, p. 229). It is clear from these conceptions of the situations facing both student and workplace writers that any description of cognitive function must attend to the instability and fluidity associated with "context." This instability leads to a sense of the writing process as a much more demanding and difficult cognitive environment, a conception that pushes the research field closer to a theory that can explain more persuasively why many people find writing difficult to master.

This work on genres of writing, and particularly the interest in how students move from classroom to workplace settings, has led to recent and current interest in transfer of learning from one academic environment to another (writing courses to discipline-specific courses) and from university to workplace environments (Artemeva, 2006; Dias et al., 1999; Dias & Paré, 2000; Giltrow & Valiquette, 1994; Smart, 1993). Transfer of learning research in writing studies builds on cognitive psychology research (Haskell, 2001; see Nelms & Dively, 2007, for an overview as it applies to writing studies).

In the United States, one of the core ideas supporting first-year writing courses is the belief that the knowledge and skills developed in those courses will transfer to courses in the rest of the students' academic programs, a view that Bergmann and Zepernick (2007) refer to as an optimistic fiction. In Canada, where there are no first-year writing requirements (with a few exceptions, such as the University of Winnipeg and the University of Prince Edward Island) and few universities with writing-intensive or writing-across-the-curriculum courses, research on transfer has been motivated more by transfer between academic settings and workplace settings and between high school contexts and university contexts for writing.

Slomp (2008) focused on problems of construct validity in standardized tests and how they then cause high school teachers to limit and constrain how they teach writing as a process in their classrooms. This limited sense of process becomes a problem at universities because students who proceed from high school to universities bring with them a reductive sense of what it means to write and a limited ability to create more sophisticated writing processes to help them succeed with the more complex demands of university writing assignments.

At the far end of the postsecondary school continuum lies doctoral student writers and the texts they create. Recently, Paré, Starke-Meyerring, and McAlpie (2009) investigated the relationship between doctoral students and the dissertations they write. They reported that meetings between students and supervisors, in which the supervisors stand in or perform the roles of other readers to demonstrate for doctoral students how others will understand their words, result in revisions that "actual readers find acceptable" (Paré et al., 2009, p. 190). Although the focus of this research is not located within cognitive research literature, it does explore cognitive functions based on shared data, that is, cognition distributed across a writer and readers. This approach to cognitive studies of writing in Anglo-Canadian research differs markedly from the traditions described below in the French-Canadian research community.

WRITING STUDIES IN QUEBEC

In Canada, and more particularly in Quebec, the teaching of writing in French is done by the arts and communication departments with the aim of training professionals in written communication. In Quebec, there is no tradition of teaching academic writing at the university level as is the case for English in Canada (Beaudet, 2010; Chartrand & Blaser, 2008). There are no writing centers in Quebec. Bachelor's degrees and professional writing certificates have sprung up throughout the French-speaking universities in Quebec since the end of the 1980s (Beaudet & Clerc, 2008). These programs that focus on professionalization have been created by linguists and literary specialists whose research focus was not professional writing. The teaching of writing was first oriented toward the description of the products stemming from professional writing rather than toward the specifics of writing per se and of the writing processes in a specific context (Plane, Olive, & Alamargot, 2010). The normative and step-wise technical approaches (Pollet, 2001) were the only two considered: Different types of professional writing were taught using compositional, stylistic, and grammatical norms with the aim of encouraging the writing of example texts based on standard models. Writing was seen as a result of linguistic and procedural knowledge of grammar, syntax, readability, and text structuring.

With the arrival of university professors and researchers specialized in writing in the 1990s and the 2000s, the teaching of professional writing has progressively based itself on concepts arising out of analytical approaches to text (linguistic analysis of discourse, text grammar, and theories of argument) (Amossy, 2000; Angenot, 2008; Bronckart, 1996; Charaudeau & Maingueneau, 2002; Ducrot & Schaeffer, 1995) as well as on the pragmatics of the written text and of professional writing (Dias et al., 1999; Ransdell & Levy, 1996; Spilka, 1993). In order to justify the updating of curricula, research first centered on the conditions of the professional practice of writing (constraint management) and the writer's competencies (what curricula should be based on), and later moved on to the description of writing strategies (Alamargot & Fayol, 2009; Chanquoy & Alamargot, 2002; Alamargot, Terrier, & Cellier, 2007; Brandt, 2009; Fayol, 1992; Piolat & Roussey, 1992). Interdisciplinarity immediately became important because the sciences of writing draw upon the sciences of information and communication, applied linguistics, the sciences of language, rhetoric, semiotics, theories of argument, and the sciences of education and cognitive psychology. This chapter's focus is on the impact cognitive psychology has had on the evolution of research on professional writing and its products in Quebec since the 1990s.

The Writer's Competencies

The initial focus on the products of professional writing, taught from a strongly normative perspective, first burst upon the scene under the momentum created by investigations into the competencies that a professional writer was expected to have, based on fact-finding surveys of employers and analyses of job postings in newspapers (Beaudet, 1998, 1999; Beaudet & Smart, 2002; Bossé-Andrieu, Cajolet-Laganière, & Grant-Russell, 1994; Clerc, 1998; Gibbs, 1998). These investigations revealed that the professional writer is a psychological, social, and emotional subject (Plane, 2006), much like a literary writer. The difference, as revealed by the survey of employers, is that the professional writer's production constraints are more numerous. Far from being only executants, writers are responsible for complex acts of professional communication.

Various successive surveys have pointed out the reductive character of the normative and technological approaches for explaining a writing activity, overdetermined by a client, having to mold itself to a great variety of types of writing, often motivated by multiple and even conflicting rhetorical and pragmatic aims; the writing activity is moreover subjected to the imperative of effective communication. In fact, the professional text, being of a utilitarian nature, is aimed at accomplishing a linguistic act such as informing, instructing, explaining, prescribing, or inciting to action, among others. That text is effective if it is read and understood and elicits the desired reaction from the reader. Communicative effectiveness corresponds to attaining pragmatic and rhetorical objectives stemming from a professional communicative act in a given situation. For example, a leaflet on the existence of a recycling program for old refrigerators will not be judged effective if the citizens continue to take their old appliances to a dump; it will also not be judged effective if the body that administers the program keeps getting phone calls from citizens wanting to know just what the program is and if they are eligible to use it. The writer is responsible for the communicative effectiveness of his or her writings.

Through these various surveys, the professional writer began to be seen not as a technician, but as a specialist whose main domain of expertise is the production of a functional text suitable for use by the reader (Bisaillon, 2007a, 2007b; Clerc, 2000; Labasse, 2008). Thus, text is a result of choices determined by ongoing interaction among the formal characteristics of the text, those of its context or social anchor, and those of the writer-reader axis that are the basis of the communicative nature of linguistic exchanges. It thus appeared very clear that all attempts to understand and explain the writing process in a professional context would have to include a comprehensive picture of the reader, for it is the reader who holds the keys to the aim of communication. In this spirit, the writing activity has been examined from the perspective of a problem-solving activity (writing to be understood), subdivided into subproblems related to textuality, communication, and comprehension (Coirier, Gaonac'h, Passerault, 1996; Fayol, 2002; Hayes, 1996; Hayes & Flower, 1980; Kellogg, 1987; Plane, 2006).

One must, however, note that the problem to be solved, an act of written communication with a goal of communicative effectiveness, remains dependent on the subjective analysis of the writing subject and on the values that connote the writer's mandate. Planning of the strategy is necessarily colored by the values and the world vision of the person who designs it. Such is not the case with solving a physiological problem: the problem-solving approach, in medicine, is applied in situations where the data and the parameters are independent of the perception and the values of the problem solver. Thus, kidney stones cannot be compared, as problems to be solved, to managing the reputation of a business accused of embezzlement or incompetence. There are well-known solutions (knowledge-based) for making kidney stones disappear whether the attending physician be left-wing or right-wing minded. Rebuilding a company's reputation is a professional communication challenge whose rationale is much more fluid and that requires value judgment.

Going from a text-based conception of writing, which starts with a subject struggling to organize his or her ideas, to a reader-based conception of writing, where the writer's ideas and writing skills are perceived in terms of their effect on the reader, did not happen without bruising a few egos. The main reason lies in the cultural origin of scientific traditions: the linguistic analysis of discourse and text grammar strongly dominated the sciences of language in France, and by ricochet, in Quebec, whereas the psychocognitive approach to the production of written texts evolved as part of the Anglo-Saxon scientific tradition. Michel Fayol (1992) was one of the first French researchers to have integrated American and British literature on writing from a psycho-cognitive perspective, and, at the same time, to make this research accessible in French.

Literacy

In the Quebec context, the professional writer who writes in French most often writes for the general public. Writers in Quebec work mainly in the fields of administration, public affairs, government relations, and institutional affairs (Clerc & Beaudet, 2008; Dumas, 2009). Technical writing is not a dominant activity because the local techno-industry produces its documents in English (Larivière, 1995; Russell, Bossé-Andrieu, & Cajolet-Laganière, 1995).

The challenge of writing utilitarian texts that are clear and understood is rendered even more difficult because the proportion of people in Quebec who are either poor readers or illiterate stands at 48%, as demonstrated by the International Adult Literacy Survey conducted by Statistics Canada in 2003, with the help of the Organisation for Economic Co-operation and Development (Bernèche & Perron, 2005). Thus the problem of literacy (Brandt, 2009; Goody, 1986; Kara & Privat, 2006; Lahire, 1999; Olson, 1994) has become the reference framework for many questions. In the professional context, the question is how do we write to be read and understood by a population of which nearly 50% are weak readers (Clerc & Beaudet, 2008)? What knowledge and what know-how must professional writers master to accomplish their mandates and to reach the objective of effectively communicating with the largest possible number of people? Communication between the government and the public has served as the experimental field for the development of a writing approach established by the Groupe Rédiger CIRAL, Université Laval, an applied research group headed by Isabelle Clerc (2006; Clerc & Kavanagh, 2006; Collette, 2008).

Previous developments in the field of textual psycholinguistics have contributed to this approach to writing, providing concepts for treating the interrelations between the contextual conditions of the production of writing, the writing processes, and the actors of the communication exchange (Coirier, Gaonac'h, & Passerault, 1996; Fayol, 2002; Kintsch, 1998; Piolat & Pélissier, 1998; Rijlaarsdam, Alamargot, & Chanquoy, 2001). In fact, a psychocognitive model of the message receiver underlies all the choices the writer makes to produce an effective text. This model will lead the writer to privilege readability, cohesion, coherence, and relevancy (Sperber & Wilson, 1995) and the ease of representation of retained information. In other words, the reader-based model makes it possible not only to orient the management of the logicolinguistic, rhetorical, and communicative constraints, but also to interrelate them.

Metacontrol

Through a reader-based approach to writing, the characteristics of institutionally constructed professional writing genres gained the attention of researchers who sought to establish a relationship between these text types and the writing processes (Alamargot, Terrier, & Cellier, 2007; Beaudet, 2005; Bisaillon, 2007a, 2007b; Clerc & Kavanagh, 2006; Collette, 2002). These publications aimed to develop an understanding of the components of a metacontrol acting on the writing processes, no matter which type of writing was undertaken. In the traditional approach to professional writing, the genre of writing, with its formal characteristics presented as fixed and decontextualized, was given as the starting point to understanding an act of professional communication (Labasse, 2006). In adopting a reader-oriented approach, a reversal in perspective became necessary in order to give the writer the place that corresponds to what is expected of a professional writer; the professional text is linked to an end purpose, and that implies numerous choices. In these publications, special attention was paid to the writing subprocesses: the mechanisms of referential continuity, thematic continuity (logical and argumentative, Amossy, 2000; Angenot, 2008), and enunciative continuity (Culioli, 1990; Kerbrat-Orecchioni, 1980). Those established mechanisms play an important role in the intelligibility (coherence and representability) and the readability (scriptovisual and lexicosyntactic) of the texts.

First studied from the angle of their textual components (Beaudet, 2001; Charolles, 1994; Gagnon, 2008; Gélinas-Chebat & C. Préfontaine, 1996; Lundquist, 1994; Pépin, 1998), the concepts of intelligibility and readability were then defined from the point of view of their effect on the reader, according to the cognitive processes implied rather than the linguistic and discursive components that actualize them. The intelligibility of the text rests on high-level cognitive processes, that is, the search for coherence and the ability to establish a representation, whereas legibility is based on low-level cognitive processes, that is, the ability to decipher and read words and to recognize the meaning of words and sentence structures (cohesion; Figure 5.1).

These definitions, based on the acquired knowledge derived from cognitive psychology, made it possible, on the one hand, to bridge the differences between

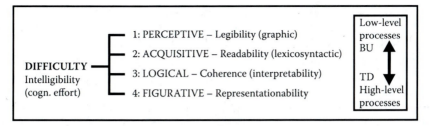

Figure 5.1   Intelligibility and cognitive processes. (From Labasse, B., in *Research Communication in the Social and Human Sciences: From Dissemination to Public Engagement*, 60–84, Cambridge University Press, Cambridge, UK, 2008.)

various approaches to text and discourse: text grammar, discourse analysis, rhetoric, information design, and writing theories. On the other hand, these definitions, based on the psycholinguistics of written text, have scientifically shed light on and legitimized the teaching of writing strategies aiming to deal with two major obstacles: the linearity of language and the limit of the reader's ability to process information. These two constraints affect the whole of the writing processes. *Écrire pour son lecteur* (Writing for one's reader) has become more than a mantra, inspired by the discourse of marketing communication, for teaching professional writing. Rather, this statement finds its basis in the constraints of language communication and the characteristics of comprehension.

Linearity of Language

The representational or mental model that the writer has of the communication situation is multidimensional. Time, space, readers, events, point of view, and the rhetorical and pragmatic aims of the writer are just some of the data processed interactively in the planning phase. These data do not pop up one after another; rather, they overlap and are interconnected in a systemic vision, producing an overall mapping of the text to be written on the level of meaning and form. This representation under construction is based on referential and linguistic knowledge and rhetorical and pragmatic schematics known to the writer. This multidimensional representation must, however, take place within a linear text, the writer having no other choice but to set out his or her ideas one after another, in a sequential chain of words.

Language linearity forces the writer to sequence the information at one level even though ideas may also be organized in a hierarchical fashion in text. The writer benefits from writing conventions relating to textual infrastructure (e.g., genres and text types) and to mechanisms for connecting ideas (e.g., textual organizers, linear integration markers, and configurational markers). Texts also have their social context (e.g., an annual report or a museum's catalog) and shared values (e.g., Catholic discourse). The more experience the writer has, the better he or she integrates these structural or semantic phenomena that characterize professional communication (Charaudeau, 1997).

Organizing by themes is done through operations that also imply certain procedural regularities: choice of information, designation, and characterization of the objects chosen. Expansions come about by repetition, description, explanation, and examples. Ideas are suggested by words, and words often come in clusters, by preferential association (the collocation phenomenon). These routine aspects of theme setting play on the predictive value of the words and, consequently, on their general clarity, because the reader recognizes the processes and shares them a priori and, therefore, pays more attention to the ideas than to the textual forms. The predictive value of theme-setting procedures is increased by the use of textual organizers, relationship markers, and metadiscursive statements, such as summarization, recontextualization, and predictive statements. All these conventionalized features of writing are attributed to the difficulty of understanding a text written in linear language and to the limits of the reader's cognitive ability.

Pedagogical Considerations

The activity of writing is monomanaged, that is, it goes on in the absence of the receiver, but must consider how to promote the reader's understanding and stimulate his or her interest. The production of meaning is admittedly dependent on the language and discourse operations that produce readability and intelligibility (Gélinas-Chabat & Préfontaine, 1996) but is effective only when they are based on a psychocognitive, contextualized model of the reader. The context of an act of professional communication includes a client, a writer, a text, and a reader whose reading process is influenced by the readability and intelligibility of the text, but also by its relevance (Figure 5.2).

In this model, each aspect of the text contains a number of variables that the writer manipulates. The professional writer's role is that of a mediator who, in a given communication situation, is trying to find common ground between the universe and constraints of the client and those of the reader. To manage the multiple levels of constraints (linguistic, discursive, rhetorical, pragmatic) that the writer must manipulate (and which the above model eloquently illustrates), we propose a list of questions that structure the professional writing process (Figure 5.3). This list integrates questions whose epistemic logic draws on cognitive psychology research (Becker, 2006), to text grammar, to rhetoric, and to the sociology of written communication (Breton, 1996).[2]

Conclusions on the Research Into Writing Studies in Quebec

This section has described the main orientation of research into professional writing in Quebec over the past 20 years. Shaped by French and Anglo-Saxon scientific traditions, this research on professional writing has drawn on two scientific traditions on text—the French tradition of studying developing writers and adults, and the Anglo-Saxon tradition in Canada and the United States of studying adult, professional writing. By organizing the SIG Writing Web site with Pietro Boscolo, in 1988,[3] as well as through his own numerous scientific writings, Michel Fayol has contributed in a very significant way to bringing together the scientific cultures

---

[2] I have used this list in a master's level course on professional writing during the winter of 2010.
[3] http://www.sig-writing.org.

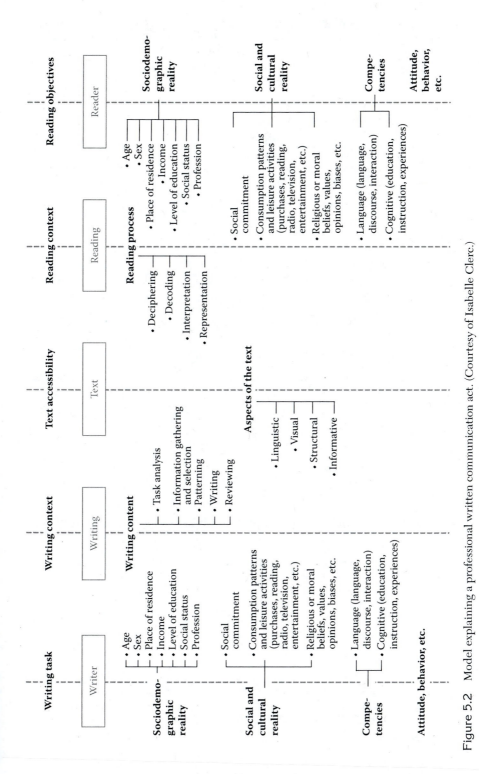

Figure 5.2   Model explaining a professional written communication act. (Courtesy of Isabelle Clerc.)

Planning		
Task analysis	In which work environment is this task situated?	
	Who is the client?	
	What is the sociodiscursive identity of the client?	
	Am I motivated by this task? Have I ever written something like this before?	
	What do I know about this topic? Do I have the resources to find the information that I need?	
	What do I think of the topic?	
	What do I think of the task given me?	
	How am I going to look for information on this topic? Where?	
	How should I organize my thoughts at this stage: taking notes, rough draft, key words?	
Rhetorical objectives	From the point of view of the client, what is the main objective of this communicative act? What are the secondary or hidden objectives?	
	What values are associated with this act?	
	Why is it important that this communicative act be accomplished at this time?	
	From the point of view of the client, why is this communicative act important?	
Pragmatic objectives	What results are expected from this act?	
	To whom is this communicative act addressed? Who will read or will use the document that I am going to produce?	
	How can this document be relevant for the receiver?	
	How can I state my task in five lines? (depiction of my task)	
Statement plan	Which type of writing best suits this situation?	
	Do I have examples of this type of writing?	
	Should I consider adding visual elements to the text?	
	What are the themes that I will address and those that I will exclude? What are the ideas to be developed?	
	Must I find information in order to write descriptions and/or explanations or to support judgments?	
Writing plan	How can I state my topic in 15 lines: introduce it, establish it, and divide it?	
	What writing superstructure best suits this situation? Plans by addition, by comparison, by opposition, by chronological order, by inverted pyramid; an analytical plan; an argumentative plan?	

Writing		
Focus	By which part of the document shall I begin?	
	Do I fully understand my topic and all of its complexities?	
	How is the topic relevant to the reader's concerns? Which aspects of my topic shall I expand upon with the reader's interests and concerns in mind?	
	Which processes should I use to take into account the appropriate density required in the development of my ideas? Description, explanation, definitions, examples, comparisons, analogies, quotes?	
	What degree of familiarity and abstraction seems appropriate? Which "voice" shall I use in the text?	
	Which style shall I give special weight to? In view of which receiver? Are the vocabulary and the syntax problematic for me?	
	How long will this document be?	
	What prompts me to separate the text into paragraphs, into parts?	

Figure 5.3   Checklist for professional writer.

	Are the ideas I am developing contained in the writing plan or will they appear during the writing? Are my ideas suggested by the words that I am using, by my prior knowledge of the subject matter, by my previous experience writing on this topic, by the text that I am actually writing?
	Am I integrating cohesion and coherence indicators as I write, or will I perform these operations during revision?
	If I feel at a standstill while developing the text, do I know why? How can I overcome this difficulty?

Revision	
Lexicosyntactic readability	What effort is required of the reader in order to <u>decode the meaning of the words</u>, the sentence structures, and the text's outline? This involves questions of vocabulary, syntax, cohesion indicators, and metatextual organizers (numbering, typography, punctuation, paragraphs, clauses, page layout processes).
	Is the vocabulary all of the same level?
	Are rules of grammar and syntax followed?
Intelligibility	Is the referential context explained in terms of the reader?
	Is the discourse easily accessible?
	Are the cultural references understandable?
	Are there coherence indicators informing the reader on: - The referential continuity (what is talked about)? - The thematic progression (how is the subject developed)? - And the enunciative continuity (who is speaking; identity, voices, and agency)?
	Is there enough information recall?
	Is the use of restatements and pronouns controlled? (e.g., correct gender for French nouns and pronouns)
	Has the degree of abstraction been evaluated?
	Are there sufficient examples, descriptions, explanations, definitions, comparisons?
	Has the density of the topic been evaluated?
	Have expressiveness and degree of proximity been evaluated in terms of the communicative situation and the genre's constraints?
Quality and relevance	Is the retained information linked to the topic?
	Is the information accurate: numerical data, proper nouns, reported facts, etc.?
	Is there sufficient information, and is that information taken from a variety of verified sources?
	Are the quotes (if any) accurate?
	Is the text interesting?
	Does the text respect the constraints of the communicative situation?

Figure 5.3   *(Continued)*

arising from the two linguistic communities that are referred to in Canada as "the two solitudes" (MacLennan, 1945).

The teaching of reader-oriented writing has been readily adopted as a model, thanks to the contributions from the field of cognitive psychology. It is obvious that rhetoric, discourse analysis, literary semiotics, textual genetics, and text grammar all contribute to our ability to explain subject-oriented writing and text-oriented writing. All of these approaches complement one another, and together allow us to conceptualize the writing activity and writing processes. However, cognitive psychology provides the two most solid explanations of the complexity of the written communication act. First, the linearity of language constitutes an important obstacle to understanding, because thought is multidimensional and not linear. Second, the writer's or the reader's ability to process and store information is limited in working memory, thus requiring the writer to develop thinking routines that rely on representations of the situation and of the task to be accomplished based on his or her own experience. These representations stored in memory have a tendency to move from one task to another (Dortier, 1998).

The construction of meaning, as in written composition for the reading audience, is a complex multidimensional activity; for example, consider Antoine Culioli's (1990) paradox that understanding is only a particular case of misunderstanding. This paradox is consistent with the relevancy theory of Sperber and Wilson (1995), according to which we understand what we hear or what we read on the basis of our cognitive schema and choose the relevant elements on the basis of our needs, interests, preferences, and obligations. Nothing can be taken for granted when meaning is at stake, nothing *tombe sous le sens* (Beaudet, 2003). Being able to reach a reader, to write to be understood, and to communicate meaning rather than words all require a long learning period. The misunderstanding suggested by Culioli is not a fatality; it is an entropic force with which the professional writer must learn to deal. Thus in the last section of this chapter Bertrand Labasse focuses on integrating metaknowledge of the written text and of writing the process into the pedagogy of writing, when applied to advanced studies in journalism and science writing for a general audience of nonscientists.

ADVANCED PROGRAMS FOR PROFESSIONAL WRITING FOR THE GENERAL PUBLIC

Research on the production of texts aims both at a theoretical level, to better understand the cognitive processes that come into play, and at an applied level, to promote new pedagogical approaches to writing (Nystrand, 2006). However, the mission of teaching workplace writing to adults differs from that of teaching writing in standard school learning situations (Boice, 1985; Davies & Birbili, 2000). This difference is accentuated when the program focuses on professional communication with the general public through journalism or popular science writing. From the experience gained from giving professional development sessions and specialized training to students in journalism and scientific communication and reviewing the research, we can examine how knowledge mainly situated in a curricular perspective (writing for one's instructor) can be inserted into the field of written communication (writing for one's readers).

The Specificities of Professional Writing

How does the development of professional communication skills (written communication) differ from learning to write from a normative point of view (written expression)? This difference can be analyzed as a reversal of priority in that the aim is not to write correctly or elegantly, but to write for one's reader in a given context.[4] This change of focus is consistent with the processes of adult skilled writing described by Hayes (1996) but also introduces some new didactic perspectives.

First, this reversal corresponds to a fundamental change in how texts are assessed. The quality of expression of a learner's text derived from linguistic indices (spelling correctness, richness of vocabulary, respect for imposed forms, etc.), the quality of a communicative text, is essentially determined by the relationship it establishes between a state of the world (the subject), an objective, and a reader. A press report, a popularized science text, or a promotional text can take a variety of different forms, and its value is not a function of its adherence or nonadherence to an expected canonical form. Thus the transposition to these domains, based only on the evaluation of language-based criteria, is insufficient. However, from an experimental point of view, studying the production of these types of texts implies having recourse to subjective judgments (expert juries) that are by nature difficult to reproduce (Hayes, Hatch, & Silk, 2000).

Second, the models developed on cognitive processes since the 1980s highlight the importance of integrating into working memory (WM) information from long-term memory (LTM)—information on the theme, the receiver, objectives, and constraints (the "issues" in Hayes and Flower's [1980] original message). That said, in professional writing situations, this information either is not available or is difficult to use (Fayol, 1997a) or even invalid (Labasse, 2001). Moreover, there is rarely one single reader: Even when the rhetorical objective is coherent, which is often not the case, texts must frequently meet highly conflicting expectations, for example, those of scientists and those of the general public in the case of a popularized text.[5] Knowledge about the theme also represents a major difficulty. The most serious problems with texts, from the perspective of the professional writer, come from either insufficient knowledge or a miscomprehension of the information being handled. For example, the professional writer may have to address ambiguous and contradictory expectations using information that is confused and incomplete.

These comments are not necessarily new (Flower, Schriver, Casey, Hass, & Hayes, 1992). Certain points have been objects of research, namely the difficulties in mobilizing knowledge on the theme at hand (Kellogg, 1987; McCutchen, 1986; Voss, Vesonder, & Spilich, 1980) and the effect of the perception of the readership (Ransdell and Levy, 1994; Swaney, Janik, Bond, & Hayes, 1981; Traxler & Gernsbacher, 1992, 1993), particularly variations in strategies for different audiences (Kirsch, 1991; Monahan, 1984). However, these projects have most often been undertaken from a developmental perspective (Alamargot & Chanquoy, 2001), whose ultimate stage would be that of a good undergraduate student. On the other hand, studying professional practices (and in particular the interactions among a lack of understanding of the theme, ill-perceived receivers, and conflicting

---

[4] For a diachronic analysis (the skills and precepts taken from ancient rhetoric) or a synchronic one, namely through the analysis of 50 contemporary textbooks for professional writing (Labasse, 2006).

[5] As Hayes (1996) pointed out, in general writers have more than one objective when they write.

objectives) remains a theoretical and experimental challenge because of the difficulty of controlling the variables.

The fundamental difficulty of studying professional writing in a realistic way has not prevented study of professional writing, which has mostly tackled rather simple texts (Taylor, 1984) or very formalized genres such as the writing of technical manuals (Ganier, 2006; Swaney et al., 1981). However, few works engaged in more complex areas of writing for adults (Alamargot & Lebrave, 2010), and even less in journalistic writing (Schumacher, Scott, Klare, Cronin, & Lambert, 1989).

Between Didactics and Instrumentalization

The syntheses that explore the pedagogical application of research on the cognitive processes of writing often contrast "product-oriented" pedagogy and "process-oriented" pedagogy (Galbraith & Rijlaarsdam, 1999; Hayes & Flower, 1986). The former (traditional) is based on the results expected in terms of criteria such as genre and style, as well as on models of "good" texts worthy of imitation. The latter is based on the cognitive skills of the writers. However, advanced courses on scientific communication and writing for the press suggest that this binary opposition does not satisfactorily do justice to the problems to be resolved.

Fundamentally, the two examples of professional training mentioned here have been guided by a single instruction that is easy to state (and to repeat, and repeat again): be *interesting and clear*. This objective, which is primarily psychological, is nevertheless subject to social constraints: accuracy of content, acceptability, and language correctness. In reality, writers had to be taught to be as interesting and as clear as possible, while knowing how to put social standards into perspective. In a contemporary society in which competition for the readers' attention is increasingly more tight (Simon, 1971), both when writing in the media (Meyer, 1996) and in scientific research articles (Frank, 1999), the *quality of writing* coalesces with its *effectiveness*. The criterion of interest (Hidi & Baird, 1986) remains spectacularly absent from much contemporary research on the written text. The Six-Subgroup Quality Scale (SSQS) for the quality of writing (Ransdell & Levy, 1996), often used in these research projects, is most striking: It describes in detailed fashion what a good dissertation is from the point of view of an academic grader, but it certainly does not describe what constitutes a text that is sociocognitively relevant in the world of professional communication.

The complexity of these writing situations obviously overcomes the opposition between "product-oriented" pedagogy and "process-oriented" pedagogy. On the one hand, adult practices and the current teaching of these practices are still largely *topic oriented*. The practitioners who teach specialized writing see it, before all else, as a sort of "packaging," a means of conveying information (journalism), erudite content, or a body of research data (science): *Scientific writing is a technique derived from science and not from literature or poetry* (Huguier et al., 1992, p. 10).

On the other hand, and mainly, as we have stated previously and shown elsewhere (Labasse, 2006), the fundamental characteristic of written communication is to be reader oriented in theory as well as in practice. If the effectiveness of a text is a result of its clarity and its interest, subsumed by its acceptability of content and form,[6] those subjective criteria depend only on the targeted audience. Even the most formal aspects of acceptability, such as spelling and syntax, vary according to the interlocutors, as is shown in the case of grammatical correctness in Internet discussion forums.

That is why the courses in question have been based first and foremost—from the skills taught to the correction criteria—on contemporary knowledge of the readers' social expectations and cognitive processes.[7] However, it is interesting to see that this approach, which on a theoretical level fits easily into Hayes and Flower's framework,[8] has, in practice, increased the need to have recourse simultaneously to reader-centered teaching: Far from being in opposition to one another, the product-oriented, topic-oriented, and especially the process-oriented and reader-oriented axes have proved to be inseparable.

In fact, a better understanding of the audience by no means simplifies the writer's task. In terms of a "didactic" analogy, we can tell a professional athlete from an amateur by the level of expertise and by the results attained, but certainly not by the fact that the activity is easier or less tiring. The directives and the constraints on the supplementary criteria of document effectiveness greatly increase the complexity of the task (Scardamalia & Bereiter, 1998) and contribute to the saturation of the writers' memorization and processing abilities (Randsell & Levy, 1996), increasing the importance of helping them to better manage their processes.

Although in the case of children, many courses use a procedural approach (creating exercises that bring the children to reinforce, without their being aware of it, one or another of their cognitive abilities), it has seemed more relevant here to use an epistemic approach: teaching writers to recognize, evaluate, and manage their own writing processes. Thus, this approach is different from that proposed by Kellogg and colleagues (Kellogg & Raulerson, 2007; Kellogg & Witheford, 2009) in that it rests at least as much on declarative knowledge as on constant and deliberate training. Paradoxically, this view converges with the approach that Graham and Harris (1989, 1993) advocate for upper elementary children with disabilities. But in the case of professional writers, it even rests on the acquisition and use by students of research-based declarative knowledge. The objective is thus to reinforce their metacognitive competencies, and more generally, their expertise, in the hope that these will help them, even long after the course, to advance steadily and thoughtfully, to adapt to new writing situations, and to see themselves as writing specialists who can, as such, draw upon specific knowledge (Beaudet, 1999).

Incidentally, drawing upon research results whenever possible is of great didactic interest: Students are sometimes more receptive to projected graphics and figures

---

[6] We are not speaking here of argumentation texts, for which a supplementary criterion, also subjective, should be added.

[7] These contents are based on the different components of the cognitive effort the text requires and the cognitive effect that it produces, as well as on the social factors that impact its reception (Labasse, 2008).

[8] Both the *task environment* and, mainly, the *audience knowledge* in long-term memory exert influences.

(Daneman & Stainton, 1993) than to verbal strategies (e.g., "Be very rigorous when revising your texts" and "Let your text sit for a while before rereading it").

Four Reference Points (Axes) for Practitioners

A first axis involves attitudes toward the written text and individual representations of writing. It draws in particular upon the many studies that establish how important writing is to achieving professional success and how dissatisfied supervisors are with their employees' performance in that area, as well as upon studies that have established a link between writers' beliefs about their own writing effectiveness, their motivation, and their real performance (Boscolo & Hidi, 2007; Meier, McCarthy, & Schmeck, 1984; Pajares, 2003). Research that stresses the high level of cognitive effort associated with writing tasks (Fayol, 1997a; Kellogg, 1994) show students that it is perfectly normal to struggle with writing—even for experienced professionals—when the task is a complex one.

A second axis centers on having writers pay attention to their metacognitive processes. These depend closely on three activities characteristic of expert professional writing: extensive preliminary planning, an ongoing recursive cycle of planning-transcription-revision throughout the writing task, and a much greater field of reevaluation, both in scope and depth, during revision (Hayes, 1996; Hayes & Flower, 1980).

The third axis, which derives from the preceding ones, focuses on the strategies themselves. To Bereiter and Scardamalia's (1987) distinction between knowledge telling and knowledge transforming, we add knowledge crafting, as suggested by Kellogg (2008). In fact, texts such as feature articles (magazines) and popularized scientific articles draw on the deep transformation of knowledge and the crafting knowledge of the professional writer.

The fourth axis, also a strategic one, involves the writer's working memory load (Bourdin & Fayol 2002; Chanquoy & Alamargot, 2002). Therefore, it is essential to encourage writers to adopt a heuristic perception of their level of cognitive load and also to propose strategies to help them manage that load so that they can allocate their resources optimally in light of the writing operation they are performing. These strategies mostly involve undertaking beforehand all the operations that can be performed before rather than during the act of writing. Such operations include, in particular, auditing the objectives (evaluating possible contradictions of the task), auditing the knowledge (ensuring that one has all the information one will need, and that one understands it clearly), and organizing these elements (linearization of thinking). This is typically a strategy of anticipated problem solving, but other methods can also serve to relieve working memory. For example, learning how, when facing a mental block, to simulate an oral dialogue ("How would you express this idea if you were simply speaking to a friend?") makes it possible to momentarily inhibit certain pragmatic and stylistic constraints and enable semantic operations that are more important at that time.

These intervention axes complement other types of teaching, theoretical (especially on sociocognitive expectations) as well as practical (e.g., case studies, exercises). However, they illustrate the possibility of using research on writing processes, not only as a source of pedagogical inspiration for teachers, which, today, is fairly mundane, but also as teaching material for students taking writing courses, which, to our knowledge, remain rather rare. Understanding the cognitive processes and deliberations of "real" experts, that is, experienced professionals facing complex writing tasks, remains a theoretical and applied frontier. This understanding will probably only be achieved by actually taking into consideration the weight of formal, pragmatic, and referential constraints, and, in particular, the role of the "reader model" in light of which the writer shapes the text; that is, the expectations of acceptability (i.e., correctness, accuracy), of clarity, but also of interest.

REFERENCES

Alamargot, D., & Chanquoy, L. (2001). *Through the models of writing in cognitive psychology*. Dordrecht: Kluwer.

Alamargot, D., & Fayol, M. (2009). Modelling the development of written composition. In R. Beard, D. Myhill, M. Nystrand, & J. Riley (Eds.), *The SAGE handbook of writing development* (pp. 23–47). Thousand Oaks, CA: Sage.

Alamargot, D., & Lebrave, J. L. (2010). The study of professional writing: A joint contribution from cognitive psychology and genetic criticism. *European Psychologist, 15*(1), 12–22.

Alamargot, D., Terrier P., & Cellier, J.-M. (Eds.). (2007). *Written documents in the workplace*. Amsterdam: Elsevier.

Amossy, R. (2000). *L'argumentation dans le discours*. Paris: Nathan Université.

Angenot, M. (2008). *Dialogue de sourds. Traité de rhétorique antilogique*. Paris: Éditions des mille et une nuits.

Artemeva, N. (2006). Approaches to learning genres: A bibliographical essay. In N. Artemeva & A. Freedman (Eds.), *Rhetorical genre studies and beyond* (pp. 9–99). Winnipeg: Inkshed.

Bazerman, C., & Paradis, J. (Eds.). (1991). *Textual dynamics of the professions*. Madison: University of Wisconsin Press.

Beaudet, C. (1998). Littératie et rédaction: vers la définition d'une pratique professionnelle. In G. Legault (Dir.), *L'intervention, usages et méthodes* (pp. 69–88). Sherbrooke: Éditions GGC, Université de Sherbrooke.

Beaudet, C. (1999). Les compétences linguistiques et discursives du rédacteur professionnel: un ensemble à circonscrire. In C. Guével & I. Clerc (Eds.), *Les professions langagières à l'aube de l'an 2000* (pp. 3–18). Ste Foy: Ciral-Université Laval.

Beaudet, C. (2001). Clarté, lisibilité, intelligibilité des textes: un état de la question et une proposition pédagogique, *Recherches en rédaction professionnelle* (Vol. 1, No. 1, pp. 1–18). Sherbrooke: Université de Sherbrooke.

Beaudet, C. (2003). Le rédacteur et la fabrication du sens d'un texte persuasif. *Communication information, médias, théories, pratiques, 22*(2), 44–62.

Beaudet, C. (2005). *Stratégies d'argumentation et impact social: le cas des textes utilitaires*. Québec: Nota bene.

Beaudet, C. (2010, April). Pour un enseignement de l'écrit par discipline à l'université. L'autre Forum, La relation professeurs-étudiants aujourd'hui. Virage ou dérives? *Le journal des professeures et professeurs de l'Université de Montréal, 14*(2), 27–29.

Beaudet, C., & Clerc, I. (2008). Enseigner la rédaction au Québec: quels fondements disciplinaires? Quelle reconnaissance institutionnelle? Actes de colloque *De la France* au Québec: l'écriture dans tous ses états, Université de Poitiers, 12–15 Novembre 2008, Actes de colloque électroniques.

Beaudet, C., & Smart, G. (Eds.). (2002). Les compétences du rédacteur professionnel/The expertise of professional writers [Special Edition]. *Technostyle, 18*(1).

Becker, A. (2006). A review of writing models research based on cognitive process. In A. Horning, A. Becker, & A. S. Horning, *Revision: History, theory, and practice* (pp. 25–49). West Lafayette, IN: Parlor Press.

Bereiter, C., & Scardamalia, M. (1987). *The psychology of written composition.* Hillsdale, NJ: Erlbaum.

Bergmann, L. S., & Zepernick, J. (2007). *Disciplinarity and transfer: Students' perceptions of learning to write.* WPA: Writing Program Administration, 31. Retrieved from http://www.wpacouncil.org/journal/index.html

Berlin, J. (1987). *Rhetoric and reality: Writing instruction in American colleges, 1900–1985.* Carbondale, IL: Southern Illinois University Press.

Bernèche, F., & Perron, B. (2005). *La littératie au Québec en 2003: faits saillants.* Enquête internationale sur l'Alphabétisation et les compétences des adultes (EIACA), Institut de la statistique du Québec.

Bisaillon, J. (2007a). Professional editing strategies used by six editors. *Written Communication, 24*(4), 295–322.

Bisaillon, J. (2007b). *La révision professionnelle: Processus, stratégies et pratiques.* Quebec: Éditions Nota Bene, Collection Rédiger.

Boice, R. (1985). The neglected third factor in writing: Productivity. *College Composition and Communication, 36*(4), 472–480.

Boscolo, P., & Hidi, S. (2007).The multiple meanings of motivation to write. In S. Hidi & P. Boscolo (Eds.),*Writing and motivation* (pp. 1–14). Oxford: Elsevier.

Bossé-Andrieu, J., Cajolet-Laganière, H., & Grant-Russell, P. (1994). La rédaction professionnelle en français au Canada, résultats d'une enquête. *Journal of Technical Writing and Communication, 24*(3), 251–263.

Bourdin, B., & Fayol, M. (2002). Even in adults, written production is still more costly than oral production. *International Journal of Psychology, 37*(4), 219–227.

Brandt, D. (2009). *Literacy and learning. Reflections on writing, reading, and society,* San Francisco: Jossey-Bass.

Breton, P. (1996). *L'argumentation dans la communication.* Paris, Éditions La Découverte.

Bronckart, J. P. (1996). *Activité langagière, textes et discours.* Lausanne: Delachaux et niestlé.

Butturff, D. R., & Sommers, N. (1980). Placing revision in a reinvented rhetorical tradition. In A. Freedman & I. Pringle (Eds.), *Reinventing the rhetorical tradition* (pp. 99–104). Conway, AR: L & S Books.

Chanquoy, L., & Alamargot, D. (2002). Working memory and writing: Model evolution and research assessment. *L'Annee Psychologique, 102,* 363–398.

Charaudeau, P. (1997). Visées discursives, genres situationnels et construction textuelle. *Revue Réseaux, 81,* http://www.patrick-charaudeau.com/Visees-discursives-genres,83.html

Charaudeau, P., & Maingueneau, D. (2002). *Dictionnaire d'analyse du discours.* Paris: Seuil.

Charolles, M. (1994). Cohésion, cohérence et pertinence du discours. *Revue internationale de linguistique française, 29,* 125–151.

Chartrand, S.-G., & Blaser, C. (2008). *Le rapport à l'écrit: un outil pour enseigner de l'école à l'Université.* Namur: Presses universitaires de Namur.

Clerc, I. (1998). L'enseignement de la rédaction professionnelle en milieu universitaire. In C. Préfontaine, L. Godard, & G. Fortier (Eds.), *Pour mieux comprendre la lecture et l'écriture* (pp. 345–370). Montréal: Éditions Logiques.

Clerc, I. (2000). *La démarche de redaction.* Québec: Éditions Nota Bene.

Clerc, I. (2005, Autumn). *Proposition d'un modèle explicatif d'un acte de communication écrite professionnelle.* Conférence donnée dans le cadre du séminaire *Langue, médiation culturelle et efficacité communicationnelle,* de la CEFAN (Chaire pour le développement de la recherche sur la culture d'expression française en Amérique du Nord), Université Laval, Québec.

Clerc, I. (2006). La simplification des écrits gouvernementaux au Québec: bilan des travaux du Groupe Rédiger et réflexion sur le rôle du chercheur dans le cadre d'un contrat de recherche. *Technostyle, 22*(1), 86–98.

Clerc, I., & Beaudet, C. (Eds.). (2008). *Langue, médiation et efficacité communicationnelle.* Québec: Presses de l'Université Laval.

Clerc, I., & Kavanagh, E. (2006). *De la lettre à la page Web. Savoir communiquer avec le grand public.* Québec: Les Publications du Québec.

Coirier, P., Gaonac'h, D., & Passerault, J.-M. (1996). *Psycholinguistique textuelle.* Colin: Armand.

Cole, M. (1991). Conclusion. In L. B. Resnick, J. M. Levine, & D. T. Teasley (Eds.), *Perspectives on socially shared cognition* (pp. 398–417). Washington, DC: American Psychological Association.

Collette, K. (2008). Qualité de la relation entre administration et usagers: la par informationnelle de l'asymétrie. *Technostyle, 22*(1), 19–38.

Collette, K., Benoît Barnet, M., Laporte, D., Pouëch, F., & Rui-Souchon, B. (2002). *Guide pratique de la rédaction administrative.* Ministère de la fonction publique et de la réforme de l'État (http://www.modernisation.gouv.fr/).

Crowley, S. (1985). The evolution of invention in current-traditional rhetoric: 1850–1970. *Rhetoric Review, 3,* 146–162.

Culioli, A. (1990). *Pour une linguistique de l'énonciation.* Paris: Ophrys.

Daneman, M., & Stainton, M. (1993). The generation effect in reading and proofreading: Is it easier or harder to detect errors in one's own writing? *Reading and Writing: An Interdisciplinary Journal, 5,* 297–313.

Davies, C., & Birbili, M. (2000). What do people need to know about writing in order to write in their jobs? *British Journal of Educational Studies, 48*(4), 429–445.

Devitt, A. J. (1991). Intertexuality in tax accounting: Generic, referential, and functional. In C. Bazerman & J. Paradis (Eds.), *Textual dynamics of the professions* (pp. 336–357). Madison: University of Wisconsin Press.

Dias, P., Freedman, A., Medway, P., & Paré, A. (Eds.). (1999). *Worlds apart. Acting and writing in academic and workplace contexts.* Mahwah, NJ: Erlbaum.

Dias, P., & Paré, A. (Eds.) (2000). *Transitions: Writing in academic and workplace settings.* Cresskill, NJ: Hampton.

Dortier, J.-F. (1998). *Le cerveau et la pensée. La révolution des sciences cognitives.* Éditions Sciences humaines.

Ducrot, O., & Shaeffer, J.-C. (1995). *Nouveau dictionnaire encyclopédique des sciences du langage.* Paris: Seuil.

Dumas, J. (2009). *La profession de rédacteur.* Montréal: Fides.

Emig, J. (1971). *The composing processes of twelfth graders.* Urbana, IL: National Council of Teachers of English.

Emig, J. (1977). Hand, eye, brain: Some "basics" in the writing process. In C. Cooper & L. Odell (Eds.), *Research on composing* (pp. 109–121). Urbana, IL: National Council of Teachers of English.

Emig, J. A. (1964). The uses of the unconscious in composing. *College Composition and Communication, 15,* 6–11.

Fayol, M. (1992). L'écrit: perspectives cognitives. In A. Bentolila (Ed.), *Les entretiens Nathan, Lecture et écriture* (pp. 101–125). Paris: Nathan.

Fayol, M. (1997a). *Des idées au texte; Psychologie cognitive de la production verbale, orale et écrite.* Paris: Presses Universitaires de France.

Fayol, M. (1997b). Écrire, orthographier et rédiger des textes. *Psychologie française, 50*(3), 391–402.

Fayol, M. (2002). *La production du langage.* Paris: Hermès.

Flower, L. S., & Hayes, R. (1977). Problem solving strategies and the writing process. *College English, 39*, 449–461.

Flower, L., & Hayes, R. (1981). A cognitive process theory of writing. *College Composition and Communication, 32*, 365–387.

Flower, L. S., Schriver, K., Carey, L., Haas, C., & Hayes, J. R. (1992). Planning in writing: The cognition of a constructive process. In S. P. Witte, N. Nakadate, & R. D. Cherry (Eds.), *A rhetoric of doing: Essays on written discourse in honor of James L. Kinneavy* (pp. 181–243). Carbondale, IL: Southern Illinois University Press.

Fogarty, D. (1959). *Roots for a new rhetoric*. New York: Teacher's College, Columbia University.

Franck, G. (1999). Scientific communication: A vanity fair? *Science, 286*, 53–55.

Freedman, A., & Pringle, I. (Eds.). (1980). *Reinventing the rhetorical tradition*. Conway, AR: L & S Books.

Gagnon, O. (2008). La cohérence du texte: mieux la définir pour mieux la maîtriser, l'enseigner, l'évaluer, Actes de colloque *De la France* au Québec: l'écriture dans tous ses états, Université de Poitiers, 12–15 Novembre 2008.

Galbraith, D., & Rijlaarsdam, G. (1999). Effective strategies for the teaching and learning of writing. *Learning and Instruction, 9*, 93–108.

Ganier, F. (2006). La révision de textes procéduraux. *Langages, 164*, 71–85.

Gélinas-Chebat, C., & Préfontaine, C. (1996). *Lisibilité et intelligibilité, Revue québécoise de linguistique*. Montreal: Université du Québec à Montréal.

Gibbs, R.-M. (1998). *Le marché de l'emploi en rédaction professionnelle*. Report presented to the Comité de programme en rédaction technique, Québec, Université Laval.

Giltrow, J. (2002). *Academic writing: Writing and reading in the disciplines*. Peterborough, ON: Broadview.

Giltrow, J., & Valiquette, M. (1994). Genres and knowledge: Students writing in the disciplines. In A. Freedman & P. Medway (Eds.), *Learning and teaching genre* (pp. 47–62). Portsmouth, NH: Boynton/Cook Heinemann.

Goody, J. (1986). *The logic of writing and the organization of society*. Cambridge: Cambridge University Press.

Graham, S., & Harris K. R. (1989). A components analysis of cognitive strategy instruction: Effects on learning disabled students' compositions and self-efficacy. *Journal of Educational Psychology, 81*, 353–361.

Graham, S., & Harris, K. R. (1993). Self-regulated strategy development: Helping students with learning problems develop as writers. *Elementary School Journal, 94*, 169–181.

Haskell, R. E. (2001). *Transfer of learning: Cognition, instruction, and reasoning*. San Diego, CA: Academic Press.

Hayes, J. R. (1996). A new framework for understanding cognition and affect in writing. In C. M. Levy & S. Ransdell (Eds.), *The science of writing: Theories, methods, individual differences and applications* (pp. 1–27). Mahwah, NJ: Erlbaum.

Hayes, J. R. (2006). New directions in writing theory. In C. A. Macarthur, S. Graham, & J. Fitzgerald (Eds.), *Handbook of writing research* (pp. 28–40). New York: Guilford Press.

Hayes, J. R., & Flower, L. S. (1980). Identifying the organization of writing processes. In L. W. Gregg & E. R. Steinberg (Eds.), *Cognitive processes in writing* (pp. 3–30). Hillsdale, NJ: Erlbaum.

Hayes, J. R., & Flower, L. S. (1986). Writing research and the writer. *American Psychologist, 41*(10), 1106–1113.

Hayes, J. R., Hatch, J. A., & Silk, C. M. (2000). Does holistic assessment predict writing performance? *Written Communication, 17*, 3–26.

Hidi, S., & Baird, W. (1986). Interestingness—A neglected variable in discourse processing. *Cognitive Science, 10*(2), 179–194.

Huguier, M., Maisonneuve, H., Benhamou, C. L., de Calan, L, Grenier, B., Franco, D., Galniche, J. P., & Lorette, G. (1992). *La rédaction médicale*. Paris: Doin.

Kara, M., & Privat J.-M. (2006). La littératie autour de Jack Goody. *Pratiques, 5–6*, 131–132.

Kellogg, R. T. (1987). Effects of topic knowledge on the allocation processing time and cognitive effort to writing processes. *Memory and Cognition, 15*(3), 256–266.

Kellogg, R. T. (1994). *The psychology of writing*. New York: Oxford University Press.

Kellogg, R. T. (2008). Training writing skills: A cognitive developmental perspective. *Journal of Writing Research, 1*(1), 1–26.

Kellogg, R. T., & Raulerson, B. A., III. (2007). Improving the writing skills of college students. *Psychonomic Bulletin and Review, 14*, 237–242.

Kellogg, R. T., & Whiteford, A. P. (2009).Training advanced writing skills: The case for deliberate practice. *Educational Psychologist, 44*(4), 250–266.

Kerbrat-Orecchioni, C. (1980). *L'énonciation*. Colin: Armand.

Kintsch, W. (1998). *Comprehension: A paradigm for cognition*. Cambridge: Cambridge University Press.

Kirsch, G. (1991). Writing up and down the social ladder: A study of experienced writers Composing for contrasting audiences. *Research in the Teaching of English, 25*(1), 33–53.

Klein, P. D. (1999a). Learning science through writing: The role of rhetorical structures. *Alberta Journal of Educational Research, 45*, 132–153.

Klein, P. D. (1999b). Reopening inquiry into cognitive processes in writing-to-learn. *Educational Psychology Review, 11*, 203–270.

Klein, P. D. (2004). Constructing scientific explanations through writing. *Instructional Science, 32*, 191–231.

Klein, P. D., Piacente-Cimini, S., & Williams, L. A. (2007). The role of writing in learning from analogies. *Learning and Instruction, 17*, 595–611.

Labasse, B. (2001). From linguistics to communication's didactics: The case of lexicology. *International Review of Applied Linguistics, 39*(9), 217–243.

Labasse, B. (2006). *La communication écrite. Une matière en quête de substance*. Lyon: Éditions Colbert.

Labasse, B. (2008). Modeling the communication of complexity in an information-saturated society. In C. Beaudet, P. Grant-Russel, & D. Starke Meyerring (Eds.), *Research communication in the social and human sciences: From dissemination to public engagement* (pp. 60–84). Cambridge: Cambridge Publishing Press.

Lahire, B. (1999). *L'invention de l'illettrisme: rhétorique publique, éthique et stigmates*. Paris: Éditions La Découverte.

Larivière, L. (1995). Situation de la rédaction professionnelle dans l'entreprise: Résultats d'une enquête effectuée en 1992 auprès de 26 entreprises de la région montréalaise. *Technostyle, 12*(1), 67–98.

Lave, J. (1991). Situating learning in communities of practice. In L. B. Resnick, J. M. Levine, & S. D. Teasley (Eds.), *Perspectives on socially shared cognition* (pp. 63–82). Washington, DC: American Psychological Association.

Lundquist, L. (1994). *La cohérence textuelle: syntaxe, sémantique, pragmatique*, Samfundslitteratur.

MacLennan, H. (1945). *Two solitudes*, Toronto, Stoddart.

McCutchen, D. (1986). Domain knowledge and linguistic knowledge in the development of writing ability. *Journal of Memory and Language, 25*, 431–444.

Meier, S., McCarthy, P. R., & Schmeck, R. R. (1984). Validity of self-efficacy as a predictor of writing performance. *Cognitive Therapy and Research, 8* (2),107–120.

Meyer, P. (1996, September). Why journalism needs PhDs. *American Editor*, 10–11.

Monahan, B. D. (1984). Revision strategies of basic and competent writers as they write for different audiences. *Research in the teaching of English*, *18* (3), 288–304.

Nelms, G., & Dively, R. L. (2007). Perceived roadblocks to transferring knowledge from first-year composition to writing-intensive major courses: A pilot study. WPA: Writing Program Administration, 31. Retrieved June 22, 2010, from http://www.wpacouncil. org/journal/index.html

Nystrand, M. (2006) The social and historical context for writing research. In C. MacArthur, S. Graham and J. Fitzgerald (Eds), *Handbook of Writing Research*. New York: Guilford Press, 11–27.

Olson, D. (1994). *The world on paper*. Cambridge: Cambridge University Press.

Orlikowski, W., & Yates, J-A. (1994). Genre repertoire: The structuring of communicative practices in organizations. *Administrative Science Quarterly*, *39*, 541–574.

Pajares, F. (2003). Self-efficacy beliefs, motivation and achievement in writing: a review of the literature. *Reading & Writing Quarterly*, *19*, 139–158.

Paré, A. (2000). Writing as a way into social work: Genre sets, genre systems, and distributed cognition. In P. Dias & A. Paré (Eds.), *Transitions: Writing in academic and work-place settings* (pp. 145–166). Cresskill, NJ: Hampton.

Paré, A., & Smart, G. (1994). Observing genres in action: Towards a research methodology. In A. Freedman & P. Medway (Eds.), *Genre and the new rhetoric* (pp. 146–155). London: Taylor & Francis.

Paré, A., Starke-Meyerring, D., & McAlpie, L. (2009). The dissertation as multi-genre: Many readers, many readings. In C. Bazerman, A. Bonini, & D. Figeiredo (Eds.), *Genre in a changing world*. Fort Collins, CO & West Lafayette, IN: WAC Clearinghouse and Parlour Press.

Pepin, L. (1998). *La cohérence textuelle. L'évaluer et l'enseigner*. Laval: Groupe Beauchemin.

Piolat, A., & Pélissier, A. (1998). *La rédaction de textes: approche cognitive*. Lausanne, Switzerland: Delachaux et Niestlé.

Piolat, A., & Roussey, J-Y. (1992). Rédaction de textes. Éléments de psychologie cognitive. *Langages*, *106*, 106–125.

Plane, S. (2006). Singularités et constantes de la production d'écrit. L'écriture comme traitement de contraintes. In J. Laffont-Terranova & D. Collin (Eds.), *Didactique de l'écrit. La construction des savoirs et le sujet-écrivant* (pp. 33–54). Namur: Presses universitaires de Namur.

Plane, S., Olive, T., & Alamargot, D. (2010, March). Traitement des contraintes de la production d'écrits: aspects linguistiques et psycholinguistiques. *Langages, 177*, 130.

Pollet, M.-C. (2001). *Pour une didactique des discours universitaires*. Bruxelles: De Boeck Université.

Ransdell, S., & Levy, C. M. (1994). Writing as process and product: The impact of tool, genre, audience knowledge, and writer expertise. *Computers in Human Behavior, 10*(4), 511–527.

Ransdell, S., & Levy, C. M. (1996). Working memory constraints on writing quality and fluency. In C. M. Levy & S. Ransdell (Eds.), *The science of writing* (pp. 93–105), Mahwah, NJ: Erlbaum.

Resnick, L. B., Levine, J. M., & Teasley, S. D. (Eds.). (1991). *Perspectives on socially shared cognition* (pp. 63–82). Washington, DC: American Psychological Association.

Rijlaarsdam, G., Alamargot, D., & Chanquoy, L. (2001). *Studies in writing:* Vol. 9. *Through the models of writing*. New York: Kluwer.

Rohman, D. G., & Wlecke, A. (1964). *Pre-writing: The construction and applications of models for concept formation in writing*. East Lansing, MI: Michigan State University Press.

Russell, P., Bossé-Andrieu, J., & Cajolet-Laganière, H. (1995). Technical writing in French in Canada: Results of two surveys. *Technostyle, 12*(2), 49–75.

Scardamalia, M., & Bereiter, C. (1998). L'expertise en lecture-rédaction. In A. Piolat & A. Pélissier (Eds.), *La rédaction de textes: Approche cognitive* (pp. 13–50). Lausanne: Delachaux & Niestlé.

Schryer, C. (1993). Records as genre. *Written Communication, 10*, 200–234.

Schumacher, G. M., Scott, B. T., Klare, G. R., Cronin, F. C., & Lambert, D. A. (1989). Cognitive processes in journalistic genres. *Written Communication, 6*, 390–407.

Selzer, J. (1983). The composing processes of an engineer. *College Composition and Communication, 34*, 178–187.

Simon, H. (1971). Designing organizations for an information-rich world. In M. Greenberger (Ed.), *Computers, communications and the public interest* (pp. 37–72). Baltimore: Johns Hopkins University Press.

Slomp, D. (2008). Harming not helping: The impact of a Canadian standardized writing assessment on curriculum and pedagogy. *Assessing Writing, 13*, 180–200.

Smart, G. (1993). Genre as community invention: A central bank's response to its executives, expectations as readers. In R. Spilka (Ed.), *Writing in the workplace: New research perspectives* (pp. 124–140). Carbondale: Southern Illinois University Press.

Smith, T. (2006). Recent trends in undergraduate writing courses and programs in Canadian Universities. In R. Graves & H. Graves (Eds.), *Writing centres, writing seminars, writing culture: Writing instruction in Anglo-Canadian Universities* (pp. 319–383). Winnipeg: Inkshed.

Sommers, N. (1980). Revision strategies of student writers and experienced adult writers. *College Composition and Communication, 31*, 378–388.

Sperber, D., & Wilson, D. (1995). *Relevance: Communication and cognition.* Oxford: Wiley-Blackwell.

Spilka, R. (Ed.). (1993). *Writing in the workplace. New research perspectives.* Carbondale: Southern Illinois University Press.

Swaney, J. H., Janik, C. J., Bond, S. J., & Hayes, J. R. (1981). *Editing for comprehension: Improving the process through reading protocols* [Technical Report No. 14]. Pittsburgh: Carnegie-Mellon University, Document Design Project.

Taylor, K. K. (1984). The different summary skills of inexperienced and professional writers. *Journal of Reading, 27*(8), 691–699.

Traxler, M. J., & Gernsbacher, M. A. (1992). Improving written communication through minimal feedback. *Language and Cognitive Processes, 7*(1), 1–22.

Traxler, M. J., & Gernsbacher, M. A. (1993). Improving written communication through perspective taking. *Language and Cognitive Processes, 8*(3), 311–334.

Voss, J. F., Vesonder, G. T., & Spilich, G. J. (1980). Text generation and recall by high-knowledge and low-knowledge individuals. *Journal of Verbal Learning and Verbal Behavior, 19*, 651–667.

Young, R. (1978). Paradigms and problems: Needed research in rhetorical invention. In C. Cooper & L. Odell (Eds.), *Research in composing: Points of departure* (pp. 29–47). Urbana, IL: NCTE.

6

Distributed Cognition as a Framework for Understanding Writing

PERRY D. KLEIN and TRACEY L. LEACOCK

WHAT IS DISTRIBUTED COGNITION?

Distributed cognition is a theoretical approach that proposes that complex human activities integrally include internal minds, external representations, and interactions among individuals (Hutchins, 1995; Zhang & Patel, 2006). Consequently, a distributed analysis identifies the ways in which members of a group use cultural practices to create, transform, and propagate representations during an activity. Distributed cognition came to the attention of social scientists through a series of publications in the early 1990s (e.g., Hutchins, 1995; Salomon, 1993; Zhang & Norman 1995). This chapter will argue that writing can be understood as distributed cognition.

External representations are a critically important resource for problem solving. These include maps, written texts, graphs, tables, diagrams, and so forth (Donald, 2001; Zhang, 1997). A distributed activity includes both external representations and internal representations, which interact continually. This distinction between internal and external representations can be illustrated using the standard multiplication algorithm (Zhang & Norman, 2005). Some information is retrieved from the long-term memory of the individual, such as arithmetic procedures, the values of individual number symbols, and addition and multiplication facts; other information is perceptually inspected from the environment, such as the shapes and positions of the number symbols in a given written arithmetic calculation. As the algorithm proceeds, partial products are encoded externally on paper, reducing working-memory load. These can then be perceptually inspected from the environment and added together to generate the final product.

A second important kind of resource for problem solving is the group of people who share a given activity. The members of a group can pool knowledge from their individual long-term memories, share cognitive load among their working memories, and check one another's processing for errors (Zhang & Patel, 2006). The classic demonstration of shared cognition is Hutchin's (1995) analysis of navigation on a naval cruiser. Hutchins documented the ways in which representations were created and propagated across the team on the ship's bridge. These two kinds of resources (external representations and people) operate in combination. External representations are used to cue individuals to tasks, coordinate their work, record the products of cognitive operations, and trace progress through an activity (Zhang & Patel, 2006). Thus, members of a group may operate face to face; or their individual operations can be distributed across time and space, using external representations to mediate their interactions.

Distribution is important because unaided human cognition in the individual mind operates under tight storage, timing, and processing constraints. These include limited working-memory capacity, slow encoding of information in long-term memory under some circumstances, and largely associative retrieval from long-term memory. External representations can support cognition in several ways (Zhang & Patel, 2006, p. 335):

- Serving as an aid to short-term memory
- Serving as an aid to long-term memory
- Providing knowledge and skills not available in internal representations
- Providing information that can be directly perceived, so that little effortful processing is needed to encode it
- Supporting perceptual operators that make inferences relatively directly
- Changing the nature of a task with efficient action sequences

DISTRIBUTED THEMES IN THE COGNITIVE PSYCHOLOGY OF WRITING

Distributed themes have been part of cognitive psychology since its inception. The classic Newell and Simon (1972) model conceived of problem solving as a search through a space comprised of the possible states of a given problem. Such a search could be partially modeled internally, in the mind of the individual. However, the small size of short-term memory and the slow rate of storing some kinds of information in long-term memory were important constraints on internal problem solving. Consequently, the authors stressed the important role of the materials used by problem solvers, which they considered to comprise an external memory. It was considered to include the elements of the problem that were in immediate view and possibly other elements in view during additional saccades. These were thought to augment short-term memory, extend its capacity, and stabilize it over time. Like internal long-term memory, external memory was thought to be "essentially infinite in its capacity" (p. 802). The problem solver's internal knowledge, plus this external memory, comprised the "extended knowledge state" (p. 585).

The classic Hayes and Flower (1980) cognitive model of writing was conceived partially in terms of internal representations and processes. The model posited that topic knowledge, audience knowledge, and writing plans are stored in long-term memory; and processes are carried out using attention and short-term memory (the concept of working memory was not yet in use at the time). However, the Hayes and Flower model also included aspects that could be conceived as distributed. First, writing processes interacted continually with the rhetorical problem, which the authors noted could be represented in a simplified, concrete form as a writing assignment (Flower & Hayes, 1981, p. 369). Second, specific processes produced external representations, which served as input to other processes. For example, the text produced so far comprised input to the reviewing process; generating could produce notes for the organizing process; and generating could provide notes for expansion through the translating process. Third, although writing processes were defined in internal terms, they were also defined at times in terms of the external representations on which they operate (e.g., see flowcharts in Hayes & Flower, 1980).

An additional type of external resource that was quickly incorporated into classical cognitive theories of writing was the source text. Flower and Hayes (1981, p. 371) considered that the writer's long-term memory "can exist in the mind as well as in outside resources such as books." In a computer-based writing activity, Schönpflug (1986) showed that when taking notes from sources, writers balance the time requirements of internal storage (memorizing) versus external storage (note taking). Subsequently, Spivey (1997) treated source texts as resources with which writers interact continually, so that they influence the content, structure, and language of product texts.

Other aspects of the cognitive psychology of writing also anticipated distributed themes. There has been a longstanding interest in the role of collaborators, particularly in educational settings (Nelson, 2008). Additionally, several cognitive psychologists have discussed ways in which writing, as an external representation, could support thinking and learning (see Klein, 1999, for a review). For example, Young and Sullivan (1984), building on the Newell and Simon model of problem solving, proposed that writing allows authors to externalize their ideas in text and repeatedly revisit them, transforming them and drawing new inferences.

COMMON WRITING PRACTICES ARE PRIMA FACIE DISTRIBUTED

Although cognitive theories of writing have always included distributed themes, we propose that it is necessary to foreground and extend these. Much cognitive research has focused on *sequestered* writing activities. Sequestered writing contrasts with distributed writing in two respects. Sequestered writing involves few external representations (e.g., only the writer's emerging text), and it minimally involves individuals other than the immediate writer. This type of writing occurs in situations such as journal writing in the elementary classroom and university essay exams.

However, sequestered writing is unrepresentative of most writing activities. Beaufort (2008) has reviewed research on writing in the workplace. She shows that practices are highly variable—but almost always social in some way. External resources support individual writing processes; for example, "boilerplate" text is used to generate content and language for multiple documents. External resources, such as e-mail, also support the distribution of writing activities across individuals, such as colleagues and supervisors. Similarly, in schools, some version of the process approach to writing is commonly used. This includes social resources, such as conferences with peers and teachers; representational resources, such as lists of prompts to support revision; and supports for regulating, such as folders with pockets for each phase of the writing process (Calkins, 1994). Similarly in schools, writing-to-learn activities may include teachers, peer collaborators, source texts, writing assignments, graphic organizers, and real audiences (Rosaen, 1990; Wright, 2008). Likewise, personal writing has become increasingly mediated by technology for supporting and sharing composition (Witte, 2007).

The prevalence of social and representational support in workplaces, schools, and homes weighs against the traditional cognitive focus on sequestered writing activities. It might be countered that writers sometimes compose alone. However, individual writing is often one phase in a more extended process that involves other people. Additionally, individual writing often involves cultural tools, such as source texts or computer software. These points are illustrated by Cronin's (2004) analysis of the recent history of academic collaboration. He documents the rising number of coauthorships, as well as the less visible presence of other contributors, including authors of previous texts that inform a given work, colleagues who casually exchange ideas in the initial stages of writing, and reviewers and editors who contribute to the publication process.

WRITING PROCESSES FROM A DISTRIBUTED COGNITIVE PERSPECTIVE

In the previous section, we noted some evidence that writing is prima facie distributed. However, to show that writing is distributed in a cognitively interesting sense, it is necessary to show that external resources complement internal cognition in ways that affect writing processes. Some ways in which external representations complement individual cognition appeared above, in the list from Zhang and Patel (2006). It could also be considered indirect evidence for distributed cognition if external resources significantly affect outcomes such as quality of text or content learning during writing. Writing could be considered to be distributed in the strong sense if, for a given writing activity, external representations and social resources substantially change or reduce the kind of information that must be stored in long-term memory or substantially change or reduce the information that must be processed in working memory. Cognition could be distributed in the weak sense if all or most information from external resources must be stored in long-term memory and retrieved into working memory to affect writing.

We will review evidence that each writing process is distributed in terms of the following five dimensions: (1) the type of writing process being distributed (Hayes & Flower, 1980); (2) the cognitive resources on which that writing process depends (e.g., long-term memory, working memory); (3) the types of external resource involved in the distribution (e.g., members of a group, external representations); (4) the practice through which the writing process is distributed; and (5) an interpretation of the way in which cognition is distributed across internal and external resources (e.g., reducing working-memory load; supplementing knowledge in long-term memory).

This last dimension requires some further clarification: What is it about written text, *as a medium*, that could support cognition? As Zhang and Patel's (2006) list, cited above, indicates, there are various possible mechanisms for distribution; perhaps the most impressive would be reduction of working-memory load, because this would most directly affect thinking during writing. The most dramatic instances of distributed cognition to date have involved physical or spatial representations that transform problem representations, allowing a solution to be generated perceptually and markedly reducing working-memory load (Larkin & Simon, 1987; Zhang & Norman, 1994). However, spatial representations are important only in some subtasks of writing, for example, the graphical organization of writing outlines.

So what is it about written text as a medium that could support elaboration of language and content reasoning? A starting point is that natural language sensitively represents concepts and the relationships among them (Gentner, 2003). Writing can record these concepts and relations so they can later be reactivated by reading. Writers could then use this knowledge to draw further inferences. Recently, Oatley and Djikic (2008) have extended this theory by incorporating long-term working memory, a set of retrieval structures comprised of content knowledge and discourse knowledge that allow concepts in long-term memory to be rapidly retrieved for processing in working memory (Ericsson & Kintsch, 1995; McCutchen, 2000). Oatley and Djikic proposed that the emerging text and long-term working memory can each cue the other, so that the text is "gradually, and thoughtfully, elaborated" (p. 15). We will now consider some evidence about how distribution operates for various kinds of writing processes.

DISTRIBUTION OF PLANNING

Goal Setting

Goal setting can address rhetoric, content, or the writing process itself. It is part of planning, which depends on the executive component of working memory (Vandenberg & Swanson, 2007). In sequestered writing, the goals that writers initially set appear to be based on the rhetorical situation and on long-term memory knowledge about texts, audiences, topics, and writing processes (Hayes & Flower, 1980).

In educational settings, goals are represented externally in the form of writing assignments. Such assignments play an active role in cognition: van den Bergh and Rijlaarsdam (2007) found that the likelihood of writers generating ideas immediately after reading the assignment is greater than the average likelihood of generating ideas after other operations. In a recent meta-analysis, Graham and Perin (2007) found that scaffolding product goal setting had large effects on text quality, both for content goals (e.g., to add three pieces of information; Graham, MacArthur, & Schwartz, 1995) and rhetorical goals (e.g., to include persuasive elements; Ferretti, Lewis, & Andrews-Weckerly, 2009).

The knowledge that underpins goal setting may be distributed between internal and external resources. Novice writers have limited knowledge of goals in long-term memory; external representations such as thinksheets provide such knowledge (Graham, MacArthur, Schwartz, & Page-Voth, 1992). Conversely, novices use knowledge in long-term memory to instantiate these goals. For example, if a thinksheet prompts the student to consider what a reader will find interesting, the student must then respond on the basis of knowledge about both the topic and the reader. With respect to process, skilled writers return to their top-level goals spontaneously, while novices may not (Flower & Hayes, 1981); an external checklist can remind them to do so (Graham et al., 1992).

The distribution of goal setting may play a role in writing to learn. In a meta-analysis of the effect of writing-intensive curriculum units on learning, a significant moderator was the teacher's provision of metacognitive writing prompts, which set for students the goal of reflecting on their own learning (Bangert-Drowns, Hurley, & Wilkinson, 2004). In another study, being assigned the goal of writing about human organ systems for peers or younger students resulted in more learning of science concepts than being assigned the goal of writing for teachers or parents, although this effect could be due to feedback as well as goal setting (Gunel, Hand, & McDermott, 2009). Generally, assigned genres that require elaborative reasoning contribute to learning during writing, although results are somewhat mixed (Klein, 1999). For example, in recent research, essay questions that set the goal of integrating information across sources produced greater transfer of content learning than questions that required processing texts separately (Cerdan & Vidal-Abarca, 2008).

Generating

In the Hayes and Flower model (1980), generating produces ideas through retrieval of information from long-term memory. Although research has not entirely separated generating from other processes, generating appears to draw on the verbal and central executive components of working memory; additionally, if content can be visualized, it also draws on visual working memory (Kellogg, Olive, & Piolat, 2007; Vandenberg & Swanson, 2007). Expert writers may have extensive topic-related retrieval structures (long-term working memory), which help them to meet these demands (McCutchen, 2000).

The generation of content in writing has been supported by several kinds of external representations. As noted above, a written assignment can prompt the generation of content (van den Bergh & Rijlaarsdam, 2007). Consistent with the conceptually based organization of information in long-term memory, content prompts are more effective than rhetorical prompts (Butcher & Kintsch, 2001), although rhetorical prompts also have significant effects (Ferretti et al., 2009). Source texts are another important external resource for generating content. Reading-to-write is a traditional school practice (Nelson, 2008). Novice writers may adopt content directly from sources, while more expert writers constructively integrate content from across multiple sources (Segev-Miller, 2007; Spivey, 1997). With the rise of the Internet, sources in a variety of modes may play an increasingly prominent role in writing (Vincent, 2007); ideas taken from multimodal sources can contribute significantly to both text quality and learning during writing (Klein & Kirkpatrick, 2010).

Cognitive psychologists have noted that external sources are analogous to long-term memory (Flower & Hayes, 1981). We would extend this observation by suggesting that external sources and internal long-term memory distribute the representation of knowledge. Externally, source texts instantiate extensive and detailed topic information; internally, skilled writers and readers form a gist that is necessary for the comprehension and effective use of multiple external sources (Schönpflug, 1986; Strømsø, Bråten, & Britt, 2010). Furthermore, the role of the source text itself is mediated by another layer of external representation, in the notes that writers take from source texts. In doing so, skilled writers respond to the storage cost, retrieval cost, and complexity of information in the source in deciding how much information to store internally in memory and how much to store externally in written notes (Schönpflug, 1986). Thus the knowledge that informs writing is a distributed, multilayered system formed by external representations in the source texts and the writer's notes, as well as internal representations in the writer's long-term memory.

Another external resource important for generating ideas is the evolving text plan or outline. Students who write from notes produce texts that are longer or higher in quality than students composing from memory alone (Benton, Kiewra, Whitfill, & Dennison, 1993; Kellogg, 1990). Benton et al. found that producing notes and access to prepared notes each affected writing. Kellogg found that producing ideas for an outline was significantly more effective than receiving ideas for an outline. He concluded that prewritten notes reduced the opportunity to engage in constructing a schema. Additionally, for writers assigned to seek intertextual relations, notes on each source improved recall of such relations (Kobayashi, 2009). Therefore, as with source texts, writing is affected *both* by the information that is distributed between internal and external representations and by the process of constructing an external representation.

In experimental studies, writers have used planning notes as a resource for generating additional ideas; for example, Re, Caeran, and Cornoldi (2008) used thinksheets to prompt students with attention deficits to generate ideas for personal letters and then to reread their ideas and select one to develop, resulting in significant positive effects on their writing (cf., Nussbaum, 2008). In this type of process, the planning notes appear to function somewhat like partial products in paper and pencil multiplication—an initial product of thought that the writer can revisit to generate further inferences.

Generating may also be distributed socially. In collaborative writing, generating ideas is a predominant process (Storch, 2005; Wigglesworth & Storch, 2009).

In a meta-analysis, the effect of peer assistance on text quality was large (Graham & Perin, 2007); however, collaborations included a variety of writing processes, so we cannot infer which ones affected text quality. Mason (1998) found that when students talked about science concepts in small groups prior to writing, they constructed new ideas, which they subsequently incorporated into their texts (cf., Jaubert & Rebiere, 2005).

A distributed view of generating helps to solve an important problem in the writing-to-learn literature. Some theories, such as the knowledge-transforming model, imply that writing should lead to learning primarily for experts; novices are thought to write simply by retrieving ideas from long-term memory and translating them directly into text (Bereiter & Scardamalia, 1987). However, the empirical literature shows that novices can learn through writing, often in brief, informal activities, which probably include little planning or revision (Bangert-Drowns et al., 2004). This finding can be explained by considering that, from a distributed perspective, generating is not simply retrieval from long-term memory: Assignment instructions, external sources (e.g., source texts, multimedia materials), and collaborators can all contribute to the generation of content. For example, in a pair of activities in which elementary students wrote about science experiments, the number of think-aloud segments—each dedicated to reviewing the experiment and generating ideas—was significantly correlated with conceptual gains during writing (Klein, 2000).

Organizing

In the Hayes and Flower (1980) model, organizing comprises selecting from the material produced by the generating process and structuring it to form temporal or hierarchical relations. It was theorized that text organization is informed by writing plans in long-term memory. Organizing can be working-memory intensive: Vandenberg and Swanson (2007) demonstrated that the executive component of working memory predicts structure in writers' analytical texts, although not in their narrative texts; and Galbraith, Ford, Walker, and Ford (2005) showed that organizing loads on spatial working memory.

External resources affect the organizing process. In educational settings, assignments may include prompts for structuring text. Additionally, source texts are external resources that writers use to organize their own texts; for example, they may use one source as a model and incorporate additional content from other texts (Segev-Miller, 2007). External resources for organizing have been investigated extensively in the instructional literature using representations such as thinksheets, computer prompts, and graphic matrices (Kirkpatrick & Klein, 2009; Re et al., 2008; Zellermayer, Salomon, Globerson, & Givon, 1991). For example, Ferretti et al. (2009) found that a writing prompt that included subgoals comprising elements of an argument was more effective than a prompt comprising the goal alone.

These resources appear to distribute cognition across internal and external representations in several ways. External representations can provide knowledge about text structure that novices may lack, such as the fact that arguments should address two sides of an issue (Klein & Kirkpatrick, 2010). External organizers can support an efficient action sequence. They encourage writers to separate the process of planning from the process of translating, improving the quality of written text, possibly by reducing working-memory demand (Kellogg, 1990). An external representation may serve as a prompt for students to make inferences from initial ideas; for example, Nussbaum (2008) used argumentation vee diagrams (AVDs)[1] to teach college writers to prepare arguments and counter-arguments and to then use these to generate a synthesis of their ideas. As with generating, both access to organized notes and the act of organizing such notes appear to contribute to writing (Benton et al., 1993; Kellogg, 1990). This suggests, again, that creating external representations is a means of forming schemata.

Initial evidence suggests that external organizers contribute to learning during writing. Hand, Hohenshell, and Prain (2007) carried out a sustained program of research on the science writing heuristic, in which students complete a science experiment or other learning experience and then receive a series of prompts that guide them in structuring their writing, producing significant effects on learning. Recently, Knückles, Hübner, and Renkl (2009) contrasted several kinds of writing prompts in a science reading–writing activity; one condition, termed "cognitive," largely focused on text structure prompts (e.g., headings, examples); it was significantly more effective than a control condition with no prompts.

DISTRIBUTION OF TRANSLATING

In the Hayes and Flower (1980) model, translating is the operation that transforms propositions into written sentences. Berninger and Swanson (1994) divided translating into two processes—text production and transcription—and we follow this distinction in our discussion. Translating imposes a load on the central executive component of working memory and on phonological working memory (Hayes & Chenoweth, 2006; Kellogg et al., 2007; Vandenberg & Swanson, 2007).

Text Generation

Several kinds of external representations support text generation. The writer's notes from the planning process embody propositional content, which the writer can reread and expand into sentences. In educational settings, teachers may support lexical knowledge with external representations, such as word lists, semantic webs, and pictionaries; writers may also draw on hardcopy or electronic dictionaries and thesauri. More recently, "Sentence Fairy" software has been used to support young writers; it creates a propositional model of the emerging text and uses it to generate a variety of syntactic options, from which the writers choose (Harbusch, Itsova, Koch, & Kuhner, 2008). In this instance, syntactic information is distributed between the external software and the long-term memory of the writer, transforming the translation process from production to recognition.

---

[1] An argumentation vee diagram (AVD) is a graphic organizer used for planning reflective opinion essays. It prompts writers to include arguments and counterarguments, to consider integrative strategies, and to include a conclusion (Nussbaum, 2008).

Collaborators also comprise an important resource for translating ideas into language. For English language learners, collaboration produces texts that are more accurate linguistically than texts composed individually (Storch, 2005; Wigglesworth & Storch, 2009). Peer collaboration in language production may also contribute to thinking and learning; Milian (2005) presented qualitative evidence that as cowriters negotiated the wording of science documents, they also refined their science knowledge.

Transcribing

Transcribing is the transformation of mental representations of language into written letters and words through handwriting, typing, or spelling. Novices are in varying stages of learning to produce letters automatically and to access word-specific spellings with links to the phonology, orthography, morphology, and semantics of the word in their mental dictionaries. For skilled writers, these same transcription processes are often but not always automatic (Berninger & Swanson, 1994; Bourdin & Fayol, 2000). Transcription can be supported externally with technologies such as predictive dictionaries and speech recognition software (MacArthur, 1999). Transcription can also be distributed to a scribe who writes for the author (MacArthur & Cavalier, 2004). The predictive dictionary illustrates the dual components of distributed cognition. As the writer begins to type a word, the software uses initial letters and other cues to generate a list of possible words, instantiating considerable orthographic knowledge. Conversely, the writer must draw on internal knowledge to produce the initial letters and then select the desired word from among the options on the menu. Thus, this software changes the spelling process from recall to recognition.

Effects of Translating

The emerging text is a resource for the subsequent generation of ideas: van den Bergh and Rijlaarsdam (2007) found that although the probability of translation-driven generating is highest early in the writing process, the correlation of translation-driven generating with text quality is highest in the middle and later parts of the writing process. This insight suggests that the cumulative influence of the emerging text is valuable. The role of translating in generating suggests that drafting could contribute to thinking and learning during writing. Klein, Piacente-Cimini, and Williams (2007) found that university students learned more by writing analogies about physics problems than by speaking about them; the students' writing processes were comprised primarily of generating and translating activities, with very little planning or revision (cf., Drabick, Weisberg, Paul, & Bubier, 2007).

DISTRIBUTION OF REVIEWING

The Hayes and Flower (1980) model proposed that reviewing includes the processes of reading and editing; it is now common to differentiate between revising the meaning of text versus editing the surface features. We will also refer here to the process of evaluating (Bereiter & Scardamalia, 1987; Hayes, Flower, Schriver, Stratman, & Carey, 1987). Reviewing is thought to draw on long-term memory knowledge about topics, texts, standards of evaluation, and revision strategies; it loads on the executive component of working memory and on verbal working memory (Hayes & Chenoweth, 2006; Vandenberg & Swanson, 2007).

Reading

An initial study found that for college students with learning disabilities, text-to-speech software significantly increased the number of errors they were able to detect in writing (Raskind & Higgins, 1995). This example shows how offloading one operation (reading) can allow writers to enact downstream processes that are dependent on it (here, evaluating).

Evaluating

Writers are better at detecting surface level and local problems than they are at detecting more global problems such as inconsistency in text (McCutchen, Francis, & Kerr, 1997). External representations of criteria for judging text, in the form of rubrics, may support evaluation; however, in a meta-analysis, the effect of scales and rubrics on text quality was small to medium in size (Hillocks, 1986). An additional caveat is that rubrics are typically available to writers prior to composing; thus, it is unclear whether they affect text quality during planning or revision (Andrade, Du, & Wang, 2008).

Bereiter and Scardamalia (1987) asked fourth-, sixth-, and eighth-grade students to review a text either while it was being drafted or after it was completed. After each sentence, writers cycled through a set of cards representing meaning-level error diagnoses (e.g., "People won't see why this is important," p. 270). For most errors, students in Grades 6 and 8 selected the same diagnosis as a semiprofessional writer. This finding suggests that the external prompt cued tacit long-term knowledge about discourse. However, students at all levels selected predominantly local error types, rather than those that affected the meaning of the text as a whole.

In a subsequent study by McCutchen et al. (1997, Study 2), dyads of seventh-grade students read brief historical narratives in which errors (spelling or inconsistencies in the timeline) were either highlighted or not highlighted. High-ability dyads were able to diagnose meaning-level errors, but low-ability dyads were not; more important, highlighting increased their tendency to focus on spelling errors instead. In McCutchen et al. (1997, Study 1), similar stimulus materials led college students to correct both spelling errors and meaning errors, but seventh-grade students were *less* likely to correct meaning-level errors if they were highlighted than if they were not. As with the Bereiter and Scardamalia (1987) study, this research reflects the influence of external representations, albeit in a negative way.

Spell-checking software and grammar-checking software have been familiar resources for supporting the orthographic and syntactic aspects of the evaluating process. Recently innovative software has begun to focus on meaning-level evaluation. Upper-year biology students wrote texts for laypeople, using software that highlighted technical terms and prompted them to rate the comprehensibility and detail of their explanations. This use of software led them to expand their explanations significantly compared to those who worked without this software (Jucks, Schulte-Löbbert, & Bromme, 2007).

Of the writing processes, evaluating is the one that we might expect to benefit most from the assistance of other individuals. Feedback from audiences affects text quality favorably (see Butterfield, Hacker, & Albertson, 1996 for a review), although in a recent meta-analysis, the effects of feedback on learning to write better text were too mixed to permit a conclusion (Graham & Perin, 2007). Greater success appears to be associated with training students to review effectively (Boscolo & Ascorti, 2004; MacArthur, Schwartz, & Graham, 1991).

In a novel approach to the evaluation process, several studies have recently examined the effects of allowing writers to see readers *act* on a text. In one study, students wrote explanations for a science experiment. They then observed a video of a reader attempting to use the written explanation to carry out the same experiment while thinking aloud. The writers then revised their texts, leading to large gains in quality (Rijlaarsdam, Couzijn, Janssen, Braaksma, & Keift, 2006; cf. Rijlaarsdam, Braaksma et al., 2008). This procedure appears to offload the reading and evaluating processes largely from the writer to the reader and to compensate for the often poor self-monitoring of comprehension in readers by externalizing it through concrete action.

Editing and Revising

Revision appears to be working-memory intensive. For example, inserting a sentence requires generating the propositional content of the sentence, translating it into language, and transcribing this to complete the translation process, all the while holding in mind the macrostructure of the text to maintain global coherence, as well as checking the previous and subsequent sentences to maintain local coherence.

In the Bereiter and Scardamalia (1987) study outlined earlier, after students evaluated each sentence, they cycled through cue cards suggesting six possible tactics for revising (e.g., "I'd better give an example"; p. 271) and made the suggested revisions or bypassed the tactic. Eighth-grade students chose the same tactics as a semiprofessional writer in most instances; fourth- and sixth-grade students chose these tactics with an above-chance frequency. For students at all three grade levels, raters judged most changes to be improvements; however, the overall texts were not judged to be better than the first drafts.

Other studies have been more successful in prompting revisions beyond a local level. Midgette, Haria, and MacArthur (2008) invited sixth-grade students to draft texts and then prompted them with one of three types of revision goals: audience goals, content goals, or general goals to revise. The audience goals and content goals led to significantly better texts overall (cf., Wallace et al., 1996). It is notable that in this study, a relatively abstract representation (a goal instruction) led to meaning-level revisions, whereas in previous studies, more concrete representations (highlighting of errors, a completed text draft) reduced meaning-level revisions (Bereiter & Scardamalia, 1987; McCutchen et al., 1997).

Reviewing and Writing to Learn

A common theoretical perspective is that writing allows ideas to be distributed between the mind and the text and iteratively elaborated or improved (Donald, 2001; Zhang, 1997). Klein (2000, 2004) found that the frequency of evaluation and revision in writing about science experiments predicted learning during writing. These revisions were at the meaning level, but local; that is, none of the students substantively revised the structure of their texts. Recently, in a more socially distributed process, Carlson and Berry (2008) found that calibrated electronic peer review improved learning in an engineering course (cf., Jaubert & Rebiere, 2005).

DISTRIBUTION OF MONITORING

In the original Hayes and Flower (1980) model, the monitor controlled transitions among other processes; it was thought to be guided by the writer's overall goals, writing plans stored in long-term memory, and goals for particular writing processes. Monitoring is clearly an executive activity, although its working-memory load has not been separated empirically from the load of the specific processes (e.g., generating) that it controls.

As we noted above, in the workplace or classroom, institutionalized practices partially control transitions among writing processes (Beaufort, 2008). Similarly, in experimental research, procedures that scaffold particular writing processes also typically control transitions among processes. For example, students may be prompted to *begin* with goal setting (Page-Voth & Graham, 1999), to *conclude* with revising (Midgette et al., 2008), or to *alternate* between translating and reviewing (Bereiter & Scardamalia, 1987). Some external representations prompt multiple transitions among operations; for example, a checklist may be used to set initial goals, to review these goals, and to check them off as they are completed (Martin & Mano, 1995; Page-Voth & Graham, 1999). Similarly, in peer collaboration studies, external representations may prompt partners to make transitions among the processes of planning, translating, and revising (Nelson & Schunn, 2009; Yarrow & Topping, 2001). Prompting transitions can result in improved writing, presumably because it allocates working-memory resources efficiently (Kellogg, 1990).

FUTURE DIRECTIONS: COMPUTER-SUPPORTED COLLABORATIVE LEARNING AND WRITING

In considering future directions for distributed cognition, we focus on the need for additional research to better understand how the rapid spread of computer-supported collaborative learning (CSCL) technologies is changing the distribution of writing processes in educational contexts (Turner & Katić, 2009; Warschauer, 2010). Examples of these technologies include asynchronous online discussions, Wikis, and a range of special-purpose tools designed specifically for educational contexts (e.g., Knowledge Forum, Scardamalia & Bereiter, 2006; SWoRD, Nelson & Schunn, 2009). Such tools facilitate the use of collaborative writing activities to share ideas and build knowledge, and they are being investigated for use in early childhood (Pelletier, Reeve, & Halewood, 2006) through to postsecondary levels (Lee, 2010).

In CSCL environments, collaboration is most often mediated by text-based communications that are stored and made available to students as an external archive of ideas that "can then become 'objects' to be acted and improved upon" (Chai & Tan, 2009, p. 1305). In other words, in addition to simply being a place where instructors can post traditional external scaffolds, such as writing assignments or grading rubrics, CSCL tools enable a new kind of external representation—a record of all individual contributions to a group writing activity. This record is available to augment the individual long-term memories of students, and, depending on the focus of the contributions, could contribute to individual writers' topic-area knowledge, genre knowledge, or writing process understanding. There is some research indicating that the record of group contributions can influence writers during online learning activities. For example, in a study of online conferencing activities with preservice teachers, Järvelä and Häkkinen (2002) noted that, particularly in higher quality discussions, participants drew on a variety of resources, including other discussants' prior contributions, when composing their own written contributions. However, more research is needed to understand the circumstances under which writers may take advantage of these possibilities and the degree to which the writing processes are distributed between individual students and the external representation of group contributions.

Another key feature of text-based CSCL tools is the nature of the medium itself—students are communicating via writing. The individual contributions combine to become a collaborative text that may progressively extend the group's collective knowledge. The organic nature of such emergent texts suggests that some of the planning processes of writing may look quite different from product-oriented writing activities, but the medium provides considerable opportunity for all writing processes to be distributed across group members. Again, there is some research to suggest that this distribution happens. University students using Wikis to complete collaborative writing assignments reported using a combination of the main Wiki content page, the history page, and the discussion page to co-create and corevise their assignments (Lee, 2010). More structured research into the impact of individual contributions on the group product would help establish if, when, and how writing processes may be distributed in such contexts.

CONCLUSIONS

In this chapter we have shown that writing is a distributed cognitive activity. Each writing process includes both compulsory and optional external representations, such as source texts, planning notes, and the emerging text. Our brief review has illustrated the various ways in which external representations distribute cognition, including aiding long-term memory, aiding working memory, providing information that is not available in long-term memory, and creating efficient action sequences. Concerning the ways in which cognitive processes can be distributed across individuals, the literature shows that collaborators pool knowledge from long-term memory (e.g., when generating content), share cognitive operations (e.g., transcribing), and correct errors (e.g., during reviewing).

How strongly distributed is the cognition of writing? This brief review indicates that for planning processes (goal setting, generating, and organizing) there appears to be a strong interdependence between external representations and internal long-term memory. This interdependence is comprised of both the information distributed across these two sites and the cognitive work of interpreting or creating these representations. The external components of these relationships may function like long-term working memory, supporting efficient retrieval of information to working memory, and so indirectly reducing working-memory load during writing. Among translating processes, it appears that spelling and transcribing words can be strongly distributed between internal representations and external computer software or human collaborators; this distribution significantly supplements knowledge in long-term memory and probably reduces working-memory load. Conversely, other translating processes, such as producing coherent discourse, appear to depend largely on the internal abilities of the writer. The reviewing processes comprise the most complex case. They are distributed in the sense that they integrally include the external text draft; additionally, basic reviewing processes such as rereading text and evaluating spelling and grammar can be partially offloaded to software. For expert writers, evaluating and revising meaning-level errors can be distributed throughout a system comprised of the author, reviewers, and the external text draft; for novice writers, this is possible with instruction, but limited knowledge and cognitive resources otherwise attenuate such distribution. In summary, planning, translating, and reviewing can be somewhat strongly distributed between internal long-term memory and external representations; and this distribution, along with human collaboration or the use of software, may reduce working-memory load. The result is that social and representational resources significantly affect text quality and, in some instances, learning during writing.

Before commenting on the advantages of a distributed cognitive approach, we should acknowledge some limitations. First, we have argued that aspects of writing can be somewhat strongly distributed; however, distribution depends on the writer's ability to incorporate external representational and social resources to form a writing system. As the literature on reviewing illustrated, this ability can vary widely across individuals. Second, the evidence reviewed in this chapter does not, in most instances, show exactly what information is represented internally and externally; so it comprises only indirect evidence for distribution. Third, although distributed cognition aspires to a description of the system formed by members of a group as well as external representations, most of the evidence presented in this chapter has addressed only two kinds of relations (writer–artifact, writer–writer) within that system. Fourth, there is some evidence that, if knowledge about writing is internalized, it has a greater effect than analogously distributed knowledge; for example, cognitive strategy instruction, which focuses on internalization, affects writing more strongly than process-writing instruction (Graham & Perin, 2007). This finding means that, fifth, from a pedagogical point of view, in many instances the distribution of knowledge about writing is a steppingstone to the internalization of the same knowledge.

Having acknowledged these limitations, we see an interrelated set of advantages to a distributed conception of writing. A distributed approach helps us to see cognitive models of writing more clearly. They have always included external resources as integral parts of writing, and the use of the term *distributed cognition* would communicate this mixture of internal and external elements clearly. In any case, this use of a common language to articulate the properties of external resources (e.g., text, collaborators) and internal resources (e.g., working memory, long-term memory) allows us to consider systematically the similarities and differences among these resources. The payoff is that we can better understand the way in which internal and external resources complement each other during writing.

The distributed model of writing as presented in this chapter is important because a certain narrative has recently emerged that claims that cognitive theories of writing have now been largely succeeded by social and cultural theories (Nystrand, 2006). In place of this succession narrative, a distributed cognitive perspective reveals the close connection between cognitive and sociocultural theories of writing. Distributed cognition is an essential complement to sociocultural theories, which otherwise would be unable to explain how it is that people can actually participate in cultural practices. Conversely, distributed cognition is a necessary extension of cognitive psychology, because it opens the door to incorporating the highly contextual and culturally contingent nature of elements such as goals, content knowledge, text structure, and audience. By retaining the key theoretical concepts of the classical cognitive models of writing and applying them to networks of people and artifacts, we can extend the scope of cognitive models to understand writing in settings such as schools and workplaces. This approach will be particularly important for understanding writing in a digital world.

REFERENCES

Andrade, H. G., Du, Y., & Wang, X. (2008). Putting rubrics to the test: The effect of a model, criteria generation, and rubric-referenced self-assessment on elementary school students' writing. *Educational Measurement: Issues and Practice, 27*(2), 3–13.

Bangert-Drowns, R. L., Hurley, M. M., & Wilkinson, B. (2004). The effects of school-based writing-to-learn interventions on academic achievement: A meta-analysis. *Review of Educational Research, 74,* 29–58.

Beaufort, A. (2008). Writing in the professions. In C. Bazerman (Ed.), *Handbook of research on writing* (pp. 221–235). New York: Erlbaum.

Benton, S. L., Kiewra, K. A., Whitfill, J. M., & Dennison, R. (1993). Encoding and external-storage effects on writing processes. *Journal of Educational Psychology, 85,* 267–280.

Bereiter, C., & Scardamalia, M. (1987). *The psychology of written composition.* Hillsdale, NJ: Erlbaum.

Berninger, V., & Swanson, H. L. (1994). Modifying Hayes and Flower's model of skilled writing to explain beginning and developing writing. In E. Butterfield (Ed.), *Children's writing: Toward a process theory of development of skilled writing* (pp. 57–81). Greenwich, CT: JAI Press.

Boscolo, P., & Ascorti, K. (2004). Effects of collaborative revision on children's ability to write understandable narrative texts. In L. Allal, L. Chanquoy, & P. Largy (Eds.), *Revision: Cognitive and instructional processes* (pp. 157–170). Boston: Kluwer.

Bourdin, B., & Fayol, M. (2000). Is graphic activity costly? A developmental approach. *Reading and Writing: An Interdisciplinary Journal, 13*, 183–196.

Butcher, K. R., & Kintsch, W. (2001). Support of content and rhetorical processes of writing: Effects on the writing process and the written product. *Cognition and Instruction, 19*, 277–322.

Butterfield, E. C., Hacker, D. J., & Albertson, L. R. (1996). Environmental, cognitive, and metacognitive influences on text revision: Assessing the evidence. *Educational Psychology Review, 8*, 239–297.

Calkins, L. M. (1994). *The art of teaching writing* (New ed). Portsmouth, NH: Heinemann.

Carlson, P. A., & Berry F. C. (2008). Using computer-mediated peer review in an engineering design course. *IEEE Transactions of Professional Communication, 51*, 264–279. Retrieved from http://ieeexplore.ieee.org

Cerdan, R., & Vidal-Abarca, E. (2008). The effects of tasks on integrating information from multiple documents. *Journal of Educational Psychology, 100*, 209–222.

Chai, C. S., & Tan, S. C. (2009). Professional development of teachers for computer-supported collaborative learning: A knowledge-building approach. *Teachers College Record, 111*, 1296–1327. Retrieved from http://www.tcrecord.org/

Cronin, B. (2004). Bowling alone together: Academic writing as distributed cognition. *Journal of the American Society for Information Science and Technology, 55*, 557–560.

Donald, M. (2001). *A mind so rare*. New York: Norton.

Drabick, D. A. G., Weisberg, R., Paul, L., & Bubier, J. L. (2007). Keeping it short and sweet: Brief, ungraded writing assignments facilitate learning. *Teaching of Psychology, 34*, 172–176.

Ericsson, K. A., & Kintsch, W. (1995). Long-term working memory. *Psychological Review, 102*, 211–245.

Ferretti, R. P., Lewis, W. E., & Andrews-Weckerly, S. (2009). Do goals affect the structure of students' argumentative writing strategies? *Journal of Educational Psychology, 101*, 577–589.

Flower, L., & Hayes, J. R. (1981). A cognitive process theory of writing. *College Composition and Communication, 32*, 365–387.

Galbraith, D., Ford, S., Walker, G., & Ford, J. (2005). The contribution of different components of working memory to knowledge transformation during writing. *L1—Educational Studies in Language and Literature, 5*, 113–145.

Graham, S., MacArthur, C., & Schwartz, S. (1995). Effects of goal setting and procedural facilitation on the revising behavior and writing performance of students with writing and learning problems. *Journal of Educational Psychology, 87*, 230–240.

Graham, S., MacArthur, C., Schwartz, S., & Page-Voth, V. (1992). Improving the compositions of students with learning disabilities using a strategy involving product and process goal setting. *Exceptional Children, 58*, 322–334.

Graham, S., & Perin, D. (2007). A meta-analysis of writing instruction for adolescent students. *Journal of Educational Psychology, 99*, 445–476.

Gentner, D. (2003). Why we're so smart. In D. Gentner & S. Goldin-Meadow (Eds.), *Language in mind: Advances in the study of language and thought* (pp. 195–235). Cambridge, MA: MIT Press.

Gunel, M., Hand, B., & McDermott, M. A. (2009). Writing for different audiences: Effects on high-school students' conceptual understanding of biology. *Learning and Instruction, 19*, 354–367.

Hand, B., Hohenshell, L., & Prain, V. (2007). Examining the effect of multiple writing tasks on year 10 biology students' understandings of cell and molecular biology concepts. *Instructional Science, 35*, 343–373.

Harbusch, K., Itsova, G., Koch, U., & Kuhner, C. (2008). The sentence fairy: A natural-language generation system to support children's essay writing. *Computer Assisted Language Learning, 21*, 339–352.

Hayes, J. R., & Chenoweth, N. A. (2006). Is working memory involved in the transcribing and editing of texts? *Written Communication, 23*, 135–149.

Hayes, J. R., & Flower, L. (1980). Identifying the organization of the writing processes. In L. W. Gregg & E. R. Steinberg (Eds.), *Cognitive processes in writing* (pp. 3–30). Hillsdale, NJ: Erlbaum.

Hayes, J. R., Flower, L. S., Schriver, K. A., Stratman, J., & Carey, L. (1987). Cognitive processes in revision. In S. Rosenberg (Ed.), *Advances in psycholinguistics:* Vol. 2: *Reading, writing and language* (pp. 176–240). Cambridge: Cambridge University Press.

Hillocks, G. (1986). *Research on written composition: New directions for teaching.* Urbana IL: ERIC Clearinghouse and the National Conference on Research in English.

Hutchins, E. (1995). *Cognition in the wild.* Cambridge, MA: MIT Press.

Järvelä, S., & Häkkinen, P. (2002). Web-based cases in teaching and learning—the quality of discussions and a stage of perspective taking in asynchronous communication. *Interactive Learning Environments, 10*, 1–22.

Jaubert, M., & Rebiere, M. (2005). Learning about science through writing. *L1–Educational Studies in Language and Literature, 5*, 315–333.

Jucks, R., Schulte-Löbbert, P., & Bromme, R. (2007). Supporting experts' written knowledge communication through reflective prompts on the use of specialist concepts. *Zeitschrift für Psychologie/Journal of Psychology, 215*, 237–247.

Kellogg, R. T. (1990). Effectiveness of prewriting strategies as a function of task demands. *American Journal of Psychology, 103*, 327–342.

Kellogg, R. T., Olive, T., & Piolat, A. (2007). Verbal, visual, and spatial working memory in written language production. *Acta Psychologica, 124*, 382–397.

Kirkpatrick, L. C., & Klein, P. D. (2009). Planning text structure as a way to improve students' writing from sources in the compare-contrast genre. *Learning and Instruction, 19*, 309–321.

Klein, P. D. (1999). Reopening inquiry into cognitive processes in writing-to-learn. *Educational Psychology Review, 11*, 203–270.

Klein, P. D. (2000). Elementary students' strategies for writing-to-learn in science. *Cognition and Instruction, 18*, 317–348.

Klein, P. D. (2004). Constructing scientific explanations through writing. *Instructional Science, 32*, 191–231.

Klein, P. D., & Kirkpatrick, L. C. (2010). A framework for content area writing: Mediators and moderators. *Journal of Writing Research, 2*, 1–46. Retrieved from http://jowr.org/

Klein, P. D., Piacente-Cimini, S., & Williams, L. A. (2007). The role of writing in learning from analogies. *Learning and Instruction, 17*, 595–611.

Knückles, M., Hübner, S., & Renkl, A. (2009). Enhancing self-regulated learning by writing learning protocols. *Learning and Instruction, 19*, 259–271.

Kobayashi, K. (2009). Comprehension of relations among controversial texts: Effects of external strategy use. *Instructional Science, 37*, 311–324.

Larkin, J. H., & Simon, H. A. (1987). Why a diagram is (sometimes) worth ten thousand words. *Cognitive Science, 11*, 65–99.

Lee, L. (2010). Exploring wiki-mediated collaborative writing: A case study in an elementary Spanish course. *CALICO Journal, 27*, 260–276. Retrieved from https://calico.org/page.php?id=5

MacArthur, C. A. (1999). Word prediction for students with severe spelling problems. *Learning Disability Quarterly, 22*, 158–172.

MacArthur, C. A., & Cavalier, A. R. (2004). Dictation and speech recognition technology as test accommodations. *Exceptional Children, 7*(1), 43–58.

MacArthur, C. A., Schwartz, S., & Graham, S. (1991). Effects of a reciprocal peer revision strategy in special education classrooms. *Learning Disability Research and Practice, 6*, 201–210.

Martin, K. F., & Mano, C. (1995). Use of check-off system to improve middle school students' story compositions. *Journal of Learning Disabilities, 28*, 139–149.

Mason, L. (1998). Sharing cognition to construct scientific knowledge in school context: The role of oral and written discourse. *Instructional Science, 26*, 359–389.

McCutchen, D. (2000). Knowledge, processing, and working memory: Implications for a theory of writing. *Educational Psychologist, 35*, 13–23.

McCutchen, D., Francis, M., & Kerr, S. (1997). Revising for meaning: Effects of knowledge and strategy. *Journal of Educational Psychology, 89*, 667–676.

Midgette, E., Haria, P., & MacArthur, C. (2008). The effects of content and audience awareness goals for revision on the persuasive essays of fifth- and eighth-grade students. *Reading and Writing, 21*, 131–151.

Milian, M. (2005). Reformulation: A means of constructing knowledge in shared writing. *L1—Educational Studies in Language and Literature, 5*, 335–351.

Nelson, M. M., & Schunn, C. D. (2009). The nature of feedback: How different types of peer feedback affect writing performance. *Instructional Science, 37*, 375–401. doi: 10.1007/s11251-008-9053-x

Nelson, N. (2008). The reading-writing nexus in discourse research. In C. Bazerman (Ed.), *Handbook of research on writing: History, society, school, individual, text* (pp. 435–450). New York: Erlbaum.

Newell, A., & Simon, H. A. (1972). *Human problem solving*. Englewood Cliffs, NJ: Prentice-Hall.

Nussbaum, E. M. (2008). Using argumentation vee diagrams (AVDs) for promoting argument-counterargument integration in reflective writing. *Journal of Educational Psychology, 100*, 549–565.

Nystrand, M. (2006). The social and historical context for writing research. In C. A. MacArthur, S. Graham, & J. Fitzgerald (Eds.), *Handbook of writing research* (pp. 11–27). New York: Guilford.

Oatley, K., & Djikic, M. (2008). Writing as thinking. *Review of General Psychology, 12*, 9–27.

Page-Voth, V., & Graham, S. (1999). Effects of goal setting and strategy use on the writing performance efficacy of students with writing and learning problems. *Journal of Educational Psychology, 91*, 230–240.

Pelletier, J., Reeve, R., & Halewood, C. (2006). Young children's knowledge building and literacy development through Knowledge Forum®. *Early Education and Development, 17*, 323–346.

Raskind, M. H., & Higgins, E. (1995). Effects of speech synthesis on the proofreading efficiency of postsecondary students with learning disabilities. *Learning Disability Quarterly, 18*, 141–158.

Re, A. M., Caeran, M., & Cornoldi, C. (2008). Improving expressive writing skills of children rated for ADHD symptoms. *Journal of Learning Disabilities, 41*, 535–544.

Rijlaarsdam, G., Braaksma, M., Couzijn, M., Janssen, T., Raedts, M., Van Steendam, E., Toorenaar, A., & van den Bergh, H. (2008). Observation of peers in learning to write, Practice and research. *Journal of Writing Research, 1*(1), 53–83. Retrieved from http://jowr.org/

Rijlaarsdam, G., Couzijn, M., Janssen, T., Braaksma, M., & Kieft, M. (2006). Writing experiment manuals in science education: The impact of writing, genre, and audience. *International Journal of Science Education, 28*, 203–233.

Rosaen, C. L. (1990). Improving writing opportunities in elementary classrooms. *Elementary School Journal, 90*, 418–434.

Salomon, G. (1993). No distribution without individuals' cognition: A dynamic interactional view. In G. Salmon (Ed.), *Distributed cognitions: Psychological and educational considerations* (pp. 111–138). New York: Cambridge University Press.

Scardamalia, M., & Bereiter, C. (2006). Knowledge building: Theory, pedagogy, and technology. In R. K. Sawyer (Ed.), *The Cambridge handbook of the learning sciences* (pp. 97–115). New York: Cambridge.

Schönpflug, W. (1986). The trade-off between internal and external information sources. *Journal of Memory and Language, 25,* 657–675.

Segev-Miller, R. (2007). Cognitive processes in discourse synthesis: The case of intertextual processing strategies. In M. Torrance, D. Galbraith, & L. Van Waes (Eds.), *Writing and cognition: research and application* (pp. 231–250). Amsterdam: Elsevier.

Spivey, N. N. (1997). *The constructivist metaphor: Writing, reading, and the making of meaning.* San Diego, CA: Academic Press.

Storch, N. (2005). Collaborative writing: Product, process and students' reflections. *Journal of Second Language Writing, 14,* 153–173.

Strømsø, H. I., Bråten, I., & Britt, M. A. (2010). Reading multiple texts about climate change: The relationship between memory for sources and text comprehension. *Learning and Instruction, 20,* 192–204.

Turner, K. H., & Katic, E. K. (2009). The influence of technological literacy on students' writing. *Journal of Educational Computing Research, 41,* 253–270.

Vandenberg, R., & Swanson, H. L. (2007). Which components of working memory are important in the writing process? *Reading and Writing, 20,* 721–752.

van den Bergh, H., & Rijlaarsdam, G. (2007). The dynamics of idea generation during writing: An online study. In G. Rijlaarsdam (Series Ed.) and M. Torrance, L. van Waes, & D. Galbraith (Volume Eds.), *Writing and cognition: Research and applications:* Vol. 20. Studies in writing (pp. 125–150). Amsterdam: Elsevier.

Vincent, J. (2007). Writing and coding: Assisting writers to cross the modes. *Language and Education, 21,* 141–157.

Wallace, D. L., Hayes, J. R., Hatch, J. A., Miller, W., Moser, G., & Silk, C. M. (1996). Better revision in eight minutes? Prompting first-year college writers to revise globally. *Journal of Educational Psychology, 88,* 682–688.

Warschauer, M. (2010). New tools for teaching writing [Invited commentary]. *Language, Learning & Technology, 14*(1), 3–8.

Wigglesworth, G., & Storch, N. (2009). Pair versus individual writing: Effects on fluency, complexity, and accuracy. *Language Testing, 26,* 445–466.

Witte, S. (2007). "That's online writing, not boring school writing": Writing with blogs and the talkback project. *Journal of Adolescent & Adult Literacy, 51*(2), 92–96.

Wright, L. J. (2008). Learning by doing: The objectification of knowledge across semiotic modalities in middle school chemistry lab activities. *Linguistics and Education, 19,* 225–243.

Yarrow, F., & Topping, K. J. (2001). Collaborative writing: The effects of metacognitive prompting and structured peer interaction. *British Journal of Educational Psychology, 71,* 261–282.

Young, R., & Sullivan, P. (1984). Why write? A reconsideration. In R. J. Conners, L. S. Ede, & A. A. Lunsford (Eds.), *Essays on classical rhetoric and modern discourse* (pp. 215–225). Carbondale, IL: Southern Illinois University Press.

Zellermayer, M., Salomon, G., Globerson, T., & Givon, H. (1991). Enhancing writing-related metacognitions through a computerized writing partner. *American Educational Research Journal, 28,* 373–391.

Zhang, J. (1997). The nature of external representations in problem solving. *Cognitive Science: A Multidisciplinary Journal, 21,* 179–217.

Zhang, J., & Norman, D. A. (1994). Representations in distributed cognitive tasks. *Cognitive Science, 18,* 87–122.

Zhang, J., & Norman, D. A. (1995). A representational analysis of numeration systems. *Cognition, 57,* 271–295.

Zhang, J., & Patel, V. L. (2006). Distributed cognition, representation, and affordance. *Pragmatics and Cognition, 14,* 333–341. Retrieved from http://www.benjamins.nl

7

Female Superiority and Gender Similarity Effects and Interest Factors in Writing

CARMEN GELATI

*T*he first part of this chapter is a review of the research on gender differences in writing. After a brief description of the early studies focused on verbal ability, research is presented that has analyzed gender differences in writing. Specific aspects of writing, in particular text quality, mechanical skills, text structure, and the processes of planning, translating, and revising, are described.[1] In the second part of the chapter the relation between gender differences and motivational factors, such as self-efficacy, gender orientation toward writing activity, and interest, are examined. In the final part of the chapter an empirical study is presented that reports new findings about the role of interest and gender in writing.

---

[1] Some researchers have focused on how males and females construct gender identities through their writing, analyzing, for example, gender stereotypes in writing related to characters and themes created by boys and girls. Although this topic is crucial to writing, it is not the aim of this chapter, and, for this reason, is mentioned only briefly here. Children often stereotype the characters in stories, assigning them socially accepted attributes and typical roles from their own culture. Males are competent, dominant, independent, brave, heroic, and have more active roles; females are sensitive, nurturing, dependent, with few occupational roles and more prosocial behaviors (Gray-Schlegel & Gray-Schlegel, 1995; Guzzetti, Peyton Young, Gritsavage, Fyfe, & Hardenbrook, 2002; Ollila, Bullen, & Collis, 1989; Peterson, 2001, 2006; Romatowski & Trepanier-Street, 1987; Trepanier & Romatowski, 1985; Tuck, Bayliss, & Bell, 1985). Moreover, females frequently write stories about their lives, related to home and school experiences; males prefer to write themes that go beyond the home and school and often include violence and crime, as well as dangerous and risky experiences (Gray-Schlegel & Gray-Schlegel, 1995; Kamler, 1994; Peterson, 2000).

GENDER DIFFERENCES IN WRITING

Two questions guided the review of the research on gender differences in writing, on which considerable research has been conducted: (1) Do males and females show different abilities in writing, and (2) if so, in which writing or writing-related abilities do they differ?

Initially, studies on gender differences were focused on verbal ability. Anastasi (1958) found that females are superior in verbal and linguistic functions from infancy to adulthood, and Tyler (1965) reported similar results. In accordance with these studies, Maccoby (1966; Maccoby & Jacklin, 1974) found that, although there are few gender differences in verbal ability from 3 to 11 years, from 11 through to college years girls outperform boys in spelling, punctuation, comprehension, and quick understanding of logical relations expressed in verbal terms. Hyde and Linn (1988) concluded that there are no gender differences in verbal ability, with the exception of speech production in which females are superior. However, in their meta-analysis of 165 studies, only five were about writing, and in four of those five (Applebee, Langer, & Mullis, 1986a; Harris & Siebel, 1976; Ramist & Arbeiter, 1986; Wormack, 1979) females received a higher rating than males. In a more recent review of gender differences in cognitive abilities, Halpern (2004) argued that females achieve better scores in verbal tests and are superior in both fluent speech production and writing.

Text Quality

Strong evidence of gender differences in text quality can be found in national writing proficiency assessments that have been conducted in many countries with thousands of students from elementary grades to high school. Students were asked to write essays that were evaluated holistically, and in these studies text quality scores showed a disparity between genders, favoring girls. In the United States, the National Assessment of Educational Progress (NAEP) monitors academic achievement in writing. Students' essays are evaluated on the basis of their ability to accomplish the specific purpose of the text, according to the conventions of written English. The latest Nation's Report Card, published in 2008, shows that girls in the 8th and 12th grades achieved higher scores in all writing tasks. They wrote better narrative, informative, and persuasive texts, confirming results found from the 1970s to the 1990s that also included elementary students (Applebee, Langer, Jenkins, Mullis, & Foertsch, 1990; Applebee et al., 1986a, 1986b, 1987; Applebee, Langer, Mullis, & Jenkins, 1990; Campbell, Voelkl, & Donahue, 1998). In line with these results, the statewide assessment of writing in Georgia showed that girls outperformed boys in middle and high school (Engelhard, Walker, Gordon, & Gabrielson, 1994). The Graduate Management Admissions Test (GMAT) Analytical Writing Assessment also showed that in three of the four ethnic groups studied (White, African American, and Hispanic/Latino), females outperformed males (Bridgeman & McHale, 1996). The differences between genders found in the United States are consistent with those found in literacy assessment in Canada by the Council of Ministers of Education (CMEC). The Report on Writing Assessment III (SAIP & CME, 2003) showed that girls surpassed boys in writing skills, and this result confirms the findings of surveys administered in the 1990s. Also the assessment of the Saskatchewan Department of Education shows a superiority of females in writing. At elementary, middle, and secondary levels, girls achieve better scores in all writing skills measured: using content, organizing written ideas, writing effective sentences, vocabulary use, and mechanical skill (Gambell & Hunter, 1999, 2000). In Italy, writing has only been assessed by a national survey since 2004. Results there show a significant difference between genders only in high school. However, it is crucial to emphasize that in their evaluations there is no direct measure of writing in the form of an essay. Writing is assessed by multiple-choice questions and by specific exercises, focused on lexicon or sentence construction. In a comparative study conducted in 14 countries, in which writing achievement in different genres was evaluated, girls outperformed boys (Purves, 1992). National writing surveys show that girls write better compositions than boys, and this result is consistent with many research findings. In particular, at elementary school, girls' essays, evaluated holistically by taking into account essential content, referential cohesion, syntactic complexity, lexical richness, and syntactic and orthographic accuracy, received higher scores for text quality than those written by boys (Vetheyden, Van den Branden, Rijlaarsdam, van den Bergh, & De maeyer, 2009). Similarly, Prater and Padia (1983), evaluating texts on a four-point holistic scale, found that girls write better expressive, expository, and persuasive compositions compared with boys. Also at the high school level, females' texts received a higher global score for text quality (Gyagenda & Engelhard, 2009). Of course, these findings do not apply to all individuals, in fact, some girls struggle with writing, some boys achieve excellent results, and, moreover, many of the world's best authors are men.

Female Superiority in Spelling, Grammar, and Sentence Structure

In many studies from elementary to high school, girls outperformed boys in the language skills related to writing. Allred (1990) showed that girls spell better than boys in Grades 1 to 6. In particular, girls are more able to write words correctly and to identify misspelled words. These findings are consistent with those of Maki, Voeten, Vauras, and Poskiparta (2001), who found that in primary school girls achieved better scores for the mechanics of writing (spelling and grammar) as evaluated by spelling tests in the first grade and by errors in a writing task in the second and third grades. Using a confirmatory factor analysis, they found that preschool phonological awareness and visual-motor skills predicted the mechanics of writing in the first and second grades and they concluded that girls' better performance for the mechanics of writing could be explained by their better phonological awareness and visual-motor skills in preschool years.

The competence of middle and high school students in explaining their own ideas through the conventions of written English was also evaluated. Middle school students were asked to write narrative, descriptive, and expository texts, whereas high school students wrote an argumentative text (Engelhard et al., 1994; Gabrielson, Gordon, & Engelhard, 1995). Scores on a 4-point scale were assigned taking into account the ability to write effective sentences (complete sentence, proper use of end punctuation, coordination, and subordination), the use of standard American English (subject–verb agreement, standard form of verbs and pronouns), and the mechanical skills (spelling, punctuation, and capitalization). The results showed that females outperformed males, attaining better scores in all grades and genres. In a study conducted with high school students, Gyagenda and Engelhard (2009) confirmed the superiority of females in writing. In accordance with these findings, Price and Graves (1980) and Roen, Peguesse, and Abordonado (1995) found that narrative and argumentative texts, as well as letters written by girls at middle and high school, adhere more to standard written English compared with boys' texts. Girls achieve better scores in both sentence structure and grammar, and in high school, girls are not only more able to use rules when they write, but they also have a better understanding of the conventions of standard written English, as measured by multiple-choice test items (Doolittle & Welch, 1989).

Female Superiority in Coherence and Text Structure

Some studies that focused on text structure have found that girls write more coherent and organized essays from second grade onward (Maki et al., 2001). A confirmatory factor analysis shows that scores for the mechanics of writing in the first grade predict second-grade text coherence. The authors concluded that girls' better performance for coherence could be explained by their superior performance in the mechanics of writing. In fact, the ability to access letter forms in memory and to produce them automatically may free attentional resources for the higher, and nonautomatic, processes of writing (Graham, Berninger, Abbott, Abbott, & Whitaker, 1997). Kamler (1994), in a longitudinal case study, explored the development of a boy and a girl from kindergarten through to second grade. She found that the girl's texts were rich in description, personal comment, and feelings integrated in the sequence of events. On the contrary, the boy's texts reported a sequence of events with few and unelaborated descriptions, comments, and feelings. Although the majority of the studies have shown that at the elementary school level girls outperform boys, some studies have not found gender differences in cohesion, text structure, and text quality (Cameron et al., 1995; Kamberelis, 1999; Kamberelis & Bovino, 1999).

More detailed studies of text structure have been conducted with middle and high school students (Engelhard et al., 1994; Gabrielson et al., 1995; Gyagenda & Engelhard, 2009). These researchers found that, although the gap between genders is higher for mechanical skills, males and females also achieve different results in their ability to develop, organize, and express ideas. The narrative, descriptive, and expository texts of middle school children and the argumentative texts of high school students were scored on a 4-point scale, using two domains: content or organization and style. The first score measured the ability to find and organize ideas and the second score the ability to control language to establish individuality. At each grade level and for each genre, girls' texts were rated higher for both content or composition and style than those written by boys. In other words, girls wrote more complete narrative, descriptive, expository, and argumentative texts.

They explained and supported their ideas better and elaborated their thoughts logically, often using examples and details to clarify concepts. Girls also showed a greater ability to use clear and descriptive language, easily readable and appropriate to the tone, topic, and purpose of the text. At the high school level they usually write texts that are better organized and more logical and have a richer vocabulary than those written by boys. Moreover, girls write essays that respond better to the task, showing a higher ability to formulate a clear thesis, support it with relevant reasons, and take into account the audience (Doolittle & Welch,1989; Roen et al., 1995).

Gender Differences in Planning, Translating, and Revising

In the cognitive processes of writing—planning, translating, and revising (Hayes & Flower, 1980)—males and females seem to develop a different approach. Based on a questionnaire administered to approximately 36,000 middle and high school students, girls plan, revise, and edit their writing more than boys, showing a more mature and reflective approach when they write (Gambell & Hunter, 2000). In order to understand better how beginner writers learn to translate ideas into written language, Berninger et al. (1992) investigated two processes involved in the translating process described in Hayes and Flower's model (1980): text generation (ideas are mapped into units of language in verbal working memory at the word-, sentence-, and text-levels) and transcription (language representations in verbal working memory are translated into orthographic symbols of letters and written spellings on paper or computer). Berninger, Whitaker, Feng, Swanson, and Abbott (1996) analyzed gender differences in the writing processes of seventh, eighth, and ninth graders. Although girls outperformed boys on many dimensions of writing, when compositional fluency (number of words produced within time limits) was used as a covariate, gender differences disappeared. Considering that earlier work in Grades 1 to 6 showed a robust relation between automatic legible alphabet letter writing and compositional fluency (and also between spelling and compositional fluency) (Graham et al., 1997), males and females appear to differ more in transcription skills (handwriting and spelling) rather than text generation. The authors concluded that boys may have the same potential for composing as girls; however, they may not achieve the same performance in school work because of problems in transcribing ideas, in particular in the earlier steps of learning to write. Berninger and Fuller (1992) found that in the first, second, and third grades, girls outperformed boys in the number of letters in alphabetic order produced correctly in the first 15 seconds, the number of words on timed text writing (compositional fluency), and the number of clauses produced in a narrative and an expository text.

In keeping with these findings, other studies have shown that females are often more fluent than males (Jewell & Malecki, 2005; Malecki & Jewell, 2003). In these studies girls at elementary and middle school levels achieved better scores in all the production-dependent measures of curriculum-based measurement (total words written, words spelled correctly, and correct writing sequences).

CAUSES OF DIFFERENCES IN WRITING BETWEEN GENDERS

As many studies reviewed in this chapter have shown, females outperform males in writing from elementary to the high school level. These findings have led researchers to investigate the reasons for such differences. Some researchers have hypothesized that gender differences in writing could be explained by biases in assessment, others have argued that genetic or biological factors play an important role. Other researchers have focused on the differences in cognitive processes of males and females, and many studies have concentrated on the close connection between the lower performance of males and motivation to write, that is, self-efficacy, gender orientation toward the activity of writing, and the role of interest in writing.

Bias in Assessment

Some studies have theorized that gender differences in writing may be due, in part, to bias in assessment rather than to actual differences between boys and girls. Evidence of evaluative bias in assessing students' essays is found in Peterson's studies (1998, 2006; Peterson & Kennedy, 2006). Teachers' evaluation was often influenced by their perception of the writer's gender. In particular, teachers scored a text higher when they thought the writer was a girl and lower when they thought the writer was a boy (Peterson, 1998). Teachers also made more corrections, criticisms, and suggestions for writing attributed to boys (Peterson, 2006; Peterson & Kennedy, 2006). Rater effect was also found by Gyagenda and Engelhard (2009). However, the gender of students still has a significant effect on writing quality after controlling for rater effect. This result seems to show that, although evaluative biases related to gender could bias writing assessment, attributing all gender differences to assessment bias is too restrictive. There are also consistent and similar findings that show and support the better writing performance of girls (Gambell & Hunter, 1999).

Biological Explanations

Some studies have hypothesized that differences in boys' and girls' writing achievement could be caused by genetic or biological differences; however, the results regarding this topic are still being investigated. Marosi et al. (1997), in a follow-up study of electroencephalogram coherences, which included normal participants and children with mild and serious reading–writing problems, did not find different maturation by gender. Skarbrevik's (2002) study seems to support the hypothesis of biological differences between the genders. He observed that in kindergarten and at upper secondary school levels, 65% of the children deemed in need of special education were boys and this percentage increased to about 70% in elementary and middle school. He concluded that in kindergarten, the higher incidence of boys in need of special education must be attributed to genetic or biological differences between genders, whereas during the school years, it could be attributed to an interaction between genetic or biological factors and the school system that seems to match better the girls' style than the educational needs of boys. Richards et al. (2009) found gender differences only in the left superior parietal area on a functional magnetic resonance finger sequencing task, after effects for motor output were removed, and brain activation in this region was related to handwriting and spelling.

Cognitive Processes

Females more often obtain college degrees, achieve higher grades in school, and better scores in writing, whereas males score better in mathematical, scientific, and visuospatial tests. Based on these different academic achievements of females and males, Halpern (1997, 2004) suggested that gender differences could be understood by analyzing the difference in cognitive processes. She found that females score higher in tasks that require rapid access to phonological, semantic, and episodic information in long-term memory, and males score higher in tasks that require transformations in visuospatial working memory. However, other studies have not found great gender differences in cognitive ability (Hyde, 1996; Rosèn, 1995). Lorna and Adams (2009), using a working memory battery that assessed verbal fluency and phonological and integrated memory capabilities, did not find any differences in the cognitive resources available for writing tasks. Like many other researchers (e.g., Maki et al., 2001; Pajares, Valiante, & Cheong, 2007), they suggested analyzing motivational and sociocultural aspects related to writing in order to understand the gender differences in writing.

MOTIVATIONAL VARIABLES

Motivation and Self-Efficacy

Studies focused on motivation and writing have shown a positive correlation between writing self-efficacy and performance and have found that writing self-efficacy predicts text quality (Pajares & Valiante, 1999, 2006). Consequently, girls' better performance in writing could be explained by their higher sense of efficacy in academic activities (Pastorelli et al., 2001). However, studies of writing self-efficacy are controversial (Pajares & Valiante, 2006). Shell, Colvin, and Bruning (1995) did not find any gender differences, but, as Klassen (2002) showed, other studies have found opposing results. Pajares and Valiante (1999) found no gender differences in writing self-efficacy for middle school students, even if girls believed they were better writers than their boy peers. As the authors asserted, it is possible that boys and girls use different approaches when they respond to the self-efficacy scale. Different findings also have emerged in more recent studies (e.g., Pajares et al., 2007; Pajares, Johnson, & Usher, 2007).

Gender-Orientation Beliefs

As Pajares et al. (2007) found, girls at elementary, middle, and high school levels report stronger writing self-efficacy. However, after controlling for gender orientation beliefs (students' stereotypic beliefs about gender), the difference in writing self-efficacy between boys and girls disappeared. This result seems to show that gender differences in writing self-efficacy may be, in part, a function of gender orientation and stereotypic beliefs rather than gender per se. The activity of writing may be associated with a feminine orientation during formal schooling because it is considered a female domain (Knudson, 1993a, 1993b; Pajares et al., 2007), but not during the adult years when many professional writers in the world of work are men. This cultural stereotype during the school years is reflected in parents', teachers', and peers' expectations. Children in Grades 2, 4, 6, and 8 and teachers in Grades 4 and 8 consider females to be better writers (Peterson, 2000; Pottoroff, Phelps-Zientarski, & Skovera, 1996). This expectation influences students' performance (Rosenthal & Jacobson, 1968) and attitudes. Millard (1997) suggested that girls' writing is more typical of the literary canon than that of boys; she presented boys as "differently literate." Girls' writing style seems to match better the expectations of teachers and, in general, the school system.

Consistent results about the more positive attitudes toward writing of girls, compared with boys, are found in the literature. Girls begin school with a higher perception of their language arts abilities (Meece, Glienke, & Burg, 2006), and from Grades 3 to 12, girls are more interested in writing, like writing more, place a higher value on writing, write more in their free time, and are more open to a career that requires the daily use of writing (Hendley, Parkinson, Stables, & Tanner, 1995; Knudson 1993a, 1993b; Meece, Glienke, & Askew, 2009). On the contrary, males experience failure and frustration more often when they write. As a consequence, they often feel themselves to be less competent than girls, are less motivated to write, and express negative writing attitudes. Compared with females, males show dissatisfaction with writing, less writing enjoyment, and place less usefulness and value on writing (Hansen, 2001; Hendley et al., 1995; Knudson, 1993a, 1993b).

How can we motivate boys (and girls) to write? As Merisuo-Storm (2006) asserted, it may be useful to select writing tasks with a meaningful purpose and a communicative function. Attractive writing tasks, as well as the writing environment, play an important role in motivating students to write (Boscolo & Gelati, 2008). For these reasons the role of interest in writing could be crucial, but is interest related to gender?

Interest

Hidi (2000) defined interest as a motivational aspect and a psychological state of writing characterized by increased attention, concentration, and affect. Hidi, Renninger, and Krapp (2004) pointed out that interest may positively influence cognitive performance. When individuals are interested in an activity, they pay more attention to a task, spend more time on it, and they enjoy themselves more than those less interested in the task (Ainley, Hidi, & Berndorff, 2002). From these studies a basic distinction emerged between situational and individual interest. Situational interest is generated by particular conditions because of their novelty and is usually transitory. Individual interest is a relatively enduring disposition to attend to events and objects, as well as to re-engage in activities.

In order to analyze how an interesting topic could influence writing performance, elementary and middle school students were asked to write a text on a topic rated as either highly interesting or not very interesting (Hidi & McLaren, 1990, 1991). Findings show that text quality was more related to the level of knowledge about the topic than to the interest in the topic itself. Although an interesting topic may increase cognitive effort, information searching, inferences drawn, and quality of ideas expressed, it cannot overcome lack of knowledge (Hidi & McLaren, 1990, 1991). Deep knowledge of the topic helps the writer retrieve information from long-term memory, positively affecting the ideas expressed (McCutchen, 1986). Benton, Corkill, Sharp, Downey, and Khramtsova (1995) found that not only knowledge of a topic, but also interest in it, influences writing performance. Ninth graders and undergraduate college students were asked to write a story about baseball. Both knowledge of, and interest in, the topic were measured. Results show that knowledge and interest influence the planning process and writing performance, that is, logical and well-organized text with content-relevant information. Albin, Benton, and Khramtsova (1996) verified how interest is related to writing, when knowledge is controlled. The findings indicate that interest influences writing, at least in producing topic-relevant ideas. Topic interest could be a good starting point for motivating children to write. In fact, pupils find that activities connected to their interests are meaningful (Merisuo-Storm, 2006).

In synthesis, topic interest may increase motivation to write and influence writing activity by improving the quality of ideas and facilitating the planning process. However, it does not necessarily improve text quality, which seems to be more affected by topic knowledge. In research with elementary and middle school students focused on an experience particularly interesting for both genders, interest positively affected writing of personal accounts. Independently of gender, students focused on events that were more interesting to them and used personal considerations, emotions, and evaluative terms to emphasize these events (Boscolo & Gelati, 2003). But what happens when boys and girls are differently interested? Does interest affect boys' and girls' writing?

NEW RESEARCH STUDY ON GENDER AND INTEREST IN WRITING

Using the results of these past studies as a starting point, I conducted research with the aim of analyzing the complex relation between writing, interest, and gender-related differences. Some of the findings of this complex research study are reported in this chapter. In the research, two events were planned to provide contrasting kinds of experience: one specifically relevant to boys (soccer), and one for girls (dance). All participants took part in both experiences and wrote a personal account of both events. Experiencing two events with different levels of interest for boys and girls, and analyzing personal accounts of these events, made it possible to verify if there are gender-related differences, and if so, how interest affects writing.

The study was based on writing personal accounts, a genre in which the writer narrates events he or she has experienced. This specific genre was chosen for two reasons:

1. The personal account is a particularly attractive genre because it gives children the opportunity to write about events that are important to them. Moreover, it allows students to express their feelings and points of view (Labov, 1972) or, using Elbow's (1981) term, their "voice." Voice has been defined as "the writer coming through the word ... the heart and soul of the writing, the magic, the wit, the feeling. ... When the writer is engaged personally with the topic, he/she imparts a personal tone and flavor to the piece that is unmistakably his/hers alone" (Northwest Regional Educational Laboratory, 2000, para. 4).
2. Compared with the expository texts used by Hidi and McLaren (1990, 1991), when writing personal accounts, the "weight" of knowledge is downsized. In fact, the writer has to narrate an event in which he or she was personally involved and which, therefore, is well known to the writer.

The personal account involves two components of the narration: the referential and the evaluative (Labov, 1972; Labov & Waletzky, 1967). The referential component includes describing events in a temporal order as well as information about the external and physical circumstances in which the events took place. The evaluative component includes information about the narrator's subjective state and personal interpretation of events. The narrator uses evaluation strategies to highlight the value and importance of what he or she is narrating. By emphasizing some elements and understating others, the narrator stresses what is most relevant and presents his or her own view of the events (Labov, 1972; Labov & Waletzky, 1967). Labov (1972) argued that a good personal account consists of the following narrative functions:

- *Abstract*—a summary of the narration in which the focus of the situation is described
- *Orientation*—a description of the initial situation, the people involved, and the time and place of the events narrated
- *Complicating action*—the focus of the narration, that is, the crucial event from which the sequence of facts follows
- *Resolution*—an explanation of how the events concluded
- *Coda*—a signal that indicates the end of the narration and connects the narration to the present
- *Evaluation*—the narrator's emphasis on some aspects of the narration

Evaluation is the most important function described by Labov (1972), and it is through the evaluation strategies that the narrator makes the narration more personal. By emphasizing some elements and understating others, the narrator stresses what is most relevant and presents his or her own view of the events. Unlike the other functions, evaluation has no fixed position in the text. It includes a variety of strategies: (a) *external evaluation*: the narrator makes comments or considerations that may interrupt the narrative flow; (b) *embedding of evaluation*: the narrator reports an evaluation, as it was expressed at the moment of the event being narrated; (c) *evaluative actions*: a protagonist action is stressed; and (d) *suspension of the action*: the narrator stops at a specific point in order to capture the listener's attention and thus put more emphasis on the following narrative. Although Labov's model was applied to oral narrations, it has also proved useful for writing personal accounts (Boscolo & Gelati, 2003; Gelati & Boscolo, 2009).

Method: Preliminary Phase to Validate Gender-Specific Interests

To identify the topics boys and girls would find more interesting, third, fifth, and seventh graders not involved in the study answered some open-ended questions explaining which topics they found interesting and uninteresting and which topics would be interesting to write about. The results showed that soccer and videogames were more interesting for boys, whereas girls were more interested in dance and volleyball. On the basis of these results, a questionnaire with 16 items on a 5-point scale related to interesting topic for boys, girls, and neutral was administered to 114 students not involved in the study. A MANOVA was carried out using the items as dependent variables. Findings showed that soccer was the more interesting topic for boys at each grade level and the least interesting for girls, $F(1, 108) = 65.88$, $p < .001$, $\eta^2_p = .38$, whereas dance was the more interesting topic for girls and less interesting for boys, $F(1, 108) = 92.70$, $p < .001$, $\eta^2_p = .46$. At the same time, soccer was the topic on which boys were more interested in writing, $F(1, 108) = 46.29$, $p < .001$, $\eta^2_p = .30$, and dance was the topic on which girls were more interested in writing, $F(1, 108) = 70.98$, $p < .001$, $\eta^2_p = .40$. Individual differences within gender emerged; however, very few boys were not interested in soccer, and a few girls were not interested in dance.

Method: Participants

One hundred and ninety-one students in a northern Italian town participated in the study: 71 third graders (M = 33, F = 38), 59 fifth graders (M = 32, F = 27), and 61 seventh graders (M = 32, F = 29).

Method: Procedures and Measures for Experiences at School and Writing Personal Accounts

Before the experience of soccer and dance, children were asked to write a personal experience about something they had done that was very satisfying (pretest). They then completed individual interest questionnaires for each topic (soccer and dance) with nine items on a 5-point scale. Experiences of soccer and dance were then organized at each grade level. All students participated in both experiences and wrote the related personal account. Experiences of soccer and dance lasted the same number of hours and activities, for a total of 20 hours for each of the 12 classes participating in the study. In the first part of each experience, children collaborated with their peers in organizing a football match (choice of the team name, identification of the role played by each participant, putting together the football kit) and a dance (watching a song video, practice, creating the costumes). In the second part, the football match was played and the dance performed.

After the experience children were asked to write about the events related to the experience of soccer and dance. In addition, they completed the situational interest questionnaires. For each topic (soccer and dance) a questionnaire with four items on a 5-point scale was administered to participants. Finally, they responded to one item on a 5-point scale for each personal account to explain the degree of their interest in writing about the soccer and dance events experienced at school.

Method: Data Analysis

Length (T-units), text quality (holistic scoring), correctness (ratio between errors and T-units), completeness (ratio between relevant written events and the total number of relevant events experienced), evaluation strategies, and narrative functions (Labov, 1972) were analyzed.

Results: Preliminary Phase[2]

A significant interaction between gender and topic emerged, $F(1, 185) = 85.24$, $p < .01$, $\eta^2_p = .31$, in an ANOVA with *individual interest* as a dependent variable. In the preliminary phase, soccer was the more interesting topic for boys and dance for girls. For an ANOVA with *situational interest* as a dependent variable, a significant interaction between gender and experience emerged, $F(1, 185) = 63.05$, $p < .01$, $\eta^2_p = .25$. As expected, the experience of soccer was the most interesting for boys and dance was the most interesting for girls. A significant interaction between gender and experience emerged, $F(1, 184) = 23.95$, $p < .01$, $\eta^2 p = .11$, in an ANCOVA with *interest in writing about the soccer and dance experiences* as a dependent variable and interest in narrative writing in general as the covariate. Boys were more interested in writing texts about soccer and girls about dance. *Independent of gender, an increase in interest in writing was observed when children wrote a text on their preferred topic and experience* (Figure 7.1). Interest in writing was related to both interest in the topic (individual interest: soccer, Pearson's $r = .217$, $p < .01$; dance, $r = .279$, $p < .01$) and, especially, to interest in the event experienced (situational interest: soccer, Pearson's $r = .330$, $p < .01$; dance, $r = .535$, $p < .01$).[3]

Results: Written Personal Account: Pretest[4]

For *length and text quality*, a MANOVA with text length and text quality as dependent variables showed that girls wrote better texts than boys, $F(1, 185) = 7.31$,

---

[2] The statistical analyses presented in the chapter were applied to all participants. The same analyses were carried out without boys interested in dance and girls interested in soccer. As expected, because very few boys were interested in dance and girls in soccer, the same results emerged.

[3] Because the variable "Interest in narrative writing" was measured by 1 item only, nonparametric tests were also applied (Mann-Whitney and Spearman's Rho). Results were confirmed.

[4] Bonferroni's correction was applied to all multivariate analyses of variance.

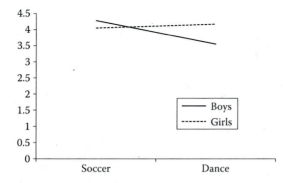

Figure 7.1   Interest in writing personal accounts.

$p < .01$, $\eta^2_p = .04$. An ANOVA with *correctness* as a dependent variable showed that girls wrote texts with fewer errors, $F(1, 185) = 4.66$, $p < .05$, $\eta^2_p = .02$. An ANCOVA with the *total number of evaluation strategies* as a dependent variable and text length as a covariate showed that girls used more evaluative strategies than boys, $F(1, 184) = 4.08$, $p < .05$, $\eta^2_p = .02$. To summarize the pretest results, in a typical and usual writing task in which students are asked to narrate a personal experience, girls outperformed boys; they wrote better and more correct texts, which were enriched with more evaluative strategies.

Results: Written Personal Accounts After Experience With Soccer and Dance

A MANCOVA with text length, completeness, and text quality as dependent variables and text length and text quality of the pretest as covariates was carried out. For *completeness*, a significant interaction between gender and experience emerged, $F(1, 183) = 14.58$, $p < .001$, $\eta^2_p = .07$. Males wrote more relevant information when they narrated the experience of the football game, and girls when they explained the experience of dance (Figure 7.2). A qualitative analysis showed that boys in the fifth and seventh grades wrote many important and

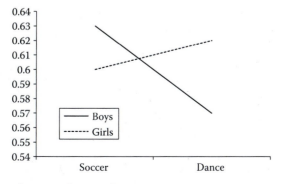

Figure 7.2   Completeness of personal accounts.

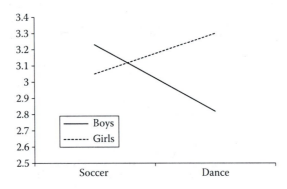

Figure 7.3   Text quality of personal accounts.

crucial details of the football match, describing in greater depth many events. On the contrary, they described the dance experience superficially. The opposite tendency was observed in girls' texts.

For *text quality*, a significant interaction between gender and experience emerged, $F(1, 183) = 31.93$, $p < .001$, $\eta^2_p = .15$. Independently of gender, interest had positive effects on text quality. Boys and girls wrote better texts when they narrated the events they found more interesting, that is, the events of soccer and dance, respectively (Figure 7.3).

In an ANCOVA, with evaluation strategies as a dependent variable and evaluation strategies of the pretest and length of texts (soccer/dance) as covariates, a significant interaction between gender and experience emerged, $F(1, 182) = 14.34$, $p < .01$, $\eta^2_p = .07$. Independent of gender, children used more evaluation strategies when they narrated the events they found more interesting (Figure 7.4), using evaluative lexicon in particular, $F(1, 182) = 22.05$, $p < .001$, $\eta^2_p = .11$.

For *narrative functions*, no gender differences occurred between boys' and girls' ability to write a coherent text. In fact, independent of topic, both males and females wrote well-structured texts with an orientation, important event, and a conclusion. In summary, the findings showed that interest affects writing a personal account. In fact, boys and girls wrote better and more complete texts, with more evaluative strategies, when they narrated the experience they found more interesting.

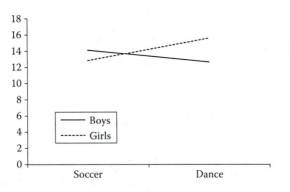

Figure 7.4   Evaluation strategies of personal accounts.

DISCUSSION

In the first part of this chapter, differences between the writing of boys and girls were discussed. The findings of most of the studies showed that females write better than males, although there is less agreement about the causes of gender differences. However, as discussed in the second part of this chapter, the importance of motivational aspects of gender differences in writing is currently being emphasized by many studies (e.g., Maki et al., 2001; Pajares et al., 2007). The relation between writing, gender differences, and interest was also presented in this chapter. To analyze if and, if so, how interest or gender-related interest may affect writing, I conducted an experiment in which children experienced two events with different levels of interest for boys and girls, analyzed the resulting personal accounts, and compared the results with scores achieved in a normal writing task (the personal account written in the pretest).

Gender Differences in Normal Writing Tasks

Analysis of a normal writing task, not "marked" in a feminine or masculine way (the pretest), showed that girls at elementary and middle school levels achieve better scores in both mechanics and higher writing skills. In fact, they wrote texts with fewer errors and higher quality. These results are consistent with the findings of many other researchers (e.g., Applebee et al., 1990; Gyagenda & Engelhard, 2009). It also seems that girls are more inclined to express their voice in writing personal accounts. An analysis of the evaluative component of the narrations, which other researchers have not carried out, showed that girls expressed their personal perspective, using evaluative strategies more than boys.

Interest and Gender Differences

Although the role of interest in writing has been analyzed by previous researchers (e.g., Albin et al., 1996; Benton et al., 1995; Hidi & McLaren, 1990, 1991), the relation between interest and gender differences in writing has not been considered. In the study reported in this chapter, the focus of analysis was on whether interest affects specific aspects of writing, and in particular text coherence, completeness, text quality, and the use of evaluation strategies (Labov, 1972). Findings revealed that interest does not influence text coherence in a gender-specific way. In fact, females' and males' texts, regardless of personal experiences provided, were well constructed. Boys and girls, in both the soccer and dance texts, started with an orientation in which the initial situation, the people involved, and the time and place were described. They then explained the most relevant activities and ended the narration with a conclusion.

However, interest seemed to influence other important aspects of writing that improved the writing performance. In fact, both boys and girls wrote more complete texts, which were enriched with more evaluative strategies and of a higher quality, when they wrote about an experience in which they were more interested, that is, soccer or dance, respectively. As a consequence, an increase in the gap between boys' and girls' performances was observed when narrating the experience girls found more interesting (dance), but a decrease in the gap emerged when pupils wrote about the events more interesting to boys (soccer).

As Benton et al. (1995; see also Albin et al., 1996) concluded, interest influences the planning process in writing, helping students to write logical and well-organized texts, with content-relevant information and ideas. The present study shows that interest influences the content of the narration; both boys and girls, when narrating the experience that was more interesting to them, wrote more relevant information and specified the events better, using greater detail, and more evaluative strategies to emphasize some events. Although a tendency to use emotions, comments, and personal considerations was observed, pupils adopted a rich, expressive, and vivid lexicon. Being interested in an event could help children write more relevant information and details because interest increases attention, concentration, and cognitive effort (Ainley et al., 2002) and influences the selection of information (Benton et al., 1995; Boscolo & Gelati, 2003). It is plausible that pupils chose to write what was relevant to them and, as Labov (1972) asserted, deserves to be reported. The complete and rich content, as well as the evaluative strategies, probably influenced text quality. In fact, writing a personal account with good and relevant ideas, enriched with feelings and points of view, made the narrative more informative, personal, and pleasing to read.

Hidi and McLaren's (1990, 1991) studies showed that, although an interesting topic may increase cognitive effort, information searching, inferencing, and idea quality, it does not necessarily improve text quality, which is more affected by knowledge. In fact, a deep knowledge of the topic may enhance information retrieval from the long-term memory during text construction (McCutchen, 1986). Two considerations are relevant when Hidi and McLaren's results are integrated with the findings of the current study. The first consideration is that, on the one hand, when writing personal accounts, the effect of knowledge is downsized because the writer narrates an event he or she has experienced and, therefore, knows. On the other hand, when asked to write an expository text, as outlined by Hidi and McLaren, having little knowledge of the topic means having nothing to express. The relation between writing and interest is complex and may also depend on genre, but differences between the findings of Hidi and McLaren and the current study may be related not only to differences between expository and personal account genres. The second important consideration is that the expository text was written as an academic task. Children were asked to write a text about a potentially interesting topic, but quite unrelated to any activity. Instead, writing a personal account related to events in which students participated enthusiastically was an occasion for reflecting on and reconstructing an enjoyable experience.

Findings show that interest in writing personal accounts could change on the basis of the topic. Independent of gender, an increase in interest in writing was observed when children wrote a text on the topic and experience they found more interesting. The interest in writing was related to both interest in the topic (individual interest) and, in particular, interest in the event experienced (situational interest).

This distinction and the differential results are important. Writing is a complex and demanding activity and often, during the school years, the will to write decreases or disappears as a function of interest and experience and not just prior knowledge; and this attitude may be difficult to change (Boscolo & Gelati, 2007). Males in particular develop negative attitudes, showing dissatisfaction with writing and less enjoyment (Hansen, 2001). Because some researchers argued that boys' poorer writing could be explained by a negative attitude toward writing (e.g., Knudson, 1993a, 1993b), it is important to try to modify this stance. Obviously, the results of the current study do not guarantee that engaging children in an interesting activity is enough to change their writing attitudes. However, although teachers cannot always create attractive and enjoyable experiences for the purpose of writing assignments, they should consider modifying, when they can, the context in which writing takes place so that students experience interesting and enjoyable events to write about.

Clearly, gender differences in writing may be only partially explained by the degree of interest in a topic or experience. As many studies have shown, they can be attributed to other factors such as transcription as well, at least early in schooling. The reasons behind the female superiority in writing deserve further research and instructional attention. A number of factors may be involved in gender differences in writing, ranging from the biological, social, and motivational to instructional factors (Gyagenda & Engelhard, 2009; Rosèn, 1995).

SUMMARY AND CONCLUSIONS

Understanding why in general boys have trouble with writing and girls achieve better in writing could help psychologists and teachers organize the curriculum and classroom practices with the primary goal of not just leveling boys' and girls' performances, but of changing negative attitudes toward writing and improving the abilities of both genders. Although boys usually achieve lower scores in writing and are more reluctant writers, some girls also struggle and some boys excel in writing. More studies are needed in order to understand all the factors and their interactions that could influence gender-related differences in writing and improve the writing ability of both boys and girls.

ACKNOWLEDGMENTS

I am infinitely grateful to Pietro Boscolo, who has guided and supervised my professional training for many years, enriching me with his invaluable precepts and suggestions.

REFERENCES

Ainley, M., Hidi, S., & Berndorff, D. (2002). Interest, learning, and the psychological processes that mediate their relationship. *Journal of Educational Psychology, 94,* 545–561.

Albin, M. L., Benton, S. L., & Khramtsova, I. (1996). Individual differences in interest and narrative writing. *Contemporary Educational Psychology, 21,* 305–324.

Allred, R. A. (1990). Gender differences in spelling achievement in grades 1 through 6. *Journal of Educational Research, 83*(4), 187–193.

Anastasi, A. (1958). *Differential psychology*. New York: Macmillan.

Applebee, A. N., Langer, J. A., Jenkins, L. B., Mullis, I., & Foertsch, M. A. (1990). *Learning to write in our nation's schools: Instruction and achievement in 1988 at grades 4, 8, and 12*. Princeton, NJ: Educational Testing Service.

Applebee, A. N., Langer, J. A., & Mullis, I. (1986a). *The writing report card: Writing achievement in American schools*. Princeton, NJ: Educational Testing Service.

Applebee, A. N., Langer, J. A., & Mullis, I. (1986b). *Writing: Trends across the decade, 1974–84*. Princeton, NJ: Educational Testing Service.

Applebee, A. N., Langer, J. A., & Mullis, I. (1987). *Grammar, punctuation and spelling: Controlling the conventions of written English at ages 9, 13, and 17*. Princeton, NJ: Educational Testing Service.

Applebee, A. N., Langer, J. A., Mullis, I., & Jenkins, L. B. (1990). *The writing report card, 1984–88: Findings from the nation's report card*. Princeton, NJ: Educational Testing Service.

Benton, S. L., Corkill, A. J., Sharp, J. M., Downey, R. G., & Khramtsova, I. (1995). Knowledge, interest, and narrative writing. *Journal of Educational Psychology, 87,* 66–79.

Berninger, V. W., & Fuller, F. (1992). Gender differences in orthographic, verbal, and compositional fluency: Implications for assessing writing disabilities in primary grade children. *Journal of School Psychology, 30,* 363–382.

Berninger, V., Whitaker, D., Feng, Y., Swanson, H. L., & Abbott, R. D. (1996). Assessment of planning, translating, and revising in junior high writers. *Journal of School Psychology, 34,* 23–52.

Berninger, V., Yates, C., Cartwright, A., Rutberg, J., Remy, E., & Abbott, R. (1992). Lower-level developmental skills in beginning writing. *Reading and Writing, 4,* 257–280.

Boscolo, P., & Gelati, C. (2003). Lo sviluppo della competenza narrativa scritta: la cronaca [The development of narrative writing: the personal account]. In M. C. Usai & M. Zanobini (Eds.), *Psicologia del ciclo di vita. Scritti in onore di Maria Teresa Bozzo* (pp. 207–226). Milano: Franco Angeli.

Boscolo, P., & Gelati, C. (2007). Best practices in promoting motivation for writing. In S. Graham, C. A. MacArthur, & J. Fitzgerald (Eds.), *Best practice in writing instruction* (pp. 202–221). New York: Guilford.

Boscolo, P., & Gelati, C. (2008). Motivating reluctant students to write: Suggestions and caveats. *Insights on Learning Disabilities, 5*(2), 61–74.

Bridgeman, B., & McHale, F. (1996). Gender and ethnic group differences on the GMAT analytical writing assessment. Princeton, NJ: Educational Testing Service.

Cameron, C. A., Lee, K., Webster, S., Munro, K., Hunt, A. K., & Linton, M. J. (1995). Text cohesion in children's narrative writing. *Applied Psycholinguistics, 16,* 257–269.

Campbell, J. R., Voelkl, K. E., & Donahue, P. L. (1998). Report in brief. NAEP 1996 trends in academic progress. Achievement of US students in science, 1969 to 1996, mathematics, 1973 to 1996, reading, 1971 to 1996, writing, 1984 to 1996. Princeton, NJ: Educational Testing Service.

Doolittle, A., & Welch, C. (1989, March). *Gender differences in performance on a college-level achievement test*. Paper presented at the AERA Annual Meeting, San Francisco.

Elbow, P. (1981). *Writing with power: Techniques for mastering the writing process*. New York: Oxford University Press.

Engelhard, G., Walker, E. V. S., Gordon, B., & Gabrielson, S. (1994). Writing tasks and gender: Influences on writing quality of black and white students. *Journal of Educational Research, 87,* 197–209.

Gabrielson, S., Gordon, B., & Engelhard, G. (1995). The effects of task choice on the quality of writing obtained in a statewide assessment. *Applied Measurement in Education, 8*(4), 273–290.

Gambell, T., & Hunter, D. (1999). Rethinking gender differences in literacy. *Canadian Journal of Education, 24*, 1–16.

Gambell, T., & Hunter, D. (2000). Surveying gender differences in Canadian school literacy. *Journal of Curriculum Studies, 32*, 689–719.

Gelati, C., & Boscolo, P. (2009). Improving the quality of primary school children's narration of personal events: An intervention study on the use of evaluation strategies. *L1—Educational Studies in Language and Literature, 9*(3), 1–28.

Graham, S., Berninger, V., Abbott, R. D., Abbott, S. P., & Whitaker, D. (1997). Role of mechanics in composing of elementary school students: a new methodological approach. *Journal of Educational Psychology, 89*, 170–182.

Gray-Schlegel, M. A., & Gray-Schlegel, T. (1995). An investigation of gender stereotypes as revealed through children's creative writing. *Reading Research and Instruction, 35*, 160–170.

Guzzetti, B., Peyton Young, J., Gritsavage, M. M., Fyfe, L. M., & Hardenbrook, M. (2002). *Reading, writing, and talking gender in literacy learning.* Newark, DE: International Reading Association.

Gyagenda, I. S., & Engelhard, G. (2009). Using classical and modern measurement theories to explore rater, domain, and gender influences on students writing ability. *Journal of Applied Measurement, 10*(3), 225–246.

Halpern, D. F. (1997). Sex differences in intelligence. *American Psychologist, 52*, 1091–1102.

Halpern, D. F. (2004). A cognitive-process taxonomy for sex differences in cognitive abilities. *Current Directions in Psychological Science, 13*(4), 135–139.

Hansen, S. (2001, July). *Boys and writing: Reluctance? Reticence? Or rebellion?* Paper presented at the Annual Meeting of the Education Research Network, Spetses, Greece.

Harris, M. B., & Siebel, C. E. (1976). Effects of sex, occupation, and confidence of model and sex and grade of subject on imitation of language behaviors. *Developmental Psychology, 12*(1), 89–90.

Hayes, J. R., & Flower, L. S. (1980). Identifying the organization of writing processes. In L. W. Gregg & E. R. Steinberg (Eds.), *Cognitive processes in writing* (pp. 3–30). Hillsdale, NJ: Erlbaum.

Hendley, D., Parkinson, J., Stables, A., & Tanner, H. (1995). Gender differences in pupil attitudes to the national curriculum foundation subjects of English, mathematics, science and technology in key stage 3 in South Wales. *Educational Studies, 21*, 85–97.

Hidi, S. (2000). An interest researcher's perspective: The effects of extrinsic and intrinsic factors on motivation. In C. Sansone & J. M. Harackiewicz (Eds.), *Intrinsic and extrinsic motivation* (pp. 309–339). San Diego, CA: Academic Press.

Hidi, S., & McLaren, J. (1990). The effect of topic and theme interestingness on the production of school expositions. In H. Mandl, E. De Corte, N. Bennett, & H. F. Friedrich (Eds.), *Learning and instruction: European research in an international context* (pp. 295–308). Oxford: Pergamon.

Hidi, S., & McLaren, J. (1991). Motivational factors and writing: The role of topic interestingness. *European Journal of Psychology of Education, 6*, 187–197.

Hidi, S., Renninger, K. A., & Krapp, A. (2004). Interest, a motivational variable that combines affective and cognitive functioning. In D. Y. Dai & R. J. Sternberg (Eds.), *Motivation, emotion, and cognition: Integrative perspectives on intellectual functioning and development* (pp. 89–115). Mahwah, NJ: Erlbaum.

Hyde, J. S. (1996). Gender and cognition: A commentary on current research. *Learning and Individual Differences, 8*(1), 33–38.

Hyde, J. S., & Linn, M. C. (1988). Gender differences in verbal ability: A meta-analysis. *Psychological Bulletin, 104*, 53–69.

Jewell, J., & Malecki, C. K. (2005). The utility of CBM written language indices: An investigation of production-dependent, production-independent, and accurate-production scores. *School Psychology Review, 34*, 27–44.

Kamberelis, G. (1999). Genre development and learning: Children writing stories, science reports, and poems. *Research in the Teaching of English, 33*, 403–460.

Kamberelis, G., & Bovino, T. D. (1999). Cultural artifacts as scaffolds for genre development. *Reading Research Quarterly, 34*, 138–170.

Kamler, B. (1994). Gender and genre in early writing. *Linguistics and Education, 6*, 153–182.

Klassen, R. (2002). Writing in early adolescence: A review of the role of self-efficacy beliefs. *Educational Psychology Review, 14*, 173–203.

Knudson, R. E. (1993a). Development of a writing attitude survey for grades 9 to 12: Effects of gender, grade, and ethnicity. *Psychological Reports, 73*, 587–594.

Knudson, R. E. (1993b). Effects of ethnicity in attitudes toward writing. *Psychological Reports, 72*, 39–45.

Labov, W. (1972). *Language in the inner city. Studies in the black English vernacular.* Philadelphia, PA: University of Pennsylvania Press.

Labov, W., & Waletzky, J. (1967). Narrative analysis: Oral versions of personal experience. In J. Helm (Ed.), *Essays on the verbal and visual arts* (pp. 12–14). Seattle: University of Washington Press.

Lorna, B., & Adams, A. M. (2009, August). *Is it differences in cognitive resources and language skills that help girls produce better writing?* Paper presented at the Writing Meeting of the European Association for Research on Learning and Instruction (EARLI), Amsterdam, Holland.

Maccoby, E. E. (1966). Sex differences in intellectual functioning. In E. Maccoby (Ed.), *The development of sex differences* (pp. 25–29). Stanford, CA: Stanford University Press.

Maccoby, E. E., & Jacklin, C. N. (1974). *The psychology of sex differences.* Stanford, CA: Stanford University Press.

Maki, H. S., Voeten, M. J. M., Vauras, M. M. S., & Poskiparta, E. H. (2001). Predicting writing skill development with word recognition and preschool readiness skills. *Reading and Writing, 14*, 643–672.

Malecki, C. K., & Jewell, J. (2003). Developmental, gender, and practical considerations in scoring curriculum-based measurement writing probes. *Psychology in the Schools, 40*(4), 379–390.

Marosi, E., Harmony, T., Reyes, A., Bernal, J., Fernández, T., Guerrero, V., Rodríguez, M., Silva, J., et al. (1997). A follow-up study of EEG coherences in children with different pedagogical evaluations. *International Journal of Psychophysiology, 25*, 227–235.

McCutchen, D. (1986). Domain knowledge and linguistic knowledge in the development of writing ability. *Journal of Memory and Language, 25*, 431–444.

Meece, J. L., Glienke, B. B., & Askew, K. (2009). Gender and motivation. In K. R. Wentzel & A. Wigfield (Eds.), *Handbook of motivation at school* (pp. 411–431). New York: Routledge.

Meece, J. L., Glienke, B. B., & Burg, S. (2006). Gender and motivation. *Journal of School Psychology, 44*, 351–373.

Merisuo-Storm, T. (2006). Girls and boys like to read and write different texts. *Scandinavian Journal of Educational Research, 50*, 111–125.

Millard, E. (1997). *Differently literate: Boys, girls and the schooling of literacy.* London: Falmer.

Northwest Regional Educational Laboratory. (2000). *6+1 Trait definitions.* Retrieved from http://educationnorthwest.org/resource/503

Ollila, L., Bullen, C., & Collis, B. (1989). Gender-related preferences for the choice of particular animals as writing topics in grade 1. *Journal of Research and Development in Education, 22*, 37–41.

Pajares, F., & Johnson, M. J., & Usher, E. L. (2007). Sources of writing self-efficacy beliefs of elementary, middle, and high school students. *Research in the Teaching of English, 42*, 104–120.

Pajares, F., & Valiante, G. (1999). Grade level and gender differences in the writing self-beliefs of middle school students. *Contemporary Educational Psychology, 24*, 390–405.

Pajares, F., & Valiante, G. (2006). Self-efficacy beliefs and motivation in writing development. In C. A. MacArthur, S. Graham, & J. Fitzgerald (Eds.), *Handbook of writing research* (pp. 158–170). New York: Guilford.

Pajares, F., Valiante, G., & Cheong, Y. F. (2007). Writing self-efficacy and its relations to gender, writing motivation, and writing competence: A developmental perspective. In S. Hidi & P. Boscolo (Eds.), *Motivation and writing: Research and instructional practice* (pp. 141–159). Oxford: Elsevier.

Pastorelli, C., Caprara, G. V., Barbaranelli, C., Rola, J., Rozsa, S., & Bandura, A. (2001). The structure of children's perceived self-efficacy: A cross-national study. *European Journal of Psychological Assessment, 17*, 87–97.

Peterson, S. (1998). Evaluation and teachers' perceptions of gender in sixth-grade student writing. *Research in the Teaching of English, 33*, 181–208.

Peterson, S. (2000). Grades four and eight students' and teachers' perceptions of girls' and boys' writing competencies. *Reading Horizons, 40*(4), 253–271.

Peterson, S. (2001). Gender identities and self-expression in classroom narrative writing. *Language Arts, 78*, 451–457.

Peterson, S. (2006). Influence of gender on writing development. In C. A. MacArthur, S. Graham, & J. Fitzgerald (Eds.), *Handbook of writing research* (pp. 311–323). New York: Guilford.

Peterson, S., & Kennedy, K. (2006). Sixth-grade teachers' written comments on student writing. *Written Communication, 23*, 36–62.

Pottoroff, D. D., Phelps-Zientarski, D., & Skovera, M. E. (1996). Gender perceptions of elementary and middle school students about literacy at school and home. *Journal of Research and Development in Education, 29*, 203–211.

Prater, D., & Padia, W. (1983). Effects of modes of discourse on writing performance in grades four and six. *Research in the Teaching of English, 17*, 127–134.

Price, G. B., & Graves, R. L. (1980). Sex differences in syntax and usage in oral and written language. *Research in the Teaching of English, 14*, 147–153.

Purves, A. (1992). *The IEA study of written composition II: Education and performance in fourteen countries.* Oxford: Pergamon.

Ramist, L., & Arbeiter, S. (1986). *Profiles, college-bound seniors.* New York: College Board Publications.

Richards, T., Berninger, V., Stock, P., Altemeier, L., Trivedi, P., & Maravilla, K. (2009). fMRI sequential-finger movement activation differentiating good and poor writers. *Journal of Clinical and Experimental Neuropsychology, 31*, 967–983.

Roen, D. H., Peguesse, C., & Abordonado, V. (1995). Gender and language variation in written communication. In D. L. Rubin (Ed.), *Composing social identity in written language* (pp. 113–131). Hillsdale, NJ: Erlbaum.

Romatowski, J. A., & Trepanier-Street, M. L. (1987). Gender perceptions: An analysis of children's creative writing. *Contemporary Education, 59*, 17–19.

Rosèn, M. (1995). Gender differences in structure, means and variance of hierarchically ordered ability dimensions. *Learning and Instruction, 5*, 37–62.

Rosenthal, R., & Jacobson, L. (1968). *Pigmalion in the classroom: Teacher expectation and pupils' intellectual development.* New York: Holt, Rinehart & Winston.

School Achievement Indicators Program (Canada), & Council of Ministers of Education (Canada). (2003). *SAIP, School Achievement Indicators Program: Student writing, the Canadian context, writing III.* Toronto, ON: Council of Ministers of Education, Canada.

Shell, D. F., Colvin, C., & Bruning, R. H. (1995). Self-efficacy, attributions, and outcome expectancy mechanisms in reading and writing achievement: Grade-level and achievement-level differences. *Journal of Educational Psychology, 87,* 386–398.

Skarbrevik, K. J. (2002). Gender differences among students found eligible for special education. *European Journal of Special needs education, 2,* 97–107.

Trepanier, M. L., & Romatowski, J. A. (1985). Attributes and roles assigned to characters in children's writing: Sex differences and sex-role perceptions. *Sex Roles, 13,* 263–272.

Tuck, D. L., Bayliss, V. A., & Bell, M. L. (1985). Analysis of sex stereotyping in characters created by young authors. *Journal of Educational Research, 78,* 248–252.

Tyler, L. E. (1965). *The psychology of human differences.* New York: Appleton-Century-Crofts.

Verheyden, L., Van den Branden, K., Rijlaarsdam, G., van den Bergh, H., & De maeyer, S. (2009, August). *Do Turkish girls outperform Flemish boys? What do their teachers expect? What do their texts tell?* Paper presented at the Writing Meeting of the European Association for Research on Learning and Instruction (EARLI), Amsterdam, the Netherlands.

Wormack, L. (1979). Cognitive predictors of articulation in writing. *Perceptual and Motor Skills, 48,* 1151–1156.

Part *III*

The Changing Nature of Teaching, Learning, and Assessing Writing Across the Life Span: K–12, Adolescence, Higher Education, and the Work World

8

The Role of Strategies, Knowledge, Will, and Skills in a 30-Year Program of Writing Research (With Homage to Hayes, Fayol, and Boscolo)

STEVE GRAHAM and KAREN R. HARRIS

A lthough 1980 had its share of unfortunate events (e.g., John Lennon was shot dead in New York City and Iran held Canadian and U.S. Embassy workers hostage), it also shined. We were captivated by the grace and skill of the Romanian gymnast Nadia Comaneci in the Summer Olympics. Voyager 1 reached Saturn and sent back data on its 14 moons and more than 1,000 rings. A phenomenal book, *A Confederacy of Dunces*, by John Kennedy Toole, was published.[1]

For us, it was a great year in several other ways. We were just starting to think about how we could combine our personal interests and expertise to develop a line of research we could pursue conjointly (see also Graham & Harris, 2009). Karen was testing the feasibility of applying a cognitive-behavioral intervention approach developed by the psychologist Don Meichenbaum (1977). Her master thesis evaluated the effectiveness of this intervention with children who were extremely shy (Harris & Brown, 1982). Steve had just completed or was in the process of completing reviews on different aspects of teaching writing (Graham, 1982; Graham & Miller, 1979, 1980). He had become increasingly interested in this topic after reading interviews with professional writers in the magazine *Paris Review*. In almost all of the articles he read, the interviewer asked the author questions about his or her writing process and craft, and Steve devoured these descriptions eagerly. The

---

[1] The author of this novel, published posthumously and considered a canonical work of modern Southern literature, was awarded a Pulitzer Prize for fiction in 1981 for a story of how true genius can be identified on the basis of the confederacy of dunces united against the person.

ultimate nexus of our interest became cognition, and we decided we would develop and test the effectiveness of a multicomponent cognitive intervention for improving the writing of students who experience learning difficulties. The decision to focus on struggling learners was strongly shaped by the fact that each of us was formerly a special education teacher, and we had (Steve) or were (Karen) in the process of pursuing a doctoral degree in special education. Over the next 30 years our decision to focus on struggling learners expanded to include more typically developing children and youngsters.

An especially fortuitous event for us in 1980 was the publication of the influential book *Cognitive Processes in Writing*, edited by Gregg and Steinberg. Although we found all of the chapters interesting and informative, a chapter by John Richard (Dick) Hayes and Linda Flower (1980) provided an anchor for our developing ideas about what a cognitive instructional approach to writing should concentrate on (Hayes went on to revise this model in 1996).

To develop their model of skilled writing, Hayes and Flower asked adults to "think aloud" while composing. They then analyzed the resulting verbal protocols to determine the types of cognitive and psychological processes involved in writing. The component of their writing model that was most salient to us was *cognitive processes*. It provided a description of the mental operations adults employed when writing. These processes included planning what to say and how to say it, translating plans into written text, and reviewing to improve existing text. Planning, in turn, involved three ingredients—setting goals, generating ideas, and organizing ideas into a writing plan—whereas reviewing included reading and editing text, which is frequently referred to as revising.

In the cognitive model of writing instruction that we developed, we placed the primary focus on teaching struggling writers strategies for planning and revising (Harris, Graham, Mason, & Friedlander, 2008). These planning strategies typically emphasized goal setting, idea generation, and text organization. It is easy to see the direct influence that the Hayes and Flower (1980) model had on our thinking. Initially, we referred to our instructional model as self-control strategy training (Harris & Graham, 1985). As the model was tweaked to make it better, we came to refer to it as self-instructional strategy training (Graham, Harris, & Sawyer, 1987), and eventually we renamed it self-regulated strategy development (SRSD; Graham & Harris, 1993) to stress the emphasis the model places on students' self-regulation (as discussed below).

Another component of the Hayes and Flower (1980) model that influenced our thinking was *writer's long-term memory*, which included the author's knowledge about the topic, the intended audience, and general plans or formulas for accomplishing various writing tasks. The plans or formulas were similar to the strategies that were emphasized in our SRSD instructional model, as they involved mental operations for carrying our specific writing tasks. Based on Stein and Glynn's (1979) seminal work on the basic structural elements included in specific types of texts (e.g., story grammars), we further decided that strategies for planning text should be genre specific in most instances (e.g., students were taught a strategy for specifically planning a persuasive text). Students needed to develop a strong knowledge of the basic qualities and attributes of the target genre.

A final element of the Hayes and Flower (1980) model that was especially important to us was their contention that the execution of the cognitive processes involved in writing were under the writer's direct control. We hardly agreed, but the rub was how to help struggling writers develop this level of control. To address this issue, we decided that we would first model how to use the target writing strategies and then provide students with any assistance they needed to use the strategies effectively, until they could do so independently. We further decided that SRSD should emphasize other self-regulation mechanisms beyond the task-specific strategies students were taught. Consequently, students were taught how to use self-regulation procedures, such as goal setting, self-assessment, self-instructions (self-talk), and self-reinforcement, to help them intelligently manage their use of target writing strategies, the writing process, and their behavior when writing (Harris & Graham, 1996, 2008). Each of these decisions was influenced by the work of Meichenbaum (1977), Alley and Deshler (1979), and Brown, Campione, and Day (1981), who were already applying some of these techniques with students.

Although we had already developed SRSD by the time we became aware of Pietro Boscolo's (1990) work, his focus on text planning and production as well as motivation in writing were compatible with our instructional model. The planning and revising strategies that we would ask students to apply required considerable persistence and effort. We thought that it was unlikely that struggling writers would continue to use such strategies if they did not view them as worthwhile. Consequently, an essential element of SRSD was for students to monitor and graph their progress as they were learning the target strategies. The emphasis of these self-evaluations was to stress that students made progress because they were effortful and used the strategies they were taught. We also asked students to set goals to improve their writing performance and apply what they were learning to new situations. Goal setting is a powerful motivator, as it directs attention to what needs to be done, provides an incentive to mobilize effort, and provides information on performance (Locke, Shaw, Saari, & Latham, 1981). Other SRSD procedures designed to enhance motivation included self-reinforcement and the development of personal self-statements that validated effort, strategy use, or both.

Obviously, we would not have been able to develop the SRSD without the pioneering work of people like John Hayes, Don Meichenbaum, Ann Brown, Donald Deshler, and others. Although the shoulders we stood on were broad, the evidence for building an instructional approach emphasizing strategies, knowledge, and will was thin. Not surprisingly, therefore, the development of our model was also influenced by what we knew about students who experience learning difficulties (based on both our experiences working with these children and the limited research base then available; Harris, 1982).

Although struggling learners form a heterogeneous group, the difficulties they face arise from multiple problems of an affective, behavioral, and cognitive nature (Harris, Graham, & Mason, 2003). They have difficulty with self-regulation (including the self-regulation of organized strategic behaviors), incomplete and even inaccurate knowledge about important academic tasks such as writing, and poor motivation (including negative attitudes, self-doubts, minimal effort, maladaptive attributions, and low self-efficacy). Consequently, SRSD was constructed on the premise that these students would benefit from an integrated instructional approach that directly addressed these issues.

From our initial development of SRSD to now, the foundational constructs of strategic behavior, knowledge, and motivation have been central to our research on writing, including but not limited to research on SRSD. Although our research in these areas at first focused on youngsters 10 to 14 years of age with learning difficulties, we have become increasingly interested in a broader range of students and ages. In addition, our research has not been limited just to these topics. We have devoted considerable attention to the role that basic skills (handwriting, spelling, sentence construction, etc.) play in writing development and writing difficulties. This interest was fueled in part by the work of Bourdin and Fayol (1993, 1994), whose research demonstrated that the process of transcribing ideas onto paper (which is dominated by handwriting and spelling) is more demanding for children than adults. Moreover, we have been increasingly pulled into the policy arena in terms of trying to make the case for why writing should be an integral part of the school reform effort in the United States. We would argue it should be an integral part of education in all countries. Before considering what our research on strategies, knowledge, will, and skills adds to knowledge about writing, writing development, and instruction, we first consider our journey into the policy arena.

INTO THE POLICY (LION'S?) DEN

What Does Contemporary Writing Instruction Look Like?

Since the turn of the millennium, we have conducted a series of surveys asking classroom teachers in the United States about their writing practices (Cutler & Graham, 2008; Gilbert & Graham, 2010; Graham, Capizzi, Hebert, & Morphy, 2010; Graham, Harris, MacArthur, & Fink-Chorzempa, 2003; Graham, Harris et al., 2008; Graham, Morphy et al., 2008; Kiuhara, Graham, & Hawken, 2009). In each of these surveys, teachers were randomly selected from across the United States. We believe that teachers who completed the survey were representative, as the response rate for most of the studies was 60% to 70%. In two investigations the response rate was below 50% (Gilbert & Graham, 2010; Graham, Capizzi et al., 2010), but responders and nonresponders did not differ on a number of important variables (expenditures per pupil, size of school, geographic location, etc.) in any of the investigations. It is important to note that the data from these surveys were self-reports, raising the possibility that teachers provided a more flattering picture of instruction than actually existed.

At first, our interest in conducting these surveys was to gain better insight into how writing was being taught to students, as we believed that such information would help us develop better writing interventions for struggling and typical writers; ones that could be successfully integrated into teachers' current writing programs. As we started tabulating the findings from these surveys, we became increasingly concerned about the quality of writing instruction students received. We became convinced that poor instruction is one of the reasons why so many students score below the proficiency level for writing on the National Assessment of Educational Progress (Salahu-Din, Persky, & Miller, 2008).

To be fair, there were some positive findings, and we share these first. Teachers of the youngest writers in our survey (Grades 1 to 3) devoted 1 hour a day to writing and writing instruction (Cutler & Graham, 2008; Graham et al., 2003). We were pleasantly surprised, as we had anticipated that less time would be allocated. For these young children, teachers placed considerable emphasis on teaching basic writing skills, devoting up to 50% of writing time to such instruction. Basic writing skills, such as sentence construction, handwriting, and spelling, play an important role in early writing development (Graham, 2006a). Furthermore, for handwriting and spelling, the amount of time primary grade teachers devoted to teaching these skills was consistent with research-based recommendations (Graham, Harris et al., 2008; Graham, Morphy et al., 2008). These young students further received considerable exposure to writing narrative text (Cutler & Graham, 2008). Finally, the majority of teachers across all grades (1 to 12) made multiple adaptations for struggling writers (Gilbert & Graham, 2010; Graham et al., 2003; Graham et al., 2010; Graham, Morphy et al., 2008; Kiuhara et al., 2009).

Beyond instruction in the first three grades and teacher adaptations for struggling writers across all grades, teachers' responses revealed that were more areas for concern than there were for celebration. First, the amount of time teachers devoted to teaching students how to write declined across the grades. These time estimates did not include how much time students spent writing (this remained fairly constant at about 20 to 25 min per day in Grades 1 to 6), just how much time the teacher spent teaching specific skills and processes. In Grades 1 to 3 about 40 min a day was spent teaching writing processes and skills (Cutler & Graham, 2008; Graham et al., 2003). By Grades 4 to 6, writing instruction was typically limited to 15 min a day (Gilbert & Graham, 2010). For students in middle and high school, most writing instruction was delivered by language arts teachers, but such teaching appeared to be infrequent based on how often they applied specific techniques for teaching writing (Graham et al., 2010; Kiuhara et al., 2009). Social studies teachers did teach writing on occasion, but much less frequently than language arts teachers, with science teachers placing little to no emphasis on writing instruction. It is also important to note that teachers across the grades devoted little time to teaching writing processes (e.g., strategies for planning and revising).

Of equal concern was how often, how much, and what students were asked to write. In Grades 1 to 6, students spent only about 20 to 30 min a day actually writing (Cutler & Graham, 2008; Gilbert & Graham, 2010; Graham et al., 2003; Graham, Harris et al., 2008), with very little emphasis on writing expository text in the first 3 years of school (Cutler & Graham, 2008). Middle and high school students also wrote infrequently (Graham et al., 2010; Kiuhara et al., 2009), with much of their writing involving very short responses (such as making lists, filling in blanks on worksheets, and writing short answers to questions on a homework assignment). Older students appeared to do very little extended writing or writing that involved analysis and interpretation. Applebee and Langer (2006) found a similar state of affairs in their recent examination of the teaching of writing nation-wide. Thus, while it is commonly assumed that students do longer and more complex school-assigned writing tasks as they move through the grades, these studies do not support that supposition.

Also problematic was teachers' evaluations of their preparation to teach writing. One third of primary grade teachers indicated that they were poorly prepared to teach writing by their college teacher preparation program (Cutler & Graham, 2008). This percentage rose to 66% in Grades 4 to 6 (Gilbert & Graham, 2010), with a drop to 47% in the middle schools (Graham et al., 2010) and a rise to 71% at the high school level (Kiuhara et al., 2009). When teachers were asked about all of their preparation (college, inservice, and personal), there was still a sizable percentage (33–50%) that indicated they were poorly prepared (Graham et al., 2010; Kiuhara et al., 2009).

Beyond these three big concerns (teaching, writing, and preparation), there were other worrisome patterns in teachers' responses. Many teachers placed considerable emphasis on teaching grammar (e.g., Cutler & Graham, 2008), even though such strategy instruction is ineffective (Graham & Perin, 2007a), at least for conventional approaches to grammar instruction (which does not include sentence combining instruction, which has been found to be effective; see Andrews et al., 2006; Graham & Perin, 2007a). There was also reason to be concerned about how some primary grade teachers taught handwriting and spelling. For instance, some teachers held a single long handwriting practice session once a week (Graham, Harris et al., 2008), even though motor (and other) skills are best learned through frequent but spaced practice distributed over time (Graham & Miller, 1980). Further, teachers indicated that students rarely used word processors as a tool for writing (Cutler & Graham, 2008; Gilbert & Graham, 2010), although students used word processors more frequently in the upper grades (Graham et al., 2010; Kiuhara et al., 2009).

Why Is Contemporary Writing Instruction So Impoverished?

As we started thinking about the findings from these surveys, the observations of others (e.g., Applebee & Langer, 2006), and our own experience in school, we had a reoccurring question: Why is writing instruction in U.S. schools so impoverished? We considered three possible reasons. First, educators, administrators, and policy makers do not believe that writing can be taught or that effective practices for teaching writing exist. Second, writing is viewed as having little or no value. Third, it is difficult to assess writing objectively and therefore it is futile to teach it as student progress cannot be determined.

To address the first question (Can writing be taught?), we conducted or are in the process of conducting a series of meta-analyses examining the effectiveness of various methods for teaching writing (e.g., Graham, 2010; Graham & Perin, 2007a, 2007b, 2007c; Morphy & Graham, 2009; Rogers & Graham, 2008; Sandmel & Graham, in press). The analyses that are currently completed have collectively focused on summarizing different kinds of research on writing interventions including true experiments, quasi-experiments, single-subject design studies, and qualitative studies examining the writing instructional practices of effective literacy teachers. This approach has resulted in the identification of 25 effective instructional practices in writing instruction. These are presented in Table 8.1. The first 11 are based on findings from true and quasi-experiments, the

TABLE 8.1   Effective Writing Practices

Writing Practices Supported by True and Quasi-Experiments[a]

1. Explicitly teach students strategies for planning, revising, and editing their compositions.
2. Explicitly teach students strategies and procedures for summarizing reading material.
3. Develop instructional arrangements where students cooperatively work together to plan, draft, revise, and edit their compositions.
4. Set clear and specific goals for what students are to accomplish in their writing.
5. Use word processing as a primary tool for writing, as it has a positive influence on what students write.
6. Explicitly teach students how to combine and write increasingly complex sentences. Implement a process writing approach.
7. Apply a process approach to writing instruction.
8. Involve students in writing activities designed to sharpen their skills of inquiry.
9. Engage students in activities that help them gather and organize ideas for their composition before they write a first draft.
10. Provide students with good models for each type of writing that is the focus of instruction.
11. Explicitly teach handwriting, spelling, and typing to students who experience difficulty acquiring these skills (moderate positive impact).

Writing Practices Supported by Single-Subject Design Research[b]

12. Encourage students to monitor one or more aspects of their writing performance to determine how well they are doing.
13. Explicitly and directly teach students basic writing skills, such as capitalization, punctuation, sentence construction, and so forth.
14. Reinforce positive aspects of students' writing.
15. Teach students strategies for writing paragraphs.

Writing Practices Used by Effective Literacy Teachers[c]

16. Dedicate time to writing and writing instruction, with writing occurring across the curriculum.
17. Involve students in various forms of writing over time.
18. Encourage students to treat writing as a process, where they plan, draft, revise, edit, and share their work.
19. Keep students engaged and on-task by involving them in thoughtful activities versus activities that do not require thoughtfulness (such as completing a workbook page).
20. Mix teaching to the whole class with teaching to small groups and one-on-one instruction.
21. Model, explain, and provide guided assistance when teaching.
22. Provide enough support so that students can make progress and carry out writing tasks and processes, but encourage students to act in a self-regulated fashion, doing as much as they can on their own.
23. Be enthusiastic about writing and create a positive environment.
24. Set high expectations for students' writing.
25. Adapt writing assignments and instruction to better meet the needs of individual students.

[a]   Graham (2010); Graham & Perin (2007a, 2007b); Morphy & Graham (2009); Sandmel & Graham (in press).
[b]   Graham & Perin (2007c); Rogers & Graham (2008).
[c]   Graham & Perin (2007c).

next 4 from single-subject design studies, and the final 10 from the study of exceptional teachers. This compilation provides credible evidence that writing can be taught and effective instructional practices exist.

To answer the second question (Is writing important?), we have conducted a meta-analysis of the impact of writing on learning content material as well as reading. Mostly replicating the 2004 meta-analysis by Bangert-Drowns, Hurley, and Wilkinson (2004), we found that having students write about the material they learn in class had a small but statistically significant and positive impact on adolescent students' learning (average weighted effect size was 0.23 across 26 studies; Graham & Perin, 2007b). We further found that writing about material read improved students' comprehension of text, that teaching writing improved students' reading skills, and that increasing how frequently students write improves how well they read (Graham & Hebert, 2010). These findings are summarized in Table 8.2. We believe that these findings provide strong support for the importance of writing, as writing can be used as a tool for enhancing reading and learning.

We are just starting to grapple with the third question (Can writing be assessed?), as we are in the process of finishing a report on this subject for the Carnegie Corporation of New York (Graham, Harris, & Hebert, 2011). Based on our knowledge of the literature at this point, the answer would be a nuanced and reserved yes, as the adequacy of current measures depends on the purpose of assessment and what is being assessed.

TABLE 8.2   The Impact of Writing and Writing Instruction on Reading

1. When students write about texts read it improves their comprehension of it (NRT ES = 0.40, 11 studies; RDT ES = 0.51, 51 studies)

Students' comprehension of language arts, social studies, and science texts is improved when they write about what they read, specifically when they:

- Respond to a text in writing by writing personal reactions, analyzing and interpreting the text: RDT ES = 0.77, 9 studies
- Write summaries of text: RDT ES = 0.52, 19 studies
- Write notes about text: RDT ES = 0.47, 23 studies
- Answer questions about text in writing or create and answer written questions about text: RDT ES = 0.27, 8 studies

2. Teach students the writing skills and processes that go into creating text

Students' reading skills are improved by learning the skills and processes that go into writing, specifically when we:

- Teach the process of writing, text structures for writing, and paragraph or sentence construction skills (improves reading comprehension: NRT ES = 0.18, 12 studies; RDT ES = 0.27, 5 studies)
- Teach spelling and sentence construction skills (improves reading fluency: NRT/RDT ES = 0.79, 4 studies)
- Teach spelling skills (improves word reading skills: NRT/RDT ES = 0.68, 5 studies)

3. Increase how much students write

- This increases students' reading comprehension: NRT ES = 0.30, 6 studies

Source: Redrawn from Graham, S., and Hebert, M., *Writing to Reading: Evidence for How Writing Can Improve Reading*, Alliance for Excellence in Education, Washington, DC, 2010.

ES, effect size; NRT, norm-referenced test; RDT, researcher-designed test.

Of course these three questions and our approach to answering them are only one aspect of the policy picture as it relates to writing. What is obvious thought is that writing is not a central part of the reform effort, at least in the United States (National Commission on Writing, 2003). If we think writing should be a major player in the educational reform movement, then it will take a concerted effort on the part of the writing community and organizations that represent this community to make this happen. We think that this is a worthy goal and hope that those interested in writing (despite ideological differences) will work together to make this happen.

OUR RESEARCH ON FOUNDATIONAL CONSTRUCTS

Underlying Self-Regulated Strategy Development

As noted earlier, SRSD was based on the premise that students would benefit from an integrated instructional approach designed to enhance their strategic behavior, knowledge, and motivation to write. Since the initial conceptualization of SRSD, we have continually returned to the question of whether these three building blocks are important ingredients in students' writing development. We have approached this question in two ways. One way is by reviewing the research literature to determine if there was support for this thesis (see Graham, 2006a; Graham & Harris, 2000) and the second way is by conducting research that tests different aspects of this thesis. In this chapter, we examine if each of our foundational constructs is indeed important to writing development, which would provide support for emphasizing them when we developed SRSD (along with support for emphasizing other instructional approaches). For this goal, we share the results of a specific literature review designed to test the thesis above (Graham, 2006a). In the process, we provide specific examples of some of the findings by referring to our own work (which included many collaborators, many of whom have contributed to this volume). It is important to note that the Graham (2006a) analysis was based on research from many different studies and investigators. It is not possible to review all of these studies here; and given space limitations, we decided only to emphasize our own research. For those who would like a broader view of the evidence on the role of strategies, knowledge, and will to writing development, we encourage you to read the original review by Graham (2006a) as well as an earlier paper by Graham and Harris (2000).

In the Graham (2006a) review, we reasoned that if any of the foundational constructs for SRSD (strategies, knowledge, or will) played an important role in writing development, then the answers to the following questions (illustrated for writing knowledge) should be yes: (a) Are skilled writers more knowledgeable about writing than less-skilled writers? (b) Do developing writers become increasingly knowledgeable about writing with age and schooling? (c) Do individual differences in knowledge about writing predict writing performance? and (d) Does teaching developing writers knowledge about writing improve their writing performance? The answer to each of these questions is examined next, starting with strategic behavior.

Strategic Behavior

Graham (2006a) found that there was enough research on two aspects of strategic writing behaviors—planning and revising—to answer the four questions posed above. First, skilled writers plan more and are better at revising than less-skilled writers. Second, planning and revising become increasingly sophisticated with age. There is considerable individual variation in these behaviors, however, especially with revising. Third, students' planning and revising behaviors generally predict writing performance, but it must be noted that correlations between planning and writing performance vary greatly from one study to the next, and revising behavior is generally not related to writing performance until high school. Fourth, teaching developing writers how to plan or revise has a strong and positive impact on their writing. Thus, the available evidence supports the proposition that both planning and revising are important ingredients in writing development.

Despite the importance of planning and revising, our own research shows that struggling writers tend to minimize each of these when composing. First, these students do little planning in advance. When we prompted weaker writers to plan before writing, they spent less than 1 min engaged in doing so (e.g., MacArthur & Graham, 1987). Second, they do little meaningful planning as they write. For example, Graham (1990) reported that struggling writers converted a persuasive essay assignment into a question-and-answer task, quickly telling whatever came to mind and abruptly ending their response. Little if any effort was directed to the needs of the reader, organization of text, establishment of rhetorical goals, or evaluation and reworking of ideas. Third, struggling writers take a least-effort approach to revising, making few meaningful changes to text. To illustrate, when we asked weaker writers to revise their papers, they mainly focused their attention on a few word changes, correcting spelling and grammar errors, and making the paper neater (MacArthur, Graham, & Schwartz, 1991).

We think that one reason for why these children are not more strategic is that they experience difficulty regulating the mental operations involved in complex processes such as planning and revising. This view was supported in several studies that focused on revising (De La Paz, Swanson, & Graham, 1998; Graham, 1997). We found that weaker writers made more and better substantive revisions when they received support designed to ensure that the separate elements of the revising process were coordinated and occurred in a regular way. This coordination happened when writers were directed to address whole text and sentence level concerns (De La Paz et al., 1998) as well as issues just at the sentence level (Graham, 1997). These findings with struggling writers and the more general conclusions drawn by Graham (2006a) support our decision to make planning and revising strategies as well as self-regulation central building blocks in the SRSD model.

Knowledge

Knowledge about writing comes in many different forms, including knowledge about the writing topic, the intended audience, and the writing process (e.g., discourse and linguistic knowledge). Although writing knowledge has been understudied, Graham (2006a) concluded that knowledge about how to write is an important ingredient in writing development. This conclusion was more tentative than the one drawn for strategic behavior, as relatively few studies addressed each of the four questions.

In terms of the first question, Graham (2006a) found skilled writers are more knowledgeable about how to write than less-skilled writers. For instance, Graham, Schwartz, and MacArthur (1993) reported that good writers have a more sophisticated conceptualization of writing than weaker writers, as was replicated by Saddler and Graham (2007). Graham further found that developing writers become increasingly knowledgeable about how to write over time. For example, Graham et al. (1993) found that older writers had a more sophisticated conceptualization of writing than younger writers. Graham also concluded that knowledge about how to write predicts how well developing writers write. Olinghouse and Graham (2009) observed that discourse knowledge (knowledge about how to write and knowledge about the characteristics of specific genres obtained by asking students questions designed to elicit such knowledge) accounted for a significant amount of variance in fourth-grade students' story quality, story length, and vocabulary diversity, when four writing (handwriting fluency, spelling, attitude toward writing, advanced planning) and three nonwriting variables (grade, gender, basic reading skills) were first controlled. Finally, Graham indicated that there was a small number of studies that demonstrated instruction aimed at enhancing writers' discourse knowledge improved their writing.

In our research with struggling writers, we found that their conceptions about how to write placed undue emphasis on form and mechanics (Graham et al., 1993; Saddler & Graham, 2007). For instance, when such students were asked to describe how good writers write, they typically responded by saying such things as: "Write neatly"; "Put their name and date on the paper"; and "Spell each word right." Their more-skilled writing peers placed greater emphasis on writing processes, indicating they "Brainstorm ideas"; "Organize their thoughts"; and "Use interesting words."

Another important finding from our ongoing research program in this area is that struggling writers' discourse knowledge about writing, its genres, devices, and conventions is quite limited. Even with a common and familiar genre like story writing, we found that weaker writers are often unable to identify basic attributes or parts (Graham, Harris, & Mason, 2005; Harris, Graham, & Mason, 2006). To illustrate, when we asked a struggling writer to tell his friend what kinds of things were included in a story, he started off in the right territory ("I would tell him main character."), but was unable to stay there ("Also, a subject, predicate, and main idea."). We have found that this incomplete knowledge is evident in weaker writers' stories, where basic elements such as the location, problem, ending, or moral are often omitted (Graham & Harris, 1989).

The conclusions drawn by Graham (2006a) and the findings from our studies included here provide support for two of the decisions we made when developing SRSD. First, the emphasis in SRSD on explicitly teaching process, including strategies for planning and revising, provided a counter to weaker writers' undue occupation with form. Second, SRSD addresses weaker writers' limited discourse knowledge, as the planning strategies that are typically taught are genre specific and students are taught the genre knowledge needed to apply these strategies effectively

Motivation

In his review, Graham (2006a) indicated that research generally supports the thesis that motivation is an important ingredient in writing development. This assertion was tenuous, however, as the amount of evidence available was very limited. It had to be combined across different motivational constructs (e.g., self-efficacy, attitude toward writing, etc.), and one of the four questions was not answered affirmatively.

For the first question, very limited and somewhat mixed evidence favored the claim that skilled writers are more motivated than less-skilled ones. A study by Graham et al. (1993) illustrates how evidence was not always consistent for different motivational constructs. We found stronger writers were more positive about their desire to write than weaker writers, but there was no difference between the two in self-efficacy for writing.

In contrast, the available evidence was not consistent enough to support a positive claim for the second question; namely, developing writers become more motivated over time. One motivational variable, students' efficacy for writing, mostly declined over time, whereas findings for other motivational variables were more variable, declining and ascending across different studies.

The available evidence mostly supported the claim (question three) that students' motivation predicts their writing performance. For example, Graham, Berninger, and Fan (2007) tested different models of the relationship between attitudes toward writing and writing performance using structural equation modeling. The model that fit the data best postulated that students' desire to write influences their writing performance.

Lastly, the available data generally support the positive assertion for the fourth question that instruction to enhance motivation improves writing performance. It must be noted that this evidence was limited just to studies where children were provided with feedback on their learning progress. This feedback was designed to enhance self-efficacy.

Unfortunately, we have conducted less research on weaker writers' motivation to write than we have on their strategic behaviors and writing knowledge. We are able to draw three conclusions from the research we have conducted (Graham & Harris, 2009). First, these students' writing persistence is limited. For instance, 10- to 12-year-old struggling writers spent only 6 min on average to write a persuasive essay, and only 1 min when they dictated such an essay (Graham, 1990). Second, weaker writers are often more confident about their writing capabilities than is warranted. For example, 10- to 14-year-old weaker writers felt they wrote just as well as stronger writing peers (Graham et al., 1993). A downside to such overconfidence is that youngsters who overestimate their capabilities may fail to allocate the needed resources and effort, believing it is unnecessary (Sawyer, Graham, & Harris, 1992). Third, weaker writers are more negative about writing than their classmates (Graham et al., 1993). These observations, and to a lesser extent the review by Graham (2006a), support our a priori decision to make motivation an SRSD building block.

SELF-REGULATED STRATEGY DEVELOPMENT

As noted earlier, SRSD involves explicitly teaching students specific writing strategies (usually strategies for planning, revising, or both), the knowledge needed to use these strategies (including genre knowledge), and procedures for regulating these strategies, the writing process, and their behavior. In addition, there are multiple procedures (e.g., self-regulation procedures) incorporated into SRSD that are designed to enhance students' motivation for writing as well as learning and using the strategies.

A key principle of SRSD and the eventual goal of instruction is students' ownership and independent use of the writing and self-regulation strategies that are taught. Students are treated as active collaborators in learning these strategies and the role of effort in learning is emphasized. Instructional support as well as level and type of feedback provided by the teacher are adjusted during instruction to be responsive to students' needs, gradually shifting responsibility for strategy use from teacher to student. Importantly, teaching is criterion based rather than time based, as students move through each stage of instruction at their own pace, not proceeding to later stages until they have met initial criteria. We have recently published two books that provide detailed descriptions of the various strategies and metascripts of the procedures used to teach them (Graham & Harris, 2005; Harris, Graham, Mason, & Friedlander, 2008). We hope that those who are interested in implementing SRSD consult these sources.

SRSD involves six stages of instruction (Table 8.3). These stages provide a general format, not a unilaterally scripted approach for teaching. They can be reordered, combined, revisited, modified, or deleted based on students' and teachers' needs.

Also please note that procedures for promoting maintenance and generalization are integrated throughout the SRSD model, including the following: (a) identifying opportunities to use the taught writing or self-regulation strategies in other situations, (b) analyzing how these procedures might need to be modified in these situations, (c) assigning homework to use the strategies in one or more of identified situations, (d) evaluating the success of such endeavors, and (e) reminders to use the strategies.

Initially, we developed SRSD for struggling writers who also experienced difficulties with learning (i.e., children with learning disabilities). Since its initial creation, however, SRSD has been applied and tested with a variety of different types of students, including regularly achieving students, students at risk for writing difficulties, and students with learning disabilities, behavior disorders, attention-deficit/hyperactivity disorder, and Asperger's syndrome (Graham & Harris, 2009). Across all of these different types of students, a variety of different writing strategies have proven effective.

In a recent meta-analysis of 15 true and quasi-experiments, Harris, Graham, Brindle, and Sandmel (2009) reported an average effect size of 1.20 for writing quality immediately following SRSD instruction (an effect size of 0.80 is considered

TABLE 8.3   Stages of SRSD Instruction

Stage 1: Develop and activate background knowledge

During this stage, background knowledge and preskills that students need to understand, learn, and apply the writing and self-regulation strategies are developed. This development may continue into subsequent stages. Students may also be asked to consider if their performance is hindered by negative self-statements, with the teacher showing them how to use more positive ones.

Stage 2: Discuss it

Teacher and students discuss the writing strategies to be learned and establish the goals and benefits of each. For each strategy, the steps are explained, as are any mnemonics used to help students remember them. Teachers and students explore how and when to apply the strategies, laying the foundation for generalization by not limiting the discussion to the current situation or task. Student effort is emphasized to enhance motivation and facilitate the development of positive, adaptive attributions. Students are asked to act as collaborative learning partners and make a commitment to learn the strategy.

At this point, students may be asked to examine and graph their current writing performance. This is done in a positive manor with emphasis on changes that will be realized by learning the strategies. Goal-setting may be introduced too, with students setting goals that can be obtained by using the strategies.

Stage 3: Model it

The teacher models how to use the strategies and self-statements or talk while writing a composition. The self-statements reflect students' needs and match their verbal style and language. These include problem definition (What is it I have to do here?), focusing attention and planning (I have to concentrate, first I need to . . . then . . .), strategy step statements (I need to write down my strategy reminder), self-evaluation and error correcting (Have I used all my parts—oops, I missed one, better add it), coping and self-control (I can handle this, go slow and take my time), and self-reinforcement (I like this ending!). The teacher typically sets goals for what he or she plans to achieve and subsequently assesses if goals were met.

Following modeling of the strategies, the benefits and challenges of using them are discussed, along with considering how they might be modified to make them more effective. Students further develop preferred, personalized self-statements. Modeling may occur multiple times.

Stage 4: Memorize it

Students participate in activities to help them memorize the strategy steps, corresponding mnemonics, and personalized self-statements. This stage is not needed by all students, but others may benefit from instructional aids (an index card that lists the strategy steps) and continued practice.

Stage 5: Support it

At this stage, teachers responsively support students' use of the writing strategies, self-statements, and other self-regulation procedures as they apply them to writing. For instance, some students may benefit from mini-lessons that target how to use one step in the strategy, additional modeling, more collaborative practice with the teacher or peers, or extra positive reinforcement and praise. These supports are faded over time, as soon as possible.

Stage 6: Independent performance

This final stage is reached when students can use the strategies independently and correctly. If students have not already transitioned to using covert ("in your head") self-statements, that is encouraged.

large), 1.23 for maintenance (based on nine studies); and 1.20 for generalization to untaught writing genres (based on five studies). In an earlier meta-analysis conducted by Graham (2006b), average effect size for writing quality for SRSD in 10 true and quasi-experiments with students with learning disabilities was 1.34. Similar positive findings were obtained in a meta-analysis of 27 single-subject design studies (Rogers & Graham, 2008). For instance, the percentage of nonoverlapping data (a single-subject design effect size) for schematic structure in 21 single-subject design studies was 97% following SRSD instruction (90% or more is considered evidence of a strong effect), 90% at maintenance (based on 18 studies), and 85% for generalization to uninstructed genres (based on 4 studies). Finally, we are not aware of any studies currently available (published or unpublished) where SRSD did not result in improved writing.

It is important to point out that many of the efficacy studies in the meta-analyses cited above were conducted by us. By the same token, many were not. For example, almost one-half (47%) of the studies in Harris et al. (2009) were conducted by experimenters other than ourselves in countries beyond the boundaries of the United States (e.g., Germany, Spain, Canada). In addition to efficacy studies examining the effectiveness of the full SRSD model, we have conducted several investigations examining the value of specific aspects of the model, including self-regulation procedures (Graham & Harris, 1989; Sawyer et al., 1992) and the maintenance and generalization procedures described above (Graham et al., 2005; Harris et al., 2006). The basic conclusion that can be drawn from these investigations is that SRSD is more effective when the full model is applied.

THE IMPORTANCE OF BASIC WRITING SKILLS IN WRITING DEVELOPMENT

When we first started working with struggling writers in the early 1980s, we noticed that an inordinate number of these students experienced difficulty with basic writing skills, such as handwriting and spelling. Until these writing skills become efficient and relatively automatic, they may exact a toll on children's writing and its development, as difficulty mastering these skills may result in three unwanted consequences. (1) Misspelling and handwriting illegibility make it more difficult to read text (Graham, 2006a). (2) Having to devote conscious attention to spelling or writing letters may interfere with other writing processes (Graham, 1990); for instance, in the process of writing it may be necessary to switch attention to how to spell a word, which may lead the writer to forget ideas or plans held in working memory. (3) Difficulties mastering handwriting and spelling may constrain students' development as writers. McCutchen (1988) argued that these skills are so demanding for beginning writers that they minimize the use of other writing processes, like planning and revising, because they exert considerable processing demands too. Berninger, Mizokawa, and Bragg (1991) also observed that difficulties with handwriting and spelling led children to avoid writing and to develop a mindset that they cannot write.

When Graham (2006a) reviewed evidence about the role of strategies, knowledge, and will in writing development, he also examined if the available evidence supported the claim that basic writing skills, such as handwriting and spelling, were important contributors too (see also Graham & Harris, 2000). In addition to the four basic questions he posed and answered for the other three constructs, he asked an additional question for handwriting and spelling skills: Does the elimination of handwriting and spelling via dictation enhance writing performance?

Graham (2006a) reported that the accumulated evidence did in fact support the claim that handwriting and spelling play an important role in writing development. He found that handwriting and spelling are easier or less cognitively demanding for more-skilled than less-skilled writers. There was a large body of research demonstrating that handwriting and spelling improves with age. For instance, in a study with students in Grades 1 to 9, we found that handwriting fluency improved about 10 letters from one grade to the next up until the last grade (Graham, Berninger, Weintraub, & Schafer, 1998). Individual differences in handwriting and spelling also predicted how well students write. In a study involving children in Grades 1 to 6, we found these two skills together accounted for 25% and 42% of the variance in writing quality at the primary and intermediate grades, and 66% and 41% of the variance in writing output at these same grade levels, respectively (Graham, Berninger, Abbott, Abbott, & Whitaker, 1997). Graham further reported that there was a small body of studies showing that handwriting and spelling instruction enhanced one or more aspects of students' writing performance. To illustrate, we found that providing extra instruction in these skills to young struggling writers increased how much they wrote and resulted in improved sentence construction skills (Graham, Harris, & Fink, 2000; Graham, Harris, & Fink-Chorzempa, 2002). Finally, Graham found that eliminating handwriting and spelling through dictation had a positive impact on the writing of specific groups of writers. For example, MacArthur and Graham (1987) reported that poor writers produced qualitatively better text when dictating stories versus writing them by hand.

Graham (2006a) offered a tentative proposition (with some reservations) about another basic writing skill: sentence construction. He indicated there is evidence that skilled writers produce more complex sentences than less-skilled ones, although these findings do not hold for all comparisons (e.g., good vs. poor readers). He further found that developing writers' sentences become increasingly complex with age, although this finding varied by writing task. Sentence skills were also correlated with writing performance (at least in some studies), but this finding appeared to vary by genre. Efforts to improve the sentence construction skills of developing writers enhanced writing performance, if the right type of instruction was provided. For instance, Saddler and Graham (2005) found that instruction for sentence combining had a positive impact on the quality of text produced by writers.

The teaching of handwriting, spelling, and sentence construction skills is not part of the SRSD model that we just reviewed. However, difficulties mastering such skills could conceivably limit the effectiveness of SRSD and other types of writing instruction, such as process writing or writers' workshop. Thus, we would argue that good writing instruction should promote the development writing constructs of strategies, knowledge, will, and skills.

CONCLUDING COMMENTS

Our writing research since the 1980s has been guided by four constructs: strategies, knowledge, will, and skills. The first three were foundational in our development of SRSD, which has been tested in over 50 experimental studies with a wide range of students at almost every grade level. These three constructs have further been instrumental in much of the other research we have conducted, as we have repeatedly examined their importance in the development of writing difficulties and typical writing development. We have also focused our attention on the role of basic writing skills, such as handwriting, spelling, and sentence construction, in students' development as writer. Of course, these are not the only aspects of writing that are important to students' progress as writers (as is aptly illustrated throughout this volume), but we would contend that our research and the research of others (Graham, 2006a) supports the argument that each is foundational.

ACKNOWLEDGMENTS

Although much remains to be learned and done in this area of research, we owe a great deal of thanks to John Hayes, Michel Fayol, and Pietro Boscolo. Without the seminal work of these great scholars, the shoulders on which all of us stand would be much narrower. We thank them for their guidance and insights.

REFERENCES

Alley, G., & Deshler, D. (1979). *Teaching the learning disabled adolescent: Strategies and methods*. Denver, CO: Love.

Andrews, R., Torgerson, C., Beverton, S., Freeman, A., Locke, T., Low, G., & Zhu, D. (2006). The effects of grammar teaching on writing development. *British Educational Research Journal, 32*, 39–55.

Applebee, A., & Langer, J. (2006). *The state of writing instruction: What existing data tell us*. Albany, NY: Center on English Learning and Achievement.

Bangert-Drowns, R. L., Hurley, M. M., & Wilkinson, B. (2004). The effects of school-based writing-to-learn interventions on academic achievement: A meta-analysis. *Review of Educational Research, 74*, 29–58.

Berninger, V., Mizokawa, D., & Bragg, R. (1991). Theory-based diagnosis and remediation of writing disabilities. *Journal of School Psychology, 29*, 57–79.

Boscolo, P. (1990). The construction of expository text. *First Language, 10*, 217–230.

Brown, A., Campione, J., & Day, J. (1981). Learning to learn: On training students to learn from text. *Educational Researcher, 10*, 14–21.

Bourdin, B., & Fayol, M. (1993). *Comparing speaking span and writing span: A working memory approach*. Paper presented at the Meeting of the European Association for Research in Learning and Instruction, Aix-en-Provence, France.

Bourdin, B., & Fayol, M. (1994). Is written language production more difficult than oral language production? A working memory approach. *International Journal of Psychology, 29*, 591–620.

Cutler, L., & Graham, S. (2008). Primary grade writing instruction: A national survey. *Journal of Educational Psychology, 100*, 907–919.

De La Paz, S., Swanson, P., & Graham, S. (1998). Contribution of executive control to the revising problems of students with writing and learning difficulties. *Journal of Educational Psychology, 90*, 448–460.

Gilbert, J., & Graham, S. (2010). Teaching writing to elementary students in grades 4 to 6: A national survey. *Elementary School Journal, 110*, 494–518.

Graham, S. (1982). Written composition research and practice: A unified approach. *Focus on Exceptional Children, 14*, 1–16.

Graham, S. (1990). The role of production factors in learning disabled students' compositions. *Journal of Educational Psychology, 82*, 781–791.

Graham, S. (1997). Executive control in the revising of students with learning and writing difficulties. *Journal of Educational Psychology, 89*, 223–234.

Graham, S. (2006a). Writing. In P. Alexander & P. Winne (Eds.), *Handbook of educational psychology* (pp. 457–478). Mahwah, NJ: Erlbaum.

Graham, S. (2006b). Strategy instruction and the teaching of writing. In C. MacArthur, S. Graham, & J. Fitzgerald (Eds.), *Handbook of writing research* (pp. 187–207). New York: Guilford.

Graham, S. (2010). Teaching writing. P. Hogan (Ed.), *Cambridge encyclopedia of language Sciences* (pp. 848–851). Cambridge: Cambridge University Press.

Graham, S., Berninger, V., Abbott, R., Abbott, S., & Whitaker, D. (1997). The role of mechanics in composing of elementary school students: A new methodological approach. *Journal of Educational Psychology, 89*, 170–182.

Graham, S., Berninger, V., & Fan, W. (2007). The structural relationship between writing attitude and writing achievement in young children. *Contemporary Educational Psychology, 32*, 516–536.

Graham, S., Berninger, V., Weintraub, N., & Schafer, W. (1998). The development of handwriting fluency and legibility in grades 1 through 9. *Journal of Educational Research, 92*, 42–52.

Graham, S., Capizzi, A., Hebert, M., & Morphy, P. (2010). *Teaching writing to middle school students: A national survey.* Paper submitted for publication.

Graham, S., & Harris, K. R. (1989). A components analysis of cognitive strategy instruction: Effects on learning disabled students' compositions and self-efficacy. *Journal of Educational Psychology, 81*, 353–361.

Graham, S., & Harris, K. R. (1993). Self-regulated strategy development: Helping students with learning problems develop as writers. *Elementary School Journal, 94*, 169–182.

Graham, S., & Harris, K. R. (2000). The role of self-regulation and transcription skills in writing and writing development. *Educational Psychologist, 35*, 3–12.

Graham, S., & Harris, K. R. (2005). *Writing better: Teaching writing processes and self-regulation to students with learning problems.* Baltimore, MD: Brookes.

Graham, S., & Harris, K. R. (2009). Almost 30 years of writing research: Making sense of it all with *The Wrath of Khan. Learning Disabilities Research and Practice, 24*, 58–68.

Graham, S., Harris, K. R., & Fink, B. (2000). Is handwriting causally related to learning to write? Treatment of handwriting problems in beginning writers. *Journal of Educational Psychology, 92*, 620–633.

Graham, S., Harris, K. R., & Fink-Chorzempa, B. (2002). Contributions of spelling instruction to the spelling, writing, and reading of poor spellers. *Journal of Educational Psychology, 94*, 669–686.

Graham, S., Harris, K. R., & Hebert, M. (2011). *Assessing writing.* Alliance for Excellence in Education. Washington, DC (commissioned by the Carnegie Corp. of New York). Manuscript in preparation.

Graham, S., Harris, K. R., MacArthur, C., & Fink-Chorzempa, B. (2003). Primary grade teachers' instructional adaptations for weaker writers: A national survey. *Journal of Educational Psychology, 95*, 279–293.

Graham, S., Harris, K. R., & Mason, L. (2005). Improving the writing performance, knowledge, and motivation of struggling young writers: The effects of self-regulated strategy development. *Contemporary Educational Psychology, 30,* 207–241.

Graham, S., Harris, K. R., Mason, L., Fink-Chorzempa, B., Moran, S., & Saddler, B. (2008). How do primary grade teachers teach handwriting: A national survey. *Reading and Writing: An Interdisciplinary Journal, 21,* 49–69.

Graham, S., Harris, K., & Sawyer, R. (1987). Composition instruction with learning disabled students: Self-instructional strategy training. *Focus on Exceptional Children, 20,* 1–11.

Graham, S., & Hebert, M. (2010). *Writing to reading: Evidence for how writing can improve reading.* Washington, DC: Alliance for Excellence in Education.

Graham, S., & Miller, L. (1979). Spelling research and practice: A unified approach. *Focus on Exceptional Children, 12,* 1–16.

Graham, S., & Miller, L. (1980). Handwriting research and practice: A unified approach. *Focus on Exceptional Children, 13,* 1–16.

Graham, S., Morphy, P., Harris, K., Fink-Chorzempa, B., Saddler, B., Moran, S., & Mason, L. (2008). Teaching spelling in the primary grades: A national survey of instructional practices and adaptations. *American Educational Research Journal, 45,* 796–825.

Graham, S., & Perin, D. (2007a). A meta-analysis of writing instruction for adolescent students. *Journal of Educational Psychology, 99,* 445–476.

Graham, S., & Perin, D. (2007b). *Writing next: Effective strategies to improve writing of adolescents in middle and high schools.* Washington, DC: Alliance for Excellence in Education.

Graham, S., & Perin, D. (2007c). What we know, what we still need to know: Teaching adolescents to write. *Scientific Studies in Reading, 11,* 313–336.

Graham, S., Schwartz, S., & MacArthur, C. (1993). Knowledge of writing and the composing process, attitude toward writing, and self-efficacy for students with and without learning disabilities. *Journal of Learning Disabilities, 26,* 237–249.

Gregg, L., & Steinberg, E. (Eds.). (1980). *Cognitive processes in writing* (pp. 3–30). Hillsdale, NJ: Erlbaum.

Harris, K., & Graham, S. (1985). Improving learning disabled students' composition skills: Self-control strategy training. *Learning Disability Quarterly, 8,* 27–36.

Harris, K., & Graham, S. (1996). *Making the writing process work: Strategies for composition and self-regulation* (2nd ed.). Cambridge: Brookline Books.

Harris, K. R. (1982). Cognitive-behavior modifications: Application with exceptional students. *Focus on Exceptional Children, 15,* 1–16.

Harris, K. R., & Brown, R. (1982). Cognitive modification and informed teacher treatments for shy children. *Journal of Experimental Education, 50,* 137–144.

Harris, K. R., & Graham, S. (2008). Self-regulated strategy development in writing: Premises, evolution, and the future. *British Journal of Educational Psychology, Monograph Series II, 6,* 113–136.

Harris, K. R., Graham, S., Brindle, M., & Sandmel, K. (2009). Metacognition and children's writing. In D. Hacker, J. Dunlosky, & A. Graesser (Eds.), *Handbook of metacognition in education* (pp. 131–153). Mahwah, NJ: Erlbaum.

Harris, K. R., Graham, S., & Mason, L. (2003). Self-regulated strategy development in the classroom: Part of a balanced approach to writing instruction for students with disabilities. *Focus on Exceptional Children, 35,* 1–16.

Harris, K. R., Graham, S., & Mason, L. (2006). Improving the writing, knowledge, and motivation of struggling young writers: Effects of self-regulated strategy development with and without peer support. *American Educational Research Journal, 43,* 295–340.

Harris, K. R., Graham, S., Mason, L., & Friedlander, B. (2008). *Powerful writing strategies for all students.* Baltimore, MD: Brookes.

Hayes, J. (1996). A new framework for understanding cognition and affect in writing. In M. Levy & S. Ransdell (Eds.), *The science of writing: Theories, methods, individual differences, and applications* (pp. 1–27). Mahwah, NJ: Erlbaum.

Hayes, J., & Flower, L. (1980). Identifying the organization of writing processes. In L. Gregg & E. Steinberg (Eds.), *Cognitive processes in writing* (pp. 3–30). Hillsdale, NJ: Erlbaum.

Kiuhara, S., Graham, S., & Hawken, L. (2009). Teaching writing to high school students: A national survey. *Journal of Educational Psychology, 101*, 136–160.

Locke, E., Shaw, K., Saari, L., & Latham, G. (1981). Goal setting and task performance: 1969–1980. *Psychological Bulletin, 90*, 125–152.

MacArthur, C., & Graham, S. (1987). Learning disabled students' composing under three methods of text production: Handwriting, word processing, and dictation. *Journal of Special Education, 21*, 22–42.

MacArthur, C., Graham, S., & Schwartz, S. (1991). Knowledge of revision and revising behavior among students with learning disabilities. *Learning Disability Quarterly, 14*, 61–74.

McCutchen, D. (1988). "Functional automaticity" in children's writing: A problem of meta-cognitive control. *Written Communication, 5*, 306–324.

Meichenbaum, D. (1977). *Cognitive behavior modification: An integrative approach*. New York: Plenum.

Morphy, P., & Graham, S. (2009). *Word processing programs and weaker writers/readers: A meta-analysis of research findings*. Submitted for publication.

National Commission on Writing (2003, April). *The neglected "R": The need for a writing revolution*. Retrieved from http://www.collegeboard.org/prod_downloads/writing-com/neglectedr.pdf

Olinghouse, N., & Graham, S. (2009). The relationship between the writing knowledge and the writing performance of elementary-grade students. *Journal of Educational Psychology, 101*, 37–50.

Rogers, L., & Graham, S. (2008). A meta-analysis of single subject design writing intervention research. *Journal of Educational Psychology, 100*, 879–906.

Saddler, B., & Graham, S. (2005). The effects of peer-assisted sentence-combining instruction on the writing performance of more and less skilled young writers. *Journal of Educational Psychology, 97*, 43–54.

Saddler, B., & Graham, S. (2007). The relationship between writing knowledge and writing performance among more and less skilled writers. *Reading and Writing Quarterly, 23*, 231–247.

Salahu-Din, D., Persky, H., & Miller, J. (2008). *The nation's report card: Writing 2007* (NCES 2008–468). Washington, DC: National Center for Education Statistics, Institute of Education Sciences, U.S. Department of Education.

Sandmel, K., & Graham, S. (in press). The process writing approach: A meta-analysis. *Journal of Educational Research*.

Sawyer, R., Graham, S., & Harris, K. (1992). Direct teaching, strategy instruction, and strategy instruction with explicit self-regulation: Effects on learning disabled students' composition skills and self-efficacy. *Journal of Educational Psychology, 84*, 340–352.

Stein, N., & Glynn, C. (1979). An analysis of story comprehension in elementary school children. In R. Freedle (Ed.), *Advances in discourse processes: Vol. 2. New directions in discourse processing*. Norwood, NJ: Ablex.

9

Phonological, Orthographic, and Morphological Word-Level Skills Supporting Multiple Levels of the Writing Process[1]

DEBORAH MCCUTCHEN

*I*n the spring of 1978 on the campus of Pittsburgh's Carnegie Mellon University, a conference convened an interdisciplinary group of researchers who were interested in the following questions: What do we know about how people write, and what do we need to know to help people write better (Gregg & Steinberg, 1980, p. ix)? One result of that conference was Gregg and Steinberg's (1980) seminal book *Cognitive Processes in Writing*. Among the many influential chapters of that book were two that reflected the collaboration between Hayes and Flower, outlining a theoretical model (Flower & Hayes, 1980; Hayes & Flower, 1980) that has influenced writing research for more than 30 years and advanced our knowledge considerably about how people write and how to help them write better. The original model comprised three primary processes: planning, translating, and reviewing.

Perhaps because Hayes and Flower (1980) were attempting to model expertise, the more clearly strategic processes of planning and reviewing have received considerable research attention (e.g., Allal, Chanquoy, & Largy, 2004; Butterfield, Hacker, & Plumb, 1994; Flower & Hayes, 1980; MacArthur, Graham, Schwartz, & Shafer, 1995). For skilled writers, other processes, such as those entailed in translating (e.g., sentence generation, spelling, handwriting), are relatively fluent and may be less obviously related to individual differences in writing skill. However, the challenge of generating coherent, grammatical sentences has long

---

[1] The opinions expressed are those of the author and do not represent views of the U.S. Department of Education or the National Institute of Child Health and Human Development.

been recognized by those who work with young or struggling writers (Bereiter & Scardamalia, 1987; Graham, 1990), or with writers working in their nonnative language (Chenoweth & Hayes, 2001).

This chapter focuses largely on translating processes, exploring linguistic skills that seem to be implicated in writing, particularly phonological and morphological skills. I review related work done by other researchers but allot considerable attention to findings from our research group regarding the linguistic skills that seem implicit in the development of children's translating processes.

In keeping with the goal of this volume, I will relate the reviewed work to larger theoretical issues. Results from work on linguistic aspects of speech production and reading have figured prominently in psychological theorizing about language and cognition in general, as well as their interactions. In addition, international research on writing, such as that done by the honorees of this volume, Boscolo, Fayol, and Hayes and Bazerman (see also Berman & Verhoeven, 2002), promises to help us understand how acquisition of skill in writing may be influenced by the characteristics of specific languages and their related orthographies, as has been found to be the case in reading (e.g., McBride-Chang, Wat, Hua, Zhou, & Wagner, 2003; Seymour, Aro, & Erskine, 2003).

THE ROLE OF LINGUISTIC KNOWLEDGE IN TRANSLATING IDEAS INTO TEXT

Based on analysis of a large cross-sectional study of writers spanning early and upper elementary to junior high (ages 6 to 15), Berninger and Swanson (1994) refined Hayes and Flower's original description of translating to better account for children's writing processes, distinguishing text generation from transcription. *Text generation* shares many cognitive components with speech production, such as content selection, lexical retrieval (see Chapter 13, this volume), phonological encoding, and syntactic formulation, as well as features specific to written texts produced at school. *Transcription* entails the cognitive, linguistic, and physical acts of producing letters by pen or keyboard and spelling written words. This distinction provided the framework for a series of studies investigating individual differences in processes contributing to transcription (handwriting and spelling) and text generation (at the word, sentence, and text levels) and how these process differences in turn contributed unique variance to the quality of children's narrative and expository texts. For example, individual differences in both handwriting and spelling explained unique variance in length and quality of composed texts in Grades 1 to 6 (age 6 to 12) (Graham, Berninger, Abbott, Abbott, & Whitaker, 1997). Although Berninger and Swanson suggested that transcription may contribute greatly at the early stages and somewhat at the middle stages of writing development, subsequent studies of the cognitive processes of translation unfolding in real time by many researchers showed that transcription processes contribute to some degree even in adult writing (see Chapter 2, this volume). In keeping with this research, Chenoweth and Hayes (2001) included transcription as an additional component to earlier descriptions of translating (Hayes & Flower, 1980; Kaufer, Hayes, & Flower, 1986). Since then, numerous studies of transcription, particularly in beginning and developing writers, have been conducted and yielded knowledge about handwriting, keyboarding, and spelling processes (see Chapters 17 and 22, this volume).

Although transcription and text generation may be distinguished conceptually, writing researchers do not claim that the temporal course of on-line processing, from idea generation to written transcription, is neatly sequential—rather the various processes related to idea generation, planning, transcription, and text generation interact and even compete for limited capacity and resources in working memory (McCutchen, 2000; see also Chapter 2, this volume). In fact, writing interventions that have proven effective in programmatic research with at-risk writers in the early grades (ages 6 to 9) (e.g., Berninger et al., 2002) and with writers with specific learning disabilities impairing writing skills (e.g., Berninger et al., 2008) intentionally take working memory issues into account and teach transcription and text generation skills close in time, so that the two processes can interact more efficiently.

Even skilled writers make frequent revisions in word choice and grammatical structure in the course of translating ideas into written text (Chenoweth & Hayes, 2001; Kaufer et al., 1986; McCutchen, 1988), much as speakers do as they generate utterances (Garrett, 1980; Levelt, 1983). Consider, for example, an excerpt from a protocol of a wine columnist whom I observed as he was writing a column about a tasting of Bordeaux wines:

> Alright, so now what we're doing is, we've got a lead-in which is obviously a pastiche of something that I heard once somewhere, "oft heard and well remembered," right? And (reading) "the names of the great chateaux of Bordeaux." Now we've got to follow it up with the names that they've heard most, which are going to be Lafite and Mouton. So (types) "Chateau Lafite and Chateau Mouton Rothchild " (stops typing) Spring to mind? Leap to mind? Come to mind? All of which are boring so I'll need another word. Again (reads and types) "Chateau Lafite and Chateau Mouton Rothchild, names that may well come ... (edits) Ok, "are those that ..." just—if I say "great chateaux" what happens? Things burst. Can we say "burst into brains first"? Terrible!

Although this expert writer could fluently generate alternative phrasings, his plans for *what* to say could be fulfilled only once he decided *how* to say it; thus translating ideas into text demands considerable linguistic fluency, even for highly skilled writers. Fluency in text generation and transcription is important due to the interactive nature of writing and to resource demands of competing processes; fluent translating processes may allow more resources to be available for the more strategic processes of planning and revising (Bourdin & Fayol, 2000; Dellerman, Coirier, & Marchand, 1996; McCutchen, 2000). Linguistic skills that may contribute to fluency in both transcription and text generation processes will be discussed in turn.

SPELLING

The contribution of linguistic knowledge to spelling—particularly phonological and morphological knowledge—has been investigated by researchers for at least four decades, but the knowledge base continues to grow. Emergent writers show considerable creativity with sound-symbol mappings, frequently described in discussions of their "invented spellings." In English, spelling is not a straightforward coding of sounds to letters because of the variable mappings of more than 40 phonemes onto the alphabet of only 26 letters. Such mapping challenges are not unique to English or to the Roman alphabet (e.g., Harris & Hatano, 1999; Sénéchal & Kearnan, 2007), but the mapping is made more complex by the fact that the orthographic rules of English represent both phonological and morphological aspects of the language (Venezky, 1970). Gentry's (1982) model of children's spelling is illustrative of how the development of spelling skill entails increasing phonological and morphological insight, although Gentry's characterization of stages is not without controversy (see also Bissex, 1980; Deacon, Kirby, & Casselman-Bell, 2009; Ehri, 1992; Henderson & Beers, 1980; Read, 1981; Sénéchal & Kearnan, 2007; Treiman, 1993). Although theorists may disagree on whether there are discrete stages or cascading development, it does appear that children progress from nonspeech, to phonetic, to phonemic representations in their spelling (Ehri, 1992; Treiman, 1993), ultimately also recognizing orthographic and morphological elements of the writing system associated with their language.

According to Gentry (1982), the earliest attempts at spelling during the *precommunicative* stage involve the child's first use of alphabetic symbols to represent language, although not necessarily at the phoneme level. As the label implies, spelling during the precommunicative stage is often undecipherable because the symbols bear little relationship to the phonological structure of the words being represented. Children may confuse the number of letters in a word with quantifiable aspects of the referent such as size or number, writing longer letter strings to represent larger objects. Such a strategy has been observed in children learning to spell across a variety of languages (Ferreiro & Teberosky, 1982; Share & Levin, 1999).

Children begin to use letters to represent some, but not necessarily all, sounds within words during the *semiphonetic* stage, as illustrated in the classic example from Bissex (1980), *RUDF* (i.e., "Are you deaf?"). Once children are attempting to represent individual sounds within words, they seem differentially sensitive to vowels and consonants, depending on the language and orthographic system. Children learning English are more likely to include letters representing initial and final consonants than other sounds within words (Ehri, 1986; Treiman, 1993), and they have more difficulty with the spellings of vowels than consonants (Varnhagen, Boechler, & Steffler, 1999). A similar tendency for consonants to be more fully represented than vowels (specifically, vowel diacritics) was observed in children learning to spell Hebrew (Share & Levin, 1999), although this may reflect the fact that diacritics reflecting vowels are not typically included in spellings after Grade 4. The reverse has been reported in studies of Spanish and Italian, with vowels being more likely represented than consonants (Ferreiro & Teberosky, 1982; Pontecovo & Zucchermaglio, 1990), perhaps influenced by the syllabic structures of these languages. More complete representations of the phonological structure of words are represented in children's spelling during the *phonetic* stage, but often unconventionally (e.g., *EGL* for *eagle*).

For languages such as English, in which spelling does not map transparently onto phonology, the later stages of spelling development (*transitional* and finally *conventional* spelling, according to Gentry, 1982) are linked to children's growing awareness of how orthography reflects word meaning (i.e., morphology) as well as sound (Carlisle, 1988; Ehri, 1992). Nunes and Bryant (2006) argued that morphological insights can demystify many peculiarities in English spelling (see also Moats, 2000; Nagy & Scott, 2000). For example, morphological knowledge can help a writer understand why the same sounds are spelled differently across words with different morphological structures (*box, socks*). Similarly, it is helpful for a writer to understand that morphemes may retain their spelling across words, despite changes in their pronunciation (*heal, health*). Furthermore, writers benefit from understanding that some morphological forms are distinguishable in writing but not in speech, for example, in English, the possessive (e.g., *the boy's box* vs. *the boys box*) and, in French, some plural markers (e.g., *il danse* vs. *ils dansent*). Evidence from English (Griffith, 1991; Treiman, 1993), French (Pacton & Fayol, 2003; Sénéchal & Kearnan, 2007), Hebrew (Share & Levin, 1999), and Greek (Bryant, Nunes, & Aidinis, 1999) indicates that children become aware of phonological aspects of spelling before morphological aspects. In addition, longitudinal studies indicate that the causal relationship between spelling skill and morphological knowledge is probably two way (Nunes, Bryant, & Bindman, 2006).

Although the development of children's spelling often follows such a trajectory, this is not to say that children learn to spell without instruction, especially in orthographies that do not represent phonology transparently, such as English and French. Exploration of the orthographic system via invented spelling together with feedback as to correct spelling has been shown to improve children's spelling more than invented spelling alone (Rieben, Ntamakiliro, Gonthier, & Fayol, 2005). Also, in consultation with Venezky (1995, 1999), Berninger and colleagues developed an approach to teaching the alternations in the alphabetic principle in English (one- or two-letter graphemes corresponding to a phoneme during reading [e.g., /sh/ and /th/] or one phoneme to corresponding one- or two-letter graphemes during spelling) that has been effective in improving the spelling skills of at-risk writers (e.g., Berninger et al., 2002) and students with writing disabilities (e.g., Berninger et al., 2008). The latter also benefit from instructional activities that develop awareness of and interrelationships among phonological, orthographic, and morphological cues in words (Berninger & Wolf, 2009).

Digital Transcription Modes

With the rise in use of digital writing technologies, keyboarding in the context of word processing has received considerable research attention as an alternative transcription mode for students. Despite initial hopes that word processing would be a panacea for writing challenges ranging from spelling to revision, early research on children's word processing showed few consistent advantages for keyboarding over handwriting (see Cochran-Smith, 1991, for a review of early work). In a more recent review, MacArthur (2009) pointed out that students' relative fluency with handwriting *and* keyboarding must be considered if we are to expect benefits over handwriting from even the increasingly sophisticated support provided by recent word-processing programs (word prediction as well as spell checks). Unless children's keyboarding is at least as fluent as their handwriting, potential gains from the tool may be overshadowed by dysfluencies in the production mode (Berninger, Abbott, Augsburger, & Garcia, 2009). Even students with writing disabilities, for whom handwriting typically presents considerable challenge, exhibit individual differences in whether they write better by keyboard than pen; however, access to word processors needs to be coupled with instruction in keyboarding as well as planning, revising, and other writing strategies, if students are to maximize the potential offered by technologies that support writing (Berninger et al., 2009; MacArthur, 2009).

Rather than a panacea to *improve* writing, more recent digital technologies have led to a concern, at least in some quarters, that some digital modes—particularly texting—have negative effects on children's conventional spelling and literacy skills. Text messages and other forms of computer-mediated communication that are used by adolescents (and increasingly by younger children) frequently contain abbreviations (e.g., *LOL, POS*) and additional "textisms" that reflect homophonic combinations of graphemes and numerals (e.g., *gr8, 2nite*) and other playful, linguistic sleights of hand (e.g., *plz, wazzup*). Although Thurlow (2006) interpreted textisms as a natural variation in language use, he reviewed more than 100 articles from popular media, many decrying the intrusions of textisms into students' other writing venues (e.g., school work) and predicting the imminent decline of conventional written English. In a recent survey, teens in the United States admitted that they sometimes incorporated textisms into their school writing, and such admissions were more likely from teens who blogged or owned cell phones compared to those who did not; however, most teens did not view their texting as writing per se (Lenhart, Arafeh, Smith, & Macgill, 2008).

Plester, Wood, and Joshi (2009) empirically examined relationships between children's texting practices and their conventional literacy skills. They asked 10- to 12-year-old British children to generate simulated text messages and examined the ratio of textisms in their written responses, as well as the nature of the textisms. Plester et al. reported a significant, positive correlation between children's density of use of textisms and their word reading and a marginally significant correlation with phonological awareness. Moreover, when they examined the kinds of textisms children used, they found the strongest relationships with word reading were with homophones (e.g., *l8r*) and stylized representations of accents (e.g., *elp* for *help*), both phonologically based. In a related study, Plester, Wood, and Bell (2008) found that the ratio of textisms to words was positively correlated with a standardized measure of verbal reasoning in one subject sample and with spelling skill in a second sample. Again, use of more phonologically based textisms (e.g., *gr8*) was more strongly related to spelling skill and to overall writing ability than were other types of textisms. Thus, in contrast to concerns that children's texting will degrade traditional literacy skills, there is growing evidence that textisms and other forms of computer-mediated communication (e.g., instant messaging) may reflect a metalinguistic exploration of written representations that support, or at minimum develop concurrent with, conventional literacy skills, especially phonological awareness (Crystal, 2008).

WRITING, WORD CHOICE, AND MORPHOLOGICAL KNOWLEDGE

Although relationships between morphological knowledge and reading have been examined extensively (Carlisle, 1995, 2000; Casalis & Louis-Alexandre, 2000; Fowler & Liberman, 1995; Mahoney, Singson, & Mann, 2000; McCutchen, Green, & Abbott, 2008; Nagy, Berninger, & Abbott, 2006; Singson, Mahoney, & Mann, 2000; Windsor, 2000), there is growing interest in the relationship between morphological knowledge and writing that extends beyond spelling. Children's control of morphological forms in their written narratives has been found to replicate patterns observed in children's speech, at least in English (Berko, 1958; Menyuk, 1988), with control over inflectional morphology, such as verb tense and plural markers, appearing earlier than control of all but the most common derivational morphemes, such as the agentive and instrumental -er marker, as in *teacher* and *eraser*, which change the meaning and the grammatical category of the affixed word (Carlisle, 1996; Green et al., 2003). Analyzing children's spontaneous use of morphological forms in their written stories, Carlisle (1996) provided evidence that between the second and third grades children increase their accurate use of morphologically complex words, consolidate their knowledge of inflections, and begin to use more derivational forms.

We observed a similar trend among students in the third and fourth grades (Green et al., 2003). Although we found that over 90% of beginning third-grade students and over 95% of beginning fourth-grade students used an accurately spelled verb inflection (e.g., *walked, was walking*) at least once in their written narratives, with average accuracy of those attempting inflections ranging from 82% (past tense inflections in Grade 3) to 93% (complex verb inflections in Grade 4), the rate of use of morphological derivations was much lower. Only 35% of beginning third-grade students used an accurately spelled derivation (e.g., *teacher, quickly*), with a mean accuracy rate 63%; and 53% of beginning fourth-grade students used a derived morphological form accurately, with a mean accuracy rate of 77%. For both grade levels, total morphological accuracy scores (based on both inflections and derivations) correlated with spelling, and in regression analyses morphological accuracy accounted for 23% of variance in spelling among third graders and 18% among fourth graders (Green et al., 2003).

When we looked more closely at the derivational morphology that the children used, we found that the majority fell into a handful of categories: forming an adverb by adding -ly (e.g., *quickly*); forming an adjective by adding either -ed (e.g., *scared*), -y (e.g., *lucky*), -ing (e.g., *missing*), or -ful (e.g., *wonderful*); and forming a noun by adding -er (e.g., *teacher, eraser*). We observed only one use of a prefix (re-, as in *rename*) in the entire sample of 247 children. Moreover, all of the derivational forms that the children used maintained the same phonological form between the stem word and the derived form; we found no instances in which the pronunciation of the derivation differed from that of the stem (e.g., *signature, sign*). Such shifts in pronunciation have been shown to decrease the accuracy and increase the time needed by children to recognize morphological relationships across words (Carlisle & Nomanbhoy, 1993; Fowler & Liberman, 1995). The findings of Green et al. (2003) suggest that such phonological shifts also make *word selection* more difficult during writing, although it is not clear whether the difficulty stems from phonological complexities in accessing the derivational form or from orthographic complexities in spelling it. In the former case, writers may not be able to find the word they are seeking because of the phonological change (a text generation issue); in the latter, writers may access the word but choose to avoid it because they are less confident of its spelling (a transcription issue).

In a recent study, Stull (2010) observed clear involvement of morphological knowledge in text generation, with her documentation of what she called invented morphology. Just as errors in children's invented spellings reflect evolution of their understanding of the orthographic rules governing English spelling (Gentry, 1982; Read, 1981), children make systematic errors as their understanding of English morphology evolves. Examples of such errors are evident in very young children's oral language with their overgeneralizations of regular inflectional markers for verb tense and noun number. Frequently cited examples of these inflectional overgeneralizations are children's use of *goed* instead of *went*, or *foots* instead of *feet* (Menyuk, 1988). Such errors may result because children have not fully internalized the morphological rules or because they lack the knowledge of specific irregular forms (Bowerman, 1982, Nunes et al., 2006), although such errors have been observed even after the irregular forms had been documented in a child's vocabulary (Menyuk, 1988). Although overgeneralizations are errors, they are recognized as evidence of developing morphological knowledge because they reflect an understanding of how inflectional morphemes are used. As Tyler and Nagy (1989) described it, "Overgeneralizations provide the clearest type of evidence that acquisition of a morphological process as a combinatory, rule-governed process is taking place" (p. 659).

Stull (2010) documented similar sorts of errors in the writing of fifth-grade children, reflecting evolution of their control over derivational morphology (in contrast to the inflectional morphology implicated in the overgeneralization in young children's speech). In tasks that invited more derivational forms than children typically include in their spontaneous writing (Green et al., 2003), Stull observed children combining stems and suffixes in unconventional ways that violated the distributional constraints of English (Tyler & Nagy, 1989). Some of the more frequent examples of such distributional errors included "*the terrored° penguins*," "*the denty° motorcycle*," "*to solidize°* (or *solidate°*) *a liquid*," and "*to make a solvation°*" by stirring salt into water. The logic in such errors is clear: By analogy, if one can be *scared*, why not *terrored°*? If motorcycles can be *rusty*, why not *denty°*? If *realize*, why not *solidize°*? And if *combination*, why not *solvation°*?

Rules governing the legal match of suffixes to stems are complex (Sénéchal & Kearnan, 2007; Tyler & Nagy, 1989), sometimes having to do with the stem's etymology, but always limited by the availability in the language of an existing word that expresses the same meaning. Thus, *denty* is illegal, in part, because the adjective *dented* is already part of the English lexicon. Tyler and Nagy documented that students continue to develop their knowledge of such distributional constraints even beyond high school, much later than they acquire knowledge of what Tyler and Nagy called relational morphology (i.e., that *teacher* is related to *teach*) or syntactic morphology (i.e., that *teach* functions as a verb). We observed the same developmental sequence in morphological knowledge and found it related to the development of children's reading (McCutchen et al., 2008), although like Tyler and Nagy, we asked students to make judgments of words presented to them.

Stull (2010) observed that children's knowledge of distributional morphology, as evidenced in their own writing, was also related to general literacy skills, although in an interesting way. The errors that Stull observed were not like those made by children with language impairments (Rubin, Patterson, & Kantor, 1991). Rather than omissions of inflectional or derivational suffixes (e.g., *miss* for *missed*) or substitutions of a related word (e.g., *interesting* for *interested*), Stull saw children using morphological knowledge to construct novel words that typically fit the sentence syntax. Just as children's invented phonetic spellings of words (e.g., *EGL* for *eagle*) reflect partial but incomplete knowledge of sound–letter correspondences, Stull hypothesized that children's invented morphology reflected more than minimal levels of morphological insight. She therefore predicted that such errors would not be present in the writing of children with little morphological knowledge. Because children with advanced morphological knowledge do not make such errors (because they use correct morphological forms), Stull observed a nonlinear relationship between children's invented morphology and their other literacy skills. Using analyses that blocked students as to (a) above or below average morphological skill (based on a traditional morphological awareness task used by Siegel, 2008), and (b) presence or absence of invented morphology in their writing, Stull examined the relationship between morphological skill and use of invented morphology.

Despite the nonlinear trends, Stull (2010) found that the high-skill group contained a significantly larger percentage of students who used invented morphology, and the low-skill group contained a larger percentage of students who did not. The pattern was markedly different for other kinds of errors, such as routine spelling errors; students with higher morphological awareness were significantly less likely to make other kinds of errors than were students with lower morphological awareness. When she blocked children on measures of word reading, vocabulary, and reading comprehension, Stull again found the high-skill groups contained a significantly larger percentage of students who used invented morphology compared to the low-skill groups. Stull's findings provide additional evidence linking children's morphological knowledge to their writing as well as to their reading.

There are compelling theoretical arguments implicating morphological skill in writing that extend beyond the previously described role in spelling. For example, children might use morphological knowledge to bootstrap vocabulary growth during reading (McCutchen & Logan, in press), inferring meanings for unfamiliar words based on familiar morphological units (e.g., *un* + *help* + *ful* + *ness*). With richer vocabulary, writers are able to retrieve more precise lexical representations for their semantic intent during writing, especially when generating the decontextualized language so common in the academic register (Beers & Nagy, 2009; Nagy & Scott, 2000). Consistent with such an argument, McCutchen, Covill, Hoyne, and Mildes (1994) found that skilled writers accessed words from memory more quickly than their less-skilled counterparts.

In addition, knowledge of morphological transformations (e.g., *nation*, *national*) could assist writers as they try to construct the more complex syntax that is characteristic of the academic register. There is an extensive literature on the general development of syntactic complexity as children mature (Hunt, 1970; Loban, 1976; O'Donnell, 1976), and although some evidence suggests that syntactic complexity correlates with text quality (Hunt, 1970), the literature is far from consistent on that point (Crowhurst, 1983). Beers and Nagy (2009) attributed much of the inconsistency to the variety of measures and genres across studies. They argued that of several widely used measures of syntactic complexity, words per clause best capture the character of the academic register, particularly of expository texts. Beers and Nagy examined texts composed by seventh- and eighth-grade students and found that words per clause correlated positively with quality of essays but not with quality of narratives, whereas clauses per T-unit (another popular measure of syntactic complexity) correlated positively with quality of narratives but negatively with quality of essays. Morphologically complex words are typical of many of the syntactic structures that characterize expository language (Scott, 2004) and written as opposed to oral language (Chafe & Danielewicz, 1987), such as complex noun phrases and nominalizations. Thus, skill with morphological transformations could assist writers in managing the syntactic complexity that characterizes the academic register.

LINGUISTIC SKILLS INTERVENTIONS AND EFFECTS ON CHILDREN'S WRITING

Extending descriptive studies of children's spontaneous use of morphological structures in their writing (Carlisle, 1996; Green et al., 2003), we recently examined whether we could influence children's use of morphologically complex words in their writing with a relatively brief intervention that called children's attention to morphological structures within words (McCutchen, Logan, Lotas, & Stull, 2010). We initially examined use of morphological markers in the writing of 175 fifth-grade students, prior to any intervention. Whereas Green et al. examined children's narratives that were written in response to picture prompts, McCutchen et al. engaged children in a more structured writing task that invited use of complex derivational forms. Because children typically include relatively few morphologically complex derivational forms in their spontaneous writing (Green et al., 2003), we were interested in whether that low rate reflected children's difficulties generating complex morphological forms in their spontaneous writing or their lack of need for complex forms, given the content they were trying to convey.

Our task was essentially a sentence-combining task, which children completed both before and after the intervention. The task consisted of multiple sentence sets, each containing three or four short sentences. For example, children were provided the following sentences and asked to combine the short sentences into a single, longer sentence:

The snake was slow.
The snake moved his coils down the tree.

The tree had moss.
The coils glistened.

Children could respond in multiple ways, but the task invited them to revise the short sentences by morphologically shifting the grammatical category of some words to create phrases such as *the mossy tree, the glistening coils, the slow snake,* or *the slowly moving snake.* Thus, the specific changes made to sentences could vary across writers, but the task invited children to attempt proportionally more morphological derivations than they typically include in their written texts. Replicating the general pattern reported by Green et al. (2003), we found that children with higher morphological awareness included more morphologically complex words in their writing and were more accurate in their spelling of those words than children with lower morphological awareness, even after reading skill and oral vocabulary were taken into account.

Following an intervention in which children in half of the participating classrooms received morphologically focused vocabulary instruction, children completed the sentence-combining task a second time. Although higher-performing students in both intervention and control classrooms were near ceiling on the sentence-combining measure, lower-performing children had room to improve and those in intervention classrooms used more morphologically complex forms at posttest and spelled them more accurately than their peers in control classrooms. The intervention effect can be illustrated by comparing the pretest and posttest responses of one low-performing student from the intervention condition. Given the item presented above, at pretest the child wrote: *Their was a slow snake, his coils moved slowly the tree, there was moss on the tree, then the coils glincesd.* Following instruction that gave her practice working with morphologically related words (not in the context of sentence combining), the child wrote: *The snake was slowly moveing slowly down the mossy tree while glistening.* Although she did not receive credit for the repetition of "slowly" or, in our most strict scoring, for the misspelling of "moving," her posttest response contained more morphological derivations than her pretest response and was clearly a better approximation of the propositionally dense language that typifies the academic register.

Sentence combining has been advocated as an instructional strategy for some time (O'Hare, 1973), and there is evidence for its effectiveness in improving writing quality (Saddler & Graham, 2005; see Graham & Perin, 2007, for a meta-analysis). Still, the mechanism underlying the effectiveness of sentence-combining instruction has been somewhat underspecified. Saddler and Graham offered a general resource-competition argument, claiming that translating fluency would increase with practice in generating longer sentences, thereby freeing cognitive resources for other processes, such as planning. The findings reported by McCutchen et al. (2010) provide additional specificity, suggesting that fluency with morphologically complex forms, which sentence-combining practice may yield, enables writers to include in their texts the more complex vocabulary and varied syntax that is characteristic of good writing (Myhill, 2008).

We have additional, although somewhat less direct, evidence linking linguistic interventions with improvements in children's writing, resulting from a series of studies in which we worked to deepen *teachers'* linguistic knowledge and then examined effects on the literacy learning outcomes of their students (McCutchen, Abbott et al., 2002; McCutchen & Berninger, 1999; McCutchen, Green, Abbott, & Sanders, 2009; McCutchen, Harry et al., 2002). Although the importance of phonological awareness, morphological awareness, and other metalinguistic skills has been discussed widely in the research literature, the concepts are not well understood by many classroom teachers, nor are their applications apparent in some classroom instruction. Consider, for example, a lesson we observed in a first-grade classroom:

> Teacher: [discussing short *u*] "It's like someone pushed you in the stomach really hard 'ugh.' How do you get *u* to say its name? By putting an *e* after it."
> Teacher writes on board two patterns: U U___E
> Teacher then asks students to use the two patterns to spell the following words (from dictation): *hunt, shush, crush, prune, stump, abuse, slump, cute, stuck, tube, truck, crunch.* (McCutchen & Berninger, 1999, p. 222)

This is a typical spelling lesson containing a common phonological mistake. Teachers frequently teach the mnemonic "long vowels say their names." In this case, however, the teacher overlooked the fact that the name of the letter /u/ actually contains two phonemes, /j/ (the International Phonetic Alphabet representation of the initial sound in *yes*) as well as /u/. These two sounds are indeed heard in the words *abuse* and *cute*, but the teacher's list also includes *prune* and *tube*, which contain only /u/, not /ju/. Thus, in *prune* and *tube* (at least in most American dialects), the letter *u* does not "say its name." The internal sounds in *cute* and *prune* are close, but not identical. (Readers who are not convinced are asked to compare the initial phonemes in *use* and *ooze*.) This teacher's oversight resulted from her phonological analysis being overshadowed by her spelling knowledge (specifically, the spelling pattern *vowel-consonant-e*). Of course, many students may have glossed over the slight phonological differences in the teacher's "long u words" and followed the spelling lesson without a hitch, but for children still struggling to identify sounds within words and map them onto spelling patterns, such unintentional misinformation can cause needless confusion.

To help teachers avoid such confusion, we worked over the course of several years with multiple cohorts of elementary school teachers, helping them develop knowledge of structural aspects of spoken and written English. Each year of the project we focused on a different grade level, kindergarten through fifth grade, and each year our primary intervention took the form of an intensive 10-day summer institute that involved daylong interactions between teachers and university researchers. Teachers assigned to the intervention condition attended the institute during the summer prior to data collection in their classrooms, and the remaining teachers served as wait-listed controls and were invited to attend the institute after data collection.

During the summer institutes we focused considerable time on deepening intervention teachers' understanding of phonology, phonological awareness, and its role in balanced literacy instruction (see McCutchen & Berninger, 1999, for a detailed description of the instruction). We began by disentangling teachers' analysis of sounds from their knowledge of spelling as we engaged them in auditory activities in which they identified phonemes in various words. We selected words in which the grapheme-to-phoneme correspondences were not simple (such as words in which single phonemes are represented by multiletter graphemes, as in the word-initial grapheme *sh* in the three-phoneme word *ship* and the word-final grapheme *ng* in the three-phoneme word *sing*; and words in which multiple phonemes are represented by a single grapheme, such as *lox*, as opposed to *locks*, which happens to also include an instance in which the single phoneme /k/ is represented by the multiletter grapheme *ch*). As teachers shared their phonological analyses of such words (which often differed dramatically across the group), they realized how profoundly their insights into word sounds were influenced by their knowledge of word spellings.

We outlined for teachers the typical sequence of development in children's phonological awareness (Rosner, 1979) and provided teachers with opportunities to first observe and then administer phonological assessments with children of various ages. We stressed the relationship between students' phonological awareness and their reading and spelling skills (Moats, 2000). We surveyed the developmental continuum of children's spelling skill (Gentry, 1982), and we helped teachers learn to use children's spelling as a diagnostic tool in assessing their students' phonological awareness.

As part of this discussion, we outlined the phonological structure of English vowels and consonants according to articulatory features (Fromkin & Rodman, 1993), and we explored with teachers many systematic errors in children's spelling that reflect phonological similarities. For example, it is not uncommon for children to spell the sounds /tr/ with the letters *ch*, as in *chran* for *train* (Treiman, 1993). After arraying English consonants in a matrix based on the articulatory features of place, manner, and voicing, teachers could see the articulatory proximity of the alveolar stop consonant represented by *t* and the alveolar affricate, typically represented by *ch*, as well as feel the similarity between /tr/ and /č/. Teachers then could understand the rationality in such a spelling error.

We also emphasized the importance of developing students' knowledge of letters (i.e., orthographic awareness), including their ability to transcribe letters fluently as well as spell words accurately. We incorporated our linguistic discussions into a broad and balanced view of literacy instruction (Pressley, 1998). We emphasized the importance of explicit comprehension instruction (Palincsar & Brown, 1984). We also stressed the importance of children's knowledge of discourse genres in their reading as well as writing development. We acknowledged that teachers hold a variety of pedagogical orientations and that developing children's phonological skills need not dictate a specific curriculum; many widely practiced classroom activities, such as encouraging children to use invented spelling in their authentic writing, can provide students with opportunities to develop their phonological awareness. However, throughout our instruction one theme was constant: Although some students seem to develop these skills spontaneously through interactions with text, many students need instruction in the alphabetic principle (but see Adams, 1990, for an analysis of that apparent "spontaneity").

In our work with kindergarten teachers (McCutchen, Abbott et al., 2002), we found that students in classrooms of intervention teachers showed increased transcription fluency (measured as fluency in writing legible letters) at the end of the year, compared to their peers in control classrooms. When we looked more closely at what teachers were actually doing in their classrooms, we found that students of kindergarten teachers (intervention or control) who spent more time on explicit phonological and orthographic activities showed increased transcription fluency and phonological awareness at the end of the year, and they could also read more words on a standardized assessment at the year end. With first-grade students we documented increased spelling skill and composition fluency (measured as longer written narratives) among students of intervention teachers, as well as increased reading gains.

In a second study (McCutchen et al., 2009), we worked with teachers of Grades 3, 4, and 5. Because many of our instructional recommendations might be considered especially relevant for struggling students in these later grades, we examined the year-end achievement of lower-performing students separately, but included a second analysis of all students to ensure that any changes in teacher practice did not help some students at the expense of others. Compared with their peers in control classrooms, lower-performing students in intervention classrooms showed significantly higher levels of performance at year end on all literacy measures, taking into account performance at the beginning of the year. We saw improved performance in intervention classrooms in multiple writing measures, including spelling (with an effect size of 0.96), writing fluency (as measured by the Woodcock-Johnson writing fluency subtest (Woodcock, McGrew, & Mather, 2001; effect size of 1.03), and composition quality (effect size of 0.96), as well as in word reading, comprehension, and vocabulary. In addition, our measure of teacher's linguistic knowledge was positively related to improved student achievement in spelling and composition quality. In addition, analyses that included everyone in the participating classrooms indicated that all students benefited, although to a somewhat lesser extent than the lower-performing students (effect sizes of 0.44, 0.48, and 0.78, respectively, for spelling, writing fluency, and composition quality).

Thus, across a relatively large number of students (1,497), we were able to document that students' writing and reading skills improved when their teachers had more literacy-relevant linguistic knowledge to inform their practice (McCutchen, Abbott et al., 2002; McCutchen et al., 2009), although phonology and morphology constituted only part of our work with teachers. Moreover, the benefits of working with more knowledgeable teachers were shared by lower-performing and higher-performing students alike.

CONCLUSIONS

The research reviewed here describes some of the underlying linguistic skills that may contribute to fluency in translating ideas into written text. Clearly, writing well entails more than phonological and morphological skill. Still, I have long argued (McCutchen, 2000) that the acquisition of fluency in translating processes may be central in enabling a writer to escape the constraints of working memory and move from what Bereiter and Scardamalia (1987) called knowledge telling to knowledge transformation or even to what Galbraith (2009) termed knowledge constitution.

To the extent that phonological and morphological skills enable more fluent spelling, word retrieval, and sentence construction, they seem important foundational skills in writing.

Writing well is also as much a social and cultural act as a cognitive act (see also Chapter 4, this volume). In the foreword of their seminal book, Gregg and Steinberg (1980) stated that work on writing would benefit from interdisciplinary collaborations across the fields of psychology, English, and linguistics. However, in the intervening years, writing research has not been characterized by the extensive interdisciplinary collaborations that Gregg and Steinberg envisioned, especially in the United States. Many North American writing researchers have taken a markedly sociocognitive or sociocultural turn (for good reason); however, rather than benefiting from interdisciplinary dialogue, the sociocultural and cognitive traditions have become rather dichotomized, with both traditions not always in touch with relevant work from linguistics, neuroscience, or clinical neuropsychology.[2] If we are going to continue to make progress in understanding how people write and how to help them write better (the questions that Gregg and Steinberg asked more than 30 years ago), the field will likely need more authentic interdisciplinary dialogue. This volume will contribute to such a dialogue.

ACKNOWLEDGMENTS

Research described here was supported in part by the Institute of Education Sciences, U.S. Department of Education (through grant R305H060073) and by the National Institute of Child Health and Human Development (through Center Grant P50HD 33812), both to the University of Washington.

REFERENCES

Adams, M. J. (1990). *Beginning to read: Thinking and learning about print.* Cambridge, MA: MIT Press.

Allal, Chanquoy, L., & Largy, P. (Eds.). (2004). *Revision: Cognitive and instructional processes.* New York: Kluwer.

Beers, S. F., & Nagy, W. E. (2009). Syntactic complexity as a predictor of adolescent writing quality: Which measures? Which genre? *Reading and Writing: An Interdisciplinary Journal, 22,* 185–200.

Bereiter, C., & Scardamalia, M. (1987). *The psychology of written composition.* Hillsdale, NJ: Erlbaum.

Berko, J. (1958). The child's learning of English morphology. *Word, 14,* 150–177.

Berman, R. A., & Verhoeven, L. (2002). Cross-linguistic perspectives on the development of text-production abilities. *Written Language and Literacy, 5,* 1–43.

Berninger, V. (1994). *Reading and writing acquisition: A developmental neuropsychological perspective.* In W. Jeffry (Series Ed.), *Developmental Psychology Series.* Madison, WI: WCB Brown & Benchmark Publishing. (Reprinted 1996, Boulder, CO: Westview)

---

[2] For an earlier attempt to integrate developmental and cognitive psychology, neuropsychology, and psycholinguistics in studying normal variation in writing acquisition, see Berninger (1994). For a more recent attempt to initiate the cross-disciplinary conversation between speech and language scientists and psychologists around the topic of writing, see Silliman and Berninger (2011).

Berninger, V., Abbott, R., Augsberger, A., & Garcia, N. (2009). Comparison of pen and key-board transcription modes in children with and without learning disabilities. *Learning Disability Quarterly, 32*, 123–141.

Berninger, V. W., & Swanson, H. L. (1994). Modifying Hayes and Flower's model of skilled writing to explain beginning and developing writing. In E. C. Butterfield (Ed.), *Advances in cognition and educational practice*, Vol. 2: *Children's writing: Toward a process theory of the development of skilled writing* (pp. 57–81). Greenwich, CT: JAI Press.

Berninger, V., Vaughan, K., Abbott, R., Begay, K., Byrd, K., Curtin, G., ... Graham, S. (2002). Teaching spelling and composition alone and together: Implications for the simple view of writing. *Journal of Educational Psychology, 94*, 291–304.

Berninger, V., Winn, W., Stock, P., Abbott, R., Eschen, K., Lin, C., ... Nagy, W. (2008). Tier 3 specialized writing instruction for students with dyslexia. *Reading and Writing. An Interdisciplinary Journal, 21*, 95–129.

Berninger, V., & Wolf, B. (2009). *Helping students with dyslexia and dysgraphia make connections: Differentiated instruction lesson plans in reading and writing*. Baltimore: Brookes.

Bissex, G. L. (1980). *GNYS AT WRK: A child learns to read and write*. Cambridge, MA: Harvard University Press.

Bourdin, B., & Fayol, M. (2000). Is graphic activity cognitively costly? *Reading and Writing: An Interdisciplinary Journal, 13*, 183–196.

Bowerman, M. (1982). Starting to talk worse: Clues to language acquisition from children's late speech errors. In S. Strauss (Ed.), *U-shaped behavioral growth* (pp. 101–145). New York: Academic Press.

Bryant, P., Nunes, T., & Aidinis, A. (1999). Different morphemes, same spelling problems: Cross-linguistic developmental studies. In M. Harris & G. Hatano (Eds.), *Learning to read and write: A cross-linguistic perspective* (pp. 112–133). New York: Cambridge University Press.

Butterfield, E. C., Hacker, D. J., & Plumb, C. (1994). Topic knowledge, linguistic knowledge, and revision skill as determinants of text revision. In J. S. Carlson (Series Ed.) & E. C. Butterfield (Vol. Ed.), *Advances in cognition and educational practice*, Vol. 2: *Children's writing: Toward a process theory of the development of skilled writing* (pp. 83–141). Greenwich, CT: JAI Press.

Carlisle, J. (1995). Morphological awareness and early reading achievement. In L. B. Feldman (Ed.), *Morphological aspects of language processing* (pp. 189–209). Hillsdale, NJ: Erlbaum.

Carlisle, J. (1996). An exploratory study of morphological errors in children's written stories. *Reading and Writing: An Interdisciplinary Journal, 12*, 61–72.

Carlisle, J. (2000). Awareness of the structure and meaning of morphologically complex words: Impact on reading. *Reading and Writing: An Interdisciplinary Journal, 12*, 169–190.

Carlisle, J., & Nomanbhoy, D. M. (1993). Phonological and morphological awareness in first graders. *Applied Psycholinguistics, 14*, 177–195.

Carlisle, J. F. (1988). Knowledge of derivational morphology and spelling ability in fourth, sixth, and eighth graders. *Applied Psycholinguistics, 9*, 247–266.

Casalis, S., & Louis-Alexandre, M. (2000). Morphological analysis, phonological analysis and learning to read French: A longitudinal study. *Reading and Writing: An Interdisciplinary Journal, 12*, 303–335.

Chafe, W., & Danielewicz, J. (1987). Properties of spoken and written language. In R. Horowitz & S. J. Samuels (Eds.), *Comprehending oral and written language* (pp. 83–113). New York: Academic Press.

Chenoweth, N. A., & Hayes, J. R. (2001). Fluency in writing: Generating text in L1 and L2. *Written Communication, 18*, 80–98.

Cochran-Smith, M. (1991). Word-processing and writing in elementary classrooms: A critical review of related literature. *Review of Educational Research, 61*, 107–155.

Crowhurst, M. (1983). Syntactic complexity and writing quality: A review. *Canadian Journal of Education, 8*, 1–16.

Crystal, D. (2008). *Txtng: The gr8 db8*. Oxford: Oxford University Press.

Deacon, S. H., Kirby, J. R., & Casselman-Bell, M. (2009). How robust is the contribution of morphological awareness to general spelling outcomes? *Reading Psychology, 30*, 301–318.

Dellerman, P., Coirier, P., & Marchand, E. (1996). Planning and expertise in argumentative composition. In G. Rijlaarsdam, H. van den Bergh, & M. Couzijn (Eds.), *Theories, models, and methodology in writing research* (pp. 182–195). Amsterdam: Amsterdam University Press.

Ehri, L. C. (1986). Sources of difficulty in learning to spell and read. In M. L. Wolraich & D. Routh (Eds.), *Advances in developmental and behavioral pediatrics* (Vol. 7, pp. 121–195). Greenwich, CT: JAI Press.

Ehri, L. C. (1992). Review and commentary: Stages of spelling development. In S. Templeton & D. R. Bear (Eds.), *Development of orthographic knowledge and the foundations of literacy: A memorial festschrift to Edmund H. Henderson* (pp. 307–332). Hillsdale, NJ: Erlbaum.

Ferreiro, E., & Teberosky, A. (1982). *Literacy before schooling*. Exeter, NH: Heinemann International.

Flower, L., & Hayes, J. R. (1980). The dynamics of composing: Making plans and juggling constraints. In L. W. Gregg & E. R. Steinberg (Eds.), *Cognitive processes in writing* (pp. 31–50). Hillsdale, NJ: Erlbaum.

Fowler, A., & Liberman, I. (1995). Morphological awareness as related to early reading and spelling ability In L. Feldman (Ed.), *Morphological aspects of language processing* (pp. 157–188). Hillsdale, NJ: Erlbaum.

Fromkin, V., & Rodman, R. (1993). *An introduction to language*. Fort Worth, TX: Harcourt Brace Javanovich.

Galbraith, D. (2009). Writing as discovery. *British Journal of Educational Psychology Monograph Series II, No. 6*, 5–26.

Garrett, M. F. (1980). Levels of processing in sentence production. In B. Butterworth (Ed.), *Language production* (pp. 177–220). New York: Academic Press.

Gentry, J. R. (1982). An analysis of developmental spelling in GNYS at WRK. *Reading Teacher, 36*, 192–200.

Graham, S. (1990). The role of production factors in learning disabled students' compositions. *Journal of Educational Psychology, 82*, 781–791.

Graham, S., Berninger, V., Abbott, R., Abbott, S., & Whitaker, D. (1997). The role of mechanics in composing of elementary school students: A new methodological approach. *Journal of Educational Psychology, 89*(1), 170–182.

Graham, S., & Perin, D. (2007). A meta-analysis of writing instruction for adolescent students. *Journal of Educational Psychology, 99*, 445–476.

Green, L. B., McCutchen, D., Schwiebert, C., Quinlan, T., Eva-Wood, A., & Juelis, J. (2003). Morphological development in children's writing. *Journal of Educational Psychology, 95*, 752–761.

Gregg, L. W., & Steinberg, E. W. (Eds.). (1980). *Cognitive processes in writing*. Hillsdale, NJ: Erlbaum.

Griffith, P. L. (1991). Phonemic awareness helps first graders invent spellings and third graders remember correct spellings. *Journal of Reading Behavior, 23*, 215–233.

Harris, M., & Hatano, G. (1999). *Learning to read and write: A cross-linguistic perspective*. New York: Cambridge University Press.

Hayes, J. R., & Flower, L. S. (1980). Identifying the organization of writing processes. In L. W. Gregg & E. R. Steinberg (Eds.), *Cognitive processes in writing* (pp. 31–50). Hillsdale, NJ: Erlbaum.

Henderson, E. H., & Beers, J. W. (Eds.). (1980). *Developmental and cognitive aspects of learning to spell: A reflection of word knowledge.* Newark, DE: International Reading Association. Cambridge: Cambridge Press.

Hunt, K. W. (1970). Syntactic maturity in school children and adults. *Monographs for the Society for Research in Child Development, 35*(1), 1–61.

Kaufer, D. S., Hayes, J. R., & Flower, L. (1986). Composing written sentences. *Research in the Teaching of English, 20,* 121–140.

Lenhart, A., Arafeh, S., Smith, A., & Macgill, A. (2008). *Writing, technology and teens.* Washington, DC: Pew Research Center.

Levelt, W. J. M. (1983). Monitoring and self-repair in speech. *Cognition, 14,* 41–104.

Loban, W. (1976). *Language development: Kindergarten through grade twelve* [Research Report No. 18]. Urbana, IL: National Council of Teachers of English.

MacArthur, C. A. (2009). Reflections on research on writing and technology for struggling writers. *Learning Disabilities Research & Practice, 24,* 93–103.

MacArthur, C. A., Graham, S., Schwartz, S. S., & Shafer, W. (1995). Evaluation of a writing instruction model that integrated a process approach, strategy instruction, and word processing. *Learning Disability Quarterly, 18,* 278–291.

Mahony, M., Singson, M., & Mann, V. (2000). Reading ability and sensitivity to morphological relations. *Reading and Writing: An Interdisciplinary Journal, 12,* 191–218.

McBride-Chang, C., Wat, C. P., Hua, S., Zhou, A., & Wagner, R. (2003). Morphological awareness uniquely predicts young children's Chinese character recognition. *Journal of Educational Psychology, 95,* 743–751.

McCutchen, D. (1988). "Functional automaticity" in children's writing: A problem of meta-cognitive control. *Written Communication, 5,* 306–324.

McCutchen, D. (2000). Knowledge acquisition, processing efficiency, and working memory: Implications for a theory of writing. *Educational Psychologist, 35,* 13–23.

McCutchen, D., Abbott, R. D., Green, L. B., Beretvas, S. N., Cox, S., Potter, N. S., … Gray, A. (2002). Beginning literacy: Links among teacher knowledge, teacher practice, and student learning. *Journal of Learning Disabilities, 35,* 69–86.

McCutchen, D., & Berninger, V. W. (1999). Those who know teach well: Helping teachers master literacy-related subject-matter knowledge. *Learning Disabilities Research and Practice, 14,* 215–226.

McCutchen, D., Covill, A., Hoyne, S. H., & Mildes, K. (1994). Individual differences in writing skill: Implications of translating fluency. *Journal of Educational Psychology, 86,* 256–266.

McCutchen, D., Green, L., & Abbott, R. D. (2008). Children's morphological knowledge: Links to literacy. *Reading Psychology: An International Journal, 29,* 289–314.

McCutchen, D., Green, L., Abbott, R. D., & Sanders, E. (2009). Further evidence for teacher knowledge: Supporting struggling readers in grades three through five. *Reading and Writing: An Interdisciplinary Journal, 22,* 401–423.

McCutchen, D., Harry, D. R., Cunningham, A. E., Cox, S., Sidman, S., & Covill, A. E. (2002). Reading teachers' knowledge of children's literature and English phonology. *Annals of Dyslexia, 52,* 207–228.

McCutchen, D., & Logan, B. (in press). Inside incidental word learning: Children's strategic use of morphological information to infer word meanings. *Reading Research Quarterly.*

McCutchen, D., Logan, B., Lotas, S., & Stull, S. (2010, May). *Effects of morphological knowledge on children's writing.* Paper presented at the annual meeting of the American Educational Research Association, Denver, CO.

Menyuk, P. (1988). *Language development: Knowledge and use.* Glenview, IL: Scott, Foresman.

Moats, L. (2000). *Speech to print: Language essentials for teachers.* Baltimore, MD: Brookes.

Myhill, D. (2008). Towards a linguistic model of sentence development in writing. *Language and Education, 22,* 271–288.

Nagy, W., Berninger, V. W., & Abbott, R. D. (2006). Contributions of morphology beyond phonology to literacy outcomes of upper elementary and middle-school students. *Journal of Educational Psychology, 98,* 134–147.

Nagy, W. E., & Scott, J. A. (2000). Vocabulary processes. In M. L. Kamil, P. B. Mosenthal, P. D. Pearson, & R. Barr (Eds.), *Handbook of reading research* (Vol. 3, pp. 269–284). Mahwah, NJ: Erlbaum.

Nunes, T., & Bryant, P. (2006). *Improving literacy by teaching morphemes.* New York: Routledge.

Nunes, T., Bryant, P., & Bindman, M. (2006). The effects of learning to spell on children's awareness of morphology. *Reading and Writing, 19,* 767–787.

O'Donnell, R. C. (1976). A critique of some indices of syntactic maturity. *Research in the Teaching of English, 10,* 31–38.

O'Hare, F. (1973). *Sentence combining.* Champaign, IL: National Council of Teachers of English.

Pacton, S., & Fayol, M. (2003). How do French children use morphosyntactic information when they spell adverbs and present participles? *Scientific Studies of Reading, 7*(3), 273–287.

Palincsar, A. S., & Brown, A. L. (1984). Reciprocal teaching of comprehension monitoring strategies. *Cognition and Instruction, 1,* 117–175.

Plester, B., Wood, C., & Bell, V. (2008). Txt msg n school literacy: Does texting and knowledge of text abbreviations adversely affect children's literacy attainment? *Literacy, 42,* 137–144.

Plester, B., Wood, C., & Joshi, P. (2009). Exploring the relationship between children's knowledge of text message abbreviations and school literacy outcomes. *British Journal of Developmental Psychology, 27,* 145–161.

Pontecovo, C., & Zucchermaglio, C. (1990). A passage to literacy: Learning in a social context. In Y. M. Goodman (Ed.), *How children construct literacy* (pp. 50–98). Newark, DE: International Reading Association.

Pressley, M. (1998). *Reading instruction: The case for balanced teaching.* New York: Guilford

Read, C. (1981). Writing is not the inverse of reading for young children. In C. H. Frederiksen & J. F. Dominic (Eds.), *Writing: The nature, development, and teaching of written communication.* Hillsdale, NJ: Erlbaum.

Rieben, L., Ntamakiliro, L., Gonthier, B., & Fayol, M. (2005). Effects of various early writing practices on reading and spelling. *Scientific Studies of Reading, 9,* 145–166.

Rosner, J. (1979). *Helping children overcome learning disabilities* (2nd ed.). New York: Walker.

Rubin, H., Patterson, P., & Kantor, M. (1991). Morphological development and writing ability in children and adults. *Language, Speech, and Hearing Services in Schools, 22,* 228–235.

Saddler, B., & Graham, S. (2005). The effects of peer-assisted sentence-combining instruction on the writing performance of more and less skilled young writers. *Journal of Educational Psychology, 97,* 43–54.

Scott, C. A. (2004). Syntactic contributions to literacy learning. In C. A. Stone, E. R. Silliman, B. J. Ehren, & K. Apel (Eds.), *Handbook of language and literacy: Development and disorders* (pp. 340–362). New York: Guilford.

Sénéchal, M., & Kearnan, K. (2007). The role of morphology in reading and spelling. In R. V. Kail (Ed.), *Advances in child development and behavior* (Vol. 35, pp. 297–325). San Diego, CA: Elsevier.

Seymour, P. H., Aro, M., & Erskine, J. M. (2003). Foundation literacy acquisition in European orthographies. *British Journal of Psychology, 94,* 143–174.

Share, D., & Levin, I. (1999). Learning to read and write in Hebrew. In M. Harris & G. Hatano (Eds.), *Learning to read and write: A cross-linguistic perspective* (pp. 89–111). New York: Cambridge University Press.

Siegel, L. S. (2008) Morphological awareness skills of English language learners and children with dyslexia. *Topics in Language Disorders, 28,* 15–27.

Silliman, E., & Berninger, V. (2011). Mobilizing professionals across disciplines to define language and learning disabilities. *Topics in Language Disorders, 31* (January to March), 6–23.

Singson, M., Mahony, D., & Mann, V. (2000). The relation between reading ability and morphological skills: Evidence from derivational suffixes. *Reading and Writing: An Interdisciplinary Journal, 12,* 219–252.

Stull, S. C. (2010). *Invented morphology: An analysis of distributional errors in children's writing* (Unpublished master's thesis). University of Washington, Seattle, Washington.

Thurlow, C. (2006). From statistical panic to moral panic: The metadiscursive construction and popular exaggeration of new media language in the print media. *Journal of Computer-Mediated Communication, 11,* 667–701.

Treiman, R. (1993). *Beginning to spell.* New York: Oxford University Press.

Tyler, A., & Nagy, W. (1989). The acquisition of English derivational morphology. *Journal of Memory and Language, 28,* 649–667.

Windsor, J. (2000). The role of phonological opacity in reading achievement. *Journal of Speech, Language, and Hearing Research, 43,* 50–61.

Woodcock, R. W., McGrew, K. S., & Mather, N. (2001–2007). *Woodcock-Johnson III tests of cognitive abilities.* Rolling Meadows, IL: Riverside.

Varnhagen, C. K., Boechler, P. M., & Steffler, D. J. (1999). Phonological and orthographic influences on children's vowel spelling. *Scientific Studies of Reading, 3,* 363–379.

Venezky, R. (1970). *The structure of English orthography.* The Hague: Mouton.

Venezky, R. (1995). From orthography to psychology to reading. In V. Berninger (Ed.), *The varieties of orthographic knowledge II: Relationships to phonology, reading, and writing* (pp. 23–46). Dordrecht, The Netherlands: Kluwer.

Venezky, R. (1999). *The American way of spelling: The structure and origins of American English orthography.* New York: Guilford.

10

Children Challenged by Writing Due to Language and Motor Difficulties

VINCENT CONNELLY, JULIE E. DOCKRELL,
and ANNA L. BARNETT

*T*here has been increased interest in recent years in the writing skills of children with specific learning or developmental difficulties such as dyslexia, specific language impairment, and developmental coordination disorder. These diagnoses refer to primary difficulties in specific domains of development, although the child's overall development and intellectual ability are typically within average range. This chapter reviews the recent work in this area and introduces issues in keeping with the goals of this volume, the application of cognitive models of writing development, which has been given insufficient attention in assessment and intervention with these clinical populations. We explain how cognitive models have shaped and influenced our ideas about how these conditions interact with both the process of learning to write and the nature of a child's language or motor difficulties. Moreover, research and clinical practices for both language and motor disorder are increasingly beginning to consider issues related to learning to write within a more complex view, integrating developmental models of writing with developmental models of oral language and motor skills.

Writing is a complex task that draws on a range of cognitive, language, motor, and social skills. Not surprisingly, given its complexity, many children struggle with writing (Graham & Harris, 2009). Difficulties in the production of legible, accurate, and coherent text can arise for different reasons, including specific patterns of difficulties experienced by the writer, limitations in teaching, or inadequate opportunities to practice producing texts. Complex effects are evident at the word, sentence, and text levels of language (Hooper, Swartz, Wakely, de Kruif, & Montgomery, 2002; MacArthur & Graham, 1987). An examination of the constraints due to individual differences, teacher variations, or differential experiences, including practice on written text production, is an essential step in developing and testing theoretical models of writing and in developing evidence-based practice to help those with writing difficulties. Although many children struggle with text production, there are particular groups of children with clinical difficulties who are especially prone to writing difficulties (Dockrell, 2009). The difficulties experienced by these children may arise in the processes that support successful text production or the cognitive representations that underpin text generation.

This longstanding interest in the writing of children with language or motor disorders can be traced back over one hundred years (Ogle, 1867, cited in Hooper et al., 2002). Although children who experience a range of developmental difficulties are at risk of writing problems (Dockrell, 2009), this chapter focuses on language difficulties, often referred to as specific language impairment (SLI)[1] or language learning disability (LLD) in the literature, specific reading difficulty or dyslexia (DYS), and developmental coordination disorder (DCD). To make the case that the cognitive tradition in writing is relevant to clinical and educational practice for children with language and motor difficulties, we will examine the writing of children who have difficulty producing and understanding oral language (children with SLI), children who have problems with spelling (children with DYS, which is a word-spelling as well as word-reading difficulty), and those with motor problems (children with DCD). Our goal is to provide insight into the difficulties these children face and elucidate the nature of the underlying cognitive, language, and motor processes involved in their written text production (Hulme & Snowling, 2009).

Poor writing is a barrier to educational progress for all children, but especially for those with SLI, DYS, or DCD. These children find it difficult to do well in public school exams that are traditionally weighted toward assessment based on producing, often extended, written responses. Children with language difficulties achieve lower levels of success in these exams than other children (Dockrell, Lindsay, Connelly, & Mackie, 2007). Moreover, writing, as a barrier to progress, continues in university students where those with DYS do less well in exams than their peers (Maughan et al., 2009; Richardson & Wydell, 2003; see Dockrell, Lindsay, & Connelly, 2009, and Scott, 1999, for the long-running writing problems of students with SLI; see Berninger, Nielsen, Abbott, Wijsman, & Raskind, 2008, Connelly, Campbell, MacLean, & Barnes, 2006, and Swanson & Hsieh, 2009, for the lifetime of writing problems in those individuals with DYS; and see Miller, Polatajko, Mandich, & Missiuna, 2001, and Barnett & Henderson, 2005, for the writing problems of children with DCD). Previous analyses have focused on the difficulties experienced by a specific group of children. Such analyses are limited in their ability to inform developmental models of writing and may imply group-specific interventions. An examination and comparison of the patterns of difficulties across these groups of children provide the opportunity to identify barriers that are general and specific and thereby provide necessary data to inform developmental models

---

[1] We use the term *specific language impairment* to reflect the most common usage in the research literature for this population.

that can link targeted interventions. This chapter briefly reviews and discusses the work related to writing in three populations of children who are significantly challenged by writing (SLI, DYS, and DCD).

To contextualize research on these three difficulties, we first consider models of writing development and identify some of the methodological difficulties of studying writing in these populations. We use a cognitive model of writing development derived from the work by Hayes and colleagues in an attempt to understand these children's difficulties in writing development, including higher-order cognitive and metacognitive processes. We then analyze the development of fluent text production from the perspective of the difficulties experienced by each group of children. The cognitive model is used to inform our understanding of both the children's specific writing difficulties and the implications of these for writing development in general. We also consider where future research efforts should be directed. The investigation of writing development in these populations is unavoidably complex, with many potential causes of their difficulties. There are a number of methodological challenges that need to be addressed if we are to understand the parameters and causes of the children's difficulties and develop effective treatment approaches, especially regarding their writing difficulties.

COGNITIVE MODELS AND METHODOLOGICAL ISSUES

The cognitive study of writing in skilled adult writers is a complex methodological task (see Flower & Hayes, 1994, for a comprehensive overview of difficulties involved). The study of children's writing is even more complex as developmental issues have to be included in the models (see Bereiter & Scardamalia, 1987, and Kellogg, 1994, for further discussions about studying writing development). In writing research, as in many areas of psychology, there is much debate about the definition of terms and reliability of methods used by researchers. For example, terms like fluency and automaticity are frequently used to describe writing performance, but these are difficult to operationalize. Do these terms mean speed of a particular rate or more than this? There has also been debate about the reliability of commonly used measures of text generation in writing research (see a number of chapters in MacArthur, Graham, & Fitzgerald, 2006, for more specific discussions).

When studying special populations of children, such as those with SLI, DYS, and DCD, the researcher must also be aware of the methodological issues relevant to this research goal (Hulme & Snowling, 2009). For example, in relation to the populations of children we discuss in this chapter, there is much discussion about differential diagnosis and comorbidity. Children with SLI can present symptoms that can lead them to be classified as children with DYS at later points in development (Bishop & Snowling, 2004). That some of these children share common phonological problems (nonword repetition) presents a serious challenge for researchers in interpreting results and comparing populations. Researchers need clear definitions, not just to design good measures for assessment, but to ensure that the conclusions they draw about difficulties and interventions can be generalized.

There are further complications in carrying out research with children with developmental difficulties. Because developmental difficulties often emerge earlier in development than when children are expected to write in school, the researcher needs to be aware of the methodological debates within, but not restricted to, cognitive psychology and other disciplines with whom psychologists often engage in interdisciplinary research (e.g., speech and language pathology, linguistics, and neuroscience). There is relatively little research linking oral language skills and written language skills in children with and without writing disabilities (see Shanahan, 2006, for a review). Therefore, interpreting links between general measures of language and general measures of writing is not straightforward.

One might find strong links between vocabulary scores and narrative writing scores in children with SLI. Thus, one could hypothesize that strong links exist between difficulty in retrieving vocabulary and successful text generation, which would impact the text produced in this population of children (Dockrell et al., 2009). However, there is much debate in the field of language development about the validity of current vocabulary measures. It is not always clear to what extent the current vocabulary measures are tapping into the breadth of children's word knowledge, the depth of their semantic representations, or the efficiency of lexical retrieval (Messer & Dockrell, 2006). Nor are all vocabulary tests measuring the same aspects of vocabulary knowledge; commonly used measures include naming a pictured word, pointing to one of several pictures portraying possible meanings, completing word analogies, and providing written or oral definitions for single words. Each of these tasks draws on different cognitive, language, executive, and motor functions. Therefore, researchers using special populations have to be aware of wider debates surrounding other related areas of psychology and have to become cognizant of the methods used in those fields as well as those in writing research.

To summarize, there are many pitfalls and difficulties associated with carrying out research with children with difficulties. However, we feel that the benefit of considering developmental difficulties in special populations outweighs these difficulties and, of course, is necessary in order to better meet these students' educational needs. Models of development and learning provide the basis for generating testable hypotheses (Morton & Frith, 1995). Detailed research undertaken to study children who are challenged by writing can add greatly to our knowledge of writing development by testing hypotheses and challenging widely held, but untested, assumptions that will ultimately enhance our understanding of all children's writing development.

RESEARCH FOCUS ON THE SINGLE WORD

Research into the writing of children with developmental difficulties has historically focused on the spelling of a single word or even the letter level in handwriting (Bishop & Clarkson, 2003; Rosenblum, Weiss, & Parush, 2003). Focusing on single-word spelling provides a starting point for research, and it is easier to examine difficulties at the single-word level because differences, when present, can be more clearly defined and potential interventions more easily targeted (Bishop &

Clarkson, 2003). The spelling of single words has dominated the majority of research on the writing of children with DYS (Jackson & Coltheart, 2001), and most of these studies have used dictation methods to examine spelling of single real words and nonwords. Fewer studies have used dictated sentences to study word spelling in sentence context; and fewer still have examined spelling during text production to evaluate word production in context, that is, self-generated by the child as a writer. However, the narrow focus on spelling only is slowly changing, and several recent studies have also examined the spelling of children with DYS related to composing (Berninger, Nielsen et al., 2008; Berninger, Winn et al., 2008). In DCD the focus has often been on even smaller units of analysis at the level of letters or strokes within letters (Smits-Engelsman, Van Galen, & Portier, 1994). In SLI the focus has been somewhat wider, but there is still a concentration of research studying spelling at the word or subword level rather than text production processes (Fey, Catts, Proctor-Williams, Tomblin, & Zhang, 2004, but for exceptions, see Scott, 1999; Scott & Windsor, 2000).

This focus on the single word has achieved much. For example, children with DYS do indeed struggle with single words. On average, they are less accurate and slower at reading single words, and they are invariably even poorer at spelling the same words (Hulme & Snowling, 2009). A large and complex literature has shown that the majority of children with DYS have difficulties with the phonological aspects of spelling (Kemp, 2009), but a growing literature across languages points to spelling problems related to orthography as well as phonology in DYS and morphology and orthography in SLI. A number of successful educational interventions for reading and spelling have been developed based on research at the single word level (Johnston, Watson, & Logan, 2009). Research on phonology at the word and subword level has contributed to understanding of spelling development in children with and without SLI and DYS (Critten & Pine, 2009; Critten, Pine, & Steffler, 2007), as has research on orthography and morphology, especially in morphophonemic orthographies such as English (Fayol, Zorman, & Lété, 2009; Nunes & Bryant, 2006, 2009). However, in order to understand writing problems we need to move beyond single words and examine how text generation develops in children. This examination must take into account the relation between text generation and contributory processes such as motor processes, language development, and reading skills.

MODELS OF WRITING DEVELOPMENT

The Hayes and Flower (1980) cognitive process model was a breakthrough in describing how the three key recursive cognitive processes involved in writing (planning, translating, and reviewing) interact within the constraints of memory and the task environment. This provided a clear framework for future research in the field. However, this is a model of skilled writing and it is increasingly accepted that models of skilled writing do not account for all aspects of writing development (Alamargot & Fayol, 2009; Berninger & Swanson, 1994). Although the theoretical factors that underpin writing have been the focus of much discussion over the past 40 years, there is no single model of writing development that provides a comprehensive analysis of all the barriers that may be experienced by children with writing difficulties.

Children's writing, just like that of adults, develops within a limited working memory capacity system (Just & Carpenter, 1992; McCutchen, 2000; Swanson & Berninger, 1996), which also has temporal constraints (Berninger, 1999). Learning to write within a limited capacity system means that children have to gradually automate low-level processes (e.g., translation skills such as handwriting and spelling) so that resources can then be freed up for more cognitively demanding and complex processes (Fayol, 1999). Low-level skills at the beginning of learning to write are very demanding and need to be taught and practiced many times before automaticity is achieved.

The model in Figure 10.1 is based on an early intervention study in writing for children who met screening criteria for very low writing fluency, constructing sentences based on provided words within a 7-min time limit (Berninger et al., 2002). Children who received transcription training in spelling improved in spelling, and children who received text generation instruction (planning, translating, reviewing, and revising) improved in composition. The model is a theoretical framework for integrating the findings of treatment studies: (a) Several studies with at-risk writers in the first three grades (ages 6 to 8) showed that treating transcription transfers to improved text generation (see Berninger & Amtmann, 2003, for review); and (b) a number of studies of self-regulated strategy instruction (planning, translating, reviewing, revising) showed transfers to improved text generation (Graham, 2006a). Thus, this model captures for at-risk

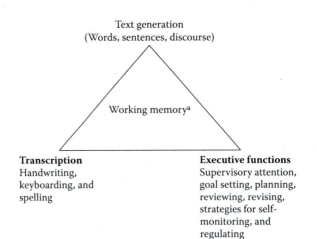

Figure 10.1 Triangle for the not-so-simple view of internal functional writing system. Modification of the simple view of writing in Berninger and Amtmann (2003). [a]Activates long-term memory during planning, composing, reviewing, and revising, and short-term memory during reviewing and revising output. (Reproduced from Berninger, V. W., and Winn, W. D., in *Handbook of Writing Research* [pp. 96–114], Guilford, New York, 2006. With permission.)

writers what prior studies of assessment have shown: Text generation is related to transcription (handwriting and spelling) and executive functions (supervisory attention—focus, switch, sustain, update, self-monitor, plan, translate, review, and revise).

CHILDREN WITH SPECIFIC LANGUAGE IMPAIRMENT

Children with SLI typically experience problems with the acquisition, processing, and production of oral language. The most commonly used core criterion to identify children with SLI is that their language problems cannot be explained in terms of other cognitive, neurological, or perceptual deficits (Leonard, 1998). Language problems are evident by a protracted rate of language development as well as difficulties with subcomponents of the language system. Measurements that tap children's proficiencies with phonological processing, sentence recall, nonword repetition, and tense marking have all demonstrated high levels of specificity and sensitivity in differentiating children with SLI from their typically developing peers (Conti-Ramsden, Botting, & Faragher, 2001). Although conventionally identified by a discrepancy between language levels and nonverbal ability, children with SLI are heterogeneous in their profile of language impairments and in terms of nonverbal ability (Botting, Faragher, Knox, Simkin, & Conti-Ramsden, 2001). Patterns of performance across measures of morphosyntax, vocabulary, and semantics in relation to receptive and expressive measures also vary over time (Botting, 2005; Conti-Ramsden & Botting, 1999). Recently Tomblin and Zhang (2006) have argued that much of the variance in standardized measures of language is attributable to a single common linguistic factor with a trend during middle childhood where grammatical abilities and vocabulary abilities become differentiated. By corollary Leonard (2009) questioned the existence of children experiencing expressive language difficulties alone.

For many young people with SLI, difficulties with spoken communication skills persist into adolescence (Beitchman, Wilson, Brownlie, Walters, & Lancee, 1996; Botting et al., 2001; Stothard, Snowling, Bishop, Chipchase, & Kaplan, 1998) and adulthood (Clegg, Hollis, Mawhood, & Rutter, 2005; Johnson et al., 1999). Older students continue to experience difficulties with reduced vocabulary levels (Johnson et al., 1999), accurate use of verb morphology (Clahsen, Bartke, & Göllner, 1997), and some syntactic structures (Norbury, Bishop, & Briscoe, 2001).

Reading, decoding, and comprehension are areas of significant weakness for these children with SLI throughout their school careers (Dockrell et al., 2007, 2009; Mackie & Dockrell, 2004; Palikara, Dockrell, & Lindsay, in press; Reilly, Tolchinsky, & Wulfeck, 2008; Scott & Windsor, 2000) and continue to be impaired even when oral language narratives become age appropriate (Palikara et al., in press; Reilly, Tolchinsky, Woolpert, & Wulfeck, 2006). For many children with SLI, spelling is also problematic (Silliman, Bahr, & Peters, 2006). Children with SLI therefore appear to exhibit problems that would impact both their text generation and the transcription aspects of their writing development.

Text Generation Problems in SLI

Figure 10.1 clearly shows that the development of good text generation skills is as important as developing good transcription skills. In fact, both transcription and text generation support overall translation, and transcription skills are related to text generation skills, as both assessment (Berninger & Swanson, 1994; Graham, Berninger, Abbott, Abbott, & Whitaker, 1997) and treatment studies (Berninger et al., 2002) have shown. Text generation involves the selection of appropriate words for sentences and discourse; so we would predict that age-appropriate language skills supported by a deep vocabulary would be related to text generation (Berninger & Swanson, 1994). Therefore, in a population of children with language problems we can expect significant difficulties with text generation, at least in relation to lexical selection and the lexical diversity used in texts.

Many children with SLI have smaller vocabularies than matched peers and can experience difficulties retrieving words they comprehend (Messer & Dockrell, 2006). A longitudinal study of a group of children with SLI in the United Kingdom revealed that at age 16 the two most significant concurrent predictors of their written text production were spelling and vocabulary[2] (Dockrell et al., 2007, 2009). The continuity of the significant role of vocabulary in relation to text quality throughout adolescence confirms the view that vocabulary provides a building block for text generation processes (Dockrell et al., 2009). Other work has also identified limitations in text generation, leading to reduced levels of lexical diversity and poorer semantic content as critical limiting factors in the written text of children with SLI (Bishop & Clarkson, 2003; Fey et al., 2004; Scott & Windsor, 2000).

However, as noted earlier in this chapter, it is not clear to what extent the vocabulary measure in these studies is tapping into the breadth of the children's knowledge, the depth of their semantic representations, or the efficiency of lexical retrieval for text generation. There is increasing evidence that measures of depth and breadth of vocabulary may have differential effects on reading, and so we might predict that similar patterns would be evident in writing (e.g., Ouellette, 2006; Tannenbaum, Torgesen, & Wagner, 2006).

Studies have also supported the view that the difficulties of children with SLI in producing written text reflect a particular vulnerability in using language structure, as evidenced by their grammatical errors (Gillam & Johnston, 1992; Mackie & Dockrell, 2004; Scott & Windsor, 2000; Windsor, Scott, & Street, 2000). These errors include both the percentage of written utterances containing grammatical errors (Gillam & Johnston, 1992; Mackie & Dockrell, 2004; Scott & Windsor, 2000) and the total number of verb composite errors. Windsor et al. (2000) carried out a further analysis on data from their cohort and reported that the children with language difficulties made more verb and noun composite errors in the spoken and written narratives than either their chronological- or language-age–matched peers did. Verb composite errors included errors with the regular past tense, third-person singular, and copula and auxiliary forms, whereas noun composite errors

---

[2] In this study measures were taken of nonverbal ability, nonword repetition, receptive and expressive grammar and reading, and spelling and vocabulary (Dockrell et al., 2007).

included the regular plural, articles, and the possessive. The rate of errors in their written narratives was much higher than that found in the spoken narratives for the children with SLI, but not for the language- and chronological-age matches. The children with SLI made 3 times as many verb as noun errors in the written narratives, but there was no difference between rate of errors in the spoken narratives. Further analysis found that most of this difference was accounted for by verb composite errors on the past tense -ed ending verbs and article errors in noun composites, a pattern that is evident in the children's oral language at a much earlier age (see Leonard, 1998, for a review of these issues), but there was substantial variability in the children's performance.

Zero marking of -ed in writing was claimed by Windsor et al. (2000) as a clinical marker of the writing of children with language impairment because typical children do not show difficulties with -ed beyond the age of 8 or 9 years. Although omitting -ed may be a failure of grammatical awareness, it may also reflect a failure to spell orthographically. When children are slow in processing language, they may experience difficulties in processing sounds with rapid acoustic transitions or perceiving phonemes with low phonetic salience (e.g., t/d and s/z). These difficulties can affect both the regular past tense (-ed) and tense agreement (plurals, for example, *plays;* Montgomery & Leonard, 1998). Despite an attempt to account for this complication in their ratings of spellings of words that should have contained -ed, Windsor et al. (2000) were not able to draw a clear conclusion from the children's errors. No spelling skill level was reported for the children in the study, and it is therefore difficult to disentangle spelling levels and language levels. Therefore, it may be that children with language impairments in this study, although matched on language levels with a comparison group, may have been poorer spellers. Problems with spelling and punctuation, as well as poorer semantic content, were reported by Bishop and Clarkson (2003) as the most commonly associated problems with poor writing in children with SLI, rather than grammatical difficulties. Moreover, Puranik, Lombardino, and Altmann (2007) suggested that children with SLI produced fewer ideas in written text than those with DYS but showed equivalent proportion of spelling errors. Therefore, the impact of poor spelling may have a wider impact on the text generated than simple misspellings.

Transcription Problems: Spelling and Handwriting in SLI

Significant proportions of children with SLI also experience phonological difficulties and thus have spelling difficulties, which influence the transcription of written text both directly and indirectly (Bishop, North, & Donlan, 1996; Briscoe, Bishop, & Norbury, 2001; Gathercole & Baddeley, 1993). In a similar way to children with DYS, the text writing of children with SLI contains many spelling errors (Bishop & Clarkson, 2003; Dockrell et al., 2007, 2009; Mackie & Dockrell, 2004). The influence of spelling difficulties is separable from those of vocabulary in the relation to or effects on text generation (Dockrell et al., 2007, 2009). Spelling error patterns in SLI can deviate from both chronological- and language-matched peers (Connelly, Dockrell, Critten, Walter, & Lindsay, 2010; Mackie & Dockrell, 2004), but differences between children with SLI and spelling-level matched peers are not always found (Silliman, Bahr, & Peters, 2006). Further complicating the picture is the prediction that their poor spelling could be influenced by an interaction between patterns of language disabilities and poor literacy skills. As for children with DYS and typically developing writers, constraints and interactions may operate at both the word and the trans-word levels and between the word and trans-word levels. Thus, poor spelling can have an impact beyond the single-word level, and the current evidence indicates that this is the case for children with SLI.

There has been a longstanding concern about the information processing constraints experienced by children with SLI (Ellis Weismer & Hesketh, 1996; Montgomery, 2000) and their reduced performance on tasks that require quick and accurate performance (Leonard et al., 2007). Measures of speed of writing and reading fluency are both significantly related—either directly or indirectly—to text production. Children with SLI are reported to have slow handwriting (Dockrell et al., 2009). Handwriting speed, as measured by a letter writing task, was a significant predictor of writing at age 16 in children with SLI. This finding occurred independently of spelling, which was also a significant predictor of writing performance. The data indicated that shorter texts were associated with reduced levels of handwriting speed. Indeed, the cohort's handwriting speed was equivalent to the average obtained for students some 7 years younger (Graham, Berninger, Weintraub, & Schafer, 1998). This finding is consistent with slow production of text, as evidenced by the few words produced per minute in text generation tasks in the same cohort. The students with slower handwriting were also more likely to show decreases in their composition standard scores over time through their teenage years.

There was also a highly significant relation between reading speed and letter-writing speed in the children with SLI (Dockrell et al., 2009). This finding suggests that there may be common factors underpinning the two measures that impact the ability to coordinate and efficiently manage linguistic information. This finding mirrors results for children with DYS who exhibited a relation between speed of naming letters in the rapid automatic naming (RAN) task and speed of handwriting (Berninger, Nielsen et al., 2008).

DYSLEXIA AND WRITING

Dyslexia is often defined as an unexplained difficulty at a word level with learning to read and spell. Most research to date has been on how individuals with DYS fail to learn to read or decode words (Hulme & Snowling, 2009). Theoretically, it is assumed that there is a biological basis for DYS related to underlying neurological factors; a comprehensive review of this rapidly growing research literature is beyond the scope of this chapter. There is a general consensus in the field that most individuals with DYS have a phonological processing deficit (Hulme & Snowling, 2009), but the research evidence is growing for other problems as well. Both difficulties in coding phonological information in memory and transforming phonological information into orthographic codes (written words) may be involved. Many individuals with DYS also have problems with RAN (rapid automatic naming of items such as letters) (for a recent study in a line of research begun four decades ago, see Jones, Branigan, Hatzidaki, & Obregon, 2010). However, most researchers agree that the difficulties faced by children with DYS when dealing with print have their impact specifically at the word or subword level (Jackson & Coltheart, 2001). These word-level deficits may in turn affect processing at other levels of language.

Results of cross-sectional studies with children in the primary grades (ages 6 to 8) and intermediate grades (ages 9 to 12) showed that child writers are initially constrained by transcription skills (handwriting and spelling; for a review, see Berninger & Amtmann, 2003; Berninger & Swanson, 1994). To transcribe some text that has been generated, a number of processes or representations need to be successfully accessed. A key point is that the appropriate spellings for words must begin to be generated. However, accurate and automatic writing also requires the integration of orthographic coding of letters in memory and motor skills for sequencing finger movements to produce the orthographic symbols for letters and words in writing. The child must also be aware of and follow the rules of basic text construction in sequencing words within sentences, capitalizing and punctuating sentences, and creating sentences that have local cohesion across sentences. Thus, there are a number of reasons to predict that children who have been diagnosed with DYS (i.e., with word-level learning problems) would experience difficulties with writing and transcription skills specifically. It is no surprise that they typically produce scripts that are shorter, contain fewer words, and are rated more poorly in general content and organization than are their age peers without DYS (Berninger, Neilsen et al., 2008).

Transcription Skills: Poor Spelling

The word-level problems of students with DYS affect spelling as well as reading (Rice, 2004). Children with DYS generally have difficulty with spelling even when their problems in reading words seem to have resolved (Kemp, 2009). Poor spelling is clearly reflected in the writing of children and adults with DYS (Berninger, Neilsen et al., 2008; Coleman, Gregg, McLain, & Bellair, 2009; Connelly et al., 2006; Puranik et al., 2007; Sterling, Farmer, Riddick, Chipchase, & Kaplan, 1998). The essays of children with DYS contain many more spelling errors compared to typically developing children of the same age (Hatcher, Snowling, & Griffiths, 2002). Berninger, Nielsen et al. (2008) found that spelling was a key predictor of overall quality of writing composition in their sample of 122 children with DYS, who were on average about 11 years of age (but ranging from 7 to 14). In a recent 5-year longitudinal study with overlapping cohorts, spelling was also consistently a predictor of composition across Grades 1 to 7 (Abbott, Berninger, & Fayol, 2010). Spelling is clearly related to quality of composing in children with and without DYS.

Misspelling has a direct influence on text quality (Berninger et al., 2002; Coleman, Gregg, McLain, & Bellair, 2009). Poor spelling leads to confusion and misreading and also frustrates the writer. Having to concentrate on spelling words takes time and effort away from the purpose of writing and means less text is produced in the equivalent time for those without spelling problems (Coleman et al., 2009; Connelly et al., 2006). In very severe cases the child may struggle to spell and produce 20 to 30 words in as many minutes (Martlew, 1992). Children with

DYS produce much less text in an equivalent time as those without DYS, which has a significant impact on what ideas the child can express in writing. There is an increasing link between text length and text quality as children make progress in writing. Over time, the constraints on writing from transcription exert less influence on text quality in typically developing children and they are able to devote more resources to higher-order cognitive processes (Gregg, Coleman, Stennett, & Davis, 2002), but children with DYS persist in their struggle with transcription.

There is also evidence that children and adults with DYS produce text with less diversity in vocabulary, probably because they are choosing to use words they can spell (Sterling, Farmer, Riddick, Morgan, & Matthews, 1997; Wengelin, 2007). Lexical diversity is an important predictor of compositional quality when writing (Beard, 1984). It demonstrates that the writer can finely tune text to the reader, which is especially important in expository writing as children progress through school. However, not all studies have found less lexical diversity in children with DYS (Puranik et al., 2007). As we have argued, measurements of vocabulary vary, but it remains a reasonable hypothesis that spelling choice can constrain the precision of the arguments that children, especially some with DYS, make when writing. The effect of poor word choice is to deny the child the opportunity to exploit precise or specialized vocabulary in writing that can lead to clearer meaning (Sterling et al., 1997).

Even adult undergraduates with DYS who have overcome reading problems to gain access to university continue to produce more spelling errors in essays than their age-matched peers (Connelly et al., 2006). These students, in fact, produced even more spelling errors in their writing than a matched control group equivalent in single-word dictated spelling. However, they were able to overcome their disability in spelling to produce coherent essays that had as many ideas and as good organization as their age-matched peers. This finding illustrates the extra pressure on individuals with DYS when having to coordinate all the tasks involved in writing. The individuals in this case study were reasonably skilled writers at the university and thus were able to work through their disability to produce good writing, but at the cost of more spelling errors than one would expect.

Other studies have also found that individuals with DYS produce more spelling errors than one would predict when asked to compose rather than just produce a dictated spelling list (Coleman et al., 2009; Hauerwas & Walker, 2003). The extra demands of text generation impact the ability to retrieve correct spellings, suggesting that the orthographic representations are not well established for these students. These studies also reported that individuals with DYS produced more morphological spelling mistakes when writing sentences or essays than age-matched peer groups. Morphological spelling components, such as written inflected forms, are complex and take time for children to master; so when working memory demands are high, these patterns are more likely to be produced incorrectly or omitted. The problem with morphological spelling is not necessarily a problem with morphology per se. There is evidence that morphological stems are correctly spelled in the same children when presented in a simple single word dictation task that demands less of the limited capacity working memory system (Hauerwas & Walker, 2003).

Transcription Skills: Slow Handwriting

A second key component of transcription is handwriting skill. Speed of handwriting is a strong predictor of written composition length and quality in typically developing children (Berninger & Swanson, 1994; Graham et al., 1997; Peverly, 2006). Children with DYS do not necessarily have impaired handwriting, but children with DYS experience difficulties with automatic legible letter writing when writing the alphabet in order, a task thought to assess the orthographic loop of working memory (Berninger, Nielson et al., 2008). Some studies have found handwriting differences and others have not for children with DYS (Hatcher, Snowling, & Griffiths, 2002; Martlew, 1992; Sovik, Arntzen, & Thygesen, 1987), and any handwriting differences found may not differ from equivalent spelling-ability matched controls (Connelly et al., 2006). A pattern of mixed results is not uncommon in research looking at DYS because there is evidence that many, but not all, children with DYS have problems with speeded tasks (Katzir et al., 2006). The RAN task and the alphabet writing task (naming and writing letters automatically and quickly), which are thought to assess the time-sensitive phonological loop and orthographic loops of working memory, were correlated in a sample of children with DYS (Berninger, Nielsen et al., 2008). Therefore, the mixed picture regarding handwriting speed could be explained by individual differences in speed of accessing letter forms in memory and integrating those with hand movements to produce letters.

Another explanation for the slow writing and the mixed handwriting fluency results in samples with DYS may be more directly related to spelling. If children with DYS are struggling with spelling, they may show more pauses in writing to try to process the spellings of words. If so, this then slows down the process of transcription, leading to slower writing than would be expected. It has been demonstrated in keystroke-logged keyboarded essays that adults with DYS produce more pauses overall and in particular more interword pauses than age-matched controls (Wengelin, 2007; Wengelin & Stromqvist, 2000). These findings need to be more widely investigated, but they do point to spelling as having an effect on transcription in a number of subtle ways that need to be taken into account when modeling the development of writing.

Impact on Writing Skills Beyond Transcription

As already mentioned, there may be an impact of spelling on vocabulary choice in writing and in pausing during writing for children with DYS. However, there is some evidence that their difficulties with writing go beyond the consequences of their transcription difficulties. Puranik et al. (2007) carried out an exploratory study to investigate this matter. They compared children with DYS to those with SLI and an age-matched control group. The children with DYS did not differ significantly from age-matched peers in the amount of ideas produced in a text but were less skilled at producing complex sentences. They linked their results with some recent studies showing differences in grammatical skills related to morphology in DYS populations. However, Connelly et al. (2006) found no difference in ratings of expository essays for ideas and development; organization, unity, and coherence; sentence structure, and grammar for their sample of university students with DYS compared to age-matched controls. However, as mentioned previously, university students may be more capable, and the measures used in this study were global and may have missed subtle grammatical differences. In addition, there may be individual differences on this aspect of writing among those with DYS.

There has been relatively little research into links between the reading and writing difficulties in DYS. Altemeier, Abbott, and Berninger (2008) did find that executive functions (for switching attention during automatic integration of orthographic and phonological name codes) uniquely predicted integration of reading and writing in children with DYS; but more research is needed on this topic. There is also the issue of reading for planning and revising, and to date there has been little research in this area on populations with DYS. Recently, in a writers workshop, children with DYS were taught planning, translating, reviewing, and revising strategies and were able to apply them to a second draft after reading and reviewing the first draft and setting goals for the revision (Berninger, Winn et al., 2008, Study 1), but again more in-depth investigation is required to follow up on this promising work. The advent of eye tracking software linked to digital writing tablets has made on-line processing studies of reading while writing possible and could open a whole new area of research linking reading to writing (e.g., see Wengelin, Leijten, & Van Waes, 2010; see also Chapter 22, this volume).

DEVELOPMENTAL COORDINATION DISORDER AND WRITING

Developmental coordination disorder (or DCD) is defined by the *Diagnostic and Statistical Manual of Mental Disorders*, fourth edition (DSM-IV) as a "marked impairment in the development of motor coordination" (APA, 2000, p. 56) that cannot be explained by a sensory, neurological, or general intellectual impairment. In the past, children with DCD have been described as "clumsy" or "physically awkward," drawing attention to the main feature of this condition, which is difficulty in the performance and learning of everyday movement tasks and very often includes specific difficulties with handwriting. Most children with DCD have difficulty with a wide range of motor tasks, including those that require fine manipulative action of the hands, gross body movements requiring balance and locomotion, and various other tasks that have precise timing and spatial demands (e.g., catching or striking a ball). Such tasks are included in tests of general motor competence such as the Movement ABC-2 (Henderson, Sugden, & Barnett, 2007) and Bruininks-Oseretsky Test of Motor Proficiency-2 (Bruininks & Bruininks, 2005), which are commonly used as part of the diagnostic process. The nature of the difficulties varies with age, but it is now well recognized that the motor difficulties often persist into adulthood (Cousins & Smyth, 2003). The lay term dyspraxia is in common usage in the United Kingdom and is often used in a more general way than DCD to include children who also have difficulties with planning and organization. Interestingly, recent work suggests that these higher level or executive control problems seem to be most prominent in adolescents and young adults with DCD (Kirby, Sugden, Beveridge, & Edwards, 2008).

Transcription Skills: Poor Handwriting

One aspect of writing is the fine motor component of physically holding the pen (sometimes referred to as pencil grasp) and manipulating it to form letters and words on the paper (orthographic-motor integration). Since handwriting involves fine motor control and coordination, it is hardly surprising that difficulty with this particular skill is noted as a common feature of DCD in the DSM-IV entry for this condition. Although some tests of general motor competence (e.g., the Movement ABC-2, mentioned above) include a pencil control (tracing or tracking) task, these are not designed to specifically assess handwriting skill. Practitioners may therefore find it useful to also use a separate test of the speed and quality of handwriting, a variety of which are available (see Rosenblum, Weiss, & Parush, 2003, for a review).

Reports of handwriting performance in children with DCD by their teachers and parents often mention poorly formed letters and words that are difficult to read. These observations are supported by more objective measures of handwriting quality or legibility (Hamstra-Bletz, De Bie, & Den Brinker, 1987; Smits-Engelsman & Schoemaker, 2010). Slow handwriting and reduced output, compared to typically developing peers, are also commonly reported (Geuze, Jongmans, Schoemaker, & Smits-Engelsman, 2001), although when measured formally there have not always been significant group differences in speed of performance (Smits-Engelsman & Schoemaker, 2010). However, most research studies and clinical reports describe handwriting difficulties in this population, with parents and teachers noting handwriting as an area needing support from early childhood and children with DCD often choosing handwriting as a task that they themselves wish to improve in intervention programs (Geuze et al., 2001; Mandich, Miller, Polatajko, & Missiuna, 2003; Miller, Polatajko, Mandich, & Missiuna, 2001). Furthermore, adults with DCD note the persistence of handwriting difficulties into later years (Cousins & Smyth, 2003).

Although it is widely recognized that handwriting difficulties can lead to low self-esteem and academic underachievement, there has been very little systematic study of their exact nature and the best ways of improving this skill in children with DCD. However, some studies have focused on a more specific group of children, those with dysgraphia, referred to in the DSM-IV as a "disorder of written expression" (APA, 2001, p. 54). Although different types of dysgraphia have been described in the literature, here we focus on children who have difficulty with the motor aspects of writing (Hamstra-Bletz & Blöte, 1993). Such children may have other fine motor control difficulties, including difficulties with the fine manipulation of small objects and producing sequential finger movements (Berninger, 2004). However, they would not perform poorly in all areas when assessed on a test of general motor competence and would not meet the formal diagnostic criteria for DCD. Interestingly, recent findings show similarities in the nature of graphic skill difficulties in children with DCD and those with dysgraphia, suggesting perhaps that these groups can be considered together (Smits-Engelsman & Schoemaker, 2010).

There has been extensive work to identify the mechanisms underlying the general motor difficulties in DCD. To date there is a consensus that these children experience information processing deficits across a range of perceptual modalities (visual, kinaesthetic, and cross-modal) and that of these deficits, problems in processing visuospatial feedback seem to be the most pronounced (Wilson & McKenzie, 1998). However, in relation to handwriting, Smits-Engelsman et al. (1994) argued that current theories of motor control place less emphasis on feedback than before, and that in handwriting, sensory feedback plays only a minor monitoring role. Therefore, to understand this specific motor skill, attention has turned to a more focused model of motor control and the particular processes involved in handwriting. This work in the field of DCD and dysgraphia could inform modeling of this aspect of the transcription process and contribute more "granularity" to future models of writing development.

Van Galen (1991) has proposed the most complete model of handwriting, which he considers as a multistage process, organized in a hierarchical manner. The initial processes in this model include intentions, semantic recovery, syntactic construction, and spelling. The remaining processes are psychomotor in nature and therefore particularly relevant when considering the handwriting of children with DCD and dysgraphia. These motor processes involve (a) motor planning or programming, or the retrieval of the action pattern for letter forms (allographs) from long-term memory; (b) parameterization, or the setting of tempo, force, and size variables of the motor program; and finally (c) muscular initiation to recruit the necessary motor units to produce an appropriate movement given the particular context. Van Galen and colleagues have used this model in an attempt to identify processing constraints underlying difficulties in the production of handwriting. Employing a series of writing tasks, they have compared the performance of children with and without handwriting difficulties under careful experimental manipulation of task demands (Smits-Engelsman et al., 1994). Using this approach they found that the two groups did not differ in terms of letter form retrieval or size control. It was in tasks designed to tap the peripheral muscular initiation process that clear group differences emerged. The poor writers had a more ballistic style, characterized by higher movement velocities and fewer final adjustments. They displayed irregularities in movement control and were particularly sensitive to increased spatial accuracy demands, showing poor error correction. A detailed analysis of the movement velocity signal (Van Galen, Portier, Smits-Engelsman, & Schoemaker, 1991) revealed significant differences between the good and poor writers in the higher frequency components of the velocity signal, showing a higher degree of neuromotor "noise." Smits-Engelsman and Van Galen (1997) suggested that in an attempt to control their distal movements within this noisy system, poor writers use the arm or wrist rather than the fingers when writing. This difference in engagement of the motor system may explain the inconsistent and poorly controlled writing so often reported in this group (Wann & Kardirkamanathan, 1991; Schoemaker, Schellekens, Kalverboer, & Kooistra, 1994).

The aim of the systematic approach described above is to identify specific difficulties, leading to a better understanding of DCD and dysgraphia and ultimately to interventions designed to improve handwriting performance levels in this group. However, certain limitations to this work have been identified, relating both to the theoretical model and to the experimental tasks employed. Research on handwriting production in children and adults reveals that higher-order linguistic units actually modulate the timing of handwriting movements (Kandel, Herault, Grosjacques, Lambert, & Fayol, 2009). It is argued, for example, that the orthographic representations activated during handwriting production are not single, linear letter strings as assumed by Van Galen's model (1991), but that letters are grouped into "linguistically coherent units, such as graphemes, syllables and morphemes" (Kandel, 2009, p. 11). This insight suggests that the model should include additional intermediate linguistic processes that have a direct impact on motor programming (this is similar to comments originally made by Abbot & Berninger, 1993).

Rosenblum and Livneh-Zirinski (2008) also argued that the brief experimental writing tasks employed in much of the research by Van Galen and colleagues lack ecological validity and that the results may not be directly applicable to longer classroom writing tasks. Although the work has provided valuable information on aspects of the quality of individual letter formation, it has not addressed aspects relating to the speed of production of whole words, sentences, and longer texts.

Selecting children with handwriting difficulties who also met the diagnostic criteria for DCD, Rosenblum and Livneh-Zirinski (2008) examined both the final handwriting product (in terms of writing speed and letter formation) and measures of the on-line movement characteristics while writing in Hebrew. In contrast to findings on short experimental writing tasks, they found a clear slowness of movement in their DCD group compared to typically developing controls, even in very familiar tasks such as writing their name. Although there were no significant group differences in overall stroke length and letter height, global spatial arrangement and legibility were significantly worse for the DCD group. More letters were also erased or overwritten in the DCD group. In terms of the on-line process of writing the DCD group spent more time both with the pen on the paper and in the air ("in-air" time). These pauses in the flow of writing have also been noted in clinical reports (Benbow, 1995), although it is not clear what they represent. These findings could reflect difficulty in visualizing the letters, difficulty retrieving motor memories for letter forms, or slow movement execution per se. General slowness of movement and difficulties with temporal control have been reported in DCD across other movement tasks (Barnhart, Davenport, Epps, & Nordquist, 2003; Missiuna, Rivard, & Bartlett, 2003), but we have yet to gain an understanding of the underlying mechanisms within the context of handwriting. However, closer examination of "in-air" samples by Rosenblum, Parush, and Weiss (2003, p. 133) revealed that these were not static pauses but "motion tours" whereby the pen is moved in a rather haphazard way over the page. This observation invokes explanations at a higher level, perhaps relating to attentional, motivational, or executive function mechanisms.

There has been very little work that has considered the impact of slow and illegible handwriting in this group more widely. For example, it is not known whether the text generation skills of children with DCD are adversely affected by their poor handwriting. There has also been debate about the phonological, spelling, and reading skills of children with DCD, but this has been inconclusive due to issues with comorbidity of samples (Hulme & Snowling, 2009; O'Hare & Khalid, 2002).

CONCLUSIONS AND QUESTIONS FOR FUTURE RESEARCH

Delayed Writing: Not Different?

What then can we say about the writing of children with SLI, DYS, and DCD who have challenges with transcription, text generation, or both? Can we say their writing is delayed and may improve to within the limits of the normal range? Can we say their writing is different and may develop but not in the usual ways?

Measures of writing of children with DYS, SLI, and DCD certainly suggest that their performance is poor in comparison to their age-matched peers and that there are similar constraints on development. The transcription and text generation constraints that hold back typically developing children are fundamentally the same constraints that hold back the writing development of children with DYS, SLI, and DCD. Poor motor skills constrain the development of handwriting in children with DCD and lead to poor transcription directly affecting their writing development. Poor spelling skills in children with DYS also have an impact on transcription skills, which feeds through into their pattern of constrained writing development. Children with SLI, meanwhile, struggle with both a text generation constraint as well as a spelling problem. As a result, children with SLI have a constraint that impacts on both text generation and transcription. This effect is reflected in the poor writing skills of this population and in direct comparisons with children with DYS whose writing is more impaired (Puranik et al., 2007). However, in order to describe performance as delayed we must be sure that it is similar in nature to that of younger children. There is evidence that on many measures performance is similar to younger children matched on target variables, for example, language or spelling. However, more fine-grained analysis of performance is lacking and it is not yet possible to differentiate between delayed or different patterns of development across the groups' performance.

Separable Processes in Writing Development: Transcription and Text Generation

Our review of children facing challenges also brings us to the second conclusion, which is that the constraints on writing development identified by Berninger and Swanson (1994) are separable, as has been shown for typically developing writers (ages 6 to 12) using a structural equation study of handwriting, spelling, and composing (Abbott & Berninger, 1993). Transcription and text generation processes have separable effects on writing development, as the contrasts discussed between children with DYS and SLI make clear. However, we would caution that more work is required in this area as the separation of transcription and text generation skills does not mean that they are not functionally integrated during on-line writing in real time and real world writing in the classroom. Children with DYS show impairments in spelling and thus transcription skills, but these may in turn have an effect on text generation. The evidence we have presented shows a direct effect on the number of spelling errors contained within text and in the number of words produced in a text. The evidence we have reviewed demonstrates that difficulties with spelling also impact wider text generation skills through having a more limited written vocabulary to draw upon and struggling to retrieve spellings, thereby affecting overall writing speed and thus ideas presented. In sum, the spelling problems have a downstream effect on the other processes required to produce text. These effects are not yet well understood beyond the prediction that a limited working memory capacity system will impact on managing multiple tasks that require much processing effort. This wider effect of poor spelling skill explains why the compositions of children with DYS are shorter, poorer in content, and rated as less adequate than peers.

Connelly et al. (2006) showed that the handwriting fluency of students with DYS was not slower than spelling matched controls, but that their spelling in a writing task was poorer. This finding is consistent with that reported for a family genetics study in which the individuals with DYS had spelling impairments but varied as to whether they also had associated handwriting (automatic alphabetic writing) problems. There are clearly close links between spelling and handwriting. Recent research has shown in typically developing children that handwriting and spelling are indeed very closely interlinked with both acting together in a cascaded function during transcription (Kandel et al., 2009); yet some children have handwriting only and not spelling problems or spelling but not handwriting problems. Spelling seems not to be fully constructed before writing begins and therefore the motor processes for handwriting are closely regulated by spelling knowledge access and may influence it. On-line access to the spellings of words could be disrupted at the word, syllable, morpheme, and grapheme levels while the word is being transcribed onto the page. More work on this aspect of the model is needed in order to demonstrate whether slow handwriting of children with DYS can be attributed to difficulties with spelling.

At the same time, there is a paucity of detailed research on handwriting in children with DCD. There should now be a focus on research in this population based on models of motor development that include, but transcend, serial finger movements and language development for orthographic coding of letters and written words as well as phonology and morphology. That would allow researchers to examine difficulties in motor function in the context of oral and written language development, and then link those findings with knowledge from the motor control literature.

Text generation processes in children with SLI are a major constraint on their writing development. There are powerful reasons to predict that oral language underpins the processes of text generation and that difficulties with oral language will constrain the development of written text production, as already explained. Specific relations between oral language competence and the production of written text have been reported both for children with continuing language problems and those with resolved language problems, showing that the development of writing skill is especially sensitive to oral language influences (Bishop & Clarkson, 2003; Fey et al., 2004). Vocabulary appears to provide a critical building block for written language (Green et al., 2003) and is a key mediator in the performance of children with SLI (Dockrell et al., 2007, 2009), whereas syntactic difficulties constrain the production of grammatically accurate written text (Scott & Windsor, 2000). Thus, the text generation processes of children with SLI are severely impaired with respect to their typically developing peers.

However, a large number of children with SLI also have concurrent difficulties with the phonological processes involved in written language. This difficulty impacts directly on the children's spelling, and thus their transcription skills are also impaired (Bishop & Clarkson, 2003; Dockrell et al., 2007, 2009; Mackie & Dockrell, 2004). This fact highlights the separable effects of text generation and transcription on the production of written text.

Beyond Writing Processes to Look at Links With Writing Foundations

The study of children with DYS, SLI, and DCD shows how different difficulties in aspects of cognitive and motor development can impact directly on the development of the writing. Text generation and transcription skills that operate within working memory and are guided by other cognitive and metacognitive processes (Berninger & Swanson, 1994) need to be mastered during the beginning and developing stages of learning to write. We have seen how problems with vocabulary, phonological knowledge, and graphomotor skills all have an impact on transcription and text generation. Writing processes are intimately linked with wider cognitive, linguistic, and motor abilities. We need more research into the specific ways in which these more general abilities affect the writing processes for children with specific problems. Studying these children allows us to begin to examine the relation between writing processes and more general cognitive, motor, and linguistic abilities in ways that inform both typical writing development and writing development in those children with challenges in learning to write.

These wider abilities have been classed as writing foundations as distinct from writing processes (Singer & Bashir, 2004). These writing foundations fall into four distinct categories: cognitive-linguistic (linguistic knowledge, meta-awareness, working memory, processing speed, conceptual ability), text production (graphomotor skills, mode of output, speed of output), social-rhetorical, and beliefs and attitudes (self-efficacy, goals, and affect). It is hypothesized that if any of these foundations are weak, the writers' capacity to meet the demands of the processes involved in composing (translation, text generation etc) will also be weakened (Singer & Bashir, 2004). That certainly is what we have found in our review of the writing development of children facing challenges such as DYS, SLI, and DCD.

We need to now take forward these ideas into further research with children who experience writing difficulties. We need to probe more deeply into the relations between writing foundations and writing processes. For example, difficulty manipulating the phonological parts of language leads to nonfluent and inaccurate spelling within texts. This inaccurate spelling has an impact on writing beyond single words that we still do not yet fully understand. On-line studies using new tools such as digital tablets may allow us to begin to see how links between writing foundations and writing processes play out in real composing time. Do children who struggle with spelling, struggle with most words or only those they do not know how to spell? What might their pattern of pauses or a linguistic analysis of spelling choices tell us about how foundations are linked to writing processes? (For some initial ideas about links between pauses and on-line writing processes, see Wengelin, Marielle, & Waes, 2010.) These and related issues now need to be specified. What impacts do writing foundations have on writing processes at the word, sentence, and text levels? Do they have different impacts, as Hayes (2009) suggested? How does on-line reading impact writing processes as a writing foundation skill? Rijlaarsdam et al. (2009) made a strong argument for how reading impacts writing processes on typical populations, but for children with DYS and SLI this very important and as yet largely unanswered question deserves investigation.

Writing researchers also have to reach into other disciplines and use the tools and techniques other disciplines, such as linguistics, have used to investigate the effects of difficulties in writing foundations on writing processes (see Hancock, 2009, and Myhill, 2009, for work using linguistic tools to investigate writing processes). Some exciting work on the links between writing foundation, general cognitive abilities, and on-line writing processes is also taking place using brain imaging to capture processes related to writing foundations in typically developing writers and comparing them to those with dysgraphia or DYS (Berninger et al., 2009; Richards, Berninger, & Fayol, 2009; see also Chapter 23, this volume). As we move further ahead in this area we can begin more confidently to develop, drawing on multiple disciplines, theoretically driven, conceptually appropriate, evidence-based assessments and interventions that can target the different constraints and challenges to writing development that these children face every day of their lives within our very literate world.

ACKNOWLEDGMENTS

Our thanks to the UK Government Department for Education and the Leverhulme Trust for funding some of the work mentioned in this chapter.

REFERENCES

Abbott, R., & Berninger, V. (1993). Structural equation modelling of relationships among developmental skills and writing skills in primary and intermediate grade writers. *Journal of Educational Psychology, 85*(3), 478–508.

Abbott, R., Berninger, V., & Fayol, M. (2010). Longitudinal relationships of levels of language in writing and between writing and reading in grades 1 to 7. *Journal of Educational Psychology, 102*, 281–298.

Alamargot, D., & Fayol, M. (2009). Modelling the development of written composition. In R. Beard, D. Myhill, M. Nystrand, & J. Riley (Eds.), *Handbook of writing development* (pp. 23–47). Thousand Oaks, CA: Sage.

Altemeier, L., Abbott, R., & Berninger, V. (2008). Executive functions for reading and writing in typical literacy development and dyslexia. *Journal of Clinical and Experimental Neuropsychology, 30*, 588–606.

American Psychiatric Association (APA). (2000). *Diagnostic and statistical manual of mental disorders*. Fourth edition. Text revision. Washington, DC.

Beard, R. (1984). *Children's writing in the primary school*. Seven Oaks: Hodder and Stoughton.

Barnett, A., & Henderson, S. E. (2005). Assessment of handwriting in children with developmental coordination disorder. In D. A. Sugden & M. E. Chambers (Eds.), *Children with developmental coordination disorder* (pp. 168–188). New York: Whurr.

Barnhart, R. C., Davenport, M. J., Epps, S. B., & Nordquist, V. M. (2003). Developmental coordination disorder. *Physical Therapy, 83*, 722–731.

Beitchman, J. H., Wilson, B., Brownlie, E. B., Walters, H., & Lancee, W. (1996). Long-term consistency in speech/language profiles: I. Developmental and academic outcomes. *Journal of the American Academy of Child and Adolescent Psychiatry, 35*(6), 804–824.

Benbow, M. (1995). Principles and practices of teaching handwriting. In A. Henderson & C. Pehoski (Eds.), *Hand function in the child* (pp. 255–281). St Louis, MO: Mosby.

Bereiter, C., & Scardamalia, M. (1987). *The psychology of written composition*. Hillsdale, NJ: Erlbaum.

Berninger, V. W. (1999). Coordinating transcription and text generation in working memory during composing: Automatic and constructive processes. *Learning Disability Quarterly, 22*, 99–112.

Berninger, V. W. (2004). Understanding the graphia in dysgraphia. In D. Dewey & D. Tupper (Eds.), *Developmental motor disorders: A neuropsychological perspective* (pp. 328–350). New York: Guilford.

Berninger V. W., & Amtmann, D. (2003). Preventing written expression disabilities through early and continuing assessment and intervention for handwriting and/or spelling problems: Research into practice. In H. L. Swanson, K. Harris, & S. Graham (Eds.), *Handbook of learning difficulties* (pp. 345–363). New York: Guilford.

Berninger, V. W., Nielsen, K. H., Abbott, R. D., Wijsman, E., & Raskind, W. (2008). Writing problems in developmental dyslexia: Under-recognized and under-treated. *Journal of School Psychology, 46*(1), 1–21.

Berninger, V., Richards, T., Stock, P., Abbott, R., Trivedi, P., Altemeier, L., & Hayes, J. R. (2009). fMRI activation related to nature of ideas generated and differences between good and poor writers during idea generation. *British Journal of Educational Psychology Monograph Series VI*, 77–93.

Berninger, V., & Swanson, H. L. (1994). Modifying Hayes & Flower's model of skilled writing to explain beginning and developing writing. In E. Butterfield (Ed.), *Children's writing: Toward a process theory of development of skilled writing* (pp. 57–81). Greenwich, CT: JAI Press.

Berninger, V., Vaughan, K., Abbott, R., Begay, K., Byrd, K., Curtin, G., … Graham, S. (2002). Teaching spelling and composition alone and together: Implications for the simple view of writing. *Journal of Educational Psychology, 94*, 291–304.

Berninger, V. W., & Winn, W. D. (2006). Implications of advancements in brain research and technology for writing development, writing instruction, and educational evolution. In C. MacArthur, S. Graham, & J. Fitzgerald (Eds.), *Handbook of writing research* (pp. 96–114). New York: Guilford.

Berninger, V. W., Winn, W. D., Stock, P., Abbott, R. D., Eschen, K., Lin, S. J., … Nagy, W. (2008). Tier 3 specialized writing instruction for students with dyslexia. *Reading and Writing. An Interdisciplinary Journal, 21*(1–2), 95–129.

Bishop, D. V. M., & Clarkson, B. (2003). Written language as a window into residual language deficits: A study of children with persistent and residual speech and language impairments. *Cortex, 39*(2), 215–237.

Bishop, D. V. M., North, T., & Donlan, C. (1996). Nonword repetition as a behavioural marker for inherited language impairment: Evidence from a twin study. *Journal of Child Psychology and Psychiatry, 37*, 391–403.

Bishop, D. V. M., & Snowling, M. J. (2004). Developmental dyslexia and specific language impairment: Same or different? *Psychological Bulletin, 130*(6), 858–886.

Botting, N. (2005). Non-verbal cognitive development and language impairment. *Journal of Child Psychology and Psychiatry, 46*(3), 317–326.

Botting, N., Faragher, B., Knox, E., Simkin, Z., & Conti-Ramsden, G. (2001). Predicting pathways of SLI: What differentiates the best and the worst outcomes. *Journal of Child Psychology and Psychiatry, 42*(8), 1013–1020.

Briscoe, J., Bishop, D. V. M., & Norbury, C. F. (2001). Phonological processing, language, and literacy: A comparison of children with mild-to-moderate sensorineural hearing loss and those with specific language impairment. *Journal of Child Psychology and Psychiatry, 42*, 329–340.

Bruininks, R. H., & Bruininks, B. D. (2005). *Bruininks-Oseretsky Test of Motor Proficiency* (2nd ed.). Windsor: NFER-Nelson.

Clahsen, H., Bartke, S., & Göllner, S. (1997). Formal features in impaired grammars: a comparison of English and German SLI children. *Journal of Neurolinguistics, 10*, 151–171.

Clegg, J., Hollis, C., Mawhood, L., & Rutter, M. (2005). Developmental language disorders—a follow-up in later adult life. Cognitive, language and psychosocial outcomes. *Journal of Child Psychology and Psychiatry and Allied Disciplines, 46*, 128–149.

Coleman, C., Gregg, N., McLain, L., & Bellair, L. W. (2009). A comparison of spelling performance across young adults with and without dyslexia. *Assessment for Effective Intervention, 34*, 94–105.

Connelly, V., Campbell, S., MacLean, M., & Barnes, J. (2006). Contribution of lower order skills to the written composition of college students with and without dyslexia. *Developmental Neuropsychology, 29*(1), 175–196.

Connelly, V., Dockrell, J. E., Critten, S., Walter, K. W., & Lindsay, G. (2010, September). Writing development in children with language difficulties and the influence of spelling skill. Paper presented at the *EARLI Special Interest Group in Writing (SIG Writing) Conference*, Heidelberg, Germany.

Conti-Ramsden, G., & Botting, N. (1999). Classification of children with specific language impairment: longitudinal considerations. *Journal of Speech, Language and Hearing Research, 42*, 1195–1204.

Conti-Ramsden, G., Botting, N., & Faragher, B. (2001). Psycholinguistic markers for SLI. *Journal of Child Psychology and Psychiatry, 42*(6), 741–748.

Cousins, M., & Smyth, M. (2003). Developmental coordination impairments in adulthood. *Human Movement Science, 22*(1), 443–459.

Critten, S., & Pine, K. J. (2009). Viewing spelling in a cognitive context: underlying representations and processes. In C. Wood & V. Connelly (Eds.), *Contemporary perspectives on reading and spelling* (pp. 91–108). London: Routledge.

Critten, S., Pine, K. J., & Steffler, D. (2007). Spelling development in young children: A case of representational redescription? *Journal of Educational Psychology, 99*, 207–220.

Dockrell, J. E. (2009). Causes of delays and difficulties in writing development. In R. Beard, D. Myhill, M. Nystrand, & J. Riley (Eds.), *Sage handbook of writing development* (pp. 489–505). London: Sage.

Dockrell, J. E., Lindsay, G., & Connelly, V. (2009). The impact of specific language impairment on adolescents' written text. *Exceptional Children, 75*(4), 427–446.

Dockrell, J. E., Lindsay, G., Connelly, V., & Mackie, C. (2007). Constraints in the production of written text in children with specific language impairments. *Exceptional Children, 73*, 147–164.

Ellis Weismer, S., & Hesketh, L. (1996). Lexical learning by children with specific language impairment: Effects of linguistic input presented at varying speaking rates. *Journal of Speech Language and Hearing Research, 39*, 177–190.

Fayol, M. (1999). From on-line management problems to strategies in written composition. In M. Torrance & G. Jeffery (Eds.), *The cognitive demands of writing. Processing capacity and working memory effects in text production* (pp. 13–23). Amsterdam: Amsterdam University Press.

Fayol, M., Zorman, M., & Lété, B. (2009). Unexpectedly good spellers too. Associations and dissociations in reading and spelling French. *British Journal of Educational Psychology, Monograph series 2—Teaching and learning writing, 6*, 63–75.

Fey, M. E., Catts, H. W., Proctor-Williams, K., Tomblin, J., & Zhang, X. Y. (2004). *Oral and written story composition skills of children with language impairment. Journal of Speech Language and Hearing Research, 47*(6), 1301–1318.

Flower, L., & Hayes, J. R. (1994). A cognitive process theory of writing. In R. B. Ruddell, M. R. Ruddell, & H. Singer (Eds.), *Theoretical models and processes of reading* (4th ed., pp. 928–950). Newark, DE: International Reading Association.

Gathercole, S. E., & Baddeley, A. D. (1993). *Working memory and language.* Hove, UK: Erlbaum.

Geuze, R. J., Jongmans, M. J., Schoemaker, M. M., & Smits-Engelsman, B. C. M. (Eds.). (2001). Developmental coordination disorder: Diagnosis, description, processes and treatment [Special issue]. *Human Movement Science, 20*(1–2).

Gillam, R. B., & Johnston, J. R. (1992). Spoken and written language relationships in language learning impaired and normally achieving school age children. *Journal of Speech and Hearing Research, 35*(6), 1303–1315.

Graham, S. (2006a). Strategy instruction and the teaching of writing: A meta-analysis. In C. MacArthur, S. Graham, & J. Fitzgerald (Eds.), *Handbook of writing research* (pp. 187–207). New York: Guilford.

Graham, S. (2006b). Writing. In P. Alexander & P. Winne (Eds.), *Handbook of educational psychology* (pp. 457–478). Mahwah, NJ: Erlbaum.

Graham, S., Berninger, V., Abbott, R., Abbott, S., & Whitaker, D. (1997). The role of mechanics in composing of elementary school students: A new methodological approach. *Journal of Educational Psychology, 89*(1), 170–182.

Graham, S., Berninger, V., Weintraub, N., & Schafer, W. (1998). The development of handwriting fluency and legibility grades 1 through 9. *Journal of Educational Research, 92*, 42–52.

Graham, S., & Harris, K. R. (2009). Evidence-based writing practices: Drawing recommendations from multiple sources. *British Journal of Educational Psychology Monograph Series VI*, 95–111.

Green, L., McCutchen, D., Schwiebert, C., Quinlan, T., Eva-Wood, A., & Juelis, J. (2003). Morphological development in children's writing. *Journal of Educational Psychology, 95*(4), 752–761.

Gregg, N., Coleman, C., Stennett, B., & Davis, M. (2002). Discourse complexity of college writers with and without disabilities: A multidimensional analysis. *Journal of Learning Disabilities, 35*, 23–38.

Hamstra-Bletz, E., & Blöte, A. W. (1993). A longitudinal study on dysgraphic handwriting in primary schools. *Journal of Learning Disabilities, 23*(10), 689–699.

Hamstra-Bletz, E., De Bie, J., & Den Brinker, B. P. L. M. (1987). *Beknopte beoordelingsmethode voor kinderhandschriften, experimentele versie.* Lisse: Swets & Zeitlinger.

Hancock, C. (2009). How linguistics can inform the teaching of writing. In R. Beard, D. Myhill, M. Nystrand, & J. Riley (Eds.), *Handbook of writing development* (pp. 194–207). Thousand Oaks, CA: Sage.

Hatcher, J., Snowling, M. J., & Griffiths, Y. M. (2002). Cognitive assessment of dyslexic students in higher education. *British Journal of Educational Psychology, 72*(1), 119–133.

Hauerwas, L. B., & Walker, J. (2003). Spelling of inflected verb morphology in children with spelling deficits. *Learning Disabilities Research and Practice, 15*, 25–35.

Hayes, J. (2009). From idea to text. In R. Beard, D. Myhill, M. Nystrand, & J. Riley (Eds.), *Handbook of writing development* (pp. 65–79). Thousand Oaks, CA: Sage.

Hayes, J. R., & Flower, L. S. (1980). Identifying the organisation of writing processes. In L. Gregg & E. R. Sternberg (Eds.), *Cognitive processes in writing* (pp. 3–30). Hillsdale, NJ: Erlbaum.

Henderson, S. E., Sugden, D. A., & Barnett, A. L. (2007). *Movement Assessment Battery for Children* [Examiner's manual]. (2nd ed.). London: Pearson Assessment.

Hooper, S., Swartz, C., Wakely, W., de Kruif, R., & Montgomery, J. (2002). Executive functions in elementary school children with and without problems in written expression. *Journal of Learning Disabilities, 35*, 57–68.

Hulme, C. J., & Snowling, M. J. (2009). *Developmental disorders of language learning and cognition.* Oxford: Blackwell/Wiley.

Jackson, N. E., & Coltheart, M. (2001). *Routes to reading success and failure.* New York: Psychology Press.

Johnson, C., Beitchman, J., Young, A., Escobar, M., Atkinson, L., Wilson, B., Brownlie, E. B., … Wang, M. (1999). Fourteen-year follow-up of children with and without speech/language impairments: Speech/language stability and outcomes. *Journal of Speech, Language and Hearing Research, 42*, 744–760.

Johnston, R. S., Watson, J. E., & Logan, S. (2009). Enhancing word reading, spelling and reading comprehension skills with synthetic phonics teaching: studies in Scotland and England. In C. Wood & V Connelly (Eds.), *Contemporary perspectives on reading and spelling* (pp. 221–238). London: Routledge.

Jones, M. W., Branigan, H. P., Hatzidaki, A., & Obregon, M. (2010). Is the 'naming' deficit in dyslexia a misnomer? *Cognition, 116*(1), 56–70.

Just, M., & Carpenter, P. (1992). A capacity theory of comprehension: individual differences in working memory. *Psychological Review, 99*, 122–149.

Kandel, S. (2009). For a psycholinguistic approach of handwriting production. *Handwriting Today, 9*, 10–15.

Kandel, S., Herault, L., Grosjacques, G., Lambert, E., & Fayol, M. (2009). Orthographic vs. phonologic syllables in handwriting production. *Cognition, 110*(3), 440–444.

Katzir, T., Kim, Y., Wolf, M., O'Brien, B., Kennedy, B., Lovett, M., & Morris, R. (2006). Reading fluency: The whole is more than the parts. *Annals of Dyslexia, 56*(1), 51–82.

Kellogg, R. (1994). *The psychology of writing.* New York: Oxford University Press.

Kemp, N. (2009). The acquisition of spelling patterns: early, late or never? In C. Wood & V. Connelly (Eds.), *Contemporary perspectives on reading and spelling* (pp. 76–91). London: Routledge.

Kirby, A., Sugden, D., Beveridge, S., & Edwards, L. (2008). Developmental co-ordination disorder (DCD) in adults and adolescents. *Journal of Research in Special Education Needs, 8* (3), 120–131.

Leonard, L. B. (1998). *Children with SLI.* Cambridge, MA: MIT Press.

Leonard, L. B. (2009). Some reflections on the study of children with specific language impairment. *Child Language Teaching and Therapy, 25*(2), 169–171.

Leonard, L. B., Ellis Weismer, S., Miller, C., Francis, D., Tomblin, B., & Kail, R. (2007). Speed of processing, working memory and language impairment. *Journal of Speech Language and Hearing Research, 50*, 408–428.

MacArthur, C. A., & Graham, S. (1987). Learning disabled students composing under three methods of text production: Handwriting, word processing and dictation. *Journal of Special Education, 21*, 22–42.

MacArthur, C. A., Graham, S., &. Fitzgerald, J. (Eds.). (2006). *Handbook of writing research.* New York: Guilford.

Mackie, C., & Dockrell, J. E. (2004). The nature of written language deficits in children with SLI. *Journal of Speech Language and Hearing Research, 47*(6), 1469–1483.

Mandich, A., Miller, L. T., Polatajko, H. J., & Missiuna, C. (2003). A cognitive perspective on handwriting: Cognitive orientation to daily occupational performance (CO-OP). *Handwriting Review, 2,* 41–7.

Martlew, M. (1992). Handwriting and spelling—Dyslexic children's abilities compared with children of the same chronological age and younger children of the same spelling level. *British Journal of Educational Psychology, 62,* 375–390.

Maughan, B., Messer, J., Collishaw, S., Pickles, A., Snowling, M., Yule, W., & Rutter, M. (2009). Persistence of literacy problems: spelling in adolescence and at mid-life. *Journal of Child Psychology and Psychiatry, 50*(8), 893–901.

McCutchen, D. (1995). Cognitive processes in children's writing-developmental and individual differences. *Issues in Education, 1,* 123–160.

McCutchen, D. (2000). Knowledge, processing, and working memory: Implications for a theory of writing. *Educational Psychologist, 35*(1), 13–23.

Messer, D., & Dockrell, J. E. (2006). Children's naming and word-finding difficulties: Descriptions and explanations. *Journal of Speech Language and Hearing Research, 49*(2), 309–324.

Miller, C., Kail, R., Leonard, L., & Tomblin, B. (2001). Speed of processing in children with specific language impairment. *Journal of Speech, Language and Hearing Research, 44,* 416–433.

Miller, L., Polatajko, H. J., Mandich, A., & Missiuna, C. (2001). A pilot trial of a cognitive treatment for children with developmental coordination disorder. Comparison of cognitive and traditional approaches to treatment of DCD. *Human Movement Science, 20,* 183–210.

Missiuna, C., Rivard, L., & Bartlett, D. (2003). Early identification and risk management of children with developmental coordination disorder. *Pediatric Physical Therapy, 15,* 32–38.

Montgomery, J. (2000). Relation of working memory to off-line and real-time sentence processing in children with specific language impairment. *Applied Psycholinguistics, 21,* 117–148.

Montgomery, J., & Leonard, L. (1998). Real-time inflectional processing by children with specific language impairment: Effects of phonetic substance. *Journal of Speech, Language and Hearing Research, 41,* 1432–1443.

Morton, J., & Frith, U. (1995). Causal modeling: A structural approach to developmental psychopathology. In D. Cicchetti & D. J. Cohen (Eds.), *Developmental psychopathology* (Vol. 2, pp. 357–390). New York: Wiley.

Myhill, D. (2009). From talking to writing: Linguistic development in writing. *British Journal of Educational Psychology Monograph Series VI,* 27–44.

Norbury, C. F., Bishop, D. V. M., & Briscoe, J. (2001). Production of English finite verb morphology: A comparison of mild-moderate hearing impairment and specific language impairment. *Journal of Speech, Language and Hearing Research, 44,* 165–178.

Nunes, T., & Bryant, P. (2006). *Improving literacy through teaching morphemes.* London: Routledge.

Nunes, T., & Bryant, P. (2009). *Children's reading and spelling.* Oxford: Wiley-Blackwell.

Ogle, J. W. (1867). Aphasia and agraphia. *Report of the Medical Research Counsel of St. George's Hospital, 2,* 83–122.

O'Hare, A., & Khalid, S. (2002). The association of abnormal cerebellar function in children with developmental coordination disorder and reading difficulties. *Dyslexia, 8*(4), 234–248.

Ouellette, G. (2006). What's meaning got to do with It: The role of vocabulary in word reading and reading comprehension. *Journal of Educational Psychology, 98*(3), 554–566.

Palikara, O., Dockrell, J. E., & Lindsay, G (in press). Patterns of change in the reading decoding and comprehension performance of adolescents with specific language impairment (SLI). *Learning Disabilities: A Contemporary Journal.*

Peverly, S. T. (2006). The importance of handwriting speed in adult writing. *Developmental Neuropsychology, 29*(1), 197–216.

Puranik, C. S., Lombardino, L. J., & Altmann, L. J. (2007). Writing through retellings: an exploratory study of language-impaired and dyslexic populations. *Reading and Writing, Interdisciplinary Journal, 20*(3), 251–272.

Reilly, J., Tolchinsky, L., Woolpert, D., & Wulfeck, B. (2006, September). *Neuroplasticity and development: Spoken and written narratives in children with early focal lesions and children with specific language impairment.* Paper presented at the 10th International Conference of the EARLI Special Interest Group on Writing. University of Antwerp, Belgium.

Reilly, J., Tolchinsky, L., & Wulfeck, B. (2008, June). *Language in older children and adolescents with language impairment.* Presented at the symposium for Lexical and Grammatical Complexity in Typical and Atypical School-Age Children and Adolescents. XI Congress of the International Association for the Study of Child Language. Edinburgh, Scotland.

Rice, M. (2004). *Developmental dyslexia in adults: A research review.* National Research and Development Centre for Adult Literacy and Numeracy. Retrieved from http://www.nrdc.org.uk/publications_details.asp?ID=11#

Richards, T., Berninger, V., & Fayol, M. (2009). FMRI activation differences between 11-year-old good and poor spellers' access in working memory to temporary and long-term orthographic representations. *Journal of Neurolinguistics, 22,* 327–353.

Richardson, J. T. E., & Wydell, T. N. (2003). The representation and attainment of students with dyslexia in UK higher education. *Reading and Writing: An Interdisciplinary Journal, 16*(5), 475–503.

Rijlaarsdam, G., Braaksma, M., Couzijn, M., Janssen, T., Kieft, M., Raedts, M., … van den Bergh, H. (2009). The role of readers in writing development: Writing students bringing their texts to the test. In R. Beard, D. Myhill, M. Nystrand, & J. Riley (Eds.), *Handbook of writing development* (pp. 436–452). Thousand Oaks, CA: Sage.

Rosenblum, S., & Livneh-Zirinski, M. (2008). Handwriting process and product characteristics of children diagnosed with developmental coordination disorder. *Human Movement Science, 27,* 200–214.

Rosenblum, S., Parush, S., & Weiss, P. L. (2003). Computerized temporal handwriting characteristics of proficient and non-proficient handwriters. *American Journal of Occupational Therapy, 57*(2), 129–138.

Rosenblum, S., Weiss, P. L., & Parush, S. (2003). Product and process evaluation of handwriting difficulties: A review. *Educational Psychology Review, 15*(1), 41–81.

Schoemaker, M. M., Schellekens, J. M. H., Kalverboer, A. F., & Kooistra, L. (1994). Pattern drawing by clumsy children: a problem of movement control? In M. L. Simner, W. Hulstijn, & P. Girouard (Eds.), *Contemporary issues in the forensic, developmental, and neurological aspects of handwriting* [Monograph] (Vol. 1, pp. 45–64). Toronto: Association of Forensic Document Examiners.

Scott, C. M. (1999). Learning to write. In H. W. Catts & A. G. Kahmi (Eds.), *Language and reading disabilities* (pp. 224–259). Boston: Allyn & Bacon.

Scott, C. M., & Windsor, J. (2000). General language performance measures in spoken and written narrative and expository discourse of school-age children with language learning disabilities. *Journal of Speech Language and Hearing Research, 43*(2), 324–339.

Shanahan, T. (2006). Relations among oral language, reading and writing development. In C. MacArthur, S. Graham, & J. Fitzgerald (Eds.), *Handbook of writing research* (pp. 171–183). New York: Guilford.

Silliman, E., Bahr, R., & Peters, M. (2006). Spelling patterns in preadolescents with atypical language skills: Phonological, morphological, and orthographic factors. *Developmental Neuropsychology, 29,* 93.

Singer, B. D., & Bashir, A. S. (2004). Developmental variations in written composition skills. In C. A. Stone, E. R. Silliman, B. J. Ehrren, & K. Apel (Eds.), *Handbook of language and literacy: Development and disorders* (pp. 559–582). New York: Guilford.

Smits-Engelsman, B., & Schoemaker, M. M. (2010). *Comparability of graphic performance in children with pure dysgraphia and children with dysgraphia as part of developmental coordination disorder (DCD)*. Manuscript submitted for publication.

Smits-Engelsman, B. C. M., & Van Galen, G. P. (1997). Dysgraphia in children: Lasting psychomotor deficiency or transient developmental delay? *Journal of Experimental Child Psychology, 67*, 164–184.

Smits-Engelsman, B., Van Galen, G., & Portier, S. (1993). Cross-sectional and longitudinal study on developmental features of psychomotor aspects of handwriting. *Proceedings of the sixth handwriting conference of the international graphonomics society. Motor Control of Handwriting*. Telecom, Paris.

Smits-Engelsman, B., Van Galen, G., & Portier, S. (1994). Psychomotor development of handwriting proficiency: A cross sectional and longitudinal study on developmental features of handwriting. In C. Faure, P. Keuss, G. Lorette, & A. Vinter (Eds.), *Advances in handwriting and drawing: A multidisciplinary approach* (pp. 187–205). Paris: Europia.

Sovik, N., Arntzen, O., & Thygesen, R. (1987). Writing characteristics of normal, dyslexic and dysgraphic children. *Journal of Human Movement Studies, 13*(4), 171–187.

Sterling, C. M., Farmer, M., Riddick, B., Morgan, S., & Matthews, C. (1997). Adult dyslexic writing. *Dyslexia, 4*, 1–15.

Stothard, S. E., Snowling, M., Bishop, D. V. M., Chipchase, B. B., & Kaplan, C. A. (1998). Language-impaired preschoolers: a follow-up into adolescence. *Journal of Speech Language and Hearing, 41*, 407–418.

Swanson, H. L., & Berninger, V. (1996). Individual differences in children's writing: A function of working memory or reading or both processes? *Reading and Writing. An Interdisciplinary Journal, 8*, 357–383.

Swanson, H. L., & Hsieh, C. J. (2009). Reading disabilities in adults: A selective meta-analysis of the literature. *Review of Educational Research, 79*(4), 1362–1390.

Tannenbaum, K., Torgesen, J., & Wagner, R. (2006). Relationships between word knowledge and reading comprehension in third-grade children. *Scientific Studies of Reading, 10*, 381–398.

Tomblin, J. B., & Zhang, X. (2006). The dimensionality of language ability in school-age children. *Journal of Speech, Language, and Hearing Research, 49*(6), 1193–1208.

Van Galen, G. P. (1991). Handwriting: Issues for a psychomotor theory. *Human Movement Science, 10*, 165–191.

Van Galen, G. P., Portier, S. J., Smits-Engelsman, B. C. M., & Schoemaker, L. R. B. (1991). Neuromotor noise and the development of optimal movement strategies in children's handwriting. In G. E. Stelmach (Ed.), *Proceedings of the fifth international conference on motor control of handwriting* (pp. 47–59). Tempe AZ: Arizona State University.

Wann, J. P., & Kardirkamanathan, M. (1991). Variability in children's handwriting: Computer diagnosis of writing difficulties. In J. Wann, A. M. Wing, & N. Sovik (Eds.), *Development of graphic skills: Research perspectives and educational implications* (pp. 224–236). London: Academic Press.

Wengelin, A. (2007). The word-level focus in text production by adults with reading and writing difficulties. In G. Rijlaarsdam (Ed.), *Writing and cognition*. Studies in Writing (Vol. 20, 68–82). Bingley: Emerald.

Wengelin, A., Leijten, M., & Van Waes, L. (2010). Studying reading during writing: New perspectives in research. *Reading and Writing: An Interdisciplinary Journal, 23*(7), 735–742.

Wengelin, A., Marielle, L., & Waes, L. V. (2010). Studying reading during writing: new perspectives in research. *Reading and Writing, 23*, 735–742.

Wengelin, A., & Stromqvist, S. (2000). Discourse level writing in dyslexics—methods, results, and implications for diagnosis. *Logopedics, Phoniatrics, Vocology, 25*(1), 22–28.

Wilson, P. H., & McKenzie, B. E. (1998). Information processing deficits associated with developmental coordination disorder: A meta-analysis of research findings. *Journal of Child Psychology and Psychiatry, 39*, 829–840.

Windsor, J., Scott, C. M., & Street, C. K. (2000). Verb and noun morphology the spoken and written language of children with language learning disabilities. *Journal of Speech, Language and Hearing Research, 43*, 1322–1336.

11

The Ordeal of Deliberate Choice
Metalinguistic Development in Secondary Writers

DEBRA MYHILL

*T*he process of creating well-crafted written text is rarely achieved without pain. The act of writing is variously described from cognitive perspectives as complex, effortful, and cognitively costly: Hayes and Flower (1980) remind us that "turning verbal thought into text is a demanding task" (Hayes & Flower, 1980, p. 39) and more recently, Kellogg (2008, p. 2) has argued that writing is as cognitively challenging as playing chess. In principle, this level of demand is conceptualized as the cost of managing competing and complementary constraints on the writer's mental resources, "the act of juggling a number of simultaneous constraints" (Hayes & Flower, 1980, p. 31). Depending on the writer's proficiency, this juggling might include, among other things, attention to transcription and the orthographic aspects of texts, the selection of appropriate words and syntactical structures, the holding of local and global ideas in harmony, and the shaping of the communicative message for the intended audience. It is a process, as Coleridge (1817/1985) lyrically depicts, "in which every line, every phrase, may pass the ordeal of deliberation and deliberate choice" (p. 485).

The act of writing is always about making choices. Whether we are novice or expert writers, we have to choose words, phrases, images, and layouts for our text production as we seek to match our written text with our rhetorical goals. Some of these choices, such as spelling, are automated in developing and expert writers; whereas for novice writers they may remain overt processes of decision making. But all writers who reflect on how they write will know about the struggle for the right word, the quest for the perfect metaphor, or the testing out of phrases to find just the right one. The nature and level of decision making varies both with the nature of the writing task and with the expertise of the writer. We may spend very little time choosing what and how to communicate if we are writing a note to a member of the family to remind them to feed the cat, or when we text a question to a colleague; but most of us will sympathize with Coleridge's ordeal as we deliberate over the phrasing and shaping of a letter of application or an academic article. Writing tasks that carry high stakes socially or academically may well demand the highest levels of expertise in making writing choices. And unlike many other activities, writing remains a complex task even as our proficiency increases because we readjust our expectations of the quality of the final product as we become more expert. Research indicates that in expert writers, planning time is longer and operates at a higher conceptual level (Haas, 1996); planning, translating, and revising interact with each other more (Berninger, Fuller, & Whitaker, 1996; Van Wijk, 1999); and expert writers "spend more time on their text and operate on more complex processes than novices" (Alamargot & Chanquoy, 2001, p. 185).

For younger and less expert writers, of course, the complexity of the writing task and the multiplicity of demands made on the writer can be frustrating and demotivating. Here the work of Boscolo has been seminal in developing understanding of the motivation to write (Boscolo, 1995; Hidi & Boscolo, 2007). Becoming a writer who can engage with a variety of written demands in social and workplace settings is critical to individuals' economic well-being and arguably also to their personal well-being. Yet across the Western world there are concerns at the national policy level about standards in writing (Machin & Macnally, 2005; NCW, 2003; Montgomery, 2008; Salahu-Din, Persky, & Miller, 2008). Understanding better how developing writers think about their emerging texts and how they make choices in the composing process is important if we are to create instructional pedagogies that support young writers in becoming confident authors of written text.

One way of theorizing about the making of choices in writing is through the conceptual construct of writing as design. This issue has been approached from different paradigmatic stances. Sharples (1999), adopting a sociocognitive stance, outlined the design processes as principally about juggling the multiple demands of writing, through "a mental dialogue between content and rhetoric" (p. 22). Social semiotic researchers have focused on the more obvious visual design demands of writing in a multimodal context (Kress & van Leeuwen, 2001). A fully realized sociocultural model of design is offered by Cope and Kalantzis (2000), although this model refers to literate practice in general, rather than specifically to writing. They see design as a transformative process, drawing on all available semiotic resources to create new combinations: "Every moment of meaning involves the transformation of the available resources of meaning" (p. 22).

I have argued elsewhere (Myhill, 2011) that the design metaphor is a helpful one for constructing both a theory and a pedagogy for decision making in writing, but that the *existing theories give insufficient attention to the linguistic and metalinguistic aspects of text production*. At the lexical, syntactical, and textual levels, writers are making multiple linguistic choices: Some of these choices are *implicit choices*, shaped by previous social and literate experiences, but others are *explicit*, brought into consciousness and deliberated over. The construct of *writing as design* views linguistic choice as a discriminating selection process from a repertoire of possibilities, creating shades of meaning that align the unfolding text with the writer's design intentions. Janks (2009) makes the point that writers who have high levels of linguistic control are able "to realise the meaning potential that language affords us. What is selected from the range of lexical and grammatical options determines how this potential is realised" (p. 131). Writing as design, therefore, involves *both* linguistic and metalinguistic competence. This chapter explores young people's thinking about design choices in writing through an analysis of their metalinguistic understanding.

DEFINING METALINGUISTIC UNDERSTANDING

It is not easy to arrive at a consensual definition of metalinguistic understanding, as the word *metalinguistic* is used across the research literature with a spectrum of meanings, an observation also made by Gombert (1992, p. 1) and Camps and Milian (1999, p. 4). It is a linguistic curiosity that, in English, we have a noun to describe *metacognition*, but no parallel noun to describe metalinguistic activity (although linguists do sometimes refer to *metalinguistics* as an abstract idea, rather like *pragmatics* or *stylistics*). Its adjectival status forces the use of a following noun, which leads to a variety of closely related terms: metalinguistic *awareness*; metalinguistic *knowledge*; metalinguistic *understanding*; metalinguistic *skill*; and metalinguistic *activity*. Gombert draws a distinction between linguistic and psychological understandings of the term *metalinguistic*. He links the term's origin to Jakobsen's (1963) use of it as one of the three secondary functions of language: the *phatic* function—the use of language in maintaining social relationships; the *ludic and poetic* function—the playful, manipulative use of language; and the *metalinguistic* function—the use of language to comment on and reflect upon itself, on language as an object. Camps and Milian describe this function as the ability "to take language as the object of observation and the referent of discourse" (p. 6), whereas Roth, Speece, Cooper, and la Paz (1996) describe it as "the ability to objectify language and dissect it as an arbitrary linguistic code independent of meaning" (p. 258). In the writing classroom, this process may be witnessed when children ask how to spell a word, or discuss where a full stop should be placed, or analyze the grammatical deletions in newspaper headlines. This kind of metalinguistic discussion, be it in a writing classroom or among linguists, is often supported by a specific metalanguage, the language of grammatical terminology or literary language, for example. So children discussing grammatical deletions in a newspaper headline may use grammatical metalanguage, such as articles, determiners, nouns, or verbs to describe how the headline is functioning, whereas children studying a poem might use literary metalanguage, such as the effect of alliteration or enjambment.

However, metalinguistic discussion can occur without use of metalanguage. For example, when a student describes the opening of a novel, he or she might talk about how the writer tries to grab the readers' attention by hinting at something dreadful that follows without using any specific metalanguage.

Psychological definitions of the term *metalinguistic* are more concerned with the processes that accompany metalinguistic activity, relating both to language production and comprehension. Gombert (1992) noted that one cluster of research focuses on metalinguistic knowledge, where the "primary criterion is provided by subjects' awareness of their declarative knowledge of language," but that others focus more on metalinguistic activity as a monitoring, regulatory function "which the subject applies to the process of attention and selection which are at work in language processing" (p. 3). In the writing classroom, declarative knowledge of language is easy to observe, centering on the range of metalanguage that relates specifically to writing (word, sentence, comma, title, paragraph, topic sentence, etc.). Metalinguistic activity as a monitoring function may be more dependent on the nature of the social environment for writing created by the teacher: One might well observe peers discussing the problem of finding the right word for a particular writing context or reviewing work together. In terms of cognitive accounts of the writing process (Berninger & Swanson, 1994; Hayes & Flower, 1980), metalinguistic monitoring is central to revision processes, when the writer checks not only linguistic accuracy but also for the match of rhetorical intention with the written output. Such monitoring would clearly be an important element of post hoc revision, but it is also a prominent process during writing, as writers pause to reread written text, deliberate over word choices or phrases, and mentally rehearse the text to come (Myhill & Jones, 2007).

Broadly speaking, for linguists, metalinguistics is concerned with language as an artifact, an object of attention in itself, whereas psychologists are more interested in the mental processes of the individual that accompany language production. For theories of writing, and teachers of writing, both are important. Writers need to understand how language functions in text, both to observe appropriate linguistic conventions and to understand how language mediates communicative messages to their intended reader. They also need to be able to manage and manipulate written language to achieve their rhetorical goals. Bialystok and Ryan (1985) seemingly draw on both linguistic and psychological definitions of metalinguistic awareness in arguing that we should think of metalinguistic ability as increased control over cognitive processes and also a growing ability to analyze language. In this chapter, I am interested in drawing on not only the linguistic and the cognitive interpretations of metalinguistic awareness, but also the sociocultural influences of contexts and writing communities, which shape such awareness. Writing is a social practice (see Prior, 2006), in which a mental dialogue occurs during writing between the writer and the imagined reader, a dialogue that is rooted in socially determined knowledge. Thus, I theorize that metalinguistic activity is the explicit bringing into consciousness of an attention to language as an artifact, and the conscious monitoring and manipulation of language to create desired meanings grounded in socially shared understandings.

METALINGUISTIC DEVELOPMENT

The most comprehensive theorization of metalinguistic development to date remains that of Gombert (1992). He distinguishes between epilinguistic and metalinguistic processes, where epilinguistic activity developmentally precedes metalinguistic activity. Like Culioli (1990), Gombert perceives epilinguistic activity as unconscious metalinguistic behaviors, not "consciously monitored," but "explicit manifestations of a functional awareness of the rules of the organization or use of language" (p. 13). In contrast, Gombert perceives metalinguistic behavior as intentional, involving "reflection on language and its use" and the monitoring of the individual's "own methods of linguistic processing" (p. 13). Van Lier (1998) critiqued Gombert's binary distinction between epi- and metalinguistic awareness as too simple and argued that there are multiple levels of awareness, from the unconscious level, to the practical and creative awareness of language, to a more academic awareness involving knowledge of the metalanguage and technical control, to the highest level, which is critical awareness. Others have also thought beyond the binary distinction: Culioli (1990) suggested three stages of developmental awareness and Karmiloff-Smith, Grant, Sims, Jones, and Cuckle (1996) suggest four. All proposed that metalinguistic behavior occurs first at an unconscious level, but they offer alternative propositions for metalinguistic development at the conscious level. Van Lier's argument for not only an acknowledgment of the role of an intuitive feel for language within the domain of metalinguistic behavior, but also for the more explicit "'attempt to control and manipulate the material at hand" (p. 136), seems important within a framework of writing as design.

Gombert (1992) offered a taxonomy of metalinguistic activity, which comprises five subdomains, each related to a specific area of knowledge and understanding. These are as follows:

- *Metaphonological development*: "[I]dentifying the phonological components in linguistic units and intentionally manipulating them" (p. 15). Metaphonological ability is one of the earliest aspects of metalinguistic development, is essential in learning oral and written language, and is an important factor in learning to read and spell.
- *Metasyntactical development*: "[T]he ability to reason consciously about the syntactic aspects of language, and exercise intentional control over the application of grammar rules" (p. 41). Gombert observed that metasyntactic ability is linked to the teaching of grammar: "It is through school work on the formal aspects of language, in particular the explicit learning of grammatical rules and in the corresponding practical exercises as well as in reading tasks focusing on comprehension, that the necessity for metasyntactic behavior … might be seen to emerge" (p. 62).
- *Metalexical and metasemantic development*: "Metasemantic awareness refers to both the ability to recognize the language system as a conventional and arbitrary code and the ability to manipulate words or more extensive signifying elements, without the signifying elements being automatically affected by this" (p. 63). Metalexical awareness, on the other hand, is "the subject's ability, on the one hand, to isolate the word and identify it as being an element of the lexicon, and on the other to endeavor to access the internal lexicon intentionally" (p. 63). Gombert saw these metalinguistic domains as very similar, so they are treated together.
- *Metapragmatic development*: "Pragmatic abilities permit the effective use of language in its (social) context, and the metapragmatic abilities allow the comprehension and control of this use" (p. 94). Metapragmatic

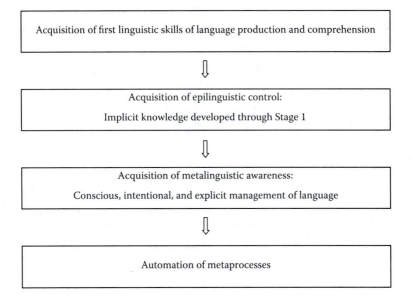

Figure 11.1 Gombert's model (1992) of metalinguistic development.

awareness goes beyond language itself to reflection on language in use in its context.

- *Metatextual development*: "Metatextual operations involved in the deliberate control, in both comprehension and production, of the ordering of utterances in larger linguistic units" (p. 121) includes the monitoring of coherence, cohesion, inference, and of the textual structure of an utterance.

Developmentally, Gombert proposed that there are four stages in acquiring a high level of metalinguistic control. The first stage, and the prerequisite for metalinguistic understanding, is learning to talk and understand spoken communication. Stage 1 generates the epilinguistic knowledge of Stage 2, which is unconscious and implicit. Stage 3, metalinguistic awareness, occurs when language is manipulated consciously and intentionally. The final stage is when this awareness becomes automated and occurs without conscious attention, except when some aspect of language is deliberately brought into consciousness for explicit attention. Gombert argues that, within this developmental framework, metaphonological, metasyntactic, and metasemantic knowledge develop first, followed by metapragmatic, and finally, metatextual knowledge (Figure 11.1).

METALINGUISTIC DEVELOPMENT IN WRITING

One problem with Gombert's (1992) taxonomy is that it focuses on speech, not on writing. It is relatively easy to see how Gombert's subdomains might be extended to include writing: for example, understanding phoneme–grapheme correspondences and reasoning about spelling would seem metaphonological, whereas adapting written text to suit its audience and purpose would seem metapragmatic in nature. However, writing development also draws on metamorphological and metaortho-graphic knowledge. There is a growing body of research signaling the significance of this knowledge (Arnback & Elbro, 2000; Bourassa, Treiman, & Kessler, 2006; Caravolas, Kessler, Hulme, & Snowling, 2005; Nunes & Bryant, 2006). Nonetheless, Gombert's model is, in essence, a model of oral development. Indeed, research in the field of metalinguistics has tended to focus on four aspects of language: early oral language development (Downing & Oliver, 1974; Karmiloff-Smith et al., 1996; Smith & Tager-Flusberg, 1982; Tunmer, Bowey, & Grieve, 1983; Tunmer & Grieve, 1980); the role of metalinguistic awareness in reading comprehension (Hiebert, Cioffi, & Antonak, 1984; MacGillivray, 1994; Zipke, 2007); the role of metalinguistic awareness in word decoding and spelling (Cassar & Treiman, 1997; Martinet, Valdois, & Fayol, 2004; Nunes, Bryant, & Bindman, 2006); and a sub-stantial body of work on metalinguistic awareness in bilingual learners (Bialystok, 2007; Cisero & Royer, 1995; Norbert, 1999).

And yet writing is a highly metalinguistic activity: As noted in the opening of this chapter, writing is cognitively effortful and more expert writers regulate and monitor their writing more effectively. The importance of metacognition in writ-ing (Butterfield, Hacker, & Albertson, 1996; Hayes & Flower, 1980; Kellogg, 1994; Martlew, 1983; Wallace & Hayes, 1991) has been discussed almost from the point Flavell (1979) first introduced the concept of metacognition. Whether metalin-guistic activity is a subset of metacognition, as argued by Allal (1999), or a separate activity, related to reflection on language, as argued by Dolz and Erard (1999), it is important to understand better the role of metalinguistic understanding in writ-ing. Camps and Milian (1999) articulate three distinct focuses for consideration in doing so: "We need to know whether and how this knowledge about language and discourse appears in the composition process, whether and how other types of knowledge appear, which type of knowledge this is, and how it is made conscious and controlled" (p. 3). These are important questions, both for theoretical elabo-ration and for pedagogical development. It is curious, then, that there is so little research on the role of metalinguistic knowledge in first language writing, given that writing is quintessentially an act of metalinguistic determination—an act of selection, choice, shaping, reflection, and revision. The study informing the analy-sis in this chapter set out to explore how metalinguistic activity is manifest in writ-ers at school. The goals were to test the ecological validity of theoretical research through "vigorous, applied research, which goes beyond the bristling defense of pedago-ideological points of view" (Gombert, 1992, p. 173) and to seek to under-stand metalinguistic development in older, adolescent writers.

RESEARCHING METALINGUISTIC DEVELOPMENT

The data in this chapter are drawn from a 3-year, nationally funded project in the United Kingdom, which investigated whether contextualized teaching of gram-mar in writing lessons improved students' writing and metalinguistic understand-ing. The study was a mixed methods design, with a randomized controlled trial

TABLE 11.1   Learning Objectives Selected as Focus for the Teaching Schemes

Key Learning Objective	Related Subsidiary Learning Objectives
Varying sentences and punctuation for clarity and effect	• Draw on the full range of punctuation, including colons and semicolons, to clarify meaning, aid cohesion, and create a variety of effects • Draw on knowledge of a wide variety of sentence lengths and structures, including complex sentences, and apply it to students' writing to clarify ideas and create a range of effects according to task, purpose, and reader
Improving vocabulary for precision and impact	• Create considered and appropriate effects by drawing independently on the range and variety of their own vocabulary and by using strategies and resources to extend students' available choices
Developing varied linguistics and literary techniques	• Draw on a repertoire of linguistic and literary techniques and select those most appropriate for creating specific effects in students' own writing

(RCT) and a complementary qualitative study. The sample comprised 31 classes of mixed-ability children aged 12 to 13 years in 31 schools from different geographic and socioeconomic backgrounds; they were randomly assigned to an intervention group or comparison group. Teachers in the Intervention Group used three detailed teaching schemes, designed by the project team, one in each term of a school year that addressed in turn the writing of narrative fiction, argument, and poetry. These schemes embedded attention to grammar within the context of writing, introducing grammatical constructions and terminology at a point in the teaching sequence that was relevant to the focus of learning. The teaching goal was to open up a repertoire of possibilities for constructing meanings and not to teach about "correct" or formulaic ways of writing. Each instructional Scheme of Work took the same set of learning objectives (Table 11.1) from the Year 8 (12- to 13-year-olds) Framework for English, a national policy guidance document in the United Kingdom, and explored them in the context of fictional narrative, argument, and poetry. The Comparison Group was also taught fictional narrative, argument, and poetry with the same learning objectives; and they completed the same writing tasks as the Intervention Group. Teachers were given the same resources that supported the intervention schemes, but no detailed instructional Schemes of Work, and the teachers were completely at liberty to teach each genre as they wished.

To determine the impact or otherwise of the intervention on students' writing attainment, pre- and posttest samples of writing were collected. The tests were designed in collaboration with Cambridge Assessment, the national test developers and markers for the National Curriculum tests of writing at age 14: The process of testing and assessment was thus very comparable with national testing procedures and outcomes. Both the pre- and posttests asked students to write a first-person narrative under controlled conditions, and a crossover design was used to avoid any test-effect bias. The marking was undertaken by Cambridge Assessment, wholly independent of the research team. Neither Cambridge Assessment nor their team of markers knew from which treatment group the writing was drawn. For each set of scripts, Cambridge Assessment provided a first marker's set of marks, a second marker's set, and a "resolution mark," adjudicated by a third senior marker if the first two marks were very different.

The pre- and posttests were both scored out of a possible 30 (as was the practice in national writing tests at age 14 in England). As might be expected, on average there was an increase between the pre- and posttest writing scores in both the Comparison and Intervention Groups. However, the mean pre- to postimprovement in scores for the comparison group (332 students) was 1.922; whereas the mean increase for the intervention group (412 students) was higher, at 3.456. The mean difference in score improvement between the Comparison Group and the Intervention Group was therefore 1.534. Taking the sizes of the Comparison and Intervention Groups into account, this estimated mean difference in score improvement has a standard error of 0.353 and therefore differs from zero with high statistical significance (a two sample t-test value of 4.347 corresponding to $p < .001$). The data from this randomized control trial thus indicate a significant positive effect size of 1.53 for the intervention terms of improvement in writing attainment.

Alongside the pre- and posttest writing attainment data for the RCT analysis, the qualitative data collected included a lesson observation of each class during the teaching of each scheme, followed by an interview with the teacher and an interview with a student. Preliminary analysis of the teacher interviews and lesson observations indicates the significance of teachers' linguistic subject knowledge in mediating grammar affects and developing writers in meaningful ways. The analysis also indicates the explicitness of the grammar focus, and teachers recognized the strong link of a grammatical feature to its possible effects in writing as departure from their usual practice, suggesting that this departure was a key factor in the positive effect size gained for the intervention.

However, the analysis of metalinguistic understanding presented here is drawn from the interviews with the students, and thus it is important to elaborate the nature of that interview in more detail. Each interview followed the observed lesson and was conducted in an informal but private space. The research team used a semistructured interview schedule (see Appendix A), which sought to investigate students' response to the lesson and their metalinguistic understanding. In particular, the interview probed students' ability to use grammatical metalanguage, their "applied" understanding of how grammar constructions can create particular effects or impacts, and their ability to talk explicitly about language choices, including without metalanguage. Prior to the interview, each student was given a prompt text to read and on which to reflect. This text also served as a stimulus for discussion in the interview. This prompt text was always in the genre under study and was not necessarily an exemplary text. That was given to the students in the form of a prompt sheet with some questions to support their reflection (see Appendices B, C, and D). The interview also probed their thinking about their own writing and how it was progressing.

The interviews were analysed inductively using the NViVO qualitative data analysis software and then a further layer of analysis utilized Gombert's (1992) taxonomy as the basis of a theoretical frame for categorizing metalinguistic understanding. Other than a few limited references to alliteration and the initial sounds of words, there were no comments that reflected metaphonological understanding. The focus of the lessons and the interviews was on creating effective texts and did not address spelling, for example, which might well have elicited more metaphonological thinking. The four remaining subdomains in Gombert's taxonomy were all evident in the students' interview discussions. In addition, the coding process led to the generation of a further category: the demonstration of metalinguistic declarative knowledge without accompanying metalinguistic understanding. Students' responses within each of these categories will be elaborated in more detail below.

METASEMANTIC AND METALEXICAL UNDERSTANDING

Gombert (1992) combines metalexical and metasemantic understanding as two aspects of closely related metalinguistic understanding: *Metalexical* relates to recognizing that words are words and being able to select words intentionally; *metasemantic* relates more to the meanings of words and the ability to manipulate words. Thus, this kind of understanding may be related to lexical diversity and vocabulary in developing writers' texts. At age 12 or 13, all of the students in this study understood the concept of *word* and were more concerned with what words can do in a text and making choices about which words to use. For example, students discussed which words were most effective in creating suspense in the opening of a narrative. This element of metalinguistic awareness appears to be the most developed in students of this age when more comments related to vocabulary choice and word effect were categorized as metasemantic or metalexical than any other category. These adolescent writers were very focused on what words can do in their writing, rather than on words as language objects.

To an extent, their metalexical understanding was demonstrated in references to explicit choices of particular words and how they talked about those words. Very common were references to *powerful* words, *descriptive* words, *strong* words, and *interesting* words. Metasemantic understanding was evident when writers articulated, or tried to articulate, the effect of word choices on shaping meaning or its intended impact on a potential reader. It is important to remember that one of the learning objectives for both the Comparison and Intervention Groups was improving vocabulary for precision and impact, so metasemantic learning was a specific teaching focus.

As shown in Table 11.2, many students selected the word *disgraceful* in response to the interview question inviting them to comment on the word choices and effectiveness of the vocabulary in the model text. The table shows the range of responses elicited and exemplifies the metalinguistic discussions about words. One strand of responses identifies *disgraceful* as an emotive word, something addressed in the teaching of argument, and many students referred to this emotive word in their interviews, both in reference to the prompt text and their own writing.

TABLE 11.2   Students' Comments About One Word in the Argument Prompt

Argument Text Prompt	
*It is **disgraceful** to see the younger generation sending their families off to old people's homes*	
Intervention	I think *disgraceful* is really good . . . because it's powerful and it's a disgrace, like that, elderly people are being treated like it when it's, maybe some of their last years alive and things, and it's horrible to think that people are doing this because that is is actually horrible to think, that that is actually happening and it's writing what's actually going on in your head. It's as if she's wrote, or he has wrote what you're thinking while you're reading it.
	Disgraceful is like a really strong word to use . . . instead of saying "Oh it's horrible," because that probably wouldn't grab your attention if you just said "it's horrible" because it's quite a common word to use, lots of people use it.
	Interviewer: Tell me why you think *disgraceful* is better.
	Student: Because it's more horrible, just sounds like horrible, like there's something horrible over there, but *disgraceful* sounds more like, angry and determined to like say it's *disgraceful* and horrible.
	Interviewer: What about *disgraceful*? (following student's selection of this word)
	Student: It sounds like they're like really angry and quite upset about it and, not too happy about the fact that it's going on.
	I think *disgraceful* is really good . . . powerful
	They're obviously trying to persuade someone because they're using really strong words like it's *disgraceful* to see the younger generation sending their families off to old people's homes.
	It's got quite a lot of emotive language in there . . . it's awful . . . *disgraceful*, that's a very powerful word.
	Disgraceful, that's sort of emotive language, a sort of put-down word.
	Instead of saying *It's really bad* which is quite boring they're saying it's *disgraceful* and it shouldn't happen, and it's really effective. If they'd put *it is bad to see the younger generation* it wouldn't have been as, like, "wow" sort of thing, but saying *it's disgraceful* is really quite strong, it's a strong opinion.
	Instead of just using *It's really bad to see*, they use a really strong word like *it's disgraceful*.
	It's disgraceful shows you how cross they are and it's really dramatic.
	Disgraceful is a tiny bit emotive.
Comparison	*Disgraceful*, like it's disgraceful about, the way they treat them.
	Here where it says *it is disgraceful to see*, they're trying to say like, how could you put them into this like after all these years and then they've got to be put into like there so they're saying like it shouldn't be really happening.
	Disgraceful, it's very, you know, it's, just saying that it's awful.
	Disgraceful, it's emotive language.

Frequently, they pointed to the power of specific word choices to have a marked effect on the reader: "words that are going to sink into the heart"; "you can make them feel guilty or sad or happy, just by using certain words"; "makes you feel something that the writer wants you to feel." In narrative, students discussed word choices they thought were more "imaginative" and helped "create a picture in your mind" or showed "what the person in the story is actually seeing."

Another strand of comments considered how word choices could increase the formality of a text, although few writers used the word *formal*. Several referred to words as more *posh*, such as the choice of *older generation* rather than *older people* in the argument model text. Sometimes, the discussion was less about formality and more about selecting less familiar words: *clambered* is a better word then just *climbed*; they have used some quite unusual words as well: "'I felt a slight pang'—I've never heard that before really." These discussions often revolve around alternatives, the possibilities that choosing different words offers to the effect of the text on the reader. The poetry prompt text instructs one student to discuss how the use of *urge* rather than *make* creates a stronger imperative to act:

> When it says "I urge you to stop dead" it's a good choice, because obviously they could say "I make you stop dead" but it doesn't sound the same. It makes you feel like, gosh, I've got to stop now, not just oh, I'll stop in a second.

One boy also realized that being deliberately colloquial can be effective. He chose to write an argument in the voice of a small child, arguing about pigs as pets: "While people say that a pig makes a lot of mess, I've heard they poo outside." In the interview afterward, he initially suggested that if he altered *poo* to *feces* it might improve his text, but decides "it doesn't really work that well" and that using *poo* "sounds like a little kid saying it."

METASYNTACTIC UNDERSTANDING

Within Gombert's (1992) taxonomy, metasyntactic understanding represents conscious reasoning about the syntax of a sentence and deliberate control over accurate use of grammar. The focus on accuracy seems to exclude how metasyntactic understanding might contribute to a writer's ability to craft and design a text to meet its rhetorical goals. For the 12- to 13-year-old writers in this study, only the weakest writers would have exhibited grammatical inaccuracies, and only on a few occasions. The teaching focus was on varying sentences and punctuation for clarity and effect, and students in the Intervention Group were taught about the possibilities of short sentences for impact, varying sentence lengths to create textual rhythm, and altering the syntactical structure of sentences to shift focus. The data suggest that students were considerably less confident in their understanding at a metasyntactic level.

The students' responses indicate an emerging understanding of why short sentences can be effective, but their understanding was often not clearly articulated. Many spoke of short sentences as "powerful," that they "grab attention" and "makes [the reader] think," conveying some understanding that short sentences tend to draw attention to themselves. One writer appeared to be suggesting that a short sentence can create tension: "when it's like a really frightening story or something a little short sentence is better." The most frequently commented-upon sentence in the narrative model text was "We had been burgled!!", which was singled out as an example of an effective "short and snappy" sentence, which created dramatic impact and tension. The two comments below show two students' thinking about this sentence:

He's got exclamation marks so it's also a very short sentence, so it's sort of suddenly whacking you and saying, what's happening and what you've been thinking all along, so I think that's quite effective.

It's sharp, so it just like hits you. When you're reading a big long sentence, and it's just dragging on, but then one comes like that, which stops you and makes you think about it.

It is also evident that students have grasped an understanding of the concept of variety in sentence length in a text, although they are much less able to articulate how that variety might link with prosody or textual rhythm. Several correctly noted that the argument prompt text used sentences of a broadly similar length and suggested the writing might be improved by judicious use of "some short blunt sentences," although this approach still shows greater understanding of short sentences than the principle of varying textual rhythm. For many, it was a superficial understanding of the principle of variety, for example, the writer who observed "I think it's good to vary it really." Some seemed to associate short sentences with interest and long sentences with boredom, thus rationalizing that "when you have a long sentence, it's more likely to be not as exciting as a short sentence," as the principle for varying sentence length. Many connect the length of the sentence more with the meaning it conveys than with the different stresses and emphases that variation can create. One writer observes that "the long ones give you more detail but then the short ones just make you think a bit more," but another associates length with reading difficulty: "If there's a really long sentence you're probably thinking, oh well I can't remember what the beginning of the sentence was."

However, metasyntactic understanding about syntactical variety was much more limited, although these writers are able to make some metasyntactic observations related to syntactical variation. The teaching scheme had taught about altering emphasis, through using nonfinite clauses, adverbials, and subordinate clauses as the start of the sentence. There were significantly fewer comments that addressed syntactical variety. Some noticed that "the sentence structures are the same" in the argument model text, and suggested "change them around a bit to make it different." Another student said, of the same text:

They're not all started with the same sort of phrases or words, so they kind of keep your attention, because if they were all started with "They ought to make" or "The elderly," it wouldn't be very exciting, it would be really quite boring.

In both cases, the writers have not understood how syntactic shifts can move reader focus. One writer, however, was very precise in describing a syntactic variation that he has used:

I've put the connective at the start like I said before and I wouldn't normally do that, normally it would be "The pig will have nowhere to sleep" or something like that, but I've put "Despite the fact that the pig will have nowhere to sleep."

However, he does not link it to any rhetorical purpose. Sometimes apparent implicit understanding is evident, as in the perceptive discussion about one sentence:

> "All they do is sit in an empty room and do nothing except sit and do nothing": They put "nothing" twice in that sentence and it doesn't sound very good, it doesn't sound like they've got a very wide range of vocabulary. So they could put, "All they do is sit in an empty room and all they do is sit and do nothing" because then they wouldn't have put "nothing" twice.

Here the writer offers an alternative that balances the repetition of the main clause on either side of the coordinating conjunction with an expansion that emphasizes the futility of their situation: "in an empty room" and "do nothing." This alternative removes the awkward repetition of "do nothing," which she has almost identified, although she has considered it as a metalexical issue. It is possible that this writer, and indeed many of the other students in the study, does not yet have sufficient explicit syntactical knowledge to articulate her emergent meta-syntactic understandings.

METATEXTUAL UNDERSTANDING

Metatextual understanding, according to Gombert (1992), moves beyond syntax-level awareness to a more global awareness of the coherence and cohesion of an utterance, which may have multiple syntactic constructions. Gombert, of course, was addressing oral performance, where metatextual monitoring is normally co-occurring with speech production. In producing a written text, however, the writer can think about and plan for the structure of a whole text before writing, and during writing is monitoring the unfolding text to check that it is developing as intended or if revisions are needed to global plan. Finally, the process of revision permits further checking that the text fulfills its communicative purpose. Different genres place different demands on metatextual understanding: Consider, for example, the simplicity of a note to a salesman left on the front door, compared with the complexity of an academic argument. There was less evidence of metatextual understanding and considerably fewer comments coded as metatextual, thus consistent with Gombert's claim that metatextual understanding develops later than metaphonological, metasemantic, or metasyntactic understanding for both oral and written productions (as in the current study).

In the current study, poetry was deliberately selected as one of the three writing genres to be taught, partly because it is frequently omitted in studies of writing, but also because the research team hypothesized that it would generate good opportunities to talk about text structure, as this is such a key aspect of poetry. In fact, students found it very difficult to respond to the text-level questions about the poetry prompt text. They were unable to articulate any clear metatextual understanding beyond visual recognition that it was a poem "because of the way it's set out" or by statements that referred to structure in terms of what it was not: "It couldn't be a story because it's too short and it couldn't just be a passage of writing, because each sentence starts the same way." One student correctly observed that the poem was "in rows of four and some poems are in rows of four, I think it's called a quatrain." The interviews prompted students to think about whether the line length and layout of the poem served any particular purpose, and beyond simple descriptions of long and short lines, students were generally at a loss how to respond to this.

With argument, the few metatextual comments tended to be about the structuring of the arguments across the text, and how "one paragraph's on one argument, and the other paragraph's a different argument." A stronger metatextual account of argument took a clearer global view of the text:

> They've put the important points at the top and important points at the bottom and in the middle they've kind of tried to persuade you it's bad. They've put a summary of the whole kind of speech in a couple of sentences at the end which is good, kind of refreshes your memory. They've used repetition ... you don't really forget what the speech is about, and it's putting across the fact that it is about the younger generation putting the older generation in care homes.... I can tell it's an argument mainly because it's all on one side ... they've put their point across really strongly.

Some students had a clear sense of the textual decisions they were making in their writing and how these related to the overall shape of their unfolding text:

> It's going to be told in first person by one of the tramps called Toby and, he's going to be like the one that had something really bad happen to him in his past and that's why he's been made homeless ...
>
> It's going to be present tense because I think if it's going to be like a diary account then, it will be past at the beginning from like, when he's telling the story of his past but like towards the main bit it will be present, so it will go from past to present.

Students were also able to comment on narrative structure and the development of plot. One student explained how he liked to create suspense by "not giving them the whole story but edging it forward slightly, the actual dilemma folding out, and not give it away straightaway." Another had learned that narrative plots can be nonchronological and "you don't necessarily have to put the opening at the beginning, you can put it in the middle."

METAPRAGMATIC UNDERSTANDING

The category of metapragmatic understanding proved more problematic in coding of the student data because Gombert's (1992) definition of it as the ability to reflect on language use in its context described what the teaching intervention was encouraging through its explicit attention to grammar in context. As writers, who principally considered the effectiveness of their own and others' written texts, a substantial number of the students made metapragmatic comments, particularly in their awareness of their intended audience or reader. Indeed, the majority of the responses already discussed could also have been coded as metapragmatic. For the purposes of this study, then, it was decided to include in this category those comments not coded elsewhere that showed understanding of language in context.

The decision whether to write in first or third person was addressed in the narrative teaching and a cluster of the metapragmatic responses related to this. In particular, although the term *omniscient narrator* was not used in the teaching, some students seemed to be grappling with articulating the way third-person viewpoints permit an all-knowing narrative stance:

> I think first person and third person depends on what you're writing, but I usually try and write in the third person because it's easier to get in everything and details, and you can sort of like show what everyone else is thinking without actually having to say it ... when you're in third person and you're looking unseen you can say, well for instance, someone rolls their eyes, you can think whatever has just happened is really, really stupid and you can kind of understand what they're talking about.
>
> If it's like the narrative viewpoint they know everything, like what's happened before, what's going to happen, and if it's like the person, they know everything as well, what's happened, but if it's a person looking at that person they don't know the full facts so they could interpret it in a different way.

Many students seemed confident in explaining their choice to use first- or third-person perspectives. One student observed: "If it's first person, you can like pretend to be the character and feel what, you feel like you're thinking if you're in his position and I found that easier," but for another it was being in "that person's eyes sort of thing, like seeing what they're seeing." For some, the choice of first person linked with the ability to express feelings more strongly; one student, responding to the poetry prompt text, reported: "I like the way it talks in first person, "I ... I" like a pen's got personal feeling and it brings everything to life.

Some students were able to explain possible genre differences in the choice of first- or third-person voice:

> If a story's like, say a birthday party, it's better to write in third person, because you get everybody's view of it, and if, say, a romantic novel, you can do it from like one person's view of what's happening around them, so you create more feelings.

Many of the writers discussed explicit choices they were making in their emerging writing that showed how they were trying to shape their texts with both audience and purpose in mind. One writer carefully used pronoun choices to position the audience, arguing that "if you use 'we' and 'I' and 'our' and 'you,' it's very personal to the audience that you're talking to, and it makes the audience a bit more involved." Another explained her choice of the modal verb "will" "because it sounds more determined and you're telling your team like you have to win, because we really want this trophy." One boy reflects on the argument letter he is writing and explains how he has shaped his opening with his reader in mind:

> "I'm writing this letter to tell you that I am very angry about the lack of enrichment week": that makes him involved, that makes him sort of interested. If

you don't put an interesting line at the beginning then they might say actually I don't want to read this, but if you've like showed what you think and then add more information in the other two (paragraphs) then he'll read it…. "It is exciting, it's enjoyable and it entertains us" gives you three reasons, so it's not just like one and it gets it into your head that we really, really like it.

METALINGUISTIC KNOWLEDGE WITHOUT METALINGUISTIC UNDERSTANDING

One category of response that was very evident in the data for this study but not addressed in Gombert's (1992) model was talking about writing with apparent metalinguistic knowledge, which was not accompanied by metalinguistic understanding. This knowledge is conscious and directly focused on talking about language, but it is not epilinguistic. In particular, when metalanguage was used it revealed either incorrect understanding or an inability to make a meaningful connection between the linguistic terminology and its possible impact in the writing.

Typically, students used the metalanguage that had been the teaching focus, but demonstrated mistaken or perhaps partial understanding. One child correctly recalled that connectives are useful in writing argument, but then suggested that "strong connectives … stand out more," but "short connectives … you can emphasise them a lot and you can put a lot more expression in." Another child argued that she was going to write in the present tense "because it's easier to understand with the problem and everything, and I might use a bit of past tense in there but I don't think I would use the past tense all the time because it's quite hard," suggesting a limited grasp of the different purposes of past and present tense. One student believed that good writing could be achieved by "using all different sorts of sentences like, compound sentences, and like short, simple ones like, that stick in your head, using a lot of repetition," but one girl, thinking about narrative, claimed that "you don't really worry about the amount of nouns because there might be a lot of people in it and you're not really sort of thinking about the nouns, but the describing words and the adjectives, well the adjectives and verbs and stuff."

One strong pattern within this category was that of writers who seemed to think that using a particular grammatical feature had merit per se, leading to metalinguistic reflections focused on identifying what was in the writing:

> He has done some short ones and some long ones which is quite good, it's good for a mix and he's used commas which is good instead of using full stops all the time, and he's used like exclamation marks and the sentences are quite well spread out.

The notion of improving writing by adding more of a particular grammar feature was also a common trend, exemplified by the following comments:

> I think I could've added, like more sentences or more, more of them words I've forgotten what they're called now.
> They could've done bigger paragraphs … and used more of the modal verbs.

> Making sure that you add in adjectives and like nouns and adverbs and verbs, because like, then you, if you do that then it makes it more interesting because … it's like describing the words, the sentence better.

Adding adjectives or adverbs seemed to be one of the most commonly stated ways to improve writing, even though the teaching focus in both narrative and poetry had been on selecting more appropriate nouns and verbs and using fewer adjectives and adverbs. The misconception that adding adjectives or adverbs was a good strategy is also implicitly evident in comments that reveal approval of rather artificial changes to a sentence, such as: "instead of just plain words like, 'I was kicking my legs back and forth,' you can say, 'I was hastily moving my legs back and forth.'"

CONCLUSIONS

Metalinguistic Development

The data presented here provide partial confirmation that the theoretical assumptions in Gombert's (1992) analysis of metalinguistic development hold true in writing. His proposition that metaphonological, metasemantic, and metasyntactic knowledge develop before metapragmatic and then metatextual knowledge is broadly confirmed in that these young writers appear to be more accomplished in discussing metasemantic decisions than metatextual ones. However, this study suggests students' metasyntactic understanding is more fragile, frequently partial, or misunderstood. In terms of syntactical variation within the sentence, it is evident that the declarative knowledge of syntactical structures such as the subject or the adverbial is often absent, which in turn limits students' ability to monitor and manipulate at a syntactical level. Gombert (1992, p. 62) suggests that metasyntactical understanding does not occur naturally but requires teaching input on the formal aspects of language, which, of course, the intervention in this study directly addressed. It may be that the teaching was not sufficient to support the development of metasyntactical understanding; however, the teacher interviews and lesson observation data suggest that teachers' linguistic subject knowledge and lack of confidence with syntactical terms were also significant influences.

The data also illustrate that metapragmatic understanding is a more significant feature of metalinguistic development than Gombert (1992) suggests. Metapragmatics may be an aspect of metalinguistic activity that is particularly important in writing, with its concern for rhetorical goals, and it may also be more significant in writers in the later stages of schooling. Certainly, the writers in this study were sharply focused toward how writers and how texts shape meaning. Indeed, it is striking how well these 12- and 13-year-olds were grappling with notions of audience and purpose and thinking about design choices. Although there was a distinct category of metapragmatic comments, there was a strong sense in the data that *all* metalinguistic discussion was moving toward metapragmatic thinking. Students were interested in what words, phrases, sentences, and texts could do and how metalinguistic choices could influence how their writing might be received by a reader.

Another aspect of metalinguistic development that Gombert's (1992) taxonomy does not capture is the issue of the use of metalanguage and of articulation of metalinguistic thinking. The data here show that writers of this age have access to a metalanguage, particularly of grammatical terminology, which they cannot always use meaningfully. Conversely, there are students who engage in high-quality metalinguistic discussion, revealing strong metalinguistic understanding, but without use of metalanguage. At times the metalanguage is unnecessary; at other times the use of metalanguage would have enabled clearer articulation of thinking. Equally, the data show how some students are struggling to articulate their metalinguistic understanding: The struggle could be due to not having the necessary metalanguage, but more often it seemed to be about the difficulty of putting emerging understanding into words, as in the example below:

> I think, umm, they've, they've put in a lot of points about, you know, umm, why, you know, why, and how, and, like they've given all the information, but I think they could've, been a bit more forceful, and a bit more, like, a bit more sort of, what's the word, you know put in, put in more language that, yeah that is like more forceful.

It seems likely that the developmental pathway from epilinguistic to metalinguistic understanding is more multilayered than Gombert proposed.

Socially Constructed Metalinguistic Understanding

This study also indicates how metalinguistic understanding is developed through socially constructed encounters with texts and communities of writers. In particular, in this dataset, young writers' metalinguistic understanding is heavily shaped by their teachers' constructions of what is valuable in writing. Many of the comments coded as metalinguistic knowledge without metalinguistic understanding reflect the teaching focus of lessons, repeated back without meaning. The tendency to see grammatical features rather formulaically as having intrinsic merit, particularly the "adding more" phenomenon, where writers have "learned" that writing is improved by adding more adjectives, or short sentences, or connectives, is learning entirely constructed in the classroom. In the United Kingdom, as in other Anglophone countries, the teaching of grammar has not been part of the language curriculum for many years. Our study has also highlighted problems for teachers in their own linguistic subject knowledge and their pedagogical knowledge of how best to teach grammar. As a consequence, the pedagogical spotlight tended to fall on the grammar feature, rather than its possible effects in writing. The greater confidence shown by students in metasemantic discussion compared with metasyntactic discussion may be a direct reflection of the teachers' knowledge. In general, teaching about vocabulary and word choice was more confident and more explicitly directed toward repertoires of meaning-making possibilities, whereas teachers lacked confidence in teaching about the syntax of the sentence.

However, students' wider cultural and linguistic experiences also shaped their metalinguistic understanding, particularly their reading experiences. One writer explained: "I normally write in first person because it's like a diary account and most of the books I read are in diary accounts"; whereas another described how she listened to her writing in her head and had "reading voices" in her head that helped her make judgments about her writing. She argued that this understanding had been developed through reading:

> I read a lot of books, I've found, so it's a bit weird but after reading quite a lot of books you can kind of, it's one of those things where you stop in the middle of a sentence and you're thinking "That doesn't sound right" and then you realise the true meaning of it and then you go back and read it … and then you reread it and then realise "Oh yeah, it's meant to be read like that."

It is important to note that the process of interviewing students about their writing may have elicited explicit articulation of metalinguistic thinking, which cannot be assumed to be paralleled or applied during writing. We cannot tell from these data if metalinguistic thinking during writing operates at an implicit or explicit level; what we can claim is that the interviews provide evidence of the nature of students' metalinguistic thinking about their writing.

FUTURE RESEARCH DIRECTIONS

Although the field of research in metalinguistic activity is a rich and growing one, it remains more focused on oral language, second language learning, and the development of reading comprehension than on writing. At the same time, the majority of studies are rooted in early years' or primary contexts. There is relatively little systematic research on metalinguistic activity in writers in the older stages of schooling, though there is substantive research on younger students' metalinguistic awareness in spelling development. There is considerable scope for future research that could extend our understanding of the metalinguistic thinking of these older writers. In particular, further research could usefully investigate whether metapragmatic understanding is a particularly critical aspect of metalinguistic understanding for writing, enabling writers to navigate and negotiate the socially determined construction of meaning in writing. Furthermore, research might investigate metalinguistic and epilinguistic dimensions specific to the academic and literary genres used in school. There is also an emerging body of literature examining the interrelationship of spoken and written discourse (Johannson, 2009; Myhill, 2009), which draws attention to the significance of discrimination between oral and written discourses: There is, to date, no research that explores writers' metalinguistic understanding of this.

SUMMARY AND CONCLUSIONS

This study of young writers who are neither novice nor yet expert writers has illuminated that, although their declarative knowledge of language, particularly metasyntactical and metatextual knowledge, may be limited, they can be engaged in rich metalinguistic activity as a monitoring and regulatory function, which may accompany the act of writing. The study is significant in extending understanding of metalinguistic activity to writers in the later stages of schooling and thus extending the conceptual framework of metalinguistic development beyond Gombert's oral model. The current study signals how metalinguistic understanding is shaped by social discourses, in this case particularly by those of the writing classroom: Students' confidence with metasemantic thinking and relative lack of metasyntactical awareness appear to be explicitly linked to the nature of the pedagogical input and the quality of their teachers' linguistic knowledge. The primacy of metapragmatic concerns cutting across all aspects of metalinguistic understanding is also a significant characteristic of this dataset, highlighting that writers of this age have developed, to differing degrees, an understanding of the relationship between the writer, the text, and the intended audience. What is clear is that the developing writers in this study were grappling with complex decision-making and design choices, rooted in socially determined understandings of texts and audiences; they were developing metalinguistic activity that "leads to knowledge of language that allows its control" (Camps & Milian, 1999, p. 13). Or, as Coleridge (1817/1985) expressed it, these are writers who are fully engaged with the ordeal of deliberate choice.

ACKNOWLEDGMENTS

Grant support funded by the Economic and Social Research Council, United Kingdom.

APPENDIX A: STUDENT INTERVIEW SCHEDULE

What is the impact of pedagogical support materials on the teaching of grammar? What is the impact of grammar teaching on pupils' metalinguistic understanding?

Preinterview: Interviewee needs time to read the stimulus text and their own text using prompt reflection card provided.

Section 1

Main construct: *Pedagogical thinking* (pupil response to teaching)
Related constructs: Planning – Lesson structure/choice of activity/grouping/terminology
Learning – Learning objective/teacher input/pupil activities
Assessment – Assessment of learning in lesson/pupil response/follow-up lessons

1. Did you enjoy today's lesson?
2. What do you think the teacher was teaching you about writing today?
3. What have you learned so far about how to write fictional narrative/argument/poetry?
4. What lesson activities do you find helpful in teaching you to write better?
5. Questions which relate to specific activities in the lesson.

Section 2

Main construct: *Metalinguistic understanding*
Relate to concepts taught in SoW:

- Ability to use terminology
- Understanding of effect/applied
- Ability to talk about language choices quite explicitly without grammar terms

Stimulus text 1: Use a model text of fictional narrative/argument/poetry to stimulate discussion on Prompt Card).
Stimulus text 2: Own writing from the SoW currently being taught.

- How well is this piece of writing progressing? What are you most pleased with?
- Does this have any of the characteristics of the opening of a story?
- What about the sentences? Can you comment on how effective the sentence structure or shaping is?
- What about the word choices? Can you comment on the effectiveness of the vocabulary?
- What would you like to change or improve?

Final question: What do you think makes good writing?

APPENDIX B: THINKING ABOUT WRITING—NARRATIVE PROMPT

The Burglary

It was November 12th, 2007. My family and I had just been to a whole family reunion in Reading. We were nearing the end of our journey home, when finally we pulled up at our house feeling happy and contented, having had a great time. We got out of the car, and walked up to our sturdy, solid gate. As I pulled the latch up and attempted to open the gate, it wouldn't budge. It wouldn't move a single inch. My mum said, "Callum, climb up the wall and check the gate from the inside." I clambered up and saw immediately that the gate was now bolted shut. A little voice in the back of my head told me, 'that wasn't bolted when we left this morning.' This was the thing that first set the alarm bells ringing. I felt a slight pang of fear and hastily unbolted the gate, and let my family through.

On approaching the back door, the security light blazed into being. We were shocked into silence. The bathroom window had been brutally smashed, so had the kitchen's windows. My mother's hands were shaking as she unlocked the back door. When my sister had finally traipsed through the door, we all stood stock-still. We had been burgled!! What a devious chap to have bolted the gate from the inside just in case we arrived home early. It would have given him the extra time to make a hasty escape.

This is the start of a story, written by someone of your age. We want to know what you think about it. Read it and then think about your answers to the following questions. We would like you to be as specific as possible in explaining and justifying your answers.

- How well do you think this opening is written?
- What makes it successful or unsuccessful as an opening for you?
- How can you tell this the opening of a story?
- What about the sentences? Can you comment on how effective the sentence structure or shaping is?
- What about the word choices? Can you comment on the effectiveness of the vocabulary?
- How could the story opening be improved?

This isn't a test and there aren't wrong or right answers—we just want to know what you think and how specific you can be in explaining your judgments.

APPENDIX C: THINKING ABOUT WRITING—ARGUMENT PROMPT

Fair Treatment for Our Elderly People

It is awful the way elderly people are treated in this day and age. They should not go to homes just because they're old.

Firstly, the younger generation owe the older generation because the older generation looked after the youger ones for at least 16 or more years, ever since they were babys. So the younger generation really should invite their parents in to there house to live with them and not be lonely in an old house or be left in some home to die.

Surely a home is no different from a boarding school. Some people argue that the homes are for caring for the eldery. But in their last years alive wouldn't you want to spend it with your family and not carted to an old home with strangers you've never met.

It is disgraceful to see the younger generation sending their families off to old peoples homes. It's not the younger generations right to control the lives of elders. They ought to make their own desicions on whether they want to go to a home or not. They've made their own decisions until now, whats changed?

To think people ever even consider placing their elderly family in a home is beyond me. All they do is sit in an empty room nothing to do exept sit and do nothing. Or the elderly could be having fun at a relitives house. So if they did stay at a home they would get very lonely indeed.

Another important point is that they might only get along with their familys because their familys are the only ones that understand them and if a nurse or someone they didn't trust or haven't met they might, not take their medicine and die. But if they were around their family they would trust them.

It is horrible to think that people are doing this, but they are. The homes could be very very dangerous, so let's end this madness now.

This is an argument, written by someone of your age. We want to know what you think about it. Read it and then think about your answers to the following questions. We would like you to be as specific as possible in explaining and justifying your answers.

- How well do you think this argument is written?
- What makes it successful or unsuccessful as an argument for you?
- How can you tell this is an argument?
- What about the sentences? Can you comment on how effective the sentence structure or shaping is?
- What about the word choices? Can you comment on the effectiveness of the vocabulary?
- How could the argument be improved?

This isn't a test and there aren't wrong or right answers—we just want to know what you think and how specific you can be in explaining your judgments.

APPENDIX D: THINKING ABOUT WRITING—POETRY PROMPT

These two poems were written by young people and we want to know what you think about them. Read them both and then think about your answers to the following questions. We would like you to be as specific as possible in explaining and justifying your answers.

- How well do you think each poem is written?
- What makes them successful or unsuccessful for you?
- How can you tell these are both poems?
- What about the sentences or lines? Can you comment on how effective the structure or shaping is?
- What about the word choices? Can you comment on the effectiveness of the vocabulary?
- How could the poems be improved?

This isn't a test and there aren't wrong or right answers—we just want to know what you think and how specific you can be in explaining your judgments.

Teacher
Lesson planner, boredom banner
Moral pillar, mayhem stiller
Concept thrower, future-sower,
Power dresser, mug obsessor,

Late night marker, silence-barker,
Blame absorber
Stress bin.

Teacher's Red Pen
I give merit where it is due
I give responses to your best guess
I give you the benefit of the doubt
I give you a qualified 'no' or a resounding 'yes'

The hand that holds me makes me tick, makes me cross
The hand that holds me is the voice I am given
The hand that holds me sorts the good from the dross
The hand that holds me writes the words that are written

I inspire you to carry on
I urge you to stop dead
I tell you to 'see me'
I force you to see red

REFERENCES

Alamargot, D., & Chanquoy, L. (2001). *Through the models of writing.* Dordrecht: Kluwer.

Allal, L. (1999). Metacognitive regulation of writing. In A. Camps & M. Milian (Eds.), *Metalinguistic activity in learning to write* (pp. 145–166). Amsterdam: Amsterdam University Press.

Arnback, E., & Elbro, C. (2000). The effects of morphological awareness training on the reading and spelling skills of young dyslexics. *Scandinavian Journal of Educational Research, 44,* 229–251.

Berninger, V. W., Fuller, F., & Whitaker, D. (1996). A process model of writing development across the life span, *Educational Psychology Review, 8*(3), 193–217.

Berninger, V. W., & Swanson, H. L. (1994). Modifying Hayes and Flower's model of skilled writing to explain beginning and developing writing. In E. C. Butterfield (Ed.), *Advances in cognition and educational practice.* Vol. 2. *Children's writing: Towards a process theory of development of skilled writing* (pp. 57–82). Greenwich: JAI Press.

Bialystok, E. (2007). Acquisition of literacy in bilingual children: A framework for research. *Language Learning, 57*(S1), 45–77.

Bialystok, E., & Ryan, E. B. (1985). Toward a definition of metalinguistic skill. *Merrill-Palmer Quarterly, 31*(3), 229–251.

Boscolo, P. (1995). The cognitive approach to writing and writing instruction: A contribution to a critical appraisal. *Cahiers de Psycologie Cognitive, 14*(4), 343–366.

Bourassa, D., Treiman, R., & Kessler, B. (2006). Use of morphology in spelling by children with dyslexia and typically developing children. *Memory and Cognition, 34*(3), 703–714.

Butterfield, E. C., Hacker, D. J., & Albertson, L. R. (1996). Environmental, cognitive, and metacognitive influences on text revision. *Educational Psychology Review, 8*(3), 239–297.

Camps, A., & Milian, M. (Eds.). (1999). *Metalinguistic activity in learning to write.* Amsterdam: Amsterdam University Press.

Caravolas, M., Kessler, B., Hulme, C., & Snowling, M. (2005). Effects of orthographic consistency, frequency, and letter knowledge on children's vowel spelling development. *Journal of Experimental Child Psychology, 92*(4), 307–321.

Cassar, M., & Treiman, R. (1997). The beginnings of orthographic knowledge: Children's knowledge of double letters in words. *Journal of Educational Psychology, 89*(4), 631–644.

Cisero, C. A., & Royer, J. M. (1995). The development and cross-language transfer of phonological awareness. *Contemporary Educational Psychology, 20,* 275–303.

Coleridge, S. T. (1817/1985). *Biographia literaria* [Literary biography]. J. Engel & W. Jackson-Bate (Eds.). Princeton: Princeton University Press.

Cope, B., & Kalantzis, M. (2000). *Multiliteracies: Literacy learning and the design of social futures*. London: Routledge.

Culioli, A. (1990). *Pour une linguistique de l'enonciation.* Vol. 1. Paris: Ophrys.

Dolz, J., & Erard, S. (1999). Metaverbal activities as an approach to teach spoken and written genres. In A. Camps & M. Milian (Eds.), *Metalinguistic activity in learning to write* (pp. 125–144). Amsterdam: Amsterdam University Press.

Downing, J., & Oliver, P. (1974). The child's concept of a word. *Reading Research Quarterly, 9,* 568–582.

Flavell, J. H. (1979). Metacognition and cognitive monitoring. *American Psychologist, 34,* 906–911.

Gombert, J. E. (1992). *Metalinguistic development.* Hemel Hempstead: Harvester Wheatsheaf.

Haas, C. (1996). *Writing technology: Studies on the materiality of literacy*. Hillsdale, NJ: Erlbaum.

Hayes, J. R., & Flower, L.S. (1980). The dynamics of composing. In L. W. Gregg & E. R. Steinberg (Eds.), *Cognitive processes in writing* (pp. 31–50). Hillsdale, NJ: Erlbaum.

Heibert, E., Cioffi, G., & Antonak, R. (1984). A developmental sequence in preschool children's acquisition of reading readiness skills and print awareness concepts. *Journal of Applied Developmental Psychology, 5,* 115–126.

Hidi, S., & Boscolo, P. (2007). *Writing and motivation.* Oxford: Elsevier.

Jakobson, R. (1963). *Essais de linguistique generale*. Paris: Editions de Minuit.

Janks, H. (2009). Writing: a critical literacy perspective. In R. Beard, D. Myhill, J. Riley, & M. Nystrand (Eds.), *International handbook of writing development* (pp. 126–136). London: Sage.

Johansson, V. (2009). *Developmental aspects of text production in writing and speech*. Lund, Sweden: Travaux de L'Institut de Linguistique de Lund.

Karmiloff-Smith, A., Grant, J., Sims, K., Jones, M-C., & Cuckle, P. (1996). Rethinking metalinguistic awareness: Representing and accessing knowledge about what counts as a word. *Cognition, 58*(2), 197–219.

Kellogg, R. T. (1994). *The psychology of writing*. Oxford: Oxford University Press.

Kellogg, R.T. (2008). Training writing skills: A cognitive developmental perspective. *Journal of Writing Research, 1*(1), 1–26.

Kress, G., & van Leeuwen, T. (2001). *Reading images: The grammar of visual design*. London: Routledge.

MacGillivray, L. (1994). Tacit shared understandings of a first-grade writing community. *Journal of Reading Behavior, 26*(3), 245–266.

Machin, S., & McNally, S. (2005). Gender and student achievement in English schools, *Oxford Review of Economic Policy, 21,* 357–372.

Martinet, C., Valdois, S., & Fayol, M. (2004). Lexical orthographic knowledge develops from the beginning of reading acquisition. *Cognition, 91,* B11–B22.

Martlew, M. (1983). *The psychology of written language: Developmental and educational perspectives.* London: Wiley.

Montgomery, D. (2008). Writing and the National Literacy Strategy: Cohort analysis of writing in year 7 following, two, four and seven years of the National Literacy Strategy. *Support for Learning, 23*(1), 3–11.

Myhill, D. A. (2009). From talking to writing: Linguistic development in writing in teaching and learning writing: Psychological aspects of education—current trends. British Psychological Society, Leicester, UK. *British Journal of Educational Psychology Monograph Series* II (6), 27–44.

Myhill, D. A. (2011). Grammar for designers: How grammar supports the development of writing. In S. Ellis, E. McCartney, & J. Bourne (Eds.), *Insight and impact: Applied linguistics and the primary school* (pp. 81–92). Cambridge: Cambridge University Press.

Myhill, D. A., & Jones, S. (2007). More than just error correction: Children's reflections on their revision processes. *Written Communication*, 24(4), 323–343.

National Commission on Writing in America's Schools and Colleges (NCW). (2003). *The neglected "R": The need for a writing revolution.* New York: College Board.

Norbert, F. (1999). Bilingualism, writing, and metalinguistic awareness: Oral-literate interactions between first and second languages. *Applied Psycholinguistics*, 20(4), 533–561.

Nunes, T., & Bryant, P. (2006). *Improving literacy by teaching morphemes.* London: Routledge.

Nunes, T., Bryant, P., & Bindman, M. (2006). The effects of learning to spell on children's awareness of morphology. *Reading and Writing, 19*, 767–787.

Prior, P. (2006). A sociocultural theory of writing. In C. Macarthur, S. Graham, & J. Fitzgerald (Eds.), *Handbook of Writing Research* (pp. 54–65). New York: Guilford.

Roth, F. P., Speece, D. L., Cooper, D. H., & de la Paz, S. (1996). Unresolved mysteries: How do metalinguistic and narrative skills connect with early reading? *Journal of Special Education, 30*(3), 257–277.

Salahu-Din, D., Persky, H., & Miller, J. (2008). *The nation's report card: Writing 2007.* Washington, DC: Institute of Education Sciences, U.S. Department of Education.

Sharples, M. (1999). *How we write: Writing as creative design.* London: Routledge.

Smith, C. L., & Tager-Flusberg, H. (1982). Metalinguistic awareness and language development. *Journal of Experimental Child Psychology, 34*, 449–468.

Tunmer, W. E., & Grieve, R. (1980). The development of the child's awareness of grammatical structure. *Educational Research and Perspectives, 7*, 47–56.

Tunmer, W. E., Bowey, J. A., & Grieve, R. (1983). The development of young children's awareness of the word as a unit of spoken language. *Journal of Psycholinguistic Research, 12*, 567–594.

Van Lier, L. (1998). The relationship between consciousness, interaction and language. *Learning, Language Awareness, 7*(2–3), 128–145.

Van Wijk, C. (1999). Identifying writing strategies through text analysis. *Written Communication, 16*(1), 51–75.

Wallace, D., & Hayes, J. R. (1991). Redefining revision for freshmen. *Research in the Teaching of English, 25*(1), 54–66.

Zipke, M. (2007). The role of metalinguistic awareness in the reading comprehension of sixth and seventh graders. *Reading Psychology, 28*(4), 375–396.

12

What We Know About Expertise in Professional Communication

KAREN SCHRIVER

P sychology has a rich tradition of studying the nature of expertise—a tradition that began with laboratory studies of skilled chess players (Charness, 1976; Chase & Simon, 1973) and continues with studies of professionals such as composers, painters (Hayes, 1985, 1989a), musicians (Lehmann & Ericsson, 1997), ocean navigators (Hutchins, 1995), and airline pilots (Schreiber et al., 2009). But with a few exceptions (Beaufort, 2000; Carter, 1990; Kellogg, 2006, 2008), studies of people who write and design[1] for a living are absent from this corpus. Research on professional communication can contribute to the study of expertise by expanding conceptions of the constructive activities that people engage in on the path toward literate expertise (Scardamalia & Bereiter, 1991). An understanding of professional communication can help us to see not only the cognitive aspects of advanced literate practices, but also the social and motivational factors that underlie the development of expertise in situated environments.

Professional communication encompasses the range of advanced writing and visual design activity in workplace settings. Surveys of adults in the workplace suggest that professionals spend on average 24% of their workweek writing (Kirtz & Reep, 1990; Mabrito, 1997; McMullen & Wellman, 1990; Reave, 2004; Tenopir & King, 2004). According to the U.S. Bureau of Labor Statistics, careers in technical communication are predicted to grow 18% from 2008 to 2018, or faster than the average of all occupations (U.S. Department of Labor, 2010). Whether adults communicate professionally as part of their jobs or work as full-time professional communicators, advanced skills in writing, speaking, and

---

[1] By "design," I refer to the constellation of choices that must be orchestrated in order to make content visually engaging, functional, legible, and rhetorically effective—from considerations of graphics, illustrations, typography, spatial arrangement, and data visualizations to visual cues such as size, position, contrast, color, grouping, or use of negative space.

visual design play an important—even crucial—role in the workplace. Even so, many preprofessional academic programs (e.g., in education, engineering, business, architecture, and medicine) include minimal, if any, education in professional communication skills. This is unfortunate because expert instruction in professional communication could help such preprofessional programs attend to aspects of learning, knowledge construction, and socialization that they might not otherwise consider (Russell, 2007). Moreover, it could help students develop the communication abilities they need in order to effect change in the workplace and the professions they serve.

This chapter reviews the literature concerning expertise in professional communication. There is much to say about developing high levels of skill in writing and visual design; here, I integrate what we know about two central questions relevant to developing expertise:

1. What are the challenges of professional writing and visual design in the workplace?
2. What knowledge underlies the development of high levels of skill in professional writing and visual design?

In addressing these questions I will argue that research on professional communication has the capacity to provide an interesting and unique window on our understanding of the nature of written and visual communication. I begin with a characterization of the challenges of professional communication, focusing on what makes writing and visual design in the workplace so difficult. Then I examine the knowledge that undergirds professional communication activity. In doing so, I elucidate some components of writing models (Hayes, 1996; Hayes & Flower, 1980) that have been largely unexplored, particularly the dynamic relationships that occur within *task environments* as individuals or teams carry out their work, especially relations between the *social environment* (the audience and collaborators) and the *physical environment* (the text-so-far and the composing medium). The chapter ends with some characteristics of high-achieving professional communicators.

WHAT IS PROFESSIONAL COMMUNICATION?

Definition

Professional communication is an umbrella term for the creative activities that adults engage in as they compose purpose-driven communications on the job. These communications take many forms—for example, reports, proposals, instructions, presentations, multimedia, Web pages—and may be displayed in a variety of media, with an increasing emphasis on Web-based presentations. To make such communications both visually engaging and rhetorically effective involves the careful integration of writing and visual design, calling on the professional to make sophisticated judgments about issues such as form, content, style, arrangement, graphics, illustrations, color, typography, and spatial display.

Cognitive Structures and Relational Networks

Although professional communication activity is often construed as merely concerned with producing work-a-day artifacts for organizations, as though the resulting artifacts were the ultimate goal, professional communication activity is actually situated in a much broader social practice; that is, *the practice of creating cognitive structures and relational networks among people through shared content (using words, pictures, sounds, or symbols).* For example, well-written and well-designed artifacts can promote comprehension of ideas in science, education, and technology, enabling people to build coherent representations of complex content, such as understanding nanotechnology or macroeconomic theory.

Mental Models

Additionally, professionally designed artifacts such as diagrams and maps can help people form accurate mental models of complex systems. For example, the redesign of the London Underground (subway) map—an icon of good information design—regularizes the appearance of subways routes to make them easy to follow by preserving some but not all geographic features. If users had to rely only on a geographically accurate map (Figure 12.1 shows a portion), they could easily be confused when trying to sort out a sensible route across the city. But Harry Beck's redesign (Figure 12.2 shows a portion) creates a more readable and understandable model of the city (for more examples, see Futrelle, 2004).

Purposes

As these examples illustrate, the cognitive and relational networks that professional communicators build are directed toward purposes such as educating, persuading, clarifying, sharing, or collaborating. In a real sense, professional communicators aim to design relationships between organizations, writers, designers, and

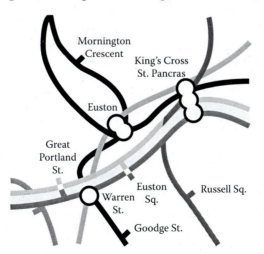

Figure 12.1   Excerpt from a geographically accurate map of the London Underground.

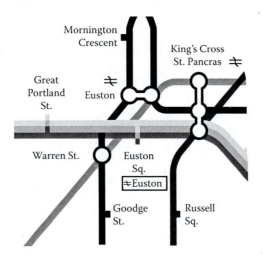

Figure 12.2   Excerpt from the redesigned London Underground map.

their constituent stakeholders (e.g., a hospital's wellness clinic and patients who have diabetes). As such, communicators construct the public face of organizations through words, images, and symbols. In designing these networks, professional communicators must be extremely knowledgeable about the social and semiotic resources they can draw on and of ways to orchestrate them.

WHO ARE PROFESSIONAL COMMUNICATORS?

Writing as a Profession Versus as a Work Tool

The field of professional communication encompasses two broad groups of working professionals. The first group centers around the literate activities of people *who write or design for a living*. This group is composed of over 100,000 people in the United States and hundreds of thousands of people around the world. It consists of information designers, journalists, editors, technical communicators, science writers, business writers, grant writers, public relations officers, communication designers, magazine writers, screenwriters, and nonfiction authors. The second group of professionals includes people who do not consider themselves as writers or designers, but *who write or design professionally as part of their work*. Again, this is also a very large group, including teachers, graduate students, professors, lawyers, researchers, scientists, politicians, architects, museum curators, engineers, doctors, nurses, computer scientists, and managers.

Professional communicators who write or design for a living typically work full time or as part-time freelancers on behalf of companies, governments, or nonprofit organizations. Although professional communicators sometimes work alone, more often they work in teams. By contrast, those who write or design as part of their professional activity tend to generate communications on an as-needed basis. For example, they may work alone or with a team on a grant proposal, a journal article, or a legal brief.

Evaluation of Professional Communication

Unlike domains in which the criteria for evaluating outstanding performance lie solely in the judgments of other experts, the quality of professional communications is judged partly by peers or domain experts, but primarily by how well the artifact(s) meets the needs of stakeholders (i.e., intended readers, users, citizens, audiences, managers, or clients). Over the past few decades, professionals have employed a variety of reader-focused evaluation methods to learn about what people think and feel as they engage with their writing and design (Schriver, 1989a). By directly collecting feedback from their intended stakeholders, professionals can acquire valuable local knowledge to underpin the cognitive and relational networks they hope to create. In doing so, they also learn that thinking about their stakeholders involves much more than projecting writer- or designer-centric representations of what people need; that is, representations created solely by the reflections of individual writers, designers, or interdisciplinary teams.

Taking stakeholders' needs seriously involves actively interacting with the range of people who may find the artifact of value—from intermediate audiences such as managers to end users such as readers of e-books. It means considering stakeholders' positive and negative evaluations in reflecting on and rerepresenting ideas for content, design, or media. And because so many of today's communications artifacts are displayed on the Web, professionals can more easily invite stakeholders to comment on their artifacts, encouraging them, for example, to participate in discussion lists, to blog or to tweet about them, or to tag them on social networks for perusal by others. In this way, serendipitous networks may be created among people designing and interpreting communications, with the roles of author and audience sometimes reversing.

Need for Experts in Professional Communication and Plain Writing

Professional communicators vary considerably—ranging from novice to expert—in how well they are able to compose artifacts that build cognitive and relational networks. As readers, we have all encountered professional communications that failed us as readers, from incomprehensible tax forms to mystifying medical information. Although we may not think about it, all of those experiences were designed by well-meaning individuals or teams. The problem of poorly designed professional communications is so severe that countries are beginning to pass *plain language* laws. Such laws have been enacted in Australia, Canada, Mexico, New Zealand, Portugal, South Africa, Sweden, the European Union, and most recently, in the United States.[2] In fact, on October 13, 2010, President Barack Obama signed into law H.R. 946, the Plain Writing Act of 2010. It requires the federal government to write all new publications, forms, and publicly distributed documents in a "clear, concise, and well-organized"

---

[2] For more information on plain language initiatives in the United States and around the world, consult the Web sites for these groups: the Center for Plain Language, a nonprofit dedicated to advocating for plain language in business and government: http://centerforplainlanguage.org; Plain, advocates who work in U.S. government agencies: http://www.plainlanguage.gov; and Clarity, an international group focused on clear legal language: http://www.clarity-international.net.

manner (Plain Writing Act of 2010, p. 1). That so many public communications from around the world disenfranchise citizens who need to use them underscores the social value of and pressing need for experts in professional communication.

Individual Differences

My work as a professor and as a consultant to organizations has given me the opportunity to be immersed in the workplace activities of professional communicators for many years. I have observed large individual differences among professionals in the workplace. Many are excellent, but many are only mediocre in professional communication. We need to characterize these differences in order to build pedagogies to help novices become more expert.

Rhetorical Goals

Whether one writes and designs for a living or as part of one's role in another career, one's professional communication activity involves the intentional design of visual and verbal artifacts for stakeholders, who bring their own purposes for engaging with the content. The rhetorical goals for communicating professionally are typically a mix of persuading, informing, explaining, or instructing. The resulting artifacts help people do things with content—understand ideas, make decisions, carry out procedures, or appreciate the value of ideas, products, or services.

To become an expert in creating rhetorically effective communications requires the development of sophisticated general knowledge about writing and visual design as well as extensive domain-specific local knowledge for carrying out writing and design activity (Carter, 1990). Experts must be able to think through complex communication challenges, while at the same time act on their thinking by employing practical knowledge and strategies for solving problems of writing and visual design. Put differently, professionals must respond creatively to ill-structured problems of design, what some have called "wicked problems" (Buchanan, 1992, p. 5; Simon, 1996, p. 129). Throughout the processes of planning, designing, and evaluating their work, professionals must anticipate how their stakeholders may respond to their solutions, adapting their writing and design activities to people's evolving needs and expectations. Although it is difficult to specify precisely how expert communicators carry out these high-wire rhetorical acts of interpretation, anticipation, production, and reflection, the existing literature offers a number of clues that shed light on the nature of expert performance.

Evolving Knowledge About Professional Communication

What we know about professional communication derives from a variety of theoretical orientations, such as cognitive theory, rhetorical theory, situated learning theory, and activity theory. An integrative view of the field needs to take a methodologically pluralistic rhetorical stance in order to bring together the sometimes theoretically incompatible research that sheds light on the nature of expertise. I turn now to the literature that uncovers the challenges of professional communication in the workplace and the knowledge that underlies developing high levels of skill in writing and visual design.

WHAT ARE THE CHALLENGES OF PROFESSIONAL WRITING AND VISUAL DESIGN IN THE WORKPLACE?

Professional writers and visual designers, like communicators in academic settings, need to draw on both subject-matter knowledge and rhetorical savvy. They need to decide what to say, how much to say, and how to say it. Expert communicators strive to provide the "right" content at an appropriate level of detail in the most suitable media for the audience. And much like students in academic settings, professional communicators often struggle with issues of content. On the one hand, professionals may feel compelled to say everything they know about a subject—an adult version of "knowledge telling" (Bereiter & Scardamalia, 1982). On the other hand, writers may assume that most stakeholders for their communication already know the basics of the subject matter, and in an interest of politeness and not wanting to be insulting, may inadvertently befuddle their readers by generating content that is overly abstruse or technical.

Either way, when writers or designers focus on displaying their mastery of the subject matter, the readers may not be provided with the content they want or need. Research suggests that experienced communicators learn to self-regulate the presentation of their subject matter knowledge in service of rhetorical goals (Ackerman, 1991; Hillocks, 1986).

Although there are many parallels between communication in classroom settings and workplace settings, there are three aspects of professional communication activity that make it quite unlike most classroom experiences in writing or visual design:

1. The need to orchestrate writing knowledge and strategy with visual design knowledge and strategy
2. The need to engage multiple stakeholders with a given body of content
3. The need to negotiate the social, political, and cultural landscapes of the workplace

ORCHESTRATING WRITING KNOWLEDGE AND STRATEGY WITH VISUAL DESIGN KNOWLEDGE AND STRATEGY

Professional communicators are skilled in integrating messages, both visually and verbally, placing emphasis on the visual display of the content (e.g., layout, figure or ground organization, grouping) and on good writing that is clear, concise, and functional. When the visual display of the message skillfully reveals the structure of the content, the design is more likely to afford stakeholders with multiple ways of engaging with the content—searching, skimming, comprehending, learning, or analyzing.

Because professional communicators recognize that stakeholders come to their messages with different purposes, they design with an eye toward flexible access of the content—expecting that sometimes stakeholders will seek to extract the gist or main point, while at other times stakeholders may seek to comprehend the content.

To be effective in designing for stakeholders' on-the-fly purposes, professional communicators need to coordinate their subject-matter knowledge with their rhetorical knowledge. They must possess both declarative and procedural knowledge of writing and visual design, being able to move from diagnosing rhetorical problems to solving them (Flower, Hayes, Carey, Schriver, & Stratman, 1986). In diagnosing visual or verbal problems of design, professionals rely on highly accomplished reading strategies for assessing the quality of the text produced so far (Quinlan & Alamargot, 2007). Professionals not only monitor their own comprehension in solving text problems, but they also strive to anticipate stakeholders' likely reading processes (Schriver, 2010). Professional communicators employ these representations as they make choices in deciding what content to keep, what to delete, what to say verbally, and what to say visually.

Design Decisions

These communication design decisions involve a host of *writing issues* such as content selection, logic, modularization, coherence, style, voice, and persona. They also involve *visual design issues* such as format, hierarchy, shape, emphasis, contrast, typography, and legibility. (For an extended treatment of writing and designing professional communications, see Schriver, 1997; for analysis of how people read online and the ways in which the quality of their engagement is mediated by the quality of writing and visual design, see Schriver, 2010.) Whether designing for print media or for the Web, professionals need to orchestrate their knowledge and strategies for writing with their knowledge and strategies for design—integrating visual and verbal content into a single coherent artifact. Experts draw on their in-depth knowledge and strategies in turning their plans and intentions into well-formed artifacts (Flower, 1989; Flower & Hayes, 1984; Flower, Schriver, Haas, Carey, & Hayes, 1992; Witte, 1987).

ENGAGING MULTIPLE STAKEHOLDERS WITH A GIVEN BODY OF CONTENT

Multiple Audiences

One of the hallmarks of writing professionally is the ability to shape the same content for different audiences, for example, for people with or without disciplinary expertise in the subject matter. Early views of professional communication tended to construe the audience as rather one dimensional, as either expert or novice. But as Holland, Charrow, and Wright (1988) pointed out more than two decades ago, there is rarely a single constituency for the work of professional communicators. More typically, there are a variety of stakeholders, audiences, critics, bosses, clients, and colleagues whose expectations need to be met. Shaping content in ways that can engage multiple stakeholders is a complex act of composing and visual design, particularly when different groups have different expectations for the same body of content. For example, professional communicators designing Web-based instructional content may attempt to reduce information overload while simultaneously maintaining the attention of multiple stakeholders by employing design strategies such as *progressive disclosure* (Lidwell, Holden, & Butler, 2003). In this strategy, communicators structure the content into layers in order to modularize and sequence it over a number of screens, segmenting abstract from concrete, easy from difficult, and basic from complex.

Gap Between Thinking About an Audience and Taking Action

Professional communicators must be sensitive both to the means of discovering stakeholders' diverse needs and to considering options for presenting content. Although "audience analysis and user-centered design" have long been cornerstones of educational programs in professional communication, students often have difficulty moving from thinking about the audience to acting on their needs (Blakeslee, 2010), especially when multiple audiences are involved (Albers, 2003; Spilka, 1990). My own research indicates that when professional communication students engage in extensive practice in learning about how people interpret text and graphics, they can develop mental models of how readers may interact with their content (Schriver, 1992a), models that can help them adapt their writing and design to the stakeholders and situation at hand. In order to close the gap between thinking about the audience and taking action, students can profit from extensive practice in observing people's moment-by-moment interpretations of text and graphics.

NEGOTIATING THE SOCIAL AND CULTURAL LANDSCAPES OF THE WORKPLACE

Persuasion Expertise

Developing expertise in professional communication requires exceptional capabilities in writing, visual design, and stakeholder analysis. But as important as these communication abilities are, they are not enough. Professional communicators work in organizations in which goals, priorities, stakeholders, funding, and deadlines for their work shift according to local political, cultural, and economic forces. Shifting constraints make writing and designing in organizations rhetorically challenging and calls on communicators to develop keen negotiation skills. Professionals must not only be able to solve problems of writing and visual design, but also to argue cogently (in writing and orally) for their plans and solutions, articulating why a particular communication problem should be solved in ways they envision. Put differently, they need to be able to persuade others in the workplace of the value of their contributory expertise (Henry, 1998). Managers, for example, may believe that "anyone who can speak a language can also write well," or "anyone who can use page layout software can design skillfully," dismissing the expertise of professional communicators as obvious and uninteresting.

Constraints and Challenges

Although communication designers view their task as a goal-oriented activity in which they imagine effective communication solutions for their stakeholders, the organizations in which they work often make it difficult to act on the behalf of those people who will use the artifact. As Hovde (2000) pointed out, sometimes organizations will not allow professional communicators to gain access to their stakeholders, believing that direct contact with the audience is unnecessary. As a type of problem-solving activity in the real world, professional communication is constrained by ambiguous missions and changing local circumstance—writing and design in the wild. Although writing and visual design of any sort are complex constraint-satisfaction and representational tasks (Visser, 2006), professional communication seems to emphasize constraint-driven design because it routinely takes place in rather volatile organizational contexts. Alamargot and Chanquoy (2001) observed that until researchers have a better understanding of the nature of constraints on writing processes, it will be difficult to model the development of expertise.

Effectiveness Within Constraints

Despite the significant constraint-based nature of workplace communication design, expert professionals often exert profound influence on how communications are created and disseminated. But to be effective, professionals must learn to anticipate workplace constraints and thrive within them. In so doing, over time they become skilled at reading the embodied and material landscapes of the workplace, gradually understanding the implicit and explicit rules for "getting things done" (Beaufort, 2000; Haas & Witte, 2001; Henry, 2000; Winsor, 1996). Professional communicators learn how the artifacts they create interface with larger systems of organizational activity (Russell, 1997), learning to use the material resources, communication tools, and representational technologies within an environment in order to collaborate and "work the system" (Bazerman, 1988; Spinuzzi, 2003; Wegner, 2004; Winsor, 2001). Research clearly suggests that to become expert in professional communication one must excel in negotiating the social, political, and cultural landscapes of workplace environments.

As we have seen, it takes exceptional sensitivity, metacognitive awareness, and knowledge in order to be able to create communications while contending with these sorts of issues. The existing literature indicates that the acquisition of professional communication expertise cannot be reduced to a set of neatly isolated and easily teachable skills. Rather, we must account for a dynamic and mutually constitutive constellation of forces and processes that enable (and sometimes disable) the development of expertise. In the next section, I explore the knowledge that professional communicators need to acquire on the road to expertise.

WHAT KNOWLEDGE UNDERLIES THE DEVELOPMENT OF HIGH LEVELS OF SKILL IN PROFESSIONAL WRITING AND VISUAL DESIGN?

To understand how professional communicators develop their expertise, it is useful to identify the knowledge that underlies skilled writing and visual design activity. To address this issue, I first characterize the types of rhetorical and social knowledge that communicators must develop. Then I detail some components of writing models (Hayes, 1996; Hayes & Flower, 1980) that have been largely unexplored, particularly the interactive relationships that occur within *task environments* as individuals or teams carry out their work, especially relations between the *social environment* (the audience and collaborators) and the *physical environment* (the text so far and the composing medium). By considering the dynamic forces that mediate the production of professional communication artifacts, we can better see how cognitive and relational networks of shared content are developed.

Rhetorical Knowledge

Perhaps the most important aspect of a professional communicator's growth is the development of rhetorical knowledge, that is, knowledge of the ways that stakeholders may engage with the writing and visual design. A key aspect of rhetorical knowledge is the ability to anticipate how the intended stakeholders (i.e., readers, users, audiences, or viewers) may think or feel about the content, a concern for both cognitive and emotional responses to the message and its presentation (Schriver, 1997). As Kellogg (2008) pointed out, professional communicators must hold a representation of the reader in memory and apply it as they craft what to say and how to say it.

After considerable experience in observing how readers actually respond to text and graphics—for example, through practice in usability testing— professional communicators may develop an image of readers that can become a working mental model, providing them with cues about what readers want and expect (Schriver, 1992b). But these working mental models that guide reader-focused writing and visual design are difficult to develop, even with explicit instruction in doing so.

For example, I compared more traditional methods of teaching audience analysis used in the professional writing classroom (e.g., audience-analysis heuristics, role playing, peer response, checklists) with a method I called protocol-aided audience modeling (PAM), a method that teaches students to analyze the transcripts of think-aloud protocols of readers at work (Schriver, 1997). Writers in my study took part in 10 lessons in PAM, which entailed reading and evaluating 10 poorly written and badly designed two-page excerpts from computer manuals intended for novice users. After reading one of the lessons, students then detected and diagnosed readers' likely difficulties with the content. Next, I provided students with a think-aloud protocol from a novice struggling to understand the text, followed by asking students to again revisit the text and identify the nature of the problems, this time with the help of the reader.

I found that students did not show signs of improvement until lessons five or six. But this immersion in reader response gradually did significantly broaden their view of what to focus on during revision. Early in the training (roughly lessons one to four), writers tended to focus on rule-governed problems at the sentence level rather than on more thorny problems of comprehension and usability at the whole-text level. Gradually—from lessons 5 through 10—novice designers changed their view of what to focus on. By the end of the 10 lessons students directed their attention not only to problems of *commission* (problems created for readers by what the text said or by how visuals were displayed) but also to problems of *omission* (problems created by what was missing visually or verbally).

Students in experimental classes (unlike those in classes using traditional methods) expanded their view of how to improve the content: from editing microlevel issues (such as diction or phrasing) to revising whole-text issues (such as organization and structure). Moreover, students were able to transfer their knowledge of audience from instructional texts (manuals) to expository science texts (articles in *Newsweek* magazine). Several students who participated in the PAM method reported that after going through the training they could no longer read their drafts without hearing "readers in their heads" saying, "I'm confused! What do you mean by that?" The PAM method helped novice professional writers to acquire a model of the reader and a critical awareness for developing their expertise.

Friess (2008) studied the workplace practices of 20 novice designers who had taken a course in user-centered design. Designers took the course and then worked on a task for a client who expected them to carry out detailed investigations of what users needed and to employ that rhetorical knowledge to derive an evidence-based solution. However, even with a semester-long course intended to help these novice designers develop skill in collecting evidence and advocating for users, 40% of the time students supported their decisions with vague opinions and hypothetical stories that were not grounded in evidence-based rhetorical knowledge, but were merely idiosyncratic designer-centric claims about what they thought would work.

Making Assumptions About Stakeholders' Reading Processes

Expert professional writers assume there will be inexpert reading strategies brought to bear in consuming their texts. Unlike expert readers who read to understand by making deliberate use of the linguistic context to monitor their comprehension—text structure, lexical repetitions, topic sentences, transitional signals, and other metadiscursive cues (Crismore, 1989)—less-skilled readers tend to interpret individual text elements immediately without necessarily considering how they fit together, without asking themselves whether they are understanding the main point, and without reflecting on how the message speaks to what they already know (Summers & Summers, 2005).

Because most professional communication is intended for reading on the job, professional communicators must anticipate readers who are in a hurry and who are likely to bring inexpert reading strategies to the task, even if they are subject-matter experts. Online readers are often multitasking, which leads them to abandon the reading process they would employ in leisurely situations (Redish, 2007). Instead, online readers are likely to adopt a strategy in which they follow their best guess about where to begin, then follow the "scent of information"—drawing on relevant macrolevel semantic cues such as menu items, links, labels, and headings (Pirolli & Card, 1999). This means that if the artifact does not provide good macrolevel cues, readers will likely miss key parts of the content or simply abandon the text.

Torrance (2007) suggested that "successful text must incorporate sophisticated structures for maintaining both cohesion and coherence if readers are to experience sentence-to-sentence flow and gain a global understanding of the writer's message" (p. 1). Although this suggestion is an excellent description of an academic writer's task, it is less of a priority for professional writers who need to focus on the macrostructure as much if not more than the microstructure.

THE ROLE OF EXPERIENCE IN PROFESSIONAL COMMUNICATION

Experience and Expertise

Since the 1970s psychologists have been interested in the nature of skill acquisition, in how long experts spend learning about their field, and in the nature of the effort required to excel. Chase and Simon (1973) were curious about just how much effort was required to become a chess master. They found that experts practiced for roughly a decade before reaching the grand master level. Simon and Chase (1973) argue that there is no such thing as instant expertise; "it requires about a decade of intense preoccupation ... perhaps 10,000 to 50,000 hours staring at chess positions" (p. 402). Becoming an expert "takes time—years—to build the thousands of chunks needed for ... building up recognition memory for many familiar chess patterns" (p. 403).

Their finding led researchers to study world-class musicians and painters (Hayes, 1985, 1989a). Parallel to Chase and Simon's findings, Hayes found that composers such as Mozart did not begin to produce world-class works until about 10 years into their careers. Although some composers and painters did produce good work early in their careers, very few produced world-class work until they had been working intensively for nearly a decade. Similarly, Wishbow (1988) studied the biographies of 66 poets whose poems were part of the literary canon found in the *Norton Anthology of Poetry*. She found that in 83% of the cases, poets whose works appeared in the anthology were composed 10 or more years into their careers. These findings suggest that extensive experience in one's domain is absolutely crucial to developing expertise, but as I will discuss next, investing a great deal of time may not always produce outstanding performance.

Cultivating Expertise

A common assumption about expertise is that the more experience one accumulates in a given field, the more expert one becomes; thus, experience cultivates expertise. In workplace settings, this translates into "the longer you are on the job, the better you get." But research on expertise tells a different story.

An intriguing observation made by Bereiter and Scardamalia (1993) is that experience *does not* necessarily lead to expertise. They concluded that although most people who are experts have extensive experience in their field(s), not all people with extensive experience are experts. In fact, people with years of experience may operate at roughly the same level as those with minimal experience.

Experience Necessary but Not Sufficient

My ongoing research into the nature of expertise in information design supports the contention that experience is necessary but insufficient to acquire expertise. On the one hand, information designers who work a long time in the same organization may get better, much better, and even exceptionally so. On the other hand, information designers might perform at roughly the same level of competence as when they started and merely repeat that level of performance again and again.

In fact, some seasoned professionals may not be much better than new graduates of academic programs in professional communication. Regrettably many workplaces for writers and designers do not provide the conditions that encourage employees to innovate and do their best work. Because the field is relatively new and often misunderstood, many workplaces fail to nurture information design expertise. Many experienced professionals who write or design for a living work on familiar sets of problems (often the same genres for the same audiences for years on end). The tendency is to address these common challenges with well-rehearsed routines. Many work environments reward their employees for being quick in learning new software and using those tools to carry out well-practiced routines rather than for working at the edge of their competence. Put differently, many workplaces fail to support the development of expertise, which can lead writers and designers to experience burn out, frustration, or complacency.

This sort of problem led Bereiter and Scardamalia (1993) to coin the term *experienced nonexperts* (p. 11) to describe people with extensive experience who tend to employ routine solutions to problems that call for novel approaches. Experienced nonexperts tend to embrace familiar and often conventional approaches to problem solving and rarely modify what worked the previous time. Although using a status quo strategy may be efficient for producing text quickly (and may please the boss or gatekeepers), it rarely leads to an optimal design for stakeholders.

Competing Hypotheses About the Nature of Expertise

If experience is not the whole story, then what is it that distinguishes the expert from the experienced nonexpert? Two competing hypotheses profile how people get better at what they do. The first, the *individual talent hypothesis*, asserts that people are born with gifts, genius, talent, or creativity that predispose them to greatness in their field (Winner, 1996). This hypothesis aligns with the romantic tradition, which assumes that writing and visual design are mysterious and cannot be taught explicitly (Young, 1980). Romantic assumptions about the nature of expertise may play out in writing and design classrooms in the form of "critique" sessions, in which students are encouraged to find their inner voice and to derive their personal standards for evaluating what good is. Such models of teaching promote a disabling designer-centric view of professional communication activity (Frascara, 1995).

A second competing conception of expertise is the *deliberate practice hypothesis*, which asserts that people need not be born with special gifts; rather, individuals must work hard—very hard—on developing knowledge, skills, and sensitivities in their domain. In short, it is not enough to simply practice or gain experience in one's chosen field, one must practice aspects of the field one has not yet mastered with the intention to improve.

THE ROLE OF DELIBERATE PRACTICE IN DEVELOPING EXPERTISE

Deliberate Practice

According to Ericsson, Krampe, and Tesch-Römer (1993), a key feature of deliberate practice is that one consciously seeks to work at the edge of one's current competence. Ericsson and his colleagues asserted that to become an expert requires considerable intrinsic motivation to engage with hard tasks in one's domain and, particularly, to sustain one's interest over the long haul (about a decade). In order to move to the "next level" in one's domain, the "expert-in-training" must both practice at the edge of his or her mastery and focus on the appropriate next level within reach.

As they work on developing their knowledge and skill, experts-in-training grow more sensitive to monitoring their own progress—figuring out what they do well and not so well. In many domains, deliberate practice involves high levels of repetition in order to achieve mastery, a fact that leads many experts-in-training to quit. A different and quite important aspect of deliberate practice is that people need external feedback about their performance. Studies show that a mentor's critical eye can help experts-in-training to see their shortcomings and recognize where they need to focus their practice next.

The studies of deliberate practice across many domains show that experts work intensively on developing their knowledge, skills, and perceptions before being able to perform at the top of their field. For example, Ericsson et al. (1993) asked the question, "How long do musicians practice en route to becoming expert?" (p. 379). They studied four groups of expert violinists: (1) the best experts, (2) the good experts, (3) professionals (people who perform in bands or orchestras), and (4) the least accomplished experts.

Researchers found that by the time musicians reached the age of 20 the "best experts" and the "good experts" had practiced more than the "professionals" and the "least accomplished experts." The two best groups of violinists practiced close to 10,000 hours, professionals about 8,000 hours, and the least accomplished experts about 5,000 hours. These results give credence to the old adage "practice makes perfect," which could be better said, "deliberate practice makes perfect."

As Anderson (2009) pointed out, all of the evidence indicates that genius is 90% perspiration and 10% inspiration (p. 263).

How Deliberate Practice Leads to Expertise

The results of many studies of experts suggest that one of the most important things experts acquire as a result of deliberate practice is *extensive pattern knowledge about their domain*. Chess is a game that demands considerable complex thinking, and like information design, it involves a great deal of visual and perceptual processing.

That humans are remarkably good at pattern recognition has implications for many fields of endeavor. In a study of how expert radiologists interpret chest X-rays, researchers showed 10 expert radiologists a series of 10 normal and 10 abnormal chest X-ray films in two viewing conditions: (1) 200 ms, and (2) an unlimited viewing time (Kundel & Nodine, 1975). Researchers found that experts could detect and name 70% of the abnormalities in the films in the 200-ms condition. Their performance improved to 97% when they could view the radiographs for an unlimited time. The researchers suggested that experts' visual search begins with a global scan that classifies the content they are looking at, detects gross deviations from normal patterns, and organizes subsequent checking to examine ambiguities in more detail.

How Expertise Acquired Depends on the Field

Research suggests that expertise develops differently, depending on the individual, the discipline, and the context. Some people get better at what they do largely by working alone; others immerse themselves in teamwork en route to gaining expertise. Perhaps more people engage in both individual effort and teamwork as they develop in their field. For example, concert pianists tend to develop their expertise as they practice in relative isolation (Sosniak, 1985, 1990). But pianists also usually practice under the guidance of a mentor who provides feedback about how to improve (Sosniak, 1990). The mentor provides one-on-one critical guidance designed to encourage developing musicians to persist in their training and to push the pianists to the next level (Howe & Davidson, 1993). Other professionals, such as commanders in the military, develop their expertise as they work in groups. Reflecting on the diverse feedback from colleagues helps them to make changes in how they perform (Fletcher, 2009).

Research also reminds us that "what constitutes expertise" is socially constructed, with criteria shifting depending on who is doing the evaluating. For example, academics who teach poetry tend to bring different criteria to bear in evaluating the skill of a poet than people outside of the academy who enjoy reading poetry. People in different settings bring their own values to bear in judging what counts. This makes the assessment of expertise a rather slippery enterprise because the definition of an expert for any given field may change from context to context (see the anthology by Ericsson, Charness, Feltovich, & Hoffman, 2006, which brings together the work on expertise from 15 domains).

WHAT MIGHT DELIBERATE PRACTICE DO FOR PROFESSIONAL COMMUNICATORS?

Taken together the research shows that sustained practice in working at the edge of one's ability gives experts sophisticated knowledge of their domain, rich schematic knowledge of typical problems in their domain, and keen perceptual skills that enable experts to recognize and judge meaningful patterns in their domain (Ericsson, 1996, 2009; Ericsson et al., 1993). Over time experts develop the ability to draw on more patterns, larger patterns, and patterns within patterns. They also learn useful strategies and procedures for working in their domain (Chase & Ericsson, 1982).

It seems reasonable to believe that deliberate practice would also provide such benefits for professional communicators, and that they would acquire deep interconnected knowledge of visual and verbal language patterns and structures. We can hypothesize that experts might display marked ability in recognizing visual or verbal patterns when they evaluate poorly designed communications, patterns that novices may not notice. These patterns would range from macrolevel visual and verbal concerns (e.g., logic and layout) to microlevel concerns (e.g., sentence style and typographic choice). In fact, information designers likely acquire many more patterns than the 100,000 required in skilled chess, particularly given that chess is a game played in a limited space (an 8-by-8 board) with a limited set of pieces and a small set of rules. The game of professional communication is played in a much larger space. The following is a list of a few of the patterns that professional communicators might acquire along their road to expertise:

- Linguistic (active vs. passive voice, simple vs. complex structures)
- Structural (hierarchy, inductive, deductive, problem solution, narrative, expository)
- Genre (procedures, advice, reviews, reports, forms, diagrams, animations)
- Spatial (position, size, weight, saturation, shape, contrast, juxtaposition)
- Graphic (grouping, size, repetition, alignment, proximity, position, color)
- Typographic (type families, style, size, weight, position, contrast, spacing)

Information designers gain rhetorical flexibility in employing these patterns while designing print or online communications, learning to detect when patterns are effective and diagnosing when they are not (Schriver, 2009). Expert information designers gain skill in replicating patterns that work and repairing patterns that do not; and they develop particular facility in rerepresenting and combining patterns in skilled ways. When professional communicators revise, the text produced so far serves as a catalyst, which triggers visual and verbal associations from the designer's long-term memory and enables creative responses to practical problems of communication. To do so requires enormous sensitivity not only to language patterns but also to the audiences for whom the visual and verbal patterns are intended to shape meaning (Sadoski & Paivio, 2001; Schriver & Hayes, 2009).

We can hypothesize then that experts' knowledge of visual and verbal language, along with their understanding of stakeholders' likely expectations for content, will make them more effective than novices at fundamental skills in professional communication, such as the following:

- Empathizing with stakeholder's cognitive and emotional responses to content
- Considering optional paths toward generating prototypes or revisions
- Distinguishing among visual or verbal features of artifacts that align with stakeholders' needs and those that do not
- Diagnosing problems of text design or integration of word and image
- Taking textual action to solve problems of poor writing or visual design

CONTEXTUAL KNOWLEDGE

As I emphasized previously, an important part of professionals' abilities lies in the development of contextual knowledge about how to make an impact within a given workplace. To be effective, professionals need to acquire sophisticated knowledge about the social networks and structures of the workplace (Beaufort, 2008). Winsor (1998) found that professionals who worked in a for-profit organization learned how to take action and make their contributions visible within the social structure of the workplace, recognizing how to negotiate the social system of the organization.

As professional communicators develop their contextual knowledge, they learn to "read" the "information ecology"—the complex interconnections among people, activities, tools, values, and practices that distinguish one context from the next (Nardi & O'Day, 1999). Acquiring deep local knowledge about the typical patterns of decision making within the organizational context becomes integral in carrying out knowledge work that coworkers and other insiders will view as constructive. Figure 12.3 depicts my view of the interactive relationships among three important processes in professional communication:

- Constructing content (generating ideas for visual and verbal artifacts)
- Connecting content to stakeholders (shaping artifacts rhetorically to build cognitive structures and relational networks)
- Contextualizing design activity (making design activity visible and valued within the context of ongoing organizational activity)

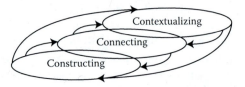

Figure 12.3   Three interactive processes in professional communication.

In my experience in working with professional communicators, I have observed, not surprisingly, that practitioners vary considerably in how well they negotiate the rhetorical space of constructing, connecting, and contextualizing. For example, they may have outstanding abilities in constructing texts, but may not be very skilled in knowing how to assess visual and verbal design, and completely unaware of the need to contextualize their work. They may be very good at analyzing readers' needs, but lack advanced skills in writing and visual design, making the resulting artifact well intended, but poorly executed. They may be rhetorically savvy in contextualizing their work, but unable to design artifacts that actually help people build cognitive structures or relational networks. Or they may be very skilled in all three processes: constructing, connecting, and contextualizing.

These interactive processes illustrate Winsor's (2001) contention that workplace design is firmly embedded in a social web, and that to participate in systems of distributed cognition, professionals need more than rhetorical and subject-matter knowledge. Professional communicators must be creative in negotiating the constellation of factors that shape and are shaped by literacy practices within organizational contexts.

CONSTELLATION OF FACTORS SHAPING COMMUNICATION WITHIN ORGANIZATIONAL CONTEXTS

Planning Ideas

Kellogg (2006) reminded us that professional writing is at once "a thinking task, a language task, and a memory task. A professional communicator can hold multiple representations in mind while adeptly juggling the basic processes of planning ideas, generating sentences, and reviewing how well the process is going" (p. 389). For example, Schumacher, Scott, Klare, Cronin, and Lambert (1989) studied journalists as they planned and composed news stories. They reported that experienced journalists imagined the structure of what they wanted to say, held that structure in mind as they went to a telephone, and then dictated the story over the phone without ever writing down or typing their plan. Similarly, Flower et al. (1992) found that expert writers created more goals than did novices; they also integrated those goals for themselves and maintained an eye on those goals, monitoring their progress during acts of planning. Haas (1996) observed that writers using a computer to write planned less than when using pen and paper, reminding us that technology mediates processes of writing and design.

Generating Content

In reviewing the research on how writers move from "idea to text," Hayes (2009) examined the bursts of words writers produce as they compose. He described a study that compared the burst length of freshmen and graduate student writers. More experienced writers (graduate students) were found to have generated twice as many words per burst (10 to 12) compared with less-experienced writers (5 to 6 words for freshmen). In other words, the increased number of words per burst meant that experienced writers could retrieve words more quickly, could form complete phrases faster, and could shape complex grammatical structures from memory more rapidly.

McCutchen, Covill, Hoyne, and Mildes (1994) found that skilled writers were faster and more accurate than less-skilled writers in accessing the words they wanted to say. Skilled writers were also better able to access representations of the text structure and to use story grammars or genre schemata as they composed.

According to McCutchen (2010), here lies a paradox: If adult experienced writers are faster at accessing what they propose to say and can also monitor how audiences might react to their content—prompting them to revise, for example, the syntax, semantics, or tone—then why do experienced writers seem to take longer to write, even the first sentence of a simple narrative (Scardamalia & Bereiter, 1991)? That expert writers may take longer and work harder to accomplish quality work runs counter to previous research on expertise in other domains, which suggests that as individuals or teams gain experience in their domain, they tend to speed up and employ their processes for doing their work more efficiently and with less conscious effort (Ericsson, 2009).

Torrance (2007) hypothesized that the extra time expert writers spend in constructing good content is related to their use of more complex and more sophisticated writing processes. As Scardamalia and Bereiter (1991) noted, experienced writers typically bring to mind a great deal of information as they plan what to say, including content they often toss out later. In fact, transcripts of think-aloud protocols of experienced writers show that they propose much more content than they actually commit to (McCutchen, 2010). Indeed, experienced writers tend to entertain more optional content, generate more revisions, take longer to write, and exert more effort than inexperienced writers (Scardamalia & Bereiter, 1991).

Although novices' speed can be attributed to their propensity to write down the first thing that comes to mind, experienced writers construct more elaborate mental representations of the communication problem at hand. We can hypothesize that for experienced communicators on the job, those more complex processes are related mainly to two difficult aspects of professional communication, discussed earlier: (1) thinking about the multiple audiences for their work and imagining content they might expect, and (2) managing the social and pragmatic constraints of the workplace.

Evaluating Content

Experienced communicators recognize the importance of evaluating their work with the intended stakeholders for the artifact. Although professionals strive to tailor their artifacts to meet stakeholders' cognitive and affective needs, they also recognize the difficulty in meeting those needs without actually talking with stakeholders. Indeed, the field of professional communication has for a long time recognized that the best way to assess an artifact is through reader-focused testing rather than by employing methods such as expert reviews, readability formulas, or focus groups (Schriver, 1989a). Usability testing of professional communication artifacts is now commonplace in many forward-thinking organizations. But even today, expert professionals still need to be able to make persuasive arguments about why assessment is valuable. Some experts in professional communication are also developing sophisticated skills in managing usability testing and evaluation efforts within organizations—framing the right questions, choosing appropriate methodologies, managing tests, analyzing results, sharing the results, and moving from analysis to subsequent revision.

Monitoring Text Production and Revising

Although skilled professional writers may take longer to accomplish their work (this observation needs further empirical testing), their final products are typically measurably better in quality from the perspective of readers (Schriver, 1993a). Skilled writers are better able to revise their texts for meaning, taking a top-down approach to text revision, improving the quality of the macrostructure before attending to editing the microstructure (Schriver, 1989b). Experienced professionals' ability to monitor their revision activity and to reflect on the quality of their writing or visual design is related to how they define revision. Experienced writers differ from inexperienced writers in that they see revision as a whole-text task that requires evaluating the text, extracting its gist, and comparing that meaning to the text produced so far, asking how well the text realizes the goals and intentions for readers (Hayes, Flower, Schriver, Stratman, & Carey, 1987).

DRAWING ON SUBJECT-MATTER KNOWLEDGE: HELP AND A HINDRANCE

Possessing subject-matter knowledge without rhetorical and cultural knowledge can inhibit professional communicators from accomplishing their goals. Indeed, people's everyday experience with instructions for cell phones, letters from lawyers, or explanations from engineers suggests that subject-matter knowledge can be a hindrance as much as a help. A central problem for many subject-matter experts lies in being able to take the perspective of people who do not share that knowledge.

Research suggests that when students acquire disciplinary knowledge, that knowledge may sometimes act as a blinder to recognizing the needs of people who do not possess that disciplinary knowledge. As mentioned earlier, one of the hallmarks of writing professionally is the ability to shape the content for different audiences, for example, for people with disciplinary expertise or people without such knowledge. Paradoxically, as students gain more sophistication in the subject matter of their field of study, they may experience more difficulty with making what they know clear for novice audiences. Learning to imagine the audience is a challenging rhetorical task for many college-aged writers and does not get easier when they enter the workplace (Smart & Brown, 2002)

Hayes (1989b) found that when college-aged writers read poorly written texts about topics they already knew well, those writers found it difficult to anticipate the comprehension problems that readers without knowledge of the subject matter might experience. Similarly, undergraduate engineering students had difficulty predicting a lay audience's ability to understand words that were part of their field's everyday vernacular (Hayes & Bajzek, 2008).

Although acquiring sophisticated subject-matter knowledge is requisite for expert-to-expert communication in any discipline, there are usually many other audiences the professional communicator must reach. For example, in his advice to scientists and researchers trying to reach broader audiences, Meredith (2010) pointed out that to have the most impact, researchers must disseminate their work beyond their network of peers to potential collaborators in other disciplines, administrators, funding agencies, private donors, prospective students, legislators, and the general public.

Not surprisingly, evidence suggests that professional communication is difficult for college-aged writers and may remain so as they make the transition to the workplace (Beaufort, 1999; Smart & Brown, 2002). For example, in a study of the professional communication skills of undergraduate bioengineers, my colleague and I studied how students' creation of technical reports, scientific posters, and oral presentations evolved from their sophomore to senior year (Schriver & Hayes, 2009). We found that early in students' coursework, bioengineers at the sophomore level necessarily focused on acquiring in-depth knowledge about their discipline. They tended to "tell their knowledge" to their professor rather than transform what they knew to a general audience or another specialized audience. Later in their coursework (by senior year), students broadened the audiences for whom they created their technical reports, scientific posters, and oral presentations. They moved from producing artifacts that were clearly oriented to the "teacher as audience" to creating artifacts shaped explicitly for people outside their field—stakeholders such as venture capitalists who could fund their research. But the transition from knowledge telling to knowledge transforming did not come easily nor did it come smoothly.

SETTING GOALS

On the one hand, organizational goals may be as simple as providing stakeholders with "accurate and helpful information" about a product or service. In this case, the professional communicator might be asked to design clear procedural information about a piece of software. A relational network might develop if stakeholders act on the procedures, have a good experience, think better of the organization, and possibly refer others to the organization. On the other hand, organizational goals for the artifact may be more complex, such as providing patients with usable information about understanding medical tests. In this case, the communicator might be challenged to invent novel visual displays for depicting the results of medical tests (e.g., decision aids about how to lower cholesterol; see Leckart, 2010, for some excellent examples).

As these examples show, professional communication tasks differ markedly in the complexity of the artifacts and in their intended rhetorical scope and temporal impact. Professional communication artifacts can be used to organize people's activity over brief periods of time (e.g., the time it takes to read a manual or inspect a Web page) or over much larger reaches of time and space (e.g., the time it takes to change a parent's thinking about the role of diet on health and the impact of parental behavior on family health). Put differently, the goals that professional communicators set for their communications may have short- or long-term motives (Russell, 1997).

RECOGNIZING RHETORICAL OPPORTUNITIES

From a rhetorical perspective, the idea of *kairos* or timing (from the Greek meaning the right or opportune moment to say or do the appropriate thing) is very important to professional communication activity. Experts in professional communication face the rhetorical demand of needing to recognize the "right time" for a particular message, a sensitivity that reminds us that expertise is much more than a collection of technical skills. As Kinneavy (2002) put it, kairos was the basis for an art of rhetoric, in which discerning the right time for a rhetorical act was crucial. Professional communicators both create these kairotic moments and seize rhetorical opportunities as they arise.

Sometimes professional communicators create their own kairos by imparting a topic with such saliency that relational networks can be built as a result of people experiencing the artifact. For example, since 1978—when communications designer Burkey Belser created the "Energy Guide label" to help consumers easily identify energy-efficient products—consumers have been able to use the Energy Guide label to make comparisons about energy savings when they bought household products (like a refrigerator). Multiplied by millions of refrigerators, the energy savings have been enormous, and companies with the best energy-savings models have built loyal customer networks that continue to grow (for a discussion, see Emerson, 2005).

Other times professional communicators build rhetorical relationships with potential stakeholders by generating a novel design in response to a kairotic moment. For example, in 2000 after the U.S. Bush versus Gore election and the Florida "butterfly ballot" fiasco—in which many voters made incorrect choices because of poor ballot design—the idea of socially conscious design gained prominence in writing and visual design circles. This consciousness prompted communication design firms to develop capabilities in ballot design and laid the groundwork for igniting the Design for Democracy Movement (Lausen, 2007).

REPRESENTING PROFESSIONAL COMMUNICATION TASKS

As we can see, the goals that organizations, individual designers, or collaborative teams set for themselves and the kairos—the rhetorical opportunities that are present or discovered in a particular situation—will influence the professional communicator's representation of the task as well as their motivation for the task. From a cognitive perspective a communicator's *task definition* (or *task representation*) is fundamental in setting in motion strategies for writing and visual design as well as for prompting the communicator to access relevant prior knowledge for generating a plan, producing an artifact, and judging its relative success (Hayes et al., 1987; Wallace & Hayes, 1991).

Previous accounts of the cognitive processes in writing focused mainly on modeling writers in academic settings, environments in which the goals for writing tasks were typically established by teachers or researchers. By contrast, the representations of professional communication tasks are set by interactions among individual writers or designers, design teams, and organizations sponsoring or requesting the work.

Task representations are constrained by opportunities and limitations posed by the genre, the media available, and the material and political conditions of the rhetorical situation. For example, an individual professional communicator might set a goal to write a scientific exposé on global warming for the print version of *National Geographic* magazine. Because she wants to reduce the risk of having the article rejected due to excessive length, she might define her task as "write a tight, compelling article in no more than three pages including images." But in talking with the magazine's editor, she may learn that if the editor likes the print version, she or he will invite her to expand the story for the Web-based version of the magazine.

Being immersed in the rhetorical situation causes the professional to modify her representation of the task and to view the smaller task in relation to the larger task. The professional communicator's rerepresentation raises her evaluative standards for what would make for an effective short article and changes her view of the whole task, altering her notion of what is possible. In this way, situated knowledge and motives for writing and visual design interact and serve a heuristic function, influencing how designers represent opportunities and the shape of their communication activity (Bazerman & Russell, 2002).

When organizations establish the goals for a task, they vary a lot in terms of their specificity. For example, the task can be quite constrained (e.g., create a step-by-step diagram to help immigrants understand the process of becoming a citizen; use a brochure format; do not use color). Organizations may also frame the task in a rather open-ended fashion (e.g., develop a communication system for helping new home buyers to understand the intricacies of financing a mortgage; design with an eye toward adding to the system other types of financial documents such as credit card agreements; create both print and Web versions). In the latter example, the professional has considerably more latitude in how the task can be represented.

In either case, professional communicators strive to define their task in ways that will allow them to shape artifacts so they adhere to their preferred representations of what to do. Put differently, experts in design are concerned with how things might be or ought to be (Simon, 1996).

THE TASK ENVIRONMENT OF PROFESSIONAL COMMUNICATION

Because the nature of professional communication is not yet well researched and its rhetorical exigencies have received little attention, it is not surprising that current models do not adequately capture the cognitive and rhetorical activity of professional communication, but they do provide important points of departure, particularly the influential models proposed by Hayes and his colleagues (Chenoweth & Hayes, 2001; Hayes, 1996; Hayes & Flower, 1980; Hayes et al., 1987).

In particular, Hayes's 1996 model of composing (shown in Figure 12.4) portrayed some of the characteristics of individuals as they engage in skilled writing. The *task environment* locates the social, cultural, and material resources for professional

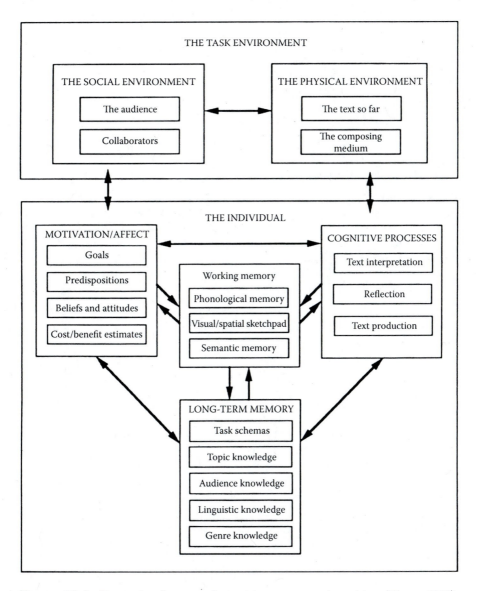

Figure 12.4 Interactive features of cognitive processes in writing (Hayes, 1996). (Courtesy of Karen Schriver.)

communication activity. The model illustrates the reciprocal and mutually constitutive relations among the social environment, the physical environment, and the writer's motivation, memory, and cognitive processes. By task environment Hayes refers to everything outside the writer's skin—the complex interactive systems of activity that shape the process and are shaped by the process.

The task environment of the workplace is parallel to classroom settings in that both the cultural context and the people who work there—peers, collaborators, and superiors—exert direct and indirect influence on the design processes. Moreover, both classroom and workplace settings are sites of highly intense collaborative activity, often mediated by advanced computing technologies. But workplace task environments are different from classroom settings in several important ways, including the following:

- Procedures for providing feedback
- How individuals or teams develop a sense of agency in their environment
- Support for writing and visual design processes
- Processes of planning, revising, and collaborating

Differences in Feedback

Educators in professional communication pride themselves on providing helpful and useful feedback on student writing and design. However, the feedback that professional communicators in the workplace receive is considerably less supportive, and it often comes as a shock to students entering the workforce to find that colleagues and superiors may be more concerned with critiquing what's wrong with their writing or design than with discussing how to improve it.

Researchers investigating teacher-feedback practices in college-level design classes found that although design studios emphasized the "critique," teachers rarely gave substantive negative feedback and tended to socialize students to assume egalitarian relationships and autonomous decision making (Dannels & Martin, 2008). When academics idealize the professional workplace, they may complicate students' ability to respond constructively to negative feedback.

Differences in Agency

In modern student-centered classrooms, learners are encouraged to develop their personal sense of agency in various ways; for example, by asking challenging questions, by defending their ideas during collaborative activities, by taking a critical rhetorical stance, or by deliberately changing the focus of class discussion in productive ways. But in the workplace, these strategies that work well in inclusive classroom settings may be viewed as annoying, insubordinate, or presumptuous. As Spilka (1993) pointed out, professional communication students often need specific instruction in analyzing the social situation at work and in using strategies for social accommodation.

Agency in organizations is not a personal attribute or a property of teams that can be deployed; rather, it is an interactive accomplishment that is constructed in real time as professionals work together with other professionals, mediated by their culture's artifacts and technologies (see Engeström, 1992). Expertise in professional communication calls on keen social skills and extensive local knowledge in order to cultivate one's agency and authority. If writers and designers are to be heard in workplace cultures organized primarily around the activities of scientists, engineers, and technology experts, they need to position themselves as central rather than as peripheral to an organization's key activities, seizing rhetorical opportunities for moment-by-moment agency. They need to read the task environment in order to learn the social norms, values, and practices for getting things done (Smart & Brown, 2002). In this way they will develop expert practices for contextualizing their work, recognizing conditions and opportunities in the local situation that may enable agency, either individually or as a team. As discussed earlier, the key for professional communicators lies in perceiving the moment (kairos) to exert their agency so they have the best chance of making a long-term impact.

Differences in Supporting Writing and Visual Design Processes

Although most writing and visual design classrooms support an optimal design process—from planning to evaluation—many corporate environments fail to understand what professional writers and information designers do and treat them more as wordsmiths and data decorators than as rhetorical problem solvers (Flower, 1989). This problem of professional identity that I described over a decade ago (Schriver, 1997) still persists and influences design processes in negative ways. A professional writing student from Carnegie Mellon University reported to me in her internship report, "my boss at IBM Boca Raton told me that planning a writing task is a waste of time; he wants me to get writing fast and stop fooling around." Comments such as these remind us that workplaces may not provide the resources for supporting an expert design process, forcing writers and designers to focus on efficiency of production over communication quality.

Because workplaces differ markedly in how they conceive of writing and design processes, professional communicators must be skilled in recognizing the characteristics of the process that can impede the creation of well-designed artifacts. They must be able to audit how design activity takes place in the local situation, considering the range of tools and practices that mediate design work—policies, methods, informal protocols, sign-offs, technologies, and reward structures. Moreover, experts must be able to persuasively argue for the cultural and material benefits of producing high-quality professional communications, especially for the long-term benefits of building cognitive structures and relational networks for stakeholders.

Differences in Planning

Students in writing and design classrooms typically begin their planning with metacognitive reflection on the best way to proceed for a design project. By contrast, professional communicators in the workplace often engage in preplanning by conducting interviews with subject-matter experts. In making the transition to the workplace, professional communication students may find the process of planning to be stressful because it is often very difficult to gain access to subject-matter experts, such as computer scientists or lawyers, whose understanding of the content they need in order to get started. Planning in the workplace demands refined skills in asking questions that will elicit the content professionals need to work with. Professionals need to reflect on their subject-matter knowledge, gauging the distance between what they know and what they need to know.

Like the plans of student writers or designers, professionals' plans usually take the form of words, images, diagrams, or sketches (Flower & Hayes, 1984; Witte, 1987). But unlike academic environments, where the plan is usually a response to a well-designed assignment, the professional's plan is more of a social negotiation among team members in response to an ill-defined problem. Professionals require keen planning skills not only to ensure the quality of their own projects, but also for contextualizing their work within the larger activities of the organization.

Differences in Revision

When students revise in classroom settings, revision is usually an activity carried out by writers or designers working on their own writing and visual design. Their efforts are guided by the assignment and by their own goals. In contrast, the workplace calls for revising texts written or visualized by other people in order to achieve goals that have been determined by negotiating with others in the organization. It is common in workplace settings for many individuals to have authority over artifacts created—demanding rewrites, revisualizations, or complete overhauls of writing and visual design. One writer in the U.S. Internal Revenue Service told me that as many as 28 people had authority to edit what he had written. To be effective, professional communicators must have strategies for evaluating, consolidating, and taking action on the contradictory feedback they will likely receive.

There is also a difference in what motivates revision in the classroom and the workplace. In the classroom, the assignment and students' personal goals shape their objectives for revision. In the workplace, revision is typically initiated when the organization recognizes a gap between the communications they have and those they need, often prompted by negative feedback from internal or external stakeholders (e.g., managers, sales representatives, users, readers). Revision in the workplace involves iterative redesign until stakeholders' needs are met or until the artifact is approved for publication. In forward-thinking organizations, professionals evaluate the quality of their artifacts through methods such as preference tests, comprehension tests, or usability tests, leaning on stakeholders' cognitive and affective constructions of the content to guide revision of the text so far.

Differences in Collaboration

In many writing and visual design classrooms, collaborative activities focus on joint projects among students in the same class who share similar goals for the task to be accomplished. In contrast, workplace collaboration is characterized by cross-disciplinary efforts in distributed work environments (separated by time, space, geography, allegiances, subject-matter expertise, or sense of mission; for a discussion, see Spinuzzi, 2007). In workplace collaboration, team members from different fields may hold radically different goals for the problem to be solved, requiring participants to engage in substantial negotiation, coordination, and conflict resolution (Burnett, 1991). For example, in an effort to introduce college students to workplace issues of collaboration, Wojahn, Dyke, Riley, Hensel, and Brown (2001) studied students who majored in engineering and technical communication as they worked together on client-based projects. They found that engineering and technical communication students experienced difficulty in collaborating because the engineering students tended to privilege their own discipline and view the task of communicating technically as a mere "add on." They also found that technical communication students were unable to articulate persuasively to engineers the value of their discipline and what they added to the project. Unlike students in a writing or design class, professional communicators often find themselves needing to make clear to their interdisciplinary collaborators the usefulness of the expertise they bring to solving problems. In doing so experienced professional communicators invent and reveal their own disciplinary identity as they engage in multidisciplinary activity.

In the classroom, students typically work face to face and in groups, mediated by technologies such as computer-based discussion lists or intranets. In the workplace, professionals may never meet their collaborators in person. Instead, most of their work may be carried out in ad hoc teams who operate remotely through electronic means (e.g., e-mails, conference calls, video chats, and intranet communications). Often separated by discipline, location, and time, these fluid group ensembles must not only build communication products, they must also coordinate their decision-making activities in ways that allow them to achieve their rhetorical goals. Part of the social burden of distributed environments is that professional communicators must coordinate two goals simultaneously. First, they must articulate their ideas for solving the problem at hand in a persuasive way, bringing to bear their knowledge of writing and visual design, and when possible, by identifying empirical research or best practices to support their ideas (Schriver & Gordon, 2010). Second, professional communicators often need to establish their credibility, ethos, and work ethic with their collaborators.

Put differently, they need to construct for their collaborators a positive image of their professional identity. Paretti, McNair, and Holloway-Attaway (2007), for example, provided a case study of U.S. and Swedish engineering and digital media students who collaborated on a design project. They found that although students were very experienced in using digital technologies for their personal work, students did not do very well in using these technologies to construct and mediate their professional identity in distributed work environments. For example, engineering students paid little attention to thinking about creating positive social interactions with their distant collaborators. Students failed to consider how productive patterns of collaboration might have enhanced their problem solving. Paretti and her colleagues contend that teachers of professional communication need to devise pedagogies for teaching collaborative strategies for interacting effectively in distributed environments.

These differences between classroom and workplace task environments illustrate how communication practices in different contexts are uniquely mediated by social influences and material practices. These differences also make clear that to understand and nurture expertise in professional communication, we need detailed empirical studies of the dynamics of workplace task environments. We need to examine the interactions between individual expertise and distributed expertise. Such studies would provide a basis for developing pedagogies for educating young professionals to be more effective in the workplace.

CHARACTERISTICS OF EXPERT PROFESSIONAL COMMUNICATORS

Taken together, the literature suggests a number of typical characteristics of high-achieving professional communicators:

1. Possess rich schematic and tacit knowledge about genres, stakeholders, processes, symbols, and tools—knowledge that guides engagement with others and that influences their symbolic-analytic production of text.
2. Able to read the context and scope out social resources, noticing opportunities that can enable them to exert change.
3. Can coordinate their representations of personal knowledge, text produced so far, stakeholders' needs, and context as they design. Able to fuse disparate items of content into a coherent whole.
4. Are visually and verbally fluent, able to draw on a large repertory of semiotic resources (words, images, sounds, numbers). Comfortable with displacing one form (e.g., text) with another (e.g., visual). Not invested in one form or another, but on what meets the needs of stakeholders, their situation, and the available media.
5. Articulate *what* they know and the *why* of their choices in particular rhetorical situations.
6. Reflective on their knowledge and able to devise tactics for learning what they need to know. Are metacognitively aware of what they need to know and have strategies for getting that knowledge.
7. Possess rich rhetorical memories about the people they have designed for—readers, audiences, stakeholders, communities, or users.
8. Rhetorically perceptive of opportunities to build knowledge and to advance personal innovation and organizational agendas through formal and informal social networks within organizations.
9. Expect their work will be circulated and repurposed (Swarts, 2010) in various lengths, formats, and media—for example, circulated as an extended report and as report highlights in modular format; presented as a print publication and displayed on the Web; or deployed on high-definition television and reformatted on the fly for display on cellular technologies. Embrace the dynamics of content reuse in organizational settings and anticipate the resemiotization (Iedema, 2003) of their work (i.e., textual artifacts may change in meaning as they shift from context to context), traversing local genre ecologies (e.g., report to instructions to brochure).
10. Recognize that communication artifacts are often recontextualized in unpredictable ways (e.g., a slogan written for a public service campaign

such as "plain language is a civil right" may become a tagline for a Web site devoted to advocacy for plain language). Each time a text is reused, it becomes divorced from the social context that produced it (Mehan, 1993). Professionals are not invested in single meaning with a singular purpose.

11. Can juggle multiple organizational constraints (deadlines or lack of funding) and multiple representations of the content (what the boss wants, what the client needs, and what the author thinks is best) and still maintain a focus on the stakeholders' needs.

12. Acquire rich patterned knowledge of visual, verbal, and typographic text features. Skilled in selecting what to say, in deciding how to say it, and in combining visual and verbal resources.

13. Recognize that the texts and artifacts they create can influence how others perceive their abilities, positioning them positively or negatively for future work.

14. Adaptive to complexity in the workplace; can interpret what they need to know on the fly.

15. Strategic in building alliances with others who may help them to achieve long-term goals for design processes and products.

CONCLUSION

In this chapter I explored two questions about developing expertise in professional communication:

- What are the challenges of professional writing and visual design in the workplace?
- What knowledge underlies the development of high levels of skill in professional writing and visual design?

In addressing the first question, I characterized three challenges that make professional communication unique:

- The need to orchestrate writing knowledge and strategy with visual design knowledge and strategy
- The need to engage multiple stakeholders with a given body of content
- The need to negotiate the social, political and cultural landscapes of the workplace

This review shows clearly that addressing these challenges is difficult for anyone who writes or designs in the workplace and that skilled performance requires much more than being able to create well-written or elegantly designed artifacts. To be effective the artifacts must actually achieve their goals for stakeholders, helping them to build appropriate cognitive structures and useful relational networks. As I have shown, the rhetorical stakes are high for designing either paper-based or Web-based artifacts, as stakeholders for professional communications are an impatient lot, tending to skim and scan more often than reading for understanding—making it difficult to gain stakeholders' attention and keep it.

The second part of the chapter examined the knowledge that underlies high levels of skill in professional communication, knowledge that may distinguish experts from novices, and experts from experienced nonexperts. Existing literature suggests that experts in professional communication need not only advanced abilities in writing and visual design, but also extensive rhetorical, social, and cultural knowledge.

This chapter also contributes to our understanding of the ways in which workplace task environments differ from classroom settings:

- Procedures for providing feedback
- How individuals or teams develop a sense of agency in their environment
- Support for writing and visual design processes
- Processes of planning, revising, and collaborating

My analysis identified some of the unique features of writing and visual design in professional settings, underscoring the need for the development of new pedagogies that could ease students' transition from school to work, pedagogies that could help them more easily negotiate the fluid and often volatile context of the workplace, and provide them with strategies for developing a sense of agency in order to be more rhetorically effective.

As researchers better understand the nature of writing and visual design ability, the knowledge needed to excel, and the ecologies of workplace task environments, the field will be better positioned to suggest a path toward developing and nurturing expertise in professional communication, both in the classroom and in the world of work.

REFERENCES

Ackerman, J. M. (1991). Reading, writing, and knowing: The role of disciplinary knowledge in comprehension and composing. *Research in the Teaching of English, 25*(2), 133–178.

Alamargot, D., & Chanquoy, L. (2001). Development of expertise in writing. In D. Alamargot & L. Chanquoy (Eds.), *Through models of writing* (pp. 185–218). Dordrech: Kluwer.

Albers, M. (2003). Multidimensional audience analysis for dynamic information. *Journal of Technical Writing and Communication, 33*(3), 263–279.

Anderson, J. R. (2009). *Cognitive psychology and its implications* (7th ed.). New York: Worth Publishers.

Bazerman, C. (1988). *Shaping written knowledge: The genre and activity of the experimental article in science*. Madison, WI: University of Wisconsin Press.

Bazerman, C., & Russell, D. R. (Eds.). (2002). *Writing selves/writing societies: Research from activity perspectives*. Fort Collins, CO: WAC Clearinghouse and Mind, Culture, and Activity. Retrieved from http://wac.colostate.edu/books/selves_societies

Beaufort, A. (1999). *Writing in the real world: Making the transition from school to work*. New York: Teachers College Press.

Beaufort, A. (2000). Learning the trade: A social apprenticeship model for gaining writing expertise. *Written Communication, 17*(2), 185–223.

Beaufort, A. (2008). Writing in the professions. In C. Bazerman (Ed.), *Research on writing: History, society, school, individual, text* (pp. 221–235). New York: Erlbaum.

Bereiter, C., & Scardamalia, M. (1982). From conversation to composition: The role of instruction in a developmental process. In R. Glaser (Ed.), *Advances in instructional psychology* (Vol. 2, pp. 1–64). Hillsdale, NJ: Erlbaum.

Bereiter, C., & Scardamalia, M. (1993). *Surpassing ourselves: An inquiry into the nature and implications of expertise*. Peru, IL: Open Court.

Blakeslee, A. M. (2010). Addressing audiences in a digital age. In R. Spilka (Ed.), *Digital literacy for technical communication: 21st century theory and practice* (pp. 199–229). New York: Routledge.

Buchanan, R. (1992). Wicked problems in design thinking. *Design Issues: History, Theory, Criticism, 8*(2), 5–21.

Burnett, R. E. (1991). Substantive conflict in a cooperative context: A way to improve collaborative planning of workplace documents. *Technical Communication, 38*(4), 532–539.

Carter, M. (1990). The idea of expertise: An exploration of cognitive and social dimensions of writing. *College Composition and Communication, 41*(3), 265–286.

Charness, N. (1976). Memory for chess positions: Resistance to interference. *Journal of Experimental Psychology, 2*, 641–653.

Chase, W. G., & Ericsson, K. A. (1982). Skill and working memory. In G. H. Bower (Ed.), *The psychology of learning and motivation* (pp. 1–58). New York: Academic Press.

Chase, W. G., & Simon, H. A. (1973). The mind's eye in chess. In W. G. Chase (Ed.), *Visual information processing* (pp. 215–281). New York: Academic Press.

Chenoweth, N. A., & Hayes, J. R. (2001). Fluency in writing: generating text in L1 and L2. *Written Communication, 18*(1), 80–98.

Crismore, A. (1989). *Talking with readers: Metadiscourse as a rhetorical act*. New York: Peter Lang.

Dannels, D. P., & Martin, K. N. (2008). Critiquing critiques: A genre analysis of feedback across novice and expert design studios. *Journal of Business and Technical Communication, 22*(2), 135–159.

Emerson, J. (2005, January–February). Guns, butter and ballots: Citizens take charge by designing for better government. *Communication Arts*, 14–23. Retrieved from http://www.commarts.com/Columns.aspx?pub=1920&pageid=604

Engeström, Y. (1992). Interactive expertise: Studies in distributed working intelligence. *Research Bulletin, 83*. Retrieved from http://helda.helsinki.fi/handle/10224/3666

Ericsson, K. A. (Ed.). (1996). *The road to excellence: The acquisition of expert performance in the arts and sciences, sports and games*. Mahwah, NJ: Erlbaum.

Ericsson, K. A. (Ed.). (2009). *Development of professional expertise: Toward measurement of expert performance and design of optimal learning environments*. New York: Cambridge University Press.

Ericsson, K. A., Charness, N., Feltovich, P. J., & Hoffman, R. R. (Eds.). (2006). *The Cambridge handbook of expertise and performance*. New York: Cambridge University Press.

Ericsson, K. A., Krampe, R. T., & Tesch-Römer, C. (1993). The role of deliberate practice in the acquisition of expert performance. *Psychological Review, 100*(3), 363–406.

Fletcher, J. D. (2009). The value of expertise and expert performance: A review of evidence from the military. In K. A. Ericsson (Ed.), *Development of professional expertise* (pp. 449–469). New York: Cambridge University Press.

Flower, L. (1989). Rhetorical problem solving: Cognition and professional writing. In M. Kogan (Ed.), *Writing in the business professions* (pp. 3–36). Urbana, IL: National Council of Teachers of English and the Association for Business Communication.

Flower, L., & Hayes, J. R. (1984, January). Images, plans, and prose: The representation of meaning in writing. *Written Communication, 1*, 120–160.

Flower, L., Hayes, J. R., Carey, L., Schriver, K. A., & Stratman, J. F. (1986). Detection, diagnosis and the strategies of revision. *College Composition and Communication, 37*(1), 16–55.

Flower, L., Schriver, K. A., Haas, C., Carey, L., & Hayes, J. R. (1992). Planning in writing: The cognition of a constructive process. In S. P. Witte, N. Nakadate, & R. D. Cherry (Eds.), *A rhetoric of doing: Essays on written discourse in honor of James L. Kinneavy* (pp. 181–243). Carbondale, IL: Southern Illinois University Press.

Frascara, J. (1995). Graphic design: Fine art or social science? In V. Margolin & R. Buchanan (Eds.), *The idea of design* (pp. 44–55). Cambridge, MA: MIT Press.

Friess, E. (2008). *The user-centered design process: Novice designers' use of evidence in designing from data.* Ph.D. rhetoric dissertation, Carnegie Mellon University, Pittsburgh, PA.

Futrelle, R. P. (2004). The London Underground map—Harry Beck's design icon. Retrieved from http://diagrams.org/fig-pages/f00022.html

Haas, C. (1996). *Writing technology: Studies on the materiality of literacy.* Mahwah, NJ: Erlbaum.

Haas, C., & Witte, S. P. (2001). Writing as an embodied practice: The case of engineering standards. *Journal of Business and Technical Communication, 15*(4), 413–457.

Hayes, J. R. (1985). Three problems in teaching general skills. In S. F. Chipman, J. W. Segal, & R. Glaser (Eds.), *Teaching and learning skills: Research and open questions* (Vol. 2, pp. 391–406). Hillsdale, NJ: Erlbaum.

Hayes, J. R. (1989a). *The complete problem solver* (2nd ed.). Hillsdale, NJ: Erlbaum.

Hayes, J. R. (1989b). Writing research: The analysis of a very complex task. In D. Klahr & K. Kotovsky (Eds.), *Complex information processing: The impact of Herbert A. Simon* (pp. 209–234). Hillsdale, NJ: Erlbaum.

Hayes, J. R. (1996). A new framework for understanding cognition and affect in writing. In C. M. Levy & S. Ransdell (Eds.), *The science of writing: Theories, methods, individual differences, and applications* (pp. 1–27). Mahwah, NJ: Erlbaum.

Hayes, J. R. (2009). From idea to text. In R. Beard, D. Myhill, J. Riley, & M. Nystrand (Eds.), *The Sage handbook of writing development* (pp. 65–79). London: Sage.

Hayes, J. R., & Bajzek, D. (2008). Understanding and reducing the knowledge effect. *Written Communication, 25*(1), 104–118.

Hayes, J. R., & Flower, L. (1980). Identifying the organization of writing processes. In L. W. Gregg & E. R. Steinberg (Eds.), *Cognitive processes in writing: An interdisciplinary approach* (pp. 3–30). Hillsdale, NJ: Erlbaum.

Hayes, J. R., Flower, L., Schriver, K. A., Stratman, J. F., & Carey, L. (1987). Cognitive processes in revision. In S. Rosenberg (Ed.), *Advances in applied psycholinguistics, Vol. 2: Reading, writing, and language processing* (pp. 176–240). Cambridge, UK: Cambridge University Press.

Henry, J. (1998). Documenting contributory expertise: The value added by technical communicators in collaborative writing situations. *Technical Communication, 45*(2), 207–220.

Henry, J. (2000). *Writing workplace cultures: An archeology of professional writing.* Carbondale, IL: Southern Illinois University Press.

Hillocks, G. (1986). *Research in written composition: New directions for teaching.* Urbana, IL: ERIC Clearinghouse on Reading and Communication Skills and National Conference on Research in English.

Holland, V. M., Charrow, V. R., & Wright, W. W. (1988). How can technical writers write effectively for several audiences at once? In L. Beene & P. White (Eds.), *Solving problems in technical writing* (pp. 27–54). New York: Oxford University Press.

Hovde, M. R. (2000). Tactics for building images of audience in organizational contexts: An ethnographic study of technical communicators. *Journal of Business and Technical Communication, 14*(4), 395–444.

Howe, M. J. A., & Davidson, J. W. (1993). The early progress of able young musicians. In R. L. Sternberg & E. L. Grigorenko (Eds.), *The psychology of abilities, competencies, and expertise* (pp. 186–212). New York: Cambridge University Press.

Hutchins, E. (1995). *Cognition in the wild*. Cambridge, MA: MIT Press.

Iedema, R. (2003). Multimodality, resemiotization: Extending the analysis of discourse as multi-semiotic practice. *Visual Communication, 2*(1), 29–57.

Kellogg, R. T. (2006). Professional writing expertise. In K. A. Ericsson, N. Charness, P. J. Feltovich, & R. R. Hoffman (Eds.), *The Cambridge handbook of expertise and expert performance* (pp. 389–402). New York: Cambridge University Press.

Kellogg, R. T. (2008). Training writing skills: A cognitive developmental perspective. *Journal of Writing Research, 1*(1), 1–26.

Kinneavy, J. L. (2002). Kairos in classical and modern rhetorical theory. In P. Sipiora & J. S. Baumlin (Eds.), *Rhetoric and kairos: Essays in history, theory, and praxis* (pp. 58–76). New York: SUNY Press.

Kirtz, M. K., & Reep, D. C. (1990). A survey of the frequency, types, and importance of writing tasks in four career areas. *Business Communication Quarterly, 53*(4), 3–4.

Kundel, H. L., & Nodine, C. F. (1975). Interpreting chest radiographs without visual search. *Radiology, 116,* 527–532.

Lausen, M. (2007). *Design for democracy: Ballot and election design*. Chicago: University of Chicago Press.

Leckart, S. (2010). The blood test gets a makeover. *Wired, 18*(12). Retrieved from http://www.wired.com/magazine/2010/11/ff_bloodwork

Lehmann, A. C., & Ericsson, K. A. (1997). Research on expert performance and deliberate practice: Implications for the education of amateur musicians and music students. *Psychomusicology: Music, Mind, and Brain, 16*(1–2), 40–58.

Lidwell, W., Holden, K., & Butler, J. (2003). *Universal principles of design*. Beverly, MA: Rockport Publishers.

Mabrito, M. (1997). Writing on the front line: A study of workplace writing. *Business Communication Quarterly, 60*(3), 58–70.

McCutchen, D. (2010, September). *Language and memory processes in the development of writing skill*. Keynote presentation to the 12th International Conference of the EARLI Special Interest Group on Writing. Heidelberg University of Education. Heidelberg, Germany.

McCutchen, D., Covill, D., Hoyne, S. H., & Mildes, K. (1994). Individual differences in writing: Implications of translating fluency. *Journal of Educational Psychology, 86*(2), 256–266.

McMullen, J. Q., & Wellman, J. D. (1990). Writing programs outside the English department: An assessment of a five-year program. *Writing Program Administration (WPA), 14*(1–2), 17–25.

Mehan, H. (1993). Beneath the skin and between the ears: A case study in the politics of representation. In S. Chaiklin & J. Lave (Eds.), *Understanding practice: Perspectives of activity and context* (pp. 241–268). Cambridge, UK: Cambridge University Press.

Meredith, D. (2010). *Explaining research: How to reach key audiences to advance your work*. New York: Oxford University Press.

Nardi, B., & O'Day, V. (1999). *Information ecologies: Using technology with heart*. Cambridge, MA: MIT Press.

Paretti, M. C., McNair, L. D., & Holloway-Attaway, L. (2007). Teaching technical communication in an era of distributed work: A case study of collaboration between U.S. and Swedish students. *Technical Communication Quarterly, 16*(3), 327–352.

Pirolli, P., & Card, S. K. (1999). Information foraging. *Psychological Review, 106*(4), 643–675.

Plain Writing Act of 2010, H. R. 946, 111th Cong., 2nd session, 1–3 (2010). Retrieved from http://thomas.loc.gov/home/thomas.php

Quinlan, T., & Alamargot, D. (2007). Highly effective writers and the role of reading: A cognitive approach to composing in professional contexts. In D. Alamargot, P. Terrier, & J. M. Cellier (Eds.), *Studies in writing: Written documents in the workplace* (Vol. 21, pp. 61–74). Amsterdam: Elsevier.

Reave, L. (2004). Technical communication instruction in engineering schools: A survey of top-ranked U.S. and Canadian programs. *Journal of Business and Technical Communication, 18*(4), 452–490.

Redish, J. (2007). *Letting go of the words: Writing web content that works*. San Francisco, CA: Morgan Kaufmann.

Russell, D. R. (1997). Rethinking genre in school and society. *Written Communication, 14*(4), 504–554.

Russell, D. R. (2007). Rethinking the articulation between business and technical communication and writing in the disciplines. *Journal of Business and Technical Communication, 21*(3), 248–277.

Sadoski, M., & Paivio, A. (2001). *Imagery and text: A dual coding theory of reading and writing*. Mahwah, NJ: Erlbaum.

Scardamalia, M., & Bereiter, C. (1991). Literate expertise. In K. A. Ericsson & J. Smith (Eds.), *Toward a general theory of expertise* (pp. 172–194). Cambridge, UK: Cambridge University Press.

Schreiber, B. T., Bennett Jr., W., Colegrove, C. M., Portrey, A. M., Greschke, D. A., & Bell, H. H. (2009). Evaluating pilot performance. In K. A. Ericsson (Ed.), *Development of professional expertise* (pp. 247–270). New York: Cambridge University Press.

Schriver, K. A. (1989a). Evaluating text quality: The continuum from text-focused to reader-focused methods. *IEEE Transactions in Professional Communication, 32*(4), 238–255.

Schriver, K. A. (1989b). Moving from sentence-level to whole-text revision: Helping writers focus on the reader's needs. In K. A. McCormick (Ed.), *Reading to write: Practical approaches for the teaching of writing* (pp. 46–57). Berkeley, CA: UC Berkeley, National Center for the Study of Writing and Literacy.

Schriver, K. A. (1992a). Teaching writers to anticipate readers' needs: A classroom-evaluated pedagogy. *Written Communication, 9*(2), 179–208.

Schriver, K. A. (1992b). Teaching writers to anticipate readers' needs: What can document designers learn from usability testing? In H. Pander Maat & M. Steehouder (Eds.), *Studies of functional text quality* (pp. 141–157). Amsterdam: Rodopi Press.

Schriver, K. A. (1993a). Quality in document design: Issues and controversies. *Technical Communication, 40*(2), 239–257.

Schriver, K. A. (1997). *Dynamics in document design: Creating texts for readers*. New York: Wiley.

Schriver, K. A. (2009, December 12). Using design to get people to read and keep reading. Health Literacy Out Loud Podcast (HLOL). Retrieved from http://www.healthliteracyoutloud.com/?s=schriver

Schriver, K. A. (2010). Reading on the web: Implications for online information design. Ljubljana Museum of Architecture and Design Lecture Series on Visual Communications Theory: On Information Design. Retrieved from http://videolectures.net/aml2010_schriver_rotw

Schriver, K. A., & Gordon, F. (2010). Grounding plain language in research. *Clarity, 64* (Nov.), 33–39.

Schriver, K. A., & Hayes, J. R. (2009). Bioengineers as professional communicators: Assessing the impact of the Cain Project on undergraduate professional writing and speaking performances at Rice University. Council for Programs in Technical and Scientific Communication. Technical Report. Retrieved from http://www.cptsc.org/research-assess.html

Schumacher, G. M., Scott, B. T., Klare, G. R., Cronin, F. C., & Lambert, D. A. (1989). Cognitive processes in journalistic genres: Extending writing models. *Written Communication, 6*(3), 390–407.

Simon, H. A. (1996). *The sciences of the artificial* (3rd ed.). Cambridge, MA: MIT Press.

Simon, H. A., & Chase, W. G. (1973). Skill in chess. *American Scientist, 61*(4), 394–403.

Smart, G., & Brown, N. (2002). Learning transfer or transformation of learning?: Student interns reinventing expert writing practices in the workplace. *Technostyle, 18*(1), 117–141.

Sosniak, L. A. (1985). Learning to be a concert pianist. In B. S. Bloom (Ed.), *Developing talent in young people* (pp. 19–67). New York: Ballantine.

Sosniak, L. A. (1990). The tortoise, the hare, and the development of talent. In M. J. A. Howe (Ed.), *Encouraging the development of exceptional abilities and talents* (pp. 149–164). London: British Psychological Society.

Spilka, R. (1990). Orality and literacy in the workplace: Process- and text-based strategies for mulitple audience adaptation. *Journal of Business and Technical Communication, 4*(1), 44–67.

Spilka, R. (1993). Influencing workplace practice: A challenge for professional writing specialists in academia. In R. Spilka (Ed.), *Writing in the workplace* (pp. 207–219). Carbondale, IL: Southern University Press.

Spinuzzi, C. (2003). *Tracing genres through organizations*. Cambridge, MA: MIT Press.

Spinuzzi, C. (2007). Guest editor's introduction: Technical communication in the age of distributed work. *Technical Communication Quarterly, 16*(3), 265–277.

Summers, K., & Summers, M. (2005). Reading and navigational strategies of Web users with lower literacy skills. *Proceedings of the American Society for Information Science and Technology, 42*(1), 1–10. Retrieved from http://eprints.rclis.org/handle/10760/7038

Swarts, J. (2010). Recycled writing: Assembling actor networks from reusable content. *Journal of Business and Technical Communication, 24*(2), 127–163.

Tenopir, C., & King, D. W. (2004). *Communication patterns of engineers*. New York: Wiley and IEEE.

Torrance, M. (2007). Cognitive process in the development of writing expertise. *Encyclopedia of language and literacy development*, 1–7. Retrieved from http://literacyencyclopedia.ca/index.php?fa=items.show&topicId=254

U.S. Department of Labor. (2010). *Bureau of Labor Statistics: Occupational outlook handbook: 2010–11 edition*. Retrieved from http://www.bls.gov/oco/ocos319.htm

Visser, W. (2006). *The cognitive artifacts of designing*. Mahwah, NJ: Erlbaum.

Wallace, D., & Hayes, J. R. (1991). Redefining revision for freshmen. *Research in the Teaching of English, 25*(1), 54–66.

Wegner, D. (2004). The collaborative construction of a management report in a municipal community of practice: Text, context, genre and learning. *Journal of Business and Technical Communication, 18*(4), 411–451.

Winner, E. (1996). *Gifted children: Myths and realities*. New York: Basic Books.

Winsor, D. A. (1996). *Writing like an engineer: A rhetorical education*. Mahwah, NJ: Erlbaum.

Winsor, D. A. (1998). Rhetorical practices in technical work. *Journal of Business and Technical Communication, 12*(3), 343–370.

Winsor, D. A. (2001). Learning to do knowledge work in systems of distributed cognition. *Journal of Business and Technical Communication, 15*(1), 5–28.

Wishbow, N. A. (1988). *Studies of creativity in poets.* Unpublished doctoral dissertation, Carnegie Mellon University, Pittsburgh, PA. Dissertation Abstracts International database. Retrieved from http://proquest.umi.com/pqdweb?index=0&did=746071191&SrchMode=1&sid=19&Fmt=2&VInst=PROD&VType=PQD&RQT=309&VName=PQD&TS=1307391249&clientId=72762&cfc=1

Witte, S. P. (1987). Pre-text and composing. *College Composition and Communication, 38*(4), 397–435.

Wojahn, P., Dyke, J., Riley, L. A., Hensel, E., & Brown, S. C. (2001). Blurring boundaries between technical communication and engineering: Challenges of a multidisciplinary, client-based pedagogy. *Technical Communication Quarterly, 10*(2), 129–148.

Young, R. E. (1980). Arts, crafts, gifts, and knacks: Some disharmonies in the new rhetoric. *Visible Language, 14*(4), 341–350.

Part IV

Levels of Language Processes in Writing: Word, Sentence, and Text

13

Translating Nonverbal Pictures Into Verbal Word Names
Understanding Lexical Access and Retrieval

PATRICK BONIN, SÉBASTIEN ROUX,
and CHRISTOPHER BARRY

*T*his chapter is concerned with written naming. Cognitive neuropsychological analyses of impaired spelling and writing have made substantial contributions to the identification and characterization of the processing levels that underlie literate written word production. This chapter reviews studies of acquired writing disorders and experimental studies of healthy adults, based on real-time techniques, to discuss the following major issues relating to word naming in general (spoken and writing) and written naming in particular: (a) the number and nature of the processing levels involved; (b) the role of phonological codes in the access to and retrieval of orthographic codes; (c) the way information flows between the different processing levels; and (d) the factors influencing lexical access and naming speed.

Language can be expressed in a number of communicative modes—in speech, in gestural signs, and in writing—but most psycholinguistic research has concentrated on language comprehension rather than production. Within the realm of language production, the past decades have seen a good number of investigations into the processes and mechanisms underlying spoken word production. As a result, detailed computational accounts of speech production have been advanced (e.g., Dell, Schwartz, Martin, Saffran, & Gagnon, 1997; Levelt, Roelofs, & Meyer, 1999). In contrast, there have been few studies devoted to understanding language production in writing. This chapter focuses on *written word production*, namely, how orthographic codes corresponding to individual words are accessed and produced from semantic information, especially in naming.

The retrieval of words is a fundamental and mandatory process that is at the root of every conversation or written document. It is not possible to produce a sentence or even a phrase without retrieving individual words from lexical memory, and individuals with impaired word access have severe difficulties of language production.

The word occupies a key position in psycholinguistic research (Balota, 1994). Even though spoken word production in both brain-damaged and healthy adults has been studied extensively in recent years (Caramazza, 1997; Dell, Martin, & Schwartz, 2007; Griffin & Crew, in press; Levelt et al., 1999), few publications have involved the experimental study of written word production using real-time paradigms in healthy adults. Furthermore, many of the studies of adult written production have been largely concerned with the production of texts (Levy & Randsell, 1996; Piolat & Pélissier, 1998) or have focused on describing the motor planning of handwriting movements (Van Galen, 1991). In neither of these areas, however, has the question of lexical access in written naming been systematically addressed.

Most of the evidence concerning lexical access in the process of written word production has come from cognitive neuropsychology. Indeed, the study of brain-damaged patients with impaired spelling and writing has proved to be particularly fruitful and has provided the foundation for the most important theories concerning written naming. However, neuropsychological data cannot constitute the only approach to understanding written word production. The experimental study of accurate written production of words in healthy adults is necessary to validate and develop theories motivated by the study of neuropsychological dissociations.

The aim of this chapter is to provide an overview of the developments of written word production with an emphasis on the recent studies conducted on healthy adults using on-line, chronometric techniques. Most of the data using real-time written picture naming tasks have proved to be broadly consistent with the cognitive neuropsychological results. More importantly, however, these findings have often made it possible to both fine tune certain theoretical views as well as impose constraints upon accounts of lexical access in the spoken and written production of words.

We begin with a brief description of the processing levels that are involved in both spoken and written word production and present the major theoretical controversies concerning the processing levels involved in word production. A model of written (and spoken) word production will be presented to clarify this review. Finally, three major issues in written word production will be addressed: the role of phonological information in the access to orthographic codes; the way information flows within the conceptual-lexical production system; and the factors influencing naming speed.

PROCESSING LEVELS IN WORD PRODUCTION

Virtually all our knowledge concerning lexical access during written production has come from analyses of patterns of impaired and preserved performance in brain-damaged patients with acquired dysgraphia. Thus, it is not surprising that models of written word production have mostly been provided by cognitive neuropsychologists (Ellis, 1982; Nickels, 2002; Rapp, Epstein, & Tainturier, 2002). The processing levels that have been identified are, to some extent, similar to those involved in spoken word production (Bonin & Fayol, 2000).

Theorists of language production distinguish between three major processing levels: conceptualization, formulation, and execution (Bock & Levelt, 1994; Caramazza, 1997; Dell et al., 1997; Levelt et al., 1999). However, agreement between researchers does not extend much beyond this broad characterization. Theories of how speakers move from an activated concept to its expression in speech differ concerning the *number* of the processing stages involved and whether the temporal dynamics of processing between the stages is serial and discrete (where processing at one stage must be finished before the next begins), cascaded (where activation from one stage feeds forward to the next before processing is completed), or fully interactive (where partially activated "later" stages can feed back to affect "earlier" stages). It is not possible here to review all these issues concerning the number and nature of the levels of processing involved in language production, but we will briefly consider the most important ones.

CHARACTERIZATION OF THE LEVELS IN WORD PRODUCTION

There are many differences among theories regarding the number and nature of the processing levels involved in spoken word production (Caramazza, 1997; Nickels, 2002). There is a debate concerning the nature of the semantic representations involved and the way in which these contact lexical representations. One question is whether a lexical representation (e.g., *father*) is contacted via the activation of its component semantic primitives (e.g., *parent* and *male*) (Caramazza, 1997; Dell, 1986, 1988; Dell & O'Seaghdha, 1991, 1992) or via a unique concept (e.g., *father*) (Roelofs, 2000). Another issue is whether the structural level—which corresponds to knowledge about the canonical perceptual description of objects— forms part of the conceptual-semantic level (Levelt et al., 1999) or is distinct from it, as argued by Humphreys, Riddoch, and Quinlan (1988) and Humphreys, Lamote, and Lloyd-Jones (1995). Yet another issue is whether it is necessary to distinguish between conceptual semantics and lexical semantics as suggested by the existence of patients who, even though they are unable to retrieve the names of objects in response to pictures or definitions or who make semantic errors (e.g., *fork* produced as *knife*) in verbal tasks, appear to be able to use the corresponding objects correctly (Nickels, 2000).

Although researchers accept that there is a lexical level (where words are stored as whole representations), along with sublexical phonological (segments or individual phonemes) and orthographic (graphemes) levels, they continue to debate the number and nature of the lexical levels involved (Caramazza, 1997). There has been considerable debate as to whether speech production entails the activation of an abstract lexical level (called lemmas), which mediates between concepts and the lexical form of the words (called lexemes), or whether conceptual information maps directly onto lexemes (Caramazza 1997; Miozzo & Caramazza, 1997; Roelofs, Meyer, & Levelt, 1998). The debate is sometimes referred to as the "two-stage" versus the "single-stage" view of lexical access (Figure 13.1). Lemmas were initially referred to as semantically and syntactically specified representations (Levelt, 1989), but have later been conceived as abstract, amodal representations including or providing access to a word's grammatical features (e.g., verb or noun and grammatical gender). Lexemes are lexical phonological representations. Different types of evidence have been put forward for the lemma-lexeme distinction but the tip-of-the-tongue (TOT) phenomenon has been considered the most intuitively appealing. In a TOT state, a speaker has the feeling of knowing the meaning of a word that she or he cannot produce (Brown & McNeill, 1966; see Brown, 2008, for a review). TOT has been accounted for as reflecting a temporary failure to retrieve a lexeme in the context of the successful retrieval of a lemma (Ferrand, 2001; Vigliocco, Antonini, & Garrett, 1997). Caramazza (1997) and Caramazza and Miozzo (1997) have argued that an amodal lemma representational level is unnecessary (see more recent arguments in Caramazza, Bi, Costa, & Miozzo, 2004; Cuetos, Bonin, Ramon Alameda, & Caramazza, 2010; Miozzo & Caramazza, 2005). In Caramazza's view, grammatical features are linked to lexical forms and that, in contrast to the lemma position, word syntax is accessible from word forms (or lexemes in Figure 13.1).

As far as written production is concerned, there has been no corresponding debate of the lemma-lexeme distinction. Pickering and Branigan (1998) argued that there was no reason to deny this distinction in written production and so proposed that there are lemmas in written production as well as for phonological word production. Adjudicating between two-stage and single-stage models of lexical access is beyond the scope of this chapter. Therefore, following Rapp and Goldrick (2000), we will use the neutral term "lexical level" (the "L-level"). Theorists of spoken word production agree that, in addition to a holistic lexical level, there is also a sublexical level where individual sounds are represented, which is necessary to account, for instance, for speech errors such as phoneme exchanges (e.g., "mad banners" for "bad manners"). Thus, in written naming, we will assume that there is a lexical level, which corresponds to whole-word

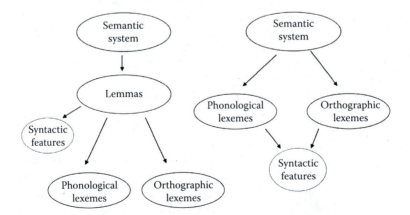

Figure 13.1   Two-stage versus single-stage models of lexical access in word production.

orthographic representations, and a sublexical level, which consists (minimally) of individual graphemes.

MODEL OF SPOKEN AND WRITTEN WORD PRODUCTION

As in spoken naming, written naming involves a conceptual level, an orthographic lexical level, and sublexical levels of representation. Sublexical levels include several dimensions, such as graphosyllables, consonant and vowel status of graphemes (Cubelli, 1991), and the identity of graphemes and geminates (Tainturier & Caramazza, 1996). In handwriting, it is possible to distinguish between several postorthographic levels: allographic (which specifies case assignment and style), letter shape assignment, graphic motor pattern retrieval, and graphic motor execution (Ellis, 1988; Rapp & Caramazza, 1997). We have outlined a theoretical framework for the processes underlying written naming in Figure 13.2, which builds in part on proposals made by Caramazza (1997), Miceli, Benvegnu, Capasso, and Caramazza (1997), and Bonin, Peereman, and Fayol (2001).

In our model of written naming shown in Figure 13.2, the first processing level is object identification, which results from the activation of stored structural descriptions (Humphreys et al., 1988, 1995). These representations send activation to semantic representations. Activation then flows, in parallel, from semantic representations to phonological and orthographic lexemes (or word forms). Finally, activation propagates from orthographic lexemes to the grapheme level, where abstract representations corresponding to individual graphemes and their positions are specified. Phonological and orthographic lexemes are not directly connected to each other, but interact via sublexical connections between phonological and orthographic units (the O → P and P → O conversion connections in Figure 13.2). Evidence for such links comes from analyses of the dysgraphic errors of brain-damaged patients (e.g., Miceli, Capasso, & Caramazza, 1999) and the naming performance in healthy adults in real-time experiments (Bonin et al., 2001). We will assume that activation is passed between different levels in a cascaded manner (Caramazza, 1997), but will return to the issue of activation dynamics later. The model assumes that the structural and semantic levels are common to both output modes. One piece of indirect evidence in favor of these shared processing levels was provided by Bonin and Fayol (2000). In this study, French participants had to produce picture names while hearing distractor words. In one experiment, distractors semantically related to the picture names yielded a semantic interference effect in both spoken and written picture naming when presented with a stimulus onset asynchrony (SOA) of –150 ms but not when an SOA of 0 ms was used.[1] The similar pattern of activation of semantic representations was taken to suggest that the semantic level was shared between speaking and writing. Indeed, Nickels (2002) claimed that "few, if any, authors would propose separate semantic information for spoken and written material" (p. 10).

---

[1] The logic behind the use of different SOAs for distractor presentations is to tap into successive stages of target processing, with "early" (i.e., more negative) SOAs tapping early stages of processing and "late" (positive) SOAs tapping later stages.

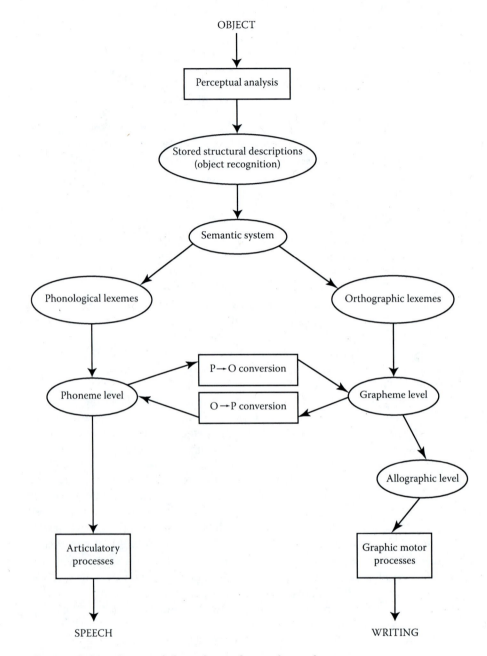

Figure 13.2 A framework for understanding spoken and written naming.

ROLE OF PHONOLOGICAL CODES IN ACCESS TO ORTHOGRAPHY IN WRITTEN WORD PRODUCTION

Obligatory Phonological Mediation Hypothesis

According to the obligatory phonological mediation (OPM) hypothesis, access to orthography is dependent on the prior access of a phonological code (Geschwind, 1969; Luria, 1970). This hypothesis (Rapp & Caramazza, 1997; Rapp, Benzing, & Caramazza, 1997) reflects the fact that spoken language precedes, both ontogenetically and phylogenetically, written language (Scinto, 1986) and is used much more frequently. It is also consistent with the presence of phonologically based spelling errors (Aitchison & Todd, 1982), such as homophone substitutions (e.g., *there* for *their*) and phonologically plausible pseudoword productions (e.g., *yot* for *yacht*), and with the introspective experience of inner speech that often accompanies writing (Hotopf, 1980).

The OPM hypothesis has been challenged by a number of neuropsychological studies of dissociations between spoken and written word production. It has been found that written naming can be relatively spared in some patients with impaired spoken production that cannot be attributed to damaged peripheral, articulatory processes (Bub & Kertesz, 1982; Rapp & Caramazza, 1997; Shelton & Weinrich, 1997). Also, some patients exhibit inconsistent lexical responses in their written and spoken responses to the same targets (e.g., a correct written response and a spoken semantic error, or the reverse; or, two distinct semantic errors to the same target, as in the spoken response "church" and the written response *piano* to the stimulus "organ"; Miceli et al., 1997; Miceli & Capasso, 1997; Miceli, Capasso, & Caramazza, 1999). Different responses in written compared to spoken picture naming cannot be explained by the OPM hypothesis, which predicts that phonology underlies both forms of language production.

Orthographic Autonomy Hypothesis

To account for the neuropsychological data, the orthographic autonomy (OA) hypothesis (Miceli et al., 1997; Rapp & Caramazza, 1997; Rapp et al., 1997) assumes that the retrieval of orthographic codes does not obligatorily require the prior access to phonology. Instead, the OA hypothesis proposes that activation from semantic representations propagates directly and in parallel to both orthographic and phonological word forms. Although the data observed in patients favor the OA hypothesis, the possibility remains that, in normal writing, phonological information might combine with semantic specifications to constrain the selection of orthographic codes.

Only a few empirical studies have addressed the relationships between phonological and orthographic codes using chronometric tasks with healthy adults. However, in one such study, Bonin, Fayol, and Peereman (1998) tested the OA hypothesis by examining the priming of real-time and accurate written word production (see also Bonin, Fayol, & Gombert, 1997). They used the masked form priming paradigm to investigate the dynamics of phonological and orthographic activation in written naming. In this technique, the visibility of the prime is reduced by using short prime durations and forward and backward masking. Ferrand, Grainger, and Segui (1994) used this procedure to investigate spoken naming using nonword primes that were (a) pseudohomophones, (b) nonhomophones, but with the same degree of orthographic overlap as the pseudohomophones (orthographic primes), or (c) nonhomophones that were orthographically and phonologically unrelated to the picture names, with the exception of the first letter (control primes). Ferrand et al. found that spoken naming latencies were faster following pseudohomophones compared to either orthographic and control primes, which did not differ. Bonin et al. (1998) used the same priming conditions but required participants to write down, rather than speak aloud, the names of pictures. Orthographic priming effects were observed with prime exposure durations of 34 and 51 ms but not with a shorter exposure duration of 17 ms. The homophony of prime words did not yield any additional priming advantage. These findings support the OA hypothesis according to which orthographic codes are retrieved directly from semantic specifications.

In a different approach, Bonin, Peereman, and Fayol (2001) investigated whether phonological codes constrain the selection of orthographic codes by studying the effect of sound-to-spelling consistency on written naming latencies. The phoneme-to-grapheme consistency of object names was manipulated at the lexical level (by comparing heterographic homophones and nonhomophones in their Experiment 1) or at the sublexical level (by comparing regular and irregular, or exception, words in their Experiments 2 and 3). Experiment 3 also manipulated the position of inconsistently spelled phonemes within the object's name (initial vs. middle or final). The most important finding was that only initial inconsistencies affected written naming latencies. The possibility that this finding merely resulted from the fact that handwriting could start before the full orthographic encoding of the endings of words was ruled out by the results of two further experiments. These found that middle and final inconsistencies *did* affect written latencies in a spelling-to-dictation task, as when stimulus words were presented in a phonological form, there would be more scope for sublexical P $\rightarrow$ O conversion to affect written latencies. Bonin, Collay, Fayol, and Méot (2005) and Delattre, Bonin, and Barry (2006) have also found effects of sound-to-spelling or P $\rightarrow$ O consistency (or regularity) on writing latencies in the spelling-to-dictation task.

Bonin et al. (2001) interpreted their results by suggesting that the buildup of orthographic activation in written picture naming is constrained by phonology. In terms of the model in Figure 13.2, the consistency effect on written latencies suggests that activation at the grapheme level is constrained by the sequential operation of sublexical P $\rightarrow$ O conversion. Encoding for written production occurs as a result of activation from both the semantics $\rightarrow$ orthographic lexemes $\rightarrow$ grapheme pathway and the sublexical P $\rightarrow$ O conversion procedure. As soon as enough information is available at the grapheme level, it is transmitted for further processing dedicated to letter-shape encoding and the peripheral motor processes of writing production. The reason why inconsistencies located in the middle or final part of words did not affect latencies to initiate written responses is because a full specification of the orthographic codes was achieved through the semantic-to-lexical pathway before there were effects of the sublexical P $\rightarrow$ O conversion of the end of the word.

Since the Bonin et al. (2001) study, very little research has examined the role of phonological codes in healthy adults undertaking semantically driven written word production in tasks such as written naming. Recently, however, Zhang and Damian (2010) used the picture–word interference paradigm to investigate the activation dynamics of phonological and orthographic codes in handwriting production. In this paradigm, participants were required to write down the name of a picture while attempting to ignore a superimposed printed distractor word presented at various SOAs. The distractor words were orthographically and phonologically related (e.g., the word *dread* on a picture of a HEAD), orthographically related only (e.g., *bead* on HEAD, *year* on BEAR), or unrelated. Uppercase is used to indicate target names of presented pictures.

As shown in Table 13.1, Zhang and Damian (2010) found a phonological facilitation effect at an early SOA of 0 ms and an orthographic effect at a later SOA of +100 ms. In a second experiment, they used concurrent articulatory suppression to diminish the contribution of phonological codes in written naming. Using the same conditions as in their first experiment, they found that the purely phonological facilitation effect was diminished with an SOA of 0 ms, but there remained (and at a similar level) a purely orthographic effect with an SOA of +100 ms. Zhang and Damian's results may be interpreted within the theoretical framework we have presented here, as follows. The phonological priming effect observed with an SOA of 0 ms suggests that there is an early stage during processing when writing is strongly affected by phonology. According to this scenario, activation from semantics via the phonological pathway is transmitted relatively rapidly to the grapheme level, whereas activation via the direct pathway arrives slightly later. As Zhang and Damian acknowledge, this interpretation needs to be strengthened by a more detailed account of the temporal dynamics of the underlying processing mechanisms. Therefore, there is a great need for more empirical studies using on-line techniques in more sophisticated experimental designs, such as various priming procedures (including masked-form priming), to better understand the time course of activation of phonological and orthographic codes in written word production. Research in visual word *recognition* has pursued such a fine-grained

TABLE 13.1   Facilitation Effects (in ms) at Different Target-Distractor of Stimulus Onset Asynchronies (SOAs)

	SOA		
	0	+100	+200
Normal writing			
Orthographic	11	55	3
Orthographic + phonological	36	43	7
Writing under articulatory suppression			
Orthographic	12	41	8
Orthographic + phonological	16	30	18

The results of Zhang and Damian (2010), shown as facilitation effects as a function of SOAs and distractor conditions (orthographic and phonological distractors), in normal writing and in writing under articulatory suppression.

study of the dynamics of access to orthographic and phonological codes, by using a wide range of SOAs and different conditions to measure facilitation and inhibition effects (Grainger, Carreiras, & Perea, 2000; Ziegler, Ferrand, Jacobs, Rey, & Grainger, 2000). Similarly detailed studies of written word naming have yet to be reported. In particular, more studies are required to better understand the role of sublexical P → O conversion and how this constrains (or interacts with) the activation and execution of orthographic lexemes.

INFORMATION FLOW WITHIN THE COGNITIVE ARCHITECTURE OF WRITTEN WORD PRODUCTION

There is very little agreement among researchers concerning how information flows within the language production system (Nickels, 2002). In the field of speech production, there has been a long debate between proponents of the discrete-serial view (Levelt et al., 1999) and cascaded and interactive views (Caramazza, 1997; Dell et al., 1997; Humphreys et al., 1988). The bulk of empirical (and computational) data from recent years seem to have favored the cascaded view of speech production. Over the past 20 years, many studies of spoken word production have tested cascading (or interactive) architectures (e.g., Jescheniak & Schriefers, 1998; Levelt et al., 1991; Peterson & Savoy, 1998). We will now focus on recent evidence concerning this issue from studies of the picture–picture interference paradigm. One crucial question concerning speech planning that has been addressed by this paradigm is whether phonological activation is confined to the selected (and eventually produced) target word or whether it also occurs for other semantically activated words.

In the picture–picture paradigm, participants are presented with two overlapping pictures (see the example in Figure 13.3), one in green ink and one in red ink, and are told to always name the object in green ink (the target) and to ignore the one in red ink (the context or distractor object). In an influential study of spoken naming, Morsella and Miozzo (2002) found that target naming latencies were facilitated when the name of the context picture was phonologically related to the target (e.g., the target object BED was named faster with the context picture BELL compared to HAT). Because this phonological facilitation effect was not shown when Italian participants (for whom the picture names had no phonological similarity) named the identical stimuli, the results could not have been due to any perceptual

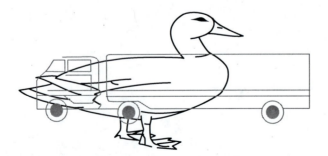

Figure 13.3   An example of a pair of superimposed pictures.

or conceptual relationships between the pictures. Morsella and Miozzo's results clearly support a cascade model of spoken word production, as they show that the phonological forms of the (irrelevant) context pictures were activated and affect target picture naming times (see also Meyer & Damian, 2007; Navarrete & Costa, 2005; Roelofs, 2008); but this effect was not replicated by Jescheniak et al. (2009). Serial-discrete models posit that phonological activation is restricted to a selected lexical unit (or a selected lemma, according to Levelt et al., 1999); however, cascade models posit that multiple lexical candidates will be phonologically activated. Recently, Oppermann, Jescheniak, Schriefers, and Görges (2010) further investigated cascading effects in spoken naming in the picture–picture paradigm that also presents additional auditory distractor words. They found that for semantically related pictures (e.g., APFEL and KIRSCHE [apple and cherry]), auditory distractor words that were phonologically related to the context (i.e., to-be-ignored) objects (e.g., "kirmes") *slowed* naming of the targets. However, there was no effect of phonological relatedness of distractor words to context objects that were semantically unrelated to the targets (e.g., APFEL and WESTE, with "wecker"). This result suggests that "not-to-be named" context objects do activate their phonological codes under certain conditions, indicative of cascaded processing.

Most of the evidence concerning the flow of information in written naming comes from analyses of the spelling and writing errors produced by brain-damaged patients. Semantic errors in written naming (e.g., writing *train* to a picture of a CAR) suggest that the names of a range of semantic neighbors, in addition to the target, are orthographically activated (Rapp et al., 1997). However, the presence of such selection errors cannot constitute direct support for the notion that there is multiple coactivation of lexical candidates by a target concept. Semantic substitution errors may be taken as evidence for cascading activation flow only when they cannot be ascribed to damage at the semantic level. Turning to chronometric data, Bonin and Fayol (2000) argued that cascaded processing does indeed occur. In their study of written naming in the picture–word interference paradigm, they found that distractor words semantically related to target pictures *slowed* written naming latencies, whereas phonologically and orthographically related distractors speeded them. This pattern of results was similar to that reported for spoken word production (Meyer & Schriefers, 1991; Schriefers, Meyer, & Levelt, 1990; Starreveld, 2000). Importantly, Bonin and Fayol (2000) also found that the semantic interference effect was reliably reduced when the distractors were both phonologically and orthographically related to the targets (e.g., the picture CHEVAL with the distractor word *chien*). The serial-discrete view (Levelt et al., 1999) proposes that the semantic interference effect occurs at the level of lemma selection, whereas the phonological facilitation effect occurs at the level of phonological encoding (Schriefers et al., 1990). Thus, this view claims that the semantic interference effect should not be modulated by a phonological relationship. The interaction between semantic and phonological relatedness found in both written (Bonin & Fayol, 2000) and spoken naming (Damian & Martin, 1999; Starreveld & La Heij, 1995) is at variance with the discrete-serial view and appears to favor a cascaded view of word production. However, this finding has given rise to a complex technical debate (Roelofs, Meyer, & Levelt, 1996; Starreveld & La Heij, 1996).

Roux and Bonin (in press) have recently used the picture–picture paradigm to investigate the cascading of information during written word production. In their first experiment, participants wrote the names of target pictures accompanied by superimposed context pictures that had phonologically and orthographically related names (e.g., COUTEAU and COURONNE; knife and crown) or unrelated names. In a second experiment, the related condition consisted of target and context pictures that shared the initial letter but not the initial sound (e.g., CIGARE and CAMION; examples in English would be CAT and KITE, and NOSE and KNIFE). Written latencies were faster in the related than in the unrelated conditions in both experiments, which suggests that activation at the object recognition level cascades (and quite quickly) to the orthographic lexeme level. Because control experiments ruled out a perceptual and conceptual contribution to the facilitation effects found in the naming experiments, these results support the view that activation within the lexical system flows in a cascaded manner for written naming.

FACTORS INFLUENCING THE SPEED OF LEXICAL ACCESS

Numerous studies have attempted to identify the various factors that affect spoken naming times (e.g., Barry, Morrison, & Ellis, 1997; Cycowicz, Friedman, Rothstein, & Snodgrass, 1997; Ellis & Morrison, 1998; Lachman, Schaffer, & Henrikus, 1974; Morrison, Ellis, & Quinlan, 1992; Snodgrass & Yuditsky, 1996; Vitkovitch & Tyrrell, 1995). These studies have helped to identify and characterize the processes and representations underlying spoken picture naming. Among the factors that have been investigated are visual complexity, image agreement, imageability, conceptual familiarity, name agreement, word frequency, age of acquisition (AoA), and different measures of word length (number of phonemes, letters, or syllables).

1. Visual complexity refers to the number of lines and details in the pictured object and is thought to index the early perceptual and structural levels of object recognition.
2. Image agreement refers to the degree to which the mental image generated by participants in response to the picture's name agrees with the actual, pictured object, and is thought to have its influence at the level of object recognition (Barry et al., 1997).
3. Imageability is a measure of the extent to which an object's name evokes a mental image and is widely recognized as indexing semantic richness (Plaut & Shallice, 1993), as high-imageability words have "richer" semantic representations than low-imageability words.
4. Concept familiarity refers to the rated familiarity of the depicted concept and is also believed to be a semantic variable.
5. Name agreement is a measure of the variability of names given to a picture across participants. Pictures that elicit many different names have lower name agreement than those that elicit single, common names.

The roles of the word frequency and AoA of object names on naming times have been investigated extensively over the past 20 years. Word frequency is a measure of the degree of use of a given word, as is generally assessed on the basis of counts of written corpora. AoA refers to the age at which words are learned and has been measured by asking adults to estimate this age (e.g., Morrison et al., 1992) or by when children of various ages can produce words as names to pictures (e.g., Morrison, Chappell, & Ellis, 1997). Studies of AoA effects go back as far as the work of Rochford and Williams (1962). Since then, numerous studies have found that early-acquired words are faster or easier to process than later-acquired words. AoA effects have been found in a variety of lexical tasks (word reading, naming, semantic categorization, etc.), in many languages with different orthographic systems (e.g., English, French, Spanish, Italian, Turkish, and Chinese), and in different populations (monolinguals, bilinguals, children, adults, and various brain-damaged patients; see Johnston & Barry, 2006, for a review). However, significant problems relating to the status of the measures of AoA have been raised by Zevin and Seidenberg (2002) and Bonin, Barry, Méot, and Chalard (2004). Zevin and Seidenberg have been extremely critical of the use of traditional AoA measures, which they argue reflect aspects of performance rather than being genuinely "independent" variables.

Alario et al. (2004) reviewed several studies of spoken naming conducted in French, English, Spanish, Italian, and even Welsh that investigated the influence of different factors in naming speed. Their review indentified the most important predictors as being AoA and name agreement, as well as, but to a lesser extent, image agreement and word frequency. The only study of written naming reviewed by Alario et al. was by Bonin, Chalard, Méot, and Fayol (2002), which was undertaken to explore the factors that affect both written and spoken naming latencies. The results of various multiple regression analyses by Bonin et al. revealed that from a set of nine independent variables, image variability, image agreement, AoA, and name agreement significantly influenced both written and spoken naming latencies. Importantly, there was a striking similarity among the percentages of variance explained by these factors in the two production modes. An AoA effect has also been replicated by Bonin, Fayol, and Chalard (2001). The findings of Bonin et al. (2002) suggest that the two production modes share some processing levels, including, of course, the structural and semantic levels. However, a general consensus concerning the effect of AoA has yet to be achieved. Different researchers have claimed that AoA effects are located at the lexical level, the semantic level, the links between different types of representations, or even links between the perceptual and structural levels. Actually, there exists a similar variety of interpretations of word frequency effects in spoken and written naming (Knobel, Finkbeiner, & Caramazza, 2008). More work is clearly needed to address the issue of the loci of AoA and word frequency effects in both spoken and written naming.

CONCLUSIONS

Analyses of the impaired performance of brain-damaged patients have provided important insights into the organization of the processes and representations involved in written word production. However, as we have emphasized throughout this chapter, it would be both unwise and incomplete to rely solely on cognitive neuropsychological data to support general theories of written naming. We claim that the experimental chronometric study of accurate written word production in healthy adults and children is also necessary to constrain, elaborate, and fine tune details of theoretical models of written word production. We hope this chapter will convince readers that the experimental study of written naming in healthy adults is indeed useful. For a long time researchers have focused on spoken language production, but even the most prominent models of speech production (i.e., Levelt et al., 1999) say very little about how spoken word production relates to written word production. As stated by Griffin and Crew (in press), "language production cannot be synonymous with speech production." We share the view proposed by Miceli et al. (1997) that certain unresolved general problems relating to the lexical system may be better understood if we take into account people's performance in both the spoken *and* written production of words.

REFERENCES

Aitchison, J., & Todd, P. (1982). Slips of the mind and slips of the pen. In B. N. Chir & W. von Raffler-Engel (Eds.), *Language and cognitive styles: Patterns of neurolinguistic and psycholinguistic development* (pp. 180–194). Swets and Zeitlinger: B.V.-Lise.

Alario, F.-X., Ferrand, L., Laganaro, M., New, B., Frauenfelder, U. H., & Segui, J. (2004). Predictors of picture naming speed. *Behavior Research Methods Instruments and Computers, 36*, 140–155.

Balota, D. A. (1994). Visual word recognition: The journey from features to meaning. In M. A. Gernsbacher (Ed.), *Handbook of psycholinguistics* (pp. 303–358). New York: Academic Press.

Barry, C., Morrison, C. M., & Ellis, A. W. (1997). Naming the Snodgrass and Vanderwart pictures: Effects of age of acquisition, frequency, and name agreement. *Quarterly Journal of Experimental Psychology, 50A*, 560–585.

Bock, J. K., & Levelt, W. J. M. (1994). Language production: Grammatical encoding. In M. A. Gernsbacher (Ed.), *Handbook of psycholinguistics* (pp. 945–984). New York: Academic Press.

Bonin, P., Barry, C., Méot, A., & Chalard, M. (2004). The influence of age of acquisition in word reading and other tasks: A never ending story? *Journal of Memory and Language, 50*, 456–476.

Bonin, P., Chalard, M., Méot, A., & Fayol, M. (2002). The determinants of spoken and written picture naming latencies. *British Journal of Psychology, 93*, 89–114.

Bonin, P., Collay, S., Fayol, M., & Méot, A. (2005). Attentional strategic control over sublexical and lexical processing in written spelling to dictation in adults. *Memory and Cognition, 33*, 59–75.

Bonin, P., & Fayol, M. (2000). Writing words from pictures: What representations are activated and when? *Memory and Cognition, 28*, 677–689.

Bonin, P., Fayol, M., & Chalard, M. (2001). Age of acquisition and word frequency in written picture naming. *Quarterly Journal of Experimental Psychology, 54A*, 469–489.

Bonin, P., Fayol, M., & Gombert, J. E. (1997). Role of phonological and orthographic codes in picture naming and writing: An interference paradigm study. *Current Psychology of Cognition, 16*, 299–320.

Bonin, P., Fayol, M., & Peereman, R. (1998). Masked form priming in writing words from pictures: Evidence for direct retrieval of orthographic codes. *Acta Psychologica, 99*, 311–328.

Bonin, P., Peereman, R., & Fayol, M. (2001). Do phonological codes constrain the selection of orthographic codes in written picture naming? *Journal of Memory and Language, 45*, 688–720.

Brown, A. S. (2008). Tip of the tongue experience. In H. L. Roediger (Ed.), *Cognitive psychology of memory*. Vol. 2: *Learning and memory: A comprehensive reference* (pp. 377–387). Oxford: Elsevier.

Brown, R., & McNeill, D. (1966). The "tip of the tongue" phenomenon. *Journal of Verbal Learning and Verbal Behavior, 5*, 325–337.

Bub, D., & Kertesz, A. (1982). Evidence for lexicographic processing in a patient with pre-served written over oral single word naming. *Brain, 105*, 697–717.

Caramazza, A. (1997). How many levels of processing are there in lexical access? *Cognitive Neuropsychology, 14*, 177–208.

Caramazza, A., Bi, Y., Costa, A., & Miozzo, M. (2004). What determines the speed of lexical access: Homophone or specific-word frequency? A Reply to Jescheniak et al. (2003). *Journal of Experimental Psychology: Learning, Memory, and Cognition, 30*, 278–282.

Caramazza, A., & Miozzo, M. (1997). The relation between syntactic and phonological knowledge in lexical access: Evidence from the 'tip-of-the-tongue' phenomenon. *Cognition, 64*, 309–343.

Cubelli, R. (1991). A selective deficit for writing vowels in acquired dysgraphia. *Nature, 353*, 258–260.

Cuetos, F., Bonin, P., Ramon Alameda, J., & Caramazza, A. (2010). The specific-word fre-quency effect in speech production: Evidence from Spanish and French. *Quarterly Journal of Experimental Psychology, 63*(4), 750–771.

Cycowicz, Y. M., Friedman, D., Rothstein, M., & Snodgrass, J. G. (1997). Picture naming by young children: Norms for name agreement, familiarity, and visual complexity. *Journal of Experimental Child Psychology, 65*, 171–237.

Damian, M. F., & Martin, R. C. (1999). Semantic and phonological codes interact in single word production. *Journal of Experimental Psychology: Learning, Memory, and Cognition, 25*, 345–361.

Delattre, M., Bonin, P., & Barry, C. (2006). Written spelling to dictation: Sound-to-spelling regularity affects both writing latencies and durations. *Journal of Experimental Psychology: Learning, Memory, and Cognition, 32*, 1330–1340.

Dell, G. S. (1986). A spreading-activation theory of retrieval in sentence production. *Psychological Review, 93*, 283–321.

Dell, G. S. (1988). The retrieval of phonological forms in production: Tests of prediction from a connectionist model. *Journal of Memory and Language, 27*, 124–142.

Dell, G. S., Martin, N., & Schwartz, M. F. (2007). A case-series test of the interactive two-step model of lexical access: Predicting word repetition from picture naming. *Journal of Memory and Language, 56*, 490–520.

Dell, G. S., & O'Seaghdha, P. G. (1991). Mediated and convergent lexical priming in language production: A comment on Levelt et al. *Psychological Review, 4*, 604–614.

Dell, G. S., & O'Seaghdha, P. G. (1992). Stages of lexical access in language production. *Cognition, 42*, 287–314.

Dell, G. S., Schwartz, M. F., Martin, N., Saffran, E. M., & Gagnon, D. A. (1997). Lexical access in aphasic and non-aphasic speakers. *Psychological Review, 104*, 801–838.

Ellis, A. W. (1982). Spelling and writing (and reading and speaking). In A. W. Ellis (Ed.), *Normality and pathology in cognitive functions* (pp. 113–146). London: Academic Press.

Ellis, A. W. (1988). Normal writing processes and peripherical acquired dysgraphias. *Language and Cognitive Processes, 3,* 99–127.

Ellis, A. W., & Morrison, C. M. (1998). Real age-of-acquisition effects in lexical retrieval. *Journal of Experimental Psychology: Learning, Memory, and Cognition, 24,* 515–523.

Ferrand, L. (2001). Grammatical gender is also on the tip of French tongues. *Current Psychology Letters, 5,* 7–20.

Ferrand, L., Grainger, J., & Segui, J. (1994). A study of masked form priming in picture and word naming. *Memory and Cognition, 22,* 431–441.

Geschwind, N. (1969). Problems in the anatomical understanding of the aphasias. In A. L. Benton (Ed.), *Contributions to clinical neuropsychology.* Chicago: Aldine.

Grainger, J., Carreiras, M., & Perea, M. (2000). A new technique for visual word recognition research: The luminance increment paradigm. *Current Psychology Letters, 1,* 107–116.

Griffin, Z. M., & Crew, C. M. (in press). Research in language production. In M. Spivey, M. Joanisse, & K. McRae (Eds.), *Cambridge handbook of psycholinguistics.* Cambridge, UK: Cambridge University Press.

Hotopf, W. H. N. (1980). Slips of the pen. In U. Frith (Ed.), *Cognitive processes in spelling* (pp. 287–307). New York: Academic Press.

Humphreys, G. W., Lamote, C., & Lloyd-Jones, T. J. (1995). An interactive activation approach to object processing: Effects of structural similarity, name frequency, and task in normality and pathology. *Memory, 3,* 535–586.

Humphreys, G. W., Riddoch, M. J., & Quinlan, P. T. (1988). Cascade processes in picture identification. *Cognitive Neuropsychology, 5,* 67–103.

Jescheniak, J. D., Oppermann, F., Hantsch, A., Wagner, V., Mädebach, A., & Schriefers, H. (2009). Do perceived context pictures automatically activate their phonological code? *Experimental Psychology, 56,* 56–65.

Jescheniak, J. D., & Schriefers, H. (1998). Discrete serial versus cascaded processing in lexical access in speech production: Further evidence from the coactivation of near-synonyms. *Journal of Experimental Psychology: Learning, Memory, and Cognition, 24,* 1256–1274.

Johnston, R. A., & Barry, C. (2006). Age of acquisition and lexical processing. *Visual Cognition, 13,* 789–845.

Knobel, M., Finkbeiner, M., & Caramazza, A. (2008). The many places of frequency: Evidence for a novel locus of the lexical frequency effect in word production. *Cognitive Neuropsychology, 25,* 256–286.

Lachman, R., Schaffer, J. P., & Henrikus, D. (1974). Language and cognition: Effects of stimulus codability, name-word frequency, and age-of-acquisition on lexical reaction time. *Journal of Verbal Learning and Verbal Behavior, 13,* 613–625.

Levelt, W. J. M. (1989). *Speaking: From intention to articulation.* Cambridge: MIT Press.

Levelt, W. J. M., Roelofs, A., & Meyer, A. S. (1999). A theory of lexical access in speech production. *Behavioral and Brain Sciences, 22,* 1–75.

Levelt, W. J. M., Schriefers, H., Vorberg, D., Meyer, A. S., Pechmann, T., & Havinga, J. (1991). The time course of lexical access in speech production: A study of picture naming. *Psychological Review, 98,* 122–142.

Levy, C. M., & Randsell, S. E. (1996). *The science of writing: Theories, methods, individual differences, and applications.* Mahwah, NJ: Erlbaum.

Luria, A. R. (1970). *Traumatic aphasia.* The Hague: Mouton.

Meyer, A. S., & Damian, M. F. (2007). Activation of distractor names in the picture-picture interference paradigm. *Memory and Cognition, 35,* 494–503.

Meyer, A. S., & Schriefers, H. (1991). Phonological facilitation in picture-word interference experiments: Effect of stimulus onset asynchrony and types of interfering stimuli. *Journal of Experimental Psychology: Learning, Memory, and Cognition, 17,* 1146–1160.

Miceli, G., Benvegnu, B., Capasso, R., & Caramazza, A. (1997). The independence of phonological and orthographic forms: Evidence from aphasia. *Cognitive Neuropsychology, 14*, 35–69.

Miceli, G., & Capasso, R. (1997). Semantic errors as neuropsychological evidence for the independence and the interaction of orthographic and phonological word forms. *Language and Cognitive Processes, 12*, 733–764.

Miceli, G., Capasso, R., & Caramazza, A. (1999). Sublexical conversion procedures and the interaction of phonological and orthographic forms. *Cognitive Neuropsychology, 16*, 557–572.

Miozzo, M., & Caramazza, A. (1997). The retrieval of lexical-syntactic features in tip-of-the tongue states. *Journal of Experimental Psychology: Learning, Memory, and Cognition, 23*, 1410–1423.

Miozzo, M., & Caramazza, A. (2005). The representation of homophones: Evidence from the distractor frequency effect. *Journal of Experimental Psychology: Language, Memory, and Cognition, 31*, 1360–1371.

Morrison, C. M., Chappell, T. D., & Ellis, A. W. (1997). Age of acquisition norms for a large set of object names and their relation to adult estimates and other variables. *Quarterly Journal of Experimental Psychology, 50A*, 528–559.

Morrison, C. M., Ellis, A. W., & Quinlan, P. T. (1992). Age of acquisition, not word frequency, affects object naming, not object recognition. *Memory and Cognition, 20*, 705–714.

Morsella, E., & Miozzo, M. (2002). Evidence for a cascade model of lexical access in speech production. *Journal of Experimental Psychology: Learning, Memory, and Cognition, 28*, 555–563.

Navarrete, E., & Costa, A. (2005). Phonological activation of ignored pictures: Further evidence for a cascade model of lexical access. *Journal of Memory and Language, 53*, 359–377.

Nickels, L. (2000). Spoken word production. In B. Rapp (Ed.), *The handbook of cognitive neuropsychology* (pp. 291–320). Philadelphia, PA: Psychology Press.

Nickels, L. (2002). Theoretical and methodological issues in the cognitive neuropsychology of spoken word production. *Aphasiology, 16*, 3–19.

Oppermann, F., Jescheniak, J. D., Schriefers, H., & Görges, F. (2010). Semantic relatedness among objects promotes the activation of multiple phonological codes during object naming. *Quarterly Journal of Experimental Psychology, 63*, 356–370.

Peterson, R. R., & Savoy, P. (1998). Lexical selection and phonological encoding during language production: Evidence for cascaded processing. *Journal of Experimental Psychology: Learning, Memory, and Cognition, 24*, 539–557.

Pickering, M. J., & Branigan, H. P. (1998). The representation of verbs: Evidence from syntactic priming in language production. *Journal of Memory and Language, 39*, 633–651.

Piolat, A., & Pélissier, A. (1998). *La rédaction de textes: Approche cognitive.* Lausanne: Delachaux et Niestlé.

Plaut, D. C., & Shallice, T. (1993). Deep dyslexia: A case study of connectionist neuropsychology. *Cognitive Neuropsychology, 10*, 377–500.

Rapp, B., Benzing, L., & Caramazza, A. (1997). The autonomy of lexical orthography. *Cognitive Neuropsychology, 14*, 71–104.

Rapp, B., & Caramazza, A. (1997). From graphemes to abstract letter shapes: Levels of representation in written spelling. *Journal of Experimental Psychology: Human Perception and Performance, 23*, 1130–1152.

Rapp, B., Epstein, C., & Tainturier, M.-J. (2002). The integration of information across lexical and sublexical processes in spelling. *Cognitive Neuropsychology, 19*, 1–29.

Rapp, B., & Goldrick, M. (2000). Discreteness and interactivity in spoken word production. *Psychological Review, 107*, 460–499.

Rochford, G., & Williams, M. (1962). Studies in the development and breakdown of the use of names. *Journal of Neurology, Neurosurgery, and Psychiatry, 25,* 222–233.

Roelofs, A. (1997). The WEAVER model of word-form encoding in speech production. *Cognition, 64,* 249–284.

Roelofs, A. (2000). WEAVER++ and other computational models of lemma retrieval and word-form encoding. In L. Wheeldon (Ed.), *Aspects of language production* (pp. 71–114). Sussex, UK: Psychology Press.

Roelofs, A. (2008). Tracing attention and the activation flow in spoken word planning using eye movements. *Journal of Experimental Psychology: Learning, Memory, and Cognition, 34,* 353–368.

Roelofs, A., Meyer, A. S., & Levelt, W. J. M. (1996). Interaction between semantic and orthographic factors in conceptually driven naming: Comment on Starreveld and La Heij (1995). *Journal of Experimental Psychology: Learning, Memory, and Cognition, 22,* 246–251.

Roelofs, A., Meyer, A. S., & Levelt, W. J. M. (1998). A case for the lemma/lexeme distinction in models of speaking: Comment on Caramazza and Miozzo (1997). *Cognition, 69,* 219–230.

Roux, S., & Bonin, P. (in press). Cascaded processing in written naming: Evidence from the picture-picture interference paradigm. *Language and Cognitive Processes.*

Schriefers, H., Meyer, A. S., & Levelt, W. J. M. (1990). Exploring the time-course of lexical access in language production: Picture-word interference studies. *Journal of Memory and Language, 29,* 86–102.

Scinto, L. F. (1986). *Written language and psychological development.* New York: Academic Press.

Shelton, J. R., & Weinrich, M. (1997). Further evidence for a dissociation between output phonological and orthographic lexicons: A case study. *Cognitive Neuropsychology, 14,* 105–129.

Snodgrass, J. G., & Yuditsky, T. (1996). Naming times for the Snodgrass and Vanderwart pictures. *Behavior Research Methods, Instruments, and Computers, 28,* 516–536.

Starreveld, P. A. (2000). On the interpretation of auditory context effects in word production. *Journal of Memory and Language, 42,* 497–525.

Starreveld, P. A., & La Heij, W. (1995). Semantic interference, orthographic facilitation and their interaction in naming tasks. *Journal of Experimental Psychology: Learning, Memory, and Cognition, 21,* 686–698.

Starreveld, P. A., & La Heij, W. (1996). The locus of orthographic-phonological facilitation: Reply to Roelofs, Meyer, and Levelt (1996). *Journal of Experimental Psychology: Learning, Memory, and Cognition, 22,* 1–4.

Tainturier, M. J., & Caramazza, A. (1996). The status of double letters in graphemic representations. *Journal of Memory and Language, 35,* 53–73.

Van Galen, G. P. (1991). Handwriting: Issues for a psychomotor theory. *Human Movement Science, 10,* 165–191.

Vigliocco, G., Antonini, T., & Garrett, M. F. (1997). Grammatical gender is on the tip of Italian tongues. *Psychological Science, 8,* 314–317.

Vitkovitch, M., & Tyrrell, L. (1995). Sources of disagreement in object naming. *Quarterly Journal of Experimental Psychology, 48A,* 822–848.

Zevin, J. D., & Seidenberg, M. S. (2002). Age of acquisition effects in word reading and other tasks. *Journal of Memory and Language, 47,* 1–29.

Zhang, Q., & Damian, M. F. (2010). Impact of phonology on the generation of handwritten responses: Evidence from picture-word interference tasks. *Memory and Cognition, 38,* 519–528.

Ziegler, J. C., Ferrand, L., Jacobs, A., Rey, A., & Grainger, J. (2000). Visual and phonological codes in letter and word recognition: Evidence from incremental priming. *Quarterly Journal of Experimental Psychology, 53A,* 671–692.

14

Why Should We Take Graphotactic and Morphological Regularities Into Account When Examining Spelling Acquisition?

SÉBASTIEN PACTON, HELENE DEACON, GAELLE BORCHARDT, JULIETTE DANJON, and MICHEL FAYOL

*M*orphophonemic writing systems like English and French lack one-to-one mappings between sounds and spellings. For example, in French, the final sound /o/ is spelled in three different ways in the words *lavabo* (washbasin), *landau* (pram), and *marteau* (hammer); many words include silent letters, especially in the final position (e.g., the unpronounced *d* in the words *bavard* and *buvard*); and most of the time, there is no phonological distinction between whether a consonant is single or double (e.g., *ule* and *ulle* are similarly pronounced in the words *bulle* [bubble] and *formule* [formula]). Consequently, although there is no ambiguity concerning how to read words such as *lavabo* that are usually categorized as regular words in reading tests, there is some uncertainty as to their spellings: For instance, *lavabo* could have been spelled *lavabau*, *lavabeau*, or *lavabot*.

Given these inconsistencies in the mapping between phonemes and graphemes, many researchers and educators assume that the only way to spell words correctly is by individually memorizing the spellings of words (Baron & Treiman, 1980). There is no doubt that the spellings of a host of words have to be memorized (Kessler & Treiman, 2001). However, these inconsistencies are not totally unpredictable nor do they represent a random set of limitless possibilities. There are several statistical regularities on which spellers can rely in order to facilitate or even avoid rote word-by-word memorization. In this chapter, we focus on regularities concerning the arrangement of letters in written words (i.e., graphotactic regularities, sometimes also referred to as orthographic or orthotactic regularities) and the representation and arrangement of the smallest meaningful units within words (i.e., morphological regularities).

We first review studies that have investigated children's knowledge about various types of graphotactic regularities. We then show that sensitivity to these orthographic/graphotactic regularities influences the spelling performance of children and adults even when it is possible to rely on graphophonological or morphological rules. Then we review studies that have investigated whether and when children use morphologically related words to spell other words. Finally, we report on recent experiments based on observation of learning of new words. Some of these studies explored the influence of general knowledge about spelling patterns on the learning of the spelling of a specific word, above and beyond frequency of exposure to this word. Other studies explored whether children benefit from information about the morphological structure of the new words embedded within stories, as if they were real words, in learning situations that allow a strict control of the number of exposures to whole words as well as to their stems.

SENSITIVITY TO GRAPHOTACTIC/ ORTHOGRAPHIC REGULARITIES

Through their readings, children not only acquire orthographic knowledge about specific words, but they also become sensitive to some graphotactic or orthographic regularities, that is, which letters or letter sequences are most likely to occur in specific positions in the words of a specific language. Determining whether correct spellings result from the use of word-specific knowledge or general orthographic knowledge turns out to be extremely difficult. Indeed, misspellings such as *mmis* for *miss* clearly indicate a lack of reliance on a rule specifying that doublets never occur in the word-initial position in English. Correct spellings, on the other hand, could reflect word-specific knowledge alone, independent of any knowledge about graphotactic regularities. That is why graphotactic knowledge has mainly been investigated with pseudoword spelling and judgment tasks. A few studies have explored whether children's misspellings tended to match the graphotactic regularities of their written language. Treiman (1993) has shown that incorrectly spelled words by first-grade U.S. children who had not received any explicit spelling teaching were compatible most of the time with the graphotactic regularities of the English written system. For instance, /k/ was sometimes erroneously written *ck*, but *ck* was used only rarely at the beginning of the words, a position where it would never appear in English.

Treiman, Kessler, and Bick (2002) explored whether adults rely on statistical regularities when they spell real words. The statistical analyses of English sound-to-spelling correspondences indicate that vowel spellings are more predictable when surrounding consonants are taken into account (Kessler & Treiman, 2001). These are not all-or-none regularities because a given vowel is not always spelled with a specific grapheme in a specific consonantal context. There are multiple graphemes that can be used to spell a given vowel sound. Although some graphemes are more likely to occur than others in specific consonant contexts, none of these occurrences is absolute. Therefore, reliance on such regularities should often lead to correct spelling, but they can also lead to misspellings of words, including letter combinations that do not match the more frequent patterns. In support of this view, Treiman et al. (2002) showed that substitution errors for vowels were more common in some consonantal contexts than in other contexts, and that this difference reflects spellers' use of their general knowledge about spelling patterns for specific words.

More evidence that children are sensitive to graphotactic regularities comes from pseudoword spelling tasks used with French-speaking children. Pacton, Fayol, and Perruchet (2002) dictated three-syllable pseudowords (e.g., /obidar/, /ribore/, /bylevo/) to second- to fifth-grade children to investigate whether they spelled /o/ differently according to its position and its consonant context. Even the youngest children employed a variety of graphemes to transcribe /o/. From the second graders, the spellings of /o/ differed according to the position and the consonantal environment. For instance, -eau was more often used in a final position than at the beginning and the middle of words. Moreover, in the final position, -eau was more often used after a v (where its appearance is frequent) than after an f (where it is rarely found). These results suggest that children are abstracting patterns of statistical regularities related to word position and letter sequences within words.

Convergent results have since been found in English by researchers who have reported that children's spellings of vowels (Treiman & Kessler, 2006) and consonants (Hayes, Treiman, & Kessler, 2006) were influenced by the surrounding consonants and vowels. As an example, Treiman and Kessler (2006) compared how children spell two kinds of pseudowords. In experimental pseudowords, consideration of the context may result in a spelling that is not necessarily typical overall (e.g., /glɛd/ with /ɛ/ spelled -ea before the coda /d/ on the basis of real words such as head and dead). In control pseudowords, consideration of the context leads to the most common spelling (e.g., /glɛp/ with /ɛ/ before the coda /p/, which does not favor -ea spelling). Children were more likely to produce the critical context-conditioned vowel spellings (-ea in the previous example) for the experimental pseudowords than for the control pseudowords (see Treiman et al., 2002, for similar results with adults).

Sensitivity to orthographic regularities has also been assessed with pseudoword judgment tasks, which require a choice between at least two possible alternatives that would not necessarily appear in children's orthographic productions. To assess children's sensitivity to graphotactic regularities, Cassar and Treiman (1997) used an orthographic constraints test (see Treiman, 1993). Children were shown a set of pairs of pseudowords such that one pseudoword in each pair conformed to a constraint of the English writing system, whereas the other pseudoword did not. For instance, to assess children's knowledge about which letters can or cannot be doubled, the material included pairs such as noss–novv and yill–yihh. Children were asked to choose which items within each pair looked more like a real word. First and second graders tended to prefer pseudowords that contained permissible doublets over pseudowords that contained doublets that never occur. For example, they judged that noss and yill look more like real words than novv and yihh. On the basis of this result, Cassar and Treiman concluded that these children were sensitive to the frequency of doubling. However, such preference could reflect children's sensitivity to the frequency of single letters, instead of sensitivity to the frequency of doubling (Pacton, Perruchet, Fayol, & Cleeremans, 2001). Indeed, as consonants such as *l* are used more frequently than consonants such as *h*, whether they are single or doubled, children could state that *yill* is a better word than *yihh* simply because *l* is a more frequently used letter than *h*, rather than because *l* is doubled more often than *h*.

In order to assess whether children are sensitive to the frequency of double consonants or only to the frequency of single consonants, Pacton et al. (2001) exploited the fact that, although there is a link between the frequency of consonants presented in isolation and in a doublet in French (e.g., *k* is rare and *kk* never occurs vs. both *l* and *ll* are frequent), some consonants occur frequently in both single and double formats (e.g., *m* or *l*) and others occur frequently only in single formats (e.g., *c* or *d*). Children were presented with pseudoword pairs such as *imose–idose* and *avumme–avudde*. Apart from the target consonants, in the single format in some pairs (*m* and *d* in the first example) and in the double format in other pairs (*mm* and *dd* in the second example), the constituent letters of the two pseudowords of a pair were the same. The hypothesis was that if children are sensitive to the frequency of single consonants alone, there should be no difference between single or double consonants for pseudowords containing consonants that are frequent in both single and double formats (e.g., *l* or *m*) or for pseudowords containing consonants that are frequent only when they are single (e.g., *c* or *d*). By contrast, if children are sensitive to the frequency of double consonants, pseudowords including *l* or *m* (rather than *c* and *d*) should be chosen more often when consonants occur in a double format than in a single format. Evidence was found for sensitivity to the frequency of double consonants when the potential confound of the component (single) consonants was removed from the first grade onward; and this sensitivity appeared to increase from the second to the third grades.

Similar conclusions have been reached by Danjon and Pacton (2009) using pairs in which the two pseudowords are pronounced similarly but spelled with the target consonant in the single format in one pseudoword (e.g., *imose*) versus in the double format in the other (e.g., *immose*). From the first grade, children more often chose pseudowords including double letters for pairs like *imose–immose*, with the target consonant *m* frequent in both single and double formats, than for pairs like *idose–iddose*, with the target consonant *d* is frequent only in the single format. The identity of the letters that may or may not be doubled constitutes an idiosyncratic property of each letter. Other orthographic regularities can be described with a rule. For instance, a single high-level rule can concisely define the position at which doublets may occur within words in many languages. For example, in English, French, and Finnish, doublets are illegal in the word-initial position.

Using the orthographic constraints test described above, Cassar and Treiman (1997) presented pairs of pseudowords such as *nuss–nnus* to test whether children know that consonants cannot double in the beginning of words. They found that even kindergarteners judged *nuss* as more wordlike than *nnus* and concluded that children knew the position at which consonants can be doubled in English. Sensitivity to the illegality of doublets in the word-initial position has also been reported as early as in the first grade in France (Pacton et al., 2001) and Finland

(Lehtonen & Bryant, 2005). Although Cassar and Treiman's study included kindergarteners, the youngest children in the experiments conducted by Pacton et al. (2001) and Lehtonen and Bryant (2005) were first graders.

Pacton et al. (2001) further investigated the degree of abstractness of children's knowledge that consonants cannot be doubled in the word-initial position. They argued that children's preference for pseudowords such as *nuss* over pseudowords such as *nnus* may be due to the learning of letter-specific features (e.g., that *nn* and *ss* occur frequently in the end of words but not at the beginning). In order to investigate the abstract character of children's orthographic knowledge about the legal position of doublets, they tested children's knowledge about the legal position of doublets with consonants that are never doubled. Cassar and Treiman (1997) argued that children's knowledge was general because, even though *j* is never doubled in English, children chose *juss* as more wordlike than *jjus* as often as they chose *nuss* as more wordlike than *nnus*. However, this finding provides only limited evidence that children's knowledge of the legal position of double consonants was general (i.e., independent of the identity of the consonants that constitute the doublets) because the preference for *juss* over *jjus* may just reflect their knowledge of the identity of allowable doublets (i.e., that *ss* is an allowable doublet but not *jj*).

In order to get around this difficulty, Pacton et al. (2001) used pseudoword pairs such as *xihhel–xxihel* to determine whether sensitivity to the legal position of double consonants extends (and in what proportions) to consonants that are never doubled. A transfer to consonants that do not allow doubling in French was observed as early as first grade. For example, although *k* and *h* never double in French, children judged pseudowords such as *xihhel* (with a doublet in a legitimate, word-medial position) as more wordlike than *xxihel* (with a doublet in a prohibited word-initial position). However, the effect for these letters remained substantially lower than for frequently doubled letters, and the magnitude of this transfer decrement remained unchanged from the first to the sixth grades. Similar results were observed with a completion task in which participants were asked to fill in blanks located in the medial position in one pseudoword and in the initial position in the other pseudoword (e.g., _uliver–mu_iver) with a single consonant and a doublet (e.g., *l* and *tt* for items without transfer; *k* and *xx* for items with transfer). Taken together, these results indicated that even after as long as 5 years of exposure to print, children's orthographic knowledge did not correspond to a general rule, such as consonants can only be doubled in medial position in French.

Studies that have investigated children's graphotactic knowledge with pseudoword judgment tasks have often only taken into account the identity of allowable doublets or the illegality of word-initial doublets (e.g., Cassar & Treiman, 1997; Cassar, Treiman, Moats, Pollo, & Kessler, 2005; Lehtonen & Bryant, 2005; Pacton et al., 2001). Sensitivity to these two regularities, reported as early as in kindergarten and first grade, clearly indicates that these two regularities are easily detected by children; however, there is evidence that this sensitivity increases when children become older (e.g., Pacton et al., 2001). Danjon and Pacton (2009) took into account a larger range of graphotactic regularities in order to investigate whether some graphotactic regularities are harder to detect and whether this possibility could explain why some mistakes are made more often in some contexts than in others. They explored first- to fifth-grade French children's knowledge of (a) the illegality of doublets in word-initial position, (b) the frequency of doubling, (c) allowable doublets being more frequent in certain contexts than in others; and (d) the rule that, within a consonant cluster, a double consonant can occur before, but not after, a single consonant. For the first two properties, the results were similar to those reported by Pacton et al. (2001). In particular, in the first five grades, children selected pseudowords including a doublet in word-medial position more often than pseudowords including a doublet in the word-initial position, even when doublets were formed with consonants that never double in French; but the scores on these items were systematically lower than when allowable doublets were used. Additional analyses further indicated that the good spellers (the 25 children of the 148 who obtained the highest scores at a standardized spelling test) performed better than poor spellers (the 25 who obtained the lowest scores at the standardized spelling test); but the amplitude of the transfer decrement did not differ as a function of spelling ability.

In order to test children's sensitivity to the fact that allowable doublets such as *nn* are more frequent in certain contexts than in others in French (e.g., *n* is frequently doubled after *o* but is never doubled after *oi*), children were presented with pseudoword pairs such as *ligédone–ligédonne* and *ligédoine–ligédoinne*. The younger children and the poor spellers did not select pseudowords such as *ligédonne* and *ligédoinne* in significantly different proportions. Children younger than third grade seemed not to be sensitive to the frequency of some doublets as a function of the left vowel, for example, that *nn* is much more frequent after the grapheme /o/ than after the grapheme /oi/.

Children's sensitivity to the fact that double consonants can occur before, but not after, single consonants in French was tested by proposing a choice between pseudowords like *apprulir* (with the doublet before the single consonant) and *aprrulir* (with the doublet after the single consonant). Furthermore, in order to assess whether children learn this orthographic rule, the consonant cluster followed a vowel after which it is frequent in French in some pairs (e.g., the cluster -ppr after the vowel *a* in the pair *apprulir–aprrulir*) versus a vowel after which it rarely or even never occurs in others (e.g., the cluster -ppr after the vowel *i* in the pair *ippraler–iprraler*). On the basis of results from Pacton et al. (2001) for the illegality of doublets in the word-initial position, it was expected that, even after prolonged exposure to print, children should perform better for pairs such as *apprulir–aprrulir* than for pairs such as *ippraler–iprraler*.

The younger children and the poor spellers did not select pseudowords with a doublet before a single consonant and pseudowords with a doublet after a single consonant in significantly different proportions, regardless of the vowel on the left. A preference for pseudowords with a doublet before a single consonant emerged in the third grade, but only for clusters that followed vowels after which they are frequent in French. Choices were at chance level for clusters that followed vowels after which they rarely or never occur in French, such as -ppr after *i*. Only the fourth and fifth graders and the good spellers were above chance level on these items. However, their performances were significantly lower for clusters that followed vowels after which they rarely or never occur in French than after vowels after which they frequently occur; and the difference between the two types of items was stable across grades.

To summarize, knowledge of certain graphotactic regularities develops as early as the first school year and increases during the following grades, but sensitivity to other aspects emerges later, suggesting that some graphotactic regularities may be easier to grasp than others. For instance, for English children, knowledge that doublets are not permissible in the word-initial position emerges earlier than knowledge about allowable doublets (as early as in the kindergarten vs. from the first grade; Cassar & Treiman, 1997). Similarly, for French children, knowledge that doublets are not permissible in the word-initial position precedes the emergence of knowledge of the order of double and single consonants within a consonant cluster (as early as first vs. from third grade; Danjon & Pacton, 2009). Thus, it might be important not to conceive of formal knowledge of print as a homogeneous entity. Just as some phonological units are easier to process than others (e.g., Treiman & Zukowski, 1991), so to some formal orthographic regularities may be easier to discover than others.

The finding that some graphotactic regularities are more difficult to learn than others may lead to reconsidering carefully the conclusions of certain studies that are intrinsically linked to the kind of graphotactic regularities studied. For example, Lehtonen and Bryant (2005) found that, at the beginning of their first school year, Finnish-speaking children were sensitive to a formal aspect of doublet use (the illegality of word-initial doublets), but ignorant of the functional connection between doublets and long consonants: Long consonants are spelled with doublets, whereas short consonants are represented by single letters. It was only from the second grade onward that Finnish children gained knowledge about the functional relation between consonant length and its representation in spelling. If this same functional knowledge had been compared to a formal aspect of print such as doublets not being permitted after single consonants —to which children are not sensitive during the first two grades—the conclusion would undoubtedly differ from the "doublet challenge: form comes before function in children's understanding of their orthography," which is the title of Lhetonen and Bryant's (2005) article. Likewise, although children with and without dyslexia performed similarly on a task to assess their sensitivity to the impermissibility of doublets in the word-initial position (Cassar et al., 2005), the issue of whether their performance differs on less salient regularities remains an open question.

Even after as long as 5 years of exposure to print, children do not seem to rely on general rules such as "doublets are impermissible in the word-initial position and after single consonants." Indeed, if children relied on such rules, their performance on pseudoword judgment tasks should not vary as a function of the frequency of the doublets used to test their knowledge of the first rule, nor as a function of the vowel left of the consonant cluster for the items used to test their knowledge of the second rule (Danjon & Pacton, 2009; Pacton et al., 2001). Thus, although children were more sensitive to the impermissibility of doublets in the word-initial position than after single consonants, their performance differed as a function of the familiarity of the material used to assess their knowledge of the two regularities. These findings echo the results of artificial grammar learning studies in which the training and test stimuli share the same underlying abstract structure but involve different surface forms (e.g., Redington & Chater, 2002). Typical results in this paradigm indicate that, although participants remain able to perform above chance on the discrimination task and their level of performance is lower than in the standard condition, the surface features do not differ between training and test. Proponents of the abstractionist view of implicit learning have suggested that this *transfer decrement* may be due to an insufficient practice to acquire the relevant rules in laboratory context, because of obvious limits with regard to the duration of experimental sessions (e.g., Manza & Reber, 1997). Performance differed as a function of the familiarity of the material used to assess knowledge of graphotactic rules, and this difference persists over extensive training, even among the better spellers, without any trend toward fading. This fact appears difficult to reconcile with the idea that implicit learning leads to the acquisition of increasingly abstract, rule-based knowledge about the regularities contained in the material over training.

INTEGRATION OF GRAPHOTACTIC REGULARITIES AND OTHER KNOWLEDGE SOURCES

The studies reported in the previous section typically investigated graphotactic knowledge in the absence of other sources of information. Here we address the issue of the integration of graphotactic knowledge with other sources of information. We consider studies suggesting that children's and adults' sensitivity to graphotactic regularities influences their spelling even when it is possible to rely on spelling sound or morphological rules.

Graphotactic Knowledge and Spelling-Sound Rules

Several studies have explored whether and when children use single versus double consonants to represent phonemic information. For instance, Cassar and Treiman (1997) explored children's knowledge about the connection between the preconsonantal vowel length and the presence of a doublet spelling. In principle, consonant doublets indicate that the preceding vowel is short (e.g., *supper*), whereas single consonants indicate that the preceding vowel is long (e.g., *super*). Children saw two pseudowords, one with a consonant doublet in the middle and the other with a single consonant (e.g., *tebbif–tebif*) while hearing a pronunciation that contained either a short or a long vowel before the medial consonant. Their task was to choose the best spelling for the word they heard. Only children aged 11 years or older were more likely than chance to take the length of the preconsonantal vowel into account when making their response, which suggests that children learn about the functional connection between phonology and doublets relatively late.

French- and Finnish-speaking children seem to learn about the functional significance of doublets in their orthography at a much younger age than the English-speaking children. Lehtonen and Bryant (2005) investigated Finnish-speaking children's knowledge that long consonants are spelled with doublets, whereas short consonants are represented by single letters in the word-medial position but not in the word-initial position (where doublets are not permissible, regardless of whether the initial phoneme is short or long). Children were presented with pairs of pseudowords such as *raissi–raisi* and *ssuono–suono* while hearing a pronunciation with either a long or a short target consonant. From the second grade on, they chose word-medial doublets significantly more often upon hearing long than short word-medial consonants, but they almost never chose word-initial doublets, whether they heard a long or a short word-initial phoneme. Thus, they applied their functional knowledge about consonant length only when this knowledge was appropriate.

In French, whether a consonant is single or double has typically no phonological counterpart, but an exception occurs for the consonant *s*, which is pronounced /z/ when single, as in the word rose (/z/), and /s/ when double, as in the word grosse (big). Crucially, *ss* is used to represent the sound /s/ only between two vowels. The phoneme /s/ is spelled with a single *s* in word-beginning positions, as in *sable* (sand), between a consonant and a vowel, as in *torse* (torso), and between a vowel and a consonant, as in *liste* (list). Alegria and Mousty (1996) have reported that 7- to 10-year-old French-speaking children who had to write down pseudowords in a dictation task almost never represented /s/ with *ss* in an initial position. On the other hand, they barely took into account the context of /s/ in a median position, using *ss* between two vowels but also between a consonant and a vowel. Danjon and Pacton (2009) have further investigated elementary school children's use of *ss* to represent the sound /s/. Children had to decide which of the two spellings was a legal orthographic production of the pseudoword pronounced by the experimenter for different types of pairs of pseudowords: *isove–issove* to represent /isov/ or /izov/ (with the alternate *s/ss* between two vowels—*ss* required for /s/; *s* for /z/); *lursir–lurssir* to represent /lyrsir/ (with *s/ss* between a consonant and a vowel -*s* required); and *sirvure–ssirvure* to represent /sirvyr/ (with *s/ss* at the initial position -*s* required). As early as in first grade, children chose the spelling *ss* more often for the intervocalic pronunciation /s/ than for the intervocalic pronunciation /z/; and the mean performance for correct spellings *s/ss* between two vowels increased all along elementary school, especially during the first three grades. However, at the same time children correctly chose the spelling *ss* to represent the intervocalic /s/, they often incorrectly chose the spelling *ss* to represent /s/ between a consonant and a vowel. Actually, throughout elementary school, the more children chose pseudowords including *ss* to represent /s/ between two vowels (which is correct), the more they chose *ss* to represent /s/ between a consonant and a vowel (which is incorrect). By contrast, throughout elementary school, children rarely selected the items with *ss* at the initial position of words.

Children's reluctance to use *ss* in the initial position of words echoes Lehtonen and Bryant's (2005) finding that Finnish children never represented long consonants with double letters in the initial position of words. According to Danjon and Pacton (2009), French children would be more likely to represent /s/ erroneously with *ss* in the word-medial position between a consonant and a vowel than in the word-initial position because they are less sensitive to the illegality of a double consonant after a single consonant than to the illegality of doublets placed at the initial position. Such a possibility is supported by another study in Danjon and Pacton (2009) in which children as well as adults more often erroneously chose pseudo-words such as *lurssir* (for the pair *lursir–lurssir*) than pseudowords like *ssirvure* (for the pair *sirvure–ssirvure*), even when they had to choose the legal spelling in a visual condition (i.e., without any pronunciation given) similar to the one used by Cassar and Treiman (1997) and Pacton et al. (2001).

Thus, Finnish children's knowledge that word-medial long consonants are represented with double letters *and* French children's knowledge that the intervocalic sound /s/ is represented with *ss* are gained much earlier than English-speaking children's knowledge that consonants are, in principle, doubled after short vowels. This discrepancy may be due to the fact that these functional aspects of doublets are taught to Finnish and French children (and from early on in life), but not to English children. A second explanation, suggested by Lehtonen and Bryant (2005), is that it could be easier to grasp the phonological rule when the format of the consonant changes the pronunciation of the consonant itself (as in Finnish and French) than the pronunciation of the preconsonantal vowel (as in English). The fact that children almost never used doublets in the initial position of words to represent long consonant sounds in Finnish and the sound /s/ in French may be due to their somewhat strong knowledge that Finnish and French words cannot begin by doublets. To the best of our knowledge, this possibility has not been explored in Finnish, but the lower sensitivity to the illegality of doublets after single consonants would explain why French children overgeneralize the use of *ss* to represent the sound /s/ far more often between a consonant and a vowel than at the beginning of words.

Graphotactic/Orthographic and Morphologic Regularities

The spelling performance of elementary school pupils and adults also seems to be influenced by their sensitivity to graphotactic regularities even when it is possible to use morphological rules that can be applied to a large sample of words (Pacton & Deacon, 2008). Pacton, Fayol, and Perruchet (2005) studied whether French pupils employed rules relative to the transcription of diminutive suffixes /o/ and /ɛt/ in French. The transcription of these two sounds can be constrained by morphology (e.g., /ɛt/ is always written *ette* when it corresponds to a diminutive suffix) and by graphotactic regularities (e.g., *ette* is more frequent after *r* than after *f*). From second grade on, pupils transcribed /ɛt/ more often *ette* when pseudowords such as /vitarɛt/ and /vitafɛt/ were inserted in sentences revealing their morphological structure (i.e., a stem + a suffix such as, "a little /vitar/ is a /vitarɛt/") than when they were dictated alone or in sentences that did not indicate diminutive suffixes. Their spelling was also influenced by graphotactic regularities since they transcribed /ɛt/ more often as *ette* for pseudowords like /vitarɛt/ than for pseudowords like /vitafɛt/, even when pseudowords were employed in sentences indicating they were diminutive suffixes. This effect, which should not have been observed if children used a rule specifying that /ɛt/ is transcribed *ette* when it corresponds to a diminutive suffix, did not differ from Grades 2 to 5. Moreover, this effect was observed even among university students.

Pacton et al. (2005) suggested that their results can be accounted for within a perspective in which statistical learning processes can apply to features that are abstracted away from their sensory context (Perruchet & Vinter, 2002; Redington & Chater, 2002). According to these authors, abstract features like "diminutiveness" can come to be associated with features like "end with *ette*." Children would learn this association, leading them to use *ette* more often when pseudowords like /vitarɛt/ are embedded within sentences like "a little /vitar/ is a /vitarɛt/." However, they would also learn associations between other features such as the fact that the spelling *ette* is far more frequent after the letter *r* than after the letter *f*. Because children and adults are sensitive to both kinds of associations, they would use *ette* less often for pseudowords like /vitafɛt/ than for pseudowords like /vitarɛt/ even when it is possible to rely on a morphological rule.

The importance of graphotactic regularities has been pointed out with a morphological rule that applies to a far larger sample of words than the morphological rule taken into account by Pacton et al. (2005): the rule specifying that the plural of regular English nouns is always written *s*, whether pronounced /s/ or /z/ (Deacon & Pacton, 2007; Kemp & Bryant, 2003). Although this morphological rule generates the correct spelling of plural nouns, graphotactic regularities can also predict the appropriate representation of many plural spellings. The /z/ sound is almost always spelled with an *s* after a consonant, but it can be written with *s*, *z*, *zz*, *ze*, or *se* after a long vowel (e.g., *fleas*, *please*, *breeze*). If spellers rely on a rule specifying the spelling of regular plurals as -s, the use of -s should not vary as a function of the nature of the sound preceding the /z/, whether it is a consonant or a long vowel. However, if they rely on graphotactic regularities, they should spell the plural form of nouns with a consonant + /z/ ending correctly without applying a morphological rule, but they should often misspell plural nouns with a long vowel + /z/ ending because /z/ can be spelled in many ways when it follows a vowel.

There was evidence to support this second hypothesis. Kemp and Bryant (2003) reported that children aged 7.6 years were better able to spell the plurals of real words when these could be determined by both morphological rules and graphotactic constraints (e.g., dogs) than when they could be determined only by morphological rules (e.g., fleas). Although on average the good spellers (spelling age = 9.6 years) correctly transcribed the final /z/ with an *s* more often than did the poor spellers (spelling age = 6.11 years), an impact of graphotactic regularities was evidenced among both poor and good spellers.

With a pseudoword spelling task, Kemp and Bryant (2003) further showed that adults' spelling of the nominal plural marker /z/ was influenced by their sensitivity to graphotactic regularities. For instance, they used *s* more often for pseudonouns like *pleens* than for pseudonouns like *prees*. An interesting result was that graphotactic constraints had a large effect on pseudoword spelling, even among adults with education beyond high school (a difference of approximately 30%). This finding does not mean that the participants did not take into account the morphological information of the sentence in which the words were embedded (e.g., that there were three *prees*). Indeed, the adults with higher education in Kemp and Bryant's study spelled the long-vowel pseudowords with an *s* more often when they were presented as plurals than when they were nonplurals that require the ending *ze* or *se* (a difference of approximately 50%). This effect was also observed in the children who were good spellers (difference of approximately 15%), but not among poor spellers.

Taken as a whole, the impact of graphotactic constraints found by Kemp and Bryant (2003) suggests that children and adults did not rely, at least exclusively, on a morphological rule. Because they compared how children and adults spell items (words and pseudowords) that can be spelled by using a morphological rule alone and items that can be spelled by relying on a morphological rule as well as on sensitivity to graphotactic regularities, their study did not allow a test of whether morphological constraints do nevertheless reduce the impact of graphotactic constraints. Such an investigation requires the comparison of a condition with only graphotactic regularities and a condition with both graphotactic and morphological constraints, as in the study of Pacton et al. (2005). Deacon and Pacton (2007) carried out such an experiment. They asked adults with education beyond high school to spell "long vowel + /z/" and "consonant + /z/" pseudowords in sentence contexts, as in Kemp and Bryant (2003), and in isolation, an added condition. For the long vowel items, they were more likely to use an -s when the item was dictated as a plural and less likely to do so when it was presented as a singular noun. There was no such difference when the items were spelled in the absence of sentence-level information, confirming Kemp and Bryant's finding that participants took into account the morphological information provided by the sentences in which pseudowords were embedded to spell them. With regard to the impact of graphotactic constraints, there was some evidence that morphological constraints did reduce the impact of graphotactic constraints. However, the main result was that the graphotactic effect (i.e., the higher use of *s* after a consonant than after a long vowel) was large in both the isolated condition (70%) and the sentence condition (52%).

Thus, the few studies that have investigated the integration of graphotactic and morphological constraints suggest that sensitivity to graphotactic regularities, which has already been well documented in isolation (e.g., Cassar & Treiman, 1997; Pacton et al., 2001), still influence the performances of spellers when they can rely on a simple, morphologically based rule. This finding appears to be fairly general given that it has been reported for (a) both children and adults, (b) both word and pseudoword spelling tasks, (c) morphological rules that applied to an important number of words, and (d) both derivations and inflections.

CHILDRENS' USE OF MORPHOLOGICAL RELATEDNESS IN SPELLING

Do children use morphologically related words to spell others? Several studies have investigated whether and when children are capable of using the morphological relations between words to guide their spelling. The principle of root consistency captures a number of morphological relationships, which specifies that the spelling of the roots of words is maintained in related words. For instance, the related words *heal* and *health* contain roots that are spelled in the same way, even though the grapheme /ea/ does not represent the same phoneme in the two words. In French, the sound /ə/, which is typically spelled with an *e* in French (e.g., *retard*, late, and *jeter*, to throw), is represented with the grapheme /ai/ in the word *faiseur* (/fəzœr/, producer) to preserve its morphological origins (derived from the verb *faire* /fɛr/, to do) at the expense of this phonological regularity. Likewise, the masculine adjective *bavard* (talkative) includes a final silent *d*, which is pronounced in morphologically related words such as the feminine adjective *bavarde*, the verb *bavarder* (to chat), and the noun *bavardage* (chatting). Such relationships are remarkably common. In English, Nagy and Anderson (1984) reported that there are approximately four related forms for each base word. In French, Rey-Debove (1984) showed that 80% of the words listed in the French dictionary *Robert-méthodique* included at least two morphemes. Notably, the principle of root consistency works well most of the time, but it is not foolproof (i.e., some words do not adhere to this principle). For example, the French noun *numéro* (/nymero/, a number) does not include a final silent consonant even though the French verb *numéroter* (/numerote/, to number) suggests the presence of a silent *t*, as is the case for the noun *sanglot* (/sãglo/, a sob) and the related verb *sangloter* (/sãglote/, to sob). Thus, it is possible that this principle is in fact overapplied, as reported for certain forms in oral language with the past tense and plural formation in English (e.g., *goed*, Marcus et al., 1992; *foots*, Clashen, Rothweiler, Woest, & Marcus, 1992).

In English, Waters, Bruck, and Malus-Abramowitz (1988) examined the use of morphological relationships in spelling. They asked 8- to 11-year-old children to spell regular, orthographic, morphological, and strange words. Regular words could be spelled correctly by simply applying phoneme-grapheme correspondences (e.g., *publish*). The orthographic words contained a portion that was determined by orthographic conventions (e.g., the spelling of /tʃ/ in *patch* depends on the vowel and the number of consonants following it). In the morphological words, spelling is determined by derivational relationships (e.g., spelling of *sign* by reference to *signal*). The strange words could only be spelled correctly by rote memorization. There was a clear hierarchy in accuracy. Regular words were the easiest to spell, followed by orthographic, then morphological, and, finally, strange words. According to Waters et al., better performance on the orthographic than on the morphological words reflects children's greater efficiency in using orthographic than morphological information. That said, greater accuracy in the morphological than the strange words demonstrates that children are capable of using morphological relationships to spell words, at least from the age of eight.

Carlisle's (1988) study also demonstrated the impact of morphology on spelling. She examined 9- to 13-year-old children's spelling of roots and their derived forms (e.g., *warm–warmth* and *heal–health*). The children were more likely to spell the derived form correctly if they had represented the root accurately, suggesting that they relied on the root in spelling the related word. Further, they had more difficulty in applying this principle with words involving phonological changes than with those that did not (e.g., *health* and *warmth*, respectively).

Perhaps surprising, given Carlisle's (1988) finding, Deacon and Bryant (2005) found that 7- to 9-year-old children had similar sensitivity to the principle that roots are represented in derived forms in words that did or did not include phonological changes. In this study, the experimenter provided a clue to the spelling of one- and two-morpheme words (such as *pot* to spell *potion* and *connect* to spell *connection*, respectively). The children used the clues to spell the two-morpheme words, but they were less likely to do so with one-morpheme words. This pattern appeared equally across the words with or without a phonological change (e.g., *objection* and *illness*, respectively). Thus, when children are provided with the spelling of the suffix, which might diminish the cognitive demands associated with spelling, they appear to have the conceptual understanding that morphemes are represented in spelling.

Several studies have explored whether children can refer to morphologically related words to help them to spell particularly difficult sounds (Kemp, 2006; Rubin, 1988; Treiman & Cassar, 1996; Treiman, Cassar, & Zukowski, 1994). For instance, Treiman et al. (1994) studied how children spelled the flap, a sound in American English that is pronounced more like /d/ than /t/. They contrasted its spelling in the word-medial position in two- and one-morpheme words, such as dirty and duty, respectively. The spelling of the flap can be elucidated by referring to the roots in the two-morpheme words (e.g., *dirt* in *dirty*), but there is no such root in the one-morpheme words. Five- to 8-year-old children were more likely to spell the flap with a *t* (correctly) in two- than in one-morpheme words. It is worth noting that children misspelled the *t* of *dirty* as *d* far more often than they did for the *t* of *dirt*, with which they were almost perfect. According to Treiman and her colleagues, these data show that although children have a ways to go in using morphological relationships to their full extent, they certainly have some sensitivity to these relationships.

Extending this line of research, Kemp (2006) asked 7-year-old children to spell words with a medial /z/ for which there are several alternative spellings (e.g., -*s*, -*z*, -*zz*). For two-morpheme words the choice between the alternatives can be determined by referring to the spelling of the root (e.g., *noisy* derived from *noise* vs. the one-morpheme word *busy* with no such root). The children were more accurate in spelling the /z/ sound in two- than in one-morpheme words. According to Kemp, this finding indicates that children used roots to choose between several phonologically plausible spellings for a particular sound in related words.

Children's use of morphologically related words to spell other words has also been reported in French. Sénéchal (2000, see also Sénéchal, Basque & Leclaire, 2006) asked 7- and 9-year-old Francophone Canadian children to spell three types of words. There were morphological words with a derived form that indicated how to spell the word-final silent consonant. For example, the words *grand* and *camp* end in a silent consonant that is pronounced in derived forms such as grande and camper. There were opaque words with no such related word (e.g., *jument*), and there were also regular words without any final silent consonant (e.g., *tiroir*). The children were most accurate in their spelling of the words without a word-final consonant. Nevertheless, they were more likely to be correct in spelling the morphological words than the opaque words. This finding suggests that they refer to related words in determining the spelling of the silent endings.

Pacton, Casalis, and Deacon (2007) explored whether French children could refer to derived words to elucidate the presence, as well as the absence, of a final silent letter (following on Sénéchal, 2000). Children are sensitive to the fact that many French words include a final silent consonant, which sometimes leads them to add a silent consonant erroneously to words that do not include such letters. However, reference to morphologically related words sometimes suggests the absence of a final silent letter. For example, children could refer to the verb *citronner* (/sitrone/, to add lemon to something) to decide that the noun *citron* (/sitrɔ̃/, lemon) is spelled with *-on*, rather than *-ond* or *-ont*. Thus, Pacton et al. hypothesized that the erroneous addition of a final silent consonant should be less frequent for morphological words without a final silent letter (e.g., *citron*) than for opaque words without a final silent letter (e.g., *caleçon*, /kalsɔ̃/) that do not have any morphologically related words suggesting this absence.

Pacton et al. (2007) also explored whether children sometimes overapply the principle of root consistency to *trap* words, which do not follow the principle of root consistency. Pacton and his colleagues' hypothesis was that children should be more likely to add a final silent consonant (erroneously) to trap words such as *numéro* (to number), which has morphologically related derived forms such as *numéroter* (/numerote/, to number) and *numérotation* (/numerotasiô/, numbering) and suggests the presence of a final silent consonant, than to the two other kinds of words, neither of which ends with a silent consonant. From Grades 3 to 5, the better scores for morphological words with a silent letter than for opaque words with a silent letter indicated that children were more likely to use appropriately a final silent consonant when words had related words that could elucidate the presence of a silent letter (as in Sénéchal, 2000, and Sénéchal et al., 2006). The better scores for morphological and opaque words without a silent letter than for morphological and opaque words with a silent letter also confirmed Sénéchal's finding that children were most accurate in their spelling of the words without a word-final consonant. This difference was observed in Grades 3 through 5, even though its size decreased as a function of grade level, mainly because of the increasing number of words correctly spelled with a final silent consonant.

The distinction of three types of words without a final silent consonant in the study by Pacton et al. (2007) extends Sénéchal's (2000) findings in two ways. First, morphological words without silent consonant were significantly more often spelled correctly without a silent letter than opaque words without silent letters, which suggests that children benefited from the existence of morphologically related words that can elucidate the absence of silent letters. The advantage of morphological over opaque words was smaller for words without silent letters than for words with silent letters, probably because the spelling of words without silent letters is easier to memorize or because it can be produced using phoneme-grapheme correspondences. Second, we used trap words, which are tricky words that pose a trap for spellers who may misspell them due to overgeneralizing a morphological rule. Indeed, these trap words were spelled correctly less often than morphological and opaque words without silent letters. Furthermore, analysis of the errors on trap words revealed that misspellings mainly resulted from overapplication of the principle of root consistency, with a mistaken reference to the morphologically related words. Indeed, the consonants added incorrectly were often those predicted from morphologically related words (e.g., addition of a *t* rather than an *s* to *numéro* by reference to *numéroter*; addition of a *d* rather than a *t* to *cauchemar* [nightmare] by reference to *cauchemardesque* [nightmarish]).

With the exception of the overapplication of the principle of root consistency to words that do not adhere to this principle, the findings reviewed above of better spelling when morphology can be used may not reflect the use of morphology, as traditionally argued, but rather a difference in the frequency of orthographic forms. Indeed, even if specific words are balanced for their frequency, the existence of morphologically related words for some words (e.g., *dirt* appearing in *dirty, dirtiness, dirtily*) and their marked absence for others (e.g., *duty*) increases the frequency of the root of words that have morphologically related words (e.g., *dirt in dirty*) beyond that of the words that do not have such morphologically related words (e.g., the first segment *dut in duty*).

Studies of Deacon and Bryant (2005, 2006a, 2006b) investigated the extent to which explanations based on the orthographic frequency of word forms account for the better spelling when morphology can be used. For example, Deacon and Bryant (2006a) compared 6- to 8-year-old children's spelling of two- and one-morpheme words that begin with the same initial letter-sound sequence (e.g., *rock* in *rocked* and *rocket*). The evaluation of the same letter-sound sequence in the two word types ensures that the frequency as well as spelling difficulty of this segment is balanced between the conditions. Children were asked to spell the initial segments of two-morpheme words (e.g., complete ___ed for *rocked*) and their one-morpheme counterparts (e.g., complete ___et for *rocket*) and they could use a clue to spell these words (e.g., *rock*). Even though the children spelled the same letter-sound sequence in the two word types, they were better able to spell these sections when they were roots than when they were not (e.g., the *rock* in *rocked* compared to *rocket*). Deacon and Bryant's findings indicate that higher performance on two-morpheme words than on their one-morpheme counterparts cannot be discounted by explanations based on the orthographic frequency of word forms.

Such a difference between one- and two-morpheme words, after careful control of the formal overlap (spelling and sound) between words with and without morphologically related words, strongly supports, according to Deacon and Bryant (2006b), the idea that children use the spelling of morphemes to determine how to spell morphologically related words from a relatively early age. However, it is worth stressing that, because one- and two-morpheme words differ in the degree of semantic overlap with the initial letter-sound segment, children may use the first section (e.g., *mess*) more often, or even only, when this segment is semantically linked to the target words being spelled (e.g., in *messy*, but not *message*). Thus, because of these differences at the semantic level, it is still possible to account for the difference between morphologically simple and complex words at a morphological level as well as in terms of convergence between different sound, spelling, and meaning (Seidenberg & Gonnerman, 2000). Thus, available studies cannot rule between alternative explanations at a morphological level or at a convergence level among spelling, sound, and meaning. However, regardless of the specific nature of the explanation, they suggest that children might find it easier to acquire letter patterns supported by multiple codes.

EXPERIMENTS THAT EXAMINE LEARNING THE SPELLING OF NEW WORDS

The studies that we reviewed investigating whether children use morphologically related words to spell others all focus on misspellings. By their design, they can reveal an impact of morphology only when children still make misspellings, by showing that they do so less when morphology can be used than when it cannot. A series of experiments that examine learning the spelling of new words (e.g., Pacton, 2010) has been recently carried out in order to go beyond limitations of studying only spelling errors. These experiments are presented later in this chapter, but first we present other experiments that examined whether learning new words influenced general knowledge about spelling patterns (graphotactic knowledge) in children's and adults' memory for specific words.

Graphotactic Regularities and the Learning of Lexical Knowledge

A few studies have investigated whether conformity to the graphotactic patterns of a given writing system influences learning of the spelling of a specific word, above and beyond frequency of exposure to this word. A first study on the impact of graphotactic knowledge on misspellings was carried out by Campbell and Coltheart (1984) soon after the release of the film *Gandhi* (Attenborough, 1982). Although the English university students of their study had probably seen the name Gandhi many times, most of them misspelled it as *Ghandi*. The lack of mistakes such as *Gandy* or *Gandi* suggests that participants knew that the word included an *h* but did not know where to place it. The misspelling *Ghandi* was more frequent than alternative misspellings such as *Ganhdi* or *Gandih* likely because this misspelling is especially consistent with the graphotactic patterns of English. Indeed, *gh* is much more frequent than *nh* or *ih*. The conclusions that can be drawn from this study are nevertheless limited given that it used only one item, and there was no control over how often participants had seen the correct spelling.

Wright and Ehri (2007) explored the influence of knowledge of graphotactic patterns on memory for spellings by 6-year-old children in the United States. The children were explicitly taught to pronounce novel spellings. Some of these spellings began with consonant doublets (e.g., *rrug*), which is illegal in English, whereas others ended with doublets, which is legal in English (e.g., *rugg*). In a subsequent spelling test, children recalled the final doublets much better than the initial doublets. For the items including an initial doublet, omission errors, which consist of spelling a word containing a doublet without any doublets (e.g., *rrug* spelled *rug*), were more frequent. However, children also made *transposition* errors, which consist of doubling the final consonant instead of the initial one (e.g., *rrug* spelled *rugg*). Importantly, they almost never doubled the initial consonant instead of the final one, and they also almost never doubled final consonants for the items that had been taught without doublets. This finding suggests that, in the same way that English university students remembered that the word *Gandhi* included an *h*, children remembered that one letter was doubled and thus doubled a consonant, but not necessary the correct one. Their trend toward doubling the consonant in a legal, rather than illegal, position suggests that their knowledge about individual spellings (that a word includes a doublet) was supplemented by general orthographic knowledge (that doublets are illegal in the word-initial position).

Fayol, Lété, and Pacton (2008) and Fayol, Treiman, Lété, and Pacton (2010) have explored the impact of adults' sensitivity to graphotactic regularities on the learning of the spelling of new words containing double letters. Whereas Campbell and Coltheart (1984) focused on the single word *Gandhi*, with the rare letter combination *dh*, Fayol and his colleagues used spellings that were more and less consistent with the graphotactic patterns of the language in order to explore whether some errors are restricted to spellings with less common patterns. Whereas the children in the Wright and Ehri (2007) study were presented with spellings of isolated words in an explicit teaching situation, in Fayol and collaborators' experiments, participants were exposed to novel spellings in the context of meaningful texts but were not explicitly asked to remember the spellings. They used an incidental learning situation, which allows a strict control over how often participants had seen the new word's spelling. This paradigm had been used previously to explore whether people can gain word-specific knowledge from reading connected texts without conscious intention to remember words' spellings (Gilbert, 1934a, 1934b, 1935; Ormrod, 1986a, 1986b; Share, 1995, 1999). Fayol and colleagues' novel adaptation of a prior paradigm assessed whether general knowledge about spelling patterns influences people's memory for specific words. Another difference of this new approach with Wright and Ehri's study is that, instead of using spellings such as *rrug* that are blatantly illegal, Fayol et al. (2010) investigated patterns that are probabilistic in nature. They exploited the fact that *n*, *r*, and *t* frequently double in French, whereas *b*, *d*, and *g* are less likely to double (35 times as many words with *nn*, *rr*, and *tt* as with *bb*, *dd*, and *gg*, according to the French lexical database LEXIQUE; New, Pallier, Ferrand, & Matos, 2001).

In the learning phase of the study by Fayol et al. (2010), university students were exposed to three types of pseudoword spellings that all corresponded to the same pronunciations: *no-doublet* items contained only single consonants (e.g., *tidunar*), *frequent-doublet* items contained one frequent consonant doublet (e.g., *tidunnar*), and *rare-doublet* items contained one rare consonant doublet (e.g., *tiddunar*). In the test phase, participants had to answer questions about the content of the stories. One required them to write the novel item. There was no explicit instruction to spell the item as it was written in the story. The results showed that participants were more accurate at spelling no-doublet and frequent-doublet items than rare-doublet items. Moreover, transposition errors were more common for rare-doublet items than frequent-doublet items. For instance, *tidunar* and *tidunnar* were more often correctly spelled than *tiddunar*, and this last word was often misspelled *tidunnar*, with transposition of the doubling from *d*, which is not often doubled in French, to *n*, which is often doubled.

The procedure used by Fayol et al. (2010) corresponds to what often happens when one spells a word without intention to spell it as it was written in the text(s) in which it has been encountered. The influence of general knowledge of spelling patterns on adults' memory for specific words could, in part, result from lack of explicit spelling instruction for specific items as they appeared in the written story. To address this issue, Borchardt et al. (2011) used the same learning phase as Fayol et al. (2010) but assessed orthographic learning with a dictation task during which university students were explicitly asked to spell the items as they were written in the story. Despite this instruction change, the results were very similar to those reported by Fayol et al. University students were less accurate at spelling the rare-doublet items than the no-doublet and frequent-doublet items in the two experiments. The only difference was that, although Fayol et al. did not find any difference between no-doublet and frequent-doublet items, Borchardt et al. (2011) found better performance for no-doublet than for frequent-doublet items. Beyond this difference, the main result was that transposition errors were frequent on rare-doublet items (e.g., *tiddunar* misspelled as *tidunnar*) but very rare on frequent-doublet items (e.g., *tidunnar* misspelled as *tiddunar*).

Borchardt et al. (2011) carried out the same experiment with third and fifth graders. The level of orthographic learning reached was higher in Grade 5 than in Grade 3. In Grade 3, misspellings were mainly omission errors (e.g., *tidunar* instead of *tiddunar* or *tidunnar*); transposition errors were very rare for both frequent-doublet and rare-doublet items. The proportion of omission errors decreased importantly from Grade 3 to Grade 5 and, conversely, transposition errors became more frequent in Grade 5. Furthermore, as for university students, transposition errors were far more frequent for rare-doublet items (doubling a consonant that is frequently doubled instead of a consonant that is rarely doubled) than for frequent-doublet items (doubling a consonant that is rarely doubled instead of a consonant that is frequently doubled). The lack of transposition errors in the third-grade children in the study by Borchardt et al. (2011) and their occurrence with younger children in the Wright and Ehri (2007) study may be explained in at least three nonexclusive ways. Learning was incidental in the former and intentional in the latter. Alternatively, frequent legal patterns were compared to rare legal patterns in the former, whereas frequent legal patterns were compared to blatantly illegal patterns in the latter. And finally, the items were longer in the former than in the latter (e.g., *tiddunar* vs. *rrug*).

Thus, these results confirm that people can gain word-specific knowledge from reading connected texts, without conscious intention to remember word-specific spellings (Gilbert, 1934a, 1934b, 1935; Omrod, 1986a, 1986b; Share, 1995, 1999). They also suggest that knowledge about individual spellings is supplemented by general orthographic knowledge, or graphotactic knowledge. This result seems to be somewhat generalizable because knowledge of graphotactic patterns appears to influence memory for the spelling of different types of words in different learning and testing situations (incidental and intentional, and words presented in isolation and in texts), different populations (beginning readers, middle and end of elementary school, and university students), and different languages (French and English).

It is important to stress that we have focused on the results showing that reliance on probabilistic patterns can yield systematic errors when a spelling includes a less common pattern. However, for the most part, such reliance leads to correct spellings, and it is very likely that many correct spellings reflect use of general knowledge about the patterns of a writing system (built up from experience with this writing system) in addition to word-specific knowledge.

Morphological Relatedness in Experiments That Examine Learning the Spelling of New Words

The studies that have investigated whether children use morphologically related words to spell others typically contrast rates of misspellings, specifically demonstrated with fewer mistakes when spellers can use morphological information than when they cannot. A straightforward consequence is that an impact of morphology can be observed only when children still make misspellings. Furthermore, in most studies, evidence of better spelling when morphological information can be used may simply reflect the higher frequency of the stem of words that can be spelled using morphology due to the presence of the stem in multiple morphologically related words. Experiments that examine learning the spelling of new words may allow us to go beyond these limitations (Pacton, 2010). They might get us closer to the process of spelling acquisition given their focus on novel words.

Pacton's (2010) experiments explored children's learning of the spelling of two kinds of pseudowords embedded within stories, as if they were real words. All the pseudowords ended with a vowel sound that could be spelled in more than one way in French. For example, given that many French words include silent letters, especially in the word-final position, the final /wa/ of the pseudowords /modwa/ and /ridwa/ can be spelled *oi* (as in *envoi*, sending off, or *paroi*, side), *oit* (as in *endroit*, place, or *exploit*, exploit), *ois* (as in *pois*, pea, or *siamois*, siamese), or *oie* (as in *joie*, joy, or *courroie*, belt). In the experiments, some children read stories with pseudowords such as *modwa* spelled as *modois*, and others spelled as *modoit*. Furthermore, pseudowords could be opaque or morphological. Opaque pseudowords were embedded within a context that provides semantic information about the pseudowords (e.g., it is a tool, a fruit, a kind of cake, a bird, a musical instrument), but no morphological information that can justify their spelling. By contrast, such a justification was available for morphological pseudowords. For example, a story including an opaque pseudoword indicated that among musical instruments, the *modwa* (spelled either *modois* or *modoit*) was probably harder to learn, that *the musician took the modwa to tidy up the modwa*, but nothing justifies the final silent -s or -t. The corresponding story that included a morphological pseudoword further indicated that the *modwatist* (or *modwazist*) was the musician who plays the *modwa* instrument and that the *modwat* (or *modwaz*) was a nice melody that was played only with a *modwa*. Thus, in the same way that morphologically related words such as *bavarder* (to chat) and *bavardage* (chatting) justify the final silent -d of the word *bavard*, the pseudowords *modwatist* and *modwat* justify the final silent -t of *modoit*; and, likewise, *modwazist* and *modwaz* justify the final silent -s of *modois*. The hypothesis was that, if children benefit from the information about the morphological structure of the pseudoword provided by the sentence, they should learn the spelling of *morphological* pseudowords better than the spelling of *opaque* pseudowords.

These learning situations further allow a strict control of the number of expositions to whole words as well as to stems. For instance, it is possible to use texts including each five occurrences of one opaque pseudoword, five occurrences of one morphological pseudoword, and one occurrence of two pseudowords morphologically related to the morphological pseudoword. In this situation, a better learning of the spelling of morphological pseudowords over opaque pseudo-words can be explained by both morphology and higher frequency of the stem for morphological than for opaque pseudowords, exactly as in studies comparing the spelling of words such as *dirt* (which also occurs in *dirty* and *dirtiness*) and *duty* (which does not occur in morphologically related words). However, if the texts include seven occurrences of one opaque pseudoword, five occurrences of one morphological pseudoword, and one occurrence of two pseudowords mor-phologically related to the morphological pseudoword, a better learning of the spelling for morphological pseudowords can no longer be explained by higher frequency of the stem.

The experiments of Pacton (2010) included these two kinds of situations. Children in the third and fourth grades had to read eight texts including in each one morphological pseudoword and one opaque pseudoword. To ensure that children did acquire word-specific knowledge, for example that *modwa* was spelled *modois*, and not simply that the (only) new word including the final sound /wa/ was spelled *ois*, only four phonological endings were used. Each of them was represented with a first spelling (e.g., *ois*) in two pseudowords and with a second spelling (e.g., *oit*) in two other pseudowords. For example, a child encountered the morphological pseudowords *modoit* and *lagois* and the opaque pseudowords *vensoit* and *ridois*, whereas another child encountered the mor-phological pseudowords *vensoit* and *ridois* and the opaque pseudowords *modoit* and *lagois*. Thus, the learning situation was made especially difficult by both the number of novel words to which children were exposed (16 new words spread over 8 texts) and the interference resulting from the fact that the four target sounds were written with one spelling in two pseudowords and with another spelling in two others.

Children received booklets that included eight stories along with a series of questions on the texts, but questions were not on the pseudowords. They were asked to read one text and move to the next page to answer questions about it, without reading the text again, and then to go to the next text, and so on. Thirty minutes after having completed this task, orthographic learning was assessed for some children with a dictation test and for others with a forced-choice test among three spellings. The three spellings were all phonologically plausible. One choice was correct (e.g., *ridois*). In one incorrect choice, the target sound was represented with the spelling used in two other pseudowords (e.g., *ridoit*). In the other incor-rect choice, it was represented with a spelling that was never in any of the four pseudowords including the same target sound (e.g., *ridoi*).

Children correctly spelled the target sound significantly more often for mor-phological pseudowords than for opaque pseudowords (58% vs. 49%). This effect occurred even when the two types of pseudowords were balanced for the number of exposures to the stem (each morphological pseudoword presented five times along with two morphologically related pseudowords and each opaque pseudo-word presented seven times).

Similar findings emerged when orthographic learning in the same learning conditions was assessed with a forced-choice test. The correct spellings were cho-sen significantly more often than expected by chance (33.33%) for morphological and opaque pseudowords, which indicates that the spellings of these two kinds of words were learned. Furthermore, the selection of the correct spelling was significantly more frequent for morphological than for opaque pseudowords (53% vs. 42%). This advantage for morphological pseudowords is important because it was found in a situation in which the stem of morphological pseudowords was not more frequent than the stem of opaque pseudowords.

To sum up, several studies have suggested that children can use morphological words to spell other words because children spell better when some morphological information can be used (e.g., using *dirt* to spell the morphologically complex word *dirty*) than when morphological information cannot be used (e.g., spelling the morphologically simple word *duty*). These studies have two limitations. First, even if the frequency of words for which morphological information can be used *and* the frequency of words for which morphological information cannot be used are controlled, the frequency of the stem of words is typically higher when morphological information can be used. Second, because these studies focused on the lower rate of misspellings when morphology can be used than when it cannot, they can reveal an impact of morphology only when children still make misspellings, which is problematic for studying how good spellers learn to spell. Experiments that watch learning of new words, embedded within little stories, as if they were real words, allow researchers to go beyond these limitations (Pacton, 2010). They show that children benefit from the information about the morphological structure of words even when the frequency of the stem does not differentiate words for which morphology can or cannot be used.

CONCLUSIONS

There is clear evidence that children are sensitive to graphotactic regularities from a young age. As early as the first grade, and sometimes even in kindergarten, children are sensitive to salient graphotactic regularities such as the illegality of doublets in word-initial position or the fact that some letters are more often doubled than others (e.g., Cassar & Treiman, 1997). However, other graphotactic regularities, such as the illegality of doublets after single letters in French, appear to be more difficult to detect. Sensitivity to these kinds of regularities might emerge later and remain less developed, even at the end of elementary school and into adulthood (Danjon & Pacton, 2009).

Sensitivity to graphotactic regularities has been mainly documented in isolation with pseudoword judgment and spelling tasks (e.g., Cassar & Treiman, 1997; Pacton et al., 2001). These tasks have been used because it is often impossible to determine whether spellers use word-specific knowledge or general orthographic knowledge by investigating the spelling of real words. A key issue concerns whether, when, and how spellers use their graphotactic knowledge when other sources of information, that is, more relevant, are available. The few studies that have addressed this issue indicate that children and even adults rely on their graphotactic knowledge even if they can rely on simple, morphologically based rules (e.g., Kemp & Bryant, 2003; Pacton et al., 2005). For instance, in English, children's and adults' sensitivity to the fact that *z* is never transcribed *ze* or *se* after a consonant leads them to use the nominal plural marker s for the plural form of nouns with a consonant + /z/ ending more often than for the plural form of nouns with a vowel + /z/ ending. Likewise, the higher sensitivity of French children and adults to the illegality of doublets in the beginning of words than in the middle of words after a consonant seems to explain that they more often spell the sound /s/ with ss (which is correct only between a vowel and a consonant) between a consonant and a vowel than in the word-initial position.

Several studies pointed out that the concordance between the orthographic structure of the words and the graphotactic regularities of the language may explain, in part, the difficulties of acquisition of lexical knowledge. Experiments that examine learning of new words allow a rigorous test of the influence of conformity to graphotactic patterns on the learning of the spelling of a specific word, above and beyond frequency of exposure to this word (Fayol et al., 2010). They are useful to better understand the integration of these two facets of orthographic knowledge, and they support recent studies that have suggested that factors other than phonology are involved in orthographic learning (e.g., Nation, Angell, & Castles, 2007).

Share (1995) conceptualized the implicit learning of specific words' spelling as a self-teaching mechanism. The practice of decoding, through which a child builds up his or her knowledge about grapheme-phonemes correspondences, would lead both to the production of an oral form likely to be connected with the verbal lexicon in which it is already known, and to the learning of the corresponding orthographic form. In support of this view, average decoding performance is positively and significantly correlated with the results from the different tests assessing the orthographic learning. However, in languages with inconsistent mappings between spellings and sounds (such as English) the correlations are modest (e.g., $r = .52$ in the study of Cunningham, Perry, Stanovich, & Share, 2002). Furthermore, the relationship between the quality of the phonological recoding and the orthographic learning is generally assessed by calculating a correlation between the mean performances of each participant for phonological recoding and for orthographic learning. This type of analysis shows a general relationship between phonological decoding and orthographic learning, but it does not assess whether the quality of the decoding of a specific item determines the level of learning of this item. In a study involving English-speaking children aged 8 to 9 years of age, Nation et al. (2007) showed that the general relationship between the phonological decoding and the orthographic spelling learning was not maintained in item-by-item analyses. According to Nation et al. (see also Castles & Nation, 2006), this finding suggests that other factors, especially graphotactic knowledge, might be involved in the orthographic learning of specific words.

After a review of several studies that have investigated whether, when, and how children use morphologically related words to spell other words, we have shown that experiments that examine learning of new words can also be used to investigate whether children benefit from the information about the morphological structure of new words. These learning situations allowed a strict control of the number of exposures to whole words as well as to stems. This control is important because prior studies contrasting the spelling of words that can and cannot be spelled using morphologically related words could balance surface frequency, but not the frequency of their stem. Further research with this paradigm should investigate the use of other kinds of morphological information and the impact of the delay on the learning of the spelling of new words. These studies should also investigate the joint influence of morphological information and graphotactic regularities (e.g., morphological information that guides toward spelling words ending in -ar with a silent /d/ or with a silent /t/ because the ending -ard is used more frequently than the ending -art in French). These interactions can best be understood in studies examining the simultaneous impact of different skills with children of varying reading and spelling abilities.

REFERENCES

Alegria, J., & Mousty, P. (1996). The development of spelling procedures in French-speaking, normal and reading-disabled children: Effects of frequency and lexicality. *Journal of Experimental Child Psychology, 63*, 312–338.

Attenborough, R. (Producer & Director). (1982). *Gandhi* [Motion picture]. United Kingdom: International Film Investors.

Baron, J., & Treiman, R. (1980). Use of orthography in reading and learning to read. In J. F. Kavanagh & R. L. Venezky (Eds.), *Orthography, reading, and dyslexia* (pp. 171–189). Baltimore: University Park Press.

Borchardt, G., Treiman, R., Fayol, M., & Pacton, S. (2011). *The influence of children's knowledge about graphotactic regularities on their learning of lexical knowledge.* Manuscript in preparation.

Campbell, R., & Coltheart, M. (1984). Gandhi: The nonviolent route to spelling reform? *Cognition, 17*, 185–192.

Carlisle, J. F. (1988). Knowledge of derivational morphology and spelling ability in fourth, sixth and eighth graders. *Applied Psycholinguistics, 9*, 247–266.

Cassar, M., & Treiman, R. (1997). The beginnings of orthographic knowledge: Children's knowledge of double letters in words. *Journal of Educational Psychology, 89*, 631–644.

Cassar, M., Treiman, R., Moats, L., Pollo, T. C., & Kessler, B. (2005). How do the spellings of children with dyslexia compare with those of typical children? *Reading and Writing, 18*, 27–49.

Castles, A., & Nation, K. (2006). How does orthographic learning happen? In S. Andrews (Ed.), *From inkmarks to ideas: Challenges and controversies about word recognition and reading* (pp. 151–179). Hove, East Sussex: Psychology Press.

Clashen, H., Rothweiler, M., Woest, A., & Marcus, G. (1992). Regular and irregular inflection in the acquisition of German noun plurals. *Cognition, 45*, 225–255.

Cunningham, A. E., Perry, K. E., Stanovich, K. E., & Share, D. L. (2002). Orthographic learning during reading: Examining the role of self-teaching. *Journal of Experimental Child Psychology, 82*, 185–199.

Danjon, J., & Pacton, S. (2009, September 2–5). *Children's learning about properties of double letters: The case of French.* Presented at the 16th European Society for Cognitive Psychology Conference (ESCOP), Kraków, Poland.

Deacon, S. H., & Bryant, P. (2005). The strength of children's knowledge of the role of roots in the spelling of derived words. *Journal of Child Language, 32*, 375–389.

Deacon, S. H., & Bryant, P. (2006a). Getting to the root: Young writers' sensitivity to the role of root morphemes in the spelling of inflected and derived words. *Journal of Child Language, 33*, 401–417.

Deacon, S. H., & Bryant, P. (2006b). This turnip's not for turning: Children's morphological awareness and their use of root morphemes in spelling. *British Journal of Developmental Psychology, 24,* 567–575.

Deacon, S. H., & Pacton, S. (2007, July 12–15). *Using spelling as an empirical test of rules versus statistics.* Presented at the Society for the Scientific Study of Reading, Prague.

Fayol, M., Lété, B., & Pacton, S. (2008, June 11–13). *On acquiring the spelling of words including silent letters. Both self-teaching and knowledge of orthographic regularities matter.* Presented at Sigwriting, The 11th International Conference of the EARLI Special Interest Group on Writing, Lund.

Fayol, M., Treiman, R., Lété, B., & Pacton, S. (2010). *Learning to spell from reading: General knowledge about spelling patterns can distort memory for specific words.* Presented at the 51st Annual Meeting of the Psychonomic Society, St. Louis, MO.

Gilbert, L. C. (1934a). Effect of reading on spelling in the ninth grade. *School Review, 42,* 197–204.

Gilbert, L. C. (1934b). Effect of reading on spelling in the secondary schools. *California Quarterly of Secondary Education, 9,* 269–275.

Gilbert, L. C. (1935). A study of the effect of reading on spelling. *Journal of Educational Research, 28,* 570–576.

Hayes, H., Treiman, R., & Kessler, B. (2006). Children use vowels to help them spell consonants. *Journal of Experimental Child Psychology, 94,* 27–42.

Kemp, N. (2006). Children's spelling of base, inflected, and derived words: Links with morphological awareness. *Reading and Writing, 19,* 737–765.

Kemp, N., & Bryant, P. (2003). Do beez buzz? Rule-based and frequency-based knowledge in learning to spell plural -s. *Child Development, 74,* 63–74.

Kessler, B., & Treiman, R. (2001). Relationships between sounds and letters in English monosyllables. *Journal of Memory and Language, 44,* 592–617.

Lehtonen, A., & Bryant, P. (2005). Doublet challenge: Form comes before function in children's understanding of their orthography. *Developmental Science, 8,* 211–217.

Manza, L., & Reber, A. S. (1997). Representing artificial grammar: Transfer across stimulus forms and modalities. In D. Berry (Ed.). *How implicit is implicit learning* (pp 73–106). Oxford: Oxford University Press.

Marcus, G. F., Pinker, S., Ullman, M., Hollander, M., Rosen, T. J., & Xu, F. (1992). Overregularization in language acquisition. *Monographs of the Society for Research in Child Development, 57*(4), 1–182.

Nagy, W. E., & Anderson, R. (1984). The number of words in printed school English. *Reading Research Quarterly, 19,* 304–330.

Nation, K., Angell, P., & Castles, A. (2007). Orthographic learning via self-teaching in children learning to read English: Effects of exposure, durability and context. *Journal of Experimental Child Psychology, 96,* 71–84.

New, B., Pallier, C., Ferrand, L., & Matos, R. (2001). Une base de données lexicales du français contemporain sur internet: LEXIQUE. [A lexical database of contemporary French on the internet: LEXIQUE]. *L'Année Psychologique, 101,* 447–462.

Ormrod, J. E. (1986a). Learning to spell: Three studies at the university level. *Research in the Teaching of English, 20,* 160–173.

Ormrod, J. E. (1986b). Learning to spell while reading: A follow-up study. *Perceptual and Motor Skills, 63,* 652–654.

Pacton, S. (2010, July). *Learning to spell from reading: Does morphological information facilitate children's memory for specific words?* Presented at the Congress of the Society for Scientific Studies of reading, Berlin, Germany.

Pacton, S., Casalis, S., & Deacon, S. H. (2007, July). *The joint influence of orthographic and morphological regularities on children's spelling: Evidence from French.* Presented at the Congress of the Society for Scientific Studies of Reading, Prague, Czech Republic.

Pacton, S., & Deacon, S. H. (2008). The timing and mechanisms of children's use of morphological information in spelling: A review of evidence from English and French, *Cognitive Development, 23*, 339–359.

Pacton, S., Fayol, M., & Perruchet, P. (2002). The acquisition of untaught orthographic regularities in French. In L. Verhoeven, C. Elbro, & P. Reitsma (Eds.), *Precursors of functional literacy* (pp. 121–136). Dordrecht: Kluwer.

Pacton, S., Fayol, M., & Perruchet, P. (2005). Children's implicit learning of graphotactic and morphological regularities. *Child Development, 76*, 324–339.

Pacton, S., Perruchet, P., Fayol, M., & Cleeremans, A. (2001). Implicit learning out of the lab: The case of orthographic regularities. *Journal of Experimental Psychology: General, 130*, 401–426.

Perruchet, P., & Vinter, A. (2002). The self-organizing consciousness. *Behavioral and Brain Sciences, 25*, 297–330.

Redington, M., & Chater, N. (2002). Knowledge representation and transfer in artificial grammar learning (AGL). In R. M. French & A. Cleeremans (Eds.), *Implicit learning and consciousness: An empirical, philosophical, and computational consensus in the making* (pp. 121–143). London: Psychology Press.

Rey-Debove, J. (1984). Le domaine de la morphologie lexicale. *Cahiers de Lexicologie, 45*, 3–19.

Rubin, H. (1988). Morphological knowledge and early writing ability. *Language and Speech, 31*, 337–355.

Seidenberg, M. S., & Gonnerman, L. M. (2000). Explaining derivational morphology as the convergence of codes. *Trends in Cognitive Sciences, 4*, 353–360.

Sénéchal, M. (2000). Morphological effects in children's spelling of French words. *Canadian Journal of Experimental Psychology, 54*, 76–85.

Sénéchal, M., Basque, M. T., & Leclaire, T. (2006). Morphological knowledge as revealed in children's spelling accuracy and reports of spelling strategies. *Journal of Experimental Child Psychology, 95*, 231–254.

Share, D. L. (1995). Phonological recoding and self-teaching: Sine qua non of reading acquisition. *Cognition, 55*, 151–218.

Share, D. L. (1999). Phonological recoding and orthographic learning: A direct test of the self-teaching hypothesis. *Journal of Experimental Child Psychology, 72*, 95–129.

Treiman, R. (1993). *Beginning to spell: A study of first-grade children*. New York: Oxford University Press.

Treiman, R., & Cassar, M. (1996). Effects of morphology on children's spelling of final consonant clusters. *Journal of Experimental Child Psychology, 63*, 141–170.

Treiman, R., Cassar, M., & Zukowski, A. (1994). What types of linguistic information do children use in spelling? The case of flaps. *Child Development, 65*, 1318–1337.

Treiman, R., & Kessler, B. (2006). Spelling as statistical learning: Using consonantal context to spell vowels. *Journal of Educational Psychology, 98*, 642–652.

Treiman, R., Kessler, B., & Bick, S. (2002). Context sensitivity in the spelling of English vowels. *Journal of Memory and Language, 47*, 448–468.

Treiman, R., & Zukowski, A. (1991). Levels of phonological awareness. In S. A. Brady & D. P. Shankweiler (Eds.), *Phonological processes in literacy: A tribute to Isabelle Y. Liberman* (pp. 67–83). Hillsdale, NJ: Erlbaum.

Waters, G., Bruck, M., & Malus-Abramowitz, M. (1988). The role of linguistic and visual information in spelling: A developmental study. *Journal of Experimental Child Psychology, 45*, 400–421.

Wright, D. M., & Ehri, E. (2007). Beginners remember orthography when they learn to read words: The case of doubled letters. *Applied Psycholinguistics, 28*, 115–133.

15

Toward a Redefinition of Spelling in Shallow Orthographies
Phonological, Lexical, and Grammatical Skills in Learning to Spell Italian

BARBARA ARFÉ, BIANCA DE BERNARDI,
MARGHERITA PASINI, and FRANCESCA POETA

O ne of the best critical appraisals of the cognitive approach to writing is reported in a paper by Pietro Boscolo (1995), who recommended it as an approach that "so convincingly described the complexity of writing" (p. 344). However, as Boscolo stressed, the complexity of writing, as documented in empirical research, does not easily transfer to models of writing and writing development. Nowadays a hierarchical model of writing processes still dominates. This model considers the linguistic process of writing as split in two: a high-level process, related to the linguistic generation of words, sentences, and paragraphs in texts (text generation), and a low-level process, related to the transcription of the text generated. This picture echoes past linguistic theories of writing, according to which the act of writing is not language, but merely a way of recording language through transcription (Bloomfield, 1970). Two characteristics of the transcription process contributed to this view: (1) transcription can be automated, and (2) transcription pertains to the processing and representation of minimal linguistic units: graphemes, words, and word parts (word bases, suffixes, and prefixes). As a result, many educators and clinicians neglect the complex linguistic nature of the transcription process related to spelling, especially in orthographies where sounds-to-letters correspondences are very predictable and regular.

Researchers who study spelling in French (Fayol, Largy, & Lemaire, 1994; Totereau, Thevenin, & Fayol, 1997) and American (Venezky, 1970, 1999) and British English (Nunes & Bryant, 2006) have long recognized that their morphophonemic languages with deep orthographies may lack simple letter–sound correspondences as in shallow orthographies, but are predictable based on the linguistic relationships underlying spelling (Ehri, 1986; Nunes, Bryant, & Bindman, 1997; Treiman & Cassar, 1997). On the one hand, the need to transcribe a predominantly silent morphology (e.g., the -s of *les chiens*) compels children to use grammatical clues and word morphology in spelling, besides phonological strategies. On the other hand, morphology helps children differentiate phonologically equivalent inputs in orthography (e.g., two vs. too). Fayol and collaborators (Fayol et al., 1994; Totereau et al., 1997) demonstrated how transcription in spelling is a high-level linguistic process, with cognitive costs not only for young spellers but also for expert adult writers. These researchers introduced the notion that the complex language knowledge of a child is utilized in the spelling transcription task.

The idea that other sources of linguistic knowledge, beyond phonology and orthography, influence spelling development has found wide consensus in the past 20 years (Metsala & Walley, 1998; Nagy, Berninger, & Abbott, 2006; Nagy, Berninger, Abbott, Vaughan, & Varmeulen, 2003; Plaza & Cohen, 2003, 2004; Richards et al., 2006; Walley, Metsala, & Garlock, 2003). However, both research data and spelling models in support of this thesis have derived from studies of nontransparent orthographies (mainly English; Plaza & Cohen, 2003, 2004; Walley et al., 2003). Their generalization to other orthographies is still open to discussion and requires some empirical evidence (Share, 2008). It is important to ascertain the extent to which results of the research and theoretical concepts of French and English scholars can be extended to more transparent orthographies or if they should be considered language specific.

The study reported in this chapter aimed to identify the role that phonological, vocabulary (semantics), and grammatical knowledge plays in Italian children's spelling development. To our knowledge, no previous research has investigated the contribution of different kinds of linguistic knowledge in the early stages of learning to spell Italian words. This chapter might then be the first contribution in this direction.

THE ROLE OF PHONOLOGICAL
PROCESSES IN SPELLING

Spelling has been traditionally conceived as a basic writing process of recoding sequential phonological segments of words into letter sequences. Especially in the early stages of learning to write, children rely on their phonological knowledge to spell written words, and their phonological abilities are important markers for the development of writing skills or disabilities (Bishop & Clarkson, 2003; Lewis, Freebairn, & Taylor, 2002; Nunes et al., 1997; Steinbrink & Klatte,

2007). For example, sensitivity to rhyme, the phonological structure of words, and phonemic awareness have been proven necessary to segmenting sublexical units in words for matching those sound segments with letters (Ouellette & Sénéchal, 2010).

Contemporary psycholinguistic spelling models assume different steps in auditory and phonological processing in the transcription of words under dictation. After speech input, the auditory information received by the ear is transformed through acoustic-to-phonological conversion routines and transferred to the phonological output buffer in working memory, a storage and processing mechanism that holds phonological information for processing it for other tasks, such as the sound-to-spelling conversion routines during writing. Alternatively, phonological short-term representations, derived from the auditory phonological analysis, are transferred to a phonological input lexicon and then to a semantic system or a phonological output lexicon, linked with an orthographic output lexicon, for written spelling (Laiacona et al., 2009; Shallice, Rumiati, & Zadini, 2000). According to these models, three processes that become related to phonological skills may constrain the functioning of the spelling system from its early phases in individuals with normal hearing: (1) an accurate analysis of the speech input (based on efficient auditory discrimination mechanisms), (2) the functioning of the mechanisms of acoustic-phonological conversion and phonological maintenance (based on an efficient use of the phonological loop of working memory), and (3) the stability and quality of the stored phonological representations of words, based on the writer's lexical knowledge and phonological sensitivity to phoneme sequence and correspondence to graphemes in word structure.

Although linguists differentiate between phonetics (production of coarticulated phones) and phonemics (abstraction of sound units that make a difference in meaning and correspond to graphemes), literacy researchers often refer to grapheme–phoneme correspondence as a phonetic strategy even though phonemes rather than phones are involved in these correspondences. From this perspective, the role of phonetic strategies in learning to write has been considered crucial in particular to shallow orthographies, such as Italian, which has a nearly perfect one-to-one phoneme–letter correspondence (Zoccolotti, Angelelli, Judica, & Luzzatti, 2005). Given the regularity of the Italian orthographic system, and the systematic correspondence between speech sounds and letters, phonemic awareness turns out to be crucial to Italian children when learning to read and write. It has been found that phonetic strategies are most successful in the early stages of spelling in Italian (in first and second grades), and only later do children learn to use orthographic and lexical strategies for reading and spelling words under dictation (third and fourth grades). Evidence in support of this developmental sequence comes from recent reading studies regarding Italian (Orsolini, Fanari, Tosi, De Nigris, & Carrieri, 2006). Results for reading are consistent with spelling under dictation data: Italian children's early spelling skills are mainly based on phonetic strategies. Nevertheless, it still seems valuable to determine the degree to which these skills are influenced by other kinds of knowledge, such as grammatical and vocabulary knowledge.

THE INTERACTION OF LINGUISTIC
REPRESENTATIONS IN SPELLING

The traditional dual-route spelling model postulates two separate and independent mechanisms (the lexical and the phonological) that contribute to the production of written nonwords (or novel pseudowords) and familiar words (Patterson, 1986). However, some recent findings contradict the assumption that the phonological mechanism represents a nonlexical process. On-line kinematic data reveal how both words and nonwords are lexically parsed in adult writers (Tucha, Trumpp, & Lange, 2004). The most recent models of spelling all assume an interaction between different spelling mechanisms and linguistic representations (phonological, lexical and semantic, morphological). Clinical data support this view. Research with dysgraphic patients, for example, suggests that lexical and sublexical processes may interact in different ways in opaque as well as transparent orthographies (Laiacona et al., 2009; McCloskey, Macaruso, & Rapp, 2006; Sage & Ellis, 2004).

Developmental models of spelling underlie the interaction and developmental relations between different kinds of linguistic representations. The lexical restructuring model (Metsala & Walley, 1998) describes the relation between the developmental construction of lexical and phonological representations of spoken words and their spelling. The model assumes a developmental link between the child's lexical knowledge (vocabulary growth), his or her construction of increasingly refined phonological word representations, and his or her subsequent reading and spelling skills. The more words a child learns, the more distinctions he or she will make between different lexical entries in memory stores and the more fine-grained his or her phonological representations of words should be, which in turn will be used to learn reading and writing. The triple word form model assumes that written words are computed and represented in three interrelated word forms (Berninger & Richards, 2002; Richards et al., 2006), which are stored and processed in working memory: phonological for spoken words, orthographic for written words, and morphological for spoken and written words (Berninger et al., 2006); the interrelationships among the three word forms are more predictive of the reading and spelling of children with and without dyslexia than are the word forms alone (Berninger, Raskind, Richards, Abbott, & Stock, 2008). It is this map of phonological-orthographic-morphological relationships that writers use to write words (Arfé, D'Ambrosio, Cona, Merella, & Cellino, 2009; Arfé, De Bernardi, Poeta, & Pasini, 2009).

Robust empirical evidence seems to support these models. Children approach the task of spelling with substantial knowledge of words in oral language; they normally have the necessary phonological, morphological, and semantic lexical knowledge to learn to read and spell words.[1] In particular, besides phonological skills, which undoubtedly play a role in the process of learning to encode and spell written words, research findings have also emphasized the contribution of vocabulary knowledge (Ouellette, 2006; Walley et al., 2003) and that of grammatical

---

[1] Young readers and writers can also use their syntactic knowledge to identify the meaning and orthographic form of homophones in the sentence context.

knowledge in learning to spell (Chliounaki & Bryant, 2007; Nagy et al., 2006; Nunes et al., 1997; Plaza & Cohen, 2004; Richards et al., 2006).

Vocabulary knowledge may be related to spelling in two ways: (1) directly, through activation of semantic knowledge stored in memory for the written or spoken word (dual route models, connectionist models; Harm & Seidenberg, 1999; Patterson, 1986; Plaut, McClelland, Seidenberg, & Paterson, 1996), and (2) indirectly, because the child's receptive vocabulary conveys relevant information about the variety of phonological structures in a language (as in the lexical restructuring model; Metsala & Walley, 1998; Walley et al., 2003).

Studies have shown that morphological knowledge also plays a role in the written spelling of deep orthographies, in particular English and French. The contribution of morphological knowledge to spelling skills has been explained as follows: Both English and French are characterized by orthographies with inconsistent sound–letter relationships. The sole use of phonological information is misleading. Morphology helps resolve some spelling inconsistencies in these two writing systems.

Research documents an increasing ability with age to use morphological and grammatical information in spelling (Beers & Beers, 1992; Pacton & Fayol, 2003). At an initial stage, spelling dwells on phonetic strategies (e.g., /wen/ may be spelled as *wen* instead of *when*), but as grammatical awareness increases, children begin to adopt morphological information to spell words conventionally and independently of phonetic properties (/wen/ spelled *when*; Chliounaki & Bryant, 2007; Nunes et al., 1997). In general, research shows that if grammatical knowledge affects spelling from its very first stages (from ages 6 and 7; Plaza & Cohen, 2003, 2004), mastery of morphological rules (both inflectional and derivational) in spelling is present only from the age of 8 or 9 in both English- and French-speaking children (Chliounaki & Bryant, 2007; Deacon & Bryant, 2005; Pacton & Fayol, 2003; Sénéchal, Basque, & Leclaire, 2006); and a functional integration of phonological, orthographic, and morphological cues in spelling is still developing among fourth graders (Nagy et al., 2003).

These data raised an important issue. The basic writing skill of spelling seems to be multifaceted, involving the use of different cues and types of knowledge. Examining the contribution of only phonology to spelling leads to an important loss of information in clinical and educational settings.

In this study we investigated the role of children's phonological, lexical, and grammatical knowledge in the early stages of learning to write Italian and the relative role of these language skills in good and poor spellers' spelling skills. We used word, nonword, and text dictation to test spelling under different conditions. Nonword spelling offers an assessment of the child's strategy for converting spoken words into written words, when the child does not have cues other than phonology, and to apply the phoneme-to-grapheme conversion. The spelling of real words activates diverse levels of knowledge of the word to be spelled: phonological, orthographic, semantic, and, probably, morphological knowledge. The spelling of words in a textual context makes it possible to assess how the child uses the linguistic context of the text as a source of semantic and grammatical information to drive his or her spelling choices.

METHOD

Participants

In this study there were 170 Italian elementary school children who participated: 39 first graders (18 boys and 21 girls), 79 second graders (34 boys, 45 girls), and 52 third graders (25 boys and 27 girls). The first language of all children was Italian, and they did not have attention or cognitive problems or other developmental disorders. Children who learned Italian as a second language, who were referred for clinical interventions, or who had significant learning problems also took part in the research activities with their classmates, but their data have not yet been analyzed and their results are not reported in this chapter.

Procedure

At the beginning of the school year, standardized tests were administered to each child individually to assess his or her auditory discrimination, nonword repetition, rhyme awareness, phonemic awareness, receptive vocabulary, and receptive grammar. In December and January, children performed three standardized spelling tasks: word and nonword dictation and dictation of a short text. First graders performed only the first two tasks 2 months after the language assessment.

Individual Language Assessment (September–October)

At the beginning of the school year children were assessed individually, during school hours. Tasks were administered in two subsequent testing sessions, about 24 hours apart. The order of the tasks was counterbalanced between participants. The following tasks were administered to each child to assess his or her linguistic skills:

1. *Auditory discrimination task* (BVN battery; Bisiacchi, Cendron, Gugliotta, Tressoldi, & Vio, 2005): The child was asked to discriminate between 37 pairs of nonwords: whether they were identical or different. Nonword pairs were of different lengths (two-, three-, and four syllables) and differed in only one sound at the beginning or in the middle. This task assesses the child's ability to detect the linguistic acoustic input and apply auditory–phonological conversions on it (Bisiacchi et al., 2005).
2. *Nonword repetition* (BVN battery; Bisiacchi et al., 2005): The child is asked to repeat orally single nonwords pronounced by the examiner. This task comprises 15 items of increasing length and difficulty (from bi- to three-syllabic nonwords) and assesses the efficiency of the child's phonological loop of working memory (Baddeley, Gathercole, & Papagno, 1998). This mechanism is considered critical in both language acquisition and reading and spelling processes. In spelling, the auditory information, once converted in a phonological representation, must be maintained as long as is necessary to perform phoneme-to-grapheme conversions and to transcribe it (Laiacona et al., 2009). Poor performance on the oral nonword repetition reflects difficulty in the phonological analysis and short-term

maintenance of phonological information that provides the input for the phoneme-to-grapheme conversions.

3. *Rhyme awareness* (CMF battery; Marotta, Trasciani, & Vicari, 2004): The task, which has 15 items, assesses the child's sensitivity to the phonological structure of language. The child is shown a picture representing the target word. The examiner names the picture aloud (e.g., va**so**/pot) and asks the child to choose among three pictures (e.g., na**so**/nose, pianta/plant, ruota/ wheel) the one that represents the rhyming word (na**so**/nose). The three pictures are named aloud by the examiner. Rhyme awareness requires the syllabic segmentation of words and is considered a good marker of the child's preliteracy skill in manipulating the phonological components of words, which is closely related to the child's experience with spoken language.

4. *Phonemic awareness* (CMF battery; Marotta et al., 2004): The child is asked to segment into phonemes a list of 15 items of increasing length (from bi- to four-syllabic words). Phonemes, unlike syllables, are not perceptual units in oral language, but rather are based on analysis of abstract sound units in words that correspond to letters. Thus, the child's knowledge of the phonemic structure of words mostly derives from his or her literacy experience (Perfetti, 1991).

5. *Peabody Picture Vocabulary Test–Revised* (Italian translation and standardization by Stella, Pizzoli, & Tressoldi, 2000): The test assesses the child's breadth of receptive vocabulary knowledge. The child is asked to choose from among four pictures the one representing the target word. Words are pronounced aloud by the examiner and no further hints are given.

6. *Receptive grammar:* Two different tests were used to assess the children's receptive grammar. The Test for the Assessment of Linguistic Comprehension (Rustioni Metz-Lancaster & Associazione, 1994) was used in Grades 1 and 2. This test assesses the comprehension of target Italian grammatical structures. Age-relevant target structures are included for each age level, from 3 to 7 years. The protocol, which has 16 items corresponding to age levels 6 and 7, was administered to first and second graders. The Test for Reception of Grammar (TROG), Italian short version (Bisiacchi et al., 2005) was administered to third graders. The TROG (Bishop, 1982) assesses the child's ability to comprehend syntactic and grammatical structures. The test, designed for English-speaking children, has been translated and adapted to Italian. Normative data on a population from 5 to 11 years old are available for a short version, including a selection of the most sensitive items for Italian (18 items; Bisiacchi et al., 2005). In language assessment, the use of tests originally designed to assess in the examinee's first language are always preferable. However, an Italian tool equivalent to Rustioni Metz-Lancaster's test for an older population was not available, and the short TROG version appeared to be the best option.

7. *Assessment of spelling skills (December–January):* Three standardized spelling tasks were administered in the classrooms, collectively, to the children in two sessions: word and nonword dictation and dictation of a short text.

7a, 7b.   *Nonword and word dictated spelling*: The nonword and word spelling subtests of the Battery for the Assessment of Developmental Dyslexia and Dysgraphia (BVDDE; Sartori, Job, & Tressoldi, 1995/2007) were administered collectively to second and third graders. The subtests are standardized on a scholastic population from second to eighth grade. The nonword spelling subtest comprises 24 nonwords of various lengths (from bi to four-syllabic) and orthographic complexity. The word spelling subtest comprises 48 words varying in length (from bi- to four-syllabic) and orthographic complexity (e.g., CVCV, CVCCV, CCVVCVCV, etc.).

To assess first graders, a list of 22 words (from bi- to three-syllabic) of varying levels of complexity (CVCV, CVCCV, etc.) and a list of 14 nonwords with similar characteristics were selected from an assessment tool designed for the early identification of risk factors for dyslexia (European Cooperation in Science and Technology [COST] action; Carriero, Vio, & Tressoldi, 2001) and two Italian lexical databases (Barca, Burani, & Arduino, 2002; Rinaldi, Barca, & Burani, 2004).

7c.   *Spelling in text dictation*: Age-appropriate standardized text dictation tasks were selected from the Battery for the Assessment of Writing and Orthographic Competence (Tressoldi & Cornoldi, 1991) and administered to second and third graders.

RESULTS

Correlations between language scores and children's spelling performance (word and nonword spelling and spelling words in text dictation) were run separately for first, second, and third graders. Table 15.1 shows the correlational matrices for each grade level. It can be seen that the relationship between oral language and spelling skills changes with grade level. Correlations between nonword and word spelling maintain their significance across the three grade levels, but their values decrease from .68 for first graders to .43 and .46 for second and third graders, respectively. This difference is statistically significant in the first case (first graders vs. second graders: $r_1 - r_2 = .25$, $p < .05$) and close to significance in the second (first graders vs. third graders: $r_1 - r_3 = .22$, $p = .07$).

To test the contribution of relevant language predictors to the children's spelling skills, we computed separate hierarchical regressions for first, second, and third graders and for each spelling task (word spelling, nonword spelling, and spelling in text under dictation).

In a first set of analyses, to test the unique contributions of phonology, vocabulary, and grammar to learning to spell in Italian, phonemic awareness, receptive vocabulary, and receptive grammar were entered separately, in this order, as independent variables. Spelling errors were the dependent variable. In a second set of hierarchical regressions, to test the unique contribution of various aspects of phonology in learning to spell in Italian, auditory discrimination, nonword repetition, rhyme, and phonemic awareness were entered separately, in this order, as independent variables. In reporting results, we first present the correlations and then the result of the regression analyses.

TABLE 15.1   Correlations Between Language Measures and Spelling Measures (First, Second, and Third Graders)

First Graders								
Variable	1	2	3	4	5	6	7	8
AD	1							
Nwrep	.40°	1						
RhyA	.37°	.38°	1	1				
PhA	.21	.28	.42°°	.07	1			
Vocab	.36°	.24	.30	.01	.27			
Gramm	.20	.03	.22	−.40°	−.33°	1		
Nwdict	−.33°	−.55°°	−.40°	−.50°°	−.12	.03	1	
Wdict	−.32°	−.32°	−.55°			.02	.68°°	1

Second Graders									
Variable	1	2	3	4	5	6	7	8	9
AD	1								
Nwrep	.13	1							
RhyA	.07	.17	1						
PhA	.04	.17	.39°	1					
Vocab	.10	.05	.18	−.07	1				
Gramm	.04	.20	.12	.10	.43°°	1			
Nwdict	−.14	−.34°	.01	.05	−.11	−.25°	1		
Wdict	−.14	−.18	−.18	−.22°	−.13	−.24°	.43°°	1	
Txtdict	−.12	−.24°	−.20	−.18	−.14	−.16	.47°°	.79°°	1

Third Graders									
Variable	1	2	3	4	5	6	7	8	9
AD	1								
Nwrep	.07	1							
RhyA	.60°°	.22	1						
PhA	.22	.00	.40°	1					
Vocab	.19	.32	.43°	.18	1				
Gramm	.22	.35°	.33°	.08	.32°	1			
Nwdict	−.14	−.07	−.20	−.12	−.23	−.40°°	1		
Wdict	−.04	−.13	−.11	−.16	−.29°	−.28°	.46°°	1	
Txtdict	−.07	−.26	−.17	−.20	−.32°	−.42°°	.50°°	.74°°	1

AD, auditory discrimination; Nwrep, nonword repetition; RhyA, rhyme awareness; PhA, phonemic awareness; Vocab, receptive vocabulary; Gramm, receptive grammar; Nwdict, nonword dictation; Wdict, word dictation; Txtdict, text dictation.
° $p < .05$, °° $p < .01$.

Correlations With First Graders' Spelling Errors

Significant negative correlations emerged between first graders' language skills (in particular phonological skills) and their spelling errors in nonword and word dictation. Nonword spelling errors showed correlations with auditory discrimination [$r(39) = -.33$, $p < .05$], nonword repetition [$r(39) = -.55, p < .001$], rhyme awareness [$r(39) = -.40$, $p < .01$], phonemic awareness [$r(39) = -.40, p < .01$], and receptive vocabulary [$r(39) = -.33, p < .05$]. Spelling errors in real word dictation negatively correlated with auditory discrimination [$r(39) = -.32, p < .05$], nonword repetition [$r(39) = -.32, p < .05$], rhyme awareness [$r(39) = -.55, p < .001$], and phonemic awareness [$r(39) = -.50, p < .001$].

Predictors in Regressions for First Graders: Phonemic Awareness, Receptive Vocabulary, and Receptive Grammar

Nonword Spelling

Because past research showed that sublexical procedures rule Italian children's spelling performance at this age, phonemic awareness was entered first in the first set of hierarchical regressions. This variable was a significant predictor of nonword spelling [$F(1, 37) = 7.23, p < .05$]. Receptive vocabulary at Step 2 resulted in a significant change in R^2 (R^2 change = .09, $p < .05$). Receptive grammar was entered at Step 3, but did not produce significant variation in R^2. The full model, accounting for 27% of variance in nonword spelling, is reported in Table 15.2a.

Real Word Spelling

Phonemic awareness at Step 1 in the first set of analyses accounted for 25% of variance in word spelling [$F(1, 37) = 12.54, p < .005$]. Receptive vocabulary at Step 2 and receptive grammar at Step 3 did not produce a further significant increase in R^2 (Table 15.2a).

Predictors in Regressions for First Graders: Auditory Discrimination, Nonword Repetition, Rhyme Awareness, and Phonemic Awareness

Nonword Spelling

Auditory discrimination was entered first in the second set of analyses, nonword repetition was entered at Step 2, rhyme awareness at Step 3, and phonemic awareness at Step 4. Results showed that, once controlling for variance due to auditory discrimination [$F(1, 37) = 4.57, p < .05$], a significant portion of variance in nonword spelling was explained by nonword repetition (R^2 change = .20, $p < .005$). Rhyme awareness and phonemic awareness did not produce significant changes in the model after the effects of the first two variables were controlled for (see Table 15.2b).

Real Word Spelling

Critically, in the second set of analyses, after auditory discrimination [$F(1, 37) = 4.19, p < .05$] and nonword repetition were controlled, rhyme awareness (Step 3) accounted for a significant portion of the variance in word spelling (R^2 change = .18, $p < .005$), and phonemic awareness (Step 4) produced a further significant increase in R^2 (R^2 change = .08, $p < .05$). Nonword repetition, at Step 2, did not account for significant changes in variance, after auditory discrimination was controlled. The full model is reported in Table 15.2b.

TABLE 15.2a   Summary of Hierarchical Regression Analyses on the Role of Phonemic Awareness, Receptive Vocabulary, and Receptive Grammar in Explaining First Graders' Spelling

| | Dependent Variable: Nonword Spelling | | | | | | | | |

Predictors	Coefficients			Change Statistics				ANOVA	
	ß	t	p	R^2	R^2 Change	F Change (df1, df2)	Sig. F Change	F (df1, df2)	p
Step 1									
Phonemic awareness	-.40	-2.69	.011	.16	.16	7.23 (1, 37)	.011	7.23 (1, 37)	.011
Step 2									
Phonemic awareness	-.38	-2.66	.012						
Receptive vocabulary	-.31	-2.12	.041	.26	.09	4.51 (1, 36)	.041	6.21 (2, 36)	.005
Step 3									
Phonemic awareness	-.38	-2.63	.013						
Receptive vocabulary	-.34	-2.26	.030						
Receptive grammar	.12	.82	.416	.27	.01	.68 (1, 35)	.416	4.33 (3, 35)	.011

| | Dependent Variable: Word Spelling | | | | | | | | |

Predictors	Coefficients			Change Statistics				ANOVA	
	ß	t	p	R^2	R^2 Change	F Change (df1, df2)	Sig. F Change	F (df1, df2)	p
Step 1									
Phonemic awareness	-.50	-3.54	.001	.25	.25	12.54 (1, 37)	.001	12.54 (1, 37)	.001
Step 2									
Phonemic awareness	-.50	-3.46	.001						
Receptive vocabulary	-.09	-.60	.556	.26	.01	.35 (1, 36)	.556	6.34 (2, 36)	.004
Step 3									
Phonemic awareness	-.50	-3.41	.002						
Receptive vocabulary	-.10	-.64	.528						
Receptive grammar	.04	.27	.791	.26	.00	.07 (1, 35)	.791	4.14 (3, 35)	.013

$N = 39$.

TABLE 15.2b   Summary of Hierarchical Regression Analyses on the Role of Auditory Discrimination, Nonword Repetition, Rhyme Awareness, and Phonemic Awareness in Explaining First Graders' Spelling

	Dependent Variable: Nonword Spelling								
Predictors	Coefficients			Change Statistics				ANOVA	
	ß	t	p	R^2	R^2 Change	F Change (df1, df2)	Sig. F Change	F (df1, df2)	p
Step 1									
Auditory discrimination	−.33	−2.14	.039	.11	.11	4.57 (1, 37)	.039	4.57 (1, 37)	.039
Step 2									
Auditory discrimination	−.14	−.89	.377						
Nonword repetition	−.49	−3.26	.002	.31	.20	10.65 (1, 36)	.002	8.20 (2, 36)	.001
Step 3									
Auditory discrimination	−.08	−.52	.605						
Nonword repetition	−.43	−2.81	.008						
Rhyme awareness	−.21	−1.39	.174	.35	.04	1.92 (1, 35)	.174	6.25 (3, 35)	.002
Step 4									
Auditory discrimination	−.07	−.47	.629						
Nonword repetition	−.41	−2.64	.012						
Rhyme awareness	−.13	−.83	.410						
Phonemic awareness	−.22	−1.47	.151	.39	.04	2.16 (1, 34)	.151	5.38 (4, 34)	.002

	Dependent Variable: Word Spelling								
Predictors	Coefficients			Change Statistics				ANOVA	
	ß	t	p	R^2	R^2 Change	F Change (df1, df2)	Sig. F Change	F (df1, df2)	p
Step 1									
Auditory discrimination	−.32	−1.63	.048	.10	.10	4.19 (1, 37)	.048	4.19 (1, 37)	.048
Step 2									
Auditory discrimination	−.23	−1.36	.181						
Nonword repetition	−.22	−1.33	−193	.14	.04	1.76 (1, 35)	.193	3.02 (2, 36)	.061
Step 3									
Auditory discrimination	−.11	−.68	.502						

TABLE 15.2b   Summary of Hierarchical Regression Analyses on the Role of Auditory Discrimination, Nonword Repetition, Rhyme Awareness, and Phonemic Awareness in Explaining First Graders' Spelling (Continued)

Predictors	Coefficients				Change Statistics			ANOVA	
					R^2	F Change	$Sig. F$	F	
	ß	t	p	R^2	Change	(df1, df2)	Change	(df1, df2)	p
Nonword repetition	−.09	−.59	.559						
Rhyme awareness	−.48	−3.10	.004	.33	.18	9.61 (1, 35)	.004	5.70 (3, 35)	.003
Step 4									
Auditory discrimination	−.10	−.65	.521						
Nonword repetition	−.05	−.34	.379						
Rhyme awareness	−.37	−2.35	.025						
Phonemic awareness	−.32	−2.14	.040	.41	.08	4.59 (1, 34)	.040	5.86 (4, 34)	.001

Dependent Variable: Word Spelling

$N = 39$.

Conclusions for First-Grade Spellers

It is interesting to note that in the first set of regressions receptive vocabulary accounted for 9% of variance in nonword spelling, after the effects of phonemic awareness were controlled. Heard names of vocabulary words require phonological processing, which surprisingly was more related to nonword spelling than real word spelling, which has a link to vocabulary meaning. However, phonemic awareness uniquely predicted real word spelling even when auditory discrimination, nonword repetition, and rhyme awareness were controlled. This finding will be discussed later in the chapter.

The second set of regressions showed that phonological skills play a major role in the spelling of both nonwords and real words at this age. First graders' phonological working memory, their sensitivity to word sounds (rhyme awareness), and their fine-grained representation of word structure (phonemic awareness) accounted for their spelling ability. Thus, multiple phonological mechanisms and strategies can be critical at this very early stage of spelling acquisition.

Interestingly, different phonological mechanisms are apparently used to spell words and nonwords: Auditory–phonological conversion and verbal working memory storage and processing mechanisms that hold phonological information contributed to first graders' nonword spelling; but ability to use structural knowledge of word phonology (rhyme awareness and phonemic awareness) was most critical in real word spelling. These data suggest the existence of two different phonological procedures for spelling words and nonwords in first graders. When words are not familiar, the ability to encode and sustain phonological information in working memory and to apply sound-to-spelling conversion procedures appears more critical to spelling, but for (familiar) real words, linguistic awareness, related to rhymes and phonemes, appears necessary.

Correlations With Second Graders' Spelling

Few correlations were significant between language and spelling skills at this grade level. Spelling errors in nonword dictation showed significant negative correlations with nonword repetition [$r(79) = -.34, p < .005$] and receptive grammar [$r(79) = -.25, p < .05$]. Spelling errors in word dictation showed significant negative correlations with phonemic awareness [$r(79) = -.22, p < .05$] and receptive grammar [$r(79) = -.24, p < .05$]; spelling errors in text dictation showed a significant correlation with nonword repetition only [$r(79) = -.24, p < .05$]. Receptive vocabulary and receptive grammar correlated positively [$r(79) = .42, p < .005$] (Table 15.1).

Predictors in Regressions for Second Graders: Phonemic Awareness, Receptive Vocabulary, and Receptive Grammar

Nonword Spelling

Phonemic awareness and receptive vocabulary did not account for variance in nonword spelling. Only receptive grammar, at Step 3, resulted in a significant increase in R^2 (R^2 change $= .06, p < .05$; see the full model in Table 15.3a).

Real Word Spelling

Phonemic awareness at Step 1 accounted for 5% of variance [$F(1, 77) = 4.03, p < .05$]. Receptive vocabulary at Step 2 and receptive grammar at Step 3 did not yield significant changes in R^2.

Text Dictation

None of the independent variables accounted for spelling in text dictation uniquely or together (Table 15.3a)

Predictors in Regressions for Second Graders: Auditory Discrimination, Nonword Repetition, Rhyme Awareness, and Phonemic Awareness

Nonword Spelling

Auditory discrimination at Step 1 did not account for variance in second graders' nonword spelling. Nonword repetition at Step 2 accounted for a significant portion of variance in nonword spelling (R^2 change $= .10, p < .005$); rhyme awareness and phonemic awareness at Steps 3 and 4 did not account for further variance.

Real Word Spelling

Auditory discrimination, nonword repetition, and rhyme awareness did not account for variance in word spelling. Phonemic awareness was the only variable showing a moderate correlation with word spelling (see Table 15.1). However, when auditory discrimination, nonword repetition, and rhyme awareness were entered first in the regression, phoneme awareness did not produce any further significant changes in R^2 (Table 15.3b).

TABLE 15.3a   Summary of Hierarchical Regression Analyses on the Role of Phonemic Awareness, Receptive Vocabulary, and Receptive Grammar in Explaining Second Graders' Spelling

Dependent Variable: Nonword Spelling

Predictors	Coefficients			Change Statistics				ANOVA		
	ß	t	p	R^2	R^2 Change	F Change (df1, df2)	Sig. F Change	F (df1, df2)		p
Step 1										
Phonemic awareness	.05	.43	.670	.002	.002	.18 (1, 77)	.670	.18 (1, 77)		.670
Step 2										
Phonemic awareness	.04	.36	.719							
Receptive vocabulary	−.10	−.91	.367	.01	.01	.82 (1, 76)	.367	.50 (2, 76)		.607
Step 3										
Phonemic awareness	.08	.66	.510							
Receptive vocabulary	.01	.08	.934							
Receptive grammar	−.26	−2.11	.038	.07	.06	4.45 (1, 75)	.038	1.84 (3, 75)		.148

Dependent Variable: Word Spelling

Predictors	Coefficients			Change Statistics				ANOVA		
	ß	t	p	R^2	R^2 Change	F Change (df1, df2)	Sig. F Change	F (df1, df2)		p
Step 1										
Phonemic awareness	−.22	−2.11	.048	.05	.05	4.03 (1, 77)	.048	4.03 (1, 77)		.048
Step 2										
Phonemic awareness	−.23	−2.11	.038							
Receptive vocabulary	−.15	−1.31	.194	.07	.02	1.72 (1, 76)	.194	2.89 (2, 76)		.061
Step 3										
Phonemic awareness	−.21	−1.88	.064							
Receptive vocabulary	−.06	−.48	.630							
Receptive grammar	−.20	−1.63	.107	.10	.03	2.66 (1, 75)	.107	2.86 (3, 75)		.043

continued

TABLE 15.3a   Summary of Hierarchical Regression Analyses on the Role of Phonemic Awareness, Receptive Vocabulary, and Receptive Grammar in Explaining Second Graders' Spelling (Continued)

Predictors	Coefficients				Change Statistics			ANOVA	
	ß	t	p	R^2	R^2 Change	F Change (df1, df2)	Sig. F Change	F (df1, df2)	p
Step 1									
Phonemic awareness	−.18	−1.64	.106	.03	.03	2.68 (1, 77)	.106	2.68 (1, 77)	.106
Step 2									
Phonemic awareness	−.20	−1.74	.085						
Receptive vocabulary	−.15	−1.38	.171	.06	.02	1.91 (1, 76)	.171	2.31 (2, 76)	.106
Step 3									
Phonemic awareness	−.18	−1.62	.110						
Receptive vocabulary	−.11	−.91	.366						
Receptive grammar	−.10	−.76	.449	.07	.01	.58 (1, 75)	.449	1.73 (3, 75)	.169

$N = 79$.

Text Dictation

Auditory discrimination at Step 1 did not account for significant variance. Nonword repetition, at Step 2, produced a significant change in R^2 (R^2 change = .05, $p < .05$). Rhyme awareness at Step 3 and phonemic awareness at Step 4 did not yield further significant increases in R^2.

Conclusions for Second Graders

The first set of regressions resulted in these findings for second graders. For nonword spelling, only receptive grammar, entered after phonological and receptive vocabulary, explained significant variance. This result will be commented on in the discussion. For real word spelling, only phonemic awareness contributed uniquely, when entered first. For these real words, children may have orthographic representations and familiar spellings based on alphabetic principle of letter–phoneme correspondence. None of the language variables assessed contributed (uniquely or together) to text dictation.

The second set of regressions resulted in these findings for second graders. After auditory discrimination was entered first, nonword repetition contributed uniquely to nonword spelling and to text dictation, that is, phonological working memory mechanisms were critical for both these tasks.

TABLE 15.3b   Summary of Hierarchical Regression Analyses on the Role of Auditory Discrimination, Nonword Repetition, Rhyme Awareness, and Phonemic Awareness in Explaining Second Graders' Spelling

	Dependent Variable: Nonword Spelling							
Predictors	**Coefficients**			**Change Statistics**			**ANOVA**	
	$ß$	t	p	R^2	R^2 Change	F Change (df1, df2)	Sig. F Change	F (df1, df2)	p
Step 1									
Auditory discrimination	−.15	−1.29	.201	.02	.02	1.66 (1, 77)	.201	1.66 (1, 77)	.201
Step 2									
Auditory discrimination	−.10	−.96	.338						
Nonword repetition	−.33	−3.01	.003	.12	.10	9.05 (1, 76)	.004	5.45 (2, 76)	.006
Step 3									
Auditory discrimination	−.11	−.99	.324						
Nonword repetition	−.34	−3.07	.003						
Rhyme awareness	.07	.66	.510	.13	.01	.44 (1, 75)	.510	3.75 (3, 75)	.014
Step 4									
Auditory discrimination	−.11	−.99	.325						
Nonword repetition	−.35	−3.13	.002						
Rhyme awareness	.04	.31	.759						
Phonemic awareness	.10	.83	.409	.14	.01	.69 (1, 74)	.409	2.97 (4, 74)	.025

	Dependent Variable: Word Spelling							
Predictors	**Coefficients**			**Change Statistics**			**ANOVA**	
	$ß$	t	p	R^2	R^2 Change	F Change (df1, df2)	Sig. F Change	F (df1, df2)	p
Step 1									
Auditory discrimination	−.14	−1.21	.230	.02	.02	1.46 (1, 77)	.230	1.46 (1, 77)	.230
Step 2									
Auditory discrimination	−.12	−1.03	.308						
Nonword repetition	−.16	−1.45	.152	.05	.02	2.10 (1, 76)	.152	1.79 (2, 76)	.174

continued

TABLE 15.3b   Summary of Hierarchical Regression Analyses on the Role of Auditory Discrimination, Nonword Repetition, Rhyme Awareness, and Phonemic Awareness in Explaining Second Graders' Spelling (Continued)

Dependent Variable: Word Spelling

Predictors	Coefficients			Change Statistics				ANOVA	
	ß	t	p	R^2	R^2 Change	F Change (df1, df2)	Sig. F Change	F (df1, df2)	p
Step 3									
Auditory discrimination	−.11	−.96	.340						
Nonword repetition	−.14	−1.22	.227						
Rhyme awareness	−.15	−1.33	.187	.07	.02	1.77 (1, 75)	.187	1.80 (3, 75)	.155
Step 4									
Auditory discrimination	−.11	−.97	.338						
Nonword repetition	−.12	−1.07	.290						
Rhyme awareness	−.09	−.75	.457						
Phonemic awareness	−.16	−1.35	.183	.09	.02	1.81 (1, 74)	.183	1.82 (4, 74)	.135

Dependent Variable: Spelling in Text

Predictors	Coefficients			Change Statistics				ANOVA	
	ß	t	p	R^2	R^2 Change	F Change (df1, df2)	Sig. F Change	F (df1, df2)	p
Step 1									
Auditory discrimination	−.12	−1.08	.284	.02	.02	1.16 (1, 77)	.284	1.16 (1, 77)	.284
Step 2									
Auditory discrimination	−.09	−.84	.406						
Nonword repetition	−.23	−2.01	.048	.07	.05	4.05 (1, 76)	.048	2.63 (2, 76)	.079
Step 3									
Auditory discrimination	−.09	−.77	.446						
Nonword repetition	−.20	−1.76	.082						
Rhyme awareness	−.17	−1.48	.144	.09	.03	2.18 (1, 75)	.144	2.51 (3, 75)	.065
Step 4									
Auditory discrimination	−.09	−.76	.448						
Nonword repetition	−.19	−1.65	.102						
Rhyme awareness	−.13	−1.07	.289						
Phonemic awareness	−.10	−.82	.417	.10	.01	.67 (1, 74)	.417	2.04 (4, 74)	.098

$N = 79$.

Correlations With Third Graders' Spelling

Both receptive vocabulary and receptive grammar correlated with spelling skills in this group. Receptive vocabulary correlated negatively with spelling errors in word dictation and in text dictation [$r(52) = -.29$, $p < .05$, and $r(52) = -.32$, $p < .05$, respectively]; receptive grammar correlated negatively with spelling errors in nonword dictation, in word dictation, and in text dictation [$r(52) = -.40$, $p < .005$, $r(52) = -.28$, $p < .05$, and $r(52) = -.42$, $p < .005$, respectively]. Other correlations emerged between phonological (nonword repetition and rhyme awareness), lexical (receptive vocabulary), and grammatical (receptive grammar) variables (see Table 15.1).

Predictors in Regressions for Third Graders: Phonemic Awareness, Receptive Vocabulary, and Receptive Grammar

Nonword Spelling

Phonemic awareness at Step 1 did not account for variance in nonword spelling. Receptive vocabulary at Step 2 did not produce significant changes in R^2, and only receptive grammar at Step 3 accounted for 12% of variance ($p = .01$) in third graders' nonword spelling (Table 15.4).

Real Word Spelling

Phonemic awareness at Step 1 did not account for variance in real word spelling. Receptive vocabulary at Step 2 accounted for 7% of variance ($p = .05$). Receptive grammar at Step 3 did not produce further significant changes in R^2.

Text Dictation

Phonemic awareness, entered first, did not account for significant variance in text dictation. Receptive vocabulary at Step 2 produced a significant increase in R^2 (R^2 change = .08, $p < .05$). Receptive grammar at Step 3 independently accounted for a further 11% of variance in spelling under text dictation ($p = .01$; Table 15.4).

In the second set of regressions, none of the phonological variables accounted for variance in nonword, real word, and text spelling.

Conclusions for Third Graders

Results for the first set of regressions were as follows. For third graders, only receptive grammar contributed uniquely to nonword spelling. Vocabulary contributed uniquely to real word spelling, after phonemic awareness had been entered. For text dictation, when receptive vocabulary and grammar were entered after phonemic awareness, both of these skills contributed uniquely to spelling during text dictation.

Results for the second set of regressions were as follows. By third grade none of the phonological skills assessed contributed to nonword or real word spelling or spelling during text dictation.

TABLE 15.4   Summary of Hierarchical Regression Analyses on the Role of Phonemic Awareness, Receptive Vocabulary, and Receptive Grammar in Explaining Third Graders' Spelling

	Dependent Variable: Nonword Spelling								
Predictors	Coefficients			Change Statistics				ANOVA	
	ß	t	p	R^2	R^2 Change	F Change (df1, df2)	Sig. F Change	F (df1, df2)	p
Step 1									
Phonemic awareness	−.12	−.88	.384	.02	.02	.771 (1, 50)	.384	.771 (1, 50)	.384
Step 2									
Phonemic awareness	−.09	−.61	.546						
Receptive vocabulary	−.21	−1.51	.137	.06	.04	2.28 (1, 49)	.137	1.54 (2, 49)	.225
Step 3									
Phonemic awareness	−.08	−.57	.573						
Receptive vocabulary	−.10	−.69	.494						
Receptive grammar	−.37	−2.64	.011	.18	.12	6.97 (1, 48)	.011	3.47 (3, 48)	.023

	Dependent Variable: Word Spelling								
Predictors	Coefficients			Change Statistics				ANOVA	
	ß	t	p	R^2	R^2 Change	F Change (df1, df2)	Sig. F Change	F (df1, df2)	p
Step 1									
Phonemic awareness	−.16	−1.13	.226	.03	.03	1.27 (1, 50)	.266	1.27 (1, 50)	.266
Step 2									
Phonemic awareness	−.11	−.79	.433						
Receptive vocabulary	−.27	−1.97	.054	.10	.07	3.90 (1, 49)	.054	2.62 (2, 49)	.083
Step 3									
Phonemic awareness	−.10	−.76	.453						
Receptive vocabulary	−.21	−1.43	.158						
Receptive grammar	−.21	−1.48	.147	.14	.04	2.17 (1, 48)	.147	2.51 (3, 48)	.070

TABLE 15.4   Summary of Hierarchical Regression Analyses on the Role of Phonemic Awareness, Receptive Vocabulary, and Receptive Grammar in Explaining Third Graders' Spelling (Continued)

					Dependent Variable: Spelling in Text				
Predictors	Coefficients				Change Statistics			ANOVA	
	ß	t	p	R^2	R^2 Change	F Change (df1, df2)	Sig. F Change	F (df1, df2)	p
Step 1									
Phonemic awareness	−.20	−1.48	.147	.04	.04	2.18 (1, 50)	.147	2.18 (1, 50)	.147
Step 2									
Phonemic awareness	−.15	−1.13	.265						
Receptive vocabulary	−.29	−2.12	.039	.12	.08	4.49 (1, 49)	.039	3.41 (2, 49)	.041
Step 3									
Phonemic awareness	−.14	−1.12	.271						
Receptive vocabulary	−.18	−1.31	.195						
Receptive grammar	−.35	−2.58	.013	.23	.11	6.66 (1,48)	.013	4.75 (3,48)	.006

$N = 51.$

PATH ANALYSES FOR STRUCTURAL MODELS OF FIRST-, SECOND-, AND THIRD-GRADE SPELLING

Because the significant contributions of language (phonology, receptive vocabulary, and receptive grammar) changed from first to second to third grades, path analyses were also conducted. Vocabulary knowledge may be related to spelling in two ways: (1) directly, in real word spelling, through the activation of word meaning and semantic knowledge in spelling (Harm & Seidenberg, 1999; Plaut et al., 1996), and (2) indirectly, in real word and nonword spelling, because the child's vocabulary knowledge conveys information about the phonological and morphological word structure (Metsala & Walley, 1998; Plaza & Cohen, 2004). Notably, morphology allows the child to store words in the orthographic lexicon on the basis of roots, derivations, and inflections (Plaza & Cohen, 2004). These meaning and grammatical representations can directly affect the spelling of real words, but also that of unfamiliar words (nonwords) that preserve some morphological features that mark grammar information. The model, reported in Figure 15.1, assumed a direct effect of vocabulary on real word dictation, a direct effect of grammar on real word and nonword dictation, and an indirect effect of vocabulary on real word and nonword dictation, through grammar. Because first graders did not perform text dictation, only path analyses for word and nonword spelling were run.

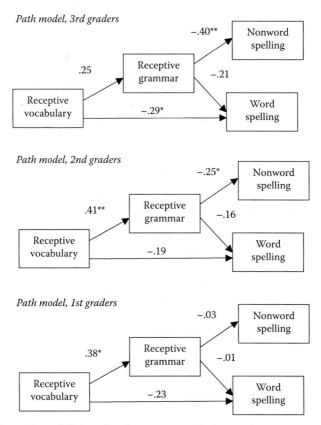

Figure 15.1 Path model: the role of receptive vocabulary and grammar in nonword and word spelling. *$p < 0.05$; **$p < 0.01$.

Overall, the model explains 24% of variance in the data ([DC] = .24) for third graders and accounts for 16% of variance in their dictated real word spelling and 16% of variance in their dictated nonword spelling. The path coefficients show only direct effects of receptive vocabulary on dictated real word spelling ($\beta = -.29$, $R^2 = .16$, $p < .05$) and grammar on dictated nonword spelling ($\beta = -.40$, $R^2 = .16$, $p < .01$).

The model globally accounts for less variance in second graders' spelling (DC = .196) than third graders' spelling. The path coefficients show a direct effect of receptive grammar on nonword spelling ($\beta = -.25$, $p < .05$) and an effect of vocabulary on grammar ($\beta = .41$, $p < .001$). The model explains 6.3% of variance in nonword spelling and 9.1% of variance in real word spelling in second graders.

For first graders, the model explained 15.5% of variance in the children's spelling performance. As Figure 15.1 shows, this variance was mainly related to the direct effect of receptive vocabulary on receptive grammar ($\beta = .38$, $p < .05$). Only 0.1% of the children's performance in nonword spelling and 4.5% of their performance in word spelling were explained by the model.

Good Versus Poor Unreferred Spellers

For each grade level, good and poor spellers were identified and their language skills compared. We used word spelling to differentiate good from poor spellers. Percentile distribution of scores in word spelling was used for this purpose. Because scores were equivalent to the number of errors, children whose scores were above the 75th percentile were considered poor spellers, and children with scores below the 25th percentile were considered good spellers.

First Graders

There were eight good spellers and nine poor spellers in this group. A t-test statistic revealed that these two groups differed significantly in nonword repetition [$t(15) = 3.04, p < .01$], rhyme awareness [$t(15) = 3.47, p < .005$], and phonemic awareness [$t(15) = 2.85, p < .01$]. No differences were found in auditory discrimination, receptive vocabulary, or receptive grammar.

Second Graders

There were 16 poor spellers and 17 good spellers. Good and poor spellers differed in auditory discrimination skills [$t(31) = 2.58, p < .05$], nonword repetition skills [$t(31) = 2.40, p < .05$], rhyme awareness skills [$t(31) = 2.55, p < .05$], and also receptive grammar skills [$t(31) = 2.37, p < .05$].

Third Graders

Only children who made no spelling errors had scores below the 25th percentile in this group. There were 9 good spellers and 13 poor spellers. Differences between these two groups were only found in rhyme awareness [$t(20) = 2.54, p < .05$] and receptive vocabulary [$t(20) = 2.09, p < .05$].

DISCUSSION

Spelling is phonologically mediated in many languages. In some, such as English, spelling may draw on the complex interrelationships of phonology, orthography, and morphology rather than single phonemes and graphemes. For a review of how children learn to spell in morphophonemic orthographies such as French and English, which are deep orthographies, see Berninger and Fayol (2008). In other languages, such as Italian, a phonological mediation is normally successful, and children may spell words correctly on the basis of an almost perfect phoneme–grapheme correspondence.

Yet the study reported in this chapter shows that, even in the case of learning a transparent, shallow written language, with simple sound–spelling correspondence, other sources of linguistic knowledge, beyond phonology (vocabulary and grammar), contribute to children's spelling. There are two possible explanations for these results. One is that the phonological features of a language cannot be artificially separated from other linguistic features. Following Ehri's amalgamation theory (Ehri & Roberts, 1979), we can describe the child's lexicon as a mental repository of words with several identities: phonological, grammatical, and semantic; these identities are amalgamated between them and with the word's orthographic representation as soon as these identities are established in the child's mental lexicon for word-specific orthographic spellings. That is, phonology in the mental lexicon is integrated with semantic and grammatical information, so one activates the other and vice versa. The other is that because spelling becomes more automatic and the child's sound-to-letter conversion more fluent, the child may shift his or her attention from a sound-by-sound analysis of the word, governed by general rules of phonetic correspondence, to spelling strategies based on a broader and more articulated knowledge of the word structure. From this moment onward, spelling could be influenced by a more complex architecture of linguistic representations, including the child's vocabulary knowledge (and the number of lexical entries that have been phonologically distinguished in the memory), and the child's morphological and grammatical knowledge (how words are morphologically structured in Italian and according to which rules).

The two possible explanations, which require further research, are compatible. Learning to spell is a linguistic achievement. The child faces this task equipped with his or her entire knowledge of word forms: their phonological, morphological, and spelling structure; their meaning and semantic associations; and their grammatical function. Spelling is the visual representation of this multifaceted linguistic knowledge (Garcia, Abbott, & Berninger, 2010). These various levels of language knowledge (sublexical, lexical, grammatical) are normally integrated in language production, in the same way they should be integrated in spelling (Abbott, Berninger, & Fayol, 2010; Richards et al., 2006; Richards, Berninger, & Fayol, 2009). The capacity to dwell on different sources of linguistic information is particularly adaptive in some languages (e.g., English and French), where the semantic and morphological knowledge of word forms may compensate for ambiguities in their phonological forms. The integrated use of different linguistic knowledge in spelling is clear in these languages. However, it is difficult to assume that children learning more transparent orthographies exploit only part of their linguistic knowledge in learning to write words. They too may draw on these integrated dimensions of language.

The findings of this first exploratory study show how, in a very shallow orthography, based on shallow correspondences between phonology and orthography, vocabulary and grammatical knowledge may also play a critical role in the acquisition of spelling skills.

Due to the transparency and regularity of the Italian orthographic system, sublexical procedures, based on the phonological analysis of word sounds and on the rehearsal mechanisms of the child's working memory system, are sufficient to correctly spell nonwords and words (Angelelli, Judica, Spinelli, Zoccolotti, & Luzzatti, 2004). Not surprisingly, these skills were critical to first graders' spelling.

Interestingly, receptive vocabulary accounted for 9% of variance in nonword spelling, but apparently it did not contribute to real word spelling at this age. Knowledge of vocabulary conveys information about phonological word forms in a language that can be exploited by sublexical spelling procedures from this very early stage. Nonwords are wordlike forms and therefore may somehow benefit from this knowledge. It is more difficult to explain the absence of effects of vocabulary on real word spelling. In the second set of our analyses, only phonemic awareness predicted first graders' real word spelling, accounting for 25% of its variance. It is likely that these beginner spellers relied on an analytic spelling procedure of one-to-one phoneme–letter conversion, rather than on lexical knowledge. The comparison between good and poor spellers confirms that Italian first graders' spelling ability is grounded in phonological mechanisms: Good and poor first-grade spellers differed in nonword repetition, rhyme awareness, and phonemic awareness.

Phonological skills (phonological working memory, in particular) also seem to play a significant role in second graders' spelling. However, by second grade, grammatical knowledge accounts uniquely for 6% of variance in nonword spelling, once phonological and vocabulary knowledge, which do not contribute uniquely, are entered. Good and poor second-grade spellers differed significantly in their phonological skills (auditory discrimination, verbal working memory, rhyme awareness), but also in their grammatical knowledge (receptive grammar). Curiously, grammatical knowledge does not yet play a unique role in spelling during text dictation in second grade: Only nonword repetition skills predicted spelling in text dictation in this group. It is possible that second graders are not yet able to shift their attention from the sound–letter conversion procedures to the semantic and grammatical context of the text produced and are thus unable to exploit a wider range of linguistic knowledge to spell words in texts (e.g., phonological, semantic, morphological, and grammatical).

At the beginning of third grade, vocabulary and grammar seem to play an increased role in spelling. Vocabulary uniquely contributed to word spelling, grammar uniquely accounted for 12% of variance in nonword spelling, after phonological and vocabulary skills were controlled, and both vocabulary and grammar accounted for spelling in text dictation. Third graders, unlike second graders, may have been able to make good use of the grammatical and semantic context of the text and of their vocabulary and grammatical knowledge to spell words in text dictation. In this group, differences between good and poor spellers were only found in phonological (rhyme awareness) and vocabulary knowledge. However, it is useful to remember that good and poor spellers were identified on the basis of their performance in word spelling, for which the child's grammatical knowledge seemed to be less influential (see also the path analysis in Figure 15.1).

One of the most interesting findings in this study was that grammar uniquely contributed to second and third graders' nonword spelling. It is possible that as the difficulty of the spelling task increases (as in nonword spelling) second and third graders exploit diverse linguistic knowledge, such as their morphological knowledge of word structure, to support their spelling. Morphological segmentation of words is as natural as phonological segmentation (Ouellette & Sénéchal, 2008; Treiman, Cassar, & Zukowski, 1994), and children can turn to this strategy to support a segmental analysis of (unfamiliar) words. As soon as the child becomes acquainted with the spelling mechanisms in her or his language, knowledge of language at various levels may contribute to spelling each new item the child encounters, not only the words the child has already (orthographically) represented in her or his mental lexicon.

The path analyses, which tested a somewhat different model than the multiple regressions, supported these conclusions (Figure 15.1): Although vocabulary showed direct effects on third graders' real word spelling, grammar showed direct effects on nonword spelling for both second and third graders.

To conclude, modern computational models and neuroscience studies have demonstrated that the creation of orthographic representations of words and their use in reading and spelling in deep, morphophonemic orthographies (mainly English and French) are linguistically complex processes based on the integration of multiple levels of language knowledge (Berninger & Richards, 2010; Harm & Seidenberg, 1999; Plaut et al., 1996; Richards et al., 2009). The current study reported evidence that this complexity may also hold for learning to spell in shallow, transparent orthographies. Even though children learn to spell words in different ways according to the characteristics of the written language there are exposed to (Cury Pollo, Kressler, & Treiman, 2009), that does not mean that the kinds of knowledge children bring to learning to spell are necessarily different.

In line with the most recent findings of cognitive writing research, researchers and educators should think of spelling as a transcription process that draws complexly on many dimensions of language (phonological, lexical, and grammatical) and different language units (phonemes, syllables, morphemes, words, and sentences), all of which interact and are integrated with the writer's thoughts, though often not in one-to-one mappings. The child brings to the task of spelling his or her implicit and explicit knowledge of words, in their different forms (oral and written), dimensions of language (phonological, orthographic, semantic, and grammatical), and language units (single words, sentences, and texts), not to mention the motor system through which the language and cognitions are expressed. Thus, writing appears to be a more complex process than the simple view (simply ideas plus spelling; Juel, 1988). Also, as shown in this chapter, spelling itself is a complex process in transparent orthographies as well as deep orthographies.

ACKNOWLEDGMENTS

This work was supported by the MIUR–PRIN 2006 grant number 111929 to Pietro Boscolo and Bianca De Bernardi. The authors thank the schools and young participants in the study and are grateful to Virginia Berninger for her helpful comments and comprehensive review.

REFERENCES

Abbott, R., Berninger, V., & Fayol, M. (2010). Longitudinal relationships of levels of language in writing and between writing and reading in grades 1 to 7. *Journal of Educational Psychology, 102,* 281–298.

Angelelli, P., Judica, A., Spinelli, D., Zoccolotti, P., & Luzzatti, C. (2004) Characteristics of writing disorders in Italian dyslexic children. *Cognitive and Behavioral Neurology, 17,* 18–31.

Arfé, B., D'Ambrosio, S., Cona, E., Merella, A., & Cellino M. R. (2009, October 23–24). *La scrittura di parole complesse nel trattamento della disortografia evolutiva* [The writing of complex words in the treatment of developmental dysorthographia]. Presented at the 18th Congresso Nazionale AIRIPA, La Spezia.

Arfé, B., De Bernardi, B., Poeta, F., & Pasini, M. (2009, August 25–29). *Phonological, lexical and grammatical skills in learning to spell Italian*. Presented at the 10th biennial EARLI conference, Amsterdam.

Baddeley, A., Gathercole, S., & Papagno, C. (1998). The phonological loop as a language learning device. *Psychological Review, 105*, 158–173.

Barca L., Burani C., & Arduino L. S. (2002). Word naming times and psycholinguistic norms for Italian nouns. *Behavior Research Methods, Instruments, and Computers, 34*, 424–434.

Beers, C. S., & Beers, J. W. (1992). Children's spelling of English inflectional morphology. In S. Templeton & D. R. Bear (Eds.), *Development of orthographic knowledge and the foundations of literacy: A memorial Festschrift for Edmund H. Henderson* (pp. 231–252). Hillsdale, NJ: Erlbaum.

Berninger, V., Abbott, R., Thomson, J., Wagner, R., Swanson, H. L., Wijsman, E., … Raskind, W. (2006). Modeling developmental phonological core deficits within a working-memory architecture in children and adults with developmental dyslexia. *Scientific Studies in Reading, 10*, 165–198.

Berninger, V., & Fayol, M. (2008). Why spelling is important and how to teach it effectively. In *Encyclopedia of language and literacy development* (pp. 1–13). London, ON: Canadian Language and Literacy Research Network. Retrieved from http://www.literacyencyclopedia.ca/pdfs/topic.php?topId=234

Berninger, V., Raskind, W., Richards, T., Abbott, R., & Stock, P. (2008). A multidisciplinary approach to understanding developmental dyslexia within working-memory architecture: Genotypes, phenotypes, brain, and instruction. *Developmental Neuropsychology, 33*, 707–744.

Berninger, V., & Richards, T. (2002). *Brain literacy for educators and psychologists*. New York: Academic Press.

Berninger, V. W., & Richards, T. (2010). Inter-relationships among behavioural markers, genes, brain and treatment in dyslexia and dysgraphia. *Future Neurology, 5*, 597–617.

Bisiacchi, P., Cendron, M., Gugliotta, M., Tressoldi, P., & Vio, C. (2005). *BVN: Batteria di valutazione neuropsicologica per l'età evolutiva* [Battery for neuropsychological assessment in children]. Trento: Erikson.

Bishop, D. V. M. (1982). *Test for reception of grammar*. Oxford: Medical Research Council.

Bishop, D. V. M., & Clarkson, B. (2003). Written language as a window into residual language deficits: a study of children with persistent and residual speech and language impairments. *Cortex, 39*, 215–237.

Bloomfield, L. (1970). *Language*. New York: Henry Holt.

Boscolo, P. (1995). The cognitive approach to writing and writing instruction: A contribution to a critical appraisal. *Current Psychology of Cognition, 14*(4), 343–366.

Carriero, L., Vio, C., Tressoldi, P. E. (2001). COST: un progetto europeo per lo studio della dislessia e la valutazione delle prime fasi di apprendimento della lettura [COST: European project for the study of dyslexia and early stages of reading acquisition]. *Psicologia clinica dello sviluppo, 2*, 261–272.

Chliounaki, K., & Bryant, P. (2007). How children learn about morphological spelling rules. *Child Development, 78*, 1360–1373.

Cury Pollo, T., Kessler, B., & Treiman, R. (2009). Statistical patterns in children's early writing. *Journal of Experimental Child Psychology, 104*, 410–426.

Deacon, S. H., & Bryant, P. (2005). What young children do and do not know about the spelling of inflections and derivations. *Developmental Science, 8*(6), 583–594.

Ehri, L. C. (1986). Sources of difficulty in learning to spell and read. In M. L. Wolraich & D. Routh (Eds.), *Advances in developmental and behavioural pediatrics* (Vol. 7, pp. 121–195). Greenwich, CT: JAI.

Ehri, L. C., & Roberts, K. T. (1979). Do beginners learn printed words better in contexts or in isolation? *Child Development, 50*, 675–685.

Fayol, M., Largy, P., & Lemaire, P. (1994). When cognitive overload enhances subject-verb agreement errors. A study in French written language. *Quarterly Journal of Experimental Psychology, 47*, 437–464.

Garcia, N., Abbott, R. D., & Berninger, V. W. (2010). Predicting poor, average and superior spellers in grades 1 to 6 from phonological, orthographic, and morphological spelling, or reading composites. *Written Language and Literacy, 13*, 61–99.

Harm, M. W., & Seidenberg, M. S. (1999). Phonology, reading acquisition and dyslexia: Insights from connectionist models. *Psychological Review, 106*, 491–528.

Juel, C. (1988). Learning to read and write: A longitudinal study of 54 children from first through fourth grades. *Journal of Educational Psychology, 80*, 437–447.

Laiacona, M., Capitani, E., Zonca, G., Scola, I., Saletta, P., & Luzzatti, C. (2009). Integration of lexical and sublexical processing in the spelling of regular words: A multiple single-case study in Italian dysgraphic patients. *Cortex, 45*, 804–815.

Lewis, B. A., Freebairn, L. A., & Taylor, H. G. (2002). Correlates of spelling abilities in children with early speech-sound disorders. *Reading and Writing, 15*, 389–407.

Marotta, L., Trasciani, M., & Vicari, S. (2004). *CMF: valutazione delle competenze meta fonologiche*. Trento: Erickson.

McCloskey, M., Macaruso, P., & Rapp, B. (2006). Grapheme-to-lexeme feedback in the spelling system: Evidence from a dysgraphic patient. *Cognitive Neuropsychology, 23*, 278–307.

Metsala, J. L., & Walley, A. C. (1998). Spoken vocabulary growth and the segmental restructuring of lexical representations: Precursors to phonemic awareness and early reading ability. In J. L. Metsala & L. C. Ehri (Eds.), *Word recognition in beginning literacy* (pp. 89–120). Mahwah, NJ: Erlbaum.

Nagy, W., Berninger, V. W., Abbott, R. D. (2006). Contributions of morphology beyond phonology to literacy outcomes of upper elementary and middle-school students. *Journal of Educational Psychology, 98*, 134–147.

Nagy, W., Berninger, V. W., Abbott, R., Vaughan, K., & Varmeulen, K. (2003). Relationship of morphology and other language skills to literacy skills in at-risk second-grade readers and at-risk fourth-grade writers. *Journal of Educational Psychology, 95*, 730–742.

Nunes, T., & Bryant, P. (2006). *Improving literacy by teaching morphemes*. London: Routledge.

Nunes, T., Bryant, P., & Bindman, M. (1997). Morphological spelling strategies: Developmental stages and processes. *Developmental Psychology, 33*, 637–649.

Orsolini, M., Fanari, R., Tosi, V., De Nigris, B., & Carrieri, R. (2006). From phonological recoding to lexical reading: a longitudinal study on reading development in Italian. *Language and Cognitive Processes, 21*(5), 576–607.

Ouellette, G. (2006). What's meaning got to do with it: The role of vocabulary in word reading and reading comprehension. *Journal of Educational Psychology, 98*, 554–566.

Ouellette, G., & Sénéchal, M. (2008). A window into early literacy: Exploring the cognitive and linguistic underpinnings of invented spelling. *Scientific Studies of Reading, 12*(2), 195–219.

Pacton, S., & Fayol, M. (2003). How do French children use morphosyntactic information when they spell adverbs and present participles? *Scientific Studies of Reading, 7*, 273–287.

Patterson, K. E. (1986). Lexical but not semantic spelling? *Cognitive Neuropsychology, 3*, 341–367.

Perfetti, C. A. (1991). Representations and awareness in the acquisition of reading competence. In L. Rieben & C. A. Perfetti (Eds.), *Learning to read: Basic research and its implications* (pp. 33–44). Hillsdale, NJ: Erlbaum.

Plaut, D. C., McClelland, J. L., Sidenberg, M. S., & Paterson, K. (1996). Understanding normal and impaired word reading: Computational principles in quasi-regular domains. *Psychological Review, 103,* 56–115.

Plaza, M., & Cohen, H. (2003). The interaction between phonological processing, syntactic awareness, and naming speed in the reading and spelling performance of first-grade children. *Brain and Cognition, 53,* 287–292.

Plaza, M., & Cohen, H. (2004). Predictive influence of phonological processing, morphological/syntactic skill, and naming speed on spelling performance. *Brain and Cognition, 55,* 368–373.

Richards, T., Aylward, E., Field, K., Grimmie, A., Raskind, W., Richards, A., . . . Berninger, W. (2006). Converging evidence from triple word form theory in children with dyslexia. *Developmental Neuropsychology, 30,* 547–589.

Richards, T., Berninger, V., & Fayol, M. (2009). fMRI activation differences between 11-year-old good and poor spellers' access in working memory to temporary and long-term orthographic representations. *Journal of Neurolinguistics, 22,* 327–353.

Rinaldi, P., Barca, L., & Burani, C. (2004). A database for semantic, grammatical and frequency properties of the first words acquired by Italian children. *Behavior Research Methods, Instruments, and Computers, 36,* 525–530.

Rustioni Metz-Lancaster, D., & Associazione. "La nostra famiglia" (1994). *Prove di valutazione della comprensione linguistica* [Test for the assessment of linguistic comprehension]. Firenze: Organizzazioni Speciali.

Sage, K., & Ellis, A. W. (2004). Lexical influences in graphemic buffer disorder. *Cognitive Neuropsychology, 21,* 381–400.

Sartori, G., Job, R., & Tressoldi, P. (1995/2007). *DDE-2: Batteria per la valutazione della dislessia e della disortografia evolutiva-2.* Firenze: Giunti O.S.

Sénéchal, M., Basque, M. T., & Leclaire, T. (2006). Morphological knowledge as revealed in children's spelling accuracy and reports of spelling strategies. *Journal of Experimental Child Psychology, 95,* 231–254.

Shallice, T., Rumiati, R. I., & Zadini, A. (2000). The selective impairment of the phonological output buffer. *Cognitive Neuropsychology, 17,* 517–546.

Share, D.L. (2008). On the Anglocentricities of current reading research and practice: The perils of overreliance on an "outlier" orthography. *Psychological Bulletin, 134,* 584–615.

Steinbrink, C., & Klatte, M. (2007). Phonological working memory in German children with poor reading and spelling abilities. *Dyslexia, 14,* 271–290.

Stella, G., Pizzoli, C., & Tressoldi, P. (2000). *PPVT-R- Peabody Picture Vocabulary Test-R.* Italian adaptation and standardization. Torino: Omega Edizioni.

Totereau, C., Thevenin, M. G., & Fayol, M. (1997). The development of the understanding of number morphology in written French. In C. A. Perfetti, L. Rieben, & M. Fayol (Eds.), *Learning to spell: Research, theory and practice across languages* (pp. 97–114). London: Erlbaum.

Treiman, R., & Cassar, M. (1997). Spelling acquisition in English. In C. A. Perfetti, L. Rieben, & M. Fayol (Eds.), *Learning to spell: Research, theory and practice across languages* (pp. 61–80). London: Erlbaum.

Treiman, R., Cassar, M., & Zukowski, A. (1994). What types of linguistic information do children use in spelling? The case of flaps. *Child Development, 65,* 1310–1329.

Tressoldi, P., & Cornoldi, C. (1991). *Batteria per la valutazione della scrittura e della competenza ortografica nella scuola dell'obbligo.* Firenze: O.S.

Tucha, O., Trumpp, C., Lange, K. W. (2004). Limitations of the dual-process-theory regarding the writing of words and non-words to dictation. *Brain and Language, 91,* 267–273.

Venezky, R. (1970). *The structure of English orthography.* The Hague: Mouton.

Venezky, R. (1999). *The American way of spelling*. New York: Guilford.

Walley, A. C., Metsala, J. L., & Garlock, V. M. (2003). Spoken vocabulary growth: Its role in the development of phoneme awareness and early reading ability. *Reading and Writing: An Interdisciplinary Journal, 15*, 5–20.

Zoccolotti, P., Angelelli, P., Judica, A., & Luzzatti, C. (2005). *I disturbi evolutivi di lettura e scrittura* [Developmental disorders in reading and writing]. Rome: Carocci.

16

Effects of Handwriting Skill, Output Modes, and Gender on Fourth Graders' Pauses, Language Bursts, Fluency, and Quality

RUI ALEXANDRE ALVES, MARTA BRANCO,
SÃO LUÍS CASTRO, and THIERRY OLIVE

*I*n a pioneering study, Kaufer, Hayes, and Flower (1986) made a seemingly evident, yet notable, observation: Writers compose in bursts, that is, written sentences are built up in a piecemeal fashion with bursts of writing activity interspersed by long production pauses (usually longer than 2 s). Whether for its apparent simplicity or for difficulties in setting up a complete scientific explanation of this otherwise exuberant writing behavior, this finding seems to have been forgotten. Only recently, Hayes has led a series of studies aimed at providing a detailed account of bursts of language production (Chenoweth & Hayes, 2001, 2003; Hayes & Chenoweth, 2006, 2007). Here, we add to this line of research by presenting a study in which, from a developmental standpoint, we argue that automatizing transcription can lead to larger language bursts and therefore to improvements in text quality.

Kaufer et al. (1986) have shown that, when producing a text, adult writers typically compose sentence parts of 9.3 words on average. They compared burst length between two groups of writers, one of expert, professional writers, and the other of graduate students, and showed that experts composed using larger bursts, an average of four words more. Moreover, the texts written by the experts were generally rated of better quality than those composed by novices, which was interpreted as evidence of more efficient translating processes. Translating refers to cognitive processes by which ideas are converted into written language (Hayes & Flower, 1980).

More recently, Chenoweth and Hayes (2001) conducted a series of studies that comprehensively characterize bursts of language production as a fundamental parameter of the translating process. In their first study, they reasoned that if writers have better translating skills in their native language than in a second, less practiced language, this relative strength with one's native language should be reflected in the length of language bursts. Indeed, they found that undergraduate students were more fluent and had larger bursts when composing in their first language rather than their second language. As in the study of Kaufer et al. (1986), better translating skills lead to larger bursts.

Translating processes have long been viewed, and studied, as partially dependent on the verbal component of working memory (Kellogg, 1996; McCutchen, 1996; McCutchen, Covill, Hoyne, & Mildes, 1994; Swanson & Berninger, 1996). Following this thread, Chenoweth and Hayes (2003) have shown that articulatory suppression, a procedure widely used to impair the rehearsal of verbal information within working memory (Baddeley, 2007), consistently decreases burst length and writing fluency. They have found an average decrease of 34% in burst length from the control condition to the articulatory suppression one. They concluded that burst length depends on available verbal working memory capacity.

In another study, Hayes and Chenoweth (2006) asked 20 highly proficient typists to transcribe six texts between two word processor windows. Three texts were copied under articulatory suppression and three under a foot tapping control. Congruent with the recruitment of verbal working memory by the transcribing task, they found a decrease in transcription fluency and an increase in mechanical errors in the articulatory suppression but not foot tapping condition. Noticeably, they did not find evidence of bursting while the expert typists were transcribing. Thus, they tentatively suggested that bursting might be dependent on the formulation of new strings of language.

More recently, Hayes and Chenoweth (2007) used a double passive-to-active sentence conversion task to test competing hypotheses regarding the sources of bursting in writing. If bursting depends on generating new ideas, then in the conversion task no bursts should be observed, because beforehand the writers knew the ideas in the sentence. Conversely, if bursting depends on generating a new linguistic structure, then bursting should be observed. They found support for the later hypothesis, yet the evidence is far from definitive. Overall, the reviewed studies have established the bursting phenomenon in writing and have convincingly related it to cognitive translating processes.

In beginning and developing writers, transcription and different levels of written language (word, sentence, and text) support the translation process (Berninger & Swanson, 1994). Text generation expresses ideas in language representations in working memory, and transcription transforms these language representations into visible letters, written spellings, and the sentences and discourse structures of written text (Berninger, Fuller, & Whitaker, 1996; Berninger & Swanson, 1994).

Transcription draws on the programming and execution of motor movements required by the particular writing tool used (e.g., pen, keyboard) to produce the letters and written spellings in the larger units of written language. The fine, automatic integration of the orthographic codes of letters and written spelling with the sequential finger movements is an early requirement for achieving automatic handwriting (for reviews, see Berninger & Amtmann, 2003; also Graham & Harris, 2000). Evidence exists that for child writers in Grades 1 to 6 (ages 6 to 12) transcription constrains fluency and quality of written texts (Bereiter & Scardamalia, 1987; Graham, Berninger, Abbott, Abbott, & Whitaker, 1997). In a large cross-sectional study with children from the primary grades, Berninger et al. (1992) found that transcription accounted for 66% of the variance in writing fluency. Similarly, Jones and Christensen (1999) found that transcription explained 67% of the variance in the quality of texts produced by a sample of second graders. Additionally, in two studies with primary school children, Connelly, Gee, and Walsh (2007) showed that limited keyboarding skill, as opposed to better handwriting skill, had a detrimental impact on text quality. Furthermore, in initial primary grades orally produced texts have been described as of better quality than written ones (Bereiter & Scardamalia, 1987; but see Hidi & Hildyard, 1983). However, a turnaround seems to occur around fourth grade in normally developing children (McCutchen, 1996) and somewhat later for children with disabilities in transcription (Graham, 1990). This change seems not to be a developmental pattern, but rather an issue of achieving relative expertise with a particular mode of composing. For instance, in a study with adult competent writers, Gould and Boies (1978) found no quality differences between commercial letters whether they were dictated or handwritten.

The release from a detrimental impact on text quality caused by poor handwriting skill is noticeably dependent on its relative automatization, which seems to be achieved earlier by girls (Berninger & Fuller, 1992). Given the limited resources of working memory, a tradeoff between formulation of content and transcription is likely to happen during written language production, as suggested by a study by Bourdin and Fayol (1994). They tested children and adults in a serial recall task, in which the response modality was spoken in some blocks and handwritten in others. For adults the response mode did not matter in that they did equally well, but children had consistently smaller spans when the response was written than when it was spoken. This detrimental impact of writing compared to speaking was attributed to the cognitive cost of transcription. Moreover, when Bourdin and Fayol asked adults to recall using an untrained uppercase cursive script, this transcription requirement had a similarly negative impact on their performance in that they did better when speaking than writing. This result has been replicated and expanded in several studies (Bourdin & Fayol, 2000, 2002; Grabowski, 2010). Additionally, Olive and Kellogg (2002) showed that in a composition task, transcription is more effortful for children than for adults, and this cost seems to alter the dynamics of activation of writing processes (see also Alves, Castro, & Olive, 2008; Olive, Alves, & Castro, 2009). Olive and Kellogg measured secondary reaction time to auditory probes while participants were copying their texts or composing them. Arguably, while copying text, writers engage only transcription; but while composing it, other processes, such as planning or revising, need to be concurrently activated. If this is the case, cognitive effort should increase from copying to composing. Indeed, Olive and Kellogg found that to be the case in their adult sample and interpreted the finding as a sign of parallel activation of writing processes. However, in their child sample handwriting was more demanding than for adults, and there was no change in cognitive effort from copying to composing tasks. This finding was interpreted as a sign of a sequential activation of writing processes. That is, when the cost of transcription is high, it might prevent the concurrent activation of other writing processes. Congruently, when adults composed or copied texts using an untrained script, as in Bourdin and Fayol's studies, they exhibited a similar pattern to children. To conclude from the reviewed studies, it is clear that when transcription is not automatized, its cognitive cost is high, which has a negative impact on fluency and text quality.

It follows that automatizing transcription might also have an impact in bursting, because bursts are closely tied to writing fluency. More efficient transcription skills might require less effort in fully capturing the language segment held in the mind and thus determine the ease and speed in which it is produced as written language. Automatic transcription processes seem to overcome some working memory limitations and enable greater support for the higher-level cognitive processes of producing written text (Berninger, 1999; Fayol, 1999; Olive & Kellogg, 2002), which might reflect in larger language bursts.

Two recent studies showed that automatizing transcription leads to larger language bursts. Alves, Castro, Sousa, and Strömqvist (2007) asked two adult groups that differed in typing proficiency to produce written narratives. They found that the highly automatic transcription group composed using larger language bursts, on average three words more. Thus, typing faster seems to allow the usage of lengthier segments while composing (see also Grabowski, 2008). Alves, Castro, and Olive (2011) randomly assigned 84 undergraduate students to one of four experimental conditions, which manipulated output modality and transcription skill. Half the participants composed by handwriting and half by typing. In handwriting, low skill was manipulated by using an uppercase cursive script or the participants' usual calligraphy. In typing, low skill was manipulated by using a scrambled keyboard or a QWERTY layout. In both modalities, handwriting and typing, the low-skill groups showed similar reliable decreases in burst length, about six words less (respectively, three vs. nine words) and received lower ratings of text quality. Alves et al. concluded that, when not well automatized, transcription creates a lower-end toll that hinders the number of words a writer can put in a written language burst.

The reviewed studies highlight the contribution of transcription skill to achieve writing fluency, text quality, and composing using longer bursts, that is, stretches of written language. In the study reported in this chapter, we extended this research to children in fourth grade (9 years old). By Grade 4 most children have relative proficiency in handwriting (Graham & Weintraub, 1996; McCutchen, 1996), but individual differences still occur (Graham et al., 1997). Thus, with initial screening one can identify groups of varying handwriting skill. Here we used the alphabet task (Berninger, Cartwright, Yates, Swanson, & Abbott, 1994) to screen for groups of low, average, and high handwriting skill. The alphabet task has been extensively used as an index of automatic handwriting, in some studies even as a solo measure to screen for children's handwriting skill (e.g., Christensen, 2005).

For this study, we screened 264 fourth graders (9 years old on average) and constituted three handwriting skill groups. The average-skill group was formed by taking the children who fell in the range between half a standard deviation below and half a standard deviation above the mean in the collected sample. The low- and high-skill groups included all children who fell one standard deviation below or above the mean, respectively. The validity of this screening was further expanded by testing if a well-established questionnaire on handwriting proficiency (Rosenblum, 2008), which we adapted to the Portuguese language, would be able to distinguish among the skill groups.

The children in this study were individually tested and asked to write two stories, one by handwriting and another by dictation to a scribe. Dictation has been extensively used to eliminate the transcription demands from written composition (for rationale, see Bereiter & Scardamalia, 1987). In normally achieving children dictating might not have clear benefits over handwriting (McCutchen, 1987; Reece & Cumming, 1996), but in learning-disabled children it is an effective way to circumvent transcription difficulties and improve text quality (De La Paz & Graham, 1997; Graham, 1990; Quinlan, 2004). In this study we were able to test written composition among three groups of differing transcription skills and across two output modalities (handwriting or dictating). Regarding transcription, we predicted that high skill should be associated with larger language bursts and better quality texts. Regarding modality, we predicted an interaction between transcription skill level versus modality (handwriting vs. dictating). Because an advantage in automatic handwriting of girls over boys is commonly reported (Alves, Branco, Pontes, & Castro, 2007; Berninger & Fuller, 1992; Graham & Weintraub, 1996), we also explored possible effects or interactions from gender.

METHOD

Participants

From the initial 264 fourth graders screened, 80 children were selected to participate in this study. On the basis of the described screening procedure, three groups were formed: 32 children of low transcription skill (mean age = 9.38 years; $SD = 0.75$; 10 girls); 27 children of average skill (mean age = 8.89 years; $SD = 0.32$; 14 girls); and 21 children of high skill (mean age = 9.05 years; $SD = 0.38$; 12 girls).

Materials

The alphabet task was adapted from Berninger, Mizokawa, and Bragg (1991). Children wrote the alphabet letters using a pen on an A4 sheet with 1-cm squares, one for each letter.

A Portuguese version of the Handwriting Proficiency Screening Questionnaire (THPQ) (Rosenblum, 2008) was adapted for this study. This 10-item questionnaire addresses issues such as handwriting speed and legibility using a 5-point Likert scale, ranging from "never" to "always." Higher scores in the scale denote less proficiency. The regular teacher of each child completed the questionnaire.

Two sets of cartoonlike pictures were used to elicit the production of written narratives. One of the sets shows a boy going for a walk. He meets a balloon seller and gets a red balloon. He is very pleased and continues strolling. Suddenly, a blast of wind takes the balloon away and the boy breaks into tears. Sadness ends when the balloon seller comes in again and offers the child a new balloon. The other set portrays a boy going to the beach with his family. On the beach, the boy decides to make a sand castle and is very pleased with his constructions. Suddenly, a girl comes running and smashes his castle. The boy gets very sad, but he finally gets through it, as the girl helps him to build a new castle.

The written productions were registered by means of a digitizing tablet (Wacom Intuos 2) connected to a Windows-compatible PC running an E-Prime script (Schneider, Eschman, & Zuccollato, 2002) that logged the handwritten trace. A 15-in screen was used to give written feedback of the orally produced stories.

Procedure

The alphabet task used for screening was administered in groups in the children's classroom during regular class time and required 5 min. The experimenter asked the children to write the lowercase cursive letters of the alphabet as fast as possible, without sacrificing legibility, during 1 min (Berninger et al., 1991). Studies in the United States have commonly asked children for manuscript letters, but here we asked for cursive letters because in Portugal the alphabet is most often taught using that script. One point was attributed for each legible letter written in the proper position within 1 min. Two weeks later, the experimenter returned to the class and asked for the participation of some selected children. One at a time, each child left the class and participated in the study. All children produced two stories, one by handwriting on a digitizing tablet and another by dictating to a typist, with written feedback given through a liquid crystal display (LCD) screen. Providing the child with written feedback while dictating renders the composition mode more similar to the handwriting condition, and it has been shown to have a positive impact on text quality (Reece & Cumming, 1996). The elicitation pictures and production modalities were counterbalanced across the whole group.

On-Line Analyses and Text Quality Measures

The handwritten productions were analyzed by pauses and language bursts. Pauses were defined as periods of handwriting inactivity lasting longer than 2 s, which is a common pause threshold (e.g., Chenoweth & Hayes, 2001; Kaufer et al., 1986; Strömqvist, Holmqvist, Johansson, Karlsson, & Wengelin, 2006). This criterion is sensitive to children's production rates and the involvement of high-level writing processes (Alves et al., 2008; Wengelin, 2006). Language bursts were defined as periods of transcription activity in between two consecutive pauses, in which at least one word was written.

All narratives produced by the children were transcribed into a word processor and then evaluated by two independent judges blind to the objectives and methods of the study. The judges assessed text quality using a 7-point scale on three criteria: formal use of language (compliance with orthographic and grammar rules), creative use of language (expressivity and originality of writing and ideas), and amount of information (detail given on the story characters and situations). A fourth score was computed from the sum of the three scales. Ratings were carried following a procedure used by Levy and Ransdell (1995). Reliable interrater agreements were found for all scales ($r > .70$, all correlations significant at $p < .01$). The two scores provided by the two raters for a text were then averaged.

RESULTS

Screening

As a consequence of the screening procedure the three transcription skill groups reliably differed in the number of alphabet letters they were able to produce per minute [$F(2, 77) = 381.86$, $p < .001$, $\eta_p^2 = .91$] (descriptive measures can be seen in Table 16.1). As expected, the teachers' evaluations of each child's handwriting proficiency (THPQ) were also reliable at the group level [$F(2, 75) = 11.21$, $p < .001$,

TABLE 16.1 Means (and Standard Deviations) of Several On-Line Written Text Production Measures Among Three Handwriting Skill Groups and Across Girls And Boys

	Low Skill		Average Skill		High Skill	
	Girls	Boys	Girls	Boys	Girls	Boys
	M (SD)	M (SD)	M (SD)	M (SD)	M (SD)	M (SD)
Alphabet task	18.70	17.68	38.43	39.46	58.75	59.00
	(5.48)	(5.47)	(4.05)	(4.22)	(6.51)	(6.78)
Composition time (min)	7.01	7.55	8.42	7.83	7.86	8.95
	(1.61)	(2.26)	(4.18)	(2.67)	(1.66)	(4.15)
Text length (words)	89.50	89.68	112.43	90.38	129.00	119.00
	(23.40)	(29.80)	(58.50)	(27.40)	(29.40)	(55.60)
Fluency (wpm)	12.30	11.64	12.79	11.46	16.00	13.33
	(2.31)	(2.63)	(2.16)	(2.50)	(2.22)	(3.08)
Number of pauses	21.60	27.36	25.86	26.23	20.83	26.00
	(8.77)	(8.92)	(10.14)	(9.82)	(6.52)	(12.33)
Pause duration (seg.)	4.31	4.89	3.96	4.70	4.16	5.80
	(0.77)	(1.30)	(0.94)	(1.55)	(0.83)	(3.03)
Burst duration (seg.)	18.70	14.00	17.53	15.86	21.65	16.79
	(7.5)	(3.75)	(8.23)	(6.24)	(7.83)	(3.81)
Burst length (words)	5.07	4.00	4.99	4.27	7.34	5.23
	(1.71)	(1.17)	(2.39)	(1.83)	(3.19)	(1.45)

wpm, words per minute.

$\eta_p^2 = .23$] and showed a moderate correlation with the alphabet task ($r = .45$, $p <$ .01). Post hoc analyses showed that THPQ was effective in distinguishing the low-skill group ($M = 10.42$, $SD = 7.77$) from the two others, but did not differentiate between the average- and high-skill groups ($M = 5.11$, $SD = 3.69$; $M = 3.60$, $SD = 2.66$, respectively). The screening procedure found some noticeable differences between the groups, namely in age [$F(2, 77) = 6.05$, $p < .01$, $\eta_p^2 = .14$] and gender. The low-skill group was slightly older than the average-skill group (Games-Howell, $p < .01$), but not significantly different from the high-skill group (Games-Howell, $p > .05$). The low-skill group had a greater proportion of boys (69%) than would be expected by chance [$\chi^2(1) = 4.5$, $p < .05$].

Handwritten Production

Table 16.1 shows several on-line text production measures across girls and boys in the three handwriting skill groups. Two-way ANOVAs were conducted, and across groups there were no reliable differences in the amount of time devoted to composition. Even if all groups spent about 8 min composing, the amount of words produced by the three groups differed [$F(2, 74) = 4.68$, $p < .01$, $\eta_p^2 = .11$], with the high-skill group producing lengthier texts than the low-skill group (Games-Howell, $p < .01$). It is not only that the children of high handwriting skill wrote longer texts, but also that they were more fluent, as shown by a main effect of skill on compositional fluency [$F(2, 74) = 8.30$, $p < .001$, $\eta_p^2 = .18$]. On average, they produced three words per minute (wpm) more than the children of low transcription skill (Scheffé, $p < .01$). This analysis also revealed a main effect of gender [$F(1, 74) = 7.16$, $p < .01$, $\eta_p^2 = .09$], showing that girls composed more fluently than boys.

The higher compositional fluency of girls can be further explored by analyzing pauses and bursts. There were no main effects of handwriting skill or gender in the number of pauses. However, boys paused for a significantly longer time than girls [$F(1, 74) = 8.12$, $p < .01$, $\eta_p^2 = .10$], and girls had longer [$F(1, 74) = 6.50$, $p < .01$, $\eta_p^2 = .08$] and lengthier bursts [$F(1, 74) = 7.74$, $p < .01$, $\eta_p^2 = .10$]. On average, girls produced bursts that were 4 s longer and contained one and a half more words than those of the boys.

Although the main effect of handwriting skill on burst duration did not reach significance, there was a main effect of handwriting on burst length [$F(1, 74) = 5.42$, $p < .01$, $\eta_p^2 = .13$]. As predicted, Scheffé post hoc analyses showed that children of high handwriting skill had lengthier bursts ($M = 6.44$, $SD = 2.75$) than children in both the average- ($M = 4.64$, $SD = 2.13$) and the low-skill handwriting groups ($M = 4.33$, $SD = 1.42$). No reliable interactions were found in the preceding analyses.

Handwritten Versus Dictated Texts

All children produced two texts (counterbalanced), one by handwriting and the other by dictation. Handwritten texts took longer to produce as evidenced by a main effect of the repeated factor in a 3 (handwriting skill) × 2 (gender) × 2 (dictation vs. handwriting modality) mixed ANOVA [$F(1, 74) = 158.97$, $p < .001$,

$\eta_p^2 = .68$]. No other effect in this analysis was significant. A similar analysis on text length showed no effect of dictation versus handwriting modality. Only an effect of handwriting skill was reliable [$F(2, 74) = 4.23$, $p < .05$, $\eta_p^2 = .10$], indicating that the high handwriting skill group wrote longer texts than the low handwriting skill group (Scheffé, $p < .01$); there were no other significant differences between groups. As expected from the large difference in composition time between dictation and handwriting modalities, composing fluency was far higher in the dictated texts [$F(1, 74) = 296.29$, $p < .001$, $\eta_p^2 = .80$]. While dictating, children produced twice as many words per minute than while handwriting ($M = 29.68$, $SD = 8.36$; $M = 12.74$, $SD = 2.85$, respectively). No other effect or interaction was observed in this analysis.

All texts were rated by two independent judges, and the means of those evaluations per groups of transcription skill and dictation versus handwriting modality can be seen in Table 16.2. Three-way mixed ANOVAs were computed on the scores of every quality scale and led to similar findings across scales. Thus, only the findings on the overall narrative quality scores are detailed next. There was no significant effect of dictation versus handwriting modality ($F < 1$), the within subjects factor, on quality. Noticeably, the handwritten or dictated texts were judged on similar quality. There was the main effect of handwriting skill [$F(2, 74) = 8.54$, $p < .001$, $\eta_p^2 = .19$]. The texts produced by the high-skill group were rated higher than those of the low-skill group (Games-Howell, $p < .001$) and also those of average skill (Games-Howell, $p < .05$). There were no differences in the quality ratings

TABLE 16.2   Means (and Standard Deviations) of Written Text Production Measures and Holistic Ratings of Text Quality Among Three Handwriting Skill Groups and Across Two Dictation and Handwriting Modes

	Low Skill		Average Skill		High Skill	
	Writing	Dictation	Writing	Dictation	Writing	Dictation
	M (SD)	M (SD)	M (SD)	M (SD)	M (SD)	M (SD)
Composition time (min)	7.38 (2.07)	3.46 (2.09)	8.14 (3.48)	3.56 (2.09)	8.33 (2.95)	4.71 (2.86)
Text length (words)	89.62 (27.57)	94.41 (55.26)	101.81 (46.75)	97.59 (56.11)	124.71 (41.67)	127.29 (67.31)
Fluency (wpm)	11.84 (2.52)	29.70 (8.03)	12.15 (2.38)	29.77 (9.74)	14.86 (2.89)	29.52 (7.26)
Formal use of language	1.98 (1.22)	2.27 (0.82)	2.52 (1.51)	2.69 (1.05)	3.31 (1.39)	3.74 (1.41)
Creative use of language	2.14 (1.17)	2.25 (.97)	2.72 (1.64)	2.59 (1.41)	3.57 (1.52)	3.52 (1.81)
Amount of information	2.13 (1.11)	2.38 (1.14)	2.59 (1.54)	2.59 (1.41)	3.52 (1.51)	3.45 (1.84)
Overall quality	6.25 (3.38)	6.89 (2.71)	7.83 (4.54)	7.87 (3.67)	10.40 (4.21)	10.71 (4.99)

wpm, words per minute.

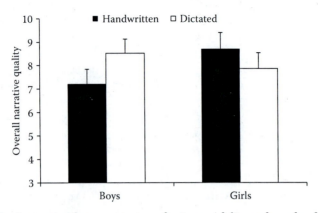

Figure 16.1   Interaction between text production modality and gender found on the overall narrative quality ratings (error bars denote standard errors).

of the low and average handwriting groups (Games-Howell, $p > .05$). This analysis also revealed a significant interaction between gender and dictation-handwriting modality [$F(1, 74) = 4.27$, $p < .05$, $\eta_p^2 = .06$], which can be seen in Figure 16.1. A simple effects analysis of the interaction showed that there were no significant differences between the texts handwritten or dictated by girls ($p > .05$), but when boys dictated the quality of their texts improved [$F(1, 78) = 4.67$, $p < .05$].

DISCUSSION

We assessed fourth graders to test if faster transcription speed would lead to larger language bursts, higher composition fluency, and overall better text quality. Indeed, the results indicate so. It is not new that handwriting speed improves composing fluency and text quality (Berninger, 1999; Graham & Harris, 2000), but, as far as we know, this is the first time that its impact on children's written language burst length is shown. In this study children of high handwriting skill showed larger written language bursts, composed text more fluently, and produced better stories.

That handwriting or typing skills contribute to burst length has also been reported in two studies with undergraduate students (Alves et al., 2007, 2011). Of interest, Hayes and Chenoweth (2006) found that written language bursts were virtually absent when the task required transcription only (typing copy task), whereas we found that when the task required transcription (handwriting) and text generation, handwriting speed was related to written language bursts. Also, the participants in the Hayes and Chenoweth study were selected for their expertise in typing (production rate higher than 40 wpm), whereas we studied good, average, and poor handwriting and not typing. In future research adult and child participants might be selected on the basis of both handwriting and typing skill and given a range of writing tasks from the alphabet (first 15 s, total time, and total legibility), to copying, to sentence writing and sentence combining, and to narrative and essay writing. The manipulation of transcription skill could be achieved experimentally, as in the Alves et al. (2011) study, or assessed for individual differences within a grade level and developmental differences across grade levels, from elementary to high school to college.

The current results are clear-cut: transcription, as assessed by handwriting skill, contributes to written language burst length in children, just as keyboarding skill did in adults (Alves et al., 2007, 2011). In the current study, the differences in handwriting skill among the groups are reliable, based on the alphabet task, which has been extensively used as an index of transcription efficiency (Christensen, 2005). Furthermore, these differences were validated by the ratings on handwriting proficiency made by the children's teachers. Similar to other studies, children showing lower handwriting proficiency were more likely boys (Graham & Weintraub, 1996) and had consistently lower scores on the Handwriting Proficiency Screening Questionnaire (HPSQ) (Rosenblum, 2008).

We expected that the quality of the texts produced by those with low handwriting skill would benefit from dictation, but this was not the case. Although this interaction was seen in beginning writers and children with learning disabilities (Bereiter & Scardamalia, 1987; MacArthur & Graham, 1987), rarely, as noted by Reece and Cumming (1996), has it been reported in normal-achieving children (see also Hidi & Hildyard, 1983; McCutchen, 1987). In the current study, the low-skill group, as a whole, cannot be described as having severe transcription difficulties, because in most of the relevant measures this group showed similar performances to that of the average group. Clearly in several measures of on-line production and text quality it was the high handwriting skill group that stood apart. We would like to point out that we screened only for handwriting speed, which if very fast and accurate, allows more efficient juggling of writing demands within working memory (McCutchen, 1996; Olive & Kellogg, 2002; Olive, Alves, & Castro, 2009). However, we cannot dismiss the possibility that fast and accurate transcription skill might also be a proxy for other abilities relevant to written composition. Keep in mind that transcription refers to both handwriting or keyboarding and spelling, and this study has not investigated whether automatic handwriting or automatic access to spelling may differentially contribute to the longer language bursts. Future research might explore this issue. Specifically, intervention studies could independently target handwriting (its accuracy or rate) or spelling and measure how each impacts burst length.

In this study, girls were more fluent than boys when using handwriting, but not when dictating. The on-line analysis of their text production revealed how deep this fluency difference runs. Girls showed smaller pauses and larger bursts. Future research could address the source of these larger bursts shown by girls during writing. Although overall girls and boys had similar scores on the alphabet task, boys were overrepresented on the low transcription skill group. Future research should investigate the differences between boys who are low and high in handwriting speed. Low handwriting speed may interfere with integration of transcription and text generation during translation. For example, one could test girls and boys in tasks like lexical decision, speaking span, or writing span (see McCutchen et al., 1994). Girls produced texts of similar quality, irrespective of dictation or handwriting modality, but boys benefited from the removal of transcription demands and produced better texts through dictation than by handwriting. In the absence of a general lower transcription skill in boys, it may be that there are individual differences variables with boys that future research should try to identify. One possibility is that some, but not all, boys have trouble connecting the language by hand system (Berninger, 2000) to their cognitions during translation. Instead of recommending dictation as a preferred way for low-skill boys to compose, they might benefit from appropriate instruction and practice in writing accurate letters automatically. It seems that the more efficient transcription gets, the more resources can readily be devoted to text generation, and the more quickly the hand will fully capture the language briefly held in the mind.

ACKNOWLEDGMENTS

This research was supported by a grant from the GRICES/CNRS agreement (Grices 01366, Proc. 4.1.1). The authors thank Lionel Granjon for the development of the handwriting logging program and Teresa Limpo and Virginia Berninger for insightful comments on previous versions of this chapter.

REFERENCES

Alves, R. A., Branco, M., Pontes, A., & Castro, S. L. (2007). Avaliação das dificuldades de leitura e escrita: Desenvolvimento da Bateria Fonológica da Universidade do Porto [Assessment of reading and writing difficulties: Development of the Phonological Battery of University of Porto]. *Educação: Temas e Problemas, 4*, 203–222.

Alves, R. A., Castro, S. L., & Olive, T. (2008). Execution and pauses in writing narratives: Processing time, cognitive effort and typing skill. *International Journal of Psychology, 43*, 969–979.

Alves, R. A., Castro, S. L., & Olive, T. (2011). Transcription skill constrains bursts of language production. In M. Torrance, D. Alamargot, M. Castelló, F. Ganier, O. Kruse, A. Mangen, L. Tolchinsky, & L. Van Waes (Eds.), *Learning to write effectively: Current trends in European research.* Brussels: OPOCE.

Alves, R. A., Castro, S. L., Sousa, L., & Strömqvist, S. (2007). Influence of typing skill on pause-execution cycles in written composition. In M. Torrance, L. van Waes & D. Galbraith (Eds.), *Writing and cognition: Research and applications* (pp. 55–65). Amsterdam: Elsevier.

Baddeley, A. (2007). *Working memory, thought, and action.* New York: Oxford University Press.

Bereiter, C., & Scardamalia, M. (1987). *The psychology of written composition.* Hillsdale, NJ: Erlbaum.

Berninger, V. W. (1999). Coordinating transcription and text generation in working memory during composing: Automatic and constructive processes. *Learning Disability Quarterly, 22*, 99–112.

Berninger, V. W. (2000). Development of language by hand and its connections with language by ear, mouth, and eye. *Topics in Language Disorders, 20*, 65–84.

Berninger, V. W., & Amtmann, D. (2003). Preventing written expression disabilities through early and continuing assessment and intervention for handwriting and/or spelling problems: Research into practice. In H. L. Swanson, K. R. Harris, & S. Graham (Eds.), *Handbook of learning disabilities* (pp. 345–363). New York: Guilford.

Berninger, V. W., Cartwright, A. C., Yates, C. M., Swanson, H. L., & Abbott, R. D. (1994). Developmental skills related to writing and reading acquisition in the intermediate grades: Shared and unique functional systems. *Reading and Writing, 6*, 161–196.

Berninger, V. W., & Fuller, F. (1992). Gender differences in orthographic, verbal, and compositional fluency: Implications for assessing writing disabilities in primary grade children. *Journal of School Psychology Review, 30,* 363–382.

Berninger, V. W., Fuller, F., & Whitaker, D. (1996). A process model of writing development across the life span. *Educational Psychology Review, 8,* 193–218.

Berninger, V. W., Mizokawa, D. T., & Bragg, R. (1991). Theory-based diagnosis and remediation of writing disabilities. *Journal of School Psychology, 29,* 57–79.

Berninger, V. W., & Swanson, H. L. (1994). Modifying Hayes and Flower's model of skilled writing to explain beginning and developing writing. In E. Butterfield (Ed.), *Children's writing: Toward a process theory of development of skilled writing* (pp. 57–81). Greenwich, CT: JAI.

Berninger, V. W., Yates, C., Cartwright, A., Rutberg, J., Remy, E., & Abbott, R. D. (1992). Lower-level developmental skills in beginning writing. *Reading and Writing, 4,* 257–280.

Bourdin, B., & Fayol, M. (1994). Is written language production more difficult than oral language production? A working memory approach. *International Journal of Psychology, 29,* 591–620.

Bourdin, B., & Fayol, M. (2000). Is graphic activity cognitively costly? A developmental approach. *Reading and Writing, 13,* 183–196.

Bourdin, B., & Fayol, M. (2002). Even in adults, written production is still more costly than oral production. *International Journal of Psychology, 37,* 219–227.

Chenoweth, N. A., & Hayes, J. R. (2001). Fluency in writing. *Written Communication, 18,* 80–98.

Chenoweth, N. A., & Hayes, J. R. (2003). The inner voice in writing. *Written Communication, 20,* 99–118.

Christensen, C. A. (2005). The role of orthographic-motor Integration in the production of creative and well-structured written text for students in secondary school. *Educational Psychology, 25,* 441–453.

Connelly, V., Gee, D., & Walsh, E. (2007). A comparison of keyboarded and handwritten compositions and the relationship with transcription speed. *British Journal of Educational Psychology, 77,* 479–492.

De La Paz, S., & Graham, S. (1997). Effects of dictation and advanced planning instruction on the composing of students with writing and learning problems. *Journal of Educational Psychology, 89,* 203–222.

Fayol, M. (1999). From on-line management problems to strategies in written composition. In M. Torrance & G. Jeffery (Eds.), *The cognitive demands of writing: Processing capacity and working memory effects in text production* (pp. 13–23). Amsterdam: Amsterdam University Press.

Gould, J. D., & Boies, S. J. (1978). Writing, dictating, and speaking letters. *Science, 201*(4361), 1145–1147.

Grabowski, J. (2008). The internal structure of university students' keyboard skills. *Journal of Writing Research, 1,* 27–52.

Grabowski, J. (2010). Speaking, writing, and memory span in children: Output modality affects cognitive performance. *International Journal of Psychology, 45,* 28–39.

Graham, S. (1990). The role of production factors in learning disabled students' compositions. *Journal of Educational Psychology, 82,* 781–791.

Graham, S., Berninger, V., Abbott, R., Abbott, S., & Whitaker, D. (1997). The role of mechanics in composing of elementary school students: A new methodological approach. *Journal of Educational Psychology, 89,* 170–182.

Graham, S., & Harris, K. R. (2000). The role of self-regulation and transcription skills in writing and writing development. *Educational Psychologist, 35,* 3–12.

Graham, S., & Weintraub, N. (1996). A review of handwriting research: Progress and prospects from 1980 to 1994. *Educational Psychology Review, 8*, 7–87.

Hayes, J. R., & Chenoweth, N. A. (2006). Is working memory involved in the transcribing and editing of texts? *Written Communication, 23*, 135–149.

Hayes, J. R., & Chenoweth, N. A. (2007). Working memory in an editing task. *Written Communication, 24*, 283–294.

Hayes, J. R., & Flower, L. S. (1980). Identifying the organization of writing processes. In L. W. Gregg & E. R. Steinberg (Eds.), *Cognitive processes in writing* (pp. 3–29). Hillsdale, NJ: Erlbaum.

Hidi, S. E., & Hildyard, A. (1983). The comparison of oral and written productions in two discourse types. *Discourse Processes, 6*, 91–105.

Jones, D., & Christensen, C. A. (1999). Relationship between automaticity in handwriting and students' ability to generate written text. *Journal of Educational Psychology, 91*, 44–49.

Kaufer, D. S., Hayes, J. R., & Flower, L. S. (1986). Composing written sentences. *Research in the Teaching of English, 20*, 121–140.

Kellogg, R. T. (1996). A model of working memory in writing. In C. M. Levy & S. Ransdell (Eds.), *The science of writing* (pp. 57–71). Mahwah, NJ: Erlbaum.

Levy, C. M., & Ransdell, S. (1995). Is writing as difficult as it seems? *Memory and Cognition, 23*, 767–779.

MacArthur, C. A., & Graham, S. (1987). Learning-disabled students composing under three methods of text production: Handwriting, word processing, and dictation. *Journal of Special Education, 21*, 23–42.

McCutchen, D. (1987). Children's discourse skill: Form and modality requirements of schooled writing. *Discourse Processes, 10*, 267–286.

McCutchen, D. (1996). A capacity theory of writing: Working memory in composition. *Educational Psychology Review, 8*, 299–325.

McCutchen, D., Covill, A., Hoyne, S. H., & Mildes, K. (1994). Individual-differences in writing: Implications of translating fluency. *Journal of Educational Psychology, 86*, 256–266.

Olive, T., Alves, R. A., & Castro, S. L. (2009). Cognitive processes in writing during pauses and execution periods. *European Journal of Cognitive Psychology, 21*, 758–785.

Olive, T., & Kellogg, R. T. (2002). Concurrent activation of high- and low-level production processes in written composition. *Memory and Cognition, 30*, 594–600.

Quinlan, T. (2004). Speech recognition technology and students with writing difficulties: Improving fluency. *Journal of Educational Psychology, 96*, 337–346.

Reece, J. E., & Cumming, G. (1996). Evaluating speech-based composition methods: Planning, dictation, and the listening word processor. In C. M. Levy & S. Ransdell (Eds.), *The science of writing* (pp. 361–380). Mahwah, NJ: Erlbaum.

Rosenblum, S. (2008). Development, reliability and validity of the handwriting proficiency screening questionnaire for handwriting proficiency (HPSQ). *American Journal of Occupational Therapy, 62*, 298–307.

Schneider, W., Eschman, A., & Zuccollato, A. (2002). *E-Prime reference guide*. Pittsburgh: Psychology Software Tools.

Strömqvist, S., Holmqvist, K., Johansson, V., Karlsson, H., & Wengelin, Å. (2006). What keystroke logging can reveal about writing. In K. Sullivan & E. Lindgren (Eds.), *Computer keystroke logging and writing: Methods and applications* (pp. 45–71). Amsterdam: Elsevier.

Swanson, H. L., & Berninger, V. W. (1996). Individual differences in children's working memory and writing skill. *Journal of Experimental Child Psychology, 63*, 358–385.

Wengelin, Å. (2006). Examining pauses in writing: Theory, methods and empirical data. In K. Sullivan & E. Lindgren (Eds.), *Computer keystroke logging and writing: Methods and applications* (pp. 107–130). Amsterdam: Elsevier.

17

Written Production of Single Words and Simple Sentences

MARK TORRANCE and GUIDO NOTTBUSCH

*I*t is normal practice for authors writing about the writing process to start with introductory remarks about how difficult it is. This perception is, no doubt, partly a reflection of the author's own immediate experience. Writing in general, and writing introductory remarks to academic papers in particular, requires high levels of sustained attention. This processing requirement is captured, for example, in Scardamalia and Bereiter's (1991) argument that, unlike development of expertise in other domains, higher expertise in writing is associated with greater, rather than less, struggle and in the frequent observation that writing makes high demands on cognitive capacity (McCutchen, 1996). Implicit within these "writing-is-difficult" arguments is a contrast with spoken language production, which seems often to proceed automatically and with relatively little need for focused attention.

Where does this writing difficulty come from? There are, broadly, two sets of processes associated with the production of coherent text. First, there is the conceptual processing required in deciding what is to be communicated. This requirement takes the writer from a general communicational goal—an intention to affect the reader's understanding in a particular way—to the intention to communicate a particular proposition in the next clause or sentence. It is these conceptual processes that were the focus of early cognitive accounts of written production (Hayes & Flower, 1980a). Conceptual processing is, at least sometimes, explicit and deliberate. This makes it accessible to the methods used in research examining complex information processing in other domains and particularly the solving of toy problems (Tower of Hanoi, the Water Jug Problem, etc.): Hayes and Flower (1980a, 1980b) explicitly identified writing as analogous to problem solving in other nonlinguistic contexts.

A second set of processes takes the output from conceptual processing—the writer's intended message—and adds the necessary lexical, syntactic, and orthographic information to turn the message into text. These psycholinguistic processes are no less complex than those associated with message generation, but are rapid, implicit, and largely automatic, at least in literate adults. They are, therefore, invisible to the self-report and think-aloud methods that have been successful in exploring writers' conceptual processing. They are also largely invisible to the writers themselves. Once a writer has decided what the next clause will say, and assuming that the necessary spelling knowledge is easily retrieved, then it will appear on the screen more or less effortlessly. To take an example from the research we report below, literate adults presented with a display showing pictures of a bird and a cat above a house have no difficulty in producing the sentence "The bird and the cat are above the house" and have no awareness of the processes underlying their ability to do so.

These low-level, postconceptual processes are the focus of the research that we review in this chapter. They have been explored extensively in the language production literature. However, in nearly all cases this research has been in the context of spoken output. A quick keyword search of volumes of the various parts of the *Journal of Experimental Psychology* for the past 20 years reveals approximately 650 articles with a specific language focus. Approximately 320 of these are concerned with spoken production (with a similar number focusing on reading). Of the remainder, 10 look at the motor-processing associated with handwriting and copy typing. Just two have a specific text-production focus. With the exception of research on the development of spelling ability, research on postconceptual processing is largely absent from the text production literature, at least in mainstream cognitive psychology—although this volume presents the efforts of three researchers trying to introduce that area of research into the cognitive psychology field (see Chapters 1–3, this volume).

This relative neglect of written production may not be a problem. It may be that the bulk of the (postconceptual) language processing associated with spoken and written output is essentially the same. Under this account, writing and speech share the same semantic, syntactic, lexical, and morphological processing and differ only in the very last stages of processing (vocalization for speech, but spelling, and inscription—also referred to in this volume as *transcription*—or typing for writing). This "language plus" account of written production has parsimony in its favor, and in the absence of evidence to the contrary it therefore makes a sensible working hypothesis. There are, however, at least three reasons why, in principle at least, we might anticipate more fundamental differences in how language processing is managed in speech and writing.

The first of these concerns differences in the relationship between output fluency and communicative effect. In speech, listeners interpret not only the words that are spoken but also the metrical structure of the utterance. The fluent utterance "I was visiting a friend" in response to the question "What were you doing last night?" means something different from "I was visiting a [pause] friend." Even when dysfluency would not result in miscommunication, there is still pressure on the speaker to avoid excessive pausing, particularly midclause. It may be that this requirement for fluency necessitates advanced planning in speech production, over and above that which is required by underlying language processes (Levelt &

Meyer, 2000; Martin, Crowther, Knight, Tamborello, & Yang, 2010). In writing, there is no such requirement for fluent output. In reporting last night's whereabouts by e-mail, a writer can, if he or she chooses, write "I was visiting a" and then leave his or her desk to make a cup of coffee before returning to complete the sentence, and this pause in writing will in no way affect the reader's understanding. This difference between speech and writing is even stronger at the word level. In almost all circumstances speakers must avoid midword pausing if what is said is to be understood. Writers are not constrained in this way.

Second, writing requires spelling. This requirement suggests that at least models of written production require an additional component dedicated to orthographic processing. These orthographic processes are explored in other chapters in this volume. However, it is possible that the need for spelling has a more general influence on language production in writing. Most obviously, spelling retrieval may draw on central attentional (or "bottleneck"; Pashler, Johnston, & Ruthruff, 2001; Welford, 1967) mechanisms that are also required by upstream language or conceptual processes. This possibility is consistent with the finding that competent adults make more errors in spelled morphology (e.g., French verb–noun agreement) when writing is combined with a secondary memory task (Fayol, Largy, & Lemaire, 1994; Totereau, Thevenin, & Fayol, 1997). If conflict between spelling retrieval and upstream processing occurs on a regular basis (and if, as seems likely, there are no similar conflicts associated with the later stages of spoken production), then language processes that are optimized for spoken production may be suboptimal when output is written. It is possible, therefore, that upstream (modality independent) conceptual and language processing are structured differently in spoken and in written production to accommodate differences in the extent to which output processing draws on central resources.

More fundamentally it may be that mental representations of written and spoken words are distinct and separate. Dominant accounts of language production, based in the study of speech (e.g., Bock, 1982; Dell & O'Seaghdha, 1992; Garrett, 1980; Levelt, 1989; Roelofs, 1992), assume two broad levels of representation between the speaker's intended meaning and spoken output. First, the speaker retrieves a semantically and syntactically defined word form—a lemma. Because lemmas do not hold phonological (or orthographic) information, they are therefore independent of output modality. This independence then permits retrieval of an associated lexeme, which provides the word's phonology and so mediates the retrieval of the individual phonemes required for articulation. Orthography, if considered at all, is theorized as being retrieved through its association with the word's phonology. Under this account, writing is not just "language plus" but "speech plus."

By contrast, Caramazza (1997), on the basis of evidence from subjects with acquired neuropsychological deficits, argued for a quite different model. He identified subjects who consistently made semantic errors in written naming but not in spoken naming, which is consistent with the traditional account, but also others who consistently showed the reverse pattern, which is incompatible with the traditional account (Caramazza & Hillis, 1990, 1991). Evidence of this kind suggests that orthographic and phonological representations are distinct and not dependent on each other for production.

The fact that errors are semantic, and, therefore, made prior to lexeme selection also casts doubt on the existence of a common lemma level representation. So, rather than a late splitting into phonemic or orthographic codes, it may be that there are distinct orthographic and phonological lexicons, activated directly from semantic memory. Under this account, written production is, at a fundamental level, distinct from speech; although of course this distinction does not preclude the possibility that speech production and written production follow very similar patterns.

Third, writing and speech afford different, but overlapping, sets of mechanisms by which the language producer can monitor his or her output for errors. Postma (2000), based on a traditional message→lemma→lexeme speech production model, identified at least 11 mechanisms by which output can be fed back to the speaker. These range from early-stage checking for syntactic feasibility through proprioceptive monitoring at output to monitoring the effects of an utterance on the listener. Writing affords some of the same feedback loops, but also some that are different. Most notably, writers have access to a permanent visible trace. This access, combined with the fact that the output fluency is independent of communicative effects, means that both error monitoring and correction can, in principle, be delayed, a phenomenon explored experimentally by Van Waes, Leijten, and Quinlan (2010).

Therefore, for reasons that have to do with output fluency, the differing demands of orthographic and phonological processing, and different feedback affordances, written and spoken production cannot simply be assumed to rely on identical underlying processes. It may well be that the language processing underlying spoken and written production, at or below the sentence level, is essentially similar. However, the question of whether this is the case requires empirical testing. Until findings based in spoken production can be reproduced in writing, researchers do not have a basis for, as often happens, treating "speech production" and "language production" as synonyms. Some of the effects they observe may result from the particular demands imposed by choosing speech as an output medium. Researchers interested in written production, therefore, have an extensive set of findings and methods from speech research begging to be replicated in the written modality. To date, few researchers have taken up this challenge.

The remainder of this chapter is divided into two main sections. First, we discuss research that has examined factors affecting the typing of single words, specifically focusing on factors affecting within-word variation in the typing time course. In the context of keyboarded production, this time course is far removed from the high-level processing that is typically the focus of writing researchers. This typing time course has, however, received concerted attention in the cognitive psychology research literature. We then describe some early experiments aimed at exploring the extent to which writers mentally plan short sentences in advance of starting to type.

WRITING SINGLE WORDS

The dynamics of typing has been studied as early as the beginning of the 20th century (Coover, 1923; Dvorak, Merrick, Dealey, & Ford, 1936; Fendrick, 1937; Wells, 1916), and the period from 1970 to 1990, especially the early 1980s, saw a surge of publications within the mainstream psychological literature on typing as a skilled motor behavior (e.g., Cooper, 1983; Gentner, 1982a, 1982b, 1983, 1987; Gentner, Grudin, & Conway, 1980; Gentner, Larochelle, & Grudin, 1988; Grudin, 1983; Larochelle, 1983, 1984; Massaro & Lucas, 1984; Norman & Rumelhart, 1983; Olsen & Murray, 1976; Ostry, 1980, 1983; Rumelhart & Norman, 1982; Sternberg, Monsell, Knoll, & Wright, 1978; Terzuolo & Viviani, 1980; Zesiger, Orliaguet, Boë, & Mounoud, 1994). This body of research now forms the basis for our present understanding of the organization of the underlying motor processes. In these studies motor processes were assumed to be largely independent of language processing, with linguistic factors having at most marginal effects on typing time course. Researchers started from the assumption that motor modules are supplied with already specified lexical-orthographic information (e.g., Sternberg et al., 1978). So, consistent with the "speech-plus" understanding of writing, typing was treated as largely independent of higher order cognitive processes.

A central concern was explanation of inter- and intrapersonal variability in typing rate. The relative lengths of an interkey interval (IKI), which is the period of time between pressing the current key and the immediately previous key, in repeated writing of the same word by the same participant is quite stable. IKIs tend to rise or fall with typing speed (the proportional duration model; Terzuolo & Viviani, 1980; Viviani & Laissard, 1996). Gentner (1982a, 1982b, 1987), however, found that this conclusion holds true in only 40% of IKIs and within a central range of typing speeds. At the extremes of the typing speed distribution the correlation between IKIs and overall speed decreases. Among writers, typing speed can vary by as much as 80% for the same short word typed at different times in the same session (Terzuolo & Viviani, 1980). Compared over different participants, the patterns for one word show a correlation of $r^2 = .50$ with a span from .25 to .68 (Gentner et al., 1988). Major differences result from the typing method that participants use—from hunt-and-peck to touch typing.

In addition to typing speed and typing method, a large number of other factors affecting the time course have been identified. One is the keyboard layout (QWERTY, QWERTZ, AZERTY, etc.). Another factor concerns where a specific key is located on the keyboard. Fingers have to move farther to strike peripheral keys, and so these tend to be associated with longer IKIs than keys that are toward the center of the keyboard. The home keys—the eight keys on which the fingers rest in touch typing—show the shortest latencies. Finger–hand combinations, which are determined by keyboard layout and individual typing method, are also important, although this effect is mediated by typing expertise. In expert (touch typing) typists, IKIs associated with keys pressed by different hands (e.g., *F* struck by the left forefinger followed by *J* struck by the right forefinger on a QWERTY keyboard) are typically shorter than when keys are pressed by the same hand, and even more so when the same key is pressed twice by the same finger. In contrast, in novice typists multiple presses on the same key by the same finger are the most rapid (Coover, 1923; Gentner, 1983; Larochelle, 1983). A computer simulation by Rumelhart and Norman (1982) successfully reproduced findings relating to digraphs requiring same finger/same key, same finger/different key, different fingers of one hand, and alternating hands. However, the model did not explain differences within one class, leading to the conclusion that there must be additional, nonbiomechanical factors that play a part in determining keystroke latencies.

One such set of factors relates to the frequency with which particular keys and key combinations are pressed. Letter, grapheme, and n-graph (digraph, trigraph, etc.) frequencies are, of course, language dependent, in that they depend on how frequently a letter combination is used in the first language of the typist (Gentner et al., 1988). The effects of these frequencies on typing rate will therefore be mediated, in part, by factors associated with psycholinguistic processing that occurs prior to motor planning. However, frequency in language will also result in frequency of use, which will mean that certain motor patterns become overlearned. Letter frequency alone plays some role in predicting IKIs (Weingarten, Nottbusch, & Will, 2004), but taking into account the context in which a keystroke occurs— which keys are pressed before and afterward—explains much more of the variability (Terzuolo & Viviani, 1980). Although there is an interaction between digraph effects and mechanical factors such as finger travel and finger-hand combination (Viviani & Laissard, 1996), digraph frequencies still show a strong effect when these other factors are held constant (e.g., as when comparing the combination *er* with *re*; Gentner, Larochelle, and Grudin, 1988). The effect is even stronger if the digraph position within the word is controlled (Massaro & Lucas, 1984). Word frequency is also a determinant of typing rate, as first identified by Fendrick (1937). Gentner et al. (1988) examined the effect by using 35 word pairs with an identical four-letter sequence (e.g., *system* vs. *oyster*), one word being frequently used and the other not. The effect on the duration of the central interval (*st* in the example) was only small (10 ms), but statistically significant. Taking into account that all word pairs were written 20 times by the participants—leading to repeated priming and therefore a probable reduction across repetitions in the effects of word frequency (Bodner & Masson, 1997)—this finding provides strong evidence for word-level effects on production rates.

There is, therefore, evidence for effects on IKI ranging from the purely mechanical to the purely linguistic. An underlying issue is the size of the basic planning unit in single word typing. Video analysis suggests that some advance planning must occur (Gentner et al., 1980; Olsen & Murray, 1976; Sternberg et al., 1978). In competent typists, movements of different fingers overlap in time. Thus, although one finger is striking a key, another finger will already have begun its trajectory toward the next key to be pressed. Larochelle (1984) compared this effect to coarticulation in overt speech. So, given the presence of advance planning, what exactly is the scope of the motor plans that typists construct?

The answer to this question has been the subject of intense debate between research teams headed by Paolo Viviani and by Don Gentner. Viviani and colleagues (Viviani & Laissard, 1996; Viviani & Terzuolo, 1982, 1983) argued, through comparison of identical trigraphs occurring within different words, that IKIs cannot be explained by the trigraph frequency alone. On the basis of this and similar findings they argued for the word as a basic planning unit, represented as a lexical item called a *motor engram*, analogous to the phonological representations (lexemes) that are accessed during spoken production.

By contrast, Gentner and colleagues argued that the same results can be explained in terms of sublexical units. Gentner (1982a) examined the effects of the keys either side of a specific key press by systematically manipulating the context size and then measuring IKI variability. The mean variability, measured in terms of interquartile range for all IKIs over all participants (expert typists), was 55.2 ms. This variability was reduced to 31.7 ms if the preceding key was taken into account. Considering the preceding two keys (so looking at variance in the final IKI in trigraphs, averaged across all trigraphs and participants) reduced variance still further, to 25.7 ms. Looking at one key forward reduced variance by an additional 9.7 ms. Crucially, this context effect also extended across word boundaries. These findings, therefore, may suggest a basic planning unit of up to four characters.

Turning to purely linguistic factors, some early work hinted at syllable-level effects, but accounts are rather vague (Ostry, 1983; Shaffer, 1978). Shaffer and Hardwick (1968) found that 5 or 15 letter strings organized into syllables were typed faster than randomly assigned letters. Thomas and Jones (1970) found that isolated syllables were typed faster than groups of four random characters or letter strings without spaces. In both cases these findings may have more to do with chunking during encoding of the to-be-typed string than with effects that occur at output.

Stronger evidence came from Massaro and Lucas (1984), who found that IKIs over syllable boundaries were longer than IKIs within syllables, although the authors compared different digraphs and did not control for digraph frequency. Finally, Zesiger et al. (1994) provided a direct comparison of the same digraphs across words in which they either did or did not span syllable boundaries (e.g., the digraph *al* in the French words *palette* and *palmier*—palette and palm). IKIs that spanned syllable boundaries were, on average, longer by 21 ms.

This paradigm was used and developed further in a series of studies by Nottbusch and colleagues (Nottbusch, 2008; Nottbusch, Grimm, Weingarten, & Will, 2005; Nottbusch, Weingarten, & Sahel, 2007; Nottbusch, Weingarten, & Will, 1998; Sahel, Nottbusch, Grimm, & Weingarten, 2008; Sahel, Nottbusch, Weingarten, & Blanken, 2005; Weingarten, Nottbusch, & Will 2004; Will, Nottbusch, & Weingarten, 2006). Nottbusch et al. (1998) compared four types of IKIs for controlled digraphs as follows: syllable and morpheme boundary (e.g., *nd* in *hindurch*/ throughout); syllable boundaries only (*nd* in *Linde*/lime tree); morpheme boundaries only (*nd* in *lachend*/laughing); and no linguistic or letter boundary (*nd* in *Kind*/ child). Findings suggested substantially longer IKIs when syllable and morpheme boundaries coincided, with similar intervals in the other three conditions (mean IKIs: syllable and morpheme boundary, 302 ms; syllable only, 215 ms; morpheme only, 198 ms; letter boundary, 206 ms). However, in this study the number of syllable-only cases was relatively low.

Later studies found a robust syllable effect. In a summary of several studies Weingarten et al. (2004) reported a strong word frequency effect on the IKI prior to striking the first key in a word and for digraphs straddling a syllable and morpheme boundary, but no word-frequency effects of IKIs at syllable-only boundaries. This pattern of findings suggests, therefore, that planning for typing, and perhaps upstream lexical retrieval processes, occurs at the start of the word, and in complex word forms, at the start of root morphemes. The pattern also lends some weight to arguments that motor planning has a word-level scope.

Where does the syllable effect come from? One possibility is that typing is accompanied by subvocal articulation of the word that is being typed, and that typing synchronizes with this subvocalization. However, Nottbusch and colleagues (Will, Weingarten, Nottbusch, & Albes, 2002) found that the syllable effect remains even under articulatory suppression conditions (participants singing a constant tone under their breath while typing), suggesting that this explanation is unlikely. Two other possibilities are that increased IKIs and syllable boundaries result from central, abstract phonological processes. Alternatively, it may be that they originate from an autonomous graphosyllabic process.

In order to decide between these two possibilities, two studies were conducted: First, the typing performance of a fluent German aphasic with an impaired lexical system and severe damage to the phoneme-grapheme-conversion system was examined (Sahel et al., 2005). Given the nature of this patient's impairment, the authors assumed that this patient's spelling ability was not phonologically mediated, either at the lexical or sublexical level. Unlike unimpaired adult controls, the patient's single word typing revealed no syllable effects. Combined syllable–morpheme boundaries, however, were prolonged as in the control group. This finding suggests that typing without phonological mediation is possible, but grouping graphemes into syllables or syllablelike units is not. In addition, typists who were born deaf showed syllabic effects similar to those found in a hearing control group (Nottbusch et al., 2005). Therefore, it can be concluded that the syllable effect is related to an abstract phonological level, independent of the complete phonological information contained in spoken language.

In summary, within-word IKIs are predicted to a large extent by physiological and biomechanical effects and very low-level features of the language being used (specifically letter and digraph frequency). Gentner et al. (1988) regressed IKIs onto a range of possible predictors and found that digraph frequency explained more unique variance in IKI than either the frequency of the word or whether the IKI represented the start of a new syllable. They also found that the combined effect of language-specific variables (word frequency, digraph frequency, and syllable boundary) was similar in size to the combined effect of physical constraints (key proximity, hand transition, etc.). The presence of a syllable effect *and* the fact that it appears to result from processing after lexical retrieval but prior to motor planning suggest that even single words are not fully planned in advance of output.

WRITING SIMPLE SENTENCES

Competent writers have no difficulty accurately and rapidly typing single-clause sentences. The question that we want to address in this section—and a question that has already been addressed in several studies in the speech production literature—is the extent to which single-clause sentences are planned in advance of output: How much of the sentence must the writer mentally prepare before being ready to start typing?

Faced with composing a sentence that describes an array of images representing, for example, a cat and a bird above a tree, one possibility is that participants mentally rehearse the full clause—*The cat and the bird are above the tree*—before they are ready to start writing. The idea that writers engage in extensive advance planning of the surface structure of their text has gained some currency in educationally focused accounts of written production. Faigley and Witte (1981) talked about "pretext," an inner-speech representation of possible text that is constructed and possibly edited prior to output. It clearly is possible for competent writers to prepare a full, phonetic representation of sentences—possibly even multiclause sentences—prior to output, although it is less clear whether this practice is typical and, if so, what function it might serve. Our present focus, however, is not on how much advance planning is possible, and not even on what typically occurs, but on how much planning is necessitated by the ways in which underlying language processes function.

Planning Scope in Spoken Production

Early evidence concerning planning scope in speech came from systematic errors in spontaneous spoken production. Errors of the form "The dog slapped the man," which involve the transposition of lemmas that share the same thematic roles, are probably much more common than cross-role transpositions ("The slap manned the dog"; Garrett, 1975, 1988; but see Harley, 1984). On the basis of this kind of evidence Garrett suggested two distinct planning stages. The first of these takes the speaker's intended message and generates an unordered set of lemmas, each mapped to thematic roles. This information is then passed on for grammatical processing in which lemmas are ordered and inflected to provide correct phrase and clause structure.

However, several findings from experimental studies have suggested a more limited scope to speech planning. Smith and Wheeldon (1999) presented participants with visual arrays that elicited sentences that were either of the form "The A and the B move above the C" (complex-simple) or "The A moves above the B and the C" (simple-complex). At the clause level, these two sentences have equivalent conceptual, syntactic, and lexical complexity. They differ just in the complexity of the initial verb-argument phrase. Participants showed substantially shorter sentence-initial latencies (time from stimulus presentation to speech onset) in the simple-complex condition. This finding suggests that, at some level, planning does not embrace the full clause, but rather a smaller phrase-level unit. This claim is consistent with results from experiments conducted in German by Schriefers, Teruel, and Meinshausen (1998) that explored the effect of introducing distractor verbs when participants produced sentences with verbs at the start of a sentence or in a later position. Schriefers and colleagues concluded that even in short sentences verbs are not necessarily processed prior to the start of articulation. In a much earlier study (Levelt & Maassen, 1981), participants required to generate sentences of the form "The A and the B move up" in response to a moving visual stimulus showed longer initial latencies than when generating sentences of the form "The A moves up and the B moves up."

Evidence from experiments exploring sentence-initial latencies therefore suggests a planning scope in spoken production that extends over units that are less than a full clause but greater than a single word. What is planned seems, however, to be dependent more on sentence position than on function. Speakers appear to preplan just the initial (possibly complex) phrase even when the initial phrase is subordinate to a subsequent phrase (Allum & Wheeldon, 2007, 2009). Similarly, there is evidence that pre–head noun modifiers are planned along with their nouns if they will appear before the noun, but are part of the initial planning unit if they appear post–head noun (Schriefers & Teruel, 1999). There is also some evidence that in some contexts speech is produced entirely incrementally, with no planning beyond the next word to be produced (Griffin, 2001; Griffin & Bock, 2000). Griffin (2001) showed participants arrays of three objects that elicited sentences of the form "The A and the B are above the C." She found that ease of retrieval of B had no effect on sentence-initial latency. Moreover, the speaker's eye movements suggested that B was typically not even looked at until output of the initial noun phrase ("The A") had been initiated. On the basis of this evidence Griffin argued that although speakers may in some context choose to plan ahead, fundamentally speech planning proceeds on a word-by-word basis.

There are two general approaches to explaining these conflicting experimental findings, both discussed by Martin et al. (2010). One is to dismiss Griffin's findings on the grounds that the task that participants performed did not require the kinds of syntactic planning that would occur in normal speech. If participants are always required to produce sentences in the same syntactic frame and name objects in the same order on the screen, then it is possible to dismiss the task as being more akin to serial picture naming than sentence production. Another possibility is that Griffin (2003) is correct in arguing that language production is essentially incremental, but when output is spoken, advance planning is necessary to maintain fluency. If so, then planning in spoken production is, in part, a function of output medium rather than language processing per se. The different requirements of written production with regard to fluency might then result in different planning behavior. Specifically, we might predict less advance planning in the kinds of tasks explored by Smith and Wheeldon (1999).

Three Studies of Planning Scope in Written Production

We now describe three studies that represent early attempts at systematically exploring planning scope in written sentence production. The first study is published. Studies 2 and 3 are reported here, in summary, for the first time.

Study 1   Nottbusch and colleagues (Nottbusch, 2010; Nottbusch et al., 2007) showed German-speaking participants arrays of colored shapes designed to elicit sentences that started either with a coordinate verb-argument phrase ("Die schwarzen Pfeile und die roten Dreiecke sind neben dem gelben Kreis"/The black arrows and the red triangles are beside the yellow circle) or a subordinate phrase ("Die schwarzen Pfeile mit den roten Dreiecken sind neben dem gelben Kreis"/ The black arrows with the red triangles are beside the yellow circle). An effect of syntactic structure (specifically, ordination) of the initial phrase on sentence-initial latency would necessarily indicate that planning extended across the whole of this phrase, not just to the first noun and its determiner. The authors hypothesized that subordination, which adds a nested structure to the syntax of the phrase, would take more planning than a coordinate structure.

In the 2007 study 19 students completed 12 trials in each of the two conditions, typing their responses. Stimulus images remained visible on the screen during typing. The authors found that sentence-initial latencies for sentences with a subordinate structure in the initial verb-argument phrase took on average 184 ms longer to plan than sentences with a coordinate structure (coordinate, $M = 2,013$ ms, $SD = 1,027$ ms; subordinate $M = 2,197$ ms, $SD = 1,169$ ms). In the 2010 study a 7-s preparation period was introduced between appearance of the stimulus display and a signal that indicated that participants could start typing, in order to reduce the influence of object recognition and lexical retrieval. This reduced the advantage of the coordinate structure to just 34 ms, and this effect was not statistically reliable.

Advance planning, however, does not necessarily occur only during pauses but may, in principle, also occur concurrently with typing. Chanquoy, Foulin, and Fayol (1990) provided some evidence to this effect. Planning, therefore, might be evidenced not only by greater pausing at particular boundaries within the text (presentence and at phrase boundaries), but also by slower typing rates for words appearing immediately prior to the structure being planned. All sentences in Nottbusch, Weingarten, and Sahel (2007) started with the same determiner (*Die*), allowing direct comparison of production fluency between the subordinate and coordinate conditions. Findings from this fluency data also showed an advantage for coordinate structures. Average IKIs for *Die* in the subordinate condition was 28 ms slower than in the coordinate condition (coordinate, $M = 319$ ms, $SD = 156$ ms; subordinate $M = 346$ ms, $SD = 205$ ms). Again this effect was absent when the 7-s preparation period was introduced.

Because coordination and subordination affect the structure of the initial verb-argument phrase, these latency effects point toward a phrasal planning scope, at least in some situations. Specifically, it may be that subordinate phrases are planned as a whole prior to typing, but coordinate constructions are planned in a more incremental fashion, with preplanning of just the first determiner adjective-noun component. If so, then we would expect slower initiation times for the second part of the phrase in the coordination condition. This effect was observed in both studies. The initiation of *und* (and) in the coordinate condition took reliably longer than the initiation of *mit* (with) in the subordination condition. Similarly preparation time for typing the space prior to *und* was reliably longer than for the space prior to *mit*. Eye-tracking data collected in the 2010 study also pointed toward a greater tendency to incremental planning of the coordinate structure. For the period after production of the initial determiner adjective-noun component up to the production of the verb, there were reliably more fixations on the stimulus images in the coordinate condition, suggesting again that the second half of the initial verb-argument phrase was less likely to be included in sentence-initial planning.

Study 2   In a second study we (Nottbusch and Torrance) adopted a similar design to Smith and Wheeldon (1999). English-speaking participants were presented with an array of pictures designed to elicit sentences in one of four forms: simple-simple (e.g., "The fish is above the star"), simple-complex ("The fish is above the tree and the star"), complex-simple ("The fish and the tree are above the star"), and complex-complex ("The fish and the tree are above the star and the ring"). The same four images were used in all trials, with order counterbalanced, and trials varied as to whether the subject was above or below the object. In each trial participants were first shown a 2 × 2 array containing all four pictures. After 2 s the images were inverted (white line drawing on a black background), and any images that were not to be featured in the sentence were hidden by imposing gray on them. Sentence-initial latency was timed from when this change was made. Our intention was that object recognition and, perhaps, lexical retrieval would occur during the initial 2-s period, making sentence-initial latency a pure measure of syntactic planning. As in the majority of Smith and Wheeldon's experiments, the stimulus array disappeared when the participant started to output his or her response (in this case when the first key was struck).

Twelve psychology undergraduates completed 12 trials in each condition. Sentence-initial latencies varied significantly with condition. We found the greatest delay in the complex-complex condition and the shortest delay in the simple-simple condition. Unexpectedly, the simple-complex condition showed slightly but significantly longer preplanning than the complex-simple condition (complex-complex, $M = 3,570$ ms, $SD = 868$ ms; complex-simple, $M = 2,759$ ms, $SD = 339$ ms; simple-complex, $M = 3,014$ ms, $SD = 292$ ms; simple-simple, $M = 1,915$ ms, $SD = 182$ ms).

These findings are clearly not consistent with planning at the phrase level. One possible explanation might be that the full sentence is planned, which would explain the large difference in planning time for the longest and shortest sentences. Alternatively, it could be that once participants realized the stimulus display disappeared at typing onset, they deliberately adopted strategies for storing stimulus information. Written production is slower than spoken production, and spelling and keyboarding are both more demanding than articulation. Adopting this strategy will increase the chances that message-level information for the latter part of the sentence will be lost during production of the first part. Participants may, therefore, have deliberately and explicitly processed images associated with the object phrase in some depth to ensure they were still available when needed. This strategy would explain differences in sentence-initial latency between the complex-complex and simple-simple conditions, and perhaps also why complex-simple stimuli were processed more quickly than simple-complex.

If need-to-store is the main reason for variation in sentence-initial latency across conditions, then removing this factor should substantially shorten latencies and remove differences across conditions. We therefore repeated the experiment with eight psychology undergraduates, but this time left the stimulus visible throughout production. This manipulation had the effect of substantially reducing both latencies and the sentence-type effect (complex-complex, $M = 845$ ms, $SD = 186$ ms; complex-simple, $M = 811$ ms, $SD = 201$ ms; simple-complex,

$M = 838$ ms, $SD = 234$ ms; simple-simple $M = 795$ ms, $SD = 184$ ms). The sample size here is clearly too small to draw conclusions on the basis of failure to find differences. However, these findings are again inconsistent with the phrase-scope hypothesis and consistent with the idea that the much longer latencies in the first Study 2 experiment were due to the need to retain information after the stimuli had disappeared.

Findings from these experiments are quite different from those found in Study 1. In the 2007 study, with stimuli remaining visible throughout, Nottbusch and co-workers found sentence-initial latencies of more than 2 s. In the Nottbusch (2010) study these were reduced to latencies similar to those found in the second experiment in Study 2. However, in the Nottbusch study this effect was achieved by showing participants the full stimulus for a very long period (7 s) before they could start writing. In the Study 2 experiment they had a 2-s preparation time during which they saw the stimuli but did not have sufficient information for syntactic planning.

We do not have an explanation for these disparate findings. They do, however, suggest that the effects we are observing, and perhaps also the effects in the speech production literature, are very sensitive to the fine details of the experimental context. This finding in turn suggests a strong strategic component in whether or not participants plan in advance.

Study 3   In a third study, we (Torrance and White) broadly replicated the design used by Griffin (2001, discussed above). Participants were shown a three-picture array, with pictures A and B placed in the upper left and right quadrants of the screen, above picture C. Unlike the previous experiment, A and B were taken from a larger pool such that each participant only saw each picture once. Picture B was manipulated both for the frequency of its name and the ease with which it could be encoded (based on the number of different names elicited by the picture during pretesting). As noted above, one of the criticisms of Griffin's design was the fact that all sentences were syntactically identical ("The A and the B are above the C") possibly bypassing the need for syntactic processing. To reduce this problem, and following Nottbusch et al. (2007), we varied ordination in the initial verb-argument phrase by inserting one of two symbols between pictures A and B: a plus sign (+) to indicate that participants should provide a coordinate initial phrase ("The A and the B") and a less than sign (<) to indicate that the second noun should be subordinated ("The A with the B").

Sixteen psychology undergraduates produced a total of 64 sentences, 32 written and 32 spoken. The stimulus display remained visible throughout, and we tracked participants' eye movements. If initial planning extended over the whole of the initial phrase, then we might expect to see effects of ease of processing of B (frequency or codability) on initial latency. We failed to find this effect in either the writing condition or (consistent with Griffin, 2001) in speech. We also failed to find an effect of ordination. This finding points toward word-by-word (incremental) planning. Data from analyses of participants' eye movements, and specifically the extent to which picture B was fixated prior to typing onset, strongly support this conclusion.

Findings were similar for spoken and written production. In the spoken condition, B was fixated during the prespeaking period in, on average, 15 of 32 trials ($SD = 9.0$) with a mean dwell time (sum of all fixation durations on B during that period, averaged across all trials and then all participants) of 299 ms ($SD = 176$). This result compared to 31 trials ($SD = 1.5$) for picture A, with a mean dwell time of 925 ms ($SD = 279$). Therefore, in replication of Griffin's (2001) findings, eye movement data point toward wholly incremental processing in at least 50% of trials. In the written condition, incremental planning was even more strongly evidenced. Picture B was fixated in a mean of just 1.3 of a possible 32 trials ($SD = 1.7$), compared to 31 trials for A ($SD = 2.3$). Mean dwell time for picture A was 544 ms ($SD = 170$), somewhat less than in the spoken condition. Mean dwell time for B was negligible.

One possibility is, as we observed in the first experiment, that processing of B occurred in parallel with output of the initial determiner. Participants might have planned the full initial phrase, but initiated output of "The" at the start of the sentence before planning was complete, because this word was common to all sentences and not dependent on ordination or other features of the initial phrase. Testing this possibility in speech requires time-consuming analysis of individual sound files, which we have not yet completed. However, one of the side benefits of studying written output is that this kind of information is easily extracted from a log of participants' keystrokes. In this instance the fifth keystroke, assuming fluent production and treating the initial shift-T combination as a single keystroke, will be associated with onset of the production of the first noun. Analysis of fixations for the period from stimulus onset to the fifth keystroke showed the same pattern as sentence-initial latency, and therefore again no evidence that B was planned prior to output of A (trials in which A was fixated, $M = 32$, $SD = 2.2$; trials in which B was also fixated, $M = 2.1$, $SD = 1.5$; dwell time for A, $M = 661$, $SD = 179$; mean dwell time for B was negligible).

Discussion   Our findings do not present a particularly clear understanding of planning scope in written sentence production. The second and third studies point toward planning that is entirely incremental. The first study could be interpreted as indicating phrase-level scope. It would be premature, and beyond our present purpose, to give a detailed discussion of the various experimental factors that might push participants toward adopting one or another planning approach (see Martin et al., 2010, for such a discussion of the much more extensive spoken production literature). It is possible that the effect of ordination found in the first experiment (Nottbusch et al., 2007) was due to perceptual grouping of the stimuli—shapes were placed on top of each other in the subordinated condition and side by side in the coordinate condition—rather than phrase-level planning. It is also possible that, despite introducing a second sentence structure into Griffin's paradigm, participants in Study 3 still treated the task as serial object recognition, bypassing the need for syntactic planning. Verb agreement errors of the form "The A with the B was above the C" were relatively common, suggesting that participants were often processing *with* as a synonym for *and*, in the sense of "The A along with the B," rather than as marking a syntactically different phrase structure.

The general pattern of findings, however, would seem to point toward relatively little advanced planning in written sentence production. Where participants were forced to process all stimuli at some level before writing—in the first experiment in Study 2—we did not find evidence that they planned the syntactic structure of the first phrase; however, findings were consistent with syntactic planning of the full sentence. When this requirement was lifted, as in the second experiment in Study 2 and in Study 3, participants appeared to process the first word without giving any attention about what was to follow. Caveats about the validity of the task aside, this finding suggests that there is nothing inherent in the language processes underlying sentence production that requires any degree of advance planning beyond the initial noun and its associated determiner. Advanced planning is clearly possible, as evidenced by findings in Study 1 and the first experiment in Study 2. However, it is possibly best thought of as a deliberate strategic activity that is not necessitated by basic psycholinguistic processes.

CONCLUDING COMMENTS

One of the purposes of this volume is to suggest an agenda for future research, both for existing writing researchers and for cognitive psychologists who might be recruited to the cause. In concluding, therefore, we want to briefly discuss what might be gained by experimental study of low-level (postconceptual) writing processes.

Turning first to potential new recruits: The research we have described here is perhaps somewhat different from that reported in the majority of the other chapters in this book in that it deliberately and explicitly looks to findings in mainstream cognitive psychology both to set research questions and to provide experimental paradigms. The work by Nottbusch and colleagues exploring latencies for single key presses builds directly on a fairly large earlier body of research. Their contribution is to show that the time course of word production is not dependent solely on motor planning and execution but is also predicted in part by underlying psycholinguistic processes. The work that we report on sentence production, although at a very early stage, closely imitates experiments from the speech literature. We found that results based on spoken production do not always simply replicate in writing. Papers exploring spoken sentence production tend to use the terms "speech production" and "language production" interchangeably (e.g., Martin et al., 2010). We tentatively suggest that, even regarding the basic, low-level processes discussed in this chapter, this use of these terms is inappropriate. Patterns in both spoken and written production are in part shaped by fundamental, and shared, language processes and in part by the specific demands and affordances of the output medium. Researchers interested in language production might usefully explore effects in both speech and writing, triangulating between the two to distinguish between medium-specific and general language effects. Written production (by keyboard) is also a particularly easy context in which to explore issues around fluency, which, as noted above, has been advanced as a possible explanation for findings that suggest phrase-level planning for spoken sentence production.

Existing writing researchers will, of course, not need convincing of the value of exploring written production. They may, however, have doubts about whether the kinds of laboratory tasks we have discussed in this chapter have anything interesting to say about more natural tasks involving production of extended (multisentence) texts. We share these concerns. There has been recent growth in research exploring keystroke patterns in extended texts (e.g., Sullivan & Lindgren, 2006), and these provide a necessary counterpart to the single-sentence and single-word research that we have described. However, findings presented in this chapter could usefully inform extended-text keystroke logging studies in at least two respects. First, most studies to date have looked at the frequency of IKIs of greater than 2,000 ms (the threshold typically adopted to define a "pause" in output). The research that we present here suggests that text production involves considerable parallelism. Important planning activity may occur concurrent with output or during pauses of much less than 2 s. Second, the research paradigm adopted in single-word production studies seeks to explain all keystroke latencies in terms of several different independent variables at the character, n-graph, and word levels. This paradigm might be usefully extended to analysis of full text, adding in variables relating to syntax and rhetorical structure.

Current understanding of the complex and multilayered cognitive processes associated with production of multisentence text is not well developed. Measurement of fluctuation in output rate, through keystroke logging, possibly combined with analysis of eye movements within the emerging text (Andersson et al., 2006; Wengelin et al., 2009), offers possibly the most powerful tool that we have available for advancing our understanding in this area. However, these studies need to take into account, and then statistically control for, a large number of determinants of IKIs, including the kinds of postconceptual factors explored in this chapter. Experimental tasks involving production of single words and short sentences, although in themselves quite removed from the complexities of extended text production, have a role in suggesting hypotheses about what these postconceptual factors might be.

REFERENCES

Allum, P. H., & Wheeldon, L. R. (2007). Planning scope in spoken sentence production: The role of grammatical units. *Journal of Experimental Psychology-Learning Memory and Cognition, 33*(4), 791–810.

Allum, P. H., & Wheeldon, L. (2009). Scope of lexical access in spoken sentence production: Implications for the conceptual-syntactic interface. *Journal of Experimental Psychology-Learning Memory and Cognition, 35*(5), 1240–1255.

Andersson, B., Dahl, J., Holmqvist, K., Holsanova, J., Johansson, J., Karlsson, H., … Wengelin, Å. (2006). Combining keystroke logging with eye tracking. In L. van Waes, M. Leijten & C. Neuwirth (Eds.), *Writing and digital media* (pp. 166–172). Amsterdam: Elsevier.

Bock, J. K. (1982). Toward a cognitive psychology of syntax: Information processing contributions to sentence formulation. *Psychological Review, 89*(1), 1–41.

Bodner, G. E., & Masson, M. E. J. (1997). Masked repetition priming of words and nonwords: Evidence for a nonlexical basis for priming. *Journal of Memory and Language, 37*, 268–293.

Caramazza, A. (1997). How many levels of processing are there in lexical access? *Cognitive Neuropsychology, 14*(1), 177–208.

Caramazza, A., & Hillis, A. E. (1990). Where do semantic errors come from? *Cortex, 26*(1), 95–122.

Caramazza, A., & Hillis, A. E. (1991). Lexical organization of nouns and verbs in the brain. *Nature, 349*(6312), 788–790.

Chanquoy, L., Foulin, J.-N., & Fayol, M. (1990). Temporal management of short text writing by children and adults. *Cahiers de psychologie cognitive, 10*(5), 513–540.

Cooper, W. E. (1983). Introduction. In W. E. Cooper (Ed.), *Cognitive aspects of skilled typewriting* (pp. 1–38). New York: Springer.

Coover, J. E. (1923). A method of teaching typewriting based upon a psychological analysis of expert typing. *National Education Association, 61*, 561–567.

Dell, G., & O'Seaghdha, P. (1992). Stages of lexical access in language production. *Cognition, 42*, 287–314.

Dvorak, A., Merrick, N. L., Dealey, W. L., & Ford, G. C. (1936). *Typewriting behavior*. New York: American Book.

Faigley, L., & Witte, S. P. (1981). Analyzing revision. *College Composition and Communication, 32*, 400–414.

Fayol, M., Largy, P., & Lemaire, P. (1994). Cognitive overload and orthographic errors—when cognitive overload enhances subject-verb agreement errors—a study in French written language. *Quarterly Journal of Experimental Psychology Section A-Human Experimental Psychology, 47*, 437–464.

Fendrick, P. (1937). Hierarchical skills in typewriting. *Journal of Educational Psychology, 28*, 609–620.

Garrett, M. F. (1975). The analysis of sentence production. In G. H. Bower (Ed.), *The psychology of learning and motivation: Advances in research and theory*. (Vol. 9, pp. 133–177). New York: Academic Press.

Garrett, M. F. (1980). Levels of processing in sentence production. In B. Butterworth (Ed.), *Language production: Speech and talk* (pp. 177–220). London: Academic Press.

Garrett, M. F. (1988). Processes in language production. In J. F. J. Newmeyer (Ed.), *The Cambridge survey of linguistics: Language, psychological and biological aspects* (Vol. 3, pp. 69–96). Cambridge, MA: Harvard University Press.

Gentner, D. R. (1982a). Evidence against a central control model of timing in typing. *Journal of Experimental Psychology: Human Perception and Performance, 8*, 793–810.

Gentner, D. R. (1982b). Testing the central control model of typing: Comments on the reply by Viviani and Terzuolo. *Journal of Experimental Psychology: Human Perception and Performance, 8*, 814–816.

Gentner, D. R. (1983). Keystroke timing in transcription typing. In W. E. Cooper (Ed.), *Cognitive aspects of skilled typewriting* (pp. 95–120). New York: Springer.

Gentner, D. R. (1987). Timing of skilled motor performance: Tests of the proportional duration model. *Psychological Review, 94*, 255–276.

Gentner, D. R., Grudin, J. T., & Conway, E. (1980). *Finger movements in transcription typing*. La Jolla, CA: University of California, San Diego, Center for Human Information Processing.

Gentner, D. R., Larochelle, S., & Grudin, J. T. (1988). Lexical, sublexical, and peripheral effects in skilled typewriting. *Cognitive Psychology, 20*, 524–548.

Griffin, Z. M. (2001). Gaze durations during speech reflect word selection and phonological encoding. *Cognition, 82*(1), B1–B14.

Griffin, Z. M. (2003). A reversed word length effect in coordinating the preparation and articulation of words in speaking. *Psychonomic Bulletin and Review, 10*(3), 603–609.

Griffin, Z. M., & Bock, J. K. (2000). What the eyes say about speaking. *Psychological Science, 11*(4), 274–279.

Grudin, J. T. (1983). Non-hierarchic specification of components in transcription typewriting. *Acta Psychologica, 54,* 249–262.

Harley, T. A. (1984). A critique of top-down independent levels models of speech production: Evidence from non-plan-internal speech errors. *Cognitive Science, 8*(3), 191–219.

Hayes, J. R., & Flower, L. S. (1980a). Identifying the organization of writing processes. In L. Gregg & E. R. Steinberg (Eds.), *Cognitive processes in writing* (pp. 3–30). Hillsdale, NJ: Erlbaum.

Hayes, J. R., & Flower, L. S. (1980b). Writing as problem solving. *Visible language, 14*(4), 288–299.

Larochelle, S. (1983). A comparison of skilled and novice performance in discontinuous typing. In W. E. Cooper (Ed.), *Cognitive aspects of skilled typewriting* (pp. 67–94). New York: Springer.

Larochelle, S. (1984). Some aspects of movement in skilled typewriting. In H. Bouma & D. G. Bouwhuis (Eds.), *Attention and performance. Control of language processes* (pp. 43–54). Hillsdale, NJ: Erlbaum.

Levelt, W. J. (1989). *Speaking: From intention to articulation.* Cambridge, MA: MIT Press.

Levelt, W. J. M., & Maassen, B. (1981). Lexical search and order of mention in sentence production. In W. Klein & W. J. M. Levelt (Eds.), *Crossing the boundaries in linguistics* (pp. 221–252). Dordrecht: Reidel.

Levelt, W. J. M., & Meyer, A. S. (2000). Word for word: Multiple lexical access in speech production. *European Journal of Cognitive Psychology, 12*(4), 433–452.

Martin, R. C., Crowther, J. E., Knight, M., Tamborello, F. P., & Yang, C. L. (2010). Planning in sentence production: Evidence for the phrase as a default planning scope. *Cognition, 116*(2), 177–192.

Massaro, D. W., & Lucas, P. A. (1984). Typing letter strings varying in orthographic structure. *Acta Psychologia, 57,* 109–131.

McCutchen, D. (1996). A capacity theory of writing: Working memory in composition. *Educational Psychology Review, 8*(3), 299–325.

Norman, D. A., & Rumelhart, D. E. (1983). Studies of typing from the LNR Research Group. In W. E. Cooper (Ed.), *Cognitive aspects of skilled typewriting* (pp. 45–65). New York: Springer.

Nottbusch, G. (2008). Handschriftliche sprachproduktion: Sprachstrukturelle und ontogenetische Aspekte [Analysis of children's handwriting movements. Orthographic and developmental aspects]. In *Linguistische Arbeiten* (Vol. 524). Tübingen: Niemeyer.

Nottbusch, G. (2010). Grammatical planning, execution, and control in written sentence production. *Reading and Writing, 23*(7), 777–801.

Nottbusch, G., Grimm, A., Weingarten, R., & Will, U. (2005). Syllabic structures in typing: Evidence from hearing-impaired writers. *Reading and Writing, 18,* 497–526.

Nottbusch, G., Weingarten, R., & Sahel, S. (2007). From written word to written sentence production. In M. Torrance, L. van Waes, & D. W. Galbraith (Eds.), *Studies in writing: Vol. 20. Writing and cognition. Research and applications* (pp. 31–53). Amsterdam: Elsevier.

Nottbusch, G., Weingarten, R., & Will, U. (1998). Schreiben mit der Hand und Schreiben mit dem Computer [Writing by hand and writing with the computer]. *Osnabrücker Beiträge zur Sprachtheorie, 56,* 11–27.

Olsen, R. A., & Murray, R. A. (1976). Finger motion analysis in typing of texts of varying complexity. In *Proceedings of the 6th Congress of the International Ergonomics Association* (pp. 446–450). University of Maryland.

Ostry, D. J. (1980). Execution-time movement control. In G. E. Stelmach & J. Requin (Eds.), *Advances in psychology: Vol. 1. Tutorials in motor behavior* (2nd ed., pp. 457–468). Amsterdam: North Holland.

Ostry, D. J. (1983). Determinants of interkey times in typing. In W. E. Cooper (Ed.), *Cognitive aspects of skilled typewriting* (pp. 225–246). New York: Springer.

Pashler, H., Johnston, J. C., & Ruthruff, E. (2001). Attention and performance. *Annual Review of Psychology, 52*, 629–651.

Postma, A. (2000). Detection of errors during speech production: a review of speech monitoring models. *Cognition, 77*(2), 97–131.

Roelofs, A. (1992). A spreading-activation theory of lemma retrieval in speaking. *Cognition, 42*, 107–142.

Rumelhart, D. E., & Norman, D. A. (1982). Simulating a skilled typist: A study of skilled cognitive-motor performance. *Cognitive Science, 6*, 1–36.

Sahel, S., Nottbusch, G., Grimm, A., & Weingarten, R. (2008). Written production of German compounds: Effects of lexical frequency and semantic transparency. *Written Language and Literacy, 11*(2), 211–228.

Sahel, S., Nottbusch, G., Weingarten, R., & Blanken, G. (2005). The role of phonology and syllabic structure in the time course of typing: Evidence from aphasia. *Linguistische Berichte, 201*, 65–87.

Scardamalia, M., & Bereiter, C. (1991). Literate expertise. In K. A. Ericsson & J. Smith (Eds.), *Toward a general theory of expertise: Prospects and limits* (pp. 172–194). Cambridge: Cambridge University Press.

Schriefers, H., & Teruel, E. (1999). The production of noun phrases: A cross-linguistic comparison of French and German. In M. Hahn & S. C. Stoness (Eds.), *Proceedings of the 21st Annual Conference of the Cognitive Science Society* (pp. 637–642). Mahwah, NJ: Erlbaum.

Schriefers, H., Teruel, E., & Meinshausen, R. M. (1998). Producing simple sentences: Results from picture-word interference experiments. *Journal of Memory and Language, 39*(4), 609–632.

Shaffer, L. H. (1978). Timing in the motor programming of typing. *Quarterly Journal of Experimental Psychology, 30*, 333–345.

Shaffer, L. H., & Hardwick, J. (1968). Typing performance as a function of text. *Quarterly Journal of Experimental Psychology, 20*, 360–369.

Smith, M., & Wheeldon, L. (1999). High level processing scope in spoken sentence production. *Cognition, 73*(3), 205–246.

Sternberg, S., Monsell, S., Knoll, R. L., & Wright, C. E. (1978). Latency and duration of rapid movement sequences: Comparison of speech and typewriting. In G. E. Stelmach (Ed.), *Information processing in motor control and learning* (pp. 117–152). New York: Academic Press.

Sullivan, K. P. H., & Lindgren, E. (Eds.). (2006). *Studies in writing 18: Computer key-stroke logging and writing: Methods and applications.* Oxford: Elsevier.

Terzuolo, C. A., & Viviani, P. (1980). Determinants and characteristics of motor patterns used for typing. *Neuroscience, 5*, 1085–1103.

Thomas, E. A. C., & Jones, R. G. (1970). A model for subjective grouping in typewriting. *Quarterly Journal of Experimental Psychology, 22*, 353–367.

Totereau, C., Thevenin, M., & Fayol, M. (1997). The development of the understanding of number morphology in written French. In C. Perfetti, L. Rieben & M. Fayol (Eds.), *Learning to spell* (pp. 97–114). Hillsdale, NJ: Erlbaum.

Van Waes, L., Leijten, M., & Quinlan, T. (2010). Reading during sentence composing and error correction: A multilevel analysis of the influences of task complexity. *Reading and Writing, 23*(7), 803–834.

Viviani, P., & Laissard, G. (1996). Motor templates in typing. *Journal of Experimental Psychology: Human Perception and Performance, 22*(2), 417–445.

Viviani, P., & Terzuolo, C. A. (1982). On the relation between word-specific patterns and the central control model of typing: A reply to Gentner. *Journal of Experimental Psychology: Human Perception and Performance, 8*(6), 811–813.

Viviani, P., & Terzuolo, C. A. (1983). The organization of movement in handwriting and typing. In B. Butterworth (Ed.), *Language production,* Vol. 2. *Development, writing and other language processes* (2nd ed., pp. 103–146). London: Academic Press.

Weingarten, R., Nottbusch, G., & Will, U. (2004). Morphemes, syllables, and graphemes in written word production. In T. Pechmann & C. Habel (Eds.), *Multidisciplinary approaches to language production* (pp. 529–572). Berlin: Mouton de Gruyter.

Welford, A. (1967). Single-channel operation in the brain. *Acta Psychologica, 27*, 5–22.

Wells, F. L. (1916). On the psychomotor mechanisms of typewriting. *The American Journal of Psychology, 27*, 47–70.

Wengelin, A., Torrance, M., Holmqvist, K., Simpson, S., Galbraith, D., Johansson, V., & Johansson, R. (2009). Combined eyetracking and keystroke-logging methods for studying cognitive processes in text production. *Behavior Research Methods, 41*(2), 337–351.

Will, U., Nottbusch, G., & Weingarten, R. (2006). Linguistic units in word typing: Effects of word presentation modes and typing delay. *Written Language and Literacy, 9*(1), 156–173.

Will, U., Weingarten, R., Nottbusch, G., & Albes, C. Linguistische rahmen und segmentale informationen bei der einzelwortschreibung: Evidenzen aus zeitstrukturen und fehlerverteilungen [Linguistic frames and segmental information in writing single words]. Retreived from http://www.guido-nottbusch.de/doc/Will_Weingarten_Nottbusch_Albes_2002.pdf

Zesiger, P., Orliaguet, J.-P., Boë, L.-J., & Mounoud, P. (1994). The influence of syllabic structure in handwriting and typing production. In C. Faure, P. Keuss, G. Lorette, & A. Vinter (Eds.), *Advances in handwriting and drawing. A Multidisciplinary approach* (pp. 389–401). Paris: Europia.

18

Information Flow Across Modalities and Text Types

AUDREY MAZUR-PALANDRE,
MICHEL FAYOL, and HARRIET JISA

*L*earning to write involves much more than learning to express ideas in an alternative medium to speech. The aim of this chapter is to outline how learning to write changes the way children process information. French-speaking monolinguals and adults were asked to produce narrative and expository texts in both written and spoken modalities. The texts are analyzed in an attempt to ascertain to what extent the predictions proposed by the theory of preferred argument structure (PAS) (Du Bois, 1987; Du Bois, Kumpf, & Ashby, 2003) hold across modalities and text types. PAS provides a framework for understanding how grammar is shaped by the communicative pressure of spoken discourse. It also provides a set of grammatical and pragmatic constraints that allow for clear measures of discourse preferences in texts. The predictions spelled out by PAS have been shown to hold for spoken narrative texts in a wide variety of languages (Du Bois et al., 2003). This chapter will add to this body of literature by questioning the extent to which the constraints proposed by PAS hold for expository texts and for the written modality. We will show how growing into literacy and academic discourse requires that children go against the natural flow of information in spoken communication. Particular attention will be given to lexical noun phrases, their distribution, as well as their syntactic architecture. A second goal of this chapter is to contribute to a body of literature that argues that lexical noun phrases provide a valid diagnostic of developing syntactic abilities and of text construction across genres and modalities (cf., Ravid & Berman, 2009).

Although written language calls upon many of the same structures that spoken language does, the two modalities differ in very important ways. In particular, the temporal constraints operating in the written and spoken modalities contrast greatly (Fayol, 1997). Producing in the written modality allows more time for planning, which results in, for example, the ability to search the mental lexicon for less frequently used words (Bonin, 2003; Gayraud, 2000) or to call upon more computationally complex syntactic structures, such as nonfinite subordination (Gayraud, Jisa, & Viguié, 2001). Producing a monologue in the spoken modality requires quick, automatic processing of linguistic resources to access lexical items, combining propositions, monitoring referential continuity, and ensuring overall text coherence (Givón, 1995; Levelt, 1989).

Recent approaches to linguistics have emphasized the role of language usage and the resulting development of grammar (Croft & Cruse, 2004). In this chapter we examine how the use of written language differs from spoken language in children, adolescents, and adults.

We begin with some general comments on language production in the spoken and written modality, attempting to underscore the fact that the written modality provides a writer with more time to devote to planning. We then move to a discussion of grammatical subjects, explaining a nonpreference in spoken language for heavy noun phrases in the subject position. Subsequently, the PAS theory (Du Bois, 1987), which proposes concrete measures of speaker preferences in spoken texts, will be presented. Following this proposal is a description of the data on which this study is based. Our results will cover the use of lexical noun phrases in spoken and written narrative and expository texts produced by French monolingual speaker and writers. In conclusion we argue that over the course of literacy development French children must learn to relax natural constraints that determine the form of information transmission in spoken language. We also emphasize that the use of heavy lexical noun phrases in the subject position of a clause is a useful diagnostic for developing syntactic and textual abilities.

SPOKEN VERSUS WRITTEN PRODUCTION

Clearly both speaking and writing require a number of shared cognitive abilities. However, writing typically allows people to devote more time and hence greater cognitive and linguistic resources to planning activities than those that can be accessed in the course of rapid on-line speech output. As a result, the study of what children know about language can be fruitfully approached by observing their text production in both written and spoken modalities. Once children are over the major hurdles of letter formation and spelling and other facets of what Ravid and Tolchinsky (2002, p. 421) refer to as "writing as a notational system," writing may actually facilitate the use of less frequent and more complex constructions and thus give a somewhat different picture of what children know about language and how to use it. Since children's knowledge of language changes as a function of their experience with how it is used in different circumstances, close examination of how children make use of language in both the spoken and written modalities seems necessary for understanding later language development in general and the process of "moving into academic language" in particular.

Crucial to understanding the forms used in a text is the time allotted to text planning. Producing language in writing alleviates some of the time pressure involved in on-line spoken language production and so allows more time for the work of converting information into words (Clark, 1996; Strömqvist et al., 2002; Strömqvist, Nordqvist, & Wengelin, 2004). Becoming a proficient writer involves gaining mastery over more compact means of establishing the flow of information, resulting in texts that show more densely integrated packages of information (Chafe, 1994). For example, syntactic subjects in written expository discourse do not necessarily obey Chafe's "light subject constraint" (1994, p. 16), which is characteristic of spoken discourse. It is for this reason, for example, that written French shows more lexical noun phrases than pronouns (Blanche-Benveniste, 1990, 1995; Lambrecht, 1987). Heavy subjects, often the result of syntactic packaging through nominalization or subordination, are characteristic of mature written expository discourse (Ravid, Van Hell, Rosado, & Zamora, 2002). In addition, written texts generally show more lexical diversity than spoken texts, since writing allows more time for planning and hence more time to search one's mental lexicon for different and less frequent lexical items (Ravid & Tolchinsky, 2002; Strömqvist et al., 2002).

Compare the following examples in which the same information is transmitted:

1. We bombed the new installation. Many people were very alarmed.
2. The bombing of the new installations alarmed many people.

In the first example two clauses are used, while the second contains a nominalization resulting in a heavy noun phrase in the subject position. Also, the second example is much more characteristic of written discourse than of spoken discourse (Biber, 1988; Chafe, 1994). And the computations necessary for generating the form observed in the second example require more time. Languages offer speakers and writers options for the expression of information, and part of becoming a proficient speaker involves learning to adapt the linguistic forms and communicative function to the situation at hand.

GRAMMATICAL SUBJECTS IN FRENCH

Written French is described as having a subject-verb-object order (Hawkins, 1983), yet in spoken French, the subject position is only rarely occupied by a lexical noun phrase. The preferred, unmarked clause structure in spoken conversational French typically involves a subject clitic pronoun and often other preverbal clitics as well. François (1974) found a total of 1,550 nouns in a long corpus of conversation between members of a working-class family, of which only 46 (about 3%) were lexical subjects as compared to the vast proportion of 1,440 clitic subjects (Lambrecht, 1987). Jeanjean (1980) confirmed this finding on the basis of a corpus of casual conversation where she found an average of approximately 11% of subject positions occupied by lexical nouns. Blanche-Benveniste's (1990) comparison of a variety of discourse types gathered from a wide range of speakers revealed that an increase in lexical nouns in the subject position is associated with a more elaborate discourse code.

Grammatical subjects or topics are important because they provide a starting point that serves as the foundation for guiding the interpretation of subsequent information (Langacker, 1998). In spoken informal French the initial position is overwhelmingly occupied by a subject pronoun clitic. Subject pronouns encode given information and thus are preferred in spoken production sequences consisting of given information (subject) followed by new information.

Tomlin (1995) proposes that the clause level subject should be understood as the linguistic reflection of a more general process of attention detection. MacWhinney (1977), using a wide variety of experimental contexts (i.e., elicited production, recall, problem solving, sentence verification), was able to show that English speakers use the first element in a sentence as the starting point for the organization of the sentence as a whole. Following Gernsbacher and Hargreaves' (1992, p. 85) "structure building framework," the initial sentential elements are privileged in memory and play a crucial role in the building of a coherent mental representation.

Not only are nouns in the subject position more typical of written French than oral French, but nouns in other syntactic positions contribute to a higher noun-per-verb ratio in written as opposed to spoken texts in general (similarly to what has been shown for other languages as well; cf. Ravid et al., 2002; Ravid & Berman, 2009). Blanche-Benveniste (1995) compared two types of accident stories, one consisting of stories recorded in oral interviews and the other of accidents reported in the press. Both types of stories obviously contained nouns, but more lexical nouns and various types of nominalizations were observed in the press reports. Where clauses consisting of a verb with a single argument were common in the spoken stories—for example, *il y avait un homme, il est tombé et il est mort* (there was a man, he fell and he died)—written stories collapsed equivalent information into a single clause (e.g., *un homme a fait une chute mortelle* [a man took a fatal fall]). The spoken version presents one new piece of information per clause, whereas the written version compacts all the information into a single clause and greatly reduces grammatical morphology.

Du Bois (1987) proposed the theory of preferred argument structure in order to study the form and flow of information in natural text production. His initial goal was to illustrate how grammar reflects information-processing constraints in discourse. The constraints determine both the quantity of information as well as the grammatical role the information plays. There are two constraints concerning quantity: Each clause will contain only one lexical argument, and each clause will carry only one new piece of information. These constraints predict that in spoken texts the first example below will be preferred to the second:

1. He bought a book.
2. A man bought a book.

The two constraints on grammatical role propose that nonlexical noun phrases will be preferred in the subject position and, consequently, given information is preferred as the subject of a transitive verb with new information introduced as a direct object or an oblique argument. These constraints predict, for example, that the first example below will be preferred to the second in naturally occurring spoken texts:

1. He bought a book.
2. The man bought a book.

These constraints have been utilized to understand the use of nouns and pronouns in early child language acquisition (Allen & Schröder, 2003; Clancy, 2003) as well as the distribution of lexical and nonlexical arguments and of information in spoken narrative discourse in a variety of languages (cf., Du Bois, 1987; Du Bois et al., 2003; Khorounjaia & Tolchinsky, 2004). The question we explore in this chapter is whether or not French speakers or writers conform to these "natural" constraints in both the spoken and written modality and in two text types: narrative and expository texts.

TWO TEXT TYPES

Two text types were chosen for this study—a personal narrative and an expository text—both of which concern interpersonal conflict situations. Narrative texts emerge early in child language within the context of highly scaffolded conversational contexts (Berman, 2009; Miller & Sperry, 1988; Ninio & Snow, 1996). However, many years of development are necessary to achieve the rhetorical expressiveness characteristic of an adult's well-organized coherent narrative text. Narratives are also a universal type of discourse, familiar to children in all cultures (Bavin, 2004; Berman, 2009). In addition, narratives have a shared canonical structure with an initial setting, episodes, resolution, and coda (Labov, 1972). Personal narratives recount specific events and involve specific characters, specific times, and specific places (Berman & Nir-Sagiv, 2007). The semantic relations underlying different segments of a personal narrative are primarily temporal and causal.

Expository texts, in contrast, develop much later than narrative texts and do not have a rigid overall canonical structure. They involve a mixture of discourse types, including claims, arguments, opinions, and reporting. They differ most clearly from personal narratives in that the speaker or writer must take a distanced discourse stance (Jisa & Tolchinsky, 2009) and present atemporal, generic, and nonspecific generalities. Expository texts are a school-situated type of text requiring more generic and abstract references.

The analyses undertaken here will compare the production of lexical noun phrases in expository and narrative texts produced by French-monolingual children, adolescents, and adults in both the spoken and written modalities. Particular interest is given to lexical noun phrases in the subject position and to their syntactic architecture.

METHODOLOGY

This section presents the participants in our study, the procedures for data collection, and the categories of analysis.

Participants

The participants in this study are 10-year-olds (fifth graders, mean age 10 years, 9 months), 12-year-olds (seventh graders, mean age 12 years, 7 months), 15-year-olds (ninth graders, mean age 15 years, 2 months), and adults (university graduate students, mean age 24). Each age group comprised 20 participants, equally divided between males and females. All of the participants are from upper middle-class backgrounds, as estimated by national INSEE (Institut National de la Statistique et des Études Économiques) statistics.

Data Collection Procedures

The participants were invited to view a video composed of various clips of moral dilemmas, such as cheating on an exam, ostracizing someone, vandalism, and so forth. After viewing the video the participants were asked to give oral and written versions of a narrative and an expository text. To elicit the narratives, participants were asked to tell or write a personal story about a conflict or an interpersonal problem they had experienced. The expository texts were elicited by asking participants to present what they know about conflicts between people.

The order of production was balanced, with half of the participants producing first the spoken and then the written text, with the other half producing first the written text and then the spoken text. Between the production of the spoken and written texts a questionnaire concerning reading practices and use of computers was completed. The data were collected over 2 weeks, with each week devoted to narrative or expository texts. The data were transcribed in CHAT format and coded using the Clan programs. Spelling and punctuation were corrected.

In total 360 texts were examined (180 spoken and 180 written). The texts differ considerably in length. Table 18.1 presents the text lengths in number of clauses for each age group, for each text type (narrative and expository), and for each modality of production (spoken and written).

TABLE 18.1   Mean Length of Texts in Clauses

	Narrative Spoken	Narrative Written	Expository Spoken	Expository Written
10-year-olds				
Mean	11.05	7.50	16.50	9.65
SD	1.24	0.98	3.10	0.88
Range	4–28	3–21	5–49	4–18
12-year-olds				
Mean	15.8	12.5	14.1	13.0
SD	1.8	1.3	1.5	1.43
Range	5–32	4–25	6–30	4–23
15-year-olds				
Mean	13.1	15.3	16.8	16.7
SD	1.2	1.2	2.4	1.73
Range	5–25	7–26	7–51	8–32
Adults				
Mean	33.95	23.75	49.75	28.45
SD	3.42	1.99	7.57	2.9
Range	14–75	10–39	15–114	13–67

Categories of Analysis

The analysis is carried out in two steps. First, we examine the distribution of lexical noun phrases in the texts. Second, we examine more specifically three features of lexical noun phrases: the number of syntactic nodes, the length in words, and the syntactic position.

Distribution of Lexical Noun Phrases   For this measure we counted the number of nouns per clause. The nouns in Example 1 are underlined, and the double slash mark indicates a clause boundary. The aim of this measure is to capture the difference between texts in terms of "nouniness."

1. Quand j'ai vu une <u>dame</u> // qui achetait des <u>babioles</u> sur la <u>chanteuse</u>, comme des <u>tee-shirts</u>, des <u>affiches</u>. (12-year-old, narrative written)
   When I saw a <u>woman</u> // who bought <u>things</u> related to the <u>singer</u> such as <u>tee-shirts</u> or <u>posters</u>.

Our methodology allows us to compare the written and spoken production of the same subject. Contrast Examples 2 and 3, produced by the same 12-year-old. In Example 2, the written version, there is one very long clause containing five nouns, while in Example 3, the five nouns are distributed over two clauses.

2. Le meilleur <u>moyen</u> de résoudre ce <u>problème</u> est la <u>paix</u> ou <u>l'ignorance</u> de <u>l'autre</u>. (12-year-old, expository written)
   The best <u>way</u> to resolve this <u>problem</u> is <u>peace</u> and <u>avoidance</u> of <u>others</u>.
3. Et euh le meilleur <u>moyen</u> de résoudre ce <u>problème</u> // et ben ben c'est de faire la <u>paix</u>. (12-year-old, expository spoken)
   And the best <u>way</u> to resolve this <u>problem</u> and well // (it) is to make <u>peace</u>.

An average number of nouns per clause was calculated for each subject and for each text.

Lexical Noun Phrases in the Subject Position   The second measure, proportion of lexical noun phrases in the subject position (underlined in Example 4), was calculated as a function of total lexical noun phrases in each text. The aim of this measure was to examine the difference between texts in terms of subject lexical noun phrases. Contrast the two following examples produced by the same 12-year-old in the written and spoken modalities.

4. <u>Le recopiage pendant un contrôle</u> peut poser beaucoup de problèmes. (12-year-old, written)
   <u>Copying during a test</u> can pose many problems.
5. <u>On</u> a pas à copier. (12-year-old, spoken)
   <u>One/We</u> must not copy.

The written version contains a long subject ("Le recopiage pendant un contrôle" [Copying during a test]), while the spoken version employs only the subject pronoun *"on"* (one, we). Similar examples are given in Examples 6 and 7, produced by the same 15-year-old participant.

6. Les bagarres commencent par des regards bizarres entre les personnes. (15-year-old, written)
   Fights begin with curious looks between people.
7. On se regarde bizarrement. (15-year-old, spoken)
   We look at each other strangely.

In the written version the writer uses a lexical noun, while in the spoken version, the same participant uses a subject pronoun. Although the information communicated is very similar, it is distributed differently in spoken and written texts.

Number of Nouns in Subject Lexical Noun Phrases   Our first measure
of the syntactic architecture examines the number of syntactic nodes, or head nouns, per lexical noun phrase in the subject position. In addition to determiners and adjectives, lexical noun phrases can be expanded by coordination as in Example 9 ("la compréhension et la fabrication" [the understanding and the making]), by a prepositional phrase in Example 9 ("de l'image" [of images]), as well as by relative clauses ("the picture that I imagined wasn't like this"). The number of nouns per lexical noun phrase in the subject position yields a measure of syntactic architecture.

8. Les personnes sont maltraitées. (9-year-old, expository written)
   People are mistreated.
9. La compréhension et la fabrication de l'image passent par cet univers. (Adult, expository written)
   The comprehension and fabricating of images passes by this universe.

A mean number of nouns per subject lexical noun phrase was established for each text and for each participant.

Number of Words Per Lexical Noun Phrase in the Nonsubject
Position   Our final measure examines the total number of words per lexical noun phrase in both subject versus object or oblique position. Example 10 shows a very long lexical noun phrase (underlined) in the oblique position, while Example 9 shows a long lexical noun phrase in the subject position. This measure aims at comparing the length or "heaviness" of lexical noun phrases in different syntactic positions. The mean number of words per lexical noun phrase was established for each text for each participant and for subject or nonsubject lexical noun phrases.

10. Les bagarres peuvent se finir en drame ou encore en dégradation des bâtiments scolaires. (9-year-old, expository written)
    Fights can finish in dramas or even in damage to school buildings.

RESULTS

Number of Nouns Per Clause

Figure 18.1 shows the average number of nouns per clause. A series of univariate ANOVAs with repeated measures indicates that with age the number of nouns per clause increases [$F(3, 303) = 70.58, p < .0001$], the number of nouns is higher in the written modality than in the spoken modality [$F(1, 303) = 7.49, p = .006$], and expository texts show more nouns per clause than do narrative texts [$F(1, 303) = 14.76, p = .0001$].

Lexical Noun Phrases in the Subject Position

Figure 18.2 presents the mean proportion of lexical noun phrases in the subject position. This proportion increases with age [$F(3, 303) = 11.77, p < .0001$]. Fisher exact analysis reveals a split between the 12-year-olds and the 15-year-olds ($p < .0001$) but no difference between the 10- and 12-year-olds or between the 15-year-olds and the adults. There is a higher proportion of lexical noun phrases in the subject position in the expository compared to the narrative texts [$F(1, 303) = 42.06, p < .0001$]. The number of lexical noun phrases in the subject position is higher for the written modality as opposed to the spoken modality [$F(1, 303) = 94.31, p < .0001$].

Number of Nouns in Subject Lexical Noun Phrases

The number of nouns in subject lexical noun phrases is shown in Figure 18.3. This number increases with age [$F(3, 303) = 18.78, p < .0001$]. Fisher texts reveal that the two youngest groups (10- and 12-year-olds) do not differ. The number of nouns

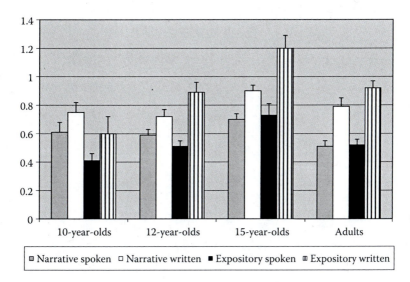

□ Narrative spoken   □ Narrative written   ■ Expository spoken   ▥ Expository written

Figure 18.1   Mean number of lexical noun phrases per clause.

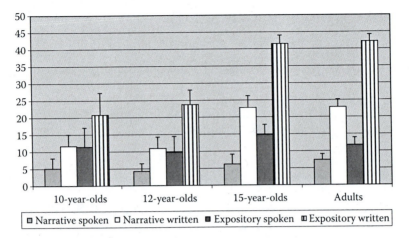

Figure 18.2   Proportion of lexical noun phrases in the subject position.

in subject lexical noun phrases is higher in the written as opposed to the spoken modality [$F(1, 303) = 65.73$, $p < .0001$] and in the expository texts as opposed to the narrative texts [$F(1, 303) = 20.69$, $p < .0001$).

Length in Words of Subject Noun Phrases

The length of subject noun phrases (measured in words) is shown in Figure 18.4. The number of words in lexical subject noun phrases increases with age [$F(3, 303) = 16.34$, $p < .0001$], is higher in expository texts as compared to narrative texts [$F(1, 303) = 15.19$, $p = .0001$], and is higher in the written as compared to the spoken modality [$F(1, 303) = 46.23$, $p < .0001$].

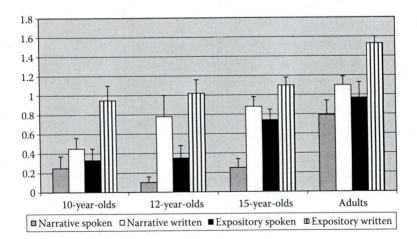

Figure 18.3   Number of nouns in subject lexical noun phrases.

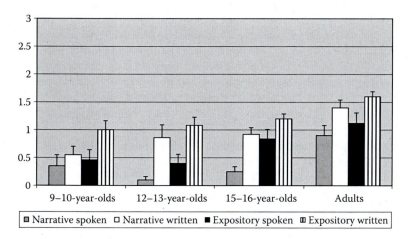

Figure 18.4   Number of words in subject lexical noun phrases.

Length in Words of Nonsubject Lexical Noun Phrases

Figure 18.5 presents the results for the measure of number of words in nonsubject (object or oblique) lexical noun phrases. The number of words increases with age [$F(3, 303) = 5.66$, $p < .0001$] and is higher in expository texts as compared to narrative texts [$F(1, 303) = 9.98$, $p < .0001$]. No difference is noted between the written and spoken modalities [$F(1, 303) = 1.23$, $p = 0.26$, NS).

DISCUSSION

Our results show that the number of lexical noun phrases per clause, the proportion of lexical noun phrases in the subject position, the number of nouns in lexical subject noun phrases, and the length of subject lexical noun phrase vary significantly

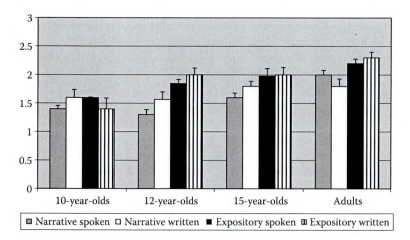

Figure 18.5   Number of words in nonsubject lexical noun phrases.

according to *age*, *text type*, and *modality*. In contrast, the length of nonsubject lexical noun phrases varies significantly for *age* and *text type*, but not for modality.

These results underscore the necessity of taking into account both *modality of production* and *text type* when studying children's language production. The number of lexical noun phrases per clause, the proportion of lexical noun phrases in the subject position, the number of nouns in lexical subject noun phrases, the length of subject lexical noun phrases, and the length of nonsubject lexical noun phrases are higher in expository texts than in narrative texts. These tendencies confirm previous studies in a number of different languages (Ravid et al., 2002; Ravid & Berman, 2009; Strömqvist et al., 2002). Indeed, expository texts and narrative texts imply two specific ways of thinking, which in turn involve different linguistic choices. Our categories of analysis (lexical noun phrases per clause, lexical noun phrases in the subject position, number of nouns in lexical subject noun phrases, length of subject lexical noun phrases, and length of nonsubject lexical noun phrases) reveal that children, even the 10-year-olds, show a sensitivity to genre appropriateness.

Lastly, our measures (except the length of nonsubject lexical noun phrases) vary significantly according to *modality of production*. Written modality has two main characteristics. The first is a relaxed temporal constraint, which provides more time for planning (Bonin, 2003; Fayol, 1997). This temporal advantage enables the production of syntactic forms whose treatment is heavier (Gayraud et al., 2001; Jisa, 2004). Second, the spoken modality, in contrast, offers less time for planning and imposes rapid constraints (Blanche-Benveniste, 1990, 1995; Fayol, 1997; Gayraud, 2000). This accounts for the higher number of lexical noun phrases per clause, proportion of lexical noun phrases in subject position, number of nouns in lexical subject noun phrases, and longer subject lexical noun phrases in written texts than in spoken texts.

By comparing the number of words in lexical noun phrases in the nonsubject (Figure 18.5) and the number of words in lexical noun phrases in the subject position (Figure 18.4), it is interesting to note that even the 10-year-olds can produce long or "heavy" noun phrases. What differs is their ability to marshal the linguistic knowledge necessary for producing heavy noun phrases as subjects, the starting point for expression. Thus, it is not simply a question of syntactic competence, but also a question of using syntactic competence in a new context—as a subject of a clause.

One of the goals of our study was to verify whether our texts conform to the predictions made by the theory of PAS (Du Bois, 1987; Du Bois et al., 2003). Our study addressed specifically two of the four proposed constraints by examining the number of lexical elements per clause and the number of lexical noun phrases in the subject position. According to PAS, only one lexical item per clause and a clear preference for pronominal subjects should be observed. Figure 18.1 illustrates that the first prediction, one lexical item per clause, calls for some revision. Written texts and expository texts conform less to these constraints. Figure 18.2 also shows that the written and the expository texts go against the "natural" preference for information transmission in spoken discourse. Even the 10-year-olds show a higher number of lexical noun phrases in the subject position in their written and expository texts.

CONCLUSIONS

Our study has shown how the choice of linguistic form is determined by the contexts of production. Thus, for example, the production of a written expository text elicits more subject lexical noun phrases than the production of a spoken narrative. One aspect of the context is the modality of production. However, our study also reveals that text type is as important as modality in defining the context of production and in determining the structures observed.

Attaining literacy involves using language in a new modality and in the production of different text types. These new language experiences necessarily impact the child's growing linguistic knowledge. Part of becoming literate involves going against the "natural" constraints that hold for face-to-face spoken discourse.

REFERENCES

Allen, S. E. M., & Schröder, H. (2003). Preferred argument structure in early Inuktitut spontaneous speech data. In J. W. Du Bois, L. E. Kumpf, & W. J. Ashby (Eds.), *Preferred argument structure: Grammar as architecture for function* (pp. 11–60). Amsterdam: Benjamins.

Ashby, W. J., & Bentivoglio, P. (2003). A comparative diachronic analysis of French and Spanish. In J. W. Du Bois, L. E. Kumpf, & W. J.Ashby (Eds.), *Preferred argument structure: Grammar as architecture for function* (pp. 61–81). Amsterdam: Benjamins.

Bavin, E. (2004). Focusing on "where," an analysis of Warlpiri Frog Stories. In S. Strömqvist & L. Verhoeven (Eds.), *Relating events in narrative: Typological and contextual perspectives* (pp. 17–35). Mahwah, NJ: Erlbaum.

Berman, R. A. (2004). Between emergence and mastery: The long developmental route of language acquisition. In R. A. Berman (Eds.), *Language development across childhood and adolescence. TILAR3 (Trends in Language Acquisition Research)* (pp. 9–34). Amsterdam: Benjamins.

Berman, R. A. (2009). Beyond the sentence: Language development in narrative contexts. In E. Bavin (Ed.), *Handbook of child language* (pp. 354–375). Cambridge: Cambridge University Press.

Berman, R., & Nir-Sagiv, B. (2007). Comparing narrative and expository text construction across adolescence: A developmental paradox. *Discourse Processes, 43*, 79–120.

Biber, D. (1988). *Variation across speech and writing.* Cambridge: Cambridge University Press.

Blanche-Benveniste, C. (1983). L'importance du français parlé pour la description du français tout court. *Recherches sur le français parlé, 5*, 23–45.

Blanche-Benveniste, C. (1985). La langue du dimanche. *Reflets, 14*, 42–43.

Blanche-Benveniste, C. (1990). *Le français parlé.* Paris: Edition du Centre National de la Recherche Scientifique.

Blanche-Benveniste, C. (1995). Le semblable et le dissemblable en syntaxe. *Recherches sur le français parlé, 13*, 7–32.

Blanche-Benveniste, C. (2000). *Approche de la langue parlée en français.* Gap, France: Ophrys.

Bonin, P. (2003). *Production verbale de mots: approche cognitive.* Bruxelles: DeBoeck.

Chafe, W. (1994). *Discourse, consciousness and time.* Chicago: University of Chicago Press.

Clancy, P. (2003). The lexicon in interaction: Developmental origins of preferred argument structure in Korean. In J. W. Du Bois, L. E. Kumpf, & W. J. Ashby (Eds.), *Preferred argument structure: Grammar as architecture for function* (pp. 81–108). Amsterdam: Benjamins.

Clark, H. (1996). *Using language*. Cambridge: Cambridge University Press.

Croft, W., & Cruse, A. (2004). *Cognitive linguistics*. Cambridge: Cambridge University Press.

Du Bois, J. W. (1987). The discourse basis of ergativity. *Language, 63*(4), 805–855.

Du Bois, J., Kumpf, L. E., & Ashby, W. J. (2003). *Preferred argument structure: Grammar as architecture for function*. Amsterdam: Benjamins.

Fayol, M. (1997). *Des idées au texte: psychologie cognitive de la production verbale orale et écrite*. Paris: PUF.

François, D. (1974). *Français parlé. Analyse des unités phoniques et significatives d'un corpus recueilli dans la région parisienne*. Paris: SELAF.

Fox, B. (1987). *Discourse structure and anaphora: Written and conversational English*. Cambridge: Cambridge University Press.

Gadet, F. (1989). *Le français ordinaire*. Paris: Armand Colin.

Gayraud, F. (2000). *Le développement de la différenciation oral/écrit vu à travers le lexique*. Doctoral thesis. Université Lyon 2.

Gayraud, F., Jisa, H., & Viguié, A. (2001). Utilisation des outils cohésifs comme indice de sensibilité au registre: une étude développementale. *Acquisition et Interaction en Langue Étrangère, 14*, 3–24.

Gernsbacher, M. A., & Hargreaves, D. (1992). The privilege of primacy: Experimental data and cognitive explanations. In D. L. Payne (Ed.), *Pragmatics of word order flexibility* (pp. 83–116). Amsterdam: Benjamins.

Givón, T. (1995). Coherence in text vs. coherence in mind. In M. Gernsbacher & T. Givón, (Eds.), *Coherence in spontaneous text* (pp. 59–116). Philadelphia: Benjamins.

Hawkins, J. (1983). *Word order universals*. New York: Academic Press.

Jeanjean, C. (1980). *Les formes sujets de type nominal: étude sur le français contemporain* (Doctoral dissertation). Linguistique: Université de Provence.

Jisa, H. (2000). Increasing cohesion in narratives: a developmental study of maintaining and reintroducing subjects in French. *Linguistics, 38*(3), 591–620.

Jisa, H. (2004). Growing into academic French. In R. A. Berman (Ed.), *Later language development: Typological and psycholinguistic perspectives. TILAR3 (Trends in Language Acquisition Research)* (pp. 135–161). Amsterdam: Benjamins.

Jisa, H., & Kern, S. (1998). Relative clauses in French children's narrative text. *Journal of Child Language, 25*, 623–652.

Jisa, H., & Tolchinsky, L. (2009). Developing a depersonalised discourse stance in typologically different languages: Written expository texts. *Written Language and Literacy, 12*, 1–25.

Jisa, H., & Strömqvist, S. (2002). Pragmatique et acquisitions tardives chez l'enfant: langage oral et langage écrit. In J. Bernicot, A. Trognon, M. Guidetti, & M. Musiol (Eds.), *La pragmatique: raisonnement, développement de l'enfant et pathologies* (pp. 257–265). Nancy: Presses Universitaires de Nancy.

Jisa, H., & Viguié, A. (2005). Developmental perspectives on the role of French *on* in written and spoken expository texts. *Journal of Pragmatics, 37*, 125–142.

Khorounjaia, E., & Tolchinsky, L. (2004). Discursive constraints on the lexical realization of arguments in Spanish. In R. A. Berman (Ed.), *Language development across childhood and adolescence. TILAR3 (Trends in Language Acquisition Research)* (pp. 83–109). Amsterdam: Benjamins.

Labov, W. (1972). *Language in the inner city*. Philadelphia: University of Pennsylvania Press.

Lambrecht, K. (1987). On the status of SVO sentences in French discourse. In R. S. Tomlin (Ed.), *Coherence and grounding in discourse* (pp. 217–261). Amsterdam: Benjamins.

Langacker, R. (1998). Conceptualization, symbolization, and grammar. In M. Tomasello (Ed.), *The new psychology of language: Cognitive and functional approaches to language structure* (pp. 1–39). Mahwah, NJ: Erlbaum.

Levelt, W. (1989). *Speaking: From intention to articulation*. Cambridge, MA: MIT Press.

MacWhinney, B. (1977). Starting points. *Language, 53*, 152–168.

Miller, P. J., & Sperry, L. L. (1988). Early talk about the past: Origins of conversational stories of personal experience. *Journal of Child Language, 15*, 293–315.

Ninio, A., & Snow, C. (1996). *Pragmatic development.* Boulder, CO: Westview.

Ravid, D. (2000). NP complexity in the development of text writing. In M. Aparici, N. Argerich, J. Perera, E. Rosado, & L. Tolchinsky (Eds.), *Developing literacy across genres, modalities and languages* (Vol. 3, pp. 163–170). Barcelona: Universitat de Barcelona.

Ravid, D., & Berman, R. A. (2009). Developing noun phrase complexity across adolescence: A text-embedded cross-linguistic analysis. *First Language, 30*, 1–24.

Ravid, D., & Tolchinsky, L. (2002). Developing linguistic literacy: A comprehensive model. *Journal of Child Language, 29*, 419–448.

Ravid, D., Van Hell, J.-G., Rosado, E., & Zamora, A. (2002). Subject NP patterning in the development of text production. *Written Language and Literacy, 5*(1), 69–93.

Strömqvist, S., Johansson, V., Kriz, S., Ragnarsdóttir, H., Aisenman, R., & Ravid, D. (2002). Toward a cross-linguistic comparison of lexical quanta in speech and writing. *Written Language and Literacy, 5*(1), 45–68.

Strömqvist, S., Nordvist, A., & Wengelin, A. (2004). Writing the frog story: Developmental and cross-modal perspectives. In S. Strömqvist & L. Verhoeven (Eds.), *Relating events in narrative: Typological and contextual perspectives* (pp. 359–394). Mahwah, NJ: Erlbaum.

Tomlin, R. S. (1995). Focal attention, voice, and word order: An experimental, cross-linguistic study. In P. A. Downing & M. Noonan (Eds.), *Word order in discourse,* (pp. 517–544). Amsterdam: Benjamins.

Part V

Cognitive Processes in Writing

19

Eye-Tracking Data During Written Recall

Clues to Subject–Verb Agreement Processing During Translation

DENIS ALAMARGOT, CHRISTEL LEUWERS,
GILLES CAPOROSSI, VIRGINIE PONTART,
KATHLEEN O'BRIEN RAMIREZ, ASCENSION PAGAN,
DAVID CHESNET, and MICHEL FAYOL

T his chapter describes how the analysis of eye-tracking data obtained during written sentence recall can contribute to understanding the nature of processing involved in the production of subject–verb agreement. Studies in this area have primarily analyzed the errors produced in response to sentences designed to trigger subject–verb agreement errors, also known as attraction errors (Francis, 1986). These errors consist of establishing agreement between the verb, conjugated in the present indicative, and the noun that immediately precedes it, such as "le chien des voisins mange(nt)" (the dog of the neighbors eats). This paradigm has led to an understanding of the influence of semantic, phonological, and syntactic processes in grammatical processing. It has provided arguments in favor of a two-level grammatical processing model in writing production. At the first level, verb-ending number agreement is automatically activated by an immediately preceding noun (e.g., "voisins" activates the plural of "mangent" in the sentence "le chien des voisins mangent"). If the preceding noun is not the subject of the verb, an attraction error is possible. The second processing level consists of pregraphic control, which detects such an error before it is written, by reiterating the appropriate agreement rule. Various studies have measured pregraphic control (see Largy, Cousin, & Dédéyan, 2005, for a summary), but neither the temporal course of the process nor the exact nature of the mechanism involved has been clearly determined.

The time course of subject–verb agreement has been partially explored by Largy and Fayol (2001), who combined a consideration of writing pauses and rates with classic error analysis. They observed a slowing down during the production of the verb ending in the most highly constrained writing condition (when the subject noun is singular and the local noun is plural, the singular-plural [SP] condition). This slow down may testify to more effortful pregraphic control processes, which limit the attraction error most frequently committed in this condition.

Although this finding sheds light on some aspects of the question of the locus of pregraphic control, the question of the exact nature of the processes involved in this control remains. Our study is based on the hypothesis that the pregraphic control of the agreement could be based, in certain circumstances, on the visual reinspection of the noun group. This reinspection should reactivate the number at the moment the verb is produced. This behavior should give rise to regressive fixations on the subject of the verb during written production of the verb. We test this hypothesis, through immediate written recall of complex sentences, such as "La fille $_{(Noun\ 1\ [N1])}$ qui regarde les garcons $_{(Noun\ 2\ [N2])}$ mange(nt)$_{(Target-Verb)}$" (The girl who watches the boys eats), in which subject number in the two nouns preceding the verb has been manipulated, providing two incongruent conditions (plural-singular [PS] and SP). Recording eye movements during writing with the Eye and Pen system (Alamargot, Chesnet, Dansac, & Ros, 2006; Chesnet & Alamargot, 2005), we were able to measure three parameters characteristic of eye behavior during graphic productions: saccades, fixations, and smooth pursuits (Gowan & Miall, 2006). We hypothesize that success in the production of verb agreement in the sentences requiring the highest level of control (sentences with the SP noun sequence) triggers saccades of greater amplitude, connected to the reinspection of N1, reiterating the verb-agreement processes with correct number.

THEORETICAL FRAMEWORK

Although subject–verb agreement errors remain rare in both oral and written language production, their frequency can be significantly increased by having subjects produce a certain type of sentence (e.g., *L'odeur des poubelles empeste*[nt] [The odor of the garbage cans infects]), where the verb can agree incorrectly with the local noun. Research using sentences of this type can highlight how subject–verb agreement is achieved and informs us, more generally, about the functioning of linguistic and cognitive systems in such a context. Over the past 20 years, the types of errors that are most frequently observed and the contexts in which they are likely to occur have been identified in several studies: in oral production (Bock, 1995; Bock & Cutting, 1992; Bock & Eberhard, 1993; Bock & Miller, 1991; Vigliocco, Butterworth, & Semenza, 1995) and in written French (Chanquoy & Negro, 1996; Fayol & Got, 1991; Fayol, Hupet, & Largy, 1999; Fayol, Largy, & Lemaire, 1994; Hupet, Fayol, & Schelstraete, 1998; Hupet, Schelstraete, Demaeght, & Fayol, 1996; Largy, Fayol, & Lemaire, 1996).

SUBJECT–VERB AGREEMENT IN ORAL PRODUCTION

Most oral production models posit three phases: (1) conceptualization, which generates the prelinguistic message, (2) the linguistic formulation of the message, and (3) the articulation of the form as sound. During formulation, a functional representation is constructed that contains each lexical item and the syntactic information associated with it, such as grammatical category (noun, verb), number, and gender (Kempen & Hoenkamp, 1987). According to Bock and Levelt (1994), in the functional representation each noun lemma is tagged for one of the grammatical functions specified by the verb lemma (e.g., subject-nominative, object-accusative). This functional representation serves as the entry for grammatical encoding, which generates a structure of fully specified constituents. Functional representation remains partial in the sense that the information concerning the hierarchical relationship between nouns and verbs is not encoded. In addition, function is attributed only to verb arguments; constituents lower in the structure (such as determiners or adjectives) are not represented functionally.

Processing is generally hypothesized to be serial (unidirectional) and autonomous (or modular), from message formulation to phonological encoding. *Serial* processing follows a precise and single order, without retroaction. This serial condition concerns each segment independently, and different portions of discourse can be processed in parallel. This hypothesis of incremental processing, proposed by Kempen and Hoenkamp (1987), has been maintained in most models of oral language production (Bock & Levelt, 1994; Dell, 1986; Lapointe & Dell, 1989; Levelt, 1989). *Autonomous* processing indicates that the different processes are hypothesized to be modular: Processes taking place at one level cannot be affected by those at other levels. In other words, processes relating to grammatical encoding would not be available to higher-level semantic factors, nor by lower-level factors, such as morphophonological irregularity. These serial and autonomous hypotheses have primarily been tested using an agreement paradigm (usually subject–verb agreement), because agreement is dependent on syntactic relationships established between the different elements in the sentence and therefore illustrates grammatical encoding. Thus, the study of agreement enables us to evaluate hypotheses concerning the autonomy of different processing levels, and, in particular, whether agreement is sensitive to information from higher (semantic) or lower (phonological) levels.

The classic paradigm used in such experimental studies induces participants to produce agreement errors. Orally, the most frequently used paradigm has the participants repeat a sentence beginning (e.g., *La porte des cabines* … [The door to the cabins]), which they must then complete, either freely or using a target verb. In general, this paradigm involves making the verb (the agreement target) agree with a head noun (HN, the agreement controller), which is part of a complex noun phrase, consisting of the HN and a prepositional phrase, which modifies the HN and also contains a local or distractor noun (LN). The main variables that are manipulated are the number (singular vs. plural) of the HN and the congruence between the number of the HN and of the LN (i.e., Example 1). The dependent variable is the number of inflectional errors observed on the agreement target.

Agreement processes are then analyzed to evaluate the influence of experimental manipulation of the preambles (or more generally of the sequences preceding the verb) and of the agreement targets on error production. These manipulations concern the syntactic, conceptual, and phonological levels.

[Le chien/Les chiens]$_{sing/pl\ HN}$ [du berger/des bergers]$_{sing/pl\ LN}$ (Example 1)

Studies using this paradigm reveal two effects on number agreement. The first is number congruence between the HN and LN, which is called the *attraction effect*. Errors are more frequent in incongruent conditions, when the LN and HN differ in number. This effect is attributed to the proximity of the LN, which "attracts" a verb-agreement error. The second effect is *asymmetry*. In the incongruent conditions (SP and PS), errors are more frequent when the HN is singular (the HN$_{sing}$ LN$_{pl}$ configuration). This effect appears to be due to the fact that the singular form is a sort of "default" setting for a noun, which is therefore marked, when plural, by a characteristic plural ending (a final -s, in English and in French). The interference provoked by discordant number in the syntactic environment of the HN is therefore greater when the HN is unmarked than when it is marked (plural). These two effects have been systematically observed in English, French, Italian, and Spanish (Bock & Cutting, 1992; Bock & Eberhard, 1993; Bock & Miller, 1991; Vigliocco et al., 1995; Vigliocco, Butterworth, & Garrett, 1996; Vigliocco, Hartsuiker, Jarema, & Kolk, 1996).

Two major criticisms can be leveled at the unidirectional-serial model. First, the sensitivity of attraction errors to conceptual influence (the *plausibility effect*) provides evidence of interaction between the conceptual and formal levels. Thornton and MacDonald (2003) showed that verb-agreement errors are more frequent when the HN is a plausible verb object (in passive sentences) than when it is not. Second, the observation of attraction errors when the LN and the HN belong to different clauses contradicts the hypothesis of clausal packaging (hierarchical vs. serial processes). Unidirectional serial production models presuppose that attraction errors would be limited to clauses in which the LN and HN are simultaneously present—the processing unit being that of the grammatical clause (Bock & Cutting, 1992). Nevertheless, Solomon and Pearlmutter (2004) and Gillespie and Pearlmutter (2009) have shown the presence of attraction errors in cases where the LN is integrated into a relative clause, which does not belong to the same syntactic unit. These two sets of data appear to support the sensitivity of agreement processes to semantic influences, as well as the importance of the linear proximity of the LN in attraction errors. Current research in oral production is exploring these questions of the permeability of processing stages, which will have major implications for models of language processing.

WRITTEN SUBJECT–VERB AGREEMENT

Although research on oral and written productions generally reflects the same general preoccupations with the architecture of the processes involved, the problems encountered by the two domains can actually be quite different. In oral production research, the modular view, considered by the majority of authors, accounts for the rapid, relatively reliable nature of the overall process (Frazier & Rayner, 1982; Green & Mitchell, 2006; Traxler, Pickering, & Clifton, 1998; Van Gompel, Pickering, Pearson, & Liversedge, 2005; but see Haskell & MacDonald, 2003; Solomon & Pearlmutter, 2004; Thornton & MacDonald, 2003, for a different perspective). In research on written production, the processes involved are examined from an interactional, capacity-based perspective. In fact, although written production relies to some extent on oral processing units, it has these unique characteristics: (a) involves specific processes, which are acquired late, over long periods of time (mechanics and orthography, Bourdin & Fayol, 2002); (b) generates a written trace, which represents an external "memory" that can be referred to during the production process; (c) is less constrained in its time course, which is much slower than that of oral production; and (d) exhibits, for these last two reasons, much greater possibility for revision of the formal trace of production. The question of maintenance and processing in working memory is, therefore, different for written than for oral production; and it is likely that the more controlled nature of written production means that the temporal distribution and economy of the processes involved are also different. All these differences between oral and written production mean that control and supervision of written agreement will differ from control and supervision during the oral production of agreement.

The study of subject–verb agreement in written production has usually relied on a double-task paradigm, in which written recall of orally presented sentences is coupled with another task (remembering words or making mathematical calculations during recall). This paradigm is particularly well adapted to French, whose verbal morphology necessitates the production (for frequent regular verbs) of a written verbal ending -ent, which is silent in spoken French (*il chante*, singular [he sings], and *ils chantent*, plural [they sing], sound the same). Studies using this paradigm have shown the permeability of agreement to semantic characteristics (Hupet et al., 1996, 1998), phonological elements (Largy & Fayol, 2001), and working memory capacity influences (Fayol et al., 1994). These factors have also been examined from a developmental perspective (Chanquoy & Negro, 1996; Fayol & Got, 1991; Fayol et al., 1999; Negro & Chanquoy, 2000a, 2000b).

In written production, it is important to understand why a secondary task significantly increases the number of attraction errors, even for adults, despite the fact that the slower speed of written production gives writers time to detect and revise possible errors. For Fayol and Got (1991), the reduction of working memory resources available, provoked by the double-task situation, should limit the engagement or the functioning of this pregraphic control. The production system, therefore, falls into the trap of the unconscious attraction error. In other words, the writer falls victim to the automatic nature of an agreement rule when the LN is neither the subject of the verb nor congruent in number with the HN, and, when cognitive resources are insufficient.

The existence of pregraphic control has been confirmed by various experimental studies (see Largy et al., 2005, for a summary). Hupet et al. (1996) showed that three parameters can modulate the way in which pregraphic control is triggered. First, the process is more difficult when the concurrent task involves executive function, such as adding numbers while writing down the recalled sentence, so pregraphic control must tap into the resources of the central executive. Second, incongruent number situations (PS, SP) generate more errors than congruent situations (singular-singular [SS], plural-plural [PP]), and the SP incongruent situation generates more errors than the PS condition. At the same time, the performance on the secondary task is also better in the SP than in the PS condition, confirming a relative lack of control in SP (leading to errors) and the executive cost of pregraphic control in PS (avoiding errors). In fact, the existence of this tradeoff between performances on the main and the secondary tasks indicates that when pregraphic control is being executed, agreement errors diminish, and this control has a cost in terms of processing resources available for the secondary task. Third, the semantic plausibility of the LN as the subject of the verb is another factor triggering pregraphic control. This effect has been observed in the case of French sentences in which only the LN precedes the verb (the HN coming after the verb, in a N1 vs. N2 configuration: *sur les moutons saute la puce* [on the sheep jumps the flea]). In incongruent number situations (SP, PS), the nonplausibility (as subject) of the noun in the N1 position is an important trigger of pregraphic control. The involvement of control is also greater in the case of nonplausibility (*sur la branche chantent les oiseaux* [on the branch sing the birds]) than in the case of plausibility (*sur le mouton sautent les puces* [on the sheep jump the fleas]). Agreement errors are therefore more frequent when the LN is a plausible verb subject, indicating that the system is proceeding automatically (without control). At the same time, performance on the secondary task is worse in the nonplausibility condition, confirming that control must have been in operation to limit errors, compared to the plausibility condition.

If the hypothesis of a two-stage process (automatic rule plus pregraphic control) appears tenable for adult written production, these various proofs of pregraphic control are in fact indirect. As Hupet et al. (1996, p. 606) state, we need real-time production studies, particularly of latency and rate of production, if we want to approach pregraphic control more directly. Largy and Fayol (2001) have attempted this approach in an initial real-time analysis of the writing rate for different phrases in targeting sentences where the production of subject–verb agreement was correct. They showed that the writing rate while the verb ending is being produced is sensitive to cognitive load and to number in incongruent cases. They report a slowdown in writing rate in the SP condition, which they attribute to the presence of heightened pregraphic control, a condition necessary for success in producing the correct ending. Their study is a first attempt to integrate real-time measures in the study of the production of written sentences. Despite this clearer picture of just where pregraphic control takes place, the nature and the time course of the precise processes involved still remain unclear.

WHY STUDY EYE MOVEMENTS DURING WRITING?

We believe that eye-tracking the written production of sentences can shed light on the nature of pregraphic control processes. Eye movements have been frequently used to study sentence comprehension by analyzing (a) which units are fixated during the reading of sentences containing syntactic, grammatical, or semantic variations (see Rayner, 1995, 1998, for summaries; and Rayner, Warren, Juhasz, & Liversedge, 2004; Staub, Rayner, Pollatsek, Hyönä, & Majewski, 2007, for studies involving semantic plausibility), or (b) which objects of a visual scene are fixated (in anticipation) while listening to a sentence (Altmann & Kamide, 2009; Kamide, Altmann, & Haywood, 2003; Knoeferle & Crocker, 2007; Knoeferle, Crocker, Scheepers, & Pickering, 2005). Eye-tracking has also been used over the past 10 years to study oral sentence production. These studies have clarified the respective time course of planning and formulating spoken sentences, in the description of simple events (Griffin, 2001; Griffin & Bock, 2000; Martin, Crowther, Knight, Tamborello, & Yang, 2010).

The study of writing production processes is more recent than reading and oral production research. As a consequence, the paradigms for studying written production are less advanced. Up to now, the study of orthographic processes, their automatic or controlled nature, has been primarily carried out through a secondary task paradigm in which the second task influences controlled processing, with an analysis of the consequences on the final written product and especially any errors generated. In the studies summarized above, the writer was asked to produce a subject–verb agreement, in written recall of a spoken sentence, while (a) maintaining in memory a series of words, (b) carrying out an addition problem (Hupet et al., 1996, 1998), or (c) counting clicks (Fayol et al., 1999). Analyses of variations in the number of agreement errors and of performance in the secondary task are characteristic of this approach (Fayol et al., 1994; Hupet et al., 1998). Despite its relevance, however, this paradigm is complicated to carry out. The secondary task must be sufficiently "costly" in attentional resources to impede pregraphic control, without interfering too much with the primary task, at the phonological level, for example, or determining a tradeoff between the two tasks. In addition, this paradigm encourages the researcher to reason in terms of processing failure, and so the strategies underlying success are not directly studied.

The simultaneous analysis of eye and graphomotor movements represents a new paradigm in research into written production and spelling. Such analysis can enable us to investigate automatic and controlled processes, without interfering with the time course of these processes. We hypothesize that, in the case of sentences triggering attraction errors, (re)fixating the HN during the production of a verb ending could contribute to the inhibition of the incorrect number reflected in the LN or to the activation of the correct number of the HN. To our knowledge, such a study has not yet been carried out, examining the process from the perceptual, attentional, and eye-movement levels.

RATIONALE

This study examines the production of relative "qui" clauses (Example 2), for which a local noun (*les papis*) incongruent in number with the head noun (*la mamie*) could induce a verb (V) agreement error on the verb (*lance*) in the main clause. The task consists of the written recall of a spoken sentence, classically used to study written production (Fayol et al., 1999; Hupet et al., 1998; Largy et al., 1996;

Negro, Chanquoy, Fayol, & Louis-Sidney, 2005), in which the participants are told to write down the previously recorded spoken sentence. Their graphomotor production is recorded using a digitizing tablet, and the simultaneous recording of their eye movements lets us determine whether each participant reinspects parts of his written text, and if so (a) at what point in time, and (b) precisely which information is inspected.

la mamie$_{HN}$ qui montre les papis$_{LN}$ lance$_V$ une balle   (Example 2)
[the grandmother who points to the grandfathers throws a ball]

When writers have to deal with a sentence with complex word order and agreement (Example 2), we expect two types of eye movements, depending on the nature of the representations activated in working memory. If the HN, LN, and V are all activated, the calculation of agreement can be carried out in working memory (HN-V agreement, inhibition of the number of the LN), and the writer's ocular focus will stay close to the pen, "following" the word being written. Alternatively, if the HN is not activated in working memory, one or more regressive fixations will be necessary to bring the HN back into attentional focus. The HN might not be activated in working memory for different reasons: syntactic distance between the HN and the V playing an especially important role (with "La mamie montre les papis$_{HN}$ qui lancent$_V$ une balle" illustrating syntactic proximity, and "La mamie$_{HN}$ qui montre les papis$_{LN}$ lance$_V$ une balle" illustrating considerable syntactic distance), as does the number of the LN, with a plural LN necessitating more effortful inhibition.

EXPERIMENTAL METHOD

Participants

Twenty-five undergraduate students enrolled in psychology courses at the University of Poitiers participated in this experiment.

Manipulated Sentences

The experimental sentences were relative subject-subject (Examples 3 and 4) in which the HN was the subject of both the main verb and the verb contained in the intervening relative clause. The grammatical number of the HN ("mamie" in Example 3 and "papis" in Example 4) and the LN ("papis" in Example 3 and "mamie" in Example 4) was always incongruent and two conditions of number were compared: HN in singular and LN in plural (condition SP, as in Example 3) or vice versa (condition PS, as in Example 4). The sentences in the two conditions were constructed by reversing the agent and patient events. Six pairs of characters (one male and one female, e.g.: *le lutin, la fée*), six "reversible" actions, which could plausibly be associated with either of the six characters (e.g., montrer [to show]), and six "nonreversible" actions (such as an action performed by a character on an object, e.g., *lancer une balle* [to throw a ball]) were used to construct six subject-subject sentences in each number condition.

The experimental sentences described above with subject-subject (SS) relative clauses were compared to controls with object-subject (OS; Examples 5 and 6) relative clauses for which the noun preceding the second verb was the subject of this verb and the direct object of the main verb, and so strictly speaking, there was no LN. These OS relatives were constructed from the same pairs of characters and the same actions as those used for constructing SS sentences, but related topic differently. The conditions of number have been built in the same way: SP in Example 5 and PS in Example 6).

SS-SP   La mamie$_{NT\text{-}sing}$ qui montre les papis$_{NL\text{-}pl}$ lance une balle   (Example 3)
        [The grandmother who points to the grandfathers throws a ball]

SS-PS   Les papis$_{NT\text{-}pl}$ qui montrent la mamie$_{NL\text{-}sing}$ lancent une balle   (Example 4)
        [The grandfathers who point to the grandmother throws a ball]

OS-SP   La reine$_{NT\text{-}sing}$ montre les rois$_{NL\text{-}pl}$ qui lancent une balle   (Example 5)
        [The queen points to the kings who throw a ball]

OS-PS   Les rois$_{NT\text{-}pl}$ montrent la reine$_{NL\text{-}sing}$ qui lance une balle   (Example 6)
        [The kings point to the queen who throws a ball]

EYE AND PEN SYSTEM

Participants wrote on a digitizing screen tablet (18p Cintiq—Wacom), coupled with an eye tracker (Eyelink II—SR-Research) via Eye and Pen software (Alamargot et al., 2006; Chesnet & Alamargot, 2005). This device manages information provided to participants (dictating items, displaying areas of writing) while recording eye movements and graphomotor behavior in synchronicity.

Procedure

After presentation of the instruction, the participants were fitted with the helmet of the eye tracker and the experimenter proceeded with the calibration (fixating successively nine points). Familiarity with the digitizing screen tablet was performed by means of two simple tasks: (1) for 1 min the participant wrote his or her own first and last name; and (2) then first and last name followed by "is in the garden." Then four practice items were proposed involving characters and actions different from the experimental items, and finally the 24 experimental items were presented via prerecorded dictation. In total, each participant was asked to recall 28 sentences.

During dictation, the participants fixated on a cross displayed on the center of the screen tablet with the digital pen held suspended over the area where writing would commence. At the end of the dictation, the listening screen was replaced by the writing screen (Figure 19.1). Participants were free to start writing (from recall of the dictation) at their own pace unconstrained by time. They could cross out and revise as they wrote. They indicated the end of the recall by pressing the tip of their pencil on a box marked "Next" at the bottom right of the screen, which prompted the display of the next item sequence (cross with simultaneous dictation, then writing area).

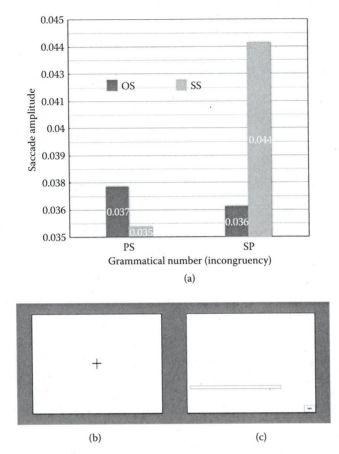

Figure 19.1   (a) Effect of relative clause and grammatical number on saccade amplitude (in centimeters; relativized by the length of the sentence as written); (b) screen displayed during dictation; and (c) screen displayed during the immediate written recall.

Measures

Quantitative Analysis of Eye Movements

Eye movements were grouped into three categories—fixations, smooth pursuits, and saccades—as a function of the speed of the eye movement. Following the work of Gowen and Miall (2006) comparing drawing and tracing of geometric forms, we characterized smooth pursuit (when the eye is in movement—following the pen—and still capable of capturing information) as comprising a displacement speed between 5.35 and 31.8 degrees per second. More rapid movements correspond to saccades. Slower movements correspond to fixations during which the eye is technically considered as immobile. In both the case of smooth pursuit and fixation, because the eye must be capable of capturing information, a minimum threshold of 75-ms duration was retained.

Six dependent variables were obtained: frequency of saccades (in hertz; i.e., number of saccades per second); amplitude of saccades (in centimeters), relativized by the length of the sentence as written (i.e., the total distance traveled by the pen because, according to the handwriting style of the participant, a sentence can be longer or shorter); the percentage of item-production time spent in smooth pursuit, the mean duration of a smooth pursuit (in milliseconds); the percentage of item-production time spent fixating, and the mean duration of fixations (in milliseconds).

Qualitative Analysis of Regressive Saccades to the Head Noun Phrase   For each sentence and each participant, the sequences of saccades and regressive fixations were analyzed; and for each, the lexical constituent from which a regressive sequence was launched was recorded, as well as the constituents, which were viewed at least once during the regressive sequence.

RESULTS

The 25 participants each produced 24 sentences, or 600 sentences in total. Twelve incomplete or incorrectly recorded items were eliminated. Of the 588 items remaining, those with at least one verbal inflection error (on either of the two verbs), lexical error (on the stem of the word), or grammatical error (on the inflectional morpheme) were removed from temporal analysis. An ANOVA, conducted on the percentage of items eliminated relative to the items remaining, resulted in OS-PS, 4.93% ($SD = 9.95$); OS-SP, 6.80% ($SD = 11.92$); SS-PS, 7.73% ($SD = 13.53$); SS-SP, 12.26% ($SD = 17.78$), which showed neither an effect of the two factors (relative clause type and grammatical number) nor an interaction.

Quantitative Analysis of Eye Movements

Analyses of variance by participants and by items were conducted for the two factors, relative clause type (object or subject: OS vs. SS), and grammatical number (singular or plural) of the first and second nouns, which were always incongruent (SP vs. PS). For each dependent variable, we present (a) the means and standard deviations for each condition (Table 19.1), and (b) the results of the ANOVAs (the effect of each factor and the interaction), as well as the results of planned comparisons when the interaction is significant (Table 19.2).

Analysis of Visual Information Intake: Saccades, Fixations, and Smooth Pursuits

For saccadic eye movements, the main effect of relative clause type is significant for saccade frequency, although only marginally by participant. Saccade frequency is greater during the production of SS clauses than during OS clauses (SS: 1.84 Hz; OS: 1.79 Hz). The main effect of number incongruence is not significant and does not interact with clause type. As for saccade amplitude (adjusted for sentence length), the main effects are both significant, although only by subjects. The interaction between the factors clause and number is marginally significant by items. The planned comparisons indicate that the effect of number is significant for SS clauses

TABLE 19.1   Temporal Characteristics of Saccades, Fixations, and Smooth Pursuits During the Production of an Item (Means and Standard Deviations)

	OS-PS	OS-SP	SS-PS	SS-SP
Frequency of saccades (Hz)	1.70 (0.60)	1.78 (0.54)	1.83 (0.54)	1.86 (0.63)
Amplitude of saccades (cm, scaled to sentence length)	0.037 (0.018)	0.036 (0.018)	0.036 (0.016)	0.044 (0.019)
Percentage of time spent in fixations (of item-production time)	26.47 (20.10)	26.79 (19.96)	26.41 (19.69)	27.63 (20.21)
Duration of fixations (ms)	247 (93)	242 (96)	240 (93)	244 (94)
Percentage of time in smooth pursuits (on the item production time)	15.93 (11.00)	14.89 (9.55)	15.35 (10.58)	14.96 (10.11)
Duration of smooth pursuits (ms)	112 (20)	107 (9)	106 (11)	110 (11)

Standard deviation is shown in parentheses. OS, object-subject; PS, plural-singular; SP, singular-plural; SS, subject-subject.

but not for OS clauses. With SS sentences, there is an augmentation of saccade amplitude in the SP number condition. These results are illustrated in Figure 19.1.

For eye fixations, concerning the percentage of time spent fixating, a trend emerged regarding number, but only in the analysis by participants. In terms of mean fixation durations, there is no significant effect.

For smooth pursuit, regarding the percentage of time spent in smooth pursuit, no effect was observed. Concerning smooth pursuit duration, only the interaction is significant. The planned comparisons indicate a significant effect of number for SS relative clauses, although only by participants. No significant effect for the OS relative clauses occurred, even though a trend emerges in the item analysis.

Qualitative Analysis of Regressive Saccades to Noun Phrases

Overall, 32.4% of experimental sentences have a regressive sequence, and in these sentences, the mean number of regressions per sentence is 2.225. From a descriptive perspective, we observe that regressive sequences are initiated most often from the beginning of the second verb (39.1%; 3.6% to 24.5% for regressions from all other constituent locations). Independent from the point of departure for regressions, the HN phrase is the most frequent landing point of regressive eye movements (refixated at least one time, 28.1%), followed by the first verb and the LN phrase (19.5% and 14.5%, respectively). Given the low rate of regressive fixations in all items, nonparametric analyses were used, which do not permit consideration of interactions; so we analyzed separately, with the help of W of Wilcoxon within participants, the effect of the relative clause and the effect of noun phrase number for each relative clause. The means and standard deviations for the different sentences are presented for each of these analyses in Table 19.3.

TABLE 19.2   Results of ANOVA

	R	N	R * N	N/OS	N/SS
Percentage of Errors					
By Participants	$F = 2.58; p < .15$	$F = 1.56; p > .20$	$F < 1; ns$		
Frequency of Saccades (Hz)					
By Participants	$F = 3.24; p < .10$ *m*	$F < 1; ns$	$F < 1; ns$		
By Items	$F = 4.5; p < .05$ °	$F = 2.45; p < .15$	$F = 1.32; p > .20$		
Amplitude of Saccades (in cm, relative to the sentence length)					
by Participants	$F = 7.86; p < .05$ °	$F = 11.46; p < .01$ °	$F = 19.67; p < .001$ °°	$F = 37.67; p < .001$ °°	$F < 1; ns$
By Items	$F = 1.64; p > .20$	$F = 2.08; p > .20$	$F = 3.49; p < .10$	$F = 5.48; p < .05$ *m* °	$F < 1; ns$
Percentage of Time Spent in Fixations (on the item production time)					
By Participants	$F < 1; ns$	$F = 3.23; p < .10$ *m*	$F < 1; ns$		
By Items	$F < 1; ns$	$F < 1; ns$	$F < 1; ns$		
Duration of Fixations (ms)					
By Participants	$F < 1; ns$	$F < 1; ns$ *m*	$F < 1; ns$		
By Items	$F < 1; ns$	$F < 1; ns$	$F < 1; ns$		
Percentage of Time Spent in Smooth Pursuits (on the Item Production Time)					
By Participants	$F < 1; ns$	$F = 2.46; p < .15$	$F = 1.13; p > .20$		
By Items	$F < 1; ns$	$F < 1; ns$	$F = 1.05; p > .20$		
Duration of Smooth Pursuits (ms)					
By Participants	$F < 1; ns$	$F < 1; ns$	$F = 5.93; p < .05$	$F = 4.86; p < .05$ °	$F = 1.79; p > .15$
By Items	$F < 1; ns$	$F < 1; ns$	$F = 6.61; p < .05$	$F = 2.86; p < .11$ °	$F = 3.77; p < .07$ *m*

By participants, $F (1, 24)$, and items, $F (1, 20)$, for the relative clause type (R) and number (N) conditions and their interaction ($R \times N$) followed, when this interaction is significant, by planned comparisons: effect on the number for the relative SS (N/SS) and the relative OS (N/OS). For each effect, the F and the significance are indicated (°°, $p < .01$; °, $p < .05$; and *m* for marginal, $p < .10$).

TABLE 19.3   Mean (SD) Regression (of Six Items Produced) from the Second Verb (V2)

	N	OS-PS	OS-SP	SS-PS	SS-SP
Overall	23	1.57 (2.13)	2.26 (2.49)	2.78 (2.89)	2.87 (2.63)
from V2 to N1	8	0.00 (0.00)	0.75 (0.71)	1.25 (1.28)	2.13 (0.64)
from V2 to N2	12	0.17 (0.58)	0.83 (1.03)	1.00 (1.21)	1.92 (1.51)

Numbers in parentheses are standard deviations. N, number of participants making regressions included in the analysis; OS, object-subject; PS, plural-singular; SP, singular-plural; SS, subject-subject.

The Occurrence of Regressive Sequences From All Departure and Landing Points

We restricted this analysis to the 23 participants displaying at least two regressive sequences on the totality of items. The effect of the relative clause is significant (normal approximation of W of Wilcoxon: $z = 2.06$, $p < .05$). Globally there is one more regressive sequence initiated from SS relative clauses ($M = 2.8$) than from OS relative clauses ($M = 1.9$). The effect of noun phrase number, however, is not significant for OS or for SS sentences ($z < 1.0$).

The Occurrence of Regressive Sequences Departing From the Second Verb

Initially we were interested in regressions originating from the second verb (V2) and identifying the landing points from these regressive saccades. We then restricted the analysis to regressions during which either the N1 phrase or the N2 phrase was fixated. These represent 84% of regressions from V2. We analyzed separately regressions departing from V2 and landing in N1 from those that landed in N2. These analyses are relatively independent because in 70% of these regressive eye movements to N1, N2 is not fixated; and in 65% of the regressions to N2, N1 is not fixated.

Regressions to Noun 1   Eight participants had at least two regressive eye movements to N1 on the total for items. For these participants, the effect of relative clause is significant [$Ws(8) = 1$, $p < .01$] and the effect of number is tangentially significant for SS relative clauses [$Ws(8) = 5$, $p < .1$] and situated near the threshold for significance for OS relative clauses [$Ws(8) = 6$, $p = .1$]. The difference between the OS-PS relatives and the SS-PS relatives is not significant [$Ws(8) = 7.5$, ns]. Thus the hierarchy in terms of regression frequency is the following: OS-PS < OS-SP = SS-PS < SS-SP.

Regressions to Noun 2   Twelve participants had at least two regressive eye movements to N2 on the totality of items. For these participants, there is a significant effect of relative clause [$Ws(12) = 9$, $p < .01$]. The effect of number, however, is neither significant for SS relative clauses [$Ws(12) = 27$, ns], nor for OS relative clauses [$Ws(12) = 28$, ns]. These effects emerge from a small quantity of regressions in the OS-PS sentences and a larger quantity of regressions in the three other conditions (all fairly equivalent). This finding is confirmed with two Friedman non-parametric ANOVAs that indicate an effect of condition: When all four conditions are taken into account, Fried(4, 12) = 12.1, $p < .01$, but is not maintained when the OS-PS condition is removed, Fried(3, 12) = 3.3, ns. Thus, when the second noun preceding the second verb is its subject and it is singular in number, regressions to this N2 are very few; the frequency of regressions is augmented and mutually similar for the three other sentence types.

DISCUSSION

The results of the quantitative analysis of the different ocular parameters involved in the written recall of sentences reveal the particularity of the SS-SP configuration, which triggers an increase in saccade amplitude. Qualitative analysis of regressive saccades shows that OS relatives give results that are the opposite of those obtained with SS relatives, when all regressive sequences have been taken into account, and that SS-SP relatives are opposed to the three other conditions when we look at regressions back to the first noun phrase initiated from V2. These results must be interpreted with caution, however, due to the low number of regressions and the small subject pool involved.

The successful production of subject–verb agreement for the second verb in an SS-SP sentence presupposes avoiding the attraction caused by the LN-V configuration—an attraction that increases in the case of a plural LN. Various studies (Fayol & Got, 1991; Largy & Fayol, 2001) have shown that the attraction is stronger in the SP than the PS condition, the reason being the required inhibition of the plural LN before the verb. It is interesting that similar results have been found, through the analysis of eye movement variables obtained during the production of successful items rather than by counting agreement errors. Pregraphic control, which might be activated to avoid error in the SS-SP condition, would therefore also involve saccades that, although not necessarily more frequent (because eye saccade frequency seemed little affected in our data), cover longer distances.

Like Largy and Fayol (2001), we consider that a significantly longer production time in the case of SP type sentences (compared with SS, PP, and PS sentences) is the proof of pregraphic control; this control implies a reinspection of the HN phrase during the production of the verbal inflection, or at least of the verb. This interpretation is corroborated by the qualitative analysis of the regressive saccades that were recorded, especially by the analysis of regressive saccades to the N1 phrase (the HN phrase in the SS relatives). For the OS-PS relatives, the agreement of V2 does not present any difficulty, because the preceding noun is the subject (short distance, no LN distractor) and because it is singular. When the LN is plural (OS-SP), however, pregraphic control is initiated, triggered by the plural noun preceding the verb. This pregraphic control is, however, more frequent in SS relatives, where the LN preceding V2 is not its subject, and particularly in the SS-SP condition, where the LN is plural. So, two factors seem to influence pregraphic control in this study: a plural noun preceding the verb, and the fact that the noun is an

LN and not an agreement controller. The influence of these two factors explains the hierarchy observed for regressive saccades to N1 initiated from V2: OS-PS < OS-SP = SS-PS < SS-SP.

Analyses of smooth pursuits do not show a contrast between SS-SP relatives and the other types of relatives (planned analyses are not congruent by subjects and by items). According to Gowen and Miall (2006), smooth pursuits during graphic execution do not correspond to higher-level cognitive processes, but simply to guide the execution of the written trace. It nevertheless remains to confirm the distribution of smooth pursuits according to the different phrases of the sentence.

CONCLUSION

Overall, the results of this experiment show that eye movements—and particularly saccades—are influenced by the grammatical configuration of sentences in immediate written recall. Sentences of the SS-SP type, which are likely to provoke attraction errors, modify the writer's eye movements, generating saccades of greater amplitude toward the HN phrase.

These initial results are encouraging and show that eye-movement research can be applied to the study of the conditions in which pregraphic control is necessary for correct subject–verb agreement in written production. In addition, these results can contribute to models of written verbal production, because they illustrate control procedures that are no doubt specific to the written modality, without counterpart in the oral modality.

Complementary studies need to be run in order to establish the time course of writing processes. The analysis of the pauses and writing rates associated with different components of the sentence, and especially during the production of the verb ending, should help reveal the nature of the processes involved as the writing process unfolds. In reference to theoretical issues concerning the architecture of the processes involved, the approach developed here should encourage us to reexamine conclusions based exclusively on error rates. Semantic and phonological effects observed during grammatical processing can express themselves through modifications of hand–eye movements, without giving rise to errors. Studying successful production of verb agreement, and the conditions underlying this success, is an important contribution of real-time analysis of written production and thus to understanding the translation process.

REFERENCES

Alamargot, D., Chesnet, D., Dansac, C., & Ros, C. (2006). Eye and Pen: A new device to study the reading during writing. *Behavior Research Methods, Instruments and Computers, 38*(2), 287–299.

Altmann, G. T. M., & Kamide, Y. (2009). Discourse-mediation of the mapping between language and the visual world: Eye movements and mental representation. *Cognition, 111*, 55–71.

Bock, J. K. (1995). Producing agreement. *Current Directions in Psychological Science, 4*, 56–61.

Bock, J. K., & Cutting, J. C. (1992). Regulating mental energy: Performance units in language production. *Journal of Memory and Language, 31*, 99–127.

Bock, J. K., & Eberhard, K. M. (1993). Meaning, sound, and syntax in English number agreement. *Language and Cognitive Processes, 8*, 57–99.

Bock, J. K., & Levelt, W. (1994). Grammatical encoding. In M. A. Gernsbacher (Ed.), *Handbook of psycholinguistics* (pp. 945–978). New York: Academic Press.

Bock, J. K., & Miller, C. A. (1991). Broken agreement. *Cognitive Psychology, 23*, 45–93.

Bourdin, B., & Fayol, M. (2002). Even in adults, written production is still more costly than oral production. *International Journal of Psychology, 37*, 219–227.

Chanquoy, L., & Negro, I. (1996). Subject-verb agreement errors in written productions: A study of French children and adults. *Journal of Psycholinguistic Research, 25*(5), 553–570.

Chesnet, D., & Alamargot, D. (2005). Analyses en temps réel des activités oculaires et graphomotrices du scripteur: intérêt du dispositif 'Eye and Pen.' *L'Année Psychologique, 105*, 477–520.

Dell, G. S. (1986). A spreading activation theory of retrieval in sentence production. *Psychological Review, 93*, 283–321.

Fayol, M., & Got, C. (1991). Automatisme et contrôle dans la production écrite. *L'Année Psychologique, 91*, 187–205.

Fayol, M., Hupet, M., & Largy, P. (1999). The acquisition of subject-verb agreement in written French: From novices to experts' errors. *Reading and Writing, 11*, 153–174.

Fayol, M., Largy, P., & Lemaire, P. (1994). When cognitive overload enhances subject-verb agreement errors. *Quarterly Journal of Experimental Psychology, 47A*, 437–464.

Francis, W. N. (1986). Proximity concord in English. *Journal of English Linguistics, 19*, 309–318.

Frazier, L., & Rayner, K. (1982). Making and correcting errors during sentence comprehension: Eye movements in the analysis of structurally ambiguous sentences. *Cognitive Psychology, 14*, 178–210.

Gillespie, M., & Pearlmutter, N. J. (2009). *Evidence against clause boundedness and hierarchical distance in subject-verb agreement production.* Poster presented at the 2009 AMLaP Conference, Barcelona, Spain.

Gowen, E., & Miall, R. C. (2006). Eye-hand interactions in tracing and drawing tasks. *Human Movement Science, 25*, 568–585.

Green, M. J., & Mitchell, D. C. (2006). Absence of real evidence against competition during syntactic ambiguity resolution. *Journal of Memory and Language, 55*, 1–17.

Griffin, Z. M. (2001). Gaze durations during speech reflect word selection and phonological encoding. *Cognition, 82*, B1–B14.

Griffin, Z. M., & Bock, J. K. (2000). What the eyes say about speaking. *Psychological Science, 11*, 274–279.

Haskell, T. R., & MacDonald, M. C. (2003). Conflicting cues and competition in subject-verb agreement. *Journal of Memory and Language, 48*, 760–778.

Hupet, M., Fayol, M., & Schelstraete, M-A. (1998). Effects of semantic variables on the subject-verb agreement processes in writing. *British Journal of Psychology, 89*, 59–75.

Hupet, M., Schelstraete, M-A., Demaeght, N., & Fayol, M. (1996). Les erreurs d'accord sujet-verbe en production écrite. *L'Année Psychologique, 96*, 587–610.

Kamide, Y., Altmann, G. T. M., & Haywood, S. L. (2003). The time-course of prediction in incremental sentence processing: Evidence from anticipatory eye movements. *Journal of Memory and Language, 49*, 133–156.

Kempen, G., & Hoenkamp, E. (1987). An incremental procedural grammar for sentence formulation. *Cognitive Science, 11*(2), 201–258.

Knoeferle, P., & Crocker, M. W. (2007). The influence of recent scene events on spoken comprehension: Evidence from eye movements. *Journal of Memory and Language, 57,* 519–543.

Knoeferle, P., Crocker, M. W., Scheepers, C., & Pickering, M. J. (2005). The influence of the immediate visual context on incremental thematic role-assignment: Evidence from eye-movements in depicted events. *Cognition, 95,* 95–127.

Lapointe, S. G., & Dell, G. S. (1989). A synthesis of some recent work in sentence production. In G. N. Carlson & M. K. Tannehaus (Eds.), *Linguistic structure in language processing* (pp. 107–156). Dordrecht: Kluwer.

Largy, P., Cousin, M. P., & Dédéyan, A. (2005). To produce and revise the inflexional morphology of number: On the access to expertise. *Psychologie Française, 50,* 339–350.

Largy, P., & Fayol, M. (2001). Oral cues improve subject-verb agreement in written French. *International Journal of Psychology, 36,* 121–132.

Largy, P., Fayol, M., & Lemaire, P. (1996). The homophone effect in written French: The case of verb–noun inflection errors. *Language and Cognitive Processes, 11,* 217–255.

Levelt, W. J. M. (1989). *Speaking: From intention to articulation.* Cambridge, MA: MIT Press.

Martin, R. C., Crowther, J. E., Knight, M., Tamborello II, F. P., & Yang, C. L. (2010). Planning in sentence production: Evidence for the phrase as a default planning scope. *Cognition, 116,* 177–192.

Negro, I., & Chanquoy, L. (2000a). Etude des erreurs d'accord sujet verbe au présent et à l'imparfait. *L'année Psychologique, 100,* 209–240.

Negro, I., & Chanquoy, L. (2000b). Subject-verb agreement with present and imperfect tenses: A developmental study from 2nd to 7th grade. *European Journal of Psychology of Education, 15,* 113–133.

Negro, I., Chanquoy, L., Fayol, M., & Louis-Sidney, M. (2005). Subject-verb agreement in children and adults: Serial or hierarchical processing? *Journal of Psycholinguistic Research, 34,* 233–258.

Rayner, K. (1995). Eye movements and cognitive processes in reading, visual search, and scene perception. *Studies in Visual Information Processing, 6,* 3–22.

Rayner, K. (1998). Eye movements in reading and information processing: 20 years of research. *Psychological Bulletin, 124,* 372–422.

Rayner, K., Warren, T., Juhasz, B. J., & Liversedge, S. P. (2004). The effect of plausibility on eye movements in reading. *Journal of Experimental Psychology: Learning, Memory, and Cognition, 30,* 1290–1301.

Solomon, E. S., & Pearlmutter, N. J. (2004). Semantic integration and syntactic planning in language production. *Cognitive Psychology, 49,* 1–46.

Staub, A., Rayner, K., Pollatsek, A., Hyönä, J., & Majewski, H. (2007). The time course of plausibility effects on eye movements in reading: Evidence from noun-noun compounds. *Journal of Experimental Psychology: Learning, Memory, and Cognition, 33,* 1162–1169.

Thornton, R., & MacDonald, M. C. (2003). Plausibility and grammatical agreement. *Journal of Memory and Language, 48,* 740–759.

Traxler, M. J., Pickering, M. J., & Clifton, C. (1998). Adjunct attachment is not a form of lexical ambiguity resolution. *Journal of Memory and Language, 39,* 558–592.

Van Gompel, R. P. G., Pickering, M. J., Pearson, J., & Liversedge, S. P. (2005). Evidence against competition during syntactic ambiguity resolution. *Journal of Memory and Language, 52,* 284–307.

Vigliocco, G., Butterworth, B., & Garrett, M. F. (1996). Subject-verb agreement in Spanish and English: Differences in the role of conceptual constraints. *Cognition, 61,* 261–298.

Vigliocco, G., Butterworth, B., & Semenza, C. (1995). Constructing subject-verb agreement in speech: The role of semantic and morphological factors. *Journal of Memory and Language, 34*, 186–215.

Vigliocco, G., Hartsuiker, R. J., Jarema, G., & Kolk, H. H. J. (1996). How many labels on the bottles? Notional concord in Dutch and French. *Language and Cognitive Processes, 11*, 407–421.

20

Evaluation and Revision

CHARLES A. MACARTHUR

U sing hyperspectral imaging, preservation scientists at the Library of Congress investigating Thomas Jefferson's original draft of the Declaration of Independence recently discovered that his initial wording of the phrase "our fellow citizens" had been "our fellow subjects" (Kaufman, 2010). This change from "subjects" of a distant monarch to "citizens" responsible to one another captures the essence of the revolutionary change taking place at that time in government. It also illustrates the importance of revision for mature writers seeking to get their meaning and style right to meet their rhetorical purposes.

From a theoretical perspective, any understanding of the cognitive processes involved in writing must include revision because writers, at least proficient writers, devote substantial time and effort to evaluating and revising their work. When writers revise, they consider whether they have met their goals for communicating with an audience, refine the style of their prose, and explore their topics in ways that may affect their own understanding. In contrast to proficient writers, inexperienced or developing writers engage in relatively little substantive revision. They revise primarily to correct surface errors and make minor changes at the local sentence level. Furthermore, when asked to revise more, they may not improve their writing. Substantial research has investigated the cognitive processes involved in revising, with the broad goals of understanding the role of revision in expert writing and how it changes as writers develop knowledge and expertise.

Revision is also a major focus of writing instruction. Aware of the importance of revising, instructors have long sought to improve writing skills by providing feedback and encouraging multiple cycles of revision. From an instructional perspective, revision is important for two reasons. First, students need to learn to revise because it is a critical aspect of skilled composing. Second, revision provides an opportunity for teachers to provide instruction and guidance about the qualities of effective writing in ways that will not only improve the current piece but also transfer to future writing tasks. Instruction in revision helps students learn to evaluate their writing, solve common writing problems, and learn about all aspects of writing from sentence structure to organization to style.

The purpose of this chapter is to explore how cognitive psychology has contributed to an understanding of revision in ways that have influenced writing instruction or that have potential to improve instruction. The chapter begins with a general review of how revision has been explained in major cognitive models of the writing processes. In the course of this review, the chapter addresses how revision has been defined, how to account for the wide variation in types of revision, and why inexperienced writers engage in so little revision. The chapter then turns to research on instruction in evaluation and revision, which has often been motivated by understandings from cognitive research. Instructional approaches considered include feedback from teachers, peers, or computers; instruction in evaluation criteria; strategy instruction; and learning to take the perspective of readers. A concluding section focuses on directions for future research and practice.

It is fitting that this chapter should appear in a book intended, in part, to honor the contributions to cognitive research in writing by John Hayes because the most prominent models of revision have been developed by Hayes and his colleagues. Three decades ago, Hayes and Flower (1980) outlined a model of the cognitive processes involved in writing that included planning, translating, and reviewing. Shortly thereafter, Hayes, Flower, Schriver, Stratman, and Carey (1987) developed a more detailed operational model of revision as a goal-directed problem-solving process involving evaluation, strategy selection, and actual changes to text. Later, Hayes (1996) developed a new model of writing processes, including revision processes, which was more consistent with research on other cognitive processes. He has continued to reflect on and revise his models in significant ways that have incorporated more recent research and perspectives (e.g., Hayes, 2004). Other researchers have also made important contributions to understanding revision processes, but all of the substantial cognitive research on revision in the past 30 years owes a direct debt to Hayes's work.

COGNITIVE MODELS OF REVISION: DEFINITION OF REVISION

As a cognitive process, revision has generally been defined quite broadly to include changes, or consideration of changes, at any point in the composing process to text or plans, whether already written or represented mentally (Fitzgerald, 1987; Hayes, 2004). There has been some discussion of alternative terminology. Bereiter and Scardamalia (1987) used the term "reprocessing" for mental processes and reserved the term revision for actual changes. Allal (2004) suggested using revision for the cognitive processes and the term "transformations" for actual changes. Rijlaarsdam, Couzijn, and van den Bergh (2004) proposed limiting revision to evaluation of already written text; evaluation of plans and evaluation of sentences during drafting would be part of planning and formulation, respectively. However, most researchers have used the broader definition. The key elements included in all definitions are evaluation and consideration of alternatives. Evaluation is most often described as a problem-solving process focused on evaluating discrepancies between the author's intentions and the actual text, though some conceptions of revision include discovery of new opportunities and ideas as well as identification and resolution of problems (Galbraith & Torrance, 2004; Hayes, 1996; Murray, 1978). The broad definition of revision processes would potentially encompass any evaluation included in the writing process. For example, writers evaluate and revise their plans, consider and evaluate alternate wordings of sentences before writing them down, more or less automatically correct some minor errors, and reflect on sections of text or the whole text with the intention of improving it. In addition, coauthors and editors also evaluate and revise texts. All of these various activities involving evaluation and consideration of alternatives fall under the broad defini- tion of revision. Although these activities have many similarities, they also have many differences. Revision processes vary considerably based on factors such as writing task and context, overall approach to writing, time in the writing process, level of text, knowledge of writing and content, understanding of revision, and writ- ing development. Descriptive models of revision need to account for this wide vari- ation. This issue will be discussed further after a brief review of cognitive models.

MAJOR COGNITIVE MODELS

Hayes

Hayes and Flower (1980) were the first to use think-aloud protocol methods from cognitive psychology to study writing as a problem-solving process. That still influ- ential model of the cognitive processes in writing included reviewing, which was proposed as a major process parallel to planning and translating. Writing was mod- eled as a recursive process in that any process could interact with or interrupt any other process at any time. For example, writers might interrupt translating to evaluate their text and consider changes; this evaluation might lead back to revi- sions in the overall plan. They described two different types of revision. *Editing* was described as a process of more or less automatic detection of problems fol- lowed by revision. *Reviewing* was described as an intentional reflective activity involving systematic evaluation of the text, or part of it, with the goal of improve- ment. In such reviewing, writers read their text and apply evaluation criteria (e.g., coherence, clarity, syntax). Hayes (2004) later discussed these two discrepant descriptions as a problem in the model, but it seems more appropriate to accept both as common types of revision (Rijlaarsdam et al., 2004). That is, expert writers detect some problems almost automatically while rereading, but other problems, and opportunities, require careful evaluation and reflection. Pertinent to issues about defining revision, it is also worth noting that this model included evaluation as a component of planning processes: The goal-setting process included setting evaluation criteria for the product, and the generating and organizing processes included evaluation of ideas generated and their arrangement, respectively. In studying the overall writing process, it is important to identify the role that evalua- tion and consideration of alternatives play within other major processes.

Hayes et al. (1987) developed a more elaborated model of revision based on continued research with expert and not-so-expert writers. In this model, revision processes include task definition, evaluation, and strategy selection, as well as actual modifications to the text. First, the task definition sets the goals and scope of revision as well as procedures for the particular occasion (e.g., fix grammatical errors, check a paragraph for coherence, review the whole paper using multiple criteria). Second, evaluation is described as an extended version of reading comprehension processes. Comprehension is modeled as based on processing text at all levels from the word and sentence to the gist and author's perspective. Revision begins with reading, and some problems will be detected because they are barriers to comprehension. In addition, revision involves reading to evaluate and define problems. Evaluation draws on the reviser's knowledge about evaluation criteria in general and goals for the particular piece. Evaluation can range from simply detecting problems to more complete diagnosis of the problems. Third, revision involves selection of strategies for dealing with problems. Strategies range from ignoring problems or delaying action to rewriting the text or revising particular problems to modifying the plans for the paper. Finally, having decided to make a change, writers modify their text or their plans. With its focus on evaluation as an expanded version of reading, this model is most appropriate for revision of already written texts.

In 1996 Hayes presented a revised cognitive model of writing intended to connect writing processes more consistently with other cognitive research. The model redefines revision as a composite of critical reading, reflection, and text production, all guided by a task schema. The new model removes revision as a basic process but preserves the components of the 1987 model. Task definition is elaborated as a task schema that includes overall goals for revising, expected activities, subgoals for what aspects of the text to consider, evaluation criteria, and typical strategies for resolving problems. Critical reading to evaluate the text is still at the heart of the revision process. However, evaluation is expanded to include not only detection of problems, as in the previous model, but also discovery of opportunities to improve the text. For example, in considering a problem of insufficient explanation a writer might discover a new example of the concept or an important exception to an idea. The inclusion of discovery as part of revision makes the model more consistent with approaches to writing that involve using multiple drafts to generate and refine ideas (e.g., Galbraith & Torrance, 2004). Strategy selection is replaced with more general reflective processes, including problem solving and decision making. Text production remains an important process that influences the success of any revision.

The models developed by Hayes and colleagues, based on think-aloud protocols, mentioned that revision could occur during planning and drafting as well as when reviewing text already written. Chenoweth and Hayes (2001, 2003) investigated the cognitive demands of evaluation and revision during drafting of sentences. In the latter study, they had adults write single sentences describing cartoons under different memory-interference conditions and with previous text visible or invisible. When adults could see the text they had written so far, they took longer to compose the sentences but made fewer errors. The time difference and errors were explained by an increase in revisions when they could see the text. The results demonstrate that substantial revision goes on even at the sentence-writing level.

Bereiter and Scardamalia

Also making significant contributions to understanding revision as part of their overall study of writing development were Bereiter and Scardamalia (1987). Their model of revision (Scardamalia & Bereiter, 1983) included three components: compare, diagnose, and operate (CDO). Writers first compare the actual text with their intentions. If a mismatch is detected, they diagnose the problem. Based on the diagnosis, they operate by choosing a tactic for revision and making the actual change. The limited revision of young and inexperienced writers might be explained by difficulties with any of these three components or by limited self-regulation for coordinating revision with the rest of composing. To test the model, they ran a simulation experiment with elementary and middle school students. They provided procedural facilitation to guide students through the hypothesized process. After reading each sentence, students selected one of several cards with general evaluations on them (compare), explained their selection (diagnose), selected one of several cards with tactics for revision, and made revisions (operate). Overall, the students made more revisions than would be expected without the procedural facilitation, and a slight majority of revisions were rated as making the paper better rather than worse, but there was no improvement in rated quality of the papers. The authors concluded that poor self-regulation was one factor limiting revision. Comparing the choices of evaluative cards, diagnostic explanations, and selected tactics for revising made by students with choices made by an experienced writer, they found that students were relatively successful with detecting overall problems but had considerable difficulty with detailed evaluation and making actual improvements.

Graham (1997) replicated this study with sixth-grade students with writing difficulties using an experimental design and found similar results. One explanation for the relatively few meaning-changing revisions and lack of improvement in overall quality in both of these studies is that the CDO procedure focused on sentence-level evaluation. De La Paz, Swanson, and Graham (1998) repeated the study, adding procedural facilitation for evaluating and revising the overall content and organization prior to sentences. Students were prompted with evaluation criteria that asked them about the overall text (e.g., "too few ideas," "ignores obvious point against my ideas"). With this support, students made more revisions of larger segments of text and improved the overall quality of their texts. Like Scardamalia and Bereiter, Graham and colleagues interpreted the results as support for the idea that weak self-regulation explains limited revision. However, the procedural support included provision of evaluation criteria, so another plausible explanation is that immature writers lack knowledge of evaluation criteria.

Bereiter and Scardamalia's (1987) dual models of the overall writing process—knowledge-telling and knowledge-transforming—are also relevant for understanding evaluation and revision. The knowledge-telling model describes writing as a relatively straightforward process in which writers use content and genre requirements to generate ideas they check for appropriateness and then write down. The process repeats until the composition is judged to be complete. The knowledge-telling model works reasonably well for knowledge that is already well organized in the writer's mind. It is characteristic of immature writers in part because it simplifies the overall composing process. In the knowledge-telling process, revision is limited primarily to evaluation of the appropriateness of content and to surface revisions.

In contrast, the knowledge-transforming model explains writing as a goal-directed, problem-solving process in which interaction between content problems and rhetorical problems leads writers to evaluate and revise their understanding. For example, in puzzling about how to explain a concept to a particular audience, a writer may further analyze that concept and discover something new about it. Composing under the knowledge-transforming model depends centrally on evaluation and revision. Writers evaluate the coherence of their content and the effectiveness of their communication and revise not only their written text but also their own understanding of the content and knowledge about effective communication. Although Bereiter and Scardamalia (1987) acknowledge that knowledge telling is sometimes used by proficient writers dealing with familiar tasks, the contrast between knowledge telling and knowledge transforming was primarily intended to explain differences between immature and proficient writers.

Galbraith and Torrance

Galbraith and Torrance (2004) have drawn a different contrast between two dramatically different approaches to composing in which both approaches are characterized as mature, effective approaches. One approach is a planning approach that resembles the model of expert writing of Hayes and Flower (1980). Writers engage in substantial planning to establish goals and select and organize content prior to writing. The other approach they call interactive and describe as similar to freewriting (Elbow, 1998). Freewriting involves writers working out what they have to say in the course of multiple drafts. Revision is substantially different in these two approaches. The models of revision developed by Hayes et al. (1987) and Bereiter and Scardamalia (1987) fit within an overall planning model of writing. In a freewriting approach, writers produce an initial draft to explore their ideas. Revision is a process of evaluation to identify valued ideas in the initial draft for exploration in further drafts. This perspective on revision is what Murray (1978) was thinking of when he defined revision as "what the writer does after a draft is completed to understand and communicate what has begun to appear on the page" (p. 87). In addition to accounts of professional writers (Murray, 1978), there is evidence of individual differences in composing processes, with some writers using a freewriting, multiple-draft strategy and others using a rhetorical planning strategy (Galbraith, 1996). Galbraith found that preferences for planning versus freewriting approaches are correlated with writers' tendency to monitor the effects of their writing on others, with high self-monitors engaging in extensive planning and evaluation and low self-monitors preferring a freewriting strategy. Revision processes within a freewriting approach have not been described in detail.

COGNITIVE VARIATIONS IN REVISION PROCESSES

Revision processes vary widely based on factors including contextual factors (topic, audience, genre), process factors (overall approach to writing, time in the writing process, level of text being evaluated), and individual factors (knowledge of writing and content, understanding of revision, writing development). From an instructional perspective, a useful model of revision needs to explain the variations, connect them to other writing processes, and help to explain writing outcomes. A few variations are considered here.

Contextual Factors

The social context for writing and the nature of writing tasks are important factors in determining the amount and type of revision. Though cognitive models do include context, this issue comes more from a sociocultural framework (Freedman, 1985; Prior, 2006). Because writing is a reciprocal process between writers and readers (Nystrand, 1986), revision is affected by anticipation of audience and actual responses from readers. From a cognitive perspective, writers set goals for communication that influence all aspects of composing including revision. Proficient writers generally have ample experience writing for authentic purposes to real audiences, whereas inexperienced writers are generally students who may not have had such experiences. School tasks may be too isolated from an authentic audience and purpose for students to have much interest in improving them once they are complete. The lack of real readers takes away much of the rhetorical or communicative purpose that drives the revision of more experienced writers. Thus, when students are asked to revise, they have little conception of how to do it.

Process Factors

Of the many cognitive process factors that influence the nature of revision, three are considered here: level of text, time in the writing process, and overall approach to the composing process. Revision varies based on the level of text evaluated. Hayes (2004) noted the difference between automatic correction of minor errors and reflective review of larger sections of text. The most prominent difference between proficient and inexperienced writers is that inexperienced writers tend to limit their revision to correction of errors and minor local changes (Fitzgerald, 1987; MacArthur, Graham, & Schwartz, 1991; McCutchen, Francis, & Kerr, 1997). Hayes's model of revision includes a model of reading comprehension with multiple levels of text, but we do not know a great deal about what guides proficient writers to focus on one level or another.

Revision also differs based on the time in the writing process and the other processes going on at the time. Scardamalia and Bereiter (1986) wrote that editing a sentence during writing involves the same cognitive processes as editing one afterward, but this is not at all obvious. Even as simple a thing as whether the text already written is visible makes a difference to sentence revision (Chenoweth & Hayes, 2003). When revising a sentence that is already part of a larger text, writers have access to a fuller representation of its meaning and the sentences both before and after the one being considered. Rijlaarsdam et al. (2004; Rijlaarsdam & van den Bergh, 2006) presented good evidence that the timing of processes within the overall time of composing, including the processes of evaluation and revision, is connected to the quality of final papers. A common recommendation in education settings is to focus on planning and text generation at first, delaying revision until later so it does not interfere with those other processes. To judge whether such a strategy makes sense, information about the timing of revision and its connection to text quality is needed.

In addition, revision differs rather dramatically depending on the overall approach to composing. The difference between the knowledge-telling and knowledge-transforming approaches to writing provides one explanation for the contrast between expert and novice writers in revision. Under the knowledge-transforming approach, writers revise their ideas in an attempt to explain them to imagined readers. The difference between a freewriting, multiple-draft approach and an advance-planning approach also leads to substantial differences in revision processes (Galbraith & Torrance, 2004). In fact, the primary rationale for freewriting is to get ideas down freely without interference from excessive evaluation. From an instructional perspective, it is important to think about how planning interacts with evaluation and revision.

Individual Factors

Perhaps the most important factors influencing revision are individual knowledge of writing and content, understanding of revision, and overall writing development. Inexperienced writers engage in minimal substantive revision, and when they are asked to revise, the changes they make often make the paper worse (Fitzgerald, 1987; MacArthur, Schwartz, & Graham, 1991). An understanding of the reasons for limited revision is important in designing instruction.

One possibility is that inexperienced writers have a limited task schema, or goals, for revision, that is, they do not understand that revision means more than correcting errors in surface features of text. In Hayes's later model (1996), the task schema includes overall goals for revising, expected activities, subgoals for what aspects of the text to consider, evaluation criteria, and typical strategies for resolving problems. Wallace and Hayes (1991; Wallace et al., 1996) induced college freshmen to engage in more global revision simply by providing them with an 8-min demonstration of revision. Graham, MacArthur, and Schwartz (1995) gave fifth- and sixth-grade students with writing problems enhanced goals for revision that asked them to add details to make their personal narrative more interesting and to fix anything that might not be clear. Compared to a group that received the general goal to improve their paper, these students made more substantive revisions and produced final drafts rated higher in quality. Midgette, Haria, and MacArthur (2008) gave fifth- and eighth-grade students either content goals or audience-awareness goals for revising persuasive essays. Students given the content or audience goals, in contrast to students given a general goal, made more substantive revisions and improved the quality of their papers. Those in the audience goal condition revised their papers to address potential opposing arguments. In both of the goal-setting studies, the enhanced revision goals were included in directions taking less than 2 min to deliver, and no examples were included. In all of these studies, very brief interventions successfully expanded students' understanding of the purpose of revision to encompass more substantive, global revisions.

The research on the modified CDO procedure discussed above (De La Paz et al., 1998) also supports the importance of overall goals or task schema for revision. This study added procedural facilitation for global revision prior to sentence-level revision and found that students made global revisions and improved the quality of their writing. This study involved more intervention than the goal-setting or task-demonstration studies, but the change in outcomes when adding facilitation for global revision supports the importance of a task schema or goals for revision. The clear implication for instruction is to focus students' attention on global revision.

A common feature across the goal-setting, task schema, and CDO studies is the provision of evaluation criteria. The prompting cards in the CDO studies were primarily evaluation criteria (e.g., from De La Paz et al., 1998, p. 451: "Ignores obvious point against my idea." "Part of the essay doesn't belong with the rest."). The goals in the goal-setting studies can be interpreted as evaluation goals (e.g., from Midgette et al., 2008, p. 138: "Think whether your reasons are clearly supported with examples or evidence." "Think about how you would defend your opinion and show that [people who disagree] are wrong."). The task schema studies demonstrated global revision in ways that referred to evaluation criteria. Of course, revision depends on evaluation, but it is interesting that revision can be affected so readily by directing students' attention to specific evaluation criteria. Evaluation criteria may be a critical aspect of the goal-structure or task schema for revision. If so, then instruction in evaluation criteria should have a positive impact on revision and writing quality, and instructional research has confirmed this hypothesis, as discussed later in the chapter.

Another possible explanation for limited revision is lack of audience awareness or difficulty in taking the perspective of potential readers. Think-aloud protocols of expert writing include frequent consideration of audience during both planning and revising (Hayes & Flower, 1980; Hayes et al., 1987), and cognitive models of writing (Bereiter & Scardamalia, 1987; Hayes & Flower, 1980; Hayes, 1996) include audience awareness as a prominent feature of expert composing. Proficient writers set rhetorical goals for communicating with an audience and use those goals in evaluating and revising their work. Learning to take the perspective of others is a challenging task for children and adolescents (Flavell, 1992) that affects writing (Clark & Delia, 1977). Writers' own understanding of the meaning of their writing may interfere with seeing comprehension problems that readers might have. Delaying revision for a few days or weeks can sometimes help readers to gain distance and see problems that were not evident at first (Daneman & Stainton, 1993). Instructional research, discussed later in the chapter, has explored the effects of giving writers experience as readers on their ability to revise.

In addition to motivation, task schema or goals for revision, and audience awareness, inexperienced writers may have difficulty with the specific skills and processes involved in revision. Models of revision processes include critical reading and evaluation of text along with generation of alternatives. Revising requires all the skills involved in reading comprehension plus application of evaluation criteria. To revise the text as a whole, writers must construct the gist of the text by attending to the main ideas and organization. To identify problems of clarity, they need sensitivity to how words and syntax convey meaning. Once writers have identified problems and diagnosed the source of the problem, they still need to generate alternative possibilities, drawing on and applying their writing skills. In addition, they need to regulate the entire process, considering alternatives in contrast to the current text in the context of the entire piece. Thus, revision is demanding of self-regulation skills, as demonstrated in the CDO studies (Graham, 1997; Scardamalia & Bereiter, 1983) Self-regulation is an important aspect of performance in most complex areas, including writing (Schunk & Zimmerman, 2007). The development of self-regulation strategies has been a significant aspect of instructional research.

In summary, research has supported a number of explanations for the limited revision of novice writers. Their goals, or task schema, for revision may be limited to correcting surface errors. They may not be able to evaluate texts due to limited knowledge of evaluation criteria for good writing. They may have difficulty taking on the perspective of a reader to see problems in their own text. They might notice problems but not be able to diagnose or fix them. Evaluation and revision may overtax limited working memory and self-regulation because so much effort is required for idea generation and transcription. They may not have clear purposes for their writing to use in evaluation. They may not be motivated to engage in the extra effort needed to revise an already completed paper. Effective instruction in writing and revising needs to take all of these factors into account.

INSTRUCTIONAL RESEARCH IN REVISION

This section reviews research on several approaches to instruction in evaluation and revision. Traditional approaches, such as instructor feedback and peer feedback, predate cognitive research on writing by centuries, but have nonetheless been influenced by research on writing processes. Approaches such as instruction in evaluation criteria, providing experience as readers, and strategy instruction build more directly on the cognitive research.

Feedback and Revision

The most common approach to teaching writing, in college composition courses, in high school English classes, and in elementary school process-writing approaches, is to provide feedback to students and engage them in writing multiple revisions. The feedback has been provided by teachers, by peers, or, more recently, by computers. Substantial research has investigated the effectiveness of teacher feedback (Beach & Friedrich, 2006). In his meta-analysis of writing instruction research 20 years ago, Hillocks (1986) reviewed the research on teacher-written feedback and concluded that it was generally ineffective. Descriptive research indicates that much teacher feedback is too general and focused on surface features to be able to help students with substantive revision (e.g., Smith, 1997). Students may not understand teachers' comments, or brief written comments may simply not provide sufficient support for students.

On the other hand, conclusions about the overall effects of teacher feedback may not be a valid guide to practice. Rather, it is important to understand how the type and quality of teacher written and oral feedback affects students' writing. A substantial body of research, most of it qualitative-interpretive in method, has analyzed the types of feedback provided and student responses to feedback. Based on a review of the literature, Beach and Friedrich (2006) drew a number of general conclusions: Effective feedback guides students in understanding the rhetorical demands of the writing task and helps students develop their self-assessment ability. It is also supportive and encouraging. Students prefer feedback that is explanatory and suggests ways of making improvements, and they are more successful in using such feedback in revising. Feedback on students' ideas and arguments may be provided more effectively in conferences where there is more opportunity for discussion.

Frequent feedback, or response, from teachers and peers is one key aspect of process approaches to writing instruction (Pritchard & Honeycutt, 2006). There is evidence that the process approach is generally effective when combined with professional development for teachers. A meta-analysis of writing instruction research for adolescents (Graham & Perin, 2007) found a moderate positive effect for process approaches with professional development (Cohen's $d = 0.45$). However, without professional development, it had only a small effect in Grades 4 to 6 and none in Grades 7 to 12. Of course, it might not be the feedback that causes the effect. Process approaches include many features, such as writing for real audiences and purposes, extended time for writing in class, and guidance in planning as well as revision.

Peer Review   Peer feedback is a common feature of writing instruction at all educational levels. Peers can provide feedback that is more frequent, extensive, and immediate than teachers. Even though peers might not have the expertise of teachers about writing or content, they may be able to detect and explain problems that writers cannot see themselves. In addition, peers may be seen more as readers providing response, compared to teachers who are seen as authorities evaluating the text. Rouiller (2004) found in a series of metacognitive interviews about revision that sixth-grade writers working collaboratively defined revision as a reconceptualization of writing, whereas sixth graders writing independently defined revision as error correction.

Furthermore, most peer review is reciprocal, with pairs or small groups of students commenting on one another's papers. Students may learn as much from giving reviews as from receiving them. Peer review engages reviewers in the cognitive processes of revising, including reading critically to detect and diagnose problems and generating potential solutions (Bereiter & Scardamalia, 1987; Hayes et al., 1987). Peer reviewing requires students to engage in a process of giving explanations, which has been shown to enhance learning in collaborative situations (Cohen, 1994). What students learn from evaluating and suggesting revisions for others may transfer to their own writing.

On the other hand, peer review presents potential difficulties as well. Students may not know how to help one another for all the reasons that they have difficulty revising their own work (e.g., focusing on surface errors). They may also be reluctant to criticize one another for social reasons or reluctant to accept feedback from their peers. Thus, training in revision and in peer interaction may be critical to the success of peer review.

Reviews of research on the effects of peer review have been conducted at the adolescent and college levels. In their meta-analysis on effective writing instruction for adolescents, Graham and Perin (2007) reported positive effects ($d = 0.75$) for peer collaboration, defined as peers working together on any stage of the writing process. All of the studies reviewed included peer evaluation for revision, but some also included assistance with planning and drafting. To give one example, Boscolo and Ascorti (2004) worked with classrooms at Grades 4, 6, and 8, teaching students to work in pairs to evaluate each other's personal narratives, looking particularly for problems of clarity. Students who practiced peer review, compared to those who only received teacher feedback, wrote personal narratives with fewer information gaps and identified more problems of clarity in standard papers.

Topping's (1998) review of peer assessment at the college level included peer review in writing. He described the literature as voluminous but largely descriptive. He reviewed eight studies in composition or technical writing classes and four in second-language (L2) writing classes that included writing outcome measures and concluded that peer assessment can yield outcomes as good as teacher assessment and sometimes better. He also reported that peer assessment results were generally reliable and valid; 18 of 25 studies that analyzed data on teacher and peer quantitative evaluations found relatively high correlations. A more recent study (Cho, 2004; Cho & MacArthur, 2010) compared three feedback conditions in a college course: teacher, single peer, or multiple peers. Students who received feedback from multiple peers wrote higher quality final drafts than those in either other condition.

Training in evaluation and review processes appears to be critical to successful peer review (Beach & Friedrich, 2006; Topping, 1998). In an experimental study with L2 classes, Berg (1999) found that students trained in peer review processes, compared to control students, made more substantive revisions and improved the quality of final drafts. In an experimental study of college composition courses (Zhu, 1995), all students received general training in peer review but some received additional guided practice in effective reviewing; the more highly trained students provided more total feedback to their peers as well as more suggestions that were specific and addressed global issues. The effects of training are also important in helping peers provide reliable and valid evaluations. Cho, Schunn, and Wilson (2006) investigated the validity and reliability of peer-generated writing grades of 708 students across 16 different courses from 4 universities in which students received training in using an evaluation rubric and incentives to take the assessment task seriously. They found that the aggregate ratings of at least four peers on a piece of writing were both highly reliable and as valid as instructor ratings.

Most research has focused on the effects of peer review on the recipients of feedback, but two studies were found that investigated the effects on reviewers of giving feedback. Lundstrom and Baker (2009) randomly assigned students in college L2 writing classes to either give feedback to peers or to receive it for a full semester. The students who gave feedback made greater gains in writing from the beginning to the end of the semester. Cho and MacArthur (in press) randomly assigned undergraduate students in a physics class to reviewing, reading, or no-treatment control conditions. Reviewers rated and commented on three papers of varying quality written by peers. Readers read the same papers without commenting. All students then wrote a paper in the same genre but on a different topic. Students in the reviewing condition significantly outperformed those in both other conditions on the quality of the report. Follow-up analysis indicated that comments coded as "problem detection" and "solution suggestions" were positively correlated with writing outcomes for students in the reviewing condition.

Computer Feedback   Some initial research has investigated the use of automated essay scoring (AES) systems to provide feedback to students. AES systems are used to rate quality in some large-scale writing assessments, and a growing body of research supports their reliability and validity for this purpose (Shermis, Burstein, & Leacock, 2006). A few studies have investigated the use of AES systems to provide frequent feedback to students as part of instruction. Questions pertain to the validity of the feedback, its comprehensibility and usefulness to students, and its effects on revision and writing quality. Two studies examined the effects of a program designed to help students write summaries by giving them feedback on content coverage and length. Students who received the feedback spent longer revising their work and received higher content and quality scores than students who worked without feedback (Franzke, Kintsh, Caccamise, Johnson, & Dooley, 2005; Wade-Stein & Kintsch, 2004).

In a recent study (Moore & MacArthur, 2008), qualitative methods were used to study the use of AES in two middle school classrooms. The AES system provided students with scores on an analytic scale and written suggestions, as well as specific feedback on grammatical and spelling errors. The study included classroom observation, interviews, and a think-aloud protocol session with each student making revisions to an essay. Students were highly motivated by the scores and engaged in frequent revision to improve their scores. On the other hand, students generally did not understand the feedback they received. Instead, in making revisions, students most often used the relatively simple criteria that they had learned from their teacher and peer evaluation sessions. Students' dominant revision strategy was to add more information or details for the purpose of clarifying their main points for the reader. Overall, the students liked using the system and were motivated to revise to improve their scores; however, they did not really understand or effectively use the feedback from the system. These problems may be resolved by better system design or better integration with classroom instruction.

TEACHING OF EVALUATION CRITERIA

One direct approach to improving revision skills is to teach students to evaluate their writing using specific evaluation criteria and then to revise their papers based on the evaluation. This approach draws directly on cognitive models that explain revision as a process of evaluation and generation of alternatives. Theoretically motivated research on goals for revision, task schema, and procedural facilitation were discussed in the section on individual factors influencing revision. All the experimental treatments in these studies involved providing participants with evaluation criteria, and one interpretation of the results is that the ability to apply evaluation criteria is critical to substantive revision.

Hillocks's (1986) meta-analysis of writing instruction included six studies in which students learned evaluation criteria and practiced applying the criteria to make revisions; the approach had moderately strong effects on revision and writing quality. The Boscolo and Ascorti (2004) study, mentioned earlier, taught students to look for problems of clarity in peers' personal narratives. Beal, Garrod, and Bonitatibus (1990) taught a process of reading comprehension focused specifically on looking for problems caused by missing information in manipulated texts and then found transfer to improved revision of texts with similar information problems. The limited research available suggests that it is important to teach specific evaluation criteria rather than general criteria such as content and organization. The limited research on teaching general analytical criteria, such as content and organization, has found very limited effects (Andrade & Boulay, 2003). Instruction in evaluation criteria is a critical component of strategy instruction in revision, considered in the next section.

STRATEGY INSTRUCTION

One of the most often studied approaches to teaching revision is cognitive strategy instruction. In strategy instruction in writing, students learn discourse knowledge and cognitive processes for applying that knowledge in meaningful writing tasks. The strategies to be taught are derived from research on the cognitive processes of proficient writers. Instruction involves a combination of explicit explanation, think-aloud modeling, guided or collaborative practice, and independent practice, often with additional self-regulation components (MacArthur, in press). Two recent meta-analytic reviews of writing instruction research found large effect sizes for strategy instruction in general (Graham, 2006; Graham & Perin, 2007). Graham's review (2006) included six studies that taught revision strategies and another five that taught revision in combination with planning. He found large and consistent effects of strategy instruction on the amount of revision and writing quality. Most of the studies combined teaching evaluation criteria with strategy instruction in the processes for applying those criteria in making revisions. For example, Graham and MacArthur (1988) taught students with learning disabilities a strategy for revising persuasive essays that focused their attention on specific criteria such as whether they had stated their position clearly, whether each reason was connected to the position, and whether they could add further reasons or examples. Following instruction, students made more substantive revisions and improved the quality of their essays. MacArthur and his colleagues (MacArthur, Schwartz, & Graham, 1991; Stoddard & MacArthur, 1993) investigated a reciprocal peer revision strategy that combined strategy instruction, peer interaction, instruction in specific evaluation criteria, and word processing. Students worked in pairs taking turns as author and editor with the strategy guiding their interaction. In preparation for the peer review process, students practiced evaluating papers written by unknown students and making revisions to improve them. Teachers modeled the process of evaluation and revision using think-aloud modeling and then provided extensive guided practice. In both studies, students made more substantive revisions and improved the quality of their papers as a result of instruction both on papers revised with peer support and on transfer to revision without support.

Several studies have investigated instruction that included both strategies for planning and strategies for revision that were conceptually linked. For example, the cognitive strategies-in-writing program (Englert, Raphael, Anderson, Anthony, & Stevens, 1991) was designed to teach expository writing to upper elementary school students. The planning strategy included graphic organizers for different text structures (e.g., comparison), and the revision strategy included evaluation criteria relevant to the text structures. Instruction emphasized explicit instruction in the strategies, peer collaboration, teacher scaffolding, and extensive dialogue about writing. Students at all ability levels made gains over the course of a year in the quality of their expository writing. No separate results were reported for revision. Combined instruction in planning and revising strategies that were both based on text structure has also been shown to be successful with adult struggling writers (MacArthur & Lembo, 2009).

EXPERIENCE AS READERS AND OBSERVATION OF READERS

The cognitive research on writing suggests that audience awareness is critical to effective revision (Bereiter & Scardamalia, 1987; Hayes & Flower, 1980; Hayes et al., 1987). In contrast to proficient writers, inexperienced writers often proceed with minimal attention to the needs of their readers. They may not see problems with their text because they have difficulty taking the perspective of their readers. Thus, providing writers with experience as readers or with the opportunity to observe readers trying to understand their writing might affect revision.

Several studies have provided writers opportunities to become readers under structured conditions (Holliway & McCutchen, 2004; Traxler & Gernsbacher, 1993). Traxler and Gernsbacher (1993) examined the effects of experience as a reader on college students' writing. Students wrote descriptions of tangrams (abstract geometric figures). Students in a reader group then read others' descriptions and matched them to tangrams, whereas students in a control group read and evaluated descriptions but without attempting to match them to tangrams. All students then revised their descriptions. The readers' revised descriptions received higher quality ratings. Holliway and McCutchen (2004) conducted a similar study with the tangram task with fifth-grade students. In their study, all groups including the controls received feedback on whether readers had been successful in matching their description to a tangram, but only the reader group had the experience of reading and matching descriptions to tangrams. As in the previous study, readers made the greatest improvements in the quality of their revised descriptions.

Another way students can learn about audience is through observing readers model their thinking processes (i.e., think aloud) as they try to comprehend text. In one such study (Couzijn & Rijlaarsdam, 2004), high school students wrote directions for conducting a laboratory experiment, which they revised later after participating in one of several experimental conditions. Some students observed readers think aloud as they attempted to follow the directions, while others received feedback or wrote self-generated comments. Students who observed readers made greater gains in the quality of their written directions, and it did not matter whether the text being read was the writer's own or another student's. The study suggests that observing readers helps writers to develop evaluation criteria for specific writing tasks that they can use in revising their own writing. Although these studies are interesting, both the tangram and the science instruction experiments were limited in that the writing task involved a very concrete and specific goal, whereas most writing tasks are less well defined.

Two studies have investigated the effects both of experience as a reader and of observing readers using more common types of writing tasks. Rijlaarsdam and Braaksma (as cited in Rijlaarsdam et al., 2008) asked junior high students to write a persuasive letter to a candy company. A group of students simulating a review board (readers) at the company read several letters and discussed which one was the most persuasive. Another group simulating researchers (observers) took notes, discussed the evaluation criteria used by the board, and presented their findings to the class. Then all students revised their own letters. Both groups improved the quality of their letters, but the observers improved more. This study did not include any analysis of revisions.

Moore and MacArthur (2011) asked fifth-grade students to write persuasive letters to their principals. Then small groups of readers discussed and evaluated a set of three letters of varying quality from unknown students. Small groups of observers took notes and had a discussion to generate a list of the criteria used by the readers. A control group practiced writing another letter. The readers produced revised drafts that were of better quality and contained more evidence of audience awareness than the controls. The observer group did not differ from either group. Argumentative elements of the letters and revisions were analyzed. In addition, think-aloud procedures were used during revision for a subset of the students, and transcripts of the discussions were analyzed qualitatively. The readers made significantly more revisions that addressed opposing positions and included significantly more elements that addressed opposing positions in their revised papers than control students. Analysis of the think-aloud protocols showed that readers discussed the audience in making revisions. Analysis of the discussions showed that the reader discussions included far more elaboration than observers' discussions.

Both of these studies demonstrate the potential value of providing students with experiences as readers or observers of readers. Common to both of these studies were group discussions focused on evaluation of papers and generation of evaluation criteria. The difference in effects on observers in the two studies may be due to the fact that observers in the Rijlaarsdam and Braaksma study were asked to organize and present their findings to the class, whereas the observers in the Moore and MacArthur study did nothing with their list. The results for both readers and observers seem to depend on the quality of the group analysis of evaluation criteria.

FUTURE DIRECTIONS FOR RESEARCH AND PRACTICE ON REVISING

Research on Cognitive Processes in Revising

Revision has been defined very broadly in writing research to include evaluation and consideration of alternatives at any point in the writing process. As discussed in the section on cognitive processes, revision processes vary widely based on contextual factors (task, audience, goals), other writing processes (time in process, level of text or pretext, overall approach), and individual factors (knowledge of writing, content knowledge, revision schema or goals, writing ability). Future descriptive studies of revision processes should more systematically consider how revision differs based on these factors.

Contextual factors, such as task, audience, and goal, affect writers' revision processes. Proficient writers may be capable of using a knowledge-transforming approach for writing, involving extensive evaluation and revision, when the task involves content knowledge that is not fully formed or important rhetorical considerations. However, Bereiter and Scardamalia (1987) acknowledged that proficient writers might also use a simpler knowledge-telling approach when writing on familiar topics for familiar audiences. Torrance (1996) has questioned whether most professional writing, at least in some fields, is not more like the knowledge-telling approach. Contextual factors also affect revision by developing writers, as shown in the study by Midgette et al. (2008), which gave students content and audience goals for revising. Contextual factors affect not only revision processes, of course, but other writing processes as well.

Revision processes operate in interaction with other writing processes, and, thus, should be studied in relationship to those other writing processes (Rijlaarsdam et al., 2004). Revision processes vary based on what level of text is evaluated and when in the overall process the revision occurs. Hayes (2004) pointed out basic differences in process between more or less automatic editing of errors and reflective review of larger segments of text. Chenoweth and Hayes (2001, 2003) demonstrated that significant amounts of revision occur at the sentence level during text production. Evaluation and revision also occur at the planning stage before actual sentences are formulated (Hayes & Flower, 1980). Galbraith (1996) has pointed out that evaluation and revision processes differ rather dramatically based on the overall approach to composing. Writers using a freewriting approach delay evaluation while writing to explore their ideas, and their evaluation begins as a process of selecting useful ideas from early drafts.

Furthermore, it is important to study variations in revision processes in relationship to their effects on writing quality. More revision is not necessarily better. Rijlaarsdam et al. (2004) have demonstrated that evaluation and revision processes have different effects on writing quality depending on when they occur in relationship to other writing processes. The types of revisions made also affect writing quality. For example, Van den Bergh, Rijlaarsdam, and Breetvelt (1993) found that revisions at the word level were negatively related to quality, whereas revisions at the sentence level were positively related to quality. MacArthur, Schwartz, and

Graham (1991) found similar results in a descriptive study of struggling writers. On the other hand, when developing writers were given more specific goals or evaluation criteria (De La Paz et al., 1998; Midgette et al., 2008), they were able to make more complex revisions that improved quality.

Individual differences in revision processes have drawn the most attention because differences between developing and proficient writers are large. However, not enough is known about how individual differences are affected by contextual factors and relationships with other writing processes. These relationships have potentially important implications for instruction. How important are authentic audiences for development of writing and revising processes? Should developing writers delay revision until after completing a draft? What are the relative benefits of freewriting and extensive preplanning?

Research on Instruction for Revising

In this chapter, instruction in revision was grouped into four categories: feedback from teacher and peers, teaching evaluation criteria, strategy instruction, and experience and readers or observation of readers. Two important factors cut across these categories: learning to use evaluation criteria and feedback or response from others. The most effective approaches combine these two factors.

More than 25 years ago, the meta-analysis by Hillocks (1986) found that teaching students evaluation criteria combined with practice in applying them to improve writing was an effective approach to improving revision and writing quality. Since then, teaching evaluation criteria for revising has been found to be effective in combination with strategy instruction for revising (Graham, 2006) and with peer review (Boscolo & Ascorti, 2004). In essence, these studies more or less directly taught the knowledge and processes included in cognitive models of revision. However, a great deal of work remains on the most effective way to teach evaluation criteria so that students are able to apply them to new writing tasks. Which evaluation criteria can be taught to students at various developmental levels? How specific do the evaluation criteria need to be? Do students learn more when they are involved in generating the evaluation criteria to be used? What is the appropriate relationship between other aspects of instruction and revision instruction? For example, should students learn about organization as part of planning before learning to revise for organization?

Feedback from others ranges on a continuum from authentic responses from readers to more consciously evaluative feedback. Response from readers without any evaluative component is possible with writing tasks with concrete goals, such as directions for a task (e.g., science experiment in Couzijn & Rijlaarsdam, 2004) or descriptions of an object to choose (e.g., tangram in Holliway & McCutchen, 2004). In these cases, writers can learn from observing readers' attempts to carry out the task. On less concrete writing tasks, peers can respond as readers by asking questions when they do not understand something, providing emotional responses, or discussing the content. However, as soon as readers start to comment on a piece of writing (e.g., to say what they like or comment on something that is confusing), an evaluative element is included. Process approaches to writing instruction encourage teachers and peers to respond to writing intuitively as readers, but they also ask teachers and peers to make suggestions for improvement. When peers are asked to provide evaluative feedback, the research indicates that training is important, and this training usually involves instruction in evaluation criteria. Even some of the studies of observing readers included evaluative components. Two studies that compared experience as readers and observing readers (Moore & MacArthur, 2011; Rijlaarsdam et al., 2008) engaged both readers and observers in reading and generating evaluation criteria for persuasive letters.

The research on peer review raises a number of questions for future research. First, is it important that writers receive feedback on their own texts or can they learn from observing or discussing evaluation of others' writing? In the Couzijn and Rijlaarsdam (2004) study, writers learned equally well whether they observed a peer reading their own paper or reading some other student's paper. In the two studies of readers and observers (Moore & MacArthur, 2011; Rijlaarsdam et al., 2008), students learned from evaluating persuasive texts written by other students. In the studies of learning evaluation scales reviewed by Hillocks (1986) and the peer revision strategy studies by MacArthur and his colleagues (MacArthur, Schwartz, & Graham, 1991; Stoddard & MacArthur, 1993), students received extensive practice in evaluating and revising papers written by unknown students before evaluating and revising their own and their peers' papers. If it is effective, learning about evaluation and revision by practicing with papers written by others would be efficient because students can quickly receive practice with multiple papers without the time required to write new papers. Using papers written by others also offers the potential of selecting papers to illustrate particular problems and opportunities.

Second, a related question is how much students can learn by giving feedback to others, alone or in combination with receiving feedback. This question is very important because peer review demands substantial time from students. If students learn from giving as well as receiving feedback, it would be a powerful reason to use peer review procedures rather than relying on teacher feedback. Only two studies were found that addressed this question (Cho & MacArthur, in press; Lundstrom & Baker, 2009), and both found positive effects of giving feedback. Note that both studies included careful procedures to train students in using an evaluation rubric.

The studies with the most consistent positive effects on the quality of writing were those using strategy instruction. Strategy instruction combines teaching evaluation criteria with strategy instruction in the processes for applying those criteria in making revisions. Many of the strategy studies included peer review as an important component or combined planning and revising instruction. Research is needed to systematically study these separate components to see what aspects are critical.

One final point to be made regards the reciprocal relationship between basic cognitive research and instructional research. Educational researchers have drawn on cognitive models to design instructional methods that help students revise more effectively. In return, the instructional research confirms and extends our understanding of the cognitive processes involved. Brief, theoretically motivated interventions have confirmed the theoretical importance of task schema for revision (Wallace et al., 1996), specific goals and evaluation criteria (Graham et al., 1995), audience awareness (Midgette et al., 2008), ability to take the perspective of reader (Holliway & McCutchen, 2004; Moore & MacArthur, 2011; Traxler & Gernsbacher, 1993), and self-regulation (Graham, 1997; Scardamalia & Bereiter, 1983). More extended and practical instructional research has confirmed the importance and value of teaching evaluation criteria (Hillocks, 1986; MacArthur, Graham, & Harris, 2004), peer feedback (Boscolo & Ascorti, 2004), and instruction in cognitive strategies (Graham, 2006). Revision is an important topic for basic cognitive research and for research on improving writing instruction.

REFERENCES

Allal, L. (2004). Integrated writing instruction and the development of revision skills. In L. Allal, L. Chanqouy & P. Largy (Eds.), *Revision: Cognitive and instructional processes* (Vol. 13, pp. 139–155). Boston: Kluwer.

Andrade, H. G., & Boulay, B. A. (2003). Role of rubric-referenced self-assessment in learning to write. *Journal of Educational Research, 97*, 21–34.

Beach, R., & Friedrich, T. (2006). Response to writing. In C. A. MacArthur, S. Graham, & J. Fitzgerald (Eds.), *Handbook of writing research* (pp. 222–234). New York: Guilford.

Beal, C. R., Garrod, A. C., & Bonitatibus, G. J. (1990). Fostering childrens' revision skills through training in comprehension monitoring. *Journal of Educational Psychology, 82*, 275–280.

Bereiter, C., & Scardamalia, M. (1987). *The psychology of written composition.* Hillsdale, NJ: Erlbaum.

Berg, E. C. (1999). The effects of trained peer response on ESL students' revision types and writing quality. *Journal of Second Language Writing, 8*, 215–241.

Boscolo, P., & Ascorti, K. (2004). Effects of collaborative revision on children's ability to write understandable narrative texts. In L. Allal, L. Chanquoy, & P. Largy (Eds.), *Revision: Cognitive and instructional processes* (Vol. 13, pp. 157–170). Boston: Kluwer.

Chenoweth, A., & Hayes, J. R. (2001). Fluency in writing: Generating text in L1 and L2. *Written Communication, 18*, 80–98.

Chenoweth, A., & Hayes, J. R. (2003). The inner voice in writing. *Written Communication, 20*, 99–118.

Cho, K. (2004). *When multi-peers give better advice than an expert: The type and impact of feedback given by students and an expert on student writing.* Unpublished doctoral dissertation, University of Pittsburgh, Pittsburgh, PA.

Cho, K., & MacArthur, C. A. (2010). Student revision with peer and expert reviewing. *Learning and Instruction, 20*, 328–338.

Cho, K., & MacArthur, C. A. (in press). Learning writing by reviewing. *Journal of Educational Psychology.*

Cho, K., Schunn, C. D., & Wilson, R. W. (2006). Validity and reliability of scaffolded peer assessment of writing from instructor and student perspectives. *Journal of Educational Psychology, 98*, 891–901.

Clark, R. A., & Delia, J. G. (1977). Cognitive complexity, social perspective-taking and functional persuasive skills in second- to ninth-grade children. *Human Communication Research, 3*, 128–134.

Cohen, E. G. (1994). Restructuring the classroom: Conditions for productive small groups. *Review of Educational Research, 64*, 1–36.

Couzijn, M., & Rijlaarsdam, G. (2004). Learning to write instructive texts by reader observation and written feedback. In G. Rijlaarsdam, H. van den Bergh, & M. Couzijn (Eds.), *Effective learning and teaching of writing: A handbook of writing in education* (2nd ed., pp. 209–240). New York: Kluwer.

Daneman, M., & Stainton, M. (1993). The generation effect in reading and proofreading. *Reading and Writing, 5,* 297–313.

De La Paz, S., Swanson, H. L., & Graham, S. (1998). The contribution of executive control to the revising by students with writing and learning difficulties. *Journal of Educational Psychology, 90,* 448–460.

Elbow, P. (1998). *Writing without teachers* (2nd ed.). Oxford: Oxford University Press.

Englert, C. S., Raphael, T. E., Anderson, L. M., Anthony, H. M., & Stevens, D. D. (1991). Making writing strategies and self-talk visible: Cognitive strategy instruction in writing in regular and special education classrooms. *American Educational Research Journal, 28,* 337–372.

Fitzgerald, J. (1987). Research on revision in writing. *Review of Educational Research, 57,* 481–506.

Flavell, J. H. (1992). Perspectives on perspective taking. In H. Beilin & P. B. Pufall (Eds.), *Piaget's theory: Prospects and possibilities* (pp. 107–139). Hillsdale, NJ: Erlbaum.

Franzke, M., Kintsch, E., Caccamise, D., Johnson, M., & Dooley, S. (2005). Summary Street: Computer support for comprehension and writing. *Journal of Educational Computing Research, 33,* 53–80.

Freedman, S. W. (Ed.). (1985). *The acquisition of written language: Response and revision.* Norwood, NJ: Ablex.

Galbraith, D. (1996). Self-monitoring, discovery through writing and individual differences in drafting strategy. In G. Rijlaarsdam, H. van den Bergh, & M. Couzijn, (Eds.), *Studies in writing: Vol. 1, Theories, models and methodology in writing research* (pp. 121–144). Amsterdam: Amsterdam University Press.

Galbraith, D., & Torrance, M. (2004). Revision in the context of different drafting strategies. In L. Allal, L. Chanqouy, & P. Largy (Eds.), *Revision: Cognitive and instructional processes* (Vol. 13, pp. 63–85). Boston: Kluwer.

Graham, S. (1997). Executive control in the revising of students with learning and writing difficulties. *Journal of Educational Psychology, 89,* 223–234.

Graham, S. (2006). Strategy instruction and the teaching of writing: A meta-analysis. In C. A. MacArthur, S. Graham, & J. Fitzgerald (Eds.), *Handbook of writing research* (pp. 187–207). New York: Guilford.

Graham, S., & MacArthur, C. (1988). Improving learning disabled students' skills at revising essays produced on a word processor: Self-instructional strategy training. *Journal of Special Education, 22,* 133–152.

Graham, S., MacArthur, C. A., & Schwartz, S. S. (1995). The effects of goal setting and procedural facilitation on the revising behavior and writing performance of students with writing and learning problems. *Journal of Educational Psychology, 87,* 230–240.

Graham, S., & Perin, D. (2007). A meta-analysis of writing instruction for adolescent students. *Journal of Educational Psychology, 99,* 445–476.

Hayes, J. R. (1996). A new framework for understanding cognition and affect in writing. In C. M. Levy & S. Ransdell (Eds.), *The science of writing: Theories, methods, individual differences, and applications* (pp. 1–27). Mahwah, NJ: Erlbaum.

Hayes, J. R. (2004). What triggers revision? In L. Allal, L. Chanqouy, & P. Largy (Eds.), *Revision: Cognitive and instructional processes* (Vol. 13, pp. 9–20). Boston: Kluwer.

Hayes, J. R., & Flower, L. (1980). Identifying the organization of writing processes. In L. W. Gregg & E. R. Steinberg (Eds.), *Cognitive processes in writing: An interdisciplinary approach* (pp. 3–30). Hillsdale, NJ: Erlbaum.

Hayes, J. R., Flower, L., Schriver, K. A., Stratman, J. F., & Carey, L. (1987). Cognitive processes in revision. In S. Rosenberg (Ed.), *Advances in applied psycholinguistics:* Vol. II. *Reading, writing, and language learning* (pp. 176–240). New York: Cambridge University Press.

Hillocks, G. (1986). *Research on written composition: New directions for teaching.* Urbana, IL: ERIC Clearinghouse on Reading and Communication Skills.

Holliway, D. R., & McCutchen, D. (2004). Audience perspective in young writers' composing and revising. In L. Allal, L. Chanqouy, & P. Largy (Eds.), *Revision: Cognitive and instructional processes* (Vol. 13, pp. 87–101). Boston: Kluwer.

Kaufman, M. (2010, July 3). With the stroke of a pen, "subjects" no more. *Washington Post*, pp. A1, A12.

Lundstrom, K., & Baker, W. (2009). To give is better than to receive: The benefits of peer review to the reviewer's own writing. *Journal of Second Language Writing, 18*, 30–43.

MacArthur, C. A. (in press). Strategies instruction. In K. R. Harris, S. Graham, & T. Urdan (Eds.), *Educational psychology handbook:* Vol. 3, *Applications of educational psychology to learning and teaching.* Washington, DC: American Psychological Association.

MacArthur, C. A., Graham, S., & Harris, K. R. (2004). Insights from instructional research on revision with struggling writers. In L. Allal, L. Chanquoy, & P. Largy (Eds.), *Revision: Cognitive and instructional processes* (pp. 125–137). Amsterdam, the Netherlands: Kluwer Academic Press.

MacArthur, C. A., Graham, S., & Schwartz, S. (1991). Knowledge of revision and revising behavior among learning disabled students. *Learning Disability Quarterly, 14*, 61–73.

MacArthur, C. A., & Lembo, L. (2009). Strategy instruction in writing for adult literacy learners. *Reading and Writing, 22*, 1021–1032.

MacArthur, C. A., Schwartz, S. S., & Graham, S. (1991). Effects of a reciprocal peer revision strategy in special education classrooms. *Learning Disabilities Research and Practice, 6*, 201–210.

McCutchen, D., Francis, M., & Kerr, S. (1997). Revising for meaning: Effects of knowledge and strategy. *Journal of Educational Psychology, 89*, 667–676.

Midgette, E., Haria, P., & MacArthur, C. A. (2008). The effects of content and audience awareness goals for revision on the persuasive essays of fifth- and eighth-grade students. *Reading and Writing, 21*, 131–151.

Moore, N., & MacArthur, C. A. (2011). The effects of being a reader and of observing readers on fifth grade students' argumentative writing and revising. *Reading and Writing.* Advance online publication. doi: 10.1007/s11145-011-9327-6

Moore, N., & MacArthur, C. A. (2008, February). *The role of automated essay scoring technology in writing instruction and learning.* Paper presented at the international Writing Research Across Borders Conference, Santa Barbara, CA.

Murray, D. (1978). Internal revision: A process of discovery. In C. Cooper & L. Odell (Eds.), *Research on composing: Points of departure* (pp. 85–103). Urbana, IL: National Council of Teachers of English.

Nystrand, M. (1986). *The structure of written communication: Studies in reciprocity between writers and readers.* New York: Academic Press.

Prior, P. (2006). A sociocultural theory of writing. In C. A. MacArthur, S. Graham, & J. Fitzgerald (Eds.), *Handbook of writing research* (pp. 54–66). New York: Guilford.

Pritchard, R. J., & Honeycutt, R. L. (2006). The process approach to writing instruction: Examining its effectiveness. In C. A. MacArthur, S. Graham, & J. Fitzgerald (Eds.), *Handbook of writing research* (pp. 275–291). New York: Guilford.

Rijlaarsdam, G., Braaksma, M., Couzijn, M., Janssen, T., Raedts, M., Van Steendam, E., … Van den Bergh, H. (2008). Observation of peers in learning to write, Practice and Research. *Journal of Writing Research, 1*(1), 53–83.

Rijlaarsdam, G., Couzijn, M., & van den Bergh, H. (2004). The study of revision as a writing process and as a learning-to-write process: Two prospective research agendas. In L. Allal, L. Chanquoy, & P. Largy (Eds.), *Revision: Cognitive and instructional processes* (Vol. 13, pp. 189–208). New York: Kluwer.

Rijlaarsdam, G., & van den Bergh, H. (2006). Writing process theory: A functional dynamic approach. In C. A. MacArthur, S. Graham, & J. Fitzgerald (Eds.), *Handbook of writing research* (pp. 41–53). New York: Guilford.

Rouiller, Y. (2004). Collaborative revision and metacognitive reflection in a situation of narrative text production. In L. Allal, L. Chanquoy, & P. Largy (Eds.), *Revision: Cognitive and instructional processes* (pp. 171–187). New York: Kluwer.

Scardamalia, M., & Bereiter, C. (1983). The development of evaluative, diagnostic, and remedial capabilities in children's composing. In M. Martlew (Ed.), *The psychology of written language: Development of educational perspectives* (pp. 67–95). London: Wiley.

Scardamalia, M., & Bereiter, C. (1986). Research on written composition. In C. Wittrock (Ed.), *Handbook of research on teaching* (3rd ed., pp. 778–803). New York: Macmillan.

Schunk, D. H., & Zimmerman, B. J. (2007). Influencing children's self-efficacy and self-regulation of reading and writing through modeling. *Reading & Writing Quarterly, 23*, 7–25.

Shermis, M., Burstein, J., & Leacock, C. (2006). Applications of computers in assessment and analysis of writing. In C. A. MacArthur, S. Graham, & J. Fitzgerald (Eds.), *Handbook of writing research* (pp. 403–416). New York: Guilford.

Smith, S. (1997). The genre of the end comment: Conventions in teacher responses to student writing. *College Composition and Communication, 33*, 148–156.

Stoddard, B., & MacArthur, C. A. (1993). A peer editor strategy: Guiding learning disabled students in response and revision. *Research in the Teaching of English, 27*, 76–103.

Topping, K. J. (1998). Peer assessment between students in colleges and universities. *Review of Educational Research, 68*, 249–276.

Torrance, M. (1996). Is writing expertise like other kinds of expertise? In G. Rijlaarsdam, H. van den Bergh, & M. Couzijn (Eds.), *Theories, models and methodology in writing research* (pp. 3–9). Amsterdam: Amsterdam University Press.

Traxler, M., & Gernsbacher, M. (1993). Improving written communication through perspective taking. *Language and Cognitive Process, 8*, 311–334.

Van den Bergh, H., Rijlaarsdam, G., & Breetvelt, I. (1993). Revision process and text quality: An empirical study. In G. Eigler & T. Jechle (Eds.), *Writing: Current trends in European research* (pp. 133–147). Freiburg: Hochschul Verlag.

Wade-Stein, D., & Kintsch, E. (2004). Summary Street: Interactive computer support for writing. *Cognition and Instruction, 22*, 333–362.

Wallace, D. L., & Hayes, J. R. (1991). Redefining revision for freshmen. *Research in the Teaching of English, 25*, 54–66.

Wallace, D. L., Hayes, J. R., Hatch, J. A., Miller, W., Moser, G., & Silk, C. M. (1996). Better revision in eight minutes? Prompting first-year college writers to revise globally. *Journal of Educational Psychology, 88*, 682–688.

Zhu, W. (1995). Effects of training for peer response on students' comments and interaction. *Written Communication, 12*, 492–528.

21

Working Memory in Writing

THIERRY OLIVE

*A*s initially noted by Flower and Hayes (1980), writers' cognitive effort is so high that they may find themselves in mental overload (Kellogg, 1987, 1994; Piolat, Olive, & Kellogg, 2005). This overload is mainly due to the large demands that the writing processes place on the cognitive system (for reviews, see Kellogg, 2008; Kellogg & Raulerson, 2007; Olive, Kellogg, & Piolat, 2002). In other words, the capacity limitation of working memory, which supports cognitive processes, may be reached when composing a text. This relationship between working memory and writing is now well documented (Gathercole & Alloway, 2008; Gathercole & Pickering, 2000a, 2000b; McCutchen, 2000; Olive, 2004; Swanson & Berninger, 1996a, 1996b).

Why is writing supported by working memory? Working memory entails the ability to temporarily store information while it is being manipulated (Baddeley & Hitch, 1974). Working memory thus provides a temporary memory register for storing transient information that results from operations of the writing processes. For example, while writers are transcribing a sentence, they may need to keep in mind an idea that they just thought about. Similarly, they may need to memorize temporarily a long sentence while beginning to write it down. Working memory also has attentional mechanisms for regulating when to activate and process knowledge necessary to compose a text. Working memory is thus the place where writing processes are activated and coordinated and where the writer's representation of the text is constructed and updated. In sum, working memory is the cognitive space where operations of the writing processes take place.

The aims of this chapter are twofold. The first is to provide a brief overview of (a) the main conceptions of working memory, (b) the models of working memory in writing, and (c) the findings that show how working memory is related to writing. The second is to delineate some issues for future research on working memory in writing, which are raised by the evolving models of working memory or by existing writing research. A glossary at the end of this chapter defines the technical terms used in this chapter.

WORKING MEMORY

The influential model of working memory proposed by Baddeley and Hitch (1974) is composed of an attentional system, the central executive, which is aided by two peripheral and code-dependent systems—the phonological loop and the visuospatial sketchpad—that temporarily store information in order to make it available for processing. The phonological loop is specialized for verbal and acoustic information. It is fractionated into a passive and temporary phonological store and an active rehearsal system. The visuospatial sketchpad performs similar functions for visuospatial information. It can be fractionated into a visual component (the visual cache), which passively stores visual information and spatial locations, and an active spatial rehearsal component (the inner scribe), which maintains sequential locations and movements and refreshes information decaying in the visual cache (Logie, 1995). The central executive in this early model was based on the supervisory attentional system model of attentional control developed by Norman and Shallice (2000) to explain how the cognitive system overrides relatively automatic behaviors when a task schema (or routine) is not available.

Evidence for separability of the subsystems of working memory is now abundant. For instance, verbal concurrent tasks affect short-term storage of verbal information but not that of visuospatial information; conversely, maintenance of visuospatial information is disrupted by concurrent visuospatial tasks but not by verbal secondary tasks (Cocchini, Logie, Della Sala, MacPherson, & Baddeley, 2002). Brain-imaging studies also indicate that the right hemisphere supports processing of visual and spatial material, whereas the left hemisphere supports verbal processing (Smith & Jonides, 1997; Smith, Jonides, & Koeppe, 1996; for a review, see Henson, 2001). More precisely, the phonological loop may involve the arcuate fasciculus tract, which connects the Broca and Wernicke areas of the brain (Baddeley, 2007; Catani, Jones, & Ffytche, 2005). For studies showing other regions that may be involved in verbal working memory, see Crosson et al. (1999). Smith and Jonides (1997) provided findings supporting the fractionation of the sketchpad. In a brain-imaging study, they showed that the dorsal areas mediate the visual (or object) working memory, and that ventral areas are activated with spatial working memory tasks. Additionally, single case studies of brain-damaged patients and of those with genetic disorders report selective loss of either verbal or visuospatial short-term memory (Jarrold, Baddeley & Hewes, 1999).

An alternative view of working memory, the capacity conception, is not based on the brain evidence but rather on the functional capacity and considers that a single system with limited resources is used for temporary storage and processing of information in working memory. Because working memory is limited in capacity, tradeoffs exist between the storage and processing capacity. When processing requires more working memory capacity, less capacity is available for storing information, and vice versa. In that perspective, Daneman and Carpenter (1980) found significant correlations between the scores on a sentence span task and reading comprehension. As the sentence span task involved reading processes, they argued that differences found in working memory measures reflected differences in efficiency of the processing component of the task (i.e., reading sentences) and was not due to differences in working memory capacity itself. Daneman and Carpenter thus assumed that working memory capacity is domain specific. Following Daneman and Carpenter, Just and Carpenter (1992) proposed a capacity theory of comprehension that explained individual differences in comprehension in terms of readers' working memory capacity and efficiency of reading processes.

However, a domain-free working memory conception has been supported by Engle and collaborators who have shown that controlling for processing time (Engle, 2002; Engle, Cantor, & Carullo, 1992) or equating demands of the processing component (Conway & Engle, 1996) did not decrease the correlation between verbal working memory span and verbal aptitude tests (see also Turner & Engle, 1989). Accordingly, Cowan (2005) proposed a model of a general and domain-free working memory. In that view, working memory involves several embedded levels: The first level consists of long-term memory representations that are activated by spreading unlimited activation. The second level has a limited focus of attention that holds up to four of the activated representations. Information on which attention is focused constitutes the content of working memory. Oberauer (2002) has also proposed including a third embedded level with a more narrow focus of attention that holds and activates the chunk of information that is processed.

WORKING MEMORY IN WRITING

References to limitations in information processing were present in Hayes and Flower's (1980; Flower & Hayes, 1980) models, even if working memory research was not explicitly mentioned. The research on working memory in writing was developed and expanded in the 1990s and reflected a convergence of research on working memory at that time. These models included working memory models grounded in either a componential or capacity perspective.

Kellogg's Componential Model of Working Memory in Writing

Kellogg's (1996, 1999) model of working memory in writing relies on Baddeley's (1986) model of working memory to delineate the relationship between each writing process and the phonological loop, visuospatial sketchpad, and central executive. Kellogg first pointed out that all writing processes place heavy demands on the central executive, which plays an important role in writers managing their cognitive effort (Olive et al., 2002). Second, he proposed that planning processes require access mainly to the visuospatial sketchpad because when planning, writers visualize images, organize diagrams, and plans. More specifically, generating figurative content would require visual working memory, and structuring the text would require spatial working memory. By contrast, translating, reading to review text produced so far, and presumably editing are expected to impose large demands on the phonological loop. Several studies have now confirmed that translating and planning, respectively, engage the phonological loop and the visuospatial sketchpad (for reviews, see Olive, 2004, in press). Finally, Kellogg proposed that the execution component does not strongly involve the slave systems, at least in writers using a well-practiced and familiar handwriting. In keeping with these theoretical developments, Hayes (1996) modified the Hayes and Flower model by giving a central place to working memory. Hayes also refers to Baddeley's model but in a slightly different way as he integrated semantic memory as well into the model. Hayes also underlines the role of visuospatial working memory in processing graphic information and in representing the text's spatial display.

McCutchen's Capacity Theory of Writing

McCutchen, Covill, Hoyne, and Mildes (1994) found that writers with high working memory capacity (assessed with a writing span task) produced better texts than writers with low working memory. Importantly, this difference was less important when working memory capacity was assessed with a reading span task, which does not rely on efficiency of sentence generation as the writing span task does. Writing span was even more closely related to writing quality when the sentences had to form a story. In addition, writing span was related to lexical retrieval. McCutchen et al. concluded that greater efficiency in translating results in freed up working memory capacity, and thus, in a better writing performance.

To account for these findings, McCutchen (1996) proposed the capacity theory of writing, which was inspired by Daneman and Carpenter (1980) and Just and Carpenter (1992). In that framework, skilled writing requires efficient management of working memory capacity to provide an opportunity for interaction among the writing processes (McCutchen, 1988, 1994). In the capacity theory of writing, such an interaction can occur only when the writing processes are sufficiently efficient to support working memory capacity.

Development of handwriting illustrates well how change in efficiency of one writing process can affect other writing processes. For example, the cost of handwriting in cursive uppercase letters reduces performance on a written serial recall task compared to an oral recall (Bourdin & Fayol, 1994; Chapter 2, this volume). In addition, if handwriting is not automatized, the efficiency of temporal management of the writing processes can be reduced (Berninger, 1999). For example, automatized handwriting allows skilled writers to activate the high-level writing processes (planning, translating, and revising) simultaneously with handwriting, whereas beginning writers can only adopt a sequential strategy consisting of thinking and then handwriting cycles (Olive, Alves, & Castro, 2009; Olive & Kellogg, 2002; for similar findings with typing, see Alves, Castro, & Olive, 2008). Accordingly, when attention is freed up from the lower-level processes of text generation and transcription, it can be devoted to higher-level processes, such as planning or revision.

Swanson and Berninger's Developmental Model

Berninger and collaborators have shown that transcription accounts for a decreasing proportion of variance of writing fluency and quality as students develop from elementary to junior high school (for Grades 1, 2, and 3, see Berninger et al., 1992; for Grades 4, 5, and 6, see Berninger, Cartwright, Yates, Swanson, & Abbott, 1994;

for Grades 7, 8, and 9, see Berninger, Whitaker, Feng, Swanson, & Abbott, 1996). Berninger and Swanson (1994) thus distinguished text generation (lexical, syntactic, and discourse schema choices) and transcription (i.e., handwriting and spelling) components to better account for translation during writing acquisition. Swanson and Berninger (1994) proposed that children learning to write are mainly constrained by working memory demands of transcription and text generation during translation. After transcription is more efficient, local planning and revision can emerge, all the cognitive components can interact in working memory, and writers are better able to take into account rhetoric constraints in their productions, which increase in length and quality.

ADVANCES IN WORKING MEMORY RESEARCH

Baddeley's Updated Model

To account for the ability of working memory to integrate information from multiple sources and to use long-term knowledge, Baddeley (2000) added a fourth component, the episodic buffer, to his model (for a review, see Baddeley, 2007). The episodic buffer is a limited-capacity component that constitutes an interface between working memory and long-term memory. This component stores and processes information retrieved in episodic (events over time) and semantic long-term memory and directly encodes information in long-term memory. The episodic buffer also integrates information of different formats (e.g., verbal and visual information) coming from the other slave systems or from long-term memory. With the episodic buffer, not only verbal and visuospatial information but also abstract or conceptual information can be manipulated in working memory. In sum, the episodic buffer provides a binding mechanism that integrates several pieces of information of different formats into a single chunk. In that sense the capacity of the episodic buffer exceeds that of the phonological loop and of the visuospatial sketchpad.

Executive Functions

Of great importance to the field of writing, Baddeley (1996) proposed a more detailed description of the central executive, which he had first conceived of as a king or homunculus that alone governed working memory. The central executive in his new model evolved to a more specified and fractionated system, performing different executive functions such as retrieval from long-term memory, selective and divided attention, task switching, and coordination of the slave systems. Executive functions are conceived as executive attention, which refers to the ability to maintain memory representations in an active state despite interference or response competition (Kane & Engle, 2002). There is abundant and convergent evidence that the central executive activates particular areas of the frontal lobes but also more posterior areas in the parietal lobes and subcortical regions such as the cingulate below the cerebral cortex (Collette, Hogge, Salmon, & van der Linden, 2006; Duncan & Owen, 2000).

Miyake et al. (2000) described three general executive functions: inhibition, shifting (or cognitive flexibility), and updating (see also Oberauer, süß, Wilhelm, & Wittmann, 2003). Inhibition entails the ability to block irrelevant information for the task at hand (e.g., intrusive thoughts) or routine procedures automatically activated (prepotent responses). It is generally assessed with tasks such as the Stroop task. Shifting refers to the ability to alternate between mental sets, retrieval plans, or strategies and is assessed by calculating shifting cost with situations in which participants either switch or not between two tasks (Rogers & Monsell, 1995). Updating, which is assessed mainly with the running memory task or with the n-back task, is the ability to update working memory with new information (Ecker, Lewandowsky, Oberauer, & Chee, 2010). It has been found to be the only executive function related to fluid intelligence (Friedman et al., 2006).

Long-Term Working Memory

Ericsson and Kintsch (1995) proposed the model of long-term working memory to describe how knowledge stored in long-term memory is used to circumvent the working memory limitations. According to that model, knowledge stored in long-term memory can be used because retrieval cues or structures linked to that knowledge are activated in working memory. Accordingly, knowledge in long-term memory can be directly and quickly accessed by working memory (Ericsson & Delaney, 1998; Kintsch, Patel, & Ericsson, 1999). The presumed effects of the limited capacity of working memory can then be reinterpreted in terms of inefficient use of knowledge stored in long-term memory, and expert performance can be explained in terms of efficient encoding and retrieval memory processes. It is, however, important to keep in mind that this model only applies to well-practiced tasks and to familiar domains. The assumption is that long-term working memory is used only in skilled or expert performance.

Development of Working Memory

Studies of working memory in children have shown that performance on complex span tasks increases with age (e.g., Case, Kurland, & Goldberg, 1982). Research on working memory development has thus investigated the basic cognitive mechanisms that account for this increase. One question is whether the increase with age of performance on complex spans is a byproduct of *improved efficiency in the processing component of working memory*, as suggested by Case et al. (1982), *or* results from an *increase in working memory capacity* as suggested by Gilchrist, Cowan, and Naveh-Benjamin (2009). Gilchrist and colleagues indeed found that the number of chunks of information that children held in working memory increases as they get older, but not the size of the chunk. Improved controlled attention is also an important factor in working memory development, as illustrated by maturation of the frontal areas of the brain (Cowan, 2010). Finally, Cowan and Alloway (2009) suggested that older children use knowledge stored in long-term working memory in a more efficient way, so that these children can use qualitatively different strategies. Other studies have shown that the basic components of working memory are present from 4 years of age and develop until adolescence (Gathercole, Pickering, Ambridge, & Wearing, 2004). Differences in the developmental trends of the phonological loop and the visuospatial sketchpad have also been observed (Pickering, Gathercole, Hall, & Lloyd, 2001). In addition, shifting seems to develop later than inhibition and updating (St. Clair-Thompson & Gathercole, 2006).

Training Working Memory

Working memory capacity is generally viewed as a constant, which is not alterable. However, recent findings show that it can be improved with specific training. Such an improvement was initially documented by Klingberg, Forssberg, and Westerberg (2002) with attention-deficient hyperactivity disorder patients who commonly present a working memory deficit. More specifically, Klingberg and collaborators designed an automated battery of tasks that were designed to train implicitly the different functions of working memory (as updating with the n-back task). They not only observed improvement in working memory capacity after training, but also transfer to other working memory tasks such as the reading span task, suggesting that specific training may result in more general advantages. Actually, working memory training increases activity in the prefrontal and parietal cortex, which has more dopamine receptors (Klingberg, 2010). The effects of working memory training suggest that such training could be used as a remedial intervention for individuals for whom low working memory capacity limits academic performance, such as writing attainment (Gathercole & Alloway, 2008).

SOME DIRECTIONS FOR RESEARCH ON WORKING MEMORY IN WRITING

Which research directions should writing studies follow? As discussed earlier, working memory models are evolving with more detailed understanding of working memory. These changes should be incorporated into writing research as they raise new questions.

Questions Raised by Working Memory Research

Executive Functions in Writing   The recursive and high working memory demands of the writing processes suggest that executive functions are fundamental in writing, as indicated by the fact that writing is more related to the attentional functions of working memory than to short-term storage of information (Vanderberg & Swanson, 2007). Hooper, Swartz, Wakely, de Kruif, and Montgomery (2002) examined various measures of executive functions in poor and good writers. They showed that all executive functions related to performance on a narrative writing task, but different facets of executive functioning affected writing of poor and good writers. Similarly, Altemeier, Jones, Abbott, and Berninger (2006) studied inhibition, switching attention, planning, and verbal fluency in children taking notes and writing a report from the notes. They found that inhibition and planning contributed to integration of writing and reading in third to fifth graders. However, Altemeier, Abbott, and Berninger (2008) found that although inhibition contributed to writing and reading in children, switching attention often contributed uniquely over and above inhibition in learning to write and read in children without and with dyslexia. A working memory model, based on three executive functions (inhibition, switching attention, and sustained attention over time), two loops (phonological and orthographic), and three word-form storage and processing systems (phonological, orthographic, and morphological) explained reading and writing in children and adults with dyslexia and reconciled competing theories of causal factors in dyslexia (Berninger et al., 2006).

One feature of skilled writing is recursion and interaction of processes in working memory (Levy & Ransdell, 1995; McCutchen, 1994). Thus, writers have to shift frequently between processes and knowledge. Shifting may thus play a fundamental role in skilled writing. Given that shifting has a cost for working memory (Rubinstein, Meyer, & Evans, 2001), writers' cognitive effort might reflect necessity of shifting. The writing processes also require inhibition, which is engaged for suppressing a dominant response that is not relevant to the writing goal at the moment. For example, inhibition may be often engaged during planning to suppress knowledge that writers do not want to include in their text but that is activated during long-term memory search (Anderson & Green, 2001). Translating content into language may also engage inhibition. Composing a good text requires writers to use language in a creative way, which means avoiding frequent forms of language in order to use sophisticated vocabulary and syntactic forms. Because frequent words are more prone to be prepotent (see Chapter 13, this volume), writers need to inhibit these frequent words and retrieve words with controlled searches in their mental lexicon. Studies of subject–verb agreement (see Chapter 19, this volume) also show how a prepotent response may lead to an error if it is not inhibited. Updating is also strongly involved in writing. For example, writers' working memory content has to be very frequently updated with new content in order to support current processing. Updating should also be involved during construction of the mental representation of the content of the text. Interference studies with the n-back task would certainly be useful to understand better the role of updating in writing. And, undoubtedly, writing research should now investigate more systematically the role of the executive functions in beginning and in skilled writers.

The Episodic Buffer   The episodic buffer is important to writing for several reasons. First, this buffer, which is connected to episodic memory, can integrate different episodic structures into a single and more coherent one. Second, because the episodic buffer allows integrating multimodal codes into unitary representations, it may be the place where the multidimensional representation of the text is constructed and updated. This representation should include the situation model (Kintsch, 1998), a semantic level representing organization of the content of the text (its macro- and microstructure), a verbal level (the text base) as suggested by studies on text recall (Kellogg, 2001a), but also a visuospatial representation of the text (Hayes, 1996; Le Bigot, Passerault, & Olive, 2009, 2011). The episodic buffer may serve to integrate these different memory traces of the text into a single integrated representation. Finally, the episodic buffer may also maintain activated retrieval cues associated with knowledge in long-term memory. Accordingly, it may be engaged differently according to the writers' level of domain knowledge.

Long-Term Working Memory

Long-term working memory is also relevant to writing. As proposed by McCutchen (2000), novice writers are limited by short-term working memory because they lack fluent text generation processes and extensive structured domain knowledge relevant to the composition. Thus, novice or beginning writers may rely on strategies that save working memory capacity, such as knowledge telling. Skilled writers, by contrast, extensively use long-term working memory to manipulate the large knowledge base they have. This strategy enables them to circumvent their short-term working memory limitations. A first experimental investigation of long-term working memory tested whether writers' degree of domain-specific knowledge interfered with a secondary reaction time task (Kellogg, 2001b). As expected, Kellogg observed that writers with high domain-specific knowledge exhibited less cognitive effort. He thus interpreted this finding as suggesting that writers with a high degree of knowledge rely on structured knowledge that is kept accessible in long-term memory.

One initial line of evidence in support of a long-term working memory comes from studies interrupting text comprehension. Glanzer and collaborators (Fischer & Glanzer, 1986; Glanzer, Dorfman, & Kaplan, 1981; Glanzer, Fischer, & Dorfman, 1984) have observed that interrupting expert readers did not affect comprehension and only slightly affected reading times after each interruption. Ericsson and Kintsch (1995) reinterpreted these results, suggesting that reading the next sentences after the interruption caused the expert readers to reactivate the situation model of the prior text, which they constructed with retrieval cues that provided direct access to the text representation. Transferring such a paradigm to writing research should shed light on the involvement of long-term working memory in writing and particularly on how writers' degree of domain knowledge affects the working memory demands of writing.

Questions Raised by Writing

The Visuospatial Dimension of Writing

Although writing is a language activity, it also requires visuospatial processing. For instance, we have found that the visual demands of text composition are equally as important as its verbal demands, and that writing requires spatial working memory, even if at a lesser extent than visual working memory (Olive, Kellogg, & Piolat, 2008). As suggested by Kellogg (1996, 1999), a series of experiments confirmed that the visual demands of writing come primarily from generating content, and that spatial demands are required for structuring the text. Kellogg, Olive, and Piolat (2007) indeed found that definitions of concrete words, but not definitions of abstract words, required visual working memory. This selective interference probably occurred during the planning phase when participants had to form a mental picture of the referent and

of the concrete name to define. Galbraith, Ford, Walker, and Ford (2005) confirmed the role of spatial working memory when structuring a text. They showed
that spatial processing during structuring allows writers to generate new ideas (for
similar results, see also Galbraith, Hallam, Olive, & Le Bigot, 2009). Additionally,
Olive, Crouzevialle, Le Bigot, and Galbraith (2010) found that structuring a text
with a diagram required more spatial working memory and resulted in discovery
of more new ideas than outlining.

As suggested by Hayes (1996), writers also engage visuospatial working memory for mentally representing the spatial layout of their text. This proposal was confirmed by Le Bigot et al. (2009, 2011), who investigated memory for word location
in writing. They showed that visual interferences (either with a secondary visual
memory task or with continuous visual noise) reduced writers' subsequent memory
for location of words on a page and concluded that writers engage visual resources
to construct the physical text representation. A visual representation of the text
also facilitates text revision by providing cues for quickly accessing information
that has already been written (Piolat, Roussey, & Thunin, 1997). The visuospatial
dimension of writing has to be more systematically studied. Several writing processes may indeed rely on the visuospatial sketchpad. For example, writers may
engage the visuospatial sketchpad when they read their text for reviewing it or for
checking spelling. Research is also needed to tease apart the differential contributions of the visuospatial sketchpad (nonverbal) and orthographic coding (of visible
language units such as letters or words) in working memory.

Developmental Changes in Writers' Cognitive Effort   If text composition is effortful for adults, it is especially so for children who rely on emerging
writing processes. Assuming that cognitive effort reflects the cognitive demands of
writing (Piolat, Olive, Roussey, Thunin, & Ziegler, 1999), then its study in children
should inform the evolving demands in working memory for writing. Olive, Favart,
Beauvais, and Beauvais (2009) studied how cognitive effort changes in children
when they composed an argumentative text or a narrative one. They observed that
cognitive effort decreased from Grades 5 to 9, but only when composing an argumentative text. This experiment indicated that children continue to improve their
skills related to writing argumentative texts between Grades 5 and 9. Conducting
equivalent studies with a larger extent of grades would be useful for determining
in which phase of writing acquisition a writer is. It is indeed probable that near the
end of an acquisition phase the overall cost of composition decreases, indicating
a release of resources resulting from automatization that precedes the establishment of a more complex process. More systematic analyses of cognitive effort of
beginning writers should help us understand how the demands of writing change
with age.

Developmental Changes in Nature of Working Memory Demands   It
also seems important to extend research based on the componential model of
working memory to a developmental approach. Skilled writers may indeed be
expected to use strategies that are different from those used by novice writers. They may require different levels of representation in working memory. For

example, Dedeyan, Olive, and Largy (2006) examined detection of subject–verb errors while participants performed verbal and visual secondary tasks. They showed that detection of subject–verb agreement errors interfered with a verbal task in novice writers, whereas it interfered with a visual secondary task in adults. The authors concluded that, in novice writers, error detection in a text is based on algorithmic procedure that relies on verbal working memory; yet, skilled writers use visual search procedures to identify in their texts surface features of morphological agreement (see Dedeyan, Largy, & Negro, 2006; Chapter 19, this volume). Similarly, detecting other types of errors such as lexical or spelling errors presumably engages visuospatial working memory when skilled writers scan the surface of their texts (Larigauderie, Gaonac'h, & Lacroix, 1998). Tracking these changes in processing may be very helpful in understanding how writing processes become more efficient with age.

Mediation of Working Memory by Social and Emotional Factors
There is abundant evidence in the literature that sociocognitive factors mediate working memory capacity (see Beilock, Rydell, & McConnell, 2007, or Schmader, Johns, & Forbes, 2008, for reviews on the effect of stereotype threat on working memory), as does processing emotion (Derakshan & Eysenck, 2010). It thus appears important for writing research to investigate how social and motivational factors and writers' emotional disposition (see Chapter 3, this volume) affect writers' cognitive functioning.

The Social Regulation of Cognition   In a series of experiments designed to study the facilitating effect of cognitive dissonance, Martinie, Olive, and Milland (2010) asked one group of writers to compose an argumentative text that presented arguments they were supporting. A second group of writers composed a text arguing against their own opinion and was not given the choice to refuse (the dissonance group). While they were composing, writers were submitted to a secondary memory load task (maintaining and recalling short and long series of digits). Interestingly, writers in the dissonance group recalled fewer items than the no-dissonance writers at the secondary memory load task, particularly when the memory load was high. This finding suggests that composing a text that contains ideas against the writer's opinion consumes more working memory resources. In addition, compositional fluency was faster in dissonance writers. It is, however, important to notice that despite the fact that the dissonance writers changed their writing behavior when composing the counter-attitudinal essay (i.e., they increased their writing rate) and had fewer available working memory resources, they composed texts that were of equivalent quality to the texts composed by the writers in the no-dissonance condition. As this example shows, a change in the writer's sociocognitive state, in the present case cognitive dissonance, affected availability of working memory capacity. Cognitive research on writing has largely ignored how these sociocognitive factors intervene in the writing process. Such a demonstration of the cognitive impact of a social factor strongly suggests that cognitive writing research should now begin to investigate this issue.

Working Memory and Writers' Emotions   Derakshan and Eysenck's (2010) review of the effects of emotion on working memory and attention clearly shows that emotion regulates or mediates working memory and particularly controlled attention. In writing, such a regulation has already been observed with expressive writing, which provides an interesting situation for examining these effects. Expressive writing refers to a writing situation in which writers are asked to compose about an emotionally intense personal event. Such an emotional disclosure has been shown to induce positive biological and psychological effects on the writer (for a meta-analysis, see Frattaroli, 2006). Klein and Boals (2001) have further observed that working memory capacity increases after a few sessions of expressive writing (see also Kellogg, Mertz, & Morgan, 2010; Yogo & Fujihara, 2008). To explain this increase in working memory capacity, it is proposed that expressive writing would help individuals to suppress the intrusive thoughts related to the stressful personal event, which would result in freeing working memory. These studies show, as in the cognitive dissonance study, that the content of the composition that writers are processing affects their working memory capacity. Such research will surely shed light on the social and emotional regulation of writers' cognition through mediation of working memory. It will also provide insight into the executive control of writing, because, if the "intrusive thoughts suppression hypothesis" is validated, it will presumably require investigating inhibition.

CONCLUSION

According to Cowan, Morey, Cheng, Gilchrist, and Saults (2008), working memory research has tried to answer two types of questions: nomothetic questions relate to how a working memory normally operates, and ideographic questions relate to how individuals (or groups) diverge from this standard functioning. Cowan et al. also indentify three types of limits in working memory: capacity limits (in number and size of chunks that can be held in working memory), energy limits (controlled attention), and time limits (related to decay in working memory). How each of these limits affects writers' processing may constitute the nomothetic questions for research on working memory in writing. How children of different ages and how different writers are constrained by these limits may constitute the ideographic questioning for writing research.

Another important issue for writing research is how writers regulate their working memory capacity and whether they can circumvent their working memory capacity limits. The fact that writing attainment in children is related to working memory capacity (Gathercole & Alloway, 2008) raises the question of interventions to increase working memory capacity. Future research on writing should particularly focus on effects of working memory training on writing performance.

GLOSSARY

Complex/simple span: These span tasks tax both the storage and processing functions of working memory (e.g., reading span); by contrast simple span tasks such as the digit span task only require short-term storage.

Intrusive thoughts: Unwelcome involuntary thoughts, activated automatically, that require controlled attention to be suppressed.

N-back task: A working memory task in which items (e.g., letters) are presented one at a time and participants must indicate whether the current item is identical to the item that occurred "n" items before its onset.

Reading span: A complex working memory task that requires participants to read lists of increasing number of sentences (load for storage) and to memorize the last word of each sentence (processing task). When a series is completed participants must recall all words.

Running memory task: In this task, a list ends unpredictably and the last n items are to be recalled. Each time a new item is presented, updating working memory content is required.

Sentence span: See *Reading span.*

Short-term working memory: Used in the framework of long-term working memory, short-term working memory refers to functions of working memory that do not rely on long-term memory.

Stroop task: An inhibition task in which participants first read names of colors printed in black. Then, they say the print colors of figures (e.g., stars). Third, they have to say the color in which the name of a color is printed. For example, if the word "Blue" is written in green, they have to say "green," but not "blue."

Supervisory attentional system: This model describes two modes of control of action. First, actions can result from automatic activation of schemas or routines by environmental triggers. Second, when routines are unsatisfactory, such as in new situations, an attentionally limited controller, the supervisory attentional system, coordinates and monitors schemas in order to achieve novel and complex tasks, acting as a general purpose planning component.

Writing span: A complex span task that requires participants to memorize lists of increasing number of words. When a series ends, participants are asked to produce one sentence (processing task) with each word memorized (load for storage). All sentences produced from a list of words may or not constitute a coherent story.

REFERENCES

Altemeier, L., Abbott, R., & Berninger, V. (2008). Executive functions for reading and writing in typical literacy development and dyslexia. *Journal of Clinical and Experimental Neuropsychology, 30,* 588–606.

Altemeier, L., Jones, J., Abbott, R. D., & Berninger, V. W. (2006). Executive functions in becoming writing readers and reading writers: Note taking and report writing in third and fifth graders. *Developmental Neuropsychology, 29,* 161–173.

Alves, R. A., Castro, S. L., & Olive, T. (2008). Execution and pauses in writing narratives: Processing time, cognitive effort and typing skill. *International Journal of Psychology, 43,* 469–479.

Anderson, M. C., & Green, C. (2001). Suppressing unwanted memories by executive control. *Nature, 410*(6826), 366–369.

Baddeley, A. D. (1986). *Working memory.* Oxford: Oxford University Press.

Baddeley, A. D. (1996). Exploring the central executive. *Quarterly Journal of Experimental Psychology, 49A*, 5–28.

Baddeley, A. D. (2000). The episodic buffer: A new component of working memory? *Trends in Cognitive Sciences, 4*, 417–423.

Baddeley, A. D. (2007). *Working memory, thought and action.* Oxford: Oxford University Press.

Baddeley, A. D., & Hitch, G. (1974). Working memory. In G. H. Bower (Ed.), *The psychology of learning and motivation* (pp. 47–90). New York: Academic Press.

Beilock, S. L., Rydell, R. J., & McConnell, A. R. (2007). Stereotype threat and working memory: Mechanisms, alleviation and spillover. *Journal of Experimental Psychology: General, 136*(2), 256–276.

Berninger, V. W. (1999). Coordinating transcription and text generation in working memory during composing: Automatic and constructive processes. *Learning Disability Quarterly, 22*(2), 99–112.

Berninger, V., Abbott, R., Thomson, J., Wagner, R., Swanson, H. L., Wijsman, E., & Raskind, W. (2006). Modeling developmental phonological core deficits within a working-memory architecture in children and adults with developmental dyslexia. *Scientific Studies in Reading, 10*, 165–198.

Berninger, V. W., Cartwright, A., Yates, C., Swanson, H. L., & Abbott, R. D. (1994). Developmental skills related to writing and reading acquisition in the intermediate grades: Shared and unique variance. *Reading and Writing, 6*, 161–196.

Berninger, V. W., & Swanson, H. L. (1994). Modifying Hayes and Flower's model of skilled writing to explain beginning and developing writing. In E. C. Butterfield (Ed.), *Advances in cognition and educational practice,* Vol. 2. *Children's writing: Toward a process theory of the development of skilled writing* (pp. 57–81). Greenwich, CT: JAI Press.

Berninger, V. W., Whitaker, D., Feng, Y., Swanson, H. L., & Abbott, R. D. (1996). Assessment of planning, translating and revising in junior high writers. *Journal of School Psychology, 34*, 23–52.

Berninger, V. W., Yates, C., Cartwright, A., Rutberg, J., Remy E., & Abbott, R. D. (1992). Lower level developmental skills in beginning writing. *Reading and Writing: An Interdisciplinary Journal, 4*, 257–280.

Bourdin, B., & Fayol, M. (1994). Is written language production more difficult than oral language production? A working memory approach. *International Journal of Psychology, 29*, 591–620.

Case, R., Kurland, D. M., & Goldberg, J. (1982). Operational efficiency and the growth of short-term memory span. *Journal of Experimental Child Psychology, 33*, 386–404.

Catani, M., Jones, D. K., & Ffytche, D. H. (2005). Perisylvian language networks of the human brain. *Annals of Neurology, 57*, 8–16.

Cocchini, G., Logie, R. H., Della Sala, S., MacPherson, S. E., & Baddeley, A. (2002). Concurrent performance of two memory tasks: Evidence for domain-specific working memory systems. *Memory and Cognition, 30*, 1086–1095.

Collette, F., Hogge, M., Salmon, E., & van der Linden, M. (2006). Exploration of the neural substrates of executive functioning by functional neuroimaging. *Neuroscience, 139*, 209–221.

Conway, A. R. A., & Engle, R. W. (1996). Individual differences in working memory capacity: More evidence for a general capacity theory. *Memory, 4*, 577–590.

Cowan, N. (2005). *Working memory capacity.* London: Psychology Press.

Cowan, N. (2010). Multiple concurrent thoughts: The meaning and developmental neuropsychology of working memory. *Developmental Neuropsychology, 35*, 447–474.

Cowan, N., & Alloway, T. (2009). Development of working memory in childhood. In M. L. Courage & N. Cowan (Eds.), *The development of memory in infancy and childhood* (pp. 303–342). Hove, East Sussex, UK: Psychology Press.

Cowan, N., Morey, C. C., Chen, Z., Gilchrist, A. L., & Saults, J. S. (2008). Theory and measurement of working memory capacity limits. In B. H. Ross (Ed.), *The psychology of learning and motivation* (Vol. 49, pp. 49–104). Amsterdam: Elsevier.

Crosson, B., Rao, S., Woodley, S., Rosen, A., Bobholz, J., Mayer, A., . . . Stein, EA. (1999). Mapping of semantic, phonological, and orthographic verbal working memory in normal adults with functional magnetic resonance imaging. *Neuropsychology, 13,* 171–187.

Daneman, M., & Carpenter, P. A. (1980). Individual differences in working memory and reading. *Journal of Verbal Learning and Verbal Behavior, 19,* 450–466.

Dedeyan, A., Largy, P., & Negro, I. (2006). Mémoire de travail et detection d'erreurs d'accord verbal: etude chez le novice et l'expert. [Working memory and detection of verbal agreement errors: A study of novices and experts]. *Langages, 164,* 57–70.

Dedeyan, A., Olive, T., & Largy, P. (2006, October). *Implication des composants de la mémoire de travail dans la détection des erreurs d'accord sujet-verbe: approche développementale* [Involvement of the different components of working memory in detecting subject-verb agreement errors: A developmental approach]. Paper presented at the International Conference on Cognitive Approach of Written Language Learning, Rennes, France.

Derakshan, N., & Eysenck, M. (2010). Introduction to the special issue: Emotional states, attention, and working memory. *Cognition and Emotion, 24,* 189–199.

Duncan, J., & Owen, A. M. (2000). Common regions of the human frontal lobe recruited by diverse cognitive demands. *Trends in Neurosciences, 23,* 475–483.

Ecker, U. K. H., Lewandowsky, S., Oberauer, K., & Chee, A. E. H. (2010). The components of working memory updating: An experimental decomposition and individual differences. *Journal of Experimental Psychology: Learning, Memory, and Cognition, 36,* 170–189.

Engle, R. W. (2002). Working memory capacity as executive attention. *Current Directions in Psychological Science, 11,* 19–23.

Engle, R. W., Cantor, J., & Carullo, J. (1992). Individual differences in working memory and comprehension: A test of four hypotheses. *Journal of Experimental Psychology: Learning, Memory and Cognition, 18,* 972–992.

Ericsson, K. A., & Delaney, P. F. (1998). Long-term working memory as an alternative to capacity models of working memory in everyday skilled performance. In A. Miyake & P. Shah (Eds.), *Models of working memory* (pp. 93–114). Cambridge: Cambridge University Press.

Ericsson, K. A., & Kintsch, W. (1995). Long-term working memory. *Psychological Review, 102*(2), 211–245.

Fischer, B., & Glanzer, M. (1986). Short-term storage and the processing of cohesion during reading. *Quarterly Journal of Experimental Psychology, 38A,* 431–460.

Flower, L. S., & Hayes, J. R. (1980). The dynamics of composing: Making plans and juggling constraints. In L. W. Gregg & E. R. Steinberg (Eds.), *Cognitive processes in writing* (pp. 31–49). Hillsdale, NJ: Erlbaum.

Frattaroli, J. (2006). Experimental disclosure and its moderators: A meta-analysis. *Psychological Bulletin, 132,* 823–865.

Friedman, N. P., Miyake, A., Corley, R. P., Young, S. E., DeFries, J. C., & Hewitt, J. K. (2006). Not all executive functions are related to intelligence. *Psychological Science, 17,* 172–179.

Galbraith, D., Ford, S., Walker, G., & Ford, J. (2005). The contribution of different components of working memory to knowledge transformation during writing. *L1-Educational Studies in Language and Literature, 5*(2), 113–145.

Galbraith, D., Hallam, J., Olive, T., & Le Bigot, N. (2009). The role of different components of working memory in writing. In N. Taatgen, H. van Rijn, L. Schomaker, & J. Nerbonne (Eds.), *Proceedings of the 31st Annual Conference of the Cognitive Science Society* (pp. 3028–3033). Amsterdam: Cognitive Science Society.

Gathercole, S. E., & Alloway, T. P. (2008). *Working memory and learning: A practical guide*. London: Sage.

Gathercole, S. E., & Pickering, S. J. (2000a). Assessment of working memory in six- and seven-year-old children. *Journal of Educational Psychology, 92*, 377–390.

Gathercole, S. E., & Pickering, S. J. (2000b). Working memory deficits in children with low achievements in the national curriculum at seven years of age. *British Journal of Educational Psychology, 70*, 177–194.

Gathercole, S. E., Pickering, S. J., Ambridge, B., & Wearing, H. (2004). The structure of working memory from 4 to 15 years of age. *Developmental Psychology, 40*, 177–190.

Gilchrist, A. L., Cowan, N., & Naveh-Benjamin, M. (2009). Investigating the childhood development of working memory using sentences: New evidence for the growth of chunk capacity. *Journal of Experimental Child Psychology, 104*, 252–265.

Glanzer, M., Dorfman, D., & Kaplan, B. (1981). Short-term storage in the processing of text. *Journal of Verbal Learning and Verbal Behavior, 20*, 656–670.

Glanzer, M., Fischer, B., & Dorfman, D. (1984). Short-term storage in reading. *Journal of Verbal Learning and Verbal Behavior, 23*, 467–448.

Hayes, J. R. (1996). A new framework for understanding cognition and affect in writing. In C. M. Levy & S. Ransdell (Eds.), *The science of writing: Theories, methods, individual differences, and applications* (pp. 1–27). Mahwah, NJ: Erlbaum.

Hayes, J. R., & Flower, L. S. (1980). Identifying the organization of writing processes. In L. W. Gregg & E. R. Steinberg (Eds.). *Cognitive processes in writing* (pp. 3–30). Hillsdale, NJ: Erlbaum.

Henson, R. (2001). Neural working memory. In J. Andrade (Ed.), *Working memory in perspective* (pp. 151–174). Hove: Psychology Press.

Hooper, S. R., Swartz, C. W., Wakely, M. B., de Kruif, R. E. L., & Montgomery, J. W. (2002). Executive functions in elementary school children with and without problems in written expression. *Journal of Learning Disabilities, 35*, 37–68.

Jarrold, C., Baddeley, A. D., & Hewes, A. K. (1999). Genetically dissociated components of working memory: Evidence from Down's and Williams syndrome. *Neuropsychologia, 37*, 637–651.

Just, M. A., & Carpenter, P. A. (1992). A capacity theory of comprehension: Individual differences in working memory. *Psychological Review, 99*, 122–149.

Kane, M. J., & Engle, R. W. (2002). The role of prefrontal cortex in working-memory capacity, executive attention, and general fluid intelligence: An individual differences perspective. *Psychonomic Bulletin and Review, 9*, 637–671.

Kellogg, R. T. (1987). Effects of topic knowledge on the allocation of processing time and cognitive effort to writing processes. *Memory and Cognition, 15*, 256–266.

Kellogg, R. T. (1994). *The psychology of writing*. New York: Oxford University Press.

Kellogg, R. T. (1996). A model of working memory in writing. In C. M. Levy & S. Ransdell (Eds.), *The science of writing: Theories, methods, individual differences, and application* (pp. 57–71). Mahwah, NJ: Erlbaum.

Kellogg, R. T. (1999). Components of working memory in writing. In M. Torrance & G. Jeffery (Eds.), *The cognitive demands of writing: Processing capacity and working memory effects in text production* (pp. 43–61). Amsterdam: Amsterdam University Press.

Kellogg, R. T. (2001a). Presentation modality and mode of recall in verbal false memory. *Journal of Experimental Psychology: Learning, Memory, and Cognition, 27*, 913–919.

Kellogg, R. T. (2001b). Long-term working memory in text production. *Memory and Cognition, 29*, 43–52.

Kellogg, R. T. (2008). Training writing skills: A cognitive development perspective. *Journal of Writing Research, 1*, 1–26.

Kellogg, R. T., Mertz, H. K., & Morgan, M. (2010). Do gains in working memory capacity explain the written self-disclosure effect? *Cognition and Emotion, 24*(1), 86–93.

Kellogg, R. T., Olive, T., & Piolat A. (2007). Verbal, visual and spatial working memory in written language production. *Acta Psychologica, 124*, 382–397.

Kellogg, R. T., & Raulerson III, B. A. (2007). Improving the writing skills of college students. *Psychonomic Bulletin and Review, 14*, 237–242.

Kintsch, W. (1998). *Comprehension: A paradigm for cognition.* New York: Cambridge University Press.

Kintsch, W., Patel, V. L., & Ericsson, K. A. (1999). The role of long-term working-memory in text comprehension. *Psychologica, 42*, 186–198.

Klein, K., & Boals, A. (2001). Expressive writing can increase working memory capacity. *Journal of Experimental Psychology: General, 130*, 520–533.

Klingberg, T. (2010). Training and plasticity of working memory. *Trends in Cognitive Science, 14*(7), 317–324.

Klingberg, T., Forssberg, H., & Westerberg, H. (2002). Training of working memory in children with ADHD. *Journal of Clinical and Experimental Neuropsychology, 24*, 781–791.

Larigauderie, P., Gaonac'h, D., & Lacroix, N. (1998). Working memory and error detection in texts: What are the roles of the central executive and the phonological loop? *Applied Cognitive Psychology, 12*, 505–527.

Le Bigot, N., Passerault, J-M., & Olive, T. (2009). Memory for words location in writing. *Psychological Research, 73*, 89–97.

Le Bigot, N., Passerault, J-M., & Olive, T. (2011). Implication of visuospatial and temporal information in memory for word location. *Journal of Cognitive Psychology.* Advance online publication. doi: 10.1080/20445911.2011.532119

Levy, C. M., & Ransdell, S. E. (1995). Is writing as difficult as it seems? *Memory and Cognition, 23*, 767–779.

Logie, R. H. (1995). *Visuo-spatial working memory.* Hove: Erlbaum.

Martinie, M.-A., Olive, T., & Milland, L. (2010). Cognitive effort of dissonance induced by the writing of a counterattitudinal essay. *Journal of Experimental Social Psychology, 46*, 587–594.

McCutchen, D. (1988). Functional automaticity in children's writing: A problem of metacognitive control. *Written Communication, 5*, 306–324.

McCutchen, D. (1994). The magical number three, plus or minus two: Working memory in writing. In J. S. Carlson (Series Ed.) & E. C. Butterfield (Vol. Ed.), *Advances in cognition and educational practice,* Vol. 2: *Children's writing: Toward a process theory of the development of skilled writing* (pp. 1–30). Greenwich, CT: JAI Press.

McCutchen, D. (1996). A capacity theory of writing: Working memory in composition. *Educational Psychology Review, 8*, 299–325.

McCutchen, D. (2000). Knowledge, processing, and working memory: Implications for a theory of writing. *Educational Psychologist, 35*, 13–23.

McCutchen, D., Covill, A., Hoyne, S. H., & Mildes, K. (1994). Individual differences in writing: Implications of translating fluency. *Journal of Educational Psychology, 86*, 256–266.

Miyake, A., Friedman, N. P., Emerson, M. J., Witzki, A. H., Howerter, A., & Wager, T. (2000). The unity and diversity of executive functions and their contributions to complex "frontal lobe" tasks: A latent variable analysis. *Cognitive Psychology, 41*, 49–100.

Norman, D. A., & Shallice, T. (2000). Attention to action: Willed and automatic control of behaviour. In M. S. Gazzaniga (Ed.), *Cognitive neuroscience: A reader* (pp. 376–390). Oxford: Blackwell.

Oberauer, K. (2002). Access to information in working memory. Exploring the focus of attention. *Journal of Experimental Psychology: Learning, Memory, and Cognition, 28,* 411–421.

Oberauer, K., Süß, H-M., Wilhelm, O., & Wittmann, W. W. (2003). The multiple faces of working memory: Storage, processing, supervision, and coordination. *Intelligence, 31,* 167–193.

Olive, T. (2004). Working memory in writing: Empirical evidences from the dual-task technique. *European Psychologist, 9,* 32–42.

Olive, T. (in press). Writing and working memory: A summary of theories and of findings. In E. Grigorenko, E. Mambrino, & D. D. Preiss (Eds.), *Writing: A mosaic of new perspectives.* New York: Psychology Press.

Olive, T., Alves, R. A., & Castro, S. L. (2009). Cognitive processes in writing during pauses and execution periods. *European Journal of Cognitive Psychology, 21,* 758–785.

Olive, T., Crouzevialle, M., Le Bigot, N., & Galbraith, D. (2010, September 8–10). *Visuospatial working memory in planning.* Paper presented at the 2010 Conference of the EARLi SIG-Writing, Heidelberg, Germany.

Olive, T., Favart, M., Beauvais, C., & Beauvais, L. (2009). Children's cognitive effort in writing: Effects of genre and of handwriting automatisation in 5th- and 9th-graders. *Learning and Instruction, 19,* 299–308.

Olive, T., & Kellogg, R. T. (2002). Concurrent activation of high and low-level production processes in written composition. *Memory and Cognition, 30,* 594–600.

Olive, T., Kellogg, R. T., & Piolat, A. (2002). The triple-task technique for studying the process of writing. In T. Olive & C. M. Levy (Eds.), *Contemporary tools and techniques for studying writing* (pp. 31–58). Dordrecht: Kluwer.

Olive, T., Kellogg, R. T., & Piolat, A. (2008). Verbal, visual and spatial working memory demands during text composition. *Applied Psycholinguistics, 29,* 669–687.

Pickering, S. J., Gathercole, S. E., Hall, M., & Lloyd, S. A. (2001). Development of memory for pattern and path: Further evidence for the fractionation of visual and spatial short-term memory. *Quarterly Journal of Experimental Psychology, 54A,* 397–420.

Piolat, A., Olive, T., & Kellogg, R. T. (2005). Cognitive effort of note taking. *Applied Cognitive Psychology, 19*(3), 291–312.

Piolat, A., Olive, T., Roussey, J.-Y., Thunin, O., & Ziegler, J. C. (1999). Scriptkell: A computer-assisted tool for measuring the relative distribution of time and cognitive effort in writing and other tasks. *Behavior Research Methods, Instruments, and Computers, 31,* 113–121.

Piolat, A., Roussey, J.-Y., & Thunin, O. (1997). Effects of screen presentation on text reading and revising. *International Journal of Human-Computer Studies, 47,* 565–589.

Rogers, R. D., & Monsell, S. (1995). Costs of a predictable switch between simple cognitive tasks. *Journal of Experimental Psychology: General, 124,* 207–231.

Rubinstein, J. S., Meyer, D. E., & Evans, J. E. (2001). Executive control of cognitive processes in task switching. *Journal of Experimental Psychology: Human Perception and Performance, 27,* 763–797.

Schmader, T., Johns, M., & Forbes, C. (2008). An integrated model of stereotype threat effects on performance. *Psychological Review, 115*(2), 336–356.

Smith, E. E., & Jonides, J. (1997). Working memory: A view from neuroimaging. *Cognitive Psychology, 33,* 5–42.

Smith, E. E., Jonides, J., & Koeppe, R. A. (1996). Dissociating verbal and spatial working memory using PET. *Cerebral Cortex, 6,* 11–20.

St. Clair-Thompson, H. L., & Gathercole, S. (2006). Executive functions and achievements in school: Shifting, updating, inhibition, and working memory. *The Quarterly Journal of Experimental Psychology, 59*(4), 745–759.

Swanson, H. L., & Berninger, V. W. (1994). Working memory as a source of individual differences in children's writing. In E. C. Butterfield (Ed.), *Advances in cognition and educational practice*, Vol. 2: *Children's writing: Toward a process theory of the devel-opment of skilled writing* (pp. 31–56). Greenwich, CT: JAI Press.

Swanson, H. L., & Berninger, V. W. (1996a). Individual differences in children's working memory and writing skill. *Journal of Experimental Child Psychology, 63*, 358–385.

Swanson, H. L., & Berninger, V. W. (1996b). Individual differences in children's writing: A function of working memory or reading or both processes? *Reading and Writing, 8*, 357–383.

Turner, M. L., & Engle, R. W. (1989). Is working memory capacity task dependent? *Journal of Memory and Language, 28*, 127–154.

Vanderberg, R., & Swanson, H. L. (2007). Which components of working memory are important in the writing process? *Reading and Writing, 20*, 721–752.

Yogo, M., & Fujihara, S. (2008). Working memory capacity can be improved by expressive writing: A randomized experiment in a Japanese sample. *British Journal of Health Psychology, 13*, 77–80.

Part VI

Applications of Technology to Studying and Teaching Writing

22

Logging Tools to Study Digital Writing Processes

LUUK VAN WAES, MARIËLLE LEIJTEN,
ÅSA WENGELIN, and EVA LINDGREN

*T*here has never been a time in which so many people have produced so much written text. The main explanation is the steady increase of written literacy all over the world, resulting to a large degree from the wide dissemination of computers and other electronic devices, which facilitated the production of written text in all kinds of new contexts (e.g., social media). However, the use of digital technology in writing has not only changed the way in which we produce texts, but these new technologies also created new possibilities for writing researchers to investigate writing as it unfolds in real time.

This chapter presents and discusses the use of keystroke logging tools in writing process research and in pedagogy. Several tools are presented and illustrated from different perspectives, including, for example, pausing, revising, and fluency in composing. Furthermore, the logging tools' advantages as pedagogical devices for raising awareness are discussed and illustrated with examples.

Several research groups developed so-called keystroke logging (KSL) tools to register writing processes (for a review, see Latif, 2009; Sullivan & Lindgren, 2006; Wengelin, 2006). Those programs enable researchers to collect very fine-grained online data because they log every keystroke in relation to a time stamp (in milliseconds), which indicates the time that a specific key was pressed (and released). KSL programs log the process in a continuous and nonobtrusive way, without interrupting the activity under way or increasing cognitive load. This capability is certainly one of the main advantages of this research method (for a discussion on reactivity, see Bowles, 2010; Greene & Higgins, 1994; Janssen, Van Waes, & Van den Bergh, 1996; Smagorinsky, 1989; Van den Haak, De Jong, & Schellens, 2004, 2006).

The data files that are collected by these programs can be used to analyze the writing process from different perspectives. Because these tools are mainly used to study cognitive processes in writing, most researchers have focused on the pausing and revising behavior. However, as some programs also have a replay function, the logging files can be used for different purposes, for instance, to show the writing process as it evolves step by step to stimulate reflection in a retrospective interview or peer interview.

One of the earliest attempts to use keystroke logging in writing research was described by Bridwell and Duin (1985). This article is a first illustration of how the advent of the personal computer not only changed the writing context radically, but also how it created new opportunities as a research tool to observe and study writing. Several tools have been developed (Latif, 2009) that have in common the ability to facilitate a fine-grained recording of every keystroke (and sometimes also mouse movements and clicks). These logged data are then made available for further analysis and they enable an exact replay of the emerging text.

Keystroke logging can be a suitable research instrument in a number of contexts (for an overview, see Sullivan & Lindgren, 2006). Research areas include, for instance, the following: studies on cognitive writing processes in general, description of writing strategies in professional writing or creative writing, the writing development of children with and without writing difficulties, spelling, first and second language writing, and the writing of expert and novice writers in professional contexts and in specialist skill areas such as translation and subtitling. Not only can keystroke logging be used in research specifically on writing, it can also be integrated in educational domains for second language learning, programming skills, and typing skills.

This chapter first presents a brief overview of the most used KSL programs. Next, to illustrate how these programs are used in several domains, we discuss the two main approaches to processing data in pause and revision analyses. In the final section we describe the use of keystroke logging data as a pedagogical tool.

OVERVIEW OF LOGGING TOOLS

Different programs have been developed to collect online processing data of writing activities. In this section we briefly describe the main programs that are actually used in writing research. The matrix in Table 22.1 presents an overview of the main functions and characteristics of the programs described in this chapter. Most of the programs have overlapping capabilities, but all of them also have very specific characteristics making them complementary in their use.

Trace-it/JEdit

Trace-it/JEdit is a set of keystroke logging programs with the longest history of use (Severinson Eklundh & Kollberg, 1992; http://www.nada.kth.se/iplab/trace-it). The programs were developed for Macintosh. The researchers at KTH in Stockholm created programs that opened new perspectives in writing research and formed the basis for all the other programs. The program used JEdit as a basic text editor and Trace-it as a separate component to analyze revisions on the basis of the so-called intermediate MID-format log file. Using the S-notation (see the section

TABLE 22.1   Matrix Describing the Main Characteristics of Keystroke Logging Tools

	Trace-it/Jedit	ScriptLog	Inputlog	Translog	uLog	EyeWrite	Eye and Pen
Logging							
Keyboard	✓	✓	✓	✓	✓	✓	✓
Mouse	✓	✓	✓	✓	✓		✓
Eye movements		✓	(✓)	✓		✓	✓
Speech			✓				
Handwriting							✓
Application identification			✓		✓		
Software and hardware							
Operating system	Macintosh	PC Windows	PC Windows	PC Windows	PC Windows	PC Windows	PC Windows Tablet
Word processor	Trace-it editor	ScriptLog text editor	Microsoft Word XP or later versions	Translog editor	All Windows programs	EyeWrite editor	Tablet
Logging environment	Trace-it editor	ScriptLog text editor	All Windows programs	Translog editor	All Windows programs	EyeWrite editor + E-Prime	Tablet
Output							
Summary process data	✓	✓	✓	✓	✓		
General file	✓	✓	✓	✓		✓	✓
Linear file	✓	✓	✓	✓			
Key transition file	✓	✓	✓				
Pause analysis	✓	✓	✓		(✓)	(✓)	
Revision analysis	(✓)		(✓)				
Process replay	✓	✓	(✓)	✓		✓	✓
Website	nada.kth.se/ iplab/trace-it/ index.html	scriptlog.net	inputlog.net	translog.dk	noldus.com		eyeandpen.net

"Keystroke Logging and Revision Analysis"), it presents all the revisions made during a computer-based writing session directly on the screen in a readable and system-independent form. The Trace-it environment also supports various types of interactive analyses and a replay of logged writing sessions. The programs have not been developed further since the late 1990s, but they can still be downloaded.

Scriptlog

Scriptlog was originally developed as a Macintosh program at the University of Gothenburg (Strömqvist & Malmsten, 1997) to study writing processes. A Windows version with more advanced analysis functions was later developed in coopera- tion between Lund University and Stavanger University (Andersson et al., 2006; Wengelin et al., 2009; http://www.scriptlog.net).[1] The program creates a writing environment with a text editor and an optional frame in which pictures or texts can be shown to elicit certain writing activities. Sound files can also be used as elicitation instruments. The setup of the environment is controlled in a design module. When activated, Scriptlog keeps a record of all events on the keyboard, the position of these events, and their temporal distribution. The analysis module enables the researcher to derive selected patterns of keystrokes, time intervals, and deletions from the data. Some of these are predefined; others can be interactively designed (e.g., the occurrence of a particular word string and its temporal distribu- tion). Scriptlog also allows one to play back a recorded session—or a selection of it—in real time on the basis of the log file. More recently, development has enabled a combination of eye-tracking data (SMI iView X) and keystroke logging data in order to enhance the study of the interplay between writing, monitoring (reading), and revision. Data on the distribution of visual attention during writing are used, for instance, in determining to what extent pauses are used for monitoring.

Inputlog

Inputlog was developed at the University of Antwerp with the aim to study online writing processes of professional writers in detail (Leijten & Van Waes, 2006; Van Waes, Leijten, & Van Weijen, 2009; http://www.inputlog.net). The main differ- ences between Inputlog and other logging programs are that (a) Inputlog logs writ- ing data in all Window applications, and (b) it executes specific analyses of writing materials that were generated in MS Word. These features enable researchers to collect data that are produced in a widely used professional editor. Moreover, the program not only logs keystrokes, mouse movements, and clicks, but also Windows events (active application and identification of URL) and dictated speech input (Dragon Naturally Speaking speech technology, Nuance). Logged data can be analyzed from different perspectives, for example, pausing or revising behavior. A replay module is under development.

---

[1] To facilitate a broad usage of Scriptlog and Inputlog, the programs are put at the disposal of the research community free of charge (http://www.scriptlog.net and www.inputlog.net), provided that reference is made to the programs (see suggested reference in program description).

Translog

Translog was developed at the Copenhagen Business School mainly to study translation processes (Jakobsen, 2006; http://www.translog.dk). It has two interdependent components: a supervisor component to prepare a logging project and replay it afterwards, and a user component. The latter displays a predefined source text in the top half of the window and a translation frame in which the target text can be edited.

uLog

Noldus (www.noldus.com) developed uLog as a tool for the automatic recording of user-system interaction as part of the Observer XT, a program used to observe, describe, and code behavior. A limited version can also be used as a separate program. With uLog, researchers can log all basic computer events such as mouse clicks, scrolling, window events, and keystrokes. One of the advantages of the program is that it can be used in a connected computer setup in a network environment (or it is possible to run the program from a USB-memory device). No keystroke analyses are provided.

EyeWrite

EyeWrite (Simpson & Torrance, 2007; Wengelin et al., 2009) aims to integrate keystroke logging with eye-movement records. The program enables researchers to log information about the location of fixations relative to the text and independently of screen coordinates. EyeWrite comprises a simple editor and an analysis program. The text editor is basic, with all cursor movements made using cursor (arrow) keys, and all delete actions made by backspacing. Eye movements are recorded using a head-mounted eye-tracker that has sufficient accuracy to permit, at least, identification of the word that the writer is fixating on at a particular moment in the writing process. The analysis program interprets the combined keystroke and eye-movement log file and generates text-relative information about the location of the fixation in a general data file for further analysis. In playback mode this program displays the text as it develops on the screen, showing both the cursor, and, when fixations are within screen coordinates, also the location of the current fixation.

Eye and Pen

Eye and Pen is not a keystroke logging program; it is designed to record writing processes in handwriting (Alamargot, Chesnet, Dansac, & Ros, 2006; Wengelin et al., 2009; http://www.eyeandpen.net). However, we include it here because the philosophy and aims of Eye and Pen are completely in line with the other tools presented here. The program was developed at the University of Poitiers. Eye and Pen synchronously logs handwriting movements and by means of a digitizing tablet coordinates the state of the pen and eye movements via a compatible optical eye-tracking system. The combination of these two types of input allows the researcher, for instance, to collect data about the synchronization between eye and pen movements during pausing and writing periods. Eye and Pen has two different modes of operation: the acquisition mode (allowing the recording of data and stimuli presentation), and the analysis mode (allowing the displaying and editing of data). A semiautomated coding system enables users to characterize and classify ocular and graphomotor events.

Table 22.1 presents a brief overview and comparison of the main characteristics and functionalities of the logging programs described above. The table shows the similarities and complementary uses among the programs for (a) the kind of logging events that are captured, (b) the required hardware and software, and (c) the type of analyses that are generated automatically. It is important to note that all programs provide a kind of general file that contains detailed information about each logging event (e.g., keystroke identification, timestamp of key-down press, position in the text, etc.). Some programs use this file to generate specific analyses (e.g., pause or revision analyses) or to input for a replay module. However, when these automatic analyses are not provided, as in uLog or Eyewrite, users can still build their own analyses on the basis of these files. Moreover, designers of the programs advise users to evaluate the output of automatic analyses very carefully before drawing conclusions. It goes without saying that the interpretation of writing process data is very complex, and therefore the automatic analyses require the critical eye and mind of the researcher. For example, the identification of pauses in relation to linguistic boundaries is sometimes very difficult because of the occurrence of incomplete words, which often occur in process data.

Advantages of these logging programs are that the underlying method itself is not reactive or obtrusive and does not interact with the writing activity itself; but the data collected require theory-based inferences on the part of the researcher. Another advantage is that it is easy to combine the logging program method with other research methods. For example, the combination of key logging with eye tracking enables better understanding of the cognitive processes that underlie written text production. It is possible to differentiate between pauses during which writers look back in their text at a local level (reading or scanning within the sentence they are currently composing) or at a more global level (looking farther back into their text). Other combinations are also possible, such as asking participants to produce a think-aloud protocol, either simultaneously or retrospectively (Leijten, Van Waes, & Janssen, 2010; Van Weijen, 2009); or combining the tool with more ethnographically oriented research techniques used to study writing, for example, of journalists (Van Hout, 2009).

KEYSTROKE LOGGING AND PAUSE ANALYSIS

The idea of analyzing pausing in writing stems from psycholinguistic analyses of the spoken language production process. In this context pauses have been considered a window to the cognitive processes underlying speech production. As early as in the 1960s, Goldman-Eisler (1961, 1968) noted that although pause durations varied across speakers, pauses tended to occur frequently at clause boundaries, sometimes within sentences, but almost never within words. Similar results were obtained for so-called filled pauses (e.g., hesitation sounds; for examples, see Swerts, 1998; Eklund & Shriberg, 1998). In the typical text production situation, as distinguished from more interactive writing situations, such as computer chats, only silent pauses are expected to occur; therefore, filled pauses will not be further dealt with in this chapter. The functions of silent pauses in spoken language production are thought to represent planning, execution, and monitoring of utterances (Brotherton, 1979).

In writing research, pauses have become an important object of study, and, as in spoken language research, are considered to be an important window on the cognitive processes that underlie language production. When pauses in keystroke logging are analyzed, they are not thought to reflect writers merely having problems finding the keys on the keyboard (e.g., Grabowski, 2008; Nottbusch, 2010). As pointed out by Spelman Miller (2006), although written and spoken language are not normally produced under the same processing conditions, the writer, like the speaker, has to move from communicative intent to production in real time. Furthermore, to our knowledge, few, if any, studies have shown any clear correlations between pause distributions during keyboarding and text quality. A keystroke logging study by Wengelin (2007) indicated that a high frequency of word-internal pauses was related to low lexical diversity in the text production processes by writers with dyslexia, but in general writers appear to be able to produce high-quality texts with very different pause distributions. Of course, much more research is needed on this topic in both typical writers and those with specific learning disabilities such as dyslexia or dysgraphia or language learning disability. As mentioned earlier, there have been many approaches to the study of pauses in writing (for a review, see Wengelin, 2006), but as far as pauses are concerned, the strength of keystroke logging method is its capability of providing detailed quantitative data of when and where pauses occur.

Most keystroke logging programs provide output that can be used for pause analysis more or less automatically (Table 22.1). At a minimum, the researcher has to have access to the time stamp for each keystroke and mouse event, which is generally provided by the general file. A linear file facilitates qualitative pause analysis, but can also, for example, be used to generate pause concordances. Example 22.1 below shows an extract of a linear file generated by a ScriptLog recording of a Swedish 10-year-old, writing in English as a foreign language (FL).

Example 22.1:   Linear file with pause criterion of 2 s

```
<START><0.03.719>It   was   Mat<BACKSPACE>y,   and   the   sun
was   <0.02.125><BACKSPACE28>   The   first   i<BACKSPACE>time
I   met   him   was<0.07.344><BACKSPACE3>I   thought   <0.04.281>
<0.37.485><BACKSPACE36>He   was   thin,   w<BACKSPACE>
vey<BACKSPACE>ry   thin   and   in   his   eyes   <0.04.484><MOUSE
EVENT>   <BACKSPACE>It was sprn<BACKSPACE>ingtime. <0.05.687>
The        su<0.08.922><0.09.641><BACKSPACE26>m<BACKSPACE>My
firs<BACKSPACE13>The first time <CAPITAL>I<BACKSPACE><CAPITAL>I
met   g<BACKSPACE>him   was   <0.03.157>in   MAy.   My   first   <MOUSE
```

```
EVENT> <DOWN><LEFT><BACKSPACE>a<MOUSE EVENT>impression of
him wasn't <0.05.718>right,
```

> Note: The angle brackets indicate pause locations and the numbers
> between them show the associated pause durations.

Some programs like ScriptLog and Inputlog provide their own pause analysis functions. For instance, ScriptLog outputs a simple list with the time stamp of each pause and its duration. ScriptLog can also output pause statistics for so-called microcontexts chosen by the researcher, such as pauses associated with a certain word or a sentence ending. ScriptLog provides a large range of predefined microcontexts, but as mentioned earlier, the analyst is also free to define his or her own microcontexts by means of regular expressions. No syntactic parsing is included. Although the current version of ScriptLog offers two preset pause criteria, 2 s and 5 s, the analyst should define his or her own pause criteria. The first question he or she needs to ask is "What is a pause?" or "What is a pause in my research?" Below we suggest some guidelines.

First, a specific characteristic of typing is that each keystroke is a discrete event and the word *pause* has by some researchers been used to describe the time that elapses between two keystrokes, the *interkey intervals* or *keystroke transitions*. Other researchers consider all keystroke transitions a *candidate* for a pause, but assume (implicitly or explicitly) that pauses are considerably longer than could be expected of a "normal" keystroke transition. The latter researchers may need to decide whether the same criterion can be used for all writers in their study. Writers of different ages and with different experiences have very different typing skills and may type with considerably different speeds. For example, young children are usually slower typists than their older peers, secretaries are typically faster than many other professionals, and people with learning difficulties are frequently slower typists than writers without learning difficulties (Wengelin, 2002, 2006). Because the question of how to adapt individual pause criteria according to different typing speeds has not been resolved, researchers need to control for typing speed in other ways. The most common way of doing so is to use a copying task in which writers either have to copy a written text or to write something from memory. See Grabowski (2008) for a more detailed discussion about keyboard skills and copying tasks.

Second, the level or nature of language in text production that is investigated will influence the choice of pause criterion. Researchers interested in content will most likely set higher pause criteria than researchers interested in typing fluency or morphological structures. For instance, Matsuhashi (1981) and Wengelin (2006), who did not use keystroke logging, but rather video recordings, used a 4-s criterion. There was no strong theoretical reason behind this choice, but as shown by Chanquoy, Foulin, and Fayol (1996), this criterion turned out to be a good cutoff point for pauses between phrases and clauses, on the one hand, and paragraphs and sentences, on the other. The mean pause durations for 10 university students in their study were 17.3 s for paragraph boundaries, 12.7 s for sentence boundaries, 2.8 s for clause boundaries, 1.2 s for phrase boundaries, and 0.9 s for word boundaries. Johansson (2009, p. 163) used a 5-s criterion "not only to exclude pauses on the micro-level, but also to include pauses expected to reflect deeper cognitive processes during text writing." Authors who have been more interested in lower-level language or cognitive processes have used a 2-s criterion (e.g., Holmqvist, Johansson, Strömqvist, & Wengelin, 2002; Spelman Miller, 2000; Sullivan & Lindgren, 2002). The important question is not what the ultimate, *absolute* pause criterion is, but how the chosen criterion suits the aim of the research. Example 22.2 below shows the same linear file as the one shown in Example 22.1, but with a 5-s pause criterion. Together, Examples 22.1 and 22.2 show how different pause criteria will answer different types of questions.

Example 22.2: Linear file with a pause criterion of 5 s

```
<START>It was Mat<BACKSPACE>y, and the sun was BACKSPACE28>The
first i<BACKSPACE>time I met him was<0.07.344><BACKSPACE3>I thought
<0.37.485><BACKSPACE36>He was thin, w<BACKSPACE>vey<BACKSPACE>ry
thin   and   in   his   eyes   <MOUSE   EVENT><BACKSPACE>It   was
sprn<BACKSPACE>  ingtime.    <0.05.687>The  su<0.08.922><0.09.6
41><BACKSPACE26>m   <BACKSPACE>My   firs<BACKSPACE13>The   first
time  <CAPITAL>I  <BACKSPACE><CAPITAL>I  met  g<BACKSPACE>him
was  in  MAy.  My  first  <MOUSE  EVENT><DOWN><LEFT><BACKSPACE>
a<MOUSE EVENT> impression of him wasn't <0.05.718>right,
```

Pause analysis by means of keystroke logging has been used to increase our knowledge in several areas. In most cases pause locations, pause durations, and pause frequencies are analyzed. One important area of research has dealt with the association between planning and pauses. Just like earlier studies of other input modes, such as handwriting (Chanquoy et al., 1996; Matsuhashi, 1981, 1987) and dictation (Schilperoord, 1996, 2002), studies conducted by means of keystroke logging have indicated that boundaries preceding higher-level units such as paragraphs are associated with longer pauses than lower-level units such as clauses, phrases, and words (Spelman Miller, 2006; Van Waes & Schellens, 2003). Wengelin (2002) could not confirm the relation between pause durations and unit size, but showed that higher-level boundaries were more likely to be associated with a pause than lower-level boundaries, a result that most likely points in the same direction. An important contribution to this field was made by Spelman Miller (2002, 2006) who addressed the dynamic nature of keystroke logging data. She pointed out (Spelman Miller, 2006, p. 133) that, although, for instance, the location of a pause immediately after the word *student* could be described as following a noun phrase, this conclusion could later be shown to be only temporarily true. The writer can, for example, add -s' to form students,' which changes the pause location from phrase final to phrase internal. In order to account for the temporary status of language produced online, Spelman Miller prefers to refer to units that may or may not survive in subsequent text modifications as potential completion points on the following levels: character, word, intermediate constituent, clause, and sentence.

Third, the question of processing units is also relevant to the internal word level. Studies of single-word typing existed already in the early 20th century (e.g.,

Coover, 1923). More recently, this type of research has been pursued by Nottbusch and colleagues who claim that within-word pauses allow for conclusions about the underlying cognitive processes (Nottbusch, 2010; Nottbusch, Grimm, Weingarten, & Will, 2005; Nottbusch, Weingarten, & Sahel, 2007; Nottbusch, Weingarten, & Will, 1998). They analyzed interkey intervals (i.e., without stipulating a pause criterion) in German and characterized word writing as "producing a hierarchically ordered set of linguistically motivated units" (Nottbusch et al., 2007, p. 33). They showed that in single-word writing, the longest pauses are always found at the initial position of the word, and that this pause duration is correlated with variables such as word frequency, word length, and task type. Interestingly, pauses in pure morpheme boundaries did not appear to be longer than in any other boundaries within words. Pauses in syllable boundaries, on the other hand, were, and combined syllable-morpheme boundaries had the longest pauses. Their results strongly suggest that the time course of motor execution in writing is dependent on linguistic processes involved in written language production.

Fourth, another important area of research for pause studies through keystroke logging is the area of fluency and execution periods (Chenoweth & Hayes, 2001; Hayes & Chenoweth, 2006; Leijten, 2007; Lindgren, Sullivan, & Spelman Miller, 2008; Spelman Miller, Lindgren, & Sullivan, 2008). This line of research is closely related to questions about the role of working memory or cognitive capacity in writing (see Chapter 21, this volume). It is well known that motor execution can have a cognitive cost (Kellogg, 2004; Kellogg, Olive, & Piolat, 2007), but few studies have explored the relation between typing skills and execution periods in text production. Alves, Castro, de Sousa, and Strömqvist (2007) showed that slow typists made more pauses and had shorter execution periods than faster typists (see Chapter 16, this volume). Alves et al. suggested that in order to cope with limited cognitive resources and high demands of execution, the slow writers might be using a serial way of composing, devoting pauses to high-level processing and execution periods to typing only.

Fifth, and finally, keystroke logging has been used to characterize and compare writers of different ages and writing experience (e.g., Johansson, 2009; Lindgren, Leijten, & Van Waes, in press; Strömqvist, Nordqvist, & Wengelin, 2004); writers with different types of language disorders (e.g., dyslexia; Wengelin, 2002, 2006, 2007); and first and second language writers (Spelman Miller, 2000, 2002; Van Weijen, 2009). Generally these studies indicate that age, experience, and language competence influence the writing process (Kellogg, 2008). Young and inexperienced writers, writers with language disorders, and second language writers appear to be less fluent writers who make more pauses in general and more word-level pauses specifically. Naturally, this finding raises the question of whether writers produce written language the same way across different types of texts and different input modes. Here an important contribution was made by Van Waes and Schellens (2003), who noticed that writers made more pauses in typing than in handwriting. By clustering pause behavior and revision behavior, they identified five different writing profiles. Interestingly, these were not stable across input modes. These results indicate that writing processes are not only dependent on individual factors but also depend greatly on the constraints of the writing environment.

KEYSTROKE LOGGING AND REVISION ANALYSIS

As explained earlier, the writing process of various writers is characterized by the varying ways they pause and revise during online writing. Although the final text product might be comparable in quality and structure, the process of planning, formulating, and revising might be quite different across writers. Keystroke logging tools that facilitate revision analysis at the moment are JEdit/Trace-it (Kollberg, 1998; Severinson Eklundh & Kollberg, 1996; Sullivan & Lindgren, 2006) and Inputlog (Leijten & Van Waes, 2006). Both tools analyze revisions as either insertions or deletions. Researchers have to refine these automated analyses in order to fully relate them to the existing writing product and process taxonomies of revisions (Faigley & Witte, 1981; Leijten, 2007; Van Waes & Schellens, 2003). In this section we provide a short overview of recent research related to online revision analysis that was conducted using keystroke logging tools. Furthermore, we describe the current status of keystroke logging tools that include automated revision analysis.

Lindgren and Sullivan (2006) stated that revisions have several functions and can represent both low-level and high-level processes. Low-level processes are the correction of typing errors (Grabowski, 2008; Inhoff & Gordon, 1997) and the influence of linguistic units within and beyond word level (Nottbusch et al., 2007; Weingarten, Nottbusch, & Will, 2004). Planning, execution, and control in written sentence production can be placed on a continuum (Leijten, Van Waes, & Ransdell, 2010; Nottbusch, 2010; Nottbusch et al., 2007). On a higher level, the revision process is influenced by the rereading and evaluation of the previously written text (Braaksma, Rijlaarsdam, Van den Bergh, & Van Hout-Wolters, 2004; Hayes, 2004; Leijten, Van Waes, & Ransdell, 2010).

The fields in which automated online revision analysis have been performed include: *developmental writing* (Grabowski, 2008; Johansson, 2009), *first and second language revisions* (Lindgren, 2005; Thorson, 2000; Van Weijen, 2009), *dyslexia and aphasia* (Wengelin, 2001; Wengelin & Strömqvist, 2000), and *professional writing* (Leijten, Van Waes, & Janssen, 2010; Perin, 2003; Sleurs, Jacobs, & Van Waes, 2003; Van Hout, 2009). The variety of kinds of research shows that keystroke logging is a powerful tool for the analysis of online revisions. Moreover, another powerful method is combining the logging data with think-aloud protocols (Stevenson, Schoonen, & de Glopper, 2006; Van Weijen, 2009) or stimulated retrospective interviews (Leijten, Van Waes, & Janssen, 2010; Lindgren & Sullivan, 2003). The cognitive effort of revisions can be isolated experimentally via the dual-task paradigm (Leijten, Van Waes, & Ransdell, 2010; Van Waes, Leijten, & Quinlan, 2010) or the triple task technique (Piolat, Kellogg, & Farioli, 2001).

As described earlier, there are two logging tools that are suitable for automated revision analysis: JEdit/Trace-it and Inputlog. Because JEdit/Trace-it is no longer being developed, we will discuss the potential of Inputlog. Moreover, the revision module of Inputlog is mainly based on the functionality of Trace-it (Kollberg, 1998; Severinson Eklundh, 1994; Severinson Eklundh & Kollberg, 1992, 1996, 2003; Spelman Miller & Sullivan, 2006). In this section we will first describe the revision module of Inputlog, which can be found under the play tab of the program. As in Trace-it, every logged writing session can be replayed in various ways. Furthermore, we elaborate on the analysis that can be performed (semi-) automatically.

In Inputlog, a recorded writing session can be replayed. The session is shown in four main windows (Figure 22.1) and users can navigate between the windows via a flexible toolbar:

1. Text process: *top left window (1)*. The writing session can be replayed at different speeds. It can be played back exactly as it was recorded (in real time); it can be replayed faster at the default speed, during which each interkey interval is limited to 150 ms, or users can replay the session at a percentage of the real-time speed or set each pause to a fixed interval.

2. Revision data: *top right window (2)*. The revision data are represented in an Excel-like matrix, showing the main characteristics of each revision (revision number, revision type, recursiveness, start time revision, end time revision, nesting depth, pause time before revision, number of characters before revision, and number of characters after revision). Besides these fixed variables, researchers can add new variables: type of error, linguistic category of error, grammatical error, and so forth. All variables—given and added—can be changed and saved. This capability creates great flexibility for researchers to analyze the data according to their research question.

3. Linear representation: *bottom left window (3)*. The linear representation of the text is based on the S-notation by Kollberg and Severinsson (Kollberg, 1998; Severinson Eklundh & Kollberg, 1996). The S-notation has been developed together with Trace-it (Severinson Eklundh & Kollberg, 1992) and has subsequently been used to describe revisions in online writing processes (Severinson Eklundh & Kollberg, 2003; Sullivan & Lindgren, 2006). An example of S-notation is presented in Figure 22.2.

4. Graphic representation: *bottom right window (4)*. Finally, we have opted for a graphical representation of the writing process. The graphical representation is a visual representation of the number of characters that are produced and deleted at each moment during the writing process. The cursor position and the pauses longer than a predefined threshold value are also shown. The graphical representation is based on a combination of Perin's (2003) progress analysis and Lindgren and colleagues' interactive representation via a geographical information system (Lindgren & Sullivan, 2002; Lindgren, Sullivan, Lindgren, & Spelman Miller, 2007). The x-axis represents the time (in seconds), whereas the y-axis indicates the number of characters that are produced effectively in the text produced so far. The top line indicates total character production including deleted characters at each point in time (cursor end position); the bottom line indicates the characters retained after deletions at each point in time. Thus, when the bottom line drops, a number of characters are deleted. The zone in between the two lines shows the increasing difference between the characters produced and the characters in the text. The

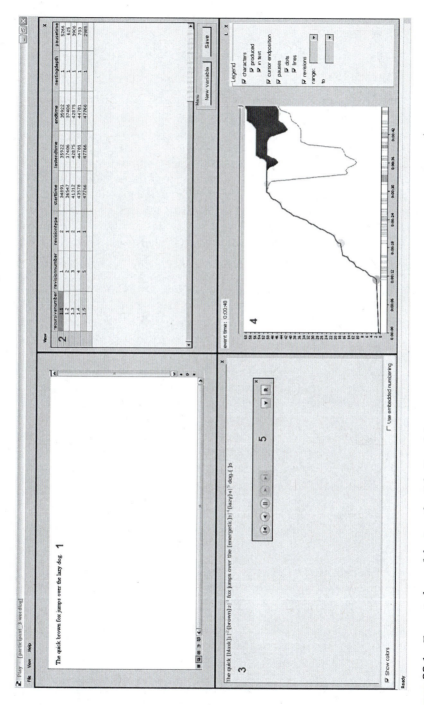

Figure 22.1   Four windows of the Inputlog "play" module.

OUTPUT:

The quick brown fox jumps over the lazy dog.

S-NOTATION:

The quick b[lack]$^{2.1}|_{2.2}${rown}$^{2.2}$ fox jump[ed$^{1.1}$]$|_{1.1}$s over the lazy dog.$|_{2.1}$

REVISIONS:
1: 1.1 - Deletion
2: 2.1 - Deletion
3: 2.2 - Insertion

Figure 22.2   Representation of revisions in S-notation via Inputlog 4 revision analysis.

small dashed lines above the *x*-axis shows all the points in time at which the writer pauses during text production and the large pauses are represented by shaded circles. The size of each circle indicates the length of the pause. The solid lines above the *x*-axis represent the location of each revision (e.g., in this case at 35 s and 37 s). Researchers can generate a graphical representation automatically or manually based on the revision data.

The revision analysis of Inputlog generates various XML files containing a basic analysis of the number, level, and kind of revision that has taken place during the writing session.[2] To define revisions Inputlog uses an algorithm and a set of rules. The revision analysis first defines critical events of nonlinearity in the writing process that can be linked to a revision and then evaluates these instances by comparing the operations in the isolated writing episode to the revision rules in the algorithm. Inputlog successively analyzes the beginning of the revision, the nesting of revisions, the selection of the text to revise or the positioning of the cursor, the (possible) deletion of the text, and the end of the revision. Inputlog treats revisions at the point of utterance differently from revisions that occur away from the point of utterance in the text produced so far. This distinction is described by Lindgren and Sullivan (2006) as precontextual and contextual revisions:

> *Pre-contextual revisions* are revisions at the point of transcription (or point of utterance) that occur when the writer notices and decides that something that has just been or is in the process of being transcribed needs to be adjusted (p. 161).
> *Contextual revisions* are revisions that are undertaken when writers move away from the point of transcription to insert new text or to delete, substitute, or rearrange already written text. When a contextual revision is undertaken, writers are operating within an externalized context (on paper/screen); a contextual revision is conducted within a previously written and completed sentence. Hence, a contextual revision is both preceded and followed by text (p. 171).

---

[2] Standardization of the XML-structure is conducted within the COST "European Research Network on Learning to Write Effectively" (http://www.cost-lwe.eu). More information about this project can also be found at http://www.writingpro.eu.

The categorization of precontextual revisions is sometimes unclear without complementary data provided via thinking-aloud or retrospective protocols. Therefore, it is often impossible to describe precisely the "range" of a revision. Because it is impossible to classify the content of a revision automatically at the point of transcription, Inputlog categorizes these revisions always as "deletions." The insertions are left aside in the analysis and considered as "new text." Of course, researchers can analyze these instances manually and could make more fine-grained interpretations. For instance, in the example in Figure 22.2 the revision of *jumped* into *jumps* is analyzed as a deletion (1.1) and not as a substitution. The other two revisions take place in the text produced so far and can be classified as deletions and insertions. (See the Appendix for detailed description.) The example shows the deletion of *lack* (2.1) followed by the insertion of *rown* (2.2). Researchers can also categorize this revision as a substitution (in the Excel-like matrix it is possible to reclassify a precoded revision).

At the moment of the revision, analysis of Inputlog calculates the number of revisions, type of revisions, level of nesting, and number of words and characters involved in the revision operation, as well as the location of the revisions in relation to the point of utterance. Figure 22.3 presents such a matrix, based on the example described above.

In the future, new technologies will create new research questions about revision strategies. The emergence of eye tracking in combination with keystroke logging especially opens new perspectives (Wengelin, Leijten, & Van Waes, 2010; Wengelin et al., 2009).[3] Because revision strategies are influenced by the rereading of the text produced so far and the cognitive resources that are available, we expect eye tracking during writing to be a main research focus in the future (Alamargot & Chanquoy, 2001; Hayes & Nash, 1996; Kellogg, 1996, 2004; Leijten, Van Waes, & Ransdell, 2010).

KEYSTROKE LOGGING AS A PEDAGOGICAL TOOL

So far this chapter has described several of the complex cognitive processes that are involved in writing and the use of keystroke logging in assisting researchers in the observation and analysis of these processes and their resultant products. However, the tools described have proven useful not only for research into the writing process but also for developing writing skills through teaching. Before moving into the specifics of keystroke logging as a pedagogical tool, we will briefly outline some general aspects of writing development.

An important aspect of writing development is to become aware of various aspects of one's own writing: "If students are not even aware of their writing strategies and their results, they can hardly be expected to evaluate—and thus deliberately change maintain or abandon—them" (Rijlaarsdam & Couzijn, 2000,

---

[3] This line of research is under development at the moment via the COST research network on learning to write effectively (COST IS0703), working group 4: technological advances in writing tools (coordinators: Luuk Van Waes & Anne Mangen, main contributors to research on reading during writing: Mariëlle Leijten, Åsa Wengelin, Victoria Johansson, Roger Johansson, Mark Torrance, Guido Nottbusch, Daniel Perin, and David Galbraith).

Revision number	Revision number (recursive)	Type of revision	Level of nesting	Start time revision episode	End time revision episode	End time revision	Pause time before revision	Number of characters produced before revision	Number of characters produced after revision	Number of characters in final text before revision	Number of characters in final text after revision
1	1.1	2	1	23562	23953	23953	734	28	31	28	25
2	2.1	2	1	34718	35406	35406	3703	52	56	49	45
3	2.2	1	1	36109	37890	37890	703	56	60	45	49

Figure 22.3 Example of list of revisions generated by Inputlog 4.

p. 176). Thus, if writers' metacognitive awareness of different writing aspects, such as language, audience, topic, genre, and structure, as well as awareness of the writing process per se can be raised, writing development is likely to occur (Galbraith & Rijlaarsdam, 1999; McCutchen, 2000). However, a successful writer has to not only master and self-regulate the components of the writing process but also acquire sufficient knowledge about how to integrate language, topic, genre, and audiences into a coherent text (Graham & Harris, 2000; McCutchen, 2000). Accordingly, it is not realistic to assume that writers are able to juggle the writing process per se and learn from it simultaneously. Separating the actual writing from the reflection and learning processes can stimulate awareness by "offer[ing] students the opportunity to 'step out' of the writing process in order to observe their activities and results, and to learn from this by verbalizing what they observe" (Rijlaarsdam & Couzijn, 2000, p. 176; Rijlaarsdam et al., 2008). Writers should be provided with a learning environment that both reduces cognitive load and affords noticing of various aspects of writing (cf., "noticing" in Schmidt, 1990).

Observational learning is a writing development method that is framed around the ideas of both cognitive capacity and metacognitive awareness (Braaksma, Rijlaarsdam, & Van den Bergh, 2002; Rijlaarsdam et al., 2008). Without writing themselves, learners observe "model" writers composing a piece of text. While watching, the learner comments and reflects on the model writer's actions. Keystroke logging is well suited as a tool for both observational learning and directing learners' attention toward the text production process rather than toward the final text product. When used with a learner's own writing, his or her own online output is used as new input that provides the writer with input at a suitable level (Rijlaarsdam & Couzijn, 2000; Swain & Lapkin, 2000), promoting inspection of writing and metacognitive awareness.

Reflection and discussion are key aspects of observational learning. When something in the writing under observation has been noticed "we can analyze it and compare it to what we have noticed on other occasions" (Schmidt, 1990, p. 132). When brought forward for reflection and discussion with someone, the social interaction further strengthens the learning process (Fortune & Thorp, 2001; Vygotsky, 1978). Hansen (2006) investigated retrospective methods in translation training at the university level. She studied two methods, one including keystroke logging as a retrospective tool for reflection and discussion. She concluded that for "preventing SD's [sources of disturbance in translation processes] and for guaranteeing a long-term effect, the dialogue and feedback seem to be crucial with both methods" (p. 27).

Typically a pedagogical session using keystroke logging as a tool for reflection starts with a "normal" writing session. The writer is informed about the procedure and provided with a topic, the logging is started, and the writer is left to compose the text. When the writer has finished writing, the logging is stopped and the text is replayed. The replay function enables the writer to see the text evolve on the screen in exactly the same way as it was inscribed. The writer is asked to talk about everything that happens on the screen, the changes that are made, and, when the cursor stops, the reason for the pause. Alternatively, the writer can be asked to focus only on revisions of a specific aspect of the writing process: language used, structural aspects of production, or other components of the writing process such as planning. Studies have shown that (a) learners benefit both from reflection on their own text and from reflection on a peer's text (Sullivan & Lindgren, 2002); and (b) some learners seem to need more prompting in order to define points of reflection (Lindgren, Sullivan, & Stevenson, 2008).

Studies using keystroke logging as a pedagogical tool have included learners from different age groups. Hansen (2006) and Lindgren, Sullivan, Deutschmann, and Steinvall (2009) used the method in translation classes with university students who were trained to translate texts from a foreign language into their mother language. Other studies have targeted the writing classroom of adults (Sullivan & Lindgren, 2002) or adolescents (Lindgren, 2004; Lindgren & Sullivan, 2003). A common denominator in all these studies is the informants' positive experiences of using the method. They find it revealing of insights into what happens during the writing process: "The log-files provide an excellent tool for revealing discrepancies between what subjects think they do and what they really do" (Hansen, 2006, p. 27).

The advantage of using keystroke logging as a pedagogical tool is primarily its capacity as an awareness-raiser. As such, it has assisted learners to detect issues in their written products and processes that need further attention and thus improve their products. Hansen (2006) reported that retrospection through the replay of a keystroke logfile "has advantages with respect to detecting SD's that can only be discovered via the combination of replay and log-file, that is, in relation to structural problems, reception problems, inappropriate changes, and revisions" (p. 27). Adult learners found the method useful in raising their awareness of various features, such as knowledge of the writing process, language, tasks, or motor skills that they believed were important in order to develop their writing (Lindgren & Sullivan, 2006). Younger writers improved their first language texts after retrospective reflection using keystroke logging (Lindgren, 2004). The method increased their awareness, in particular, of form and style when using it with foreign language writing (Lindgren, Sullivan, & Stevenson, 2008).

The form of the retrospective session and the role of the interlocutor seem important to maximize the learning effect. In the translation classroom the elements of dialogue and feedback in the retrospective session seemed to be important for a long-term effect (Hansen, 2006). However, when only peer feedback is accompanying the replay of the keystroke log, students benefit more if given feedback from someone trained in peer assessment and peer feedback prior to the reflection session (Lindgren et al., 2009). If the replay session is only guided by the replay itself, some writers may find it difficult to decide what to bring up for discussion. In these cases a more active role of a teacher, or a set of focus areas for discussion, is necessary: "The use of the computer to enhance reflection in the teaching of a foreign language, thus, needs to be directed and structured by well-organized teacher-student and student-student collaboration to maximize the student learning outcomes" (Lindgren, Sullivan, & Stevenson, 2008, p. 201).

CONCLUDING REMARKS

In this chapter we have presented a relatively new methodology for writing research and pedagogy, namely, keystroke logging (KSL). Several computer programs have been developed, and their use as research tools has expanded over the past 10 years. There is now a growing body of research in which keystroke logging has been used to investigate various aspects of text, writing processes, and writing development. This research demonstrates that the use of KSL deepens our understanding of the writing process. Transfer of this knowledge to writers who are using computers in learning to write better is very important. That these programs have been successfully used both in research and pedagogy illustrates their value for both advancing understanding of writing processes in the computer-assisted writing environment and for improving writing of developing writers across their lifespan.

Also, further technical development of KSL tools is important and should focus both on technical and contextual elements. From the technical point of view, XML standardization seems to be crucial. A common output structure and tag library would enable easily exchanged logged files between programs, enabling optimally bridging analyses of the different programs to achieve more common approaches. Also the combination or merging of data from other registration and observation tools (e.g., eye-tracking, usability programs) is high on the developers' agenda. Further integration with data from these sources would enrich the KSL data to a large extent. Finally, projects have been started to aggregate the data from the letter (keystroke) level to the word level by merging them with existing lexica and natural language processing (NLP) tools. This step in development will enrich the data with valuable grammatical and syntactical information of the process data, creating a valuable basis for more linguistically oriented writing process research, especially across languages.

Because more and more researchers are using KSL data in their research, experience and sophistication with the interpretation of this kind of process data are expanding, opening up new discussions in the writing community, for instance, related to the use of a threshold in pause analyses. It is important that the findings and consequences related to these issues are openly described and discussed and that implications are carefully considered. Also, the use of more advanced statistical techniques to explore KSL data opens new perspectives. For instance, multilevel analysis is certainly one of the techniques that has been shown to be suitable for the analyses of these kind of data (see Beers, Quinlan, & Harbaugh, 2010; Van Waes et al., 2010). It is our aim to bring together expertise on these aspects in a new online knowledge center, called WritingPro (http://www.writingpro.eu). We hope to report about this initiative in detail soon and in the meantime encourage readers to visit this site to keep up with new developments and indeed even contribute to it. In summary, for the future we hope the tools will continue to develop along the lines described above and that they become easily accessible for researchers as well as pedagogues and continue to inform research as well as help writers learn about the writing process.

APPENDIX

Time	Document	Cursor Position	Range Length	Content
0	1	1	1	
12890	2	2	1	T
13468	3	3	1	h
13890	4	4	1	e
14078	5	5	1	
15140	6	6	1	q
15453	7	7	1	u
15593	8	8	1	i
15984	9	9	1	c
16125	10	10	1	k
16531	11	11	1	
17265	12	12	1	b
17593	13	13	1	l
18047	14	14	1	a
18437	15	15	1	c
18828	16	16	1	k
19000	17	17	1	
19203	18	18	1	f
19328	19	19	1	o
19781	20	20	1	x
20000	21	21	1	
20218	22	22	1	j
20390	23	23	1	u
20703	24	24	1	m
21062	25	25	1	p
22156	26	26	1	e
22531	27	27	1	d
22828	28	28	1	
23562	27	27		
23797	26	26		
23953	25	25		
24578	26	26	1	s
24906	27	27	1	
25140	28	28	1	o
25390	29	29	1	v
25750	30	30	1	e
26078	31	31	1	r
26203	32	32	1	
26375	33	33	1	t
26562	34	34	1	h
26656	35	35	1	e
26781	36	36	1	

Time	Document	Cursor Position	Range Length	Content
26968	37	37	1	l
27703	38	38	1	a
27953	39	39	1	z
28343	40	40	1	y
28437	41	41	1	

Time	Document	Cursor Position	Range Length	Content
28828	42	42	1	d
28953	43	43	1	o
29312	44	44	1	g
30765	45	45	1	
31015	46	46	1	.
31812	46	45		
32312	46	44		
32359	46	43		
32406	46	42		
32453	46	41		
32500	46	40		
32547	46	39		
32593	46	38		
32640	46	37		
32687	46	36		
32734	46	35		
32781	46	34		
32828	46	33		
32875	46	32		
32922	46	31		
32968	46	30		
33015	46	29		
33062	46	28		
33109	46	27		
33156	46	26		
33203	46	25		
33250	46	24		
33297	46	23		
33343	46	22		
33390	46	21		
33437	46	20		
33484	46	19		
33531	46	18		

Time	Document	Cursor Position	Range Length	Content
33812	46	17		
34047	46	16		
34718	45	15		
34922	44	14		
35156	43	13		
35406	42	12		
36109	43	13	1	r
36343	44	14	1	o
37656	45	15	1	w
37890	46	16	1	n
40297	46	46		

REFERENCES

Alamargot, D., & Chanquoy, L. (Eds.). (2001). *Through the models of writing*. Dordrecht: Kluwer.

Alamargot, D., Chesnet, D., Dansac, C., & Ros, C. (2006). Eye and Pen: A new device for studying reading during writing. *Behavior Research Methods Instruments and Computers, 38*(2), 287–299.

Alves, R. A., Castro, S. L., de Sousa, L., & Strömqvist, S. (2007). Influence of typing skill on pause-execution cycles in written composition. In M. Torrance, D. Galbraith & L. Van Waes (Eds.), *Recent developpements in writing-process research* (Vol. 20, pp. 55–65). Dordrecht: Kluwer.

Andersson, B., Dahl, J., Holmquist, K., Holsanova, J., Johansson, V., Karlsson, H., ... Wengelin, Å. (2006). Combining keystroke logging with eye-tracking. In L. Van Waes, M. Leijten & C. Neuwirth (Eds.), *Writing and digital media* (Vol. 17, pp. 166–172). Oxford: Elsevier.

Beers, S., Quinlan, T., & Harbaugh, A. (2010). Adolescent students' reading during writing behaviors and relationships with text quality: an eyetracking study. *Reading and Writing, 23*(7), 743–775.

Bowles, M. (2010). *The think-aloud controversy in second language research*. New York: Routledge.

Braaksma, M. A. H., Rijlaarsdam, G., & Van den Bergh, H. (2002). Observational learning and the effects of model-observer similarity. *Journal of Educational Psychology, 94*(2), 405–415.

Braaksma, M. A. H., Rijlaarsdam, G., Van den Bergh, H., & Van Hout-Wolters, B. H. A. M. (2004). Observational learning and its effects on the orchestration of writing processes. *Cognition and Instruction, 22*(1), 1–36.

Bridwell, L. S., & Duin, A. H. (1985). Looking in-depth at writers: Computers as writing medium and research tool. In J. L. Collins & E. A. Sommers (Eds.), *Writing on-line* (pp. 115–121). Upper Montclair, NJ: Boynton/Cook.

Brotherton, P. (1979). Speaking and not speaking: Processes for translating ideas into speech. In A. W. Siegman & S. Feldstein (Eds.), *Of speech and time: Temporal speech patterns in interpersonal contexts* (pp. 179–209). Hillsdale, NJ: Erlbaum.

Chanquoy, L., Foulin, J. N., & Fayol, M. (1996). Writing in adults: A real-time approach. In G. Rijlaarsdam, H. van den Bergh, & M. Couzijn (Eds.), *Theories, models and methodology in writing research* (pp. 36–43). Amsterdam: Amsterdam University Press.

Chenoweth, N. A., & Hayes, J. R. (2001). Fluency in writing: Generating text in L1 and L2. *Written Communication, 18*(1), 80–98.

Coover, J. E. (1923). A method of teaching typewriting based upon a psychological analysis of expert typing. *National Education Association, 61*, 561–567.

Eklund, R., & Shriberg, E. (1998). *Crosslinguistic disfluency modelling: A comparative analysis of Swedish and American English human–human and human–machine dialogues.* Paper presented at the 5th International Conference on Spoken Language Processing, Sydney.

Faigley, L., & Witte, S. (1981). Analyzing revision. *College Composition and Communication, 32*, 400–414.

Fortune, A., & Thorp, D. (2001). Knotted and entangled: new light on the identification, classification and value of language related episodes in collaborative output tasks. *Language Awareness, 10*(2–3), 143–160.

Galbraith, D., & Rijlaarsdam, G. (1999). Effective strategies for the teaching and learning of writing. *Learning and Instruction, 32*(2), 93–233.

Goldman-Eisler, F. (1961). The distribution of pause durations in speech. *Language and Speech, 4*, 232–237.

Goldman-Eisler, F. (1968). *Psycholinguistics: experiments in spontaneous speech.* New York: Academic Press.

Grabowski, J. (2008). The internal structure of university students' keyboard skills. *Journal of Writing Research, 1*(1), 27–52.

Graham, S., & Harris, K. R. (2000). The role of self-regulation and transcription skills in writing and writing development. *Educational Psychologist, 35*(1), 3–12.

Greene, S., & Higgins, L. (1994). "Once upon a time": The use of retrospective accounts in building theory in composition. In P. Smagorinsky (Ed.), *Speaking about writing* (pp. 115–140). London: Sage.

Hansen, G. (2006). Retrospection methods in translator training and translation research. *Journal of Specialised Translation, 5*(1), 2–41.

Hayes, J. R. (2004). What triggers revision? In L. Allal, L. Chanquoy, & P. Largy (Eds.), *Revision: Cognitive and instructional processes* (Vol. 13, pp. 9–20). Dordrecht: Kluwer.

Hayes, J. R., & Chenoweth, N. (2006). Is working memory Involved in the transcribing and editing of Texts? *Written Communication, 23*(2), 135–141.

Hayes, J. R., & Nash, J. G. (1996). On the nature of planning in writing. In C. M. Levy & S. Ransdell (Eds.), *The science of writing: Theories, methods, individual differences, and applications* (pp. 29–55). Mahwah, NJ: Erlbaum.

Holmqvist, K., Johansson, V., Strömqvist, S., & Wengelin, Å. (2002). Studying reading and writing online. In S. Strömqvist (Ed.), *The diversity of languages and language learning* (pp. 103–123). Lund: Lund University, Centre for Languages and Literature.

Inhoff, A. W., & Gordon, A. M. (1997). Eye movements and eye-hand coordination during typing. *Current Directions in Psychological Science, 6*(6), 153–157.

Jakobsen, A. L. (2006). Research methods in translation-Translog. In K. P. H. Sullivan & E. Lindgren (Eds.), *Computer keystroke logging: Methods and applications* (Vol. 18, pp. 95–105). Oxford: Elsevier.

Janssen, D., Van Waes, L., & Van den Bergh, H. (1996). Effects of thinking aloud on writing processes. In C. M. Levy & S. Ransdell (Eds.), *The science of writing: Theories, individual differences, and applications* (pp. 233–250). Mahwah, NJ: Erlbaum.

Johansson, V. (2009). *Developmental aspects of text production in writing and speech.* Unpublished PhD thesis, University of Lund, Lund.

Kellogg, R. T. (1996). A model of working memory in writing. In C. M. Levy & S. E. Ransdell (Eds.), *The science of writing: Theories, methods, individual differences and applications* (pp. 57–71). Hillsdale, NJ: Erlbaum.

Kellogg, R. T. (2004). Working memory components in written sentence generation. *American Journal of Psychology, 117*, 341–361.

Kellogg, R. T. (2008). Training writing skills: A cognitive developmental perspective. *Journal of Writing Research, 1*(1), 1–26.

Kellogg, R. T., Olive, T., & Piolat, A. (2007). Verbal, visual, and spatial working memory in written language production. *Acta Psychologica, 124*, 382–397.

Kollberg, P. (1998). *S-notation—a computer-based method for studying and representing text composition.* Unpublished Lic thesis, Stockholm University, Stockholm.

Latif, M. M. A. (2009). A state-of-the-art review of the real-time computer-aided study of the writing process. *International Journal of English Studies, 8*(1), 29–50.

Leijten, M. (2007). *Writing and speech recognition: Observing error correction strategies of professional writers* (Vol. 160). Utrecht: LOT.

Leijten, M., & Van Waes, L. (2006). Inputlog: New perspectives on the logging of on-line writing. In K. P. H. Sullivan & E. Lindgren (Eds.), *Computer key-stroke logging and writing: Methods and applications* (Vol. 18, pp. 73–94). Oxford: Elsevier.

Leijten, M., Van Waes, L., & Janssen, D. (2010). Error correction strategies of professional speech recognition users: Three profiles. *Computers in Human Behaviour, 26*, 964–975.

Leijten, M., Van Waes, L., & Ransdell, S. (2010). Correcting text production errors: Isolating the effects of writing mode from error span, input mode, and lexicality. *Written Communication, 27*(2), 189–227.

Lindgren, E. (2004). The uptake of peer-based intervention in the writing classroom. In G. Rijlaarsdam, H. Van den Bergh, & M. Couzijn (Eds.), *Effective learning and teaching of writing* (Vol. 14, pp. 259–274). Dordrecht: Kluwer.

Lindgren, E. (2005). *Writing and revising: Didactic and methodological implications of keystroke logging (Skrifter från moderna språk, No. 18)*. Umeå, Sweden: Umeå University, Department of Modern Languages.

Lindgren, E., Leijten, M., & Van Waes, L. (in press). Adapting to the reader during writing. *Written Language & Literacy.*

Lindgren, E., & Sullivan, K. P. H. (2002). The LS graph: A methodology for visualising writing revision. *Language Learning, 52*(3), 565–595.

Lindgren, E., & Sullivan, K. P. H. (2003). Stimulated recall as a trigger for increasing noticing and language awareness in the L2 writing classroom: A case study of two young female writers. *Language Awareness, 12*, 172–186.

Lindgren, E., & Sullivan, K. P. H. (2006). Analysing on-line revision. In K. P. H. Sullivan & E. Lindgren (Eds.), *Computer keystroke logging: Methods and applications* (Vol. 18, pp. 157–188). Oxford: Elsevier.

Lindgren, E., Sullivan, K. P. H., Deutschmann, M., & Steinvall, A. (2009). Supporting learner reflection in the language translation class. In M. Chang & C.-W. Kuo (Eds.), *Handbook of research on computer enhanced language and culture learning* (pp. 21–40). Hershey, NY: Information Science Reference, IGI Global.

Lindgren, E., Sullivan, K. P. H., Lindgren, U., & Spelman Miller, K. (2007). GIS for writing: Applying geographic information system techniques to data-mine writing's cognitive processes. In M. Torrance, L. Van Waes, & D. Galbraith (Eds.), *Writing and cognition: Methods and applications* (Vol. 20, pp. 83–96). Oxford: Elsevier.

Lindgren, E., Sullivan, K. P. H., & Spelman Miller, K. (2008). Development of fluency and revision in L1 and L2 writing in Swedish high school years 8 and 9. *International Journal of Applied Linguistics, 156*, 133–151.

Lindgren, E., Sullivan, K. P. H., & Stevenson, M. (2008). Supporting the reflective language learner with computer keystroke logging. In B. Barber & F. Zhang (Eds.), *Handbook of research on computer-enhanced language acquisition and learning* (pp. 189–204). Hershey, NY: Information Science Reference, IGI Global.

Matsuhashi, A. (1981). Pausing and planning: The tempo of written discourse production. *Research in the Teaching of English, 15*(2), 113–134.

Matsuhashi, A. (1987). Revising the plan and altering the text. In A. Matsuhashi (Ed.), *Writing in real time: Modelling production processes* (pp. 197–223). New York: Academic Press.

McCutchen, D. (2000). Knowledge, processing, and working memory: Implications for a theory of writing. *Educational Psychologist, 35*(1), 13–23.

Nottbusch, G. (2010). Grammatical planning, execution, and control in written sentence production. *Reading and Writing, 23*(7), 777–801.

Nottbusch, G., Grimm, A., Weingarten, R., & Will, U. (2005). Syllabic structures in typing: Evidence from hearing-impaired writers. *Reading and Writing, 18*, 497–526.

Nottbusch, G., Weingarten, R., & Sahel, S. (2007). From written word to written sentence production. In M. Torrance, L. Van Waes, & D. Galbraith (Eds.), *Writing and cognition: Research and applications* (Vol. 20, pp. 31–54). Amsterdam: Elsevier.

Nottbusch, G., Weingarten, R., & Will, U. (1998). Schreiben mit der hand und schreiben mit dem computer. *Osnabrücker Beiträge zur Sprachtheorie, 56*, 11–27.

Perin, D. (2003). Progression analysis: Investigating writing strategies at the workplace. *Journal of Pragmatics, 35*(6), 907–921.

Piolat, A., Kellogg, R. T., & Farioli, F. (2001). The triple task technique for studying writing processes: On which task is attention focused? *Current Psychology Letters. Brain, Behavior and Cognition, 4*, 67–83.

Rijlaarsdam, G., Braaksma, M., Couzijn, M., Janssen, T., Raedts, M., Van Steendam, E., . . . Van den Bergh, H. (2008). Observation of peers in learning to write: Practice and research. *Journal of Writing Research, 1*(1), 53–83.

Rijlaarsdam, G., & Couzijn, M. (2000). Stimulating awareness of writing in the writing curriculum. In A. Camps & M. Milian (Eds.), *Metalinguistic activity in learning to write* (pp. 167–202). Amsterdam: Amsterdam University Press.

Schilperoord, J. (1996). The distribution of pause time in written text production. In G. Rijlaarsdam, H. van den Bergh, & M. Couzijn (Eds.), *Theories, models and methodology in writing research* (pp. 21–35). Amsterdam: Amsterdam University Press.

Schilperoord, J. (2002). On the cognitive status of pauses in discourse production. In T. Olive & C. M. Levy (Eds.), *Contemporary tools and techniques for studying writing* (Vol. 10, pp. 61–88). Dordrecht: Kluwer.

Schmidt, R. W. (1990). The role of consciousness in second language learning. *Applied Linguistics, 11*(2), 129–158.

Severinson Eklundh, K. S. (1994). Linear and non-linear strategies in computer-based writing. *Computers and Composition, 11*, 203–216.

Severinson Eklundh, K. S., & Kollberg, P. (1992). *Translating keystroke records into a general notation for the writing process* (IPLab-59). Stockholm: Department of Numerical Analysis and Computing Science, Royal Institute of Technology.

Severinson Eklundh, K. S., & Kollberg, P. (1996). Computer tools for tracing the writing process: From keystroke records to S-notation. In G. Rijlaarsdam, H. Van den Bergh, & M. Couzijn (Eds.), *Models and methodology in writing research* (pp. 526–541). Amsterdam: Amsterdam University Press.

Severinson Eklundh, K. S., & Kollberg, P. (2003). Emerging discourse structure: Computer-assisted episode analysis as a window to global revision in university students' writing. *Journal of Pragmatics, 35*, 869–891.

Simpson, S., & Torrance, M. (2007). *EyeWrite (Version 5.1)*. Unpublished report.

Sleurs, K., Jacobs, G., & Van Waes, L. (2003). Constructing press releases, constructing quotations: A case study. *Journal of Sociolinguistics, 7*(2), 192–212.

Smagorinsky, P. (1989). The reliability and validity of protocol analysis. *Written Communication, 6*, 463–479.

Spelman Miller, K. (2000). *Writing on-line: Temporal features of first and second language written text production.* Unpublished PhD thesis, the University of Reading.

Spelman Miller, K. (2002). Units of production in writing: Towards a discourse perspective. In S. Burgess (Ed.), *Revista Canaria de Estudios Ingleses* (Vol. 44, pp. 115–139). Tenerife: University La Laguna.

Spelman Miller, K. (2006). The pausological study of written language production. In K. P. H. Sullivan & E. Lindgren (Eds.), *Computer keystroke logging: Methods and applications* (Vol. 18, pp. 11–30). Oxford: Elsevier.

Spelman Miller, K., Lindgren, E., & Sullivan, K. P. H. (2008). The psycholinguistic dimension in second language writing: Opportunities for research and pedagogy. *TESOL Quarterly, 42*(3), 433–454.

Spelman Miller, K., & Sullivan, K. P. H. (2006). Keystroke logging—an introduction. In K. P. H. Sullivan & E. Lindgren (Eds.), *Computer keystroke logging and writing: Methods and applications* (Vol. 18, pp. 1–10). Amsterdam: Elsevier.

Stevenson, M., Schoonen, R., & de Glopper, K. (2006). Revising in two languages: A multidimensional comparison of online writing revisions in L1 and FL. *Journal of Second Language Writing, 15*(3), 201–233.

Strömqvist, S., & Malmsten, L. (1997). *Scriptlog Pro 1.04—user's manual.* Department of Linguistics, University of Göteborg.

Strömqvist, S., Nordqvist, Å., & Wengelin, Å. (2004). Writing the frog story—developmental and cross-modal perspectives. In S. Strömqvist & L. Verhoeven (Eds.), *Relating events in narrative—typological and contextual perspectives* (pp. 359–394). Mahwah, NJ: Erlbaum.

Sullivan, K. P. H., & Lindgren, E. (2002). Self-assessment in autonomous computer-aided L2 writing. *ELT Journal, 56*(3), 258–266.

Sullivan, K. P. H., & Lindgren, E. (2006). *Computer key-stroke logging and writing.* Oxford: Elsevier.

Swain, M., & Lapkin, S. (2000). Task-based second language learning: The uses of the first language. *Language Teaching Research, 4*(3), 251.

Swerts, M. (1998). Filled pauses as markers of discourse structure. *Journal of Pragmatics, 30*(4), 485–496.

Thorson, H. (2000). Using the computer to compare foreign and native language writing processes: A statistical and case study approach. *Modern Language Journal, 84*(2), 155–170.

Van den Haak, M. J., De Jong, M. D. T., & Schellens, P. J. (2004). Employing thinkaloud protocols and constructive interaction to test the usability of online library catalogues: A methodological comparison. *Interacting with Computers, 16*, 1153–1170.

Van den Haak, M. J., De Jong, M. D. T., & Schellens, P. J. (2006). Hardopdenkprotocollen en gebruikersonderzoek: Volledigheid en reactiviteit van de synchrone hardopdenk-methode. *Tijdschrift voor Taalbeheersing, 28*(3), 185–197.

Van Hout, T. (2009). *Writing form sources: Ethnographic insights into business news production.* Unpublished PhD thesis, University of Ghent, Ghent.

Van Waes, L., Leijten, M., & Quinlan, T. (2010). Reading during sentence composing and error correction: A multilevel analysis of the influences of task complexity. *Reading and Writing, 23*(7), 803–834.

Van Waes, L., Leijten, M., & Van Weijen, D. (2009). Keystroke logging in writing research: Observing writing processes with Inputlog. *GFL-German as a Foreign Language, 2*(3), 41–64.

Van Waes, L., & Schellens, P. J. (2003). Writing profiles: The effect of the writing mode on pausing and revision patterns of experienced writers. *Journal of Pragmatics, 35*(6), 829–853.

Van Weijen, D. (2009). *Writing processes, text quality, and task effects: Empirical studies in first and second language writing* (Vol. 201). Utrecht: LOT.

Vygotsky, L. S. (1978). *Mind in society: The development of higher psychological processes.* Cambridge, MA: Harvard University Press.

Weingarten, R., Nottbusch, G., & Will, U. (2004). Morphemes, syllables and graphemes in written word production. In T. Pechmann & C. Habel (Eds.), *Multidisciplinary approaches to speech production* (pp. 529–572). Berlin: Mouton de Gruyter.

Wengelin, Å. (2001). From the "dyslexia classroom" to the "classroom for reading and writing difficulties"—How do spelling difficulties influence the text production? In W. Vagle & K. Wikberg (Eds.), *New directions in Nordic text linguistics and discourse analysis: Methodological issues* (pp. 160–175). Oslo: Novus.

Wengelin, Å. (2002). *Text production in adults with reading and writing difficulties* (PhD thesis). Gothenburgh Monographs in Linguistics 20. Department of Linguistics, University of Gothenburg.

Wengelin, Å. (2006). Examining pauses in writing: Theories, methods and empirical data. In K. P. H. Sullivan & E. Lindgren (Eds.), *Computer key-stroke logging and writing: Methods and applications* (Vol. 18, pp. 107–130). Oxford: Elsevier.

Wengelin, Å. (2007). The word level focus in text production by adults with reading and writing difficulties. In D. Galbraith, M. Torrance, & L. Van Waes (Eds.), *Writing and cognition* (pp. 68–82). Oxford: Elsevier.

Wengelin, Å., Leijten, M., & Van Waes, L. (2010). Studying reading during writing: New perspectives in research. *Reading and Writing, 23*(7), 735–742.

Wengelin, Å., & Strömqvist, S. (2000). Discourse level writing in dyslexics—methods, results and implications for diagnosis. *Scandinavian Journal of Logopedics, Phoniatrics and Vocology, 25*(1), 22–28.

Wengelin, Å., Torrance, M., Holmqvist, K., Simpson, S., Galbraith, D., Johansson, V., & Johansson, R. (2009). Combined eye-tracking and keystroke-logging methods for studying cognitive processes in text production. *Behavior Research Methods, 41*(2), 337–351.

Part VII

Emerging Cognitive Neuroscience of Writing

23

The Writing Brain
Coordinating Sensory/Motor, Language, and Cognitive Systems in Working Memory

VIRGINIA WISE BERNINGER and TODD L. RICHARDS

*T*he two themes in this volume have been to make writing research more visible and central in mainstream cognitive psychology and to draw on multiple disciplines in writing research. This chapter illustrates the recent paradigm shift from cognitive psychology to cognitive neuroscience with an overview of an interdisciplinary research program on writing. A psychologist, drawing on cognitive psychology, linguistics, neuropsychology, developmental psychology, and educational psychology, and a neurophysicist in the field of radiology, with expertise in multiple imaging modalities, contributed to this programmatic research. Here we will place research on the writing brain in its historic context. We begin with pioneering studies on acquired writing disorders, based on clinical studies of lost and preserved writing functions or correlations between lost functions and abnormal structures in autopsy studies. We then proceed to more recent brain imaging of adults and children with normal writing development or with developmental writing disorders. In the final section, we discuss cutting-edge research issues that may lead to greater understanding of the writing brain.

CROSS-DISCIPLINARY COGNITIVE NEUROSCIENCE RESEARCH ON WRITING

The call at a historic research conference in 1976 for interdisciplinary research on writing (see Chapter 9, this volume; also Hooper, Knuth, Yerby, & Anderson, 2009) is as timely in the 21st century as it was in the 20th century. The following paradigm shifts have occurred within psychology: neurophysiology (wedding philosophy and experimental methods) at the end of the 19th century, to behaviorism (focusing on observable behaviors without making inferences about mediating processes) at the beginning of the 20th century, to cognitive psychology (understanding mental representations and processing in the human mind) at the middle of the 20th century, to cognitive neuroscience (understanding the brain basis of cognition) at the beginning of the 21st century. In fact, some departments of psychology in the United States have been renamed departments of cognitive neuroscience to reflect this paradigm shift.

Cognitive Neuroscience Model of the Writing Brain

Since 1995 we have collaborated on interdisciplinary brain research related to normal and disabled written language acquisition (reading and writing). Collectively, our research findings, based on developmental studies of writing, assessment studies of normal and disabled writing, instructional studies for at-risk writers or those with diagnosed writing disabilities, and brain-imaging studies, supported a model of the writing brain with the following component structures or functions of a working memory (Berninger & Richards, 2010):

1. *End organs with direct contact with external world—motor systems* (hand for writing or mouth for oral reading of one's writing to others), *sensory systems* with initial input (ears for dictated spelling) or subsequent feedback (eyes for reviewing writing produced so far), and *loops between sensory—motor systems that connect with internal language and cognitive systems*, especially a *phonological loop* (from eye to mouth in naming for cross-code integration or to internal covert phonological codes for sustaining language processing over time) and an *orthographic loop* (from ear to internal letter- or word-orthographic code representations to hand or directly from the orthographic representations to hand);

2. An *internal, multileveled language system that stores and processes phonological* (spoken), *orthographic* (written), and *morphological* (spoken and written) *word forms and their parts* and *syntax units* (for accumulating words); and

3. A panel of lower-level executive functions for supervisory attention that (a) inhibits focus on what is relevant and ignores what is irrelevant; (b) switches attention flexibly from one focus to another as needed; (c) sustains attention to stay on task over time; and (d) updates the current state of mind over time.

This working memory architecture supports the intercommunication among the sensory and motor, language, cognitive, and higher-level executive functions as they engage in language learning, language use, and cognitive processes. The higher-level executive functions include the cognitive processes of writing in the Hayes and Flower (1980) model-planning, translating, reviewing, and revising (Berninger & Richards, 2002). *Planning* allows the writer to envision goals and make a plan to achieve those goals. Translating transforms cognitive representations into language or language into cognitive representations (or cognitive into nonverbal forms of expression such as music, dance, art, and vice versa) (Berninger & Hayes, 2011). Reviewing enables self-monitoring and reflecting to modify plans and translation as needed. Revising is retranslating to modify the text produced so far to improve it (see Chapter 20, this volume).

Olive (Chapter 21, this volume) presented the history of the research on the relationship of both verbal working memory and nonverbal working memory to writing, and McCutchen (Chapter 9, this volume) provided evidence that phonological, morphological, and orthographic processing can support written expression at many levels of language. Although listening and reading comprehension and oral and written expression all draw on common language processes, they are also unique language systems, depending on the end organ (ear, eye, mouth, or hand) to which they are functionally connected for the purpose of communicating with the cognitive system (understanding or expressing ideas in a specific modality; Berninger & Abbott, 2010).

Thus, brain systems involved in writing are not insular modules but rather dynamic internal systems that interact with one another in a working memory architecture (James, 2010; Fuster, 2003). This architecture supports interactions among multiple sensory and motor systems, which communicate directly with the external environment (Eliot, 1999), but also communicate with two internal systems: the multileveled language system and the complex cognitive system with its varied, extensive, concrete, and abstract cognitive representations, which for the most part are outside conscious awareness until brought into consciousness through capacity, resource, and time-limited working memory for goal-directed activity (Goldman-Rakic, 1992). The language and cognitive systems communicate with the external world only indirectly through the sensory and motor systems (Eliot, 1999). To summarize, this working memory architecture for oral and written language has three components: (1) the loops between specific sensory and motor end organs, (2) four storage and processing units (three word form and one syntax), and (3) the panel of lower-level executive functions. Collectively these working memory components support the high-level executive functions for writing—planning, translation, reviewing, and rewriting—and other complex cognitive functions involved in human verbal development, learning, and behavior (see Cornoldi & Vecchi, 2003, for research on visual-spatial working memory, which also plays a role in writing).

In the subsections that follow we share, in the spirit of the social constructivist tradition of distributed cognition across social networks (see Chapters 4–6 and 12, this volume), how our thinking has evolved, based on collaborative research, in conceptualizing developmental and instructional issues related to the writing brain.

Building a Writing Brain Neurologically and Pedagogically

Berninger and Richards (2002), in the tradition of Bates et al. (1998), proposed a neuroconstructivist model of how the writing brain is constructed through remodeling of existing brain structures to create new functional systems during the developmental journey in learning to write. This process begins about the 10th month of the first year of life when an infant, given a writing tool and writing surface, leaves her or his first graphic trace by hand (Gibson & Levin, 1975), and then continues through adulthood. This model drew mostly on imaging studies of normal adult writers available before 2002 and explained why writing is not merely a motor act and novice writers are not merely younger expert writers—the developmental journey is not the same as the developmental outcome. Although the reconstruction to create a writing brain draws on some of the same structures as does the developing reading brain, the construction process does not evolve directly from the reading system but rather is unique to writing; that is, writing is not a mere inverse, mirror process of reading (for further discussion of this issue, see Richards, Berninger, & Fayol, in press).

Relevant brain structures and functions that are used to build the writing brain include those involved in arousal; idea generation and other kinds of cognitions; emotions and motivation; language generation; transcription (letter forms and word spellings); orthographic and phonological representations and their cross-code coordination; the word-specific orthographic lexicon; graphomotor function (e.g., not only for motor execution but also for planning and executing serial finger movements, both novel and practiced); attention and executive function systems; memory systems (short-term encoding of sensory input or plans for motor output, working memory for conscious, goal-oriented tasks, and long-term memory for more enduring storage); and learning circuits (controlled, strategic processing during learning, but after practice, automatic access or fluency in coordinating multiple processes efficiently). For details, see Table 6.2 in Berninger and Richards (2002). Ideas for future research on the biological bases of affective or language variables in writing, which may interact with cognitive processes, are presented in this volume in Chapter 7 for affect and motivation, in Chapter 13 for lexical access and naming, in Chapter 14 for abstracting statistical regularities in word spelling, in Chapter 15 for phonological, orthographic, and morphological processes in word spelling, in Chapter 16 for language bursts during writing, and in Chapters 17 and 18 for text composing.

Berninger and Richards (2002) also emphasized that both microlevel and macrolevel brain structures and functions participate in the writing brain. At the microlevel (see Figures 2.1 and 2.2 in Berninger & Richards, 2002), microscopic neurons spatially separated by small gaps create brief electrochemical functional connections with each other. Each neuron has dendrites, which receive analog signals from other neurons, a cell body with a nucleus containing an individual's DNA organized in a double helix, and an axon for sending a digital signal to another neuron (either it fires or does not and it either inhibits the receiving neuron from transmitting or excites it to transmit). The lower-order branches of the dendrites are under genetic control, whereas the upper branches are responsive to experience and education (Jacobs, Schall, & Scheibel, 1993), showing that nature–nurture interactions operate at the microlevel (Diamond & Hopson, 1998).

At the macrolevel (see Carter, Aldridge, Page, & Parker, 2009, for illustrated, interactive introduction to brain structures and functions), vast numbers of neurons are organized in pathways, that is, distributed neural networks across different spatial locations in the brain, with various neurons or pathways operating on their own time scales. Cortical computation mechanisms periodically integrate these distributed networks across spatial locations and time scales so they are synchronized, at least for a moment, in linear time perceived as real time; this synchronization gives rise to brain waves (Minsky, 1986). The periodic synchronization may give rise to sequential cycles of working memory over time (Berninger & Hayes, 2011), which in turn supports the language bursts (Chenoweth & Hayes, 2003; see also Chapters 1 and 16, this volume).

Repeated studies show an association between working memory (middle frontal gyrus, also known as *dorsal lateral prefrontal cortex* [DLPFC]), which is larger in humans than other species, and superior parietal regions; disruptions in connectivity with these working memory regions or timing mechanisms in the cerebellum can disrupt language learning (e.g., see Richards, Berninger, Winn et al., 2009). Working memory, which plays a unique role in organizing cognitive brain functions, draws on the following three pathways for orchestrating its written language activities across spatially distributed neural circuits in real time (Fuster, 1997):

1. A bottom-up pathway that originates in sensory areas in the back of the brain, which receive incoming messages from the external environment via eyes, ears, and touch, and projects messages up to the association areas in cortex that integrates them
2. A top-down pathway originating in DLPFC that projects to midlevel premotor and supplementary areas and then to primary motor area (all in frontal regions) and finally to the spinal cord, which generates the elements of movement that support behavioral acts in the external world
3. A cortical–subcortical pathway from cerebrum to cerebellum (the air traffic control of the brain; Eliot, 1999), which provides the temporal coordination for the sequential and simultaneous communication of the other pathways and thus plays a critically important role in managing working memory

Working memory supports time travel—from engagement in the present to access to the past through long-term memory activation and to the potential future through imagination of what does not exist yet—all of which may contribute to the writing process (Berninger & Richards, 2002). However, working memory is only one functional system in the working human brain, which organizes and reorganizes its components for different tasks (Luria, 1973). These components are specific brain areas distributed throughout the brain, which can participate in more than one functional system, depending on the task at hand. Each functional system may have common and unique components compared to other functional systems. This organizational capability, whereby the same components can be reorganized to perform different functions rather than having single components dedicated to a single function, is cost-efficient in terms of the energy required to fuel the activities of the whole system. For example, blood oxygen level dependent magnetic resonance imaging (BOLD MRI) is a special MRI technique that allows indirect assessment of oxygen levels in blood that are influenced by the conversion of glucose into energy (via mitochondria in individual neurons) to provide the fuel for brain activity.

Berninger and Richards (2002) also discussed (a) *nature–nurture interactions*, in which the brain is both an independent variable influencing interactions with the environment and a dependent variable influenced in turn by the environment, and (b) *brain plasticity* in response to interaction with the environment, but constrained by biologically based maturational mechanisms and in some cases neurogenetic conditions or brain injury or disease. Karmiloff-Smith (2009) presented a similar developmental perspective informing developmental and brain research.

Berninger and Richards (2002) discussed how both *other-regulation*, via explicit instruction and teacher-guided instructional support, and *self-regulation*, via writing strategies, help construct the writing brain that (a) generates ideas, (b) translates cognitions into language representations that are converted via the transcription processes of letter formation and spelling into written text, and (c) composes at multiple levels of language (word generation, syntax construction, and discourse schema organization). The word spelling processes draw on many of the same processes as the reading brain: abstracting patterns and statistical regularities in written and spoken words (see Chapter 14, this volume), becoming aware of the different kinds of language units contributing to written word representations via metacognitive reflections (linguistic awareness), and creation of multiple interconnections among the language units in word-specific spelling (see Chapter 15, this volume).

Berninger and Richards (2002, 2010), based on instructional studies conducted by the psychologists on the interdisciplinary team, highlighted the following six research-supported guidelines for creating a writing brain instructionally:

1. Teach to all levels of language (*subword* letter, *word* spelling, and *text* composing) close in time to overcome limitations of working memory and create a functional writing system in which all the language and nonlanguage components are coordinated efficiently in time for the writing task at hand.
2. Avoid habituation (nonresponding of the brain to repeated stimuli or tasks) by practicing strategies for transcription skills (handwriting and spelling) for only brief times in isolation (to automatize them); follow this "warm-up" practice with transfer writing tasks to apply transcription skills to meaningful writing tasks, including composing, which is shared with others.
3. Teach for transfer from subword skills to word skills (spelling and vocabulary choice) and from word skills to text composing.
4. Encourage high-level meaning making in the composing process so that the writer is in thinking mode in which ideas flow or can be strategically retrieved or constructed.
5. Support writing success through teacher modeling of skills, teacher-guided supportive assistance and feedback, opportunities to self-generate and self-regulate learning, and peer feedback and sharing.
6. Assess response to instruction in each lesson, graph assessment results for visible inspection to decide if reasonable progress is being made across sessions, and if not, modify instructional approach for the skill(s) not showing progress.

Several recent updates have presented evidence-based writing instruction for building writing brains (e.g., Graham & Perin, 2007; Harris, Graham, Mason, & Friedlander, 2008; Harris, Graham, & Urdan, in press; Hooper et al., 2009; Morris & Mather, 2008; Troia, 2009; see also Chapter 8, this volume).

Applications of Brain-Imaging Research for Classroom Instruction in Writing

Berninger and Richards (2009) discussed the varying reactions of educators and psychologists to the rapidly expanding brain research related to education. These reactions range from uncritical acceptance or overgeneralization of findings to skepticism or outright rejection that brain research has any relevance to classroom learning. Berninger and Richards explained that whether instructor led (or guided) or student guided, learning is mediated by the brain, even though neither the teacher nor the student has conscious awareness of how an individual's brain is involved in either teaching or learning!

At the same time, learning and teaching are not synonymous processes; teaching can be effective without knowledge of the brain; and studying brain responses to experimentally manipulated stimuli and tasks in the research laboratory may not capture all relevant aspects of brain function in the learning mechanisms by which brains self-regulate their own learning and create their own representations and procedures. That is, highly controlled imaging studies may not portray all the complexities of learning to write in the messy real world outside the research laboratory. However, although one study cannot answer all the relevant questions, as studies accumulate within and across research laboratories using different brain-imaging tools, addressing different research questions with different research methods, designs, and data analysis procedures, a body of relevant research may emerge that enhances understanding of the learning or teaching process, even if it does not provide answers for all educationally relevant issues. As with all complex questions, multiple perspectives and methods are needed to paint the complete picture and tell the whole story.

One of the intriguing findings relevant to writing acquisition is the normal variation in the white matter and gray matter structures across the brains of normally developing writers (see Figure 23.1). Although all brains have the same macrolevel structures, they vary greatly in size and patterning across individual writers. Such interindividual differences—no two brains are exactly alike in either structural neuroanatomy or history of interactions with the writing environment—may pose challenges not only for researchers but also for teachers. Increasingly teachers are expected to show that all students reach the same high level of writing achievement outcomes, despite individual differences across their brains and their brains' interactions with variable environments; all of these sources of variation may affect the rate and level of writing development.

One of the challenges still to be overcome is for preservice educators to gain access to courses that teach the concepts and terminology required to understand the brain-imaging or cognitive science studies of learning to write (or read or calculate or think mathematically), which are often available only in departments

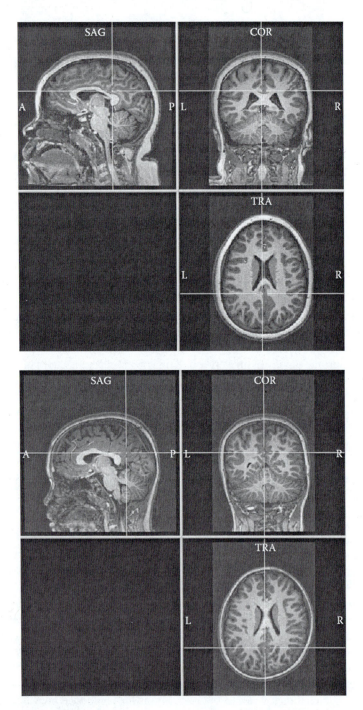

Figure 23.1 View from three imaging perspectives of two typically developing brains. SAG, sagittal side view of the brain section; COR, coronal frontal view of the brain section; RA, transverse, which means a top view of the brain section. (Courtesy of Todd Richards.)

of medicine, radiology, neuroscience, cognitive neuroscience, cognitive science, or psychology (Berninger & Richards, 2002, 2009). As pointed out in Chapter 3, this volume, the cognitive psychologists studying specific kinds of learning such as writing would benefit from more input from educators. We extend the argument to a call for more bidirectional collaboration among educators, cognitive neuroscientists, and neuroscientists. Educators could participate actively in such a bidirectional collaboration by helping to frame research questions and interpret and apply results, especially if they were given more access to courses on the brain at the preservice level. That is, education has a contribution to make to the cognitive neuroscience of writing!

Integrating Brain Imaging and Family Genetics

Berninger and Richards (2010) reviewed the results from over a decade of family genetics, brain-imaging, and treatment studies in their multidisciplinary research center on learning disabilities. In these studies the participants in the imaging and treatment studies were recruited from the family genetics study that used consistent inclusion criteria across participants. Thus, there was a rare opportunity to examine converging evidence for comparably selected participants across research grounded in four disciplines: genetics, neuroscience, psychology, and education.

1. *Phenotyping* (assessment of multiple behavioral measures shown in family aggregation studies to be probably heritable)
2. *Statistical genetics* (probable chromosome linkage and modes of genetic transmission)
3. *Molecular genetics* (replicating or identifying alleles, which are variations in sequences of the four base chemicals in DNA, that is, gene candidates associated with specific phenotypes)
4. *Brain imaging of neuroanatomy* (structural magnetic resonance imaging [MRI] and diffusion tensor imaging [DTI]) and *brain function* (blood oxygen level-dependent [BOLD] activation on functional MRI [fMRI], during tasks or task contrasts that correspond to phenotypes, or functional connections in time during a continuous task yoked to a phenotype, *fMRI connectivity*)

Converging evidence emerged across studies for a working memory architecture underlying written language, as described earlier in this chapter, which may be a language-learning mechanism (Berninger et al., 2010) for learning to write (as well as to read and use oral language) and even learn verbal labels for number concepts or write numerals during steps of written arithmetic computations (Berninger, 2007, 2011; Berninger, Rijlaarsdam, & Fayol, 2011). Variables identified in the earlier developmental studies of normal writing acquisition and used to identify at-risk writers for early intervention studies or children with diagnosable writing disabilities for treatment studies (also reviewed in Berninger & Richards, 2002, 2009, 2010) were used as phenotypes for the genetics studies. Tasks and task contrasts analogous to the phenotypes were constructed for the brain-imaging studies. One allele that has been reported across laboratories to be related to written language impairments was found to be associated with the executive function for switching attention during cross-code integration of written symbols and names; another allele also replicated in the research literature was associated with the ability to store and process spoken words in working memory (Berninger, Raskind, Richards, Abbott, & Stock, 2008).

Also reviewed by Berninger and Richards (2010) are the 10 reported gene candidates for dyslexia, a disorder of word reading and word spelling—impaired spelling is more persistent across the lifespan and often interferes with written composing, long after an affected individual learns to read sufficiently well (e.g., Berninger, Nielsen, Abbott, Wijsman, & Raskind, 2008; see also Chapter 10, this volume). Of considerable note, Roeske et al. (2009) reported the first evidence for dyslexia of gene-endophenotype linkage, that is, relationships between genes and brain activation, during an imaging task related to a phenotype (behavioral expression of an underlying gene)—genes on two chromosomes (one related to phonological storage and processing and one related to glucose utilization) and brain function during an electrophysiological task (listening to changing aural syllables) were involved. Of interest, the participants with dyslexia in the study were recruited for the persisting spelling impairment, which is also often impaired in dysgraphia and can occur without reading problems. Further research is needed to determine if the electrophysiological findings reflect only problems in phonological processing of wordlike stimuli or perhaps a more fundamental underlying executive function in detecting and adapting to change or in storing and monitoring heard aural wordlike speech stimuli from which phonotactic regularities are abstracted, which ultimately play a role in learning to spell written words (Berninger, Fayol, & Alamargot, 2011; see also Chapter 14, this volume). Whether this gene may also be involved in anomalies in detection of change in other stimuli, for example, changing letters across word position in written words and thus orthotactics (Apel, Oster, & Masterson, 2006), should also be investigated.

HISTORY OF BRAIN RESEARCH AND CURRENT KNOWLEDGE OF WRITING BRAIN

More research on acquired and developmental writing disorders and normal writing development has focused on transcription (handwriting and spelling) than composition. That is because the former is easier than the latter to study in the imaging environment; but as documented in earlier chapters in this volume (e.g., Chapters 2, 16, and 17), these transcription skills do place limits on composing.

Tools for Identifying Brain Regions
Discussed in Writing Research

Schemes for naming regions visible from the surface of the brain include (a) names of the four lobes of cerebral cortex on each side of the brain (occipital, temporal, parietal, and frontal), and (b) adjectives that indicate where a gyrus (ascending up like a mountain) or sulcus (ascending below like a valley) occur in the convolutions (gray folds in cortex) surrounding the cerebrum—on top (dorsal), bottom (ventral), back (posterior), or front (anterior). Not all cerebral structures can be viewed from the surface; medial structures include many other regions and white fiber tracts not visible on the brain's surface. When region is used rather than gyri or sulci, it may be that the relevant structure or correlated function involves a broader area than the one containing the gyrus or only part of a region near or including the gyrus.

Another scheme uses the numbers a neurosurgeon named Brodmann assigned to specific regions, for example, Brodmann's area (BA) 8 in the left frontal lobe, which is Exner's area, one of the writing centers in the brain. Both text and the CD in Carter et al. (2009) can be used in the overview of research findings that follows to associate the names, BA numbers, and spatial locations of cortical regions in the brain, both on the surface and below, when they are mentioned in the overview of research.

Acquired Writing Disorders

For clues to the specific brain structures or functions underlying writing, neurologists and neuropsychologists study individuals who had normal writing skills but lost them through stroke, tumor, disease, brain injury, or another source of brain damage. Acquired writing disorders have been found to be associated with three brain regions, which together may participate in distributive pathways supporting writing functions: (1) *left posterior middle frontal gyrus* (Exner's area BA8; Exner, 1881), which Anderson, Damaisio, and Damaisio (1990) found supports coactivation of movement sequences during letter generation; (2) *left superior parietal lobule*, which Basso, Taborelli, and Vignolo (1978) reported supports formation of internal letter codes in preparation for production; and (3) *left premotor region* (BA6), which Brain (1967) showed stores the graphomotor codes for writing letters. Thus, by inference, parietal and frontal regions contribute to the preparation for and production of letter forms whether alone, in words, or in text; interfering with these regions can cause breakdowns in specific processes contributing to letter writing.

Four general principles emerged from the early brain research on acquired writing disorders (Richards et al., 2011). First, the brain draws on different neural circuits in learning a novel writing-related motor skill than when the skill is no longer novel and is practiced sufficiently to be automatic. For example, prefrontal cortex and cingulate are involved in controlled, strategic processes, whereas subcortical striatum is involved in automatic processes. Second, graphomotor tasks involve not only motor execution but also motor planning and motor control, all mediated by frontal areas. Third, the three brain regions discussed earlier that are associated with specific kinds of acquired letter writing disorders also activate in typically developing writers or those with developmental writing disorders, depending on which fMRI writing tasks and writing task contrasts are employed in a particular study. Fourth, a close relationship exists between letter production and letter perception, as discussed in the next subsection on normal writing development.

In a recent study conducted prior to surgery for patients with tumors, both fMRI and direct cortical stimulation were used to study Exner's BA6 (Roux et al., 2009). Results showed that this area in the middle frontal gyrus, which is associated with working memory function, supports the bridging of orthography to motor programs specific to handwriting. These authors conceptualize Exner's area as a graphemic motor region where orthographic representations are converted to motor representations, which then support production of a sequence of hand movements. Thus, these investigators may have identified a neural pathway underlying the *orthographic loop* of working memory, which Berninger, Nielsen et al. (2008) have studied at the behavioral level. Accumulating research is showing that working memory has not only a phonological loop (Baddeley, Gathercole, & Papagno, 1998) but also an orthographic loop (Berninger & Richards, 2010).

Normal Writing Development: Letter Writing and Letter Perception

Flowers et al. (2004) studied normal adult writers in an fMRI study and identified a portion of a left extrastriatal area (BA37) that was sensitive to single letter forms in contrast to fusiform gyrus, which was sensitive to written word forms (Cohen et al., 2002; Dehaene, 2002). Although other researchers have found fusiform activation associated with single letters, research has shown that letters and letter strings activate different neural circuits (James, James, Jobard, Wong, & Gauthier, 2005), letters activate different neural circuits than do other visual stimuli such as shapes, and both alphabetic and nonalphabetic writing systems activate occipital-temporal areas (for review, see Wong, Jobard, James, James, & Gauthier, 2009). Forming letters by handwriting results in better letter recognition than selecting letters on keyboards in both 4-year-old children (Longcamp, Zerbato-Poudou, & Velay, 2005) and adults (Longcamp et al., 2008). Forming letters by hand recruited different neural circuits than did naming letters (James & Atwood, 2009). Developmental research has shown children wrote more words and wrote words faster (Berninger, Abbott, Augsburger, & Garcia, 2009) and expressed more ideas (Hayes & Berninger, 2010) when composing essays by pen than by computer keyboard; see comparable findings by Connelly et al. (2006). (For the cognitive costs for adults of word retrieval without handwriting transcription, see Chapter 13, this volume, and of keyboarding to generate letters, compared to more automatic speech, to produce words and sentences, see Chapter 17, this volume.)

At the same time, a growing body of brain research on normal writing development in children or adults has identified a close relationship between letter production and letter perception—both motor and visual regions are involved in handwriting or outputting the letter form, which enhances visual perception of letters (James & Gauthier, 2006; Longcamp, Anton, Roth, & Velay, 2003). Simply seeing a letter activates motor regions (James & Gauthier, 2009; Longcamp, Anton, Roth, & Velay, 2003; Longcamp et al., 2005). In fact, in normal adult writers, neural pathways engaged in letter writing are connected to brain regions involved in letter perception; a concurrent letter-writing task impaired letter perception, but not shape perception, indicating that not only storage but also on-line processing were impaired by the motor interference (James & Gauthier, 2009). Preschoolers showed activation in fusiform gyrus after experience in letter writing (copying lower- and uppercase letters and words), but not letter or word naming; this finding held only for letter, not pseudoletter or shape, stimuli (James, 2010).

James and colleagues' findings (e.g., James, 2010; James & Gauthier, 2009) are also relevant to action-perception cycles and the recent research in mainstream psychology on embodied cognition, according to which humans internally perceive the external world on the basis of their interactions with it. That is, they learn to understand the visual world by acting on it and then motor systems associated with learning the visual perception may be activated solely by the reoccurrence of the visual perception. For example, James and Maouene (2009) reported intriguing findings between verbs and adjectives in normally developing 4- and 5-year-olds: (a) verbs, which are related to motor acts in the external world, activated frontal motor regions (bilateral middle frontal area and bilateral supplementary motor area cortex), but adjectives, which are not related to motor acts, did not activate those motor regions; (b) no differences were found between verbs and adjectives in superior temporal gyri (auditory cortex); and (c) hand and leg verbs differed as to which motor regions were engaged (e.g., right premotor for hand verbs and bilateral premotor and precentral gyri for leg verbs). Similar findings have also been reported for adults.

Normal Writing Development: Spelling

Word spelling in normal adults also draws more on networks other than primary visual areas. During spelling tasks adult writers activated inferior temporal regions (e.g., fusiform gyrus) more robustly than primary visual (occipital) brain regions in response to linear arrays of visual elements that could be linguistically coded into visible language (Cohen et al., 2002; Dehaene, 2002). Spelling is visible language for a single word (lexical) unit, which in normally developing writers has also been shown to activate left fusiform gyrus (Booth et al., 2002), associated with *orthographic coding*, posterior parietal cortex (Bitan et al., 2007), associated with *phonological-orthographic integration*, and left inferior frontal gyrus (Booth, Cho, Burman, & Bitan, 2007), associated with *executive functions for language*. Thus, underlying normal spelling may be an unfolding temporal course of processing along a neural pathway proceeding from visual processing in occipital visual association areas to orthographic processing in fusiform gyrus in lower temporal areas to sound-meaning mapping in Wernicke's area in posterior parietal areas, to executive integration of orthographic, phonological, and semantic codes in left inferior frontal gyrus (Dhond, Buckner, Dale, Marinkovic, & Halgren, 2001). Consistent spelling-to-sound and sound-to-spelling relationships were associated with more activation in precuneus and posterior cingulate, whereas inconsistent relationships were associated with greater activation in left inferior frontal gyrus, medial frontal gyrus, and anterior cingulate (Bolger, Hornickle, Cone, Burman, & Booth, 2007).

Comparison of Normal and Disabled Child Writers on Handwriting, Spelling, Orthographic Coding, Finger Sequencing, and Idea Generation

In the brain-imaging studies conducted at the end of the 5-year longitudinal writing study when children had completed fifth grade, both good writers and poor writers, who met research-supported criteria for dysgraphia, were identified. In this section we report findings from those brain-imaging studies with the same participants but five varying tasks. Results are reported for good child writers or comparisons between the good writers without dysgraphia and the poor writers with dysgraphia.

Individual fifth-grade children without handwriting problems activated many brain regions, but fewer than those with dysgraphia on an fMRI BOLD *contrast between novel and familiar letter writing*, with letters equated on motor movements for formation (Richards, Berninger, Stock, Altemeier, Trivedi, & Maravilla, 2009b, see Table 1); but on a *contrast between familiar and novel letter writing* equated on motor movements, they activated many fewer brain regions, probably because the familiar, more practiced letter was written more automatically (Jones, 2004; Jones & Christensen, 1999). On the familiar automatic letter writing contrast, the good handwriters differed significantly from poor handwriters only in left fusiform gyrus (Richards, Berninger, Stock et al., 2009b), which is associated with orthographic coding in fMRI research, consistent with the developmental behavioral research findings that orthographic coding and letter analysis in written words uniquely predict handwriting even when fine motor finger skills are included in the structural model (Abbott & Berninger, 1993).

These findings provide cross-disciplinary converging evidence that handwriting is not just a motor skill. They also suggest that fewer brain regions may be activated for familiar, practiced letter forms than for novel letter forms that are being learned. With practice, the brain may become more efficient in how many brain regions are used, thus safeguarding its limited energy resources. It is also the case that real letters, but not novel letter forms, could be phonologically coded (associated with a single phoneme). Thus, the alphabetic principle for mapping graphemes onto phonemes may have a brain advantage for more efficient letter writing. However, more research is needed on how brains may become more efficient when skills become automatic and what the advantages of orthographic–phonological correspondences may be in creating more efficient brains for handwriting.

The hand may also play a special role in spelling development as James and Longcamp and colleagues have found to be the case for handwriting. On a word-specific orthographic spelling judgment task, children without dysgraphia activated more than those with dysgraphia in the left precentral gyrus (primary motor area), postcentral gyrus (primary somatosensory area), inferior frontal gyrus (executive language area), and right superior frontal gyrus (cognitive area) (Richards, Berninger, & Fayol, 2009). The first three brain regions—left precentral, left inferior frontal gyrus pars triangularis, and left postcentral—were significantly correlated with a normed behavioral measure of dictated spelling; but the activation in right superior frontal gyrus serves as a reminder that written spellings are associated with underlying cognitive representations (Stahl & Nagy, 2005).

Based on activation in the first two regions, Richards, Berninger, and Fayol (2009) proposed that graphomotor envelopes (analogous to the intonational or musical melodies in oral expressive language) play a role in learning to spell through the motor act of writing letters in word units and the kinesthetic sensory feedback from producing the written word by hand. Consistent with this proposal, Lambert, Kandel, Fayol, and Esperet (2008) reported that adults group letters into syllable-size chunks, which are orthographically rather than phonologically defined units (Kandel, Herault, Grosjacques, Lambert, & Fayol, 2009) to optimize both retrieving word spellings from memory and programming motor output efficiently (see Chapter 2, this volume). The graphomotor envelope may support the kinetic melody described by Luria (1973), which involves not only the motor output system but also the sequential touch sensation (kinesthesia) as the letters are produced and receive somatosensory touch feedback. The kinetic melody for writing may function in analogous fashion to the oral-motor functions of mouth that support the intonation of spoken language and package words in musical melodies.

On the fMRI contrast for word-specific spelling compared to letter strings, children with dysgraphia activated more than good writers in the left precentral (primary motor) and left superior and middle frontal (cognitive and working memory, respectively) areas, and left fusiform and lingual and right cuneus-occipital and middle temporal (word form) areas (Richards, Berninger, & Fayol, 2009). They appeared to rely more than did good writers on posterior word form brain regions rather than frontal executive functions in left inferior frontal gyrus, which may explain their inefficient engagement of working memory. Four brain regions differed from good writers—left superior frontal, left middle frontal, right cuneus, and left lingual—and were negatively correlated with scores on a standardized, normed test of dictated spelling (the more the activation the lower the spelling score). Also, the children with dysgraphia activated more in a different part of the primary motor region than did the children without dysgraphia, but did not activate in the primary somatosensory region of the brain, consistent with not receiving touch sensation from experience in writing words (Richards, Berninger, & Fayol, 2009). Faulty kinesthetic feedback may explain the widespread belief that students with learning disabilities require special multisensory teaching with a large kinesthetic component. In addition, children with dysgraphia activated superior frontal gyrus on the left side, but the good spellers activated this structure on the right, consistent with more difficulty accessing word meanings, which are often in nonverbal format but related to written spelling (Stahl & Nagy, 2005).

Children with dysgraphia also differed significantly from those without dysgraphia in left anterior cingulate (executive functions), calcarine (visual), and bilateral precuneus (orthographic coding and processing) on an orthographic coding task contrast for storing and processing written pseudowords in temporary working memory, with letter string processing as a control. This finding is consistent with developmental findings discussed earlier that orthographic coding in working memory contributes uniquely to developing transcription skills (handwriting and spelling; Abbott & Berninger, 1993).

On the fMRI contrast for serial finger tapping (sequencing) compared to a single finger tap (no sequencing), children without dysgraphia activated robustly in widely distributed regions associated with thinking, working memory, executive functions, and language, but those with dysgraphia hardly activated (Richards, Berninger, Stock, Altemeier, Trivedi, & Maravilla, 2009a). These findings are consistent with Lashley's (1951) conceptual insight, which contributed to the transition from the behavioral to cognitive paradigm in psychology, that serial organization underlies human cognition. Moreover, behavioral measures of handwriting, spelling, and composing significantly predicted the amount of BOLD activation during this finger sequencing task, with effects due to motor output alone controlled, consistently in the same five brain regions in individual brains—right and left inferior temporal, right precuneus, left superior parietal, and right inferior frontal orbital (Berninger, Richards, & Abbott, 2009). Serial organization is fundamentally important in writing: Handwriting requires serial organization of component letter strokes. Spelling requires serial organization of letters in a word. Composing requires serial organization of words in syntax and sentence units, serial organization of sentences, and serial organization within and across structures in discourse schema.

In a departure from exclusive focus on transcription skills, Berninger, Richards, Stock et al. (2009) assessed idea generation in fifth graders (average age 11) before they composed outside the scanner. Based on 24 coded categories of generated ideas on oral protocols, hypotheses were generated, tested, and confirmed about regions where child writers would show fMRI BOLD activation during idea generation. Good writers showed more fMRI BOLD activation than poor writers during idea generation in brain regions associated with visual imagery (left occipital gyrus), nonverbal cognition (right superior and middle temporal gyri), affect (left posterior cingulate), language (left inferior frontal gyrus), executive functions (left anterior cingulate), and working memory, higher order cognition, and metacognition (left middle frontal gyrus; see Chapter 11, this volume, for the importance of metacognition in writing assessment and instruction).

The children with dysgraphia activated significantly more than did those without dysgraphia in fMRI BOLD activation during the idea generation to baseline rest contrast. The children with dysgraphia activated only in the left and not the middle frontal gyrus, whereas those without dysgraphia activated bilaterally in both the left and right frontal gyrus, consistent with their drawing on both verbal and nonverbal concepts; also those with and without dysgraphia activated more than each other in a different location within the middle frontal gyrus (Berninger, Richards, Stock et al., 2009). Overall results showed that those with dysgraphia engaged brain regions associated with working memory differently than did those who were good writers.

Developmental Writing Disorders: Dyslexia

As already discussed, dyslexia is a writing as well as a reading disorder; children whose development is otherwise normal have word reading and word spelling impairment, and the spelling problems can interfere with their composing (Berninger, Nielsen et al., 2008). Richards et al. (2005) investigated their brain activation on phonological, orthographic, and morphological tasks (related to the three word-form storage and processing units of working memory) before and after spelling instruction. Berninger, Nagy, Richards, and Raskind (2008) presented an overview of the neurolinguistic findings from all the interdisciplinary studies related to spelling. In addition, Berninger and Nagy (2008) presented a multifaceted discussion of why flexibility (the lower order executive function of switching attention) is just as important as automaticity, which has often been emphasized in the recent literacy research to the exclusion of other important executive functions. (Also see Chapter 3, this volume, on the relevance of flexibility to cognitive instruction for writing and Hooper, Swartz, Wakely, de Kruif, & Montgomery, 2002.) Swanson (2006) provided evidence that reading disability is caused by not only phonological deficits but also impaired working memory, which of course can interfere with writing development as well as reading development. Thus, it is not surprising to find that many individuals may have both reading and writing disabilities, although writing disabilities can also occur without reading disability as shown in a population-based epidemiological study (Katusic, Colligan, Weaver, & Barbaresi, 2009).

Relationship Between Writing and Math in Normal Writing and Disabled Writing and Calculation

Writing, reading, and math are often considered separate domains of learning. In recent years educators have emphasized the importance of instruction across the curriculum (e.g., reading or writing in the content areas) and learning across curriculum domains (e.g., integrated reading and writing). However, insufficient attention has been given to the interrelationships between writing and math—both for learning and for instruction. Zago et al. (2008) presented evidence that working memory also supports the learning of arithmetic calculation—but calculation draws on both verbal and nonverbal storage and processing units. (See Chapter 1, this volume, for a discussion of how writing draws on both imagery as well as language.) However, the orthographic loop also plays a role in learning math and written calculations. Berninger (2007) discussed diagnosing and treating orthographic loop problems that may interfere with learning to do math in general or written calculations in particular, for example, in (a) writing numerals legibly and automatically; (b) drawing conceptual links between finger counting forward (addition, multiplication) and backward (subtraction, division) along the number line and summary written "math facts" used in the calculation operations; (c) arranging numerals in unidimensional sequenced spaces to represent the place value system for expressing an infinite number of numbers with just 10 written symbols, at least in base 10; (d) arranging single-digit and multidigit numerals into two-dimensional space to perform addition, subtraction, multiplication, and division; and (e) linking the concept of part-whole relationships to writing fractions, decimals, and mixed numbers.

Significance of the Brain Research for Writing Development

Overall the results in this overview are of interest to the field of writing research for four reasons. First, the subword orthographic coding (letter form and word form) storage and analysis systems have separate neural circuits in the left posterior region of the brain, consistent with a levels-of-language framework for writing. Second, although neural circuits for storing and processing letter forms in normal writing development are in the back of the brain, those revealed in acquired writing disorders are in frontal and parietal (not far from the frontal) regions in preparation for and written production of letters. However, in both normal development and acquired disorders, regardless of whether activation is in the back or front of the brain, the activation is on the left. Thus, there may be a left posterior-to-anterior pathway for letter forms, proceeding from initial representation in the back to preparation for production and finally execution of production of the letter form in the front. Considering that frontal regions are more vulnerable to brain injury, those regions may be more likely to be damaged and result in specific kinds of acquired disorders compared to the posterior regions where occipital association areas blend into lower temporal regions. Third, the findings show that writing cannot be explained solely on the basis of phonological codes for spoken words—orthographic representations (letters) are also involved, which are not visual percepts received or stored in primary visual area, but rather are visible language representations that can be both imaged in the mind's eye and correspond to other kinds of language representations in temporal and parietal regions. Fourth, these results are also relevant to research showing that the hand (including its orthographic loop to internal orthographic codes) may uniquely engage working memory to gain access to cognitive representations, both for writing and nonwriting goals (Berninger, Richards, & Abbott, 2009).

CUTTING-EDGE ISSUES FOR FUTURE OF RESEARCH ON WRITING BRAIN

New Approaches Needed for Research Questions Requiring Multivariate Answers

In its early years, science emphasized the contributions of the individual investigator and put a premium on being the first to discover new knowledge. In the 21st century, science benefits more from going beyond the "not invented here mentality" to developing ways to make sense of the rapidly expanding volume of data from many disciplines and traditions or perspectives within and across those disciplines. What is at stake is construction of a science that has conceptual frameworks and methods to make sense of multiple variables that exert their effects within a system of interrelated and often interacting components. Whether science has applications to the pressing needs of society at this stage of human evolution will depend greatly on the collective efforts of scientists to begin to create a multivariate systems approach. An indication that it can be done is the inspiring leadership of Leroy Hood in modeling this approach for systems biology and personalized medicine.

Berninger and Richards (2002, 2009, 2010) offered suggestions, based on the writing brain (as well as reading and math brains), for how psychologists might begin to integrate what has been learned from the various paradigms—physiology and neuroscience, behavior analysis, and cognitive—about the human brain, behavior, and mind for over a century. Their proposal to begin to develop systems models with multiple interacting components at multiple levels of analysis is a modest beginning to which hopefully others will contribute to construct a multivariate systems approach with potential applications to improve services for biological, behavioral, and mental disorders. Ultimately psychology needs to evolve beyond the paradigms described in this chapter to encompass all relevant approaches to understanding human cognition, behavior, and development, including writing.

Mesulam (1990), who envisioned a triangle with three sides—the biological properties and neurological structures of an individual's brain, the mental representations and functions supported by that brain, and the individual's behavior—provided guidance for developing viable paradigms. The first two constructs are internal to the individual, and the third to the individual operating in the external physical and social environment. Thus, the most powerful paradigms will integrate the neurophysiological, behavioral, and cognitive paradigms to create new interdisciplinary ones grounded in the individual's internal environment interacting with the external environment and also in the information age using technology (see Chapters 19 and 22, this volume). At the same time, other writing implements such as pencils, pens, crayons, chalk, and markers are not dinosaurs yet, and indeed using them appears to have brain advantages for letter formation, for which evidence was presented in this chapter.

Definitional Issues

One of the major problems hindering progress in creating such an interdisciplinary, systems approach is the inability of researchers (and clinicians) to define with consensus what the concepts are, how they can be measured reliably and validly, what is normal, and what departs from normal, and if so, how. Connelly, Dockrell, and Barnett (Chapter 10, this volume), who collectively represent the fields of educational psychology, speech and language, and developmental psychology with expertise in reading, writing, oral language, and motor development, have made a truly pioneering contribution to beginning to address across disciplines the complex but important issues for dealing with the definitional issues. The challenge for the professionals is that the individuals studied in research and served clinically present with multidimensional profiles of abilities and disabilities or relative strengths and weaknesses across many facets of brain, behavior, and mental functioning. Not only individual data points but the contexts in which they occur across multiple domains or dimensions need to be taken into account.

Integration of Molecular Genetics, Brain, Behavior, and Mental Functioning

Adding to the complexity is an emerging consensus, after completing studies that swept the genome to sequence the four base chemicals in DNA, that sequencing alone does not explain everything. Not only is there much empty space (junk DNA), but the potential for computation at the molecular biology level is also mind-boggling. Much is being learned about the biochemical transcription and translation processes of mRNA from DNA into the mechanisms that affect the functioning of each neuron (for an introduction to the protein chemistry at the molecular level involving 14 peptides and 4-level protein structures, see Bear, Connors, & Paradiso, 2007). Moreover, the new field of epigenetics (chemical modification of the behavioral expression of underlying gene sequences as organisms interact with the environment) is rapidly expanding (see Cassiday, 2009, and the special section on epigenetics in *Science, 330*, from October 15, 2010).

However, Berninger and Richards (2010) pointed out that it is unknown if instruction can really modify the gene expression (e.g., through methylation, as has been found for other environmental interventions; see Cassiday, 2009). Accumulating studies show that children with gene variants associated with specific learning disabilities respond to instruction in that they improve in taught skills and sometimes transfer skills. But did the instruction translate into epigenetic modifications that ensure there will be no learning problems in the future? The possibility remains that individuals with genetically based specific learning disabilities may respond to instructionally appropriate treatment at one time in development, but still face challenges later in development because the underlying genetic vulnerability has not been altered—gene variants or sequencing is unchanged as curriculum requirements increase in volume and complexity across the grades. Future research should address the possible interrelationships among teaching, learning, and epigenetics. The results could have enormous applications for providing free and appropriate educational services for all students, including those with writing (or reading and math brain) skills constrained by genetic variation, which make it more difficult for them to learn the curriculum in the instructional and learning environment in their educational settings.

Multilevel Models That Incorporate DNA and mRNA Computations at the Neuronal Level

Now that the sequencing of the human genome has been completed and research on the epigenetic modification of the behavioral expression is under way, we need to revise our multilevel models of writing to incorporate computations at the molecular chemical level in individual neurons. Such widespread molecular computations at the microlevel may explain the biological basis of the vast unconscious human mind. In contemporary cognitive psychology, there does appear to be a consensus that the human mind has conscious awareness of only a fraction of its representations at any one time, and many of these representations are in implicit memory outside conscious awareness, unless they are accessed via working memory mechanisms for specific goals or tasks. Berninger, Fayol, and Alamargot (2011) further explored the nature and implications of these possibilities. Of relevance to the writing brain is that the act of writing, which externalizes cognition by bringing into conscious awareness that which heretofore was not available at a conscious level (see Hayes & Flower, 1980, for this initial insight), has and will continue to play an important role in helping the human mind gain conscious access to its cognitions, including those that are represented and influence our mental functions and behavior without our conscious attention (see Koch, 2004, for further insight into the neurobiological basis of the unconscious and Galbraith, 2009, for further ideas about the role of writing in gaining access to cognitions in implicit, unconscious memory).

Role of the Episodic Buffer in Abstracting Statistical Regularities in Implicit Working Memory

Episodic memory stores ongoing events in time, including not only life events in each individual's personal narrative but also exposure to spoken and written words and their constituent parts, which have not only semantic associations (Stahl & Nagy, 2005) but also morphological forms (bases with or without prefixes or inflectional or derivational suffixes). An analyzer may operate outside conscious awareness on this episodic storage system and abstract frequency of words and word parts, occurrence of word parts in word positions, and sequencing of the parts across word units (Berninger et al., 2011). The outputs of this analyzer may, in turn, contribute to the fast mapping (McGregor, 2004) underlying lexical-level mapping, which supplements the slower subword phonological to orthographic mapping (Bahr, Silliman, & Berninger, 2009).

Advantages and Disadvantages of a Brain With Vast Storage and Processing in Molecular Computational Mechanisms

A multilevel system in which most storage and processing is outside conscious awareness, but can be brought into consciousness for specific tasks, which require a limited amount of time (not unlike the computer user who stores most files on a server and calls up only those files needed for specific daily purposes because the number of files exceeds storage capacity), has fuel-conserving advantages. Less glucose needs to be burned and therefore the brain does not have to work as hard to gain access to the oxygen—its fuel for burning the glucose that fuels the brain at work.

Another advantage of a leveled arrangement is the greater freedom for interactions and thus conversations among cognitive representations and thinking operations in the unconscious mind. Numerous combinations and permutations may occur across the multilevel space–time continua of the unconscious mind with periodic excursions into consciousness, resulting in a richer and more powerful and adaptable mind than if what is represented and what is processed are restricted to what appears at a conscious level to be relevant to the task at hand or socially acceptable.

However, this kind of brain organization—mostly unconscious in implicit memory (never or only occasionally brought to consciousness)—relies greatly on the ability of the human brain to self-regulate itself. Indeed, the brain needs to not only self-program itself to learn and function but also to reprogram itself as it continues to learn and adapt and, when necessary, modify its environment. In the process of performing a variety of tasks for variable goals and plans, and as necessary, gaining or trying to gain access to relevant declarative and procedural representations in implicit memory, an individual brain faces enormous challenges in self-regulation. Posner and Rothbart (2007a, 2007b) presented their pioneering contributions to understanding the attentional mechanisms and self-regulation abilities required for managing brains across development and for skilled performance. Although we know a great deal about effective self-regulation strategies to teach developing writers (Harris, Graham, Mason, & Friedlander, 2008; Harris, Graham, & Urdan, in press), we have much to learn about how the writing brain supports its own self-regulation processes (Altemeier, Abbott, & Berninger, 2007) during specific developmental windows (Rogers, 2010) in the lifespan developmental journey in learning and perfecting writing skills.

ACKNOWLEDGMENTS

The interdisciplinary research on writing featured in this chapter was supported by grants HD25858 and P50 33812 from the National Institute of Child Health and Human Development (NICHD). The authors thank Karin Harman James for helpful comments about a prior version of the chapter.

REFERENCES

Abbott, R., & Berninger, V. (1993). Structural equation modeling of relationships among developmental skills and writing skills in primary and intermediate grade writers. *Journal of Educational Psychology, 85*(3), 478–508.

Altemeier, L., Abbott, R., & Berninger, V. (2007). Executive functions for reading and writing in typical literacy development and dyslexia. *Journal of Clinical and Experimental Neuropsychology, 30*, 588–606.

Anderson, S., Damasio, A., & Damasio, H. (1990). Troubled letters but not numbers: Domain specific cognitive impairments following focal damage in frontal cortex. *Brain, 113*, 749–760.

Apel, K., Oster, J., & Masterson, J. (2006). Effects of phonotactic and orthotactic probabilities during fast-mapping on five-year-olds' learning to spell. *Developmental Neuropsychology, 29*, 21–42.

Baddeley, A., Gathercole, S., & Papagno, C. (1998). The phonological loop as a language learning device. *Psychological Review, 105*, 158–173.

Bahr, R. H., Silliman, E. R., & Berninger, V. (2009). What spelling errors have to tell about vocabulary learning. In C. Wood & V. Connelly (Eds.). *Reading and spelling: Contemporary perspectives* (pp. 177–210). London: Routledge EARLI Writing Series.

Basso, A., Taborelli, A., & Vignolo, L. (1978). Dissociated disorders of speaking and writing in aphasia. *Journal of Neurology, Neurosurgery, and Psychiatry, 41*, 556–563.

Bates, E., Elman, J., Johnson, M., Karmiloff-Smith, A., Parisi, D., & Plunkett, K. (1998). Innateness and emergentism. In W. Berchet & G. Graham (Eds.), *A companion to cognitive science* (pp. 590–601). Oxford: Blackwell.

Bear, M. F., Connors, B., & Paradiso, M. (2007). *Neuroscience: Exploring the brain* (3rd ed.). Philadelphia: Lippincott Williams & Wilkins.

Berninger, V. (2007). *Process assessment of the Learner II User's Guide*. San Antonio, TX: Pearson. (CD format) Second revision issued August 2008.

Berninger, V. (2011). Process assessment of the learner, 2nd edition (PAL II) comprehensive assessment for evidence-based, treatment-relevant differential diagnosis of dysgraphia, dyslexia, oral and written language learning disability (OWL LD), and dyscalculia. In N. Mather & L. Fuchs (Eds.), *Comprehensive evaluations from experts in psychology and special education*. New York: Wiley.

Berninger, V., & Abbott, D. (2010). Listening comprehension, oral expression, reading comprehension and written expression: Related yet unique language systems in grades 1, 3, 5, and 7. *Journal of Educational Psychology, 102*, 635–651.

Berninger, V., Abbott, R., Augsburger, A., & Garcia, N. (2009). Comparison of pen and keyboard transcription modes in children with and without learning disabilities affecting transcription. *Learning Disability Quarterly, 32*, 123–141.

Berninger, V., Abbott, R., Swanson, H. L., Lovitt, D., Trivedi, P., Lin, S., ... Amtmann, D. (2010). Relationship of word- and sentence-level working memory to reading and writing in second, fourth, and sixth grade. *Language, Speech, and Hearing Services in Schools, 41*, 179–193.

Berninger, V., Fayol, M., & Alamargot, D. (2011). Contribution of the pattern analyzer, oracle, cross-code talker, cross-code scribe, and silent portal of mind in learning to transcribe and translate at the word-level. In M. Fayol, D. Alamargot, & V. Berninger (Eds.), *Translation of thought to written text while composing: Advancing theory, knowledge, methods, and applications*. New York: Psychology Press/Taylor & Francis Group/Routledge.

Berninger, V., & Hayes, J. R. (2011). 20 children on writing treks: Their developing translation processes. In M. Fayol, D. Alamargot, & V. Berninger (Eds.), *Translation of thought to written text while composing: Advancing theory, knowledge, methods, and applications*. New York: Psychology Press/Taylor & Francis Group/Routledge.

Berninger, V., & Nagy, W. (2008). Flexibility in word reading: Multiple levels of representations, complex mappings, partial similarities, and cross-modality connections. In K. Cartwright (Ed.), *Flexibility in literacy processes and instructional practice: Implications of developing representational ability for literacy teaching and learning* (pp. 114–139). New York: Guilford.

Berninger, V., Nagy, W., Richards, T., & Raskind, W. (2008). Developmental dyslexia: A developmental neurolinguistic approach. In G. Rickheit & H. Strohner (Eds.), *Handbook of communicative competence. Handbook of applied linguistics* (Vol. 1, pp. 397–440). Germany: Mouton de Gruyter.

Berninger, V., Nielsen, K., Abbott, R., Wijsman, E., & Raskind, W. (2008). Writing problems in developmental dyslexia: Under-recognized and under-treated. *Journal of School Psychology, 46*, 1–21.

Berninger, V., Raskind, W., Richards, T., Abbott, R., & Stock, P. (2008). A multidisciplinary approach to understanding developmental dyslexia within working-memory architecture: Genotypes, phenotypes, brain, and instruction. *Developmental Neuropsychology, 33*, 707–744.

Berninger, V., & Richards, T. (2002). *Brain literacy for educators and psychologists*. New York: Academic Press.

Berninger, V., & Richards, T. (2009). Brain and learning. In E. Anderman & L. Anderman (Eds.), *Psychology of classroom learning: An encyclopedia* (Vol. 1, pp. 15–22). Detroit: Macmillan Reference USA.

Berninger, V., & Richards, T. (2010). Inter-relationships among behavioral markers, genes, brain, and treatment in dyslexia and dysgraphia. *Future Neurology, 5*, 597–617.

Berninger, V., Richards, T., & Abbott, R. (2009). The role of the hand in written idea expression. In D. Alamargot, J. Bouchand, E. Lambert, V. Millogo, & C. Beaudet (Eds.), Proceedings of the International Conference de la France au Québec: l'Ecriture dans tous ses états, University of Poitiers, France, 12–15 November 2008. Retrieved from http://www.poitou-charentes.iufm.fr/IMG/pdf/BerningerRichards AbbottCONF.pdf

Berninger, V., Richards, T., Stock, P., Abbott, R., Trivedi, P., Altemeier, L., & Hayes, J. R. (2009). fMRI activation related to nature of ideas generated and differences between good and poor writers during idea generation. *British Journal of Educational Psychology Monograph Series II, 6*, 77–93.

Berninger, V. Rijlaarsdam, G., & Fayol, M. (2011). Mapping models, measures, and methods to writing research questions. In M. Fayol, D. Alamargot, & V. Berninger (Eds.), *Translation of thought to written text while composing: Advancing theory, knowledge, methods, and applications*. New York: Psychology Press/Taylor & Francis Group/Routledge.

Bitan, T., Cheon, J., Lu, D., Burman, D., Gitelman, D., Mesulam, M., & Booth, J. R. (2007). Developmental changes in activation and effective connectivity in phonological processing. *NeuroImage, 38*, 564–575.

Bolger, D., Hornickel, J., Cone, N., Burman, D., & Booth, J. (2007). Neural correlates of orthographic and phonological consistency effects in children. *Human Brain Mapping, 29*(12), 1416–1429.

Booth, J., Cho, S., Burman, D., & Bitan, T. (2007). Neural correlates of mapping from phonology to orthography in children performing an auditory spelling task. *Developmental Science, 10*, 441–451.

Booth, J. R., Burman, D. D., Meyer, J. R., Gitelman, D. R., Parrish, T. B., & Mesulam, M. M. (2002). Functional anatomy of intra- and cross-modal lexical tasks. *Neuroimage, 16*(1), 7–22.

Brain, L. (1967). *Speech disorders: Aphasia, apraxia, and agnosia*. London: Butterworth.

Carter, R., Aldridge, S., Page, M., & Parker, S. (2009). *The human brain: An illustrated guide to the structure, function, and disorders* [Includes DVD-ROM]. London: DK Publishing.

Cassiday, L. (2009, September 14). *Mapping the epigenome: New tools chart chemical modifications of DNA and its packaging proteins*. Retrieved from http://pubs.acs.org/cen/coverstory/87/8737cover.html

Chenoweth, N., & Hayes, J. R. (2003). The inner voice in writing. *Written Communication, 20*, 99–118.

Cohen, L., Lehèricy, S., Chochon, F., Lemer, C., Rivaud, S., & Dehaene, S. (2002). Language-specific tuning of visual cortex? Functional properties of the visual word form area. *Brain, 125*, 1054–1069.

Connelly, V., Campbell, S., MacLean, M., & Barnes, J. (2006). Contribution of lower-order skills to the written composition of college students with and without dyslexia. *Developmental Neuropsychology, 29*, 175–196.

Cornoldi, C., & Vecchi, T. (2003). *Visuo-spatial working memory and individual differences. Essays in cognitive psychology*. New York: Psychology Press.

Dehaene, S. (2002). Language-specific tuning of visual cortex? Functional properties of the visual word form area. *Brain, 125*, 1054–1069.

Dhond, R., Buckner, R., Dale, A., Marinkovic, K., & Halgren, E. (2001). Spatiotemporal maps of brain activity underlying word generation and their modification during repetition priming. *Journal of Neuroscience, 21*, 3564–3571.

Diamond, M., & Hopson, J. (1998). *Magic trees of mind. How to nurture your child's intelligence, creativity, and healthy emotions from birth to adolescence*. New York: Penguin.

Eliot, L. (1999). *What's going on in there? How the brain and mind develop in the first five years of life*. New York: Bantam.

Exner, S. (1881). *Untersuchungen uber die Lokalisation der Funktionen in der Grossshirnrinde des Menschen*. Vienna: Wilhelm Braumuller.

Flowers, D. L., Jones, K., Nobel, K., VanMeter, J., Zeffiro, T., Wood, F., & Eden, G. (2004). Attention to single letters activates left extrastriate cortex. *NeuroImage, 21*, 829–839.

Fuster, J. (1997). *The prefrontal cortex. Anatomy, physiology, and neuropsychology of the frontal lobe* (3rd ed.) (pp. 205–252). New York: Raven.

Fuster, J. (2003). *Cortex and mind: Unifying cognition*. Oxford: Oxford University Press.

Galbraith, D. (2009) Writing as discovery. *British Journal of Educational Psychology Monograph Series II, 6*, 1–23.

Gibson, E., & Levin, H. (1975). *The psychology of reading*. Cambridge, MA: MIT Press.

Goldman-Rakic, P. (1992). Working memory and the mind. *Scientific American, 267*, 111–117.

Graham, S., & Perin, D. (2007). A meta-analysis of writing instruction for adolescent students. *Journal of Educational Psychology, 99*, 445–476.

Harris, K. R., Graham, S., Mason, L., & Friedlander, B. (2008). *Powerful writing strategies for all students*. Baltimore, MD: Brookes.

Harris, K., Graham, S., & Urdan, T. (Eds.). (in press). *Educational psychology handbook, Vol. 3, Applications of educational psychology to learning and teaching*. Washington, DC: American Psychological Association.

Hayes, J. R., & Berninger, V. (2010). Relationships between idea generation and transcription: How act of writing shapes what children write. In C. Brazerman, R. Krut, K. Lunsford, S. McLeod, S. Null, P. Rogers, & A. Stansell (Eds.), *Traditions of writing research* (pp. 166–180). New York: Taylor & Frances/Routledge.

Hayes, J. R., & Flower, L. S. (1980). Identifying the organization of writing processes. In L.W. Gregg & E. R. Steinbert (Eds.), *Cognitive processes in writing* (pp. 3–30). Hillsdale, NJ: Erlbaum.

Hooper, S., Knuth, S., Yerby, D., & Anderson, K. (2009). A review of science supported writing instruction with implementation in mind. In S. Rosenfield & V. Berninger (Eds.), *Implementing evidence-based interventions in school settings* (pp. 49–83). New York: Oxford University Press.

Hooper, S. R., Swartz, C. W., Wakely, M. B., de Kruif, R. E. L., & Montgomery, J. W. (2002). Executive functions in elementary school children with and without problems in written expression. *Journal of Learning Disabilities, 35*, 37–68.

Jacobs, B., Schall, M., & Scheibel, A. (1993). A qualitative dendritic analysis of Wernicke's area in humans. II. Gender, hemispheric, and environmental factors. *Journal of Comparative Neurology, 327*, 97–111.

James, K. (2010). Sensori-motor experience leads to changes in visual processing in the developing brain. *Developmental Science, 13*(2), 279–288.

James, K., & Atwood, T. (2009). The role of sensorimotor learning in the perception of letter-like forms: Tracking the causes of neural specialization for letters. *Cognitive Neuropsychology, 26*, 91–110.

James, K. H., & Gauthier, I. (2006). Letter processing automatically recruits a sensory–motor brain network. *Neuropsychologia, 44*, 2937–2949.

James, K., & Gauthier, I. (2009). When writing impairs reading: Letter perception's susceptibility to motor interference. *Journal of Experimental Psychology: General, 138*, 416–431.

James, K., James, T., Jobard, G., Wong, A., & Gauthier, I. (2005). Letter processing in the visual system: Different activation patterns for single letters and strings. *Cognitive, Affective, and Behavioral Neuroscience, 5*, 452–466.

James, K., & Maouene, J. (2009). Auditory verb perception recruits motor systems in the developing brain: An fMRI investigation. *Developmental Science, 12*(6), F26–F34.

Jones, D. (2004). *Automaticity of the transcription process in the production of written text*. Unpublished doctoral dissertation. Graduate School of Education, University of Queensland, Australia, Brisbane.

Jones, D., & Christensen, C. (1999). The relationship between automaticity in handwriting and students' ability to generate written text. *Journal of Educational Psychology, 91*, 44–49.

Kandel, S., Herault, L., Grosjacques, G., Lambert, E., & Fayol, M. (2009). Orthographic vs. phonologic syllables in handwriting production. *Cognition, 110*, 440–444.

Karmiloff-Smith, A. (2009). Preaching to the converted: From constructivism to neo-constructivism. *Child Development Perspectives, 3*, 99–102.

Katusic, S., Colligan, R., Weaver, A., & Barbaresi, W. (2009). The forgotten learning disability: Epidemiology of the written-language disorder in a population-based birth cohort (1976–1982), Rochester, Minnesota. *Pediatrics, 123*(5), 1306–1313.

Koch, C. (2004). *The quest for consciousness. A neurobiological approach*. Englewood, CO: Roberts & Company Publishers.

Kolb, B., & Whishaw, I. (2009). *Fundamentals of neuropsychology* (6th ed.). New York: Worth Publishers.

Lambert, E., Kandel, S., Fayol, M., & Esperet, E. (2008). The effect of the number of syllables on handwriting production. *Reading and Writing, 21*, 859–883.

Lashley, K. S. (1951). The problem of serial order in behavior. In L. A. Jeffress (Ed.), *Cerebral mechanisms in behavior* (pp. 112–131). New York: Wiley.

Longcamp, M., Anton, J. L, Roth, M., & Velay, J. L. (2003). Visual presentation of single letters activates a premotor area involved in writing. *NeuroImage, 19*, 1492–1500.

Longcamp, M., Bourcard, C., Gilhodes, J.-C., Anton, J. L., Roth, M., Nazarian, B., & Velay, J.-L. (2008). *Journal of Cognitive Neuroscience, 20*, 802–815.

Longcamp, M., Zerbato-Poudou, M.-T., & Velay, J-L. (2005). The influence of writing practice on letter recognition in preschool children: A comparison between handwriting and typing. *Acta Psychologica, 119*, 67–79.

Luria, A. R. (1973). *The working brain. An introduction to neuropsychology.* New York: Basic Books.

McGregor, K. (2004). Developmental dependencies between lexical semantics and reading. In C. A. Stone, E. Silliman, B. Ehren, & K. Apel (Eds.), *Handbook of language and literacy* (pp. 302–317). New York: Guilford.

Mesulam, M. (1990). Large-scale neurocognitive networks and distributed processing for attention, language, and memory. *Annals Neurology, 28*, 597–613.

Minsky, M. (1986). *Society of mind.* New York: Simon and Schuster.

Morris, R., & Mather, N. (Eds.). (2008). *Evidence-based interventions for students with learning and behavioral challenges.* Mahwah, NJ: Erlbaum-LEA.

Posner, M., & Rothbart, M. (2007a). Research on attention networks as a model for the integration of psychological science. *Annual Review of Psychology, 58*, 1–23.

Posner, M., & Rothbart, M. (2007b). *Educating the human brain.* Washington, DC: American Psychological Association.

Richards, T., Berninger, V., & Fayol, M. (2009). fMRI activation differences between 11-year-old good and poor spellers' access in working memory to temporary and long-term orthographic representations. *Journal of Neurolinguistics, 22*, 327–353.

Richards, T., Berninger, V., & Fayol, M. (in press). The writing brain of normal child writers and children with writing disabilities: Generating ideas and transcribing them through the orthographic loop. In E. Grigorenko, E. Mambrino, & D. D. Preiss (Eds.), *Writing: A mosaic of perspectives and views.* New York: Psychology Press.

Richards, T., Berninger, V., Nagy, W., Parsons, A., Field, K., & Richards, A. (2005). Brain activation during language task contrasts in children with and without dyslexia: Inferring mapping processes and assessing response to spelling instruction. *Educational and Child Psychology, 22*(2), 62–80.

Richards, T., Berninger, V., Stock, P., Altemeier, L., Trivedi, P., & Maravilla, K. (2009a). fMRI sequential-finger movement activation differentiating good and poor writers. *Journal of Clinical and Experimental Neuropsychology, 29*, 1–17.

Richards, T., Berninger, V., Stock, P., Altemeier, L., Trivedi, P., & Maravilla, K. (2009b). Differences between good and poor child writers on fMRI contrasts for writing newly taught and highly practiced letter forms. *Reading and Writing. An Interdisciplinary Journal, 24*(5), 493–516.

Richards, T., Berninger, V., Winn, W., Swanson, H. L., Stock, P., Liang, O., & Abbott, R. (2009). Differences in fMRI activation between children with and without spelling disability on 2-back/0-back working memory contrast. *Journal of Writing Research, 1*(2), 93–123.

Roeske, D., Ludwig, K., Neuhoff, N., Becker, J., Bartling, J., Bruder, J., … Schulte-Körne, G. (2009). First genome-wide association scan on neurophysiological endophenotypes points to trans-regulation effects on SLC2A3 in dyslexic children. *Molecular Psychiatry, 16*(1), 97–107.

Rogers, P. M. (2010). The contributions of North American longitudinal studies of writing in higher education to our understanding of writing development. In C. Bazerman, R. Krut, K. Lunsford, S. McLeod, S. Null, P. M. Rogers, & A. Stansell (Eds.), *Traditions of writing research* (pp. 365–377). Oxford: Routledge.

Roux, F.-E., Dufor, O., Giussani, C., Wamain, Y., Draper, L., Longcomp, M., & Démonet J. F. (2009). The graphemic/motor frontal area Exner's area revisited. *Annals of Neurology, 66*, 537–545.

Stahl, S., & Nagy, W. (2005). *Teaching word meaning.* Mahwah, NJ: Erlbaum.

Swanson, H. L. (2006). Working memory and reading disabilities: Both phonological and executive processing deficits are important. In T. Alloway & S. Gathercole (Eds.), *Working memory and neurodevelopmental conditions* (pp. 59–88). London: Psychology Press.

Troia, G. (Ed.). (2009). *Instruction and assessment for struggling writers. Evidence-based practices.* New York: Guilford.

Wong, C.-N., Jobard, G., James, K., James, T., & Gauthier, I. (2009). Expertise with characters in alphabetic and nonalphabetic writing systems engage overlapping occipito-temporal areas. *Cognitive Neuropsychology, 26*(1), 111–127.

Zago, L., Petit, L., Turbelin, M-R., Andersson, F., Vigneau, M., & Tzourio-Maxoyer, N. (2008). How verbal and spatial manipulation networks contribute to calculation: An fMRI study. *Neuropsychologia, 46*, 2403–2414.

Visions of the Future of Writing Research

Perspectives From the New Generation of Writing Researchers and Contemporary Leaders

Through the Models of Writing
Ten Years After and Visions for the Future

DENIS ALAMARGOT and LUCILE CHANQUOY

*D*uring the 1998 SIG Writing meeting, Gert Rijlaarsdam, who was at that time an editor for the EARLI Writing Series, invited us to write *Through the Models of Writing* (Alamargot & Chanquoy, 2001). Our goal in writing this book was to synthesize the various definitions and theoretical ideas about writing processes. During the process of writing our book, we became more and more aware of the necessity to analyze the different writing models precisely and to compare them. Indeed, since the publication of Hayes and Flower's (1980) model, many criticisms and revisions occurred and progress emerged, occasionally introducing some conceptual misunderstandings, which made it increasingly difficult to compare empirical results and theoretical ideas. From Hayes and Flower's model, "new" models have been built but sometimes without any consideration to their validation or heuristic interest. After 20 years of "model building," the writing community lacked a unifying theoretical background.

When, 10 years later, we considered these issues, it was clear that progress toward a unified model of writing processes remains limited, despite the fact that the field of writing research is maturing. It is today less important to build a model than to collect empirical data and, gradually, to advance a deeper understanding of the specific writing mechanisms. With this in mind, it is likely that future models will be less theoretical constructs and more predictive computer-generated models. The now old formula that asserted that *writing is a complex activity whose study is difficult* is no more defendable. To begin with, the complexity of writing is today fairly well clarified; the components, processes, and constraints are clearly identified if not yet totally explained. Moreover, more than 30 years of research cannot be considered only a first step toward discovery.

After early work on description, the focus is switching from description to explanation. As emphasized by Alamargot and Fayol (2009):

> Put rather simplistically, there are two main lines of research on verbal production. The first one, involving research of a largely fundamental nature, is inspired mainly by generativist-type linguistic models and seeks to establish an integrative psycholinguistic theory of verbal production. It focuses almost exclusively on the production of words and sentences, the basic units of formal linguistics. The aim of the second one, which is initially more reliant on social demand, is to form one or several production models in order to improve the

> way in which utterances or texts are organized, and therefore the way in which they are processed by those who are called upon to perceive and understand them. These two approaches mirror the opposition between the two categories of units constituted by the sentence and the discourse. They correspond to two linguistic conceptions and essentially remain juxtaposed, each conducting its own research without paying much attention to the data and models generated by the other's research. (p. 23)

This mutual ignorance of these two psycholinguistic and cognitive fields is problematic and has most certainly contributed to the weak advances in this field of research. There is a paradox: Much research on handwriting, spelling, and text production does not take the other into account, although research that succeeded in integrating these approaches in the study of writing development has emerged (e.g., Chanquoy, Foulin, & Fayol, 1990; Fayol, Largy, & Lemaire, 1994; Graham, 1990; McArthur, Graham, & Fitzgerald, 2006; McCutchen, Covill, Hoyne, & Mildes, 1994; Swanson & Berninger, 1996). The major interest of these works was to consider a system made of several constraints between low levels of processing—handwriting and spelling—and high levels of cognitive processes in written text production. It is therefore important to consider what is unique about writing: a language code that is different from oral language because its "physical" organ is the hand rather than the mouth.

The developmental approach to writing research contributes by describing, explaining, and understanding writing processes and their constraints through a lifespan perspective. This approach leads to more precise analysis and understanding of the nature of writing units and operations than did merely describing the main cognitive processes as had been done before. However, this approach—the offline analysis of products, that is, characteristics of the written messages—can be combined with analysis in real time of the processing (time durations, eye fixations, or reaction times) that led to these products.

Advances in on-line methodology and the increase in real-time studies over the past 5 to 6 years have increased understanding of writing. However, in combining this off-line and on-line approach, certain pitfalls should be avoided. Method should not be confused with objective. For instance, describing pause durations only makes sense if the underlying writing operations have been identified. A strict chronometric approach, conceived as a kind of "psychophysics" approach, is really not interesting regarding the highly controlled and metacognitive activities involved during writing unless the experimental design allows for that in some clever way. Nor does a pause or an eye fixation have significance in and of itself apart from the processes that led to the pause or the eye fixation (or what follows them). This use of on-line dependent variables needs to result in very precise hypotheses; otherwise, it will be time consuming with no research contribution.

However, identifying that a specific writing operation (process or subprocess), in a given context, results in a longer pause or an additional eye fixation is a new and important step in the discovery of the dynamics of writing. Few on-line studies have addressed the study of written production within this double perspective. To do so requires the conjunction of the two main research approaches, one more psycholinguistic and the other more centered on cognition. We believe that the future of research on writing relies on this trilogy: (1) identification of linguistic units and operations (psycholinguistic approach), (2) activation of units and operations in a constraining system of information processing (cognitive approach), and (3) linking the text and its processing (real-time approach).

Methodologically, the collection of eye movements (fixations or gaze durations) during writing appears to be one of the more promising advances. As noted by Salvucci and Anderson (2001), the use of eye-tracking systems has become considerably widespread—and that was a decade ago! These systems have become increasingly robust and integrated, but equally more ergonomic and less expensive. In this context, the creation of the Eye and Pen software is a major advance in the study of handwriting (Alamargot, Chesnet, Dansac, & Ros, 2006; Caporossi, Alamargot, & Chesnet, 2004; Chesnet & Alamargot, 2005). It has already helped us to reconsider the dynamics of text processing and spelling, actually by identifying the conditions for the appearance of parallel visual processing during writing (Alamargot, Dansac, Chesnet, & Fayol, 2007; Alamargot, Plane, Lambert, & Chesnet, 2009; Lambert, Alamargot, Laroque, & Caporossi, in press). Considering eye movements during handwriting, Chesnet and Alamargot (2005) showed that, with a variety of perspectives (also see Chapter 22, this volume), various research questions and issues can be explored and investigated. The studies could be carried out in two main directions:

1. Eye movements can be used and validated as indicators of different writing processes. Largely studied in the field of reading research, eye movements—saccades, fixations, and gazes—can be fruitfully adapted to writing research. In order to do this, researchers must consider the specific eye behaviors created by writing, which have to be defined and collected. These include eye microsaccades and eye pursuits, which could be engaged for tracking the writing trace that develops slowly. In addition, it is not certain that writing requires the writer to look continually at the text that is created, but when writers do, such looking may reveal clues about the writing process. Tactile and kinesthetic pieces of information from the hand activity may be sufficient for adults or teenagers to write properly, at least during a certain time and within a certain space and a certain time. Similarly, the act of voluntarily stopping to look at the text during writing (averting the gaze) has to be analyzed because it is possible that this behavior could reflect specific aspects of cognitive processing.

2. The particularly fine-grained measures of eye movements have led to reconsideration of the timescale that had been adopted earlier to assess written production (see Anderson, 2002, for the presentation of a timescale of mental events). Research findings may necessitate a change in the conceptions of the temporal dimensions of writing processes, and thereby, how the temporal dimensions are modeled.

Some preliminary results show that decisive information can be processed within a few hundred milliseconds, in parallel with the writing execution. This kind of information is really useful to understand, for instance, where and how the computation of an agreement between subject and verb is realized (see Chapter 19, this volume). This new methodology can help us to answer this question, and, more importantly, to see, for example, if the computation of an agreement is systematically realized before or during the writing of the concerned word or is elaborated while the whole sentence is mentally built. However, it seems that there is no one answer to this particular crucial question: It depends on the expertise of the writer and on her or his familiarity with the topic. Indeed, the timescale requires questioning the nature and the role of pieces of information that, when extracted from the task environment, may, at any time during the writing process, reactivate or modify a given process. In this sense, it is possible that the design of the research on writing dynamics and its management over the next few years should be reviewed again at the end of the next decade to evaluate how much progress has been made.

It is now clear and fairly convincing that the coupling of a digital tablet, a computer screen, and an eye-tracker apparatus is particularly useful to allow researchers to both study the writing time course and to assess in real time the effect of interactive environments built to help writers (such as spelling supports). This possibility increases the opportunity for many applications. Handwriting studies have become of interest because new media make it possible to use pen and handwriting as an interface between man and machine (such as PDAs, electronic notebooks, electronic binders). Thus, new methodological paradigms should be developed to study writing "on" or "with" these new devices. For instance, is it functionally the same thing to write on a paper with an ordinary pen as it is to write with a specific pen on a digital tablet? Is it the same thing to type on an "ordinary" computer keyboard and to type on a "screen" keyboard of an iPad? Are the same processes in play? Do writers manage their cognitive processes in the same way? Is there the same interplay between controlled and automated processes with these devices? There are many studies to carry out in this field in the future, especially for comparing traditional writing and technologically advanced writing.

Nevertheless, despite the very sophisticated technology and devices that are increasingly available, writing researchers must not forget the practical applications of writing research so it is viewed as useful or valuable. Writing is a crucial tool during the school years and after, during the professional years (see Chapters 5 and 12, this volume). In this way, writing researchers can help not only adults but also children to write better (see Chapters 8 and 11, this volume). For examples of how writing research is being applied to improve children's spelling, including its phonological, orthographic, and morphological bases, see the research by McCutchen and Arfé et al. (Chapters 9 and 15, this volume). For the impact of motivation and affect on writing, see the research by Boscolo and Gelati (Chapters 3 and 7, this volume).

With all this in mind, is it possible, today, to draw a new model of writing that integrates all the criticisms and all the progress made during these past 20 or 30 years? Because writing is a composite process, it is unlikely to be modeled in four or fives boxes connected with several arrows. Indeed, to draw a complete picture of writing we would have to consider (a) all the parameters of "cold" cognition—attention, memory, cognitive resources; (b) all the parameters of "warm" cognition—emotion, motivation, and affects; (c) the relationships of (a) and (b) to each other and to the different writing processes and subprocesses; (d) the relationships of the writing processes to spelling processes; (e) the output modes of writing such as handwriting, or typewriting, or texting (or new technology that appears) and their underlying motor processes; (f) the relationships of writing to grammar conventions; and (g) the relationships of writing processes to reading processes. Other issues that need to be taken into account in the model include metacognitive awareness, intra- and interindividual differences, gender, and expertise. An integrated model of writing will look like a big planet with many, many satellites. Is this kind of model helpful for future research? It first must be drawn by a very expert and skillful designer; then, it must be experimentally validated; and what results is another story to be told by the current and future generation of writing researchers.

REFERENCES

Alamargot, D., & Chanquoy, L. (2001). *Through the models of writing.* Dordrecht: Kluwer.

Alamargot, D., Chesnet, D., Dansac, C., & Ros, C. (2006). Eye and Pen: A new device to study reading during writing. *Behavior Research Methods, 38*(2), 287–299.

Alamargot, D., Dansac, C., Chesnet, D., & Fayol, M. (2007). Parallel processing before and after pauses: A combined analysis of graphomotor and eye movements during procedural text production. In M. Torrance, L. van Waes, & D. Galbraith (Eds.), *Writing and cognition: Research and applications* (pp. 13–29). Amsterdam: Elsevier.

Alamargot, D., & Fayol, M. (2009). Modelling the development of written composition. In R. Beard, D. Myhill, M. Nystrand, & J. Riley (Eds.), *Handbook of writing development* (pp. 23–47). London: Sage.

Alamargot, D., Plane, S., Lambert, E., & Chesnet, D. (2009). Using eye and pen movements to trace the development of writing expertise: Case studies of a seventh, ninth and twelfth grader, graduate student, and professional writer. *Reading and Writing, 23*(7), 853–888.

Anderson, J. R. (2002). Spanning seven orders of magnitude: A challenge for cognitive modeling. *Cognitive Science, 26*(1), 85–112.

Caporossi, G., Alamargot, D., & Chesnet, D. (2004). Using the computer to study the dynamics of handwriting processes. *Lecture Notes in Computer Science, 3245,* 73–78.

Chanquoy, L., Foulin, J. N., & Fayol, M. (1990). Temporal management of short text writing by children and adults. *Cahiers de Psychologie Cognitive, 10*(5), 513–540.

Chesnet, D., & Alamargot, D. (2005). Analyse en temps réel des activités oculaires et graphomotrices du scripteur. Intérêt du dispositif 'Eye and Pen'. *L'Année Psychologique, 105*(3), 477–520.

Fayol, M., Largy, P., & Lemaire, P. (1994). When cognitive overload enhances subject-verb agreement errors. *Quarterly Journal of Experimental Psychology, 47A,* 437–464.

Graham, S. (1990). The role of production factors in learning-disabled students' compositions. *Journal of Educational Psychology, 52*(4), 781–791.

Hayes, J. R., & Flower, L. S. (1980). Identifying the organization of writing processes. In L. W. Gregg & E. R. Steinberg (Eds.), *Cognitive processes in writing* (pp. 3–30). Hillsdale, NJ: Erlbaum.

Lambert, E., Alamargot, D., Laroque, D., & Caporossi, G. (in press). Dynamics of spelling process during a copy task. Effect of frequency and regularity. *Canadian Journal of Experimental Psychology.*

MacArthur, C. A., Graham, S., & Fitzgerald, J. (Eds.). (2006). *Handbook of writing research.* New York: Guilford.

McCutchen, D., Covill, A., Hoyne, H. S., & Mildes, K. (1994). Individual differences in writing: Implications of translating fluency. *Journal of Educational Psychology, 86*(2), 256–266.

Salvucci, D. D., & Anderson, R. J. (2001). Automated eye-movement protocol analysis. *Human Computer Interaction, 16*(1), 39–86.

Swanson, H. L., & Berninger, V. W. (1996). Individual differences in children's working memory and writing skill. *Journal of Experimental Child Psychology, 63,* 358–385.

Looking Into the Text Generation Box to Find the Psycholinguistic (Cognitive–Language) Writing Processes

BARBARA ARFÉ

*T*he writing models that have illuminated writing research and the teaching of writing in the past 30 years were inspired by the pioneering intuition that writing is a cognitive process (Hayes & Flower, 1980; Kellogg, 1996). Undeniably, writing—the production of written language—is cognitive in many respects, with a variety of processes contributing: existing or created representations of knowledge, mental imagery, visual cognition, memory, attention, planning, and a monitoring system to orchestrate all these processes. Nevertheless, a full understanding of writing, including its difficulties and disorders, must consider in detail the language processes and language mechanisms underlying the generation, formulation, and production of written text to communicate thoughts. More explicit integration of language into the cognitive writing models will (a) contribute to explaining how writing skill develops, because a large part of writing development involves the growing ability of translating ideas into linguistic representations (Chenoweth & Hayes, 2001; Dockrell, Lindsay, & Connelly, 2009; Fayol, Alamargot, & Berninger, 2011); and (b) account for a broad class of errors in writing due to problems in choosing words; encoding and selecting syntactic and grammatical structures; and programming words, phrases, and sentences, which result in dysfluencies and disruptions (Arfé, Dockrell, & Berninger, in press). Other chapters in this volume make the case that writing models need to incorporate language variables (see Chapters 9, 10, and 11, this volume; see also Alves' Vision, "The Future Is Bright for Writing Research," this volume, which discusses the need, pointed out by Alamargot & Fayol, 2009, to integrate more meaningfully cognitive and psycholinguistic traditions in writing).

Despite this emerging and converging recognition of the need for models that more meaningfully integrate cognitive and language processes, mainstream writing research still lacks a formal psycholinguistic model of text generation. Models of expert writing conceptualize translation as the process through which prelinguistic ideas are converted into strings of language but do not specify the language processes with precision (Chenoweth & Hayes, 2001; Hayes & Flower, 1980). All too often the text generation processes of translation are portrayed as a box or insular module without capturing the dynamic interacting cognitive and linguistic processes involved.

One approach toward characterizing the language processes involved in text generation was the 20-year programmatic research of Berninger and colleagues, which was grounded in a *levels of language theoretical framework* for written language generation—ranging from *subword* letter writing to *word* spelling to *syntactic* construction to *text production*, each of which maps onto different kinds of cognitive representations (for review of cross-sectional and longitudinal assessment, instructional, family genetics, and brain imaging studies, focused on typically developing and disabled writers, see Berninger, 2009 and Berninger & Richards, 2010). Cognitive neuroscience research also points to a writing brain with interacting cognitive and language systems that work together (see Chapter 23, this volume).

VISION FOR A MODEL FOR TEXT GENERATION RESEARCH

Future research should focus on the additional issue of how the cognitive and linguistic systems interact with each other during translation and text generation, especially at the higher levels; these interactions play an important role in written communication of thoughts. A model of language production guiding future writing research ought to address three issues: (1) how specific oral or written language processes (e.g., lexical selection, grammatical encoding, encoding of syntactic relations) are organized within the architecture of the written text generation system, which also includes cognitive processes; (2) how processes of written language production are transformed and constrained by the mechanisms of transcription or the specific communication demands of writing; and (3) how language processes (e.g., grammatical encoding) develop in writing and constrain, along with their cognitive interactions, writing and the writing product at different ages.

To date, models of writing focused on spelling explain language mechanisms that drive the process of writing single words. These models can satisfy conditions in (1) and at least partially in (2) (Laiacona et al., 2009; Patterson, 1986). Of course no one study can address all three areas in the model above or all the interesting and important aspects of oral or written language that may contribute to all aspects of writing. However, an important step forward beyond the focus on word level only is the study of how words are combined in the writer's mind and arranged in chunks of text while writing (Arfé, De Bernardi, & Pasini, 2010). More research is needed on how cognition and language interact as developing and skilled writers translate thoughts in language units. Such research is necessary if the field of writing is to acquire comprehensive answers to questions (1), (2), and (3) as articulated earlier in this section.

ADVANCING KNOWLEDGE OF NORMAL WRITING DEVELOPMENT

Some research on text generation focuses on description of what is observed in the writing product for individual writers or writers in general at a particular age or grade. Some focuses on relationships between coded cognitive and linguistic variables in written language productions. This descriptive or univariate/multivariate correlational research, which concentrates on individual differences in skills related to writing processes rather than on processes unfolding in real time (on-line), is sometimes interpreted as if text generation is a simple module composed of static components, which I refer to as the *text generation box*. Experimental research that studies on-line processing (see Chapters 2, 16, 17, and 19, this volume) and draws inferences about multiple underlying processes in real time or instructional research holds promise for learning more about how the higher-level cognitive and language processes interact in writing. Results of developmental studies of interactions among levels of language (e.g., syntax and genre; see Beers & Nagy, 2011) and metalinguistic strategies in writing (see Chapter 11, this volume) might inform the research questions addressed by experimental and instructional research methodologies, which inform understanding of the complexity and plasticity in the processes of learning to generate written text.

Toward this goal, writing researchers must look inside the text generation box to define a comprehensive representation of how language processes for generating words in sentences and producing sentences in relation to previous text are incorporated and organized in the process of writing. This analysis will represent a necessary integration of the developmental models of writing (Abbott, Berninger, & Fayol, 2010; Juel, 1988) and of our knowledge of writing disorders (see Chapter 10, this volume), which are discussed next. Developmental writing models concern periods in the development of writing skills in which the ability to generate text linguistically is central and writing is developing at the sentence and text as well as word levels (Abbott et al., 2010; Arfé et al., 2010). On the other hand, clinicians and educators need a model capable of deepening the understanding of the language mechanisms at the basis of written language production and its disturbances.

UNDERSTANDING WRITING PROBLEMS IN CHILDREN WITH ORAL LANGUAGE PROBLEMS

Written-language disorders represent a clinical and educational emergency, with incidence rates varying from 6.9% to 14.7% (Katusic, Colligan, Weaver, & Barbaresi, 2009). These problems seem strongly related to oral language difficulties (Berninger, Nielsen, Abbott, Wijsman, & Raskind, 2008; Dockrell, Lindsay, Connelly, & Mackie, 2007; Dockrell et al., 2009) and can be resistant to instructional intervention unless tailored to individual needs.

There is a largely unexplored field at the boundaries between written and oral language production. Many questions arise from a consideration of the oral language (and related speech) processes in writing. Speech is a rapid process; adults produce an average of 270 words per minute during conversational speech (Calvert & Silverman, 1983), and children from 6 to 11 years produce an average of 120 to 140 words per minute (Purcell & Runyan, 1980). Production rates appear to be slower for translating thought into written rather than oral language. Important unanswered questions include the following: How do language processes change in writing when language production is slowed by transcription times? How does the necessity to coordinate graphomotor sequences and language bursts affect the process of language production in writing (see Chapters 1 and 16 and the Vision "The Future Is Bright for Writing Research," this volume)? Are alternative lexical and grammatical formulations of an idea encoded in parallel or sequentially in the writer's memory buffer, and if so, how does this affect text generation (Coppock, 2009)? How and when do syntactic, grammatical, and lexical errors emerge in writing, and do the same error patterns characterize writing as speech (Coppock, 2009)? Psycholinguistics has a long tradition of studies investigating the mechanisms of lexical selection and syntagmatic and paradigmatic interference in language production (Dell, Oppenheim, & Kittredge, 2008). These studies represent an unexplored potential field of investigation for writing research.

Two important innovations can contribute to the future research on writing: On the one hand, the technical advancements allow researchers to capture on-line processes of the writing task (e.g., digital tablets, eye tracking, keystroke logging; see Chapters 19 and 22, this volume). On the other hand, a conceptual advancement that integrated thought and language could reduce the distance between researchers in two fields that have been traditionally separated by theoretical and methodological barriers—language and writing research. Language research has been oriented to oral rather than written language. The second innovation is more critical, because research questions normally originate from the exploration and broadening of the conceptual field. To date, the two fields of language and writing research remain inexplicably separated. An overview of the papers presented at the 16th annual conference on Architectures and Mechanisms for Language Processing (York, September 6–8, 2010) revealed only one contribution on writing.

In a very thought-provoking paper on language production, Bock and Huitema (1999) commented that a psycholinguistic theory of language must be concerned with "real speakers who are vulnerable to memory limitations, distractions, shifts of attention and interest, and errors (random or characteristic) in applying their knowledge of language" (p. 365). This recommended point of view can also characterize a model of written text generation, capable of explaining how real writers, in real time, produce language units while transcribing texts and generating meaning, and which typical errors distinguish such a system, developmentally and clinically. It is difficult to predict where writing research will move in the next years, but writing researchers can wish and hope that because the barriers between the fields of writing and language research are not impenetrable (indeed, language can be processed and produced both orally and in writing) researchers and approaches from these two fields can communicate with each other and enrich each other.

REFERENCES

Abbott, R., Berninger, V., & Fayol, M. (2010). Longitudinal relationships of levels of language in writing and between writing and reading in grades 1 to 7. *Journal of Educational Psychology, 102,* 281–298.

Alamargot, D., & Fayol, M. (2009). Modeling the development of written composition. In R. Beard, D. Myhill, J. Riley, & M. Nystrand (Eds.), *The Sage handbook of writing development* (pp. 23–47). London: Sage.

Arfé, B., De Bernardi, B., & Pasini, M. (2010, September 8–10). *Assessing text generation in expressive writing difficulties.* Paper presented at the 12th SIG Writing conference, Heidelberg.

Arfé, B., Dockrell, J., & Berninger, V. (Eds.). (in press). *Writing development and instruction in children with hearing, speech, and language disorders.* New York: Oxford University Press.

Beers, S., & Nagy, W. (2011). Writing development in four genres from grades three to seven: Syntactic complexity and genre differentiation. *Reading and Writing: An Interdisciplinary Journal, 24,* 183–202.

Berninger, V. (2009). Highlights of programmatic, interdisciplinary research on writing. *Learning Disabilities. Research and Practice, 24,* 68–79.

Berninger, V., & Abbott, D. (2010). Listening comprehension, oral expression, reading comprehension and written expression: Related yet unique language systems in grades 1, 3, 5, and 7. *Journal of Educational Psychology, 102,* 635–651.

Berninger, V., Nielsen, K., Abbott, R., Wijsman, E., & Raskind, W. (2008). Writing problems in developmental dyslexia: Under-recognized and under-treated. *Journal of School Psychology, 46,* 1–21.

Berninger, V., Raskind, W., Richards, T., Abbott, R., & Stock, P. (2008). A multidisciplinary approach to understanding developmental dyslexia within working-memory architecture: Genotypes, phenotypes, brain, and instruction. *Developmental Neuropsychology, 33,* 707–744.

Berninger, V., & Richards, T. (2010). Inter-relationships among behavioral markers, genes, brain, and treatment in dyslexia and dysgraphia. *Future Neurology, 5,* 597–617.

Bock, J. K., & Huitema, J. (1999). Language production. In S. Garrod & M. Pickering (Eds.), *Language processing* (pp. 365–388). Hove: Psychology Press.

Calvert, D. R., & Silverman, S. R. (1983). *Speech and deafness.* Washington, DC: Alexander Graham Bell Association for the Deaf.

Chenoweth, N. A., & Hayes, J. R. (2001). Fluency in writing. Generating text in L1 and L2. *Written Communication, 18*(1), 80–98.

Coppock, E. (2009). Parallel grammatical encoding in sentence production: Evidence from syntactic blends. *Language and Cognitive Processes, 25*(1), 38–49.

Dell, G. S., Oppenheim, G. M., & Kittredge, A. K. (2008). Saying the right word at the right time: Syntagmatic and paradigmatic interference in sentence production. *Language and Cognitive Processes, 23,* 583–608.

Dockrell, J. E., Lindsay, G., & Connelly, V. (2009). The impact of specific language impairment on adolescents' written text. *Exceptional Children, 75,* 427–426.

Dockrell, J. E., Lindsay, G., Connelly, V., & Mackie, C. (2007). Constraint in the production of written text in children with specific language impairments. *Exceptional Children, 73,* 147–164.

Fayol, M., Alamargot, D., & Berninger, V. (Eds.). (2011). *Translation of thought to written text while composing: Advancing theory, knowledge, methods, and applications.* New York: Psychology Press.

Hayes, J. R., & Flower, L. S. (1980). Identifying the organization of writing processes. In L. W. Gregg & E. R. Steinberg (Eds.), *Cognitive processes in writing* (pp. 3–30). Hillsdale, NJ: Erlbaum.

Juel, C. (1988). Learning to read and write: A longitudinal study of 54 children from first through fourth grades. *Journal of Educational Psychology, 80,* 437–447.

Katusic, S. K., Colligan, R. C., Weaver, A. L., & Barbaresi, W. J. (2009). The forgotten learning disability: Epidemiology of written-language disorder in a population based birth cohort (1976–1982), Rochester, Minnesota. *Pediatrics, 123,* 1306–1313.

Kellogg, R. T. (1996). A model of working memory in writing. In C. M. Levy & S. Ransdell (Eds.), *The science of writing: Theories, methods, individual differences and applications* (pp. 57–71). Mahwah, NJ: Erlbaum.

Laiacona, M., Capitani, E., Zonca, G., Scola, I., Saletta, P., & Luzzatti, C. (2009). Integration of lexical and sublexical processing in the spelling of regular words: A multiple single-case study in Italian dysgraphic patients. *Cortex, 45,* 804–815.

Patterson, K. E. (1986). Lexical but not semantic spelling? *Cognitive Neuropsychology, 3,* 341–367.

Purcell, R., & Runyan, C. M. (1980). Normative study of speech rates of children. *Journal of the Speech and Hearing Association of Virginia, 21,* 6–14.

Writing Research
Where to Go To?

GERT RIJLAARSDAM and HUUB VAN DEN BERGH

*I*n Michael Levy and Sarah Ransdell's book *Science of Writing* (1996) we outlined a research agenda for writing research (Rijlaarsdam & Van den Bergh, 1996; Van den Bergh & Rijlaarsdam, 1996). Then we focused on writing process research, setting up an agenda that is more or less summarized in Figure V3.1.

We agree that the scheme is simple and general. In fact, one may say nothing in the scheme refers to writing. We agree this is also true. Nevertheless, it contains the most relevant sets of variables if one wants to know more about what processes lead to certain results ("products"): this might be reading (i.e., literary texts), history (i.e., historical thinking), or learning (i.e., learning from multiple sources). We must get insight into the components or constituent elements of the processes, including the way they are organized, the way this organization is monitored, the stability or variability of this process for provided task variables (topic, genre, sources, etc.), and the configuration between task variables, processes, and products when learner or writer variables are taken into account. This model can be used to guide research and help us to understand the differences between more and less effective processes.

For writing, we now know much about the processes and how variations in processes relate to the quality of the outcome (Rijlaarsdam & Van den Bergh, 2006; Van den Bergh et al., 2009). We know now that we must collect at least four task executions or processes to get a more or less stable view from an individual writer (Van Weijen, 2009). We know that nowadays relevant task parameters are language (writing in one's first language [L1] or in global English) and its effect on how writers adapt the writing process to the task parameters (Van Weijen, 2009). We know more about *relevant writer variables* that affect the course of the writing process and the relation between processes and resulting text quality: (1) *self-monitoring* (Galbraith, 2009; Galbraith & Rijlaarsdam, 1999); (2) *revising and planning skill* (Van der Hoeven, 1997); (3) *writing style* as measured with an offline inventory (Tillema, Van den Bergh, & Rijlaarsdam, 2011); and (4) L1-writing skill and second language (L2) vocabulary when writing in L2 (Van Weijen, 2009; Van Weijen, Van den Bergh, Rijlaarsdam, & Sanders, 2009). Yet, writer variables and task variables are too seldom included in writing process research as relevant factors.

At the same time, there is certainly a need to get more knowledge about writer-learner variables that interact with the relations between task variables and processes; we need to know more about why some writers provide more stable patterns in their processes across tasks than do other writers. Why is it that some writers

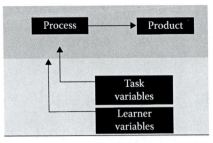

Figure V3.1   Research agenda 1: What do effective writing processes entail?

adapt quite easily to new tasks while other writers show a sharp decrease in performance? Our first point in agenda setting as the field moves beyond writing process research is that the research agenda should include (a) studying multiple task executions per individual writer, (b) studying learning to write, and (c) studying multiple task executions with learner variables.

Studying multiple task executions reflects an old but nowadays neglected psychometric issue in writing research: measuring writing skill. This issue has been taken up relatively recently by Schoonen (2005) but was also an issue studied in the 1960s and 1970s (Coffman, 1966). From these studies, we know that for a reliable estimate of an individual's writing skill we need, depending on the kind of tasks, at least 4 (in case of essaylike texts) to 14 (short functional writing tasks) tasks (Van den Bergh, 1988). And now that we have found that the same holds for writing processes, we are thrown back to the past, being punished by having neglected valid research from an earlier time. If we consider that 50% of the variance in text scores is due to the typical task, and that therefore about 50% of the scores do not reflect the writers' skill, how valid then were conclusions in writing process research with single tasks per individual? But there is more that was neglected in writing research. It seems that as a research community we dived in eagerly to observe and analyze processes, and although we now know quite a lot about swimming, we still do not know how not to sink or drown or at least keep our heads out of the water. Writing research was going deep into processes, but we took for granted that the ultimate variable, the quality of the resulting text, is something understudied.

Our second point in agenda setting is that it is essential that more attention in writing process research should be focused on the concept of writing skill, that is, text quality (Rijlaarsdam et al., in press). This issue is multifaceted because we need to define the concept of writing skill for a contemporary world, which is global and digitalized: "Print culture sans print" (Baron, 2006, p. 28). The world of texts has changed dramatically since this issue was studied in the 1960s (Bezemer & Kress, 2008). The world of written information is so very different nowadays for children than 20 years ago when most authors of this volume started their research careers. And yet we still design research studies in which we ask subjects to write ordinary texts, by handwriting or on the computer (very modern!). It is really about time to reconsider the concept of writing—if we can use the word *writing* in future times—and to validate concurrent concepts with psychometric stringent studies, which asks for componential analyses. This issue must also deal with writing in various languages (L1, L2) because multilingualism is nowadays the default situation of language users in our world. Measuring L1 writing and L2 writing on a congeneric scale will be quite a challenge.

Our third issue in agenda setting is that the writing research community will expand theory building and educational practice with what we call full intervention studies: Testing educational interventions under experimental conditions, in school settings, that use process and product measures and take into account learner variables. The concept of text is also the main object when we focus on intervention research, again presented in simplified fashion in Figure V3.2. Practitioners need validated short courses on interventions that were shown to work. Researchers need data to study (a) the effect of interventions on processes and product, (b) the relations between processes and products, and (c) the effect of learner variables on these outcome variables. Torrance, Fidalgo, and Garcia (2007) and Braaksma, Rijlaarsdam, Van den Bergh, and Van Hout-Wolters (2004) are studies in which process measures were included; the research by Braaksma et al. also studied the relations between text quality and process outcomes as a result of the intervention.

We know that learner variables interact with the interventions, for instance (a) general academic aptitude (Braaksma, Rijlaarsdam, & Van den Bergh, 2002), and (b) writing style (Kieft, Rijlaarsdam, Galbraith, & Van den Bergh, 2007; Kieft, Rijlaarsdam, & Van den Bergh, 2008). Differentiation instruction and feedback are major issues in classrooms that become more and more heterogeneous in social and linguistic background. Interventions studies must accommodate for these situations.

Now we make the case for our final point of agenda setting: involvement of teachers in research and improving teacher education. Pietro Boscolo explained in Chapter 3 of this volume how he moved from teaching into research and now back into teaching, and that his teaching nowadays is informed by his research background. In our institutional setting, we learned that student teachers who became involved in our research, as they had to do for their graduation, an instructional design research study (for design research, see Chapter 3, this volume), changed and enriched their thinking about writing education. They too had to measure processes (mostly by observing task executions) and they reported impressive learning experiences from these observations. They also

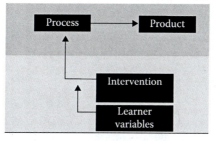

Figure V3.2   Research agenda 2: What do effective writing instruction processes entail?

learned from our institutional setting, in the research group, what the effect was on teachers who participated in the design of interventions we wanted to test empirically. Design experiments can be quite a strong vehicle to teach teachers (and researchers!) to consider and take all variables into account when designing specific lessons (interventions). On the one hand, it seems that researchers can study what they want, but the findings of the writing research community as a whole provide a wealth of knowledge that can serve educational practice. On the other hand, there is much teaching in academia that is not informed by research and that does not contribute to research or practice. When we sent an open call for a special issue on L2 learning and writing, we received many papers from L2-university teachers who wanted to share their insights from experiences (Van Weijen, Van Steendam, & Rijlaarsdam, 2008). In some cases, we published these papers as vignettes; but we could have published more if the research to warrant the experiences had been done more stringently.

Now that the costs of university teaching are increasing, we should not expect that university boards will lower the teaching load and increase the research time. The tendency to separate research and teaching will probably continue, but creative ways to integrate them for some purposes may be discovered. At the same time, teaching, in all stages of education, will become more complex as recognition increases that the school population has become more heterogeneous. The way we envision creating strong relations between research and teaching is through extended teacher training, which includes doing empirical research, in initial as well as in-service education. Design research is then a good option to explore in future writing research and teaching.

REFERENCES

Baron, N. (2006). The future of written culture: Envisioning language in the new millennium. *Iberuca, 9,* 7–31

Bezemer, J., & Kress, G. (2008). Writing in multimodal texts: A social semiotic account of designs for learning. *Written Communication, 25,* 166–195.

Braaksma, M. A. H., Rijlaarsdam, G., & Van den Bergh, H. (2002). Observational learning and the effects of model-observer similarity. *Journal of Educational Psychology, 94,* 405–415.

Braaksma, M., Rijlaarsdam, G., Van den Bergh, H., & Van Hout-Wolters, B. H. A. M. (2004). Observational learning and its effects on the orchestration of the writing process. *Cognition and Instruction, 22,* 1–36.

Coffman, W. E. (1966). On the validity of essay tests of achievement. *Journal of Educational Measurement, 3,* 151–156.

Galbraith, D. (2009). Writing as discovery. Teaching and learning writing: Psychological aspects of education: Current Trends. *British Journal of Educational Psychology, Monograph Series II, 6,* 5–26.

Galbraith, D., & Rijlaarsdam, G. (1999). Effective strategies for the teaching and learning of writing. *Learning and Instruction, 2,* 93–108.

Kieft, M., Rijlaarsdam, G., Galbraith, D., & Van den Bergh, H. (2007). The effects of adapting a writing course to students' writing strategies. *British Journal of Educational Psychology, 77,* 565–578.

Kieft, M., Rijlaarsdam, G., & Van den Bergh, H. (2008). An aptitude–treatment interaction approach to writing-to-learn. *Learning and Instruction, 18*, 379–390.

Levy, C. M. & Ransdell, S. (Eds.). (1996). *The science of writing.* New York: Lawrence Erlbaum Associates.

Rijlaarsdam, G., & Van den Bergh, H. (1996). An agenda for research into an interactive compensatory model of writing. Many questions, some answers. In C. M. Levy & S. Ransdell (Eds.), *The science of writing* (pp. 107–126). New York: Erlbaum.

Rijlaarsdam, G., & Van den Bergh, H. (2006). Writing process theory: A functional dynamic approach. In C. A. MacArthur, S. Graham, & J. Fitzgerald (Eds.), *Handbook of writing research* (pp. 1–53). New York: Guilford.

Rijlaarsdam, G., Van den Bergh, H., Couzijn, M., Janssen, T., Braaksma, M., Tillema, M., ... & Raedts, M. (in press). Writing. In S. Graham, A. Bus, S. Major, & L. Swanson (Eds.), *Application of educational psychology to learning and teaching* (Vol. 3). Washington, DC: APA.

Schoonen, R. (2005). Generalizability of writing scores: An application of structural equation modelling. *Language Testing, 22*, 1–30.

Tillema, M., Van den Bergh, H., & Rijlaarsdam, G. (2011). Metacognitive skill during writing. Relating self reports of writing behaviour and online task execution using a temporal model. *Metacognition and Learning.* Advance online publication. doi: 10.1007/s11409-011-9072-x

Torrance, M., Fidalgo, R., & García, J. N. (2007). The teachability and effectiveness of cognitive self-regulation in sixth-grade writers. *Learning and Instruction, 17*, 265–285.

Van den Bergh, H. (1988). Schrijven en schrijven is twee: Een onderzoek naar de samenhang tussen prestaties op verschillende schrijftaken [Writing and writing makes two: An investigation into the relation between performances on different writing tasks]. *Tijdschrift voor Onderwijsresearch, 13*(6), 311–324.

Van den Bergh, H., & Rijlaarsdam, G. (1996). The dynamics of composing. Modeling writing process data. In C. M. Levy & S. Ransdell (Eds.), *The science of writing* (pp. 207–232). New York: Erlbaum.

Van den Bergh, H., Rijlaarsdam, G., Janssen, T., Braaksma, M., van Weijen., D., & Tillema, M. (2009). Process execution of writing and reading: Considering text quality, learn and task characteristics. In M. C. Shelley II, L. D. Yore, & B. Hand (Eds.), *Quality research in literary and science education* (pp. 399–425). Boston: Springer.

Van der Hoeven, J. (1997). *Children's composing. A study into the relationships between writing processes, text quality, and cognitive and linguistic skills.* Vol. 12. Utrecht Studies in Language and Communication. Amsterdam: Rodopi.

Van Weijen, D. (2009). *Writing processes, text quality, and task effects: Empirical studies in first and second language writing.* Utrecht, the Netherlands: LOT Dissertation Series.

Van Weijen D., Van den Bergh, H., Rijlaarsdam G., & Sanders, T. (2009). L1 use during L2 writing: An empirical study of a complex phenomenon. *Journal of Second Language Writing, 18*(4), 235–250.

Van Weijen, D., Van Steendam, E., & Rijlaarsdam, G. (2008). Special issue on learning and teaching L2 writing [editorial]. *International Journal of Applied Linguistics, 156*, 1–12.

Evolving Integration and Differentiation in Cognitive and Sociocultural-Historical Writing Research

PAUL M. ROGERS

*T*he contemporary field of writing research includes substantial contributions from the disciplines and subdisciplines of education, psychology, linguistics, anthropology, cultural studies, computer science, communication, and composition. This research activity has illuminated the deeply interconnected grouping of cognitive processes and multilayered social, cultural, historical, and linguistic activities that make writing a complex and worthwhile human endeavor and object of study. The specialization of researchers and the differentiation of research within each of these fields have raised the awareness of the value of writing in the many arenas where writing is practiced and taught, and have helped set writing on an equal footing with reading in the literacy curriculum of schools today. Results of these studies have acted as qualifiers for each other and as warnings against the tendency toward reductionist approaches to writing. However, this wide range of approaches to writing research has created an enormous amount of data that can be difficult to synthesize. They have also called to attention the nontrivial and potentially problematic differences in the ways different disciplines think about writing theory, research, and practice.

Cognitive research, which is the primary focus of this volume, is itself an interdisciplinary field of its own (Gardner, 1985), which has, since its early investigations of writing, made many critical contributions to our understanding of writing along a number of lines, including describing the central elements of the writing process, interactions among writing processes, and the recursive interplay between writing and thinking. In addition, the fundamental structure of cognitive research, with its emphasis on empiricism and methodological sophistication, along with researchers' willingness to experiment and revise models as new findings emerge (e.g., Hayes, 1996), has set a high standard for all writing researchers.

The cognitive writing research tradition has focused a great deal on the stable features of task representation and memory processes, and individual components of the writing process, especially planning, text production, and revision. For cognitive researchers, writing development is linked to cognitive apparatus, and individual traits, which may to a large degree be stable structures, such as long-term and working memory, information processing, problem solving, concept development, motivation, perceptual development, theory of mind, and domain-specific knowledge (Flavell, 1996). Yet, in spite of this relatively tight focus, researchers in the cognitive tradition have recognized the value of other research methods to the overall project of writing research.

Pioneering cognitive writing researchers, Bereiter and Scardamalia (1987, p. 34), for example, provided a description of six levels of inquiry into the composing process:

1. Reflective inquiry
2. Empirical variable testing
3. Text analysis
4. Process description
5. Theory embedded experimentation
6. Simulation

These levels of inquiry span a wide range of research questions and methods ranging from introspection to simulation by intervention. This holistic approach has characterized the tremendous growth and expansion of approaches to writing research in recent years, both sociocultural and cognitive.

From the sociocultural perspective, individual cognitive psychological processes emerge through culturally mediated, historically developing practical activity (Cole, 1997, p. 108), rather than a natural progression through fixed stages or steps. Writing, from this perspective, is seen as a higher-order psychological process and is always situation and time bound, that is, writing activities are contingent and stand in direct relation to tools that are embedded in particular historical, social, and cultural circumstances. Research from this sociocultural point of view has been highly attuned to the contexts in which individuals and aspects of writing systems—content, forms, and uses—are situated. The social view conceives of learning to write as a process of enculturation into particular communities of practice (Lave & Wenger, 1991), where knowledge is distributed and mediated by cultural tools, including language, technologies, and other affordances, a significant difference from the cognitive views that have viewed writing as somewhat an autonomous skill rooted in fixed mental structures and language conventions (see Chapters 4–6, this volume).

The sociocultural view emphasizes writing development over time and across grade levels, arguing that growth in writing must be viewed in direct relation to writers' interactions with the symbolic world that surrounds them, and in particular their interactions with teachers and curriculum. Print literacy development does not occur in isolation from social influences, but in brains or minds functioning within sociocultural contexts, and hence is social, cultural, historical, and cognitive.

Efforts continue to connect the social and cognitive theoretical and research traditions, which at times have blended well into hybrid sociocognitive models of writing (Flower, 1994; Purcell-Gates, Jacobsen, & Degener, 2004). In the hybrid views, the development of individual writing abilities can be characterized as a dialectical process of negotiation between social and cultural inputs and individual dispositions and abilities, with the emphasis on the dynamic change at all levels

(Berninger, Fuller, & Whitaker, 1996). Furthermore, development lies neither in the individual alone nor in the social group, but rather in the dialectical interaction of both.

Fortunately, for those interested in ensuring that the power of writing is made available to all, the leaders of major writing research networks, regardless of their individual research specialties, including the editors of recent handbooks of writing research (Bazerman, 2008; MacArthur, Graham, & Fitzgerald, 2006) and a variety of journals that publish writing research, have recognized the value of diverse approaches to writing and have, in many cases, integrated and acknowledged the diversity of approaches in ways that have made the knowledge from these varied approaches available to graduate students, teachers at all grade levels, and researchers, providing an expansive vision of the universe of writing. Without contradiction we have learned to appreciate the historical emergence of writing in Samaria, China, and Mesoamerica, the nuances and importance of visual and verbal working memory in the composing process, the layers of intertext and oral conversation found in revisions of graduate students, the roles advanced forms of writing play in individuals' enculturation to professional communities of practice, the ways genres of writing have morphed across time in the service of different audiences and purposes, and much more.

This kind of integration represents the true development of the field. For just as the human embryo develops through the differentiation of new organs and limbs and the simultaneous integration of these structures into a functional whole, writing research has advanced steadily over the past 50 years to the point where teachers can now turn to a substantive base of evidence to inform their curricular judgments in many areas (see Chapter 3, this volume, for this perspective plus the perspective that researchers can also learn from teacher knowledge based on teaching writing). Arguably, true development always proceeds along such a course. For it is only when an entire activity system reorganizes that a developmental step has occurred.

A case in point is Janet Emig (1971), who, when she published her landmark study on the composing process of 12th graders, moved the field forward: A new nub had emerged in the field with the shift of attention in writing from product to process. Researchers were quick to recognize the potential value of this approach and borrowed emergent methods in psychology, leading to new frameworks for thinking about the composing process. Soon, the notion of the writing process began to cross the networks of professional teachers at all grade levels. The process model of writing is now represented in most elementary, secondary, and higher education textbooks on writing.

Recent advances in cognitive writing research hold out similar promise for advancement of educational theory and practice. For example, Rijlaarsdam and Van den Bergh's (2006) research aimed at understanding the nature and timing of writing processes suggests that "at different points in writing different cognitive activities dominate" (p. 43). This work, in addition to informing theory-building activities and future research, can help those responsible for instruction think more carefully about the kinds and amounts of support that are provided at different stages of the writing process. Many more examples can be found, including the eye-tracking and keyboard logging studies of the writing process (see Chapters 19 and 22, this volume, as well as functional magnetic resonance imaging and other studies of the writing brain; e.g., Berninger & Richards, 2002; Chapter 23, this volume).

Among the many vibrant areas of sociocultural research today, two areas of work stand out as having particularly high potential for improving educational practice. First are longitudinal studies of the kind Emig called for in 1971:

> Longitudinal case studies of a given sample of students, following them from the time they begin to write in the earliest elementary grades throughout their school careers, up to and including graduate school ... would make better known the developmental dimensions of the writing process, both for the individual and for members of various chronological and ability age groups. (p. 95)

Though they are expensive, time consuming, subject to high degrees of attrition, and produce slow results, these kinds of studies are essential if we are to develop a robust lifespan approach to writing development (Rogers, 2010).

Additionally, studies that investigate the interaction and impact of various instructional approaches, in particular studies of response and feedback on real writing tasks that account for all viewpoints (multiple and individual writers, students, teachers, and peers), text types, and interactions (audio, video, and face-to-face conferencing, peer review, interlinear, marginal, and end comments, etc.), are needed to advance this important and ubiquitous element of writing instruction.

If the past is indeed a prologue, for the field of writing research to maintain its momentum and progress further in bringing support to learners and teachers, we must continue to encourage ever-finer differentiation of writing research, that is, investigations that recognize the increased specializations of researchers within the various disciplines and subdisciplines that study writing. We must be willing to encourage and support many pilot studies and experiments across levels of inquiry into composing processes. Simultaneously we must continue to follow the lead of the pioneers of our field who have established a scholarly and humane discourse across research traditions and methodologies, attending to the findings of researchers in traditions that differ radically from our own, and we must work to translate our research findings to teachers who need an evolving and solid evidence base.

In addition to delving deeper in our own areas of research, we should welcome new approaches to writing research, particularly those with potential to improve writing instruction (brain research and research on writing and technology stand out as two key areas). We must also engage in multiple, joint projects across disciplinary boundaries with the deliberate aim of influencing educational policy. Recent reports by Graham and Perin (2007), Graham and Hebert (2010), the National Commission on Writing (2003), and the College Board (2004, 2005) have provided those fighting for increased investments in writing education and research with some of our most powerful arguments. We must continue to marshal and leverage our collective research capacity, as the European Research Network on Learning to Write Effectively (ERN-LWE) has done in Europe, in order to tackle the most pressing challenges associated with writing, especially providing access to high-quality writing instruction for underserved populations.

Although the bulk of the capacity-building activity in support of research takes place in the many graduate programs that produce writing researchers, the field of writing research must create more forums for ongoing professional development for early career researchers looking to expand their work and influence (such as the Research Network Forum at the Conference of College Composition and Communication organized by Charles Bazerman). We also need more meetings and workshops focused on methodology, like the Summer Seminar for Composition Research (organized by Christiane Donahue and held from July 31 through August 12, 2011). Additionally, we must create online and face-to-face forums that can facilitate opportunities for mentoring by senior researchers. Journal editors too can nurture early-stage researchers by taking time to work with projects and manuscripts that show promise but need additional support to reach their potential.

ACKNOWLEDGMENTS

My heartfelt thanks to the inimitable Charles Bazerman for his many contributions to my life and work.

REFERENCES

Bazerman, C. (Ed.). (2008). *Handbook of research on writing: History, society, school, individual, and text.* Mahwah, NJ: Erlbaum.

Bereiter, C., & Scardamalia, M. (1987). *The psychology of written composition.* Hillsdale, NJ: LEA.

Berninger, V. W., Fuller, F., & Whitaker, D. (1996). A process model of writing development across the life span. *Educational Psychology Review, 8,* 193–218.

Berninger, V. W., & Richards, T. (2002). *Brain literacy for educators and psychologists.* New York: Academic Press.

Cole, M. (1997). *Cultural psychology: A once and future discipline.* Cambridge: Harvard University Press.

College Board. (2004). *Writing: A ticket to work … or a ticket out. A survey of business leaders.* Retrieved from http://www.collegeboard.org/prod_downloads/writingcom/writing-ticket-to-work.pdf

College Board. (2005). *Writing: A powerful message from state government.* Retrieved from http://www.collegeboard.org/prod_downloads/writingcom/powerful-message-from-state.pdf

Emig, J. (1971). *The composing process of twelfth graders.* Urbana, IL: NCTE.

Flavell, J. H. (1996). Piaget's legacy. *Psychological Science, 7*(4), 200–203.

Flower, L. (1994). *The construction of negotiated meaning: A social cognitive theory of writing.* Carbondale: Southern Illinois University Press.

Gardner, H. (1985). *The mind's new science.* New York: Basic Books.

Graham, S., & Hebert, M. A. (2010). *Writing to read: Evidence for how writing can improve reading.* A Carnegie Corporation Time to Act Report. Washington, DC: Alliance for Excellent Education.

Graham, S., & Perin, D. (2007). *Writing next: Effective strategies to improve writing of adolescents in middle and high schools.* A report to Carnegie Corporation of New York. Washington, DC: Alliance for Excellent Education.

Hayes, J. R. (1996). A new framework for understanding cognition and affect in writing. In C. M. Levy & S. E. R. Steinberg (Eds.), *The science of writing: Theories, methods, individual differences and applications* (pp. 1–27). Mahwah, NJ: Erlbaum.

Lave, J., & Wenger, E. (1991). *Situated learning.* New York: Cambridge University Press.

MacArthur, C. A., Graham, C., & Fitzgerald, J. (2006). *The handbook of writing research.* New York: Guilford.

National Commission on Writing. (2003). *The neglected "R": The need for a writing revolution.* Retrieved from http://www.collegeboard.org/prod_downloads/writingcom/neglectedr.pdf

Purcell-Gates, V., Jacobsen, E., & Degener, S. (2004). *Print literacy development: Uniting cognitive and social practice theories.* Cambridge, MA: Harvard University Press.

Rijlaarsdam, G., & Van den Bergh, H. (2006). Writing process theory: a functional dynamic approach. In C. A. MacArthur, S. Graham, & J. Fitzgerald (Eds.), *The handbook of writing research* (pp. 41–53). New York: Guilford.

Rogers, P. M. (2010). The contributions of North American longitudinal studies of writing in higher education to our understanding of writing development. In C. Bazerman, R. Krut, K. Lunsford, S. McLeod, S. Null, P. M. Rogers, & A. Stansell (Eds.), *Traditions of writing research* (pp. 365–377). Oxford, UK: Routledge.

The Future Is Bright for Writing Research

RUI ALEXANDRE ALVES

B ecause writing is a complex and powerful tool, multiple disciplines, research traditions, and diverse scholars are needed to understand it fully. Landmark volumes in writing (Bazerman, 2008; MacArthur, Graham, & Fitzgerald, 2006) and cognitive science (Gardner, 1985) and several chapters in this volume (see Chapters 9 and 23) have emphasized that even as writing research becomes more established in mainstream psychology, it is important that cognitive psychologists draw on multiple disciplines to advance writing research. However, for this interdisciplinary effort to be maximally valuable, it is necessary that across disciplines a common vocabulary emerges to discuss and synthesize findings and guide future scientific inquiry on writing.

As cognitive psychology, in collaboration with other disciplines, moves forward to expand the field of writing research, where is this community heading? I envision and forecast five themes to which a cognitive writing science might fruitfully devote time and effort.

THE NEGLECTED *R* IS NO LONGER BEING NEGLECTED

For some time *'riting* has been neglected by cognitive psychology (Levy, 1997). However, even if there are relatively fewer writing research publications than for the two other Rs (*readin'* and *'rithemetic*), still a substantial body of writing research exists and is greatly increasing. In 1997, Levy has counted 31,000 publications in reading, 14,000 in mathematics and arithmetic, and only 1,050 in writing. A similar current survey on indexed keywords at PsycInfo database found for reading, arithmetic, and writing, respectively, 36,176, 15,193, and 9,824 publications. These comparisons may underestimate the amount of writing research if they did not comprehensively sample all the traditions in writing research and cover the late 19th century (Rice, 1897) when writing research began before Huey (1908/1968) published his famous volume on reading in the first decade of the 20th century.

Not only are more and more researchers studying writing, but also a strong societal demand for knowledge about writing is emerging, particularly for better writing instruction to be in place. Following a general concern in several Western countries with reading and mathematics instruction (e.g., see the reports of the National Reading Panel, 2000, and of the National Mathematics Advisory Panel, 2008), a similar demand about raising the standards of writing instruction is gaining public recognition (e.g., National Commission on Writing in America's Schools and Colleges, 2003). As policymakers become more and more aware of the pivotal role played by writing in societies, we will see an increase in global writing research funding. A recent European example of this alliance between writing researchers and societal demands was the funding of an interdisciplinary research network on writing by the European Union (COST Action IS0703, 2007). There is also recognition of the need for more writing research globally by the National Institutes of Health in the United States (Miller & McCardle, 2011). To deal with societal concerns with populations' writing skills, researchers are summing up the best current evidence-based practices that promote writing (for a meta-analysis, see Graham & Perin, 2007; see also Graham, MacArthur, & Fitzgerald, 2007). As the education field adopts and promotes these practices, writing researchers are left with the task of further developing new and more effective writing practices, which will emerge as scientific knowledge of writing unfolds.

A DEVELOPMENTAL MODEL OF WRITING EXPERTISE

In the late 20th century the focus of writing research that had the broadest impact was that on the adult skilled writer (Emig, 1971; Hayes & Flower, 1980). This line of writing research, typically based on college students, never lost sight of the learner and had implications for process-oriented writing instruction (Hayes & Flower, 1986). Yet, studies of writing development also emerged, for example, the influential contributions of Bereiter and Scardamalia (1987), who emphasized the differences between learners and expert writers. Detailed accounts of human cognition, writing components, and writing strategies set the stage for thorough explorations of writing development (e.g., Berninger, 1994; Berninger & Swanson, 1994; McCutchen, 1996). Although much of the research on writing development has drawn on multiple disciplines (e.g., developmental psychology; neuropsychology; psycholinguistics; speech, hearing, and language sciences; education; social cognition; and technology; for examples, see chapters in this volume; Abbott, Berninger, & Fayol, 2010; Beard, Myhill, Riley, & Nystrand, 2009; Berninger & Abott, 2010; Connelly, Barnett, Dockrell, & Tolmie, 2009; Kellogg, 2008), the dual challenges remaining are to establish (a) writing research as mainstream cognitive psychology, and (b) a well-integrated, interdisciplinary framework for cognitive writing research at a time when cognitive psychology increasingly draws on multiple disciplines, including neuroscience and technology.

THE NEGLECTED WRITING PROCESS—TRANSLATING

The empirical research on writing that rose in the 1970s in North America and its first formal cognitive accounts were hugely influential not only for the innovative process view of writing but also for the vocabulary that legions of researchers adopted (for a historical account, see Nystrand, 2006). The construction of any science needs precise concepts and concise word tags. Such verbally labeled concepts as *planning, revising,* and *translating* introduced by Hayes and Flower (1980) provided the field with a common terminology and research targets that could be operationalized. Nevertheless, over the past 30 years attention to this triad of cognitive processes was unequally distributed. Compared to planning (Hayes & Nash, 1996) and revision (Allal, Chanquoy, & Largy, 2004), translating was relatively neglected. Three reasons seem to account for this neglect.

First, the early focus was on expert writers, for whom language processes were thought to be automatic and not as easily studied using the think-aloud protocols that were widely used then. However, see Chapter 2, this volume, for the introduction of on-line experiments to investigate the not always automatic processes of language.

Second, the concept of translating as a basic cognitive process has evolved since it was first proposed by Hayes and Flower (1980). Much of the research on translation in both children and adults has investigated transcription and text generation processes (e.g., see Parts I, III, and IV, this volume). However, in some recent models of the cognitive processes of writing, transcription is treated as a separate cognitive process from translation (see Hayes' perspective in Chapter 1, this volume). In addition, an emerging view is that translation may be bidirectional cognitive ← → linguistic transformation processes, which are supported by transcription and result in text generation, but are not merely transcription and text generation (see Fayol, Alamargot, & Berninger, 2011). In-progress and future research on the cognitive and language processes in writing may further clarify and resolve these contrasting perspectives as well as the fundamental nature of translation.

Third, as noted by Alamargot and Fayol (2009), research on the language component of writing has been fundamentally divided by two main cognitive research approaches that have progressed rather independently. One is based on psycholinguistics and focused on lexical production. The other is based on cognitive problem solving and focused on written discourse production. Integration between these two strands is needed and is a promising research avenue for writing, a topic explored in Fayol et al. (2011) and illustrated in Fayol's programmatic research (see Chapter 2, this volume).

The study of language bursts is a promising way to investigate text production (see Chapter 16, this volume). Kaufer, Hayes, and Flower's (1986) detailed account of text production showed that writers compose in bursts of language in between pauses. Recently the research on language bursts is expanding and considered a cutting-edge issue in the field of cognitive research. Several experiments have shown that domain expertise (Kaufer et al., 1986), language skill (Chenoweth & Hayes, 2001), available working memory capacity (Chenoweth & Hayes, 2003; Hayes & Chenoweth, 2006), and transcription skill contribute to burst length (Alves, Castro, & Olive, 2011; Alves, Castro, Sousa, & Strömqvist, 2007). Although other factors are likely to play a role, relation of bursts to writing quality, fluency, writing difficulties, and crucially syntactic units remain largely unexplored. Research on bursts might help to bridge the gap between the two aforementioned traditions devoted to the psycholinguistics and words versus cognitive problem solving and written discourse production. Furthermore, as we know more about bursts' development, potential for conducting new interventions on text production might well be uncovered.

RELATIVE NEGLECT OF AFFECT AND MOTIVATION IN WRITING RESEARCH

Although affect and motivation have not been totally ignored (see Chapters 3 and 7, this volume; Hidi & Boscolo, 2006), future cognitive research should increasingly investigate the interrelationships among cognition, affect, and motivation. Hayes (1996) did add affect in his revised model, and Hidi and Boscolo (2006) made an important contribution in bringing attention to those writing researchers who have considered the emotions and motivations related to the writing process (Zajonc & Markus, 1984; see also Chapter 3, this volume).

This neglect is curious because in contrast to the behavioral pathway, which is not connected to brain regions associated with affect, the brain's cognitive pathway is highly interconnected with the limbic system (emotional brain) (Mishkin & Appenzeller, 1987). Pessoa (2008) further discussed the false distinction between cognition and emotion at the brain and behavioral levels. Writing researchers will hopefully create collaborations with researchers in other disciplines that study emotions, feelings, moods, attitudes, beliefs, motivations, and evaluations to situate these affect variables within the writing process. Hopefully in the future researchers focused on affective and motivational (and sociocultural) variables in writing will learn more about the cognitive writing research and vice versa, in keeping with the call for a conceptual framework with greater interdisciplinary integration.

IMPLICIT AND EXPLICIT ACCOUNTS OF WRITING

New conceptualizations of written composition are emerging. Galbraith and Torrance (1999) made a strong case for a fundamental shift in writing research from a metaphor of writing as explicit problem solving to one of writing as autonomous text production that also draws on implicit processing. Galbraith and Torrance situated the studies in their edited volume as representative of this shift. To this day the best representative of this new breed of models of writing is Galbraith's (1999, 2009) knowledge-constituting model.

These accounts are grounded in basic, implicit processes that operate autonomously of explicit writing processes, but the implicit and explicit processes might interact and define the shape of the emerging text. One example of such implicit processes is the so-called priming effects in writing fluency (Alves, Branco, Limpo, & Castro, 2008; Limpo, Alves, & Galbraith, 2010). In a nutshell, Alves and colleagues have found that fundamental attributes of the writing theme (e.g., slowness in the stereotype of the elderly) on which a writer is composing may inadvertently affect writing fluency. For instance, writing about a typical elderly man reduced written fluency in comparison to writing about a nontypical elderly man. It seems that we are only scratching the surface of these interesting writing effects. Likely, as writing researchers learn more from these effects related to implicit knowledge influencing explicit language production, they might flesh out a rather different view of writing.

FUTURE VISION OF WRITING RESEARCH

Taleb (2010) made a compelling case that science, like many other human ventures, is governed by large-scale, deeply consequential, unpredictable ideas and original discoveries, for which he coined the term "black swans." Taleb further argues that humans are fundamentally blind to black swans, that is, before they happen, few, if any, would have predicted their appearance and far-reaching consequences. Who had predicted the highly influential role of Hayes and Flower's (1980) writing model? Yet, with hindsight it all makes perfect sense. Furthermore, one can climb on top of these ideas and look confidently farther ahead, make predictions, and imagine the future. However, we must not forget that experts seem generally no better at predictions than your casual taxi driver, yet they tend to be more confident (Tetlock, 1999). This does not mean that one should suspend from envisioning the future, but only that we should be ready for a surprise. Thus, following Taleb's advice, if you want to be ready for the future "be a fox with an open mind" (p. 154). In science this often means standing on the shoulders of giants. Present-day cognitive writing researchers stand on the shoulders of giants like the ones honored in this volume. From such heights the future looks bright for writing research, even if one cannot ascertain where we, the contemporary writing researchers, are leading it.

Indeed, I feel like the dwarf Cedalion standing on the shoulders of blind giant Orion. From where I stand the future is bright for cognitive writing research.

ACKNOWLEDGMENTS

References cited are one way of acknowledging one's giants. I thank Dick Hayes in particular for allowing me to stand on his shoulders and for giving me vision of what might be as writing research goes forward to discover the future.

REFERENCES

Abbott, R., Berninger, V., & Fayol, M. (2010). Longitudinal relationships of levels of language in writing and between writing and reading in grades 1 to 7. *Journal of Educational Psychology, 102*, 281–298.

Alamargot, D., & Fayol, M. (2009). Modeling the development of written composition. In R. Beard, D. Myhill, J. Riley, & M. Nystrand (Eds.), *The Sage handbook of writing development* (pp. 23–47). London: Sage.

Allal, L., Chanquoy, L., & Largy, P. (Eds.). (2004). *Revision: Cognitive and instructional processes.* Dordrecht: Kluwer.

Alves, R. A., Branco, M., Limpo, T., & Castro, S. L. (2008, June). *Priming effects on writing fluency.* Paper presented at the Writing 2008 11th International Conference of the Special Interest Group on Writing of the European Association for Research on Learning and Instruction, Lund.

Alves, R. A., Castro, S. L., & Olive, T. (2011). Transcription skill constrains bursts of language production. In M. Torrance (Ed.), *Learning to write effectively: Current trends in European research.* Brussels: OPOCE.

Alves, R. A., Castro, S. L., Sousa, L., & Strömqvist, S. (2007). Influence of typing skill on pause-execution cycles in written composition. In M. Torrance, L. van Waes, & D. Galbraith (Eds.), *Writing and cognition: Research and applications* (pp. 55–65). Amsterdam: Elsevier.

Bazerman, C. (Ed.). (2008). *Handbook of research on writing: History, society, school, individual, text*. New York: Erlbaum.

Beard, R., Myhill, D., Riley, J., & Nystrand, M. (Eds.). (2009). *The Sage handbook of writing development*. London: Sage.

Bereiter, C., & Scardamalia, M. (1987). *The psychology of written composition*. Hillsdale, NJ: Erlbaum.

Berninger, V. (1994). *Reading and writing acquisition: A developmental neuropsychological perspective*. Developmental Psychology Series, Wendell Jeffry (Ser. Ed.). Madison, WI: WCB Brown & Benchmark Publishing. (Reprinted 1996, Boulder, CO: Westview.)

Berninger, V., & Abbott, D. (2010). Listening comprehension, oral expression, reading comprehension and written expression: Related yet unique language systems in grades 1, 3, 5, and 7. *Journal of Educational Psychology, 102*, 635–651.

Berninger, V. W., & Swanson, H. L. (1994). Modifying Hayes and Flower's model of skilled writing to explain beginning and developing writing. In E. Butterfield (Ed.), *Children's writing: Toward a process theory of development of skilled writing* (pp. 57–81). Greenwich, CT: JAI Press.

Chenoweth, N. A., & Hayes, J. R. (2001). Fluency in writing. *Written Communication, 18*, 80–98.

Chenoweth, N. A., & Hayes, J. R. (2003). The inner voice in writing. *Written Communication, 20*, 99–118.

Connelly, V., Barnett, A. L., Dockrell, J., & Tolmie, A. (Eds.). (2009). Teaching and learning writing. *British Journal of Educational Psychology Monograph Series II, 6*.

COST Action IS0703. (2007). Memorandum of Understanding (MoU) for the implementation of a European Concerted Research Action designated as COST Action IS0703: The European Research Network on Learning to Write Effectively (ERN-LWE). Retrieved from http://www.cost-lwe.eu/spip.php?article88&lang=en

Emig, J. (1971). *The composing processes of twelfth graders*. Urbana, IL: National Council of Teachers of English Research.

Fayol, M., Alamargot, D., & Berninger, V. (Eds.). (2011). *Translation of thought to written text while composing: Advancing theory, knowledge, methods, and applications*. New York: Psychology Press.

Galbraith, D. (1999). Writing as a knowledge-constituting process. In M. Torrance & D. Galbraith (Eds.), *Knowing what to write: Conceptual processes in text production* (pp. 139–159). Amsterdam: Amsterdam University Press.

Galbraith, D. (2009). Writing as discovery. *British Journal of Educational Psychology Monograph Series II, 6*, 5–26.

Galbraith, D., & Torrance, M. (1999). Conceptual processes in writing: From problem solving to text production. In M. Torrance & D. Galbraith (Eds.), *Knowing what to write: Conceptual processes in text production* (pp. 1–12). Amsterdam: Amsterdam University Press.

Gardner, H. (1985). *The mind's new science: A history of the cognitive revolution*. New York: Basic Books.

Graham, S., & Perin, D. (2007). A meta-analysis of writing instruction for adolescent students. *Journal of Educational Psychology, 99*, 445–476.

Graham, S., MacArthur, C., & Fitzgerald, J. (Eds.). (2007). *Best practices in writing instruction*. New York: Guilford.

Hayes, J. R. (1996). A new framework for understanding cognition and affect in writing. In C. M. Levy & S. Ransdell (Eds.), *The science of writing: Theories, methods, individual differences, and applications* (pp. 1–27). Mahwah, NJ: Erlbaum.

Hayes, J. R., & Chenoweth, N. A. (2006). Is working memory involved in the transcribing and editing of texts? *Written Communication, 23*, 135–149.

Hayes, J. R., & Flower, L. S. (1980). Identifying the organization of writing processes. In L. W. Gregg & E. R. Steinberg (Eds.), *Cognitive processes in writing* (pp. 3–29). Hillsdale, NJ: Erlbaum.

Hayes, J. R., & Flower, L. S. (1986). Writing research and the writer. *American Psychologist, 41*, 1106–1113.

Hayes, J. R., & Nash, J. G. (1996). On the nature of planning in writing. In C. M. Levy & S. Ransdell (Eds.), *The science of writing: Theories, methods, individual differences, and applications* (pp. 29–55). Mahwah, NJ: Erlbaum.

Hidi, S., & Boscolo, P. (Eds.). (2006). *Writing and motivation.* Emerald, Australia: Elsevier.

Huey, E. G. (1908). *The psychology and pedagogy of reading.* New York: Macmillan. (Reprinted by MIT Press, 1968.)

Kaufer, D. S., Hayes, J. R., & Flower, L. S. (1986). Composing written sentences. *Research in the Teaching of English, 20*, 121–140.

Kellogg, R. (2008). Training writing skills: A cognitive developmental perspective. *Journal of Writing Research, 1*(1), 1–26.

Levy, C. M. (1997). The "R" that psychology forgot: Research on writing processes. *Behavior Research Methods, Instruments, and Computers, 29*, 137–145.

Limpo, T., Alves, R. A., & Galbraith, D. (2010, September). *Priming effects on writing are moderated by empathy and self-monitoring.* Paper presented at the 12th International Conference of the Special Interest Group on Writing of the European Association for Research on Learning and Instruction, Heidelberg.

MacArthur, C. A., Graham, S., & Fitzgerald, J. (2006). *Handbook of writing research.* New York: Guilford.

McCutchen, D. (1996). A capacity theory of writing: Working memory in composition. *Educational Psychology Review, 8*, 299–325.

Miller, B., & McCardle, P. (2011). Reflections on the need for continued research on writing. *Reading and Writing, 24*(2), 121–132.

Mishkin, M., & Appenzeller, T. (1987). The anatomy of memory. *Scientific American, 256*, 80–89.

National Commission on Writing in America's Schools and Colleges. (2003). *The neglected "R": The need for a writing revolution.* New York: College Entrance Exam Board.

National Mathematics Advisory Panel. (2008). *Foundations for success: The final report of the National Mathematics Advisory Panel.* Washington, DC: U.S. Department of Education.

National Reading Panel. (2000). *Teaching children to read: An evidence-based assessment of the scientific research literature on reading and its implications for reading instruction.* Washington, DC: National Institute of Child Health and Development.

Nystrand, M. (2006). The social and historical context for writing research. In C. A. MacArthur, S. Graham, & J. Fitzgerald (Eds.), *Handbook of writing research* (pp. 11–27). New York: Guilford.

Pessoa, L. (2008). On the relationship between emotion and cognition. *Nature Reviews Neuroscience, 9*, 148–158.

Rice, J. (1897). The futility of the spelling grind. *Forum, 23*, 163–172.

Simon, H. (1967). Motivational and emotional controls of cognition. *Psychological Review, 74*, 29–39.

Taleb, N. N. (2010). *The black swan: The impact of the highly improbable*. London: Penguin.

Tetlock, P. (1999). Theory-driven reasoning about plausible pasts and probable futures in world politics: Are we prisoners of our preconceptions? *American Journal of Political Science, 43*(2), 335–366.

Zajonc, R. B., & Markus, H. (1984). Affect and cognition: The hard interface. In C. Izard, J. Kagan, & R. B. Zajonc (Eds.), *Emotion, cognition, and behavior* (pp. 73–102). Cambridge, UK: Cambridge University Press.

Author Index

Subject Index

A

Acquired writing disorders, 547–548
Affective decision mechanisms (ADM), 20
Age-of-acquisition (AoA), 326, 327
  effect, 43
Agreement spelling, management of, 38
Argument prompt, students' comments about
  one word in, 257

B

Baddeley's updated model, working memory
  research, 489–490
Basic *vs.* applied writing research, 63
Bereiter and Scardamalia's cognitive models,
  465–466
Bereiter and Scardamalia's knowledge-telling
  model, 12
Brain research
  current knowledge of the writing brain, 546
    acquired writing disorders, 547–548
    developmental writing disorders:
      dyslexia, 552–553
    letter writing and letter perception,
      548–549
    normal *vs.* disabled child writers,
      549–552
    relationship between writing/math
      in normal and disabled writing/
      calculation, 553
    significance of brain research for writing
      development, 553–554
    spelling, 549
    tools for identifying brain regions
      discussed in writing research,
      546–547
Brains, developing, 544
Brain scanning studies, 14–15

C

Capacity theory of writing, 37, 38, 42
  McCutchen's, 488
Children challenged by writing due to language,
  217–219
  cognitive models/methodological issues,
    219–223
  delayed writing, 234
  developmental coordination disorder and
    hand writing, 230, 231–233

links with writing foundations, 236–237
separable processes in writing development,
  234–236
single word, 220–221
Children's writing processes, modeling, 12–14
Children with oral language and writing
  problems, 575–576
Children with specific language impairment,
  223
  text generation problems, 224–225
  transcription problems, 225–226
Cognition, social regulation of, 495
Cognitive and affective complexity of situated
  writing, 95–98
Cognitive architecture of written word
  production, information flow,
  324–326
Cognitive decision mechanisms, 20
Cognitive neuroscience model of the writing
  brain, 538–539
Cognitive processes in writing
  evolution of text composition, ages 6 to 11,
    28–29
    analyzing already produced texts, 29–30
    components of composing, 37–40
    coordinating low-level and high-level
      processes, 36
    experimental studies, 30–36
    producing texts, 47–50
    producing words, 43–44
    spelling: lexicon and sublexicon
      problems, 40–41
    studying components, 42–43
    from words to sentences, 44–46
  interactive features of, 299
  translating thought to written language,
    27–28
Cognitive psychology of writing, distributed
  themes in, 134–135
Cognitive resources in writing, 18
Cognitive/sociocultural-historical writing
  research, 585–589
Cognitive variations in revision processes,
  466–467
  contextual factors, 467
  individual factors, 468–470
  process factors, 467–468
Common writing practices, prima facie
  distributed, 135–136
Communication, professional. *See* Professional
  communication